Major Opponents			Electoral Vote		Popular Vote
For President	Party				
			Washington	69	Electors selected
			J. Adams	34	by state legislatures
George Clinton	Democratic-Republican		Washington	132	Electors selected
			J. Adams	77	by state legislatures
			Clinton	50	
Thomas Pinckney	Federalist		J. Adams	71	Electors selected
Aaron Burr	Democratic-Republican		Jefferson	68	by state legislatures
			Pinckney	59	
John Adams	Federalist		Jefferson	73	Electors selected
Charles Cotesworth Pinckney	Federalist		J. Adams	65	by state legislatures
Charles Cotesworth Pinckney	Federalist		Jefferson	162	Electors selected
			Pinckney	14	by state legislatures
Charles Cotesworth Pinckney	Federalist		Madison	122	Electors selected
			Pinckney	47	by state legislatures
George Clinton	Eastern Republican				
De Witt Clinton	Democratic-Republican (antiwar faction) and Federalist		Madison	128	Electors selected
			Clinton	89	by state legislatures
Rufus King	Federalist		Monroe	183	Electors selected
			King	34	by state legislatures
			Monroe	231	Electors selected
			J. Q. Adams	1	by state legislatures
Andrew Jackson	Democratic		J. Q. Adams	84	113,122
Henry Clay	Democratic-Republican		Jackson	99	151,271
			Clay	37	47,531
William H. Crawford	Democratic-Republican		Crawford	41	40,856
John Quincy Adams	National Republican		Jackson	178	642,553
			J. Q. Adams	83	500,897
Henry Clay	National Republican		Jackson	219	701,780
William Wirt	Anti-Masonic		Clay	49	482,205
			Wirt	7	100,715
			*Floyd (Ind. Dem.)	11	*Delegates chosen by South Carolina legislature

Presidential Election Year	Elected to Office			
	President	Party	Vice-President	Party
1836	Martin Van Buren	Democratic	Richard M. Johnson First and only vice-president elected by the Senate (1837), having failed to receive a majority of electoral votes.	Democratic
1840	William Henry Harrison	Whig	John Tyler	Whig
1844	James K. Polk	Democratic	George M. Dallas	Democratic
1848	Zachary Taylor	Whig	Millard Fillmore	Whig
1852	Franklin Pierce	Democratic	William R. King	Democratic
1856	James Buchanan	Democratic	John C. Breckinridge	Democratic
1860	Abraham Lincoln	Republican	Hannibal Hamlin	Republican
1864	Abraham Lincoln	National Union/ Republican	Andrew Jackson	National Union/ Democratic
1868	Ulysses S. Grant	Republican	Schuyler Colfax	Republican
1872	Ulysses S. Grant	Republican	Henry Wilson	Republican
1876	Rutherford B. Hayes Contested result settled by special election commission in favor of Hayes	Republican	William A. Wheeler	Republican
1880	James A. Garfield	Republican	Chester A. Arthur	Republican

Major Opponents		Electoral Vote		Popular Vote
For President	**Party**			
Daniel Webster	Whig	Van Buren	170	764,176
Hugh L. White	Whig	W. Harrison	73	550,816
William Henry	Anti-Masonic	White	26	146,107
Harrison		Webster	14	41,201
		*Mangum	11	*Delegates chosen by South Carolina legislature
		(Ind. Dem.)		
Martin Van Buren	Democratic	W. Harrison	234	1,274,624
James G. Birney	Liberty	Van Buren	60	1,127,781
Henry Clay	Whig	Polk	170	1,338,464
James G. Birney	Liberty	Clay	105	1,300,097
		Birney	—	62,300
Lewis Cass	Democratic	Taylor	163	1,360,967
Martin Van Buren	Free-Soil	Cass	127	1,222,342
		Van Buren	—	291,263
Winfield Scott	Whig	Pierce	254	1,601,117
John P. Hale	Free-Soil	Scott	42	1,385,453
		Hale	—	155,825
John C. Fremont	Republican	Buchanan	174	1,832,955
Millard Fillmore	American	Fremont	114	1,339,932
	(Know-Nothing)	Fillmore	8	871,731
John Bell	Constitutional Union	Lincoln	180	1,865,593
Stephen A. Douglas	Democratic	Breckinridge	72	848,356
John C. Breckinridge	Democratic	Douglas	12	1,382,713
		Bell	39	592,906
George B. McClennan	Democratic	Lincoln	212	2,218,388
		McClennan	21	1,812,807
		*Eleven secessionist states did not participate.		
Horatio Seymour	Democratic	Grant	286	3,598,235
		Seymour	80	2,706,829
		*Texas, Mississippi, and Virginia did not participate.		
Horace Greeley	Democratic and Liberal Republican	Grant	286	3,598,235
		Greeley	80*	2,834,761
Charles O'Conor	Democratic	*Greeley died before the Electoral College met. His electoral votes were divided among the four minor candidates.		
James Black	Temperance			
Samuel J. Tilden	Democratic	Hayes	185	4,034,311
Peter Cooper	Greenback	Tilden	184	4,288,546
Green Clay Smith	Prohibition	Cooper	—	75,973
Winfield S. Hancock	Democratic	Garfield	214	4,446,158
James B. Weaver	Greenback	Hancock	155	4,444,260
Neal Dow	Prohibition	Weaver	—	305,997

continued at back

American Government

American Government

Policy and Politics

Third Edition

Neal Tannahill
Houston Community College

Wendell M. Bedichek

■ HarperCollins*Publishers*

Sponsoring Editor: Lauren Silverman
Project Coordination, Text and Cover Design: Carnes-Lachina
    Publication Services
Cover Photo: Patricia Fisher/Folio Inc.
Photo Research: Kelly Mountain
Production: Michael Weinstein
Compositor: Beacon Graphics Corporation
Printer and Binder: R. R. Donnelley & Sons Company
Cover Printer: The Lehigh Press, Inc.

American Government: Policy and Politics, Third Edition
Copyright © 1991 by HarperCollins Publishers Inc.

Library of Congress Cataloging-in-Publication Data

Tannahill, Neal R.
    American government: policy and politics/Neal Tannahill,
  Wendell M. Bedichek.—3rd ed.
        p.   cm.
    Includes bibliographical references and index.
    1. United States—Politics and government.   I.
Bedichek, Wendell M.   II. Title.
JK274.T36   1991
320.473—dc20   90-42114
                                                CIP

ISBN: 0-673-38805-0

90 91 92 93 9 8 7 6 5 4 3 2 1

To all high emprise

CONTENTS

PERSPECTIVES

PREFACE

This is the third edition of *American Government: Policy and Politics*. When the late Wendell Bedichek and I first began work on an American government text about a decade ago, we wanted to produce a book that would explain the basics of American government in a fashion that was both easy to understand and interesting to read. We knew from experience in the classroom that many of today's students are poorly informed about government. To paraphrase a line that is now popular among educators, many students are politically illiterate. Consequently, Wendell and I set out to explain our subject clearly, assuming our audience of student readers would have little prior knowledge of American government or political science.

Wendell and I wanted to produce a text that was both readable and attractive. Good scholarship and good writing are not incompatible. This generation of students is the generation of music videos, stereo headsets, and cinematic extravaganzas. Never has the written word faced such stiff competition for attention. If scholarly writing is to be read by anyone other than die-hard academics, it must be sharp and crisp. Bland, colorless language dulls student interest, undermining motivation for learning. If students are to learn from a text, they must be motivated to read it with their full attention and interest.

Since the first edition was published in 1985, I have done a good deal of thinking about teaching American government. I now have a more fully developed teaching philosophy, and this textbook reflects that philosophy. I have kept the first edition's emphasis on clear writing and interesting presentation, and have added to it a commitment to upgrade the text's political-science scholarship and to involve students more actively in the learning process.

I still believe that textbooks should be written clearly and written well. In this text I have tried to explain every concept and idea fully, in language that students can understand. In each chapter I have highlighted key vocabulary terms, defined them in the text, and then listed them at the end of the chapter for study reference. Each key term is also found in a glossary at the end of the text. At the front of each chapter, meanwhile, I have included a set of learning objectives that students can use to guide their study.

To catch students' interest, I have begun each chapter with an illustration of some recent political event or policy issue, such as the Supreme Court's abortion decision in *Webster* v. *Reproductive Health Services* or the gun-control controversy. To hold students' attention, I have tried to use prose that is both crisp and clear, and to employ current-events examples with which students may be somewhat familiar. Moreover, I have illustrated each chapter with pictures, graphs, and cartoons.

In this edition of *American Government*, my major substantive goal has been to strengthen the text's overall level of political-science scholarship. This reflects my commitment to upgrading academic standards and my continued growth as a political scientist. In each chapter, the text introduces students to the vocabulary of the discipline and explains the basic processes of government. With this foundation laid, the text identifies and discusses some of the issues addressed by political-science scholarship.

This textbook also reflects my strong commitment to critical thinking and active learning. My definition of *critical thinking* is any thought process that goes beyond simple memorization. *Active learning*, meanwhile, refers to students' participation in exercises that allow them to "discover" ideas and develop concepts themselves. Although most critical-thinking/active-learning exercises begin in the classroom, the textbook can be an important resource for the teacher. Moreover, I have prepared an instructor's manual filled with active-learning activities, critical-thinking exercises, and suggestions for classroom research to assess teaching effectiveness.

Many persons contributed significantly to the writing and production of this book. Bruce Boreland, Karen Bednarski, Greg Odjakjian, Melissa J. Gulley, and Lauren Silverman of HarperCollins Publishing Company gave me sympathetic and professional help from the edition's beginning to its completion. I am also grateful to a number of scholars here at Houston Community College who read portions of the manuscript and shared with me the benefit of their political-science scholarship and teaching expertise. They include Cecile Artiz, Evelyn Ballard, Carol Brown, Stephen Coates, Dale Foster, Larry Gonzalez, Edmund "Butch" Herod, Brenda Jones, Woody Latham, Raymond Lew, David Ngene, James Patterson, Donna Rhea, James Steele, Mark Tiller, Randolph Wagner, Marcella Washington, Linda Webb, and Bob Wightman.

A number of scholars and friends helped me gather information and gave me useful advice on how best to use it. These include Robert Stein, Chandler Davidson, and Ferne Hyman of Rice University; Michael Adams, Franklyn Jones, Marva Johnson, and Glenn Nichols of Texas Southern University; Irving O. Dawson of the University of Texas at Arlington; Marshall de Rosa of Louisiana State University; William F. West of Texas A&M University; Warren Anderson and Virginia Perrenod of North Harris County Community College; Greg Thielemann of the University of Texas at Dallas; George Cvejanovich of Barry University; John Patrick Plumlee of the University of North Florida; and Roderick A. Stamey Jr., now retired.

Some individuals deserve special mention. Dr. Sue Cox, Dean of Social Sciences at Houston Community College, was supportive and encouraging. Mary Davis, Susan Howard, and Jeanelle Gunn of the college's clerical staff were cheerful and helpful. I am thankful to my mother, Mrs. Roy A. (Ruby) Tannahill, who faithfully clipped information from the newspapers. Her efforts proved indispensable to the book's timely completion.

Finally, I am grateful to my friends for reminding me that there is more to life than writing a textbook. Thank you Mike McKinney, Walt Griffin, Kim Galle, Don Lapin, Bruce Felgar, Mark Nash, Anthony Faulise, Morgan Slusher, Warren Holleman, Peter Armato, Steve Darby, Dick Holloway, Ron Rueckert, Larry Leutwyler, Greg Parnell, Margaret Hebert, Kevin Wallace, Clare Giesen, Marian McWhorter, Jeff Lindemann, David Gersh, Patricia Johnson, Manuel Reyes, Hal Stockbridge, and the good folks in the Rice NBA.

NEAL TANNAHILL

American Government

INTRODUCTION

POLITICAL SCIENCE AND PUBLIC POLICY

WHY STUDY GOVERNMENT?
POLITICAL SCIENCE
THE PUBLIC POLICY APPROACH

LEARNING OBJECTIVES

1. To understand why studying government is important for everyone, not just political science majors.
2. To explain how political scientists use the scientific method to study their subject.
3. To identify the five stages of the public policy approach and discuss their usefulness for the study of government and politics in America.

For Yolanda Perez, a Mexican-born housekeeper living in Houston, the law was a godsend: "I'm so happy. I prayed and prayed the INS [Immigration and Naturalization Service] wouldn't find me. Now I'll be able to make plans for the future."[1]

But not everyone was so pleased. Ed Angstadt, the president of a vegetable grower-shipper association in California, complained that the law created an administrative nightmare for employers. "The biggest problem," he said, "is the increased paperwork and the increased problems employers will have in documenting people they hire."[2]

Ms. Perez and Mr. Angstadt were reacting to the Immigration Reform and Control Act, the most important revision in American immigration policy in over twenty years. In 1986, Congress passed, and the president signed, the measure into law with the twin goals of first, stemming the flow of illegal immigration, and second, affording millions of people who had been working in this country illegally for many years the opportunity to achieve legal status. On one hand, the act made it a crime for employers knowingly to hire illegal aliens. On the other hand, it offered amnesty to illegal immigrants who could prove they had been permanent residents of the United States since January 1, 1982.

WHY STUDY GOVERNMENT?

The Immigration Reform and Control Act illustrates the relevance of American government. For Yolanda Perez and other undocumented workers, the law promised the hope of escaping the shadows of illegal worker status and becoming citizens. For Ed Angstadt and other employers, however, the measure threatened a blizzard of paperwork and the prospect of being unable to find sufficient numbers of workers. What's more, illegal immigrants and employers weren't the only ones affected by the act. The law required everyone seeking employment in the United States, including native-born Americans, to prove their eligibility to work in this country.

It is important to study government because it affects us all through services, regulations, and taxes. First, we all benefit from government services. We are born in hospitals that probably receive government assistance, either directly or indirectly. As youngsters, we attend public grade schools and high schools. Even if we go to private schools, we may receive government aid in the form of free transportation, textbooks, or school lunches. Many of us enroll in public community colleges or state universities, often with the help of student loans. Eventually, some of us will work for the government, while others will take jobs with private companies doing contract work for government agencies or departments. All the while, we drive on government-built streets and highways and ride on publicly subsidized mass transit. We are protected by local police and fire departments and rely on the national government to guard our nation's security. The government collects garbage, delivers mail, vaccinates children, and insures bank deposits against loss or theft. If we fall on hard times, government can help with unemployment compensation, food stamps, and Medicaid. When we retire, we collect Social Security and receive Medicare benefits.

Second, government regulates many aspects of our lives, either directly or indirectly. We must follow the criminal law, of course, but government also establishes educational and technical requirements for practicing many occupations and professions. Government even sets the proportion of meat byproducts that processors may include in a frankfurter. Government regulations affect the quality of air and water, gasoline-mileage performance of automobiles, and working conditions in factories. Regulation attempts to protect us from unsafe products, untested drugs, misleading package labels, deceptive advertising, and discrimination based on race, color, gender, religion, national origin, or age.

Third, all of us share in the cost of government. Our employers withhold income and Social Security taxes from our paychecks. We pay sales taxes on many retail purchases and excise taxes on a variety of products, including tobacco, alcohol, tires, and gasoline. We pay property taxes directly on our homes and businesses or indirectly through our rent.

Government not only touches our lives as individuals; it affects society as a whole. Education, health care, welfare assistance, roads, public transportation, sanitation, recreation facilities, law enforcement, consumer-protection laws, occupational licensing regulations, and other services and regulations have a major impact on the quality of life in the United States. Moreover, the tax system influences the distribution of wealth in society and affects the nation's economy as a whole.

Studying American government is important because of its great impact on us as individuals and on society as a whole. If we understand the workings of government, we will be better equipped to take advantage of the benefits and services government provides and to prepare ourselves to live effectively under government regulation and taxation. We will also have a clearer idea of

how we can influence government policies through our votes, our participation in political organizations, and our personal communications with
policymakers.

POLITICAL SCIENCE

This is a political science textbook, centering on the study of American government. **Government** is the institution with authority to set policy for society. **Political science**, meanwhile, is the academic discipline that deals with
the theory and practice of politics and the description and analysis of political
systems and political behavior. We can elaborate by first defining politics and
then discussing science.

Politics is the process that determines who shall occupy the roles of
leadership in government and how the power of government shall be exercised. It involves competition, bargaining, negotiation, and compromise. In
some quarters, politics has gotten a bad name. When we believe we have
been shortchanged in our dealings with government, we may write off the experience by saying, "That's politics." Sometimes public officials promise reform by taking some area of policymaking "out of politics." In fact, however,
politics is an essential, inevitable part of decision making. In today's diverse
society, a multitude of contending groups and interests hold different views
about governmental policy. Politics determines whose views will prevail and
what policies will be enacted. Politics is neither good nor bad; it is a process.
Complex society could not exist without it.

Science is a method of study concerned with describing and explaining
certain phenomena through the formulation of theories and laws. Scientists
begin with an interest in some aspect of the world around them, such as animal life, the movement of subatomic particles, or child psychology. Natural
science, including physics, biology, and chemistry, deals with matter and energy. Social science, including economics, sociology, and psychology, is concerned with human behavior. Political science is a social science that deals
with the scientific study of political behavior.

The scientific method has three components: description, discovery of
regularity, and formulation of scientific theories and laws. Scientists carefully
observe a phenomenon in order to describe it and to identify patterns of regularity. The ultimate goal of the scientist is to develop theories and laws. A
scientific theory is a general, logical statement of relationships among characteristics and events that explains a particular range of phenomena. In short,
a theory is an attempt to explain why something happened. Once a theory has
been proposed, scientists derive hypotheses to test it. A **hypothesis** is a
specific prediction about events that can be tested by experimentation and
the collection and analysis of data. In general, before a hypothesis can be
tested, it must be made operational. **Operationalization** is the process

through which a hypothesis is stated in terms that can be tested experimentally. Scientists do this by identifying indicators that can be collected and analyzed to test the hypothesis. A **scientific law** is a theory that has not been disproved and is generally accepted as correct.

Suppose, for example, that a group of political scientists decides to study voter turnout. During a discussion of the subject, several scholars mention that they have observed that voter turnout seems lower when it rains on election day than when the weather is fair. After some thought and discussion, the political scientists pose the following theory: Voter-turnout rates are positively related to convenience. This theory satisfies the criteria used for evaluating theories: It is *general* and *logical*, and it *explains* the observed phenomenon. The theory is general in that it encompasses more than just rainy weather to include all sorts of factors that could inconvenience voters, from snowstorms to registration requirements to the time elections are held. Moreover, the theory logically explains why voter turnout falls when it rains.

Having proposed a theory, the political scientists derive a hypothesis for testing: The farther citizens must travel to cast their ballots, the less likely they are to vote. (Hypotheses, you recall, are more specific than theories.) The political scientists operationalize their hypothesis by measuring the distance between the homes of a cross section of registered voters and their polling places. Then, the scholars examine election records to determine which of the citizens cast ballots in recent elections and which did not. Based on their theory, the scholars predict that citizens having to travel the farthest would be less likely to vote than people closer to the polling place. The political scientists can use the results of their research to evaluate their original theory. Before the scholars can be confident in the correctness of their theory, they will want to test a number of hypotheses using a variety of research methods.

In general, political science and the other social sciences are not as well developed as most of the natural sciences. Political science can offer no equivalent of Newton's law of gravity or Einstein's general and special theories of relativity. Perhaps the best explanation for this state of affairs is that political science is a young discipline. Although the study of government in its broadest sense dates from Plato and Aristotle, Greek philosophers who lived several hundred years before Christ, the scientific study of political behavior did not begin until the mid-twentieth century. Social scientists also believe that the subject matter of their disciplines—human behavior—is more complex and therefore more difficult to study than the subject matter of the natural sciences.

THE PUBLIC POLICY APPROACH

Although political scientists employ a number of approaches for studying their subject, we believe the public policy approach is particularly helpful. Public means governmental, while policy refers to the decision-makers' response, or lack of response, to an issue. **Public policy**, then, is the response, or lack of response, of governmental decision-makers to an issue. The process through which public policy is made is known as the **public policy process**.

The Five Stages of the Process

The public policy process has five stages: agenda building, policy formulation, policy adoption, policy implementation, and policy evaluation. **Agenda building** is the process through which issues become matters of public concern and governmental action. Political leaders, government agencies, interest-group spokespersons, scientists, individual citizens, and the media can all bring issues to the public's attention. In the mid-1980s, for example, individual members of Congress, state and local governments located along the Mexican border, a number of interest groups, and the media all played a role in placing the issue of immigration reform on the policy agenda.

The set of problems that are raised to public concern are known as the **public agenda**, while the set of problems that government actually chooses to attempt to remedy are called the **official agenda**. The issue of immigration reform, for example, was an item on the public agenda for several years before it became part of the official agenda. As students of the public policy process, we may be as interested in which problems are *not* raised to public attention and debate as in those issues that are.

Policy formulation, the second stage of the policy process, involves the development of courses of action for dealing with problems on the official agenda. A wide range of governmental and nongovernmental actors may participate in policy formulation. For example, congressional committees, the INS, various business groups, organized labor, Hispanic-rights groups, and a number of state and local governments all played a role in formulating the revision in immigration policy embodied in the Immigration Reform and Control Act.

Policy adoption is the official decision of a governmental body to accept a particular policy and put it into effect. Congress may pass legislation to reform immigration policy. The president may negotiate a trade agreement with Japan. The Food and Drug Administration (FDA) may approve the use of an experimental drug for treating Acquired Immune Deficiency Syndrome (AIDS). The Supreme Court may rule on the constitutionality of state restrictions on abortion.

Policy implementation is the stage of the policy process in which policies are carried out. Governmental bureaucracies and private parties may both be involved in the implementation process. While Congress assigned the INS the task of creating a form to document individual employees' eligibility status for working in the United States (called the I–9 Form), Congress required individual employers to perform the actual task of verifying the employment eligibility of their prospective workers.

Policy evaluation is concerned with the assessment of policy. It involves questions of cost, efficiency, honesty, fairness, and effectiveness measured in terms of policy goals. The Immigration Reform and Control Act, you recall, was passed with the aims of controlling illegal immigration and offering amnesty to undocumented persons who had lived in the United States since 1982. Measured in light of these goals, the act was only a partial success, at best. By the end of the 1980s, the INS admitted that the new law had done little to slow the flow of illegal immigrants because undocumented workers simply used fake information to qualify for jobs.[3] The amnesty program, meanwhile, fell short of original expectations. Although nearly 1.5 million persons applied for amnesty, the government estimated that perhaps another 1.5 to 3.5 million individuals were eligible for the program but failed to apply.[4]

A number of important points need to be made about the nature of policy evaluation. First, we must draw a distinction between policy outputs and policy outcomes. **Policy outputs** refer to governmental policies themselves. **Policy outcomes**, meanwhile, are the situations that arise as a result of the impact of policy in operation. Policies often have wide-ranging effects that may be unexpected. One unanticipated consequence of immigration reform, for example, was the appearance in the United States of thousands of immigrants from Mexico and Central America asking for political asylum so they could stay legally in this country.[5]

Second, evaluation can be made from either an empirical or normative standpoint. An **empirical analysis** is a method of study that relies on experience and scientific observation. It is objective and factually based. We can count, for example, the number of persons qualifying for amnesty, and we can survey employers about the time it takes to complete paperwork required by the new law. Many questions, however, are more subjective, requiring a normative focus. A **normative analysis** is a method of study that is based on certain values. We may endorse amnesty for illegal aliens, for example, because we believe that it is humane, or we may oppose the policy because we think that it unfairly rewards those who entered the country illegally. In either case, we are making a value judgment. As human beings, we have values and make normative judgments. As political scientists, however, our focus is primarily empirical.

Policymaking in Practice

In practice, policymaking is more complex than the model suggests at first glance. First, keep in mind that the public policy process is not just another way of describing "how bills become laws." Not all policies are drafted into formal legislation (as was immigration reform). Judicial rulings make policy, as do presidential orders and decisions made by bureaucratic agencies. Congress, for example, left some of the more important aspects of immigration reform for the INS to settle, such as the decision on how to handle a family when one spouse qualifies for amnesty but the other does not. (The INS decided that non-qualifying family members would be subject to deportation unless there were humanitarian reasons for them to stay, such as illness or disability.)

Second, each stage of the policy process does not neatly match up one-to-one with a different governmental institution or political actor. Interest groups, the president, or big-city mayors may raise issues to the public agenda. Congress, the federal bureaucracy, or the White House staff may formulate policy. Federal bureaucracies, state agencies, and even private firms may be involved in policy implementation.

Third, no clear lines of demarcation can be drawn among the five stages of the policy process. Agenda setting and policy formulation sometimes overlap. Policy implementation often has an aspect of policy adoption to it as agencies fill in the details of policies adopted by legislative bodies. Moreover, policy evaluations occur throughout the policy process, not just at its end. Evaluation may then lead to demands for more government action, and the process begins anew. By the end of the 1980s, for example, Congress was considering legislation to reform American immigration policy once again.

Finally, the public policy approach is not a completely rational path leading inevitably to the "ideal public policy." After all, public policy is made by humans operating within complicated political structures. In an ideal process, policymakers would act to identify policy issues before they reached the crisis stage. They would emphasize problem prevention, not just problem solution. In reality, however, policymakers don't tackle problems until they are clearly identified as problems and placed on the public agenda. Little energy is directed toward problem prevention. In an ideal process, policymakers would examine all possible policy options to determine the best possible solution. In reality, though, policymakers tend to settle upon the first policy that appears workable. In an ideal process, policymakers would adopt the best possible policy without regard for past practices and procedures. In reality, however, policymakers first consider modifications of current programs and policies instead of turning to dramatic new approaches. Policymakers tend to retain practices that once proved successful even if the nature of the problem has changed. Consequently, public policy usually changes incrementally—slowly, by bits and pieces—rather than dramatically.

Real-life policymaking usually falls short of the ideal, but it isn't because public officials are necessarily lazy, careless, and uninformed about scientific, systematic approaches to policy analysis. Most governmental decision-makers know full well that their approaches to policymaking often fall short of the ideal. The ideal method, however, requires more time and resources than public officials usually have at their disposal. Moreover, political leaders often face pressures from interest groups, the media, and the general public. As a result, governmental officials often settle on seemingly plausible policies that fit within available resources and that are politically acceptable.

KEY TERMS

agenda building

empirical analysis

government

hypothesis

normative analysis

official agenda

operationalization

policy adoption

policy evaluation

policy formulation

policy implementation

policy outcomes

policy outputs

political science

politics

public agenda

public policy

public policy process

science

scientific law

scientific theory

NOTES

1. Quoted in *Time*, 4 May 1987, p. 17.
2. Ibid.
3. Jacob V. Lamar, "The Immigration Mess," *Time*, 27 February 1989, pp. 14–15.
4. Ibid.; Zita Arocha, "For Those Still Not Legal, It's Too Late," *Washington Post*, National Weekly Edition, 9–15 May 1988, p. 32.
5. Lamar.

SUGGESTED READINGS

Anderson, James E. *Public Policy-Making*, 2d ed. New York: Praeger, 1990.

Finer, Ada W. *Political Science: The State of the Discipline*. Washington, DC: American Political Science Association, 1983.

Goggin, Malcolm L.; Bowman, Ann O.; Lester, James T.; and O'Toole, Lawrence J., Jr. *Implementation Theory and Practice*. Glenview, IL: Scott, Foresman and Company, 1990.

Johnson, Janet Buttolph, and Joslyn, Richard A. *Political Science Research Methods*. Washington, DC: Congressional Quarterly Press, 1986.

Kaplan, Morton A. *Science, Language and the Human Condition*. New York: Paragon House, 1984.

Kingdon, John W. *Agendas, Alternatives, and Public Policy*. Boston: Little, Brown, 1984.

Lawson, Kay. *The Human Polity: An Introduction to Political Science*, 2d ed. Boston: Houghton Mifflin Co., 1989.

Nagel, Stuart S. *Policy Evaluation*. New York: Praeger, 1982.

Nakamura, Robert T., and Smallwood, Frank. *The Politics of Policy Implementation*. New York: St. Martin's Press, 1980.

Van Horn, Carl E.; Baumer, Donald C.; and Gornley, William T., Jr. *Politics and Public Policy*. Washington, DC: Congressional Quarterly Press, 1989.

1

AMERICA AND THE WORLD

LEARNING OBJECTIVES

1. To describe the United States in terms of geographic size and location, natural resources, and population size and composition.
2. To compare and contrast the major economic and political systems found in the world today, giving examples of nations representing each type.
3. To describe the American economy, identifying indicators of both strength and weakness.
4. To summarize the argument advanced by various observers that the United States is in decline and evaluate the accuracy of that assessment.
5. To describe the origin and content of America's political culture and evaluate its impact on the policymaking process.
6. To compare and contrast liberalism and conservatism, discussing the position of each on various policy issues.
7. To discuss the relationship between socioeconomic and cultural factors and the public policymaking process.

In 1986 the *National Journal*, a weekly periodical of public affairs, published an issue on the "baby-bust generation."[1] The title was ironic. In the late 1940s, 1950s, and early 1960s, the birthrate soared as Americans who had postponed having children during the Great Depression and World War II made up for lost time. The exceptionally large number of Americans born during this period was known as the **baby-boom generation**. Since the early 1960s, however, birthrates have fallen dramatically. As a result, the number of Americans today under the age of eighteen is seven million less than in 1970.[2]

Stories about demographic trends are more than just entertaining reading; they contain information vitally important to policymakers. Because of lower birthrates in the late 1960s and 1970s, state colleges and universities must compete to attract students from a smaller population of young people of traditional college age. Military recruiters face a smaller pool from which to enlist volunteers. Policymakers, meanwhile, must devise a plan to keep the Social Security system solvent after the baby-boom generation has retired, leaving a smaller generation behind in the work force to pay taxes to fund retirement checks.

As these examples demonstrate, policymaking takes place within the broad context of national life. The country's population make-up, economy, and political culture all influence the policymaking process. In this chapter, we describe the socioeconomic and cultural setting for politics in America and discuss its influence on the nation's policymaking process.

AMERICA AND ITS PEOPLE

Among the world's nations, the United States stands fourth in terms of both land area and population size. The Soviet Union (USSR), Canada, and the People's Republic of China (Mainland China) are geographically larger. China, India, and the USSR have larger populations.

Natural Resources

America benefits from an abundance of natural resources. Rich soil and a temperate climate have combined to make the United States one of the world's foremost agricultural producers. America is also among the leaders in the production of a broad range of minerals. Until recent years, the United States was virtually self-sufficient in terms of agricultural goods and mineral resources. Because of declining domestic oil production and increased demand, though, America is now one of the world's largest oil importers, purchasing more than half of its petroleum needs from abroad.

Historically, America benefited from geographic isolation. Because it had the good fortune to be relatively isolated from areas of major world conflict, the United States was able to develop its resources and build its industrial base without an overriding concern for national defense against hostile neighbors. Today, however, intercontinental ballistic missiles and nuclear weapons diminish the importance of geographic isolation.

Population

The Census Bureau estimates the population of the United States at roughly 250 million.[3] Although the nation's population has grown by about a hundred million since the 1940s, the rate of growth has decreased. As we noted in the introduction to this chapter, soaring birthrates produced a baby boom in the years after World War II. Thereafter, birthrates fell until the mid-1970s, when the baby-boom generation began having children of their own, producing an echo effect from the original boom. Nonetheless, the birthrate has declined below the population-replacement rate. The Census Bureau reports that American women now average 1.8 children in their lifetimes, while it takes about 2.1 births per woman to keep the population stable. Were it not for the large number of baby-boom-generation women of childbearing age, the population would be declining. As it is, experts predict that the nation's population will peak at some point in the next century and then begin to decline. Future population estimates depend, of course, upon such factors as birthrates, death rates, and immigration (which now adds more than a million legal and illegal newcomers to the population every year).[4]

America has a diverse population. Although a majority of the nation's people are whites of European descent, the population includes a sizable

proportion of African-Americans (blacks), Hispanic-Americans, Asian-Americans, and American Indians. African-Americans, who make up about 12 percent of the population, are found in largest numbers in the South and the Northeast. Meanwhile, Hispanic-Americans, who compose roughly 4 percent of the population, are concentrated in New York City, South Florida, and the western United States. Because of relatively high birth and immigration rates, America's nonwhite population is growing at a faster rate than its white population.

The Census Bureau has uncovered some interesting population shifts within the United States. In recent decades, the South and Southwest, the region known as the **Sunbelt**, have grown faster than the Northeast and Midwest, the **Frostbelt**. In fact, the latest census data show that, for the first time in history, the Sunbelt has a larger population than the Frostbelt. The Census Bureau has also learned that America's suburbs are growing more rapidly than inner-city or rural areas. Indeed, many of the nation's inner cities have been declining in population since the 1970s.

WORLD ECONOMIC AND POLITICAL SYSTEMS

Political scientists classify nations according to their economic and political systems. **Economics** is the process that determines the production, distribution, and consumption of goods and services in a society. In contrast, **politics** is the process that determines who shall occupy the roles of leadership in government and how the power of government shall be exercised.

Economic Systems

Two general economic models compete for supporters in today's world: capitalism and socialism. **Capitalism** is an economic system based on individual and corporate ownership of the means of production and a market economy based on supply and demand. Under capitalism, the marketplace, in which buyers and sellers freely exchange goods and services, determines what goods and services are to be produced, how they are to be produced, and for whom they are produced. Private business people or groups of private investors own natural resources and industrial plants. Most workers are employed by private enterprises which compete to provide goods to consumers at prices consumers are willing to pay. The proponents of capitalism believe that the profit motive leads to an efficient distribution of economic resources with strong economic growth.

Socialism is an economic system based on governmental ownership of the means of production, such as factories, land, banks, and businesses. In a socialist economy, the government decides what to produce, how to produce, and how goods and services will be distributed. Since the government owns the nation's natural resources and industrial plants, most workers are government employees. A central planning commission draws up an economic master plan which regional and local agencies then implement. The advocates of socialism believe that the capitalist free market is chaotic, conflictual, and, therefore, inefficient. They believe that socialism replaces the competition of capitalism with cooperation, thus promoting a better society, a more productive economy, and a more even distribution of income and opportunity.

In practice, no country's economy conforms exactly to either capitalism or socialism. Instead, each nation has a **mixed economy**, that is, an economy that combines some aspects of a capitalist economy with some features of socialism. The nature of that mix, however, varies from country to country. The Soviet economy, for example, remains basically socialist, despite the presence of limited free-market activity in agriculture and the introduction of additional competitive features under the more recent economic reforms instituted by Soviet leader Mikhail Gorbachev. In contrast, the American economy, which is predominantly capitalist, features extensive government regulation of economic activity. Moreover, government in the United States spends hundreds of billions of dollars annually on a vast network of social-welfare programs. In sum, then, both the United States and the Soviet Union have mixed economies, despite clear leanings toward capitalism in one case and socialism in the other.

For other nations, the mixture of capitalist and socialist elements is more balanced than it is in the United States or the USSR. In a number of Western European nations, for example, the government owns many basic industries, usually including transportation, communications, energy, and finance. Other industries and most smaller businesses, however, are privately owned. Moreover, market forces determine most production and pricing decisions, rather than a government-established planning commission.

Our capitalist/socialist division doesn't necessarily apply to the economies of many developing countries. Most of the world's poorer nations have dual economies, with a modern sector found in the cities and a traditional, preindustrial sector functioning in the countryside. Developing countries that are socialist, such as Ethiopia, institute socialism only in the modern segments of their economy. Underdeveloped nations that are capitalist, such as El Salvador, have capitalist modern sectors.[5]

The Soviet Union, once the world's most ardent anti-capitalist state, has recently permitted some changes in its economic system—as demonstrated by this McDonald's restaurant in Moscow.

Political Systems

We can classify political systems as democratic or authoritarian. A **democracy** is a system of government in which the people hold ultimate political power. In a democracy, citizens have the right to vote periodically in fair elections for candidates representing different political groups and/or expressing different political views. Democratic governments honor the will of the people, allowing election winners to replace election losers in office. Democracies also guarantee civil liberties to their citizens, including freedom of expression, organization, assembly, press, and religion.[6]

Authoritarianism is the concentration of political power in one person or a small group of persons. Authoritarian regimes emphasize the obedience of citizens to their rulers and the absolute authority of rulers over their subjects. The power of the government takes precedence over individual rights and liberties. Authoritarian governments include one-party communist countries (such as the People's Republic of China), nations ruled by military strongmen (such as Iraq), and monarchies (such as Saudi Arabia).

Authoritarian regimes vary in the degree to which they control the lives of their citizens. **Totalitarianism** is a form of authoritarianism in which the government controls nearly every aspect of people's lives. Totalitarian regimes do not tolerate criticism or permit the formation of organizations not controlled by the government. Totalitarian dictators maintain their control by means of secret police and the use of terrorism against opponents, real and suspected. Nazi Germany and the Soviet Union under Stalin were examples of totalitarian regimes.

Totalitarian is too strong a word to describe most authoritarian governments. Because of either a lack of will or a lack of resources, most authoritarian governments fall short of exercising total control over their citizens' lives. Moreover, a number of scholars believe that totalitarian systems may not control as thoroughly as the term implies, since several groups—the army, political leaders, industrialists, and others—compete for influence.

A number of nations fall somewhere along the scale between democracy and authoritarianism. These nations combine some aspects of democratic political systems with other features of authoritarian regimes. Mexico, for example, holds regular elections in which opposition parties run candidates for the presidency and other important public offices. Nonetheless, opposition candidates have never captured the presidency and many observers question the fairness of government vote counts.

Over the last decade or so, many of the nations that were once clearly authoritarian have adopted at least some of the features of democracy. The Soviet Union and the nations of Eastern Europe have relaxed restrictions on political freedom and held free elections to fill some offices. In Latin America, meanwhile, most of the military regimes that had ruled in the region have been replaced by democratically elected civilian governments.

Political scientist Lucian Pye has described recent events as a "crisis of authoritarianism." He believes that authoritarian governments are under attack around the world because of their failure to provide a favorable environment for economic growth. According to Pye, economic progress in today's world depends upon a society's openness to international trade and investment, the spread of science and technology, and modern communication. These factors, however, are incompatible with centralized authoritarian rule. Consequently, many authoritarian governments have either relaxed political control voluntarily or been forced to reform by citizens' impatience with economic stagnation. Pye believes that authoritarian governments will not necessarily become democracies. Instead, he says they will adopt political systems which are part free, part authoritarian.[7]

Classifying Nations

As we have noted, all national economies are mixed economies, at least to some degree, and a number of nations fall somewhere between democracy and authoritarianism. Nonetheless, we can use general tendencies to devise a classification scheme. Figure 1.1 creates four categories into which nations may be classified. The vertical axis places democracy at the top, authoritarianism at the bottom. The horizontal axis lists socialism on the left and capitalism on the right. The figure also gives an example of a country that can be placed in each of the four quadrants. As you can see, not all democracies are predominantly capitalist, and not all predominantly capitalist countries are democracies.

FIGURE 1.1
Political and Economic Systems of Selected Nations

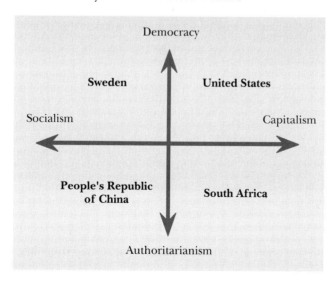

ECONOMIC DEVELOPMENT

Economics affects politics and politics affects economics. The United States' dependence on imported oil, for example, influences American foreign policy and public policies affecting domestic energy production. Conversely, when Congress debated immigration reform in the late 1980s, a major concern was the possible impact of changes in immigration laws on wage rates and the labor supply. Let's consider the economic context of policymaking in America.

The American Economy

The United States economy is by far the largest in the world, nearly twice the size of the economies of Japan and the Soviet Union. By the beginning of the 1990s, America's **gross national product (GNP)**, which is the total value of goods and services produced by an economy in a year (and a standard measure of an economy's size), exceeded $5 trillion. The United States economy alone accounted for roughly 22 percent of the entire world GNP. American economic strength is impressive when measured on a per capita (per person) basis as well. Although Switzerland and a number of tiny oil-producing nations can boast higher figures, America's GNP per capita exceeds that of all other major industrial nations, including Japan.

Nevertheless, critics of American economic performance identify a number of weaknesses in the nation's economy. As you can see from Table 1.1, economic growth rates in the United States have generally lagged behind economic growth rates of Japan and the combined nations of Western Europe since the early 1960s. Moreover, Congressional Budget Office statistics show that between 1977 and 1988 average family income in the United States fell by about $1,000 a year (after discounting for inflation).[8] Family income would have declined even more had it not been for an increase in the number of two-income families.

TABLE 1.1
Average Annual Growth Rate of Real GNP

Years	U.S.	Japan	Western Europe
1961–65	4.6%	12.4%	4.9%
1966–70	3.0	11.0	4.6
1971–75	2.2	4.3	2.9
1976–80	3.4	5.0	3.0
1981–85	2.6	4.0	1.5
1986–87	2.9	3.1	2.5

Note: Real GNP refers to the rate of economic growth after controlling for inflation.
Source: Annual Report of the Council of Economic Advisers, in *Economic Report of the President* (Washington, DC: United States Government Printing Office, 1988), based on Table B-111, p. 374.

Many observers are troubled by statistics showing that the gap between the rich and the poor in America is widening. A recent congressional study found that between 1977 and 1988 the wealthiest 5 percent of American families increased their after-tax earnings (after adjusting for inflation) by 37 percent, from $94,476 a year to $129,762. In contrast, the poorest 10 percent of the population saw their income fall by 11 percent, dropping from $3,673 a year to $3,286.[9]

The number of Americans living in poverty has also risen. The government measures poverty on the basis of subsistence. The **poverty line** is the amount of money an individual or family needs to purchase basic necessities, such as food, clothing, health care, shelter, and transportation. The actual dollar amount varies with family size and rises with inflation, but in 1988 the poverty line was $12,092 for a family of four. By this standard, nearly 32 million Americans lived in poverty, roughly 13.1 percent of the population. This represented an increase of about 20 percent over the late 1970s.[10] (See the Perspective on page 22 for a discussion of the problem of defining poverty.)

The burden of poverty falls more heavily upon racial minorities, children, and families headed by women. Although the majority of Americans living below the poverty line are white (most Americans, after all, are white), the incidence of poverty is much higher *on a percentage basis* for racial minority groups. In 1988, the poverty rate for African- and Hispanic-Americans stood at 32 and 27 percent, respectively, compared to 10 percent for whites.[11] Poverty also affects children and families headed by women in disproportionate numbers. More than 20 percent of the nation's children under eighteen are growing up in poverty, while as many as 40 percent of families headed by women have incomes below the poverty line.[12]

In recent decades, American economic strength has been sapped by a number of problems. In the late 1970s, the United States experienced several years of high inflation. **Inflation** is a decline in the purchasing power of the currency. The annual inflation rate was about 5 percent in the early 1970s, but soared to more than 13 percent a year by the end of the decade. Although inflation cooled during the 1980s, a number of economists worry about the possibility of rising inflation rates once again.

The American economy has suffered periodic recessions. A **recession** is an economic slowdown characterized by declining economic output and rising unemployment. Between 1970 and the end of the 1980s, the United States experienced recessions in 1974, 1979, and 1982. Moreover, the 1982 recession was the nation's most severe economic slump since the Great Depression, with unemployment rising above 10 percent.

Even in times of general prosperity, certain segments of the American economy have fared poorly. The auto, textile, electronics, shoe, and shipbuilding industries have not performed well against foreign competition for years. Moreover, during the middle years of the 1980s, the oil industry and the farming sector of the nation's economy slumped because of falling international prices and, in the case of some farming areas, poor weather. As a result, farm states in the Midwest and oil states in the Southwest suffered regional recessions.

The inability of some American industries to compete effectively against foreign competition has helped produce a record trade deficit for the United States. The term **trade deficit** refers to the amount by which the value of a nation's imports exceeds its exports. Throughout the 1980s, Americans purchased considerably more imported goods and services than they sold abroad. In 1987, the trade deficit peaked at a record high of $152 billion.[13] Although economists agree that international trade benefits all nations involved, many economists think that the $100-billion-plus trade deficits the United States ran for most of the 1980s will have a negative long-term impact on the country's standard of living. As one economist phrased it, "While you are borrowing you do very well, but when you have to pay it back it starts to hurt."[14]

Economists believe that declining labor productivity is an important underlying weakness of America's economy. **Labor productivity** refers to the amount of output generated per worker. Productivity increases are important

PERSPECTIVE

Defining Poverty

The government first defined poverty and began measuring its extent in the early 1960s using a process that is remarkably simple and unscientific. Mollie Orshansky, an official in the Social Security Administration, calculated the cost of the minimum diet judged nutritionally acceptable by the Agriculture Department. Since studies of consumer spending showed that the average American family spent about a third of its income on food, Ms. Orshansky established the official poverty line by multiplying the cost of the minimum diet by three. She adjusted the figure to take into account differences in family size. Since the 1960s, Molly Orshansky's poverty line has remained unchanged except for annual adjustments to compensate for the effects of inflation.

The government's method of measuring poverty is controversial. One group of critics argue that the government overestimates poverty because it only counts cash when assessing family income, omitting in-kind benefits such as Medicaid and food stamps. One study estimates that the poverty rate would be only 10.5 percent were the government to include the value of non-cash benefits in family income. In contrast, another group of critics believe that Ms. Orshansky's system for measuring poverty has been left behind by changing times. According to government figures, today's consumers spend less than a fifth of family income on food, not a third, as did families in the early 1960s. Were the government to use a multiplier of five instead of three, critics point out that the proportion of Americans below the poverty line would rise to more than 24 percent.

The debate over measuring poverty is more than just theoretical. A high poverty rate increases public pressures for government to offer more problems to benefit low-income people, while a low poverty rate makes poverty seem less a problem. What's more, the government uses the poverty rate in a state or locality to determine eligibility for certain benefits.

Source: Spencer Rich, "Defining Poverty: A Science or an Art?" *Washington Post*, National Weekly Edition, 6–12 November 1989, p. 31.

because they are the primary source of rising standards of living. If labor productivity is flat or grows slowly, a nation's standard of living will stagnate. Since the mid-1970s, American labor productivity has grown at the relatively slow rate of only about 1 percent a year.[15] To a large extent, productivity increases depend on industrial modernization and technological advances which, in turn, depend upon investment. Much of the money that could go into business investment, however, has been diverted to finance the federal budget deficit.

A **budget deficit** refers to the amount by which budget expenditures exceed budget receipts. Federal budget deficits aren't a new phenomenon, but during the 1980s the red ink hit record-high levels, exceeding $200 billion in each of several years during the middle of the decade. The origin of the record-setting deficits lay in political decisions made in the early 1980s when President Ronald Reagan persuaded Congress to reduce federal taxes by hundreds of billions of dollars. Congress, however, did not enact (nor did the president request) spending cuts sufficient to offset the tax reductions.

Although some economists warn that the budget deficit could precipitate an economic crisis, other scholars believe that the real danger from the deficit lies in its effect on future economic growth. Because of the deficit, billions of dollars that could go into business investment go to finance the deficit instead. Consequently, business doesn't expand and doesn't modernize, or, if it does, the money to finance the expansion and/or modernization comes from foreigners (who have plenty of dollars to spend because of the American trade deficit). In the first instance, the American economy doesn't grow; in the second, most of the profits from that growth go to foreign investors. In either case, future generations of Americans are worse off economically than they would have been had there been no deficit. Economist Herbert Stein summarizes the deficit problem as follows: "For every $100 billion of deficit we run, we reduce national income by $15 billion a year forever."[16]

Is the United States in Decline?

The American economy is an economy in transition. In the years following World War II, the emergence of the United States as the world's foremost power was based on economic strength. Today, however, the nation's smokestack industries, such as steel and automobile manufacturing, have shrunk in importance. America's economy is becoming more oriented toward services (health care, fast food, and the like) and high-technology industries, such as computers and telecommunications.

This transition has not been painless. Many industrial jobs have been eliminated, displacing thousands of workers and harming the communities where they live. In some cases, the new jobs created by service and high-technology companies have not paid as well as the old manufacturing jobs that were lost. As a result, family incomes have shrunk, the nation's middle class has been squeezed, and the ranks of the poor have swollen.

In fact, some observers believe that the United States is a nation in decline. Historian Paul Kennedy analyzes the last five centuries of world history to identify a cycle of national growth and decline. Through a combination of innovation and investment, Kennedy says, a nation achieves a spurt of economic growth. Economic power enables the nation to expand its investments and interests abroad and become a world power. As the nation expands its international commitments, however, it must spend more and more of its resources on the military in order to protect its global interests. Eventually, this diversion of resources to the military detracts from the investment needed to maintain economic growth. As a result, the nation's economy begins to slip and it eventually falls behind its international competitors.

Kennedy believes that this description of a nation's rise and fall applies equally well to sixteenth-century Spain, nineteenth-century Britain, and twentieth-century America. After World War II, the United States was the world's leading nation, but, Kennedy argues, the costs of world leadership have been high. The United States has spent billions of dollars on defense, he says, leaving relatively little money for the investment needed to maintain a healthy rate of economic growth. Consequently, the American economy has begun to slide and the United States is in decline. The only real question for American policymakers, Kennedy says, is whether the United States will experience a gradual, smooth decline from its position of world leadership or whether the nation's fall will be sharp and abrupt.[17]

Although Kennedy may be correct in saying that America is in decline, his explanation of the cause of a decline seems unsupported. Kennedy says that great nations fall because they spend too much for the military, leaving too few resources for investment. The United States, however, devotes only about 7 percent of its GNP to defense. That is a smaller proportion than went for defense during the early 1960s, a time that Kennedy recognizes as a high point of American power. Kennedy's model for national decline seems to apply more closely to the Soviet Union, which devotes 18 percent of its GNP to military spending.[18]

At least when judged on a comparative basis, the United States' problem isn't excessive spending on defense, but excessive spending on short-term consumption of goods and services. Instead of saving money for the investment needed to finance economic growth and development, Americans have been borrowing money to purchase imported consumer goods; hence, the trade deficit. In the meantime, many of the dollars Americans do manage to save have gone to the national government to finance huge federal budget deficits.

Critics of American economic policy believe that the United States has been living beyond its means. In the early 1970s, you recall, the rate of American labor productivity growth fell off sharply, a condition that would soon lead to a halt in increases in the nation's standard of living. America could have responded to the situation by accepting slower growth or by forgoing some short-term pleasures in order to devote more resources to the economic

A Hispanic organization distributes food to needy families in Chicago.

modernization necessary for long-term productivity growth. Instead, the nation responded by borrowing to maintain the current standard of living.[19]

Not all observers believe that the United States is in decline. Indeed, some scholars make a strong argument that America hasn't slipped and isn't slipping. First, they believe that many of the statistics indicating economic weakness are misleading. Consider the data showing increasing disparities between rich and poor Americans. The number of families in upper-income categories has risen, they argue, because the number of two-income families has increased as more and more women have entered the work force. At the other end of the income scale, meanwhile, the number of low-income wage earners has grown because, as the baby-boom generation has come of age, the number of inexperienced, unskilled workers earning low wages has increased. Similarly, the nation's poverty rate has increased as the number of teenage mothers has risen and the percentage of single-parent families has grown.[20]

Second, those scholars who believe that America is not in decline point out that, by nearly every measure of national strength (population size, economic strength, military power, natural resources, technological advancement, political stability, and the like), the United States stands at, or near, the forefront of the world's nations. No other country enjoys such a distinction. Japan is an economic powerhouse, but spends little on defense, relying instead on American protection. The Soviet Union is a military giant, but its economy is a shambles. The United States is like a decathlon athlete: perhaps not the best on every measure of achievement, but superior overall. No other nation can claim that distinction. Moreover, America's defenders argue that the openness of United States society makes America less likely to suffer long-term decline than any other nation.[21]

And so the debate goes on. One group of observers reviews the nation's economic statistics and concludes that the United States is in decline. In contrast, another group, looking at the same data, argues that not only does the United States have the world's richest, most dynamic economy, but its prospects for the future are bright as well. It is too early to predict which group's view of the nation and its future is more likely to prove true. Indeed, a good case can be made that America's future may depend on international developments and technological advances that have not yet taken place and policy decisions yet to be made.

POLITICAL CULTURE

Political culture refers to the widely held, deeply rooted political values of a society. These values are important for the policymaking process because they define the terms of political debate and establish the range of acceptable policy options available to policymakers. Let's consider the origins of America's political culture, its content, its impact on the policymaking process, and its role in defining the contemporary policy debate between liberalism and conservatism.

Origins of America's Political Culture

Scholars identify a number of sources of America's political culture. One source is the nation's Puritan heritage. The **Puritans** were seventeenth-century English religious reformers. When their efforts to reform the Church of England failed, many of them emigrated to America, where they founded the Massachusetts Bay Colony. Their moralistic and idealistic values became an important part of America's political inheritance. The nation's Puritan heritage may explain, for example, the tendency of many Americans to view such matters as gambling and the use of alcohol from a moralistic perspective.

A second source of America's political culture is the absence of a feudal tradition. **Feudalism** was the system of political organization found in Europe from the ninth to about the fifteenth century that provided for a hierarchical class structure with lords, vassals, and serfs. Its legacy in much of Europe was a social structure characterized by rigid class distinctions. In contrast, America was settled by persons fleeing the oppression of the Old World. They created a political culture that cherished the values of political openness and equality. As a result, the United States lacks the rigid class structure of much of Europe and its political system is more open to participation and leadership by persons from a broad range of social groups.[22]

Finally, some scholars believe that the American environment has been important in shaping the nation's political culture, especially the American ideals of equality and individualism. For Americans, the concept of equality doesn't refer to mathematical equality in which everyone enjoys the same status, nor is it an equality of results in which all persons receive the same rewards for their labors. Instead, it is *equality of opportunity*. In America, the concept of equality includes a recognition of differences among individuals in ability and achievement. Americans believe that people succeed or fail on the basis of their own merit as individuals; hence the emphasis on **individualism**, which is the concept that places primary emphasis on the individual rather than the group or society as a whole.

Historian Frederick Jackson Turner believes that the frontier played a major role in shaping the American ideals of equality and individualism. The frontier was a harsh place, he says, where class status counted for little in the face of drought, disease, flood, Indian attack, and other hardships.[23] Another historian, David M. Potter, contends that America's material wealth allowed for social mobility. This was a land of great economic opportunity in which everyone, even the children of the poor, could succeed with hard work. For many Americans, then, the notion of equality of opportunity seemed an accurate description of the world in which they lived.[24]

The Content of America's Political Culture

Attitudes toward democracy and capitalism constitute the core of America's political culture. A democracy, you recall, is a system of government in which ultimate political authority is vested in the people. America's democratic values include the belief that all people possess equal worth, with equal rights and equal opportunities; that the nation's political leaders are accountable to the people; and that government should respect such individual rights as freedom of speech, press, assembly, and worship. In short, America's democratic values stress liberty and equality.

You also remember from our earlier discussion that capitalism is an economic system based on individual and corporate ownership of the means of production and a supply-demand market economy. America's political culture includes the following capitalist elements: belief in private ownership of property; acceptance of the pursuit of profit by entrepreneurs; and support for the right to unlimited gain through economic effort. Capitalist values include hard work, competition, and rewards based on achievement.[25]

Political Culture and Policymaking

Political culture is important for the policymaking process because it helps determine what problems make the policy agenda and sets the boundaries of permissible solutions available to policymakers for dealing with those problems. For example, a series of airplane accidents in the United States would lead to calls for tougher safety standards and closer inspections of airplanes. It would not lead, however, to serious demands that the government take over the airline industry, even though most of the world's airlines outside the United States are government owned and operated. Government ownership of airlines (or most major industries in general) is not a policy option within the permissible limits of America's political culture.

Political scientists believe that political culture provides an orientation, or a framework, through which people interpret and respond to political events and issues.[26] When a political event occurs, such as a terrorist bombing, the nation's political culture shapes the way Americans interpret and react to that event. Similarly, citizen response to political issues, such as the question of mandatory testing for illegal drug use, is influenced by political culture as well.

Liberalism and Conservatism

Although the values of democracy and capitalism set the boundaries for political debate in America, these two elements of the nation's political culture are too general to provide specific solutions to most policy problems. Moreover, tensions exist between America's democratic and capitalist values, and these tensions are the basis for a good many policy conflicts. While the goal of democracy is to maximize freedom, equality, and the public good, capitalism aims at maximizing private profit. Consequently, many contemporary policy problems are the focus of ongoing policy debates.

In American politics today, major policy controversies are often debated from the perspectives of liberalism and conservatism. **Liberalism** can be defined as the political view that seeks to change the political, economic, or social status quo to foster the development and well-being of the individual. Liberals believe that government can (and should) foster social progress by promoting social justice, political equality, and economic prosperity. In contrast, **conservatism** is the defense of the status quo against major changes in political, economic, or social institutions of society. Conservatives want to conserve the positive aspects of the present system.

Ironically, both liberals and conservatives criticize government. Liberals often argue that government doesn't do enough to promote equality by helping disadvantaged individuals and groups gain economic and political power. Moreover, when government does act, liberals say that it often favors the interests of the rich and powerful. Conservatives, meanwhile, think that society as it is rewards those who work hard and punishes those who do not, and, they say, that is how it should be. At any rate, conservatives argue, when government intervenes in the marketplace, it interferes with the efficient workings of the free enterprise system, lowering economic productivity. In the long run, they argue, that hurts everyone, including the poor.

Let's compare the positions of liberalism and conservatism on some of the major policy issues of our day.

Social-Welfare Policies

Liberals advocate government action to benefit disadvantaged groups in society, such as the elderly, the poor, and minorities. They generally favor such programs as Social Security, Medicare, housing assistance for the poor, federal aid to education, and affirmative-action programs for women and minorities.

In contrast, conservatives argue that government, especially the national government, is too inefficient to solve the nation's social problems. Conservatives believe that private initiative, private charities, and, when need be, state and local governments are better able to solve the country's social problems. As President Reagan once phrased it, "The best anti-poverty program is a job."

Business Regulation

Liberals believe in the use of government power to regulate business in the "public interest," as *they* define the term, of course. Consequently, liberals support environmental-protection laws to safeguard air and water quality, consumer-protection laws to protect the buying public, occupational safety and health standards to ensure good working conditions, and careful regulation of utilities to guarantee efficiency. Liberals are also more likely than conservatives to endorse trade restrictions to protect American companies and workers from foreign competition.

Conservatives, meanwhile, warn that government regulations usually involve undue interference with the free-market economy. They believe that regulation is often beset by red tape, inefficiency, and higher costs for consumers. In this policy area, at least, conservatives agree with the motto: The Government That Governs Least, Governs Best.

Social Policy

Some of the more controversial issues in American politics today are social issues, such as pornography, abortion, gay rights, school prayer, and women's rights. Liberals see these issues in terms of individual rights, while conservatives regard them as matters of traditional morality and family values. Liberals argue that adults should be free to decide for themselves what books to read or films to watch. Women should be allowed to pursue the career goals they choose and should be treated the same as men under the law. Women should not be forced to bear unwanted children; gays and lesbians should not suffer discrimination; and the government should not prescribe prayers to be recited in public schoolrooms.

In contrast, conservatives define social issues in terms of traditional family values. They see pornography, gay rights, abortion, some aspects of the feminist movement, and the Supreme Court's refusal to allow government-mandated spoken prayer in public schoolrooms as direct assaults on God, family, and country. As a result, conservatives tend to support the rigorous enforcement of pornography laws and the adoption of a constitutional amendment against abortion and another amendment permitting school prayer. At the same time, conservatives oppose the feminist movement and equal rights for homosexuals.

Foreign and Defense Policy

As with other issue areas, liberal/conservative disagreements over foreign and defense policies reflect differing images of the world. Conservatives see the Soviet Union as the chief threat to world peace and national security. They have little faith in the effectiveness of international organizations such as the United Nations and they are pessimistic about negotiating evenhanded arms-control agreements with the Soviets. They favor increasing U.S. defense spending and generally support foreign military aid to friendly governments or "freedom fighters" in the front lines against communism. Conservatives tend to be less supportive of foreign economic aid.

Liberals, meanwhile, regard poverty, illiteracy, disease, and political oppression from communist and noncommunist governments alike as the major threats to world peace and national security. They have more faith than do conservatives in the ability of international organizations to resolve disputes, and they are more optimistic about prospects for arms control. Liberals are less supportive of defense spending than are conservatives and are also less likely to favor foreign military aid, preferring economic assistance instead.

Qualifications

Although the terms liberal and conservative help define the contours of the policy debate in America, their usefulness is limited. First, the real-life differences between liberals and conservatives are often matters of degree and emphasis rather than dramatic contrast. Second, a number of policy issues, including honesty in government, cannot really be defined in liberal/conservative terms. Finally, few Americans are consistently liberal or conservative, with most of us holding conservative views on some issues, liberal opinions on others.

CONCLUSION: THE CONTEXT OF POLICYMAKING

Public policymaking takes place within the socioeconomic and cultural context of American society and the international environment. Politics, demographics, economics, and political culture are closely entwined, so much so that one cannot be understood apart from the others. Several points deserve special notice.

First, demographic changes can affect policymaking. In the introduction to this chapter, we discussed some of the policy effects of changes in birthrates—what might be called the politics of fertility. There's also a politics of aging. Today, more than 25 million Americans are age sixty-five and over, representing 11 percent of the population. In the future, the number and percentage of older Americans will increase, especially when the baby-boom generation reaches old age after the year 2000.[27] As a result, the policy agenda will increasingly reflect the interests and demands of the elderly. Health care and retirement-income security, for example, will claim a higher place on the policy agenda. Moreover, we can expect to see an increase in the size and influence of interest groups organized by and for older Americans.

A second point concerns the relationship between prosperity and policymaking. The United States has been the beneficiary of an abundance of natural and human resources. Because of the nation's wealth, public policy decisions in America have been less agonizing than they have been in poorer nations. The workplace could more easily be opened to greater participation by racial minorities and women because the economy was expanding. Because the economy produced more jobs, new workers could be added without taking jobs from older workers. Moreover, economic growth generated tax revenues that could finance federal social-welfare programs. Thus, part of the nation's economic surplus could be used to help the poor. Charity comes easier to a wealthy people whose income is growing than to a poor people whose income is shrinking.

Third, America's political culture helps set boundaries for the policy agenda and significantly affects policy formulation. The American definition of equality in terms of equality of opportunity rather than equality of results, for example, helps determine the acceptance of policy proposals designed to deal with poverty. Policy proposals that emphasize education and job training find greater acceptance than do proposals that call for redistributing income by taxing the well-to-do and giving cash to the poor.

Finally, the relationship between socioeconomic factors, political culture, and public policy is not a one-way street. As we have seen, public policymaking in America is shaped by the socioeconomic and cultural context in which it takes place. It is also true, however, that public policies affect the nation's economy, social structure, and political culture. Earlier in this chapter, for example, we presented data showing that the gap between rich and poor Americans has grown in recent years. To be sure, this will have its effects on the policy process. To at least some degree, however, the gap itself is the result of government policy. In the early 1980s, President Reagan and Congress enacted a major tax cut while eliminating a number of domestic spending programs. The tax cut benefited middle- and upper-income taxpayers more than people at the lower end of the economic ladder. The spending cuts, meanwhile, fell more heavily on programs aimed at helping the poor. The net im-

Since the 1970s, the areas of greatest population growth have been the suburbs.

pact of government policy, then, was to shift wealth from the lower to the upper end of the income ladder.[28]

In sum, policymaking in America takes place within the broad context of America and the world. The socioeconomic and cultural environment of American life affects the public policy process and vice versa. It's impossible to understand one without understanding the other.

KEY TERMS

authoritarianism

baby-boom generation

budget deficit

capitalism

conservatism

democracy

economics

feudalism

Frostbelt

gross national product (GNP)

individualism

inflation

labor productivity

liberalism

mixed economy

political culture

politics

poverty line

Puritans

recession

socialism

Sunbelt

totalitarianism

trade deficit

NOTES

1. *National Journal*, 8 March 1986.
2. Ann Cooper and Julie Kosterlitz, "Baby Boom Coming of Age," *National Journal*, 8 March 1986, pp. 546–55.
3. "U.S. Population to Shrink As Boomers Go Gray, Expert Says," *Houston Post*, 1 February 1989, p. A-13.
4. Ibid.
5. Raymond D. Gastil, *Freedom in the World: Political Rights and Civil Liberties 1984–1985* (Westport, CT: Greenwood Press, 1985), p. 53.
6. Ibid., pp. 132–35.
7. Lucian W. Pye, "Political Science and the Crisis of Authoritarianism," *American Political Science Review* 84 (March 1990), pp. 3–19.
8. Cited in Michael Harrington, "The Middle Class Is Under an Unfair Tax Assault," *Houston Chronicle*, 15 February 1988, sec. 2, p. 7.
9. *Time*, 10 October 1988, p. 29.
10. Spencer Rich, "And the Poor Keep Getting...," *Washington Post*, National Weekly Edition, 3–9 August 1989, p. 34.
11. "U.S. Economic Expansion Fails to Improve Poverty Rate in 1988," *Houston Chronicle*, 19 October 1989, p. 4A.
12. Andrew Mollison, "Two-Thirds of Poor Are Whites," *Houston Chronicle*, 4 September 1985, sec. 1, p. 1.

13. "U.S. Trade Deficit Up by 20.9 Percent," *Houston Chronicle*, 14 April 1989, p. 4A.
14. Walter Joelson, quoted in Hugh Hickery, "Experts: U.S. Trade Deficit to Nip Living Standard," *Houston Chronicle*, 13 March 1989, p. 2B.
15. John M. Berry, "The Legacy of Reaganomics," *Washington Post*, National Weekly Edition, 19–25 December 1988, p. 6.
16. Quoted in George Will, "Administration's Figures Wrong," *Houston Chronicle*, 17 March 1989, p. 8B.
17. Paul Kennedy, *The Rise and Fall of Great Nations: Economic Change and Military Conflict from 1500 to 2000* (New York: Random House, 1987).
18. Samuel P. Huntington, "The U.S.—Decline or Renewal?" *Foreign Affairs* 67 (Winter 1988/89): 76–96.
19. Jonathan Rauch, "Is the Deficit Really So Bad?" *Atlantic Monthly*, February 1989, pp. 36–42.
20. Fabian Linden, "Interpreting Income Data," *Public Opinion*, November/December 1988, pp. 19, 57–58.
21. Huntington.
22. Louis Hartz, *The Liberal Tradition in America* (New York: Harcourt, Brace & World, 1955).
23. Frederick Jackson Turner, *The Frontier in American History* (New York: Henry Holt & Co., 1920).
24. David M. Potter, *People of Plenty* (Chicago: University of Chicago Press, 1954).
25. Herbert McCloskey and John Zaller, *The American Ethos: Public Attitudes Toward Capitalism and Democracy* (Cambridge, MA: Harvard University Press, 1984), pp. 1–31.
26. Harry Eckstein, "A Culturalist Theory of Political Change," *American Political Science Review* 82 (September 1988): 789–804.
27. *National Journal*, 25 March 1989, p. 734.
28. Joel Havemann, "Sharing the Wealth: The Gap Between Rich and Poor Grows Wider," *National Journal*, 23 October 1983, pp. 1788–95.

SUGGESTED READINGS

Brown, Thad A. *Migration and Politics: The Impact of Population Mobility on American Voting Behavior.* Chapel Hill, NC: University of North Carolina Press, 1988.

Gastil, Raymond D. *Freedom in the World: Political Rights and Civil Liberties 1984–1985.* Westport, CT: Greenwood Press, 1985.

Huntington, Samuel P. *The Promise of Disharmony.* Cambridge, MA: Harvard University Press, 1981.

Kennedy, Paul. *The Rise and Fall of Great Nations: Economic Change and Military Conflict from 1500 to 2000.* New York: Random House, 1987.

Lindblom, Charles E. *Politics and Markets: The World's Political Economic Systems.* New York: Basic Books, 1977.

McCloskey, Herbert, and Zaller, John. *The American Ethos: Public Attitudes Toward Capitalism and Democracy.* Cambridge, MA: Harvard University Press, 1984.

Olson, Mancur. *The Rise and Decline of Nations.* New Haven, CT: Yale University Press, 1982.

2

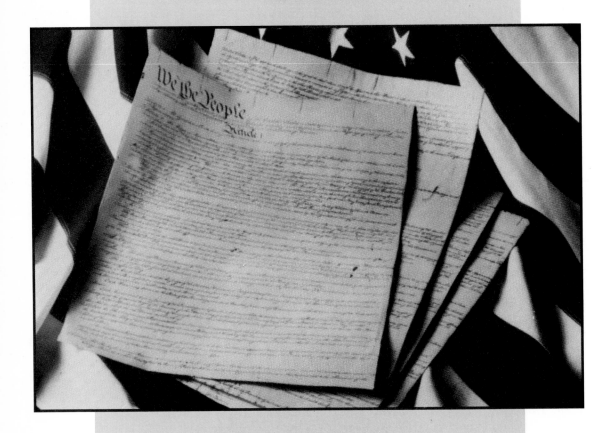

THE AMERICAN CONSTITUTION

LEARNING OBJECTIVES

1. To evaluate the adequacy of America's constitutional system for dealing with today's policy problems, considering separation of powers with checks and balances, and the modern phenomenon of divided party control of the executive and legislative branches.
2. To trace the historical background of the Constitution, describing the governments under which Americans lived before the ratification of the Constitution in 1789.
3. To identify the elements of American political thought that had the greatest impact on the writing of the Constitution.
4. To outline the major features of the Constitution.
5. To define the following constitutional principles and identify their significance for contemporary policymaking: popular sovereignty, representative democracy, rule of law, limited government, separation of powers with checks and balances, federalism, and bicameralism.
6. To discuss the concept of majestic vagueness as it applies to constitutional development.
7. To describe the processes of constitutional change.
8. To discuss and evaluate arguments for and against America's constitutional system.

The United States has become a nation of divided government, in which one political party holds the presidency while the other controls Congress. By 1993, when George Bush ends the four-year presidential term he began in 1989, Republicans will have occupied the White House for twenty of the last twenty-four years. Throughout the same period, however, Democrats will have controlled the House of Representatives continuously and held a majority of seats in the Senate in all but the first six years of the Reagan administration (1981–87). In 1989, for example, when George Bush began his presidency, Democrats outnumbered Republicans 260 to 175 in the House, 55 to 45 in the Senate.

The phenomenon of divided party control of the executive and legislative branches of government was once unusual. In the nineteenth century, the party occupying the White House enjoyed a majority in the Senate almost 90 percent of the time, and in the House more than two-thirds of the time.[1] Then, in the twentieth century, the same party controlled both the executive and legislative branches 79 percent of the time, from 1900 to 1968. Only since 1968 has divided party control of government become commonplace.

The authors of the American Constitution created a political system in which the branches of government would check and balance one another. If the president, Congress, or the judiciary attempted to increase power, the members of the other branches of government would oppose the action in order to defend their own authority. Thus, the Constitution's framers hoped to prevent any one political leader or group of leaders from becoming powerful enough to threaten the liberty of the people.

Some observers believe that today's system of divided party control of government is beneficial because it enhances checks and balances. The president and Congress will be especially watchful of one another because of party rivalries. What's more, they argue, since American national government is larger today than ever before, this additional check and balance is particularly important.

In contrast, other observers think that divided party control of the executive and legislative branches cripples the government's ability to deal with major national problems. Each side is more interested in blaming the other, they say, than in working out policy agreements. As a result, pressing policy problems, such as the federal budget deficit, illegal drug use, and environmental preservation, aren't resolved because the president and Congress cannot agree on workable solutions.

Are America's constitutional arrangements adequate for dealing with the policy problems of the 1990s? We consider the controversy as we study the American Constitution and its role in the policymaking process.

THE BACKGROUND OF THE CONSTITUTION

A **constitution** is the fundamental law by which a state or nation is organized and governed. It establishes the framework of government, assigns the powers and duties of governmental bodies, and defines the relationship between the people and their government. The United States Constitution, at two hundred years of age, is the oldest written national constitution still in effect in the world today.

Historical Setting

The Americans who wrote the Constitution of 1787 had lived through two rather difficult periods: the late colonial period under British rule and the time under the government created by the Articles of Confederation. To a considerable degree, the Constitution was their reaction to these two experiences.

The American colonists were initially satisfied with their political relationship with Great Britain. Preoccupied with matters at home, the British authorities allowed the colonists a good measure of self-government. Each colony had a governor, appointed by the king, and a legislative assembly whose members were locally elected. The colonial assemblies could levy taxes, appropriate money, approve appointments, and pass laws for the colony. Although the governor had the power to veto legislation, the assemblies exercised considerable leverage over the governor by virtue of their control of the budget. This **power of the purse** (the control of the finances of government) made the locally elected legislative assemblies the dominant bodies of colonial government.

After 1763, however, the British authorities chose to reorganize their colonial system. The French and Indian War (1756–63), which the British and Americans fought against the French and their Indian allies for control of North America, left London with a sizable war debt. The British also faced the problem of governing Canada and enforcing treaties with the Indians, which limited westward expansion by the colonists.

London officials decided that the American colonists would have to pay part of the cost of defending and administering the empire in North America. The British imposed new taxes, such as the Stamp Act of 1765, and attempted to crack down on smuggling. To accomplish these goals, London increased the number of officials in North America and permanently stationed troops in the colonies.

To the surprise of the British, the Americans were outraged. Over the years, the colonists had grown accustomed to a large measure of self-government, and they were unwilling to surrender that privilege. They regarded the new policies as a violation of local traditions and an abridgment of their rights as British subjects. Before 1763, the only taxes the Americans paid to London were duties on trade, and the colonists interpreted them as measures to regulate commerce. Now, however, London attempted to impose levies that were clearly taxes (such as the Stamp Act). The Americans argued that as English citizens they could only be taxed by their own elected representatives and not by the British Parliament. No taxation without representation, they said. To the British, this argument made no sense. In their view, every member of Parliament represented every British citizen; the fact that no Americans sat in Parliament was irrelevant. The disputes over taxation (and other issues) worsened, leading eventually to revolution and American independence.

During the Revolutionary War, the American colonies became the United States, loosely allied under the leadership of the Continental Congress, which was a **unicameral** (one-house) legislature in which each state had a single vote. Although the Continental Congress had no official governing authority, it declared America's independence, raised an army, appointed George Washington its commander in chief, coined money, and negotiated with foreign nations. The Continental Congress also drafted a plan for national union. This plan, known as the Articles of Confederation, went into effect in 1781, upon approval by the thirteen states.

The Americans who wrote the Articles of Confederation were determined to create a national government whose powers would be strictly limited. They had recently experienced a period of governance by a central government they considered too strong, the British, and did not want to repeat the experience. The government they established under the Articles was a league of friendship, a "perpetual union" of states, with a unicameral congress. Although state legislatures could send as many as seven delegates to the Congress, each state possessed a single vote, and nine states (out of thirteen) had to approve decisions. The Articles provided for no independent national executive or national judiciary.

Since the Confederation was weak, the states were the primary units of government in the new nation. Each of the thirteen states had its own state constitution that established a framework for state government. These state constitutions typically provided for a **bicameral** (two-house) legislature, a governor, and a judicial system. Because Americans feared executive power as a source of tyranny, they adopted state constitutions that limited the powers of state governors, making legislatures the dominant branch of state government.[2]

Experience proved the Confederation too weak to deal effectively with the new nation's problems. It did not possess the power to collect taxes from individuals, having to rely instead upon contributions from the states. When states failed to pay—as many did—the national government was left without financial support. The government under the Articles also lacked the power to regulate commerce, prohibit states from printing worthless currency, or even enforce the provisions of the peace treaty with Great Britain. To make matters worse, amending the Articles to correct the problems required unanimous approval of the thirteen states and—thanks to stubborn Rhode Island—unanimity could not be achieved. Before long, the United States treasury was empty, the economy was slumping, the nation's foreign affairs were in disarray, and most Americans had lost respect for their government.

The two houses of America's bicameral Congress meet in a joint session.

American Political Thought

Historians refer to the epoch in which the founders lived as the Enlightenment. It was the Age of Reason, a time of abiding faith in the capacity of people to solve their problems in a rational manner. The philosophers of the Enlightenment—Montesquieu, David Hume, Voltaire, and others—believed that everything in nature from the solar system to human society operated according to natural laws. Just as there was a law of gravity, there was a natural law of human behavior that could be identified through reason. According to the natural-law philosophers, all that was necessary to achieve human perfection was for mankind to discover these natural laws and then follow them.

The Americans who wrote the Constitution of 1787 were learned individuals who had studied the important political writings of their day. They engaged in great debates about the nature of government and, in keeping with the perspective of the Enlightenment, they sought the scientific principles that would guide mankind's political and social behavior.

The writings of Englishman John Locke (1632–1704) were particularly important for Americans contemplating revolution. In his *Second Treatise on Government* (1689), Locke assumed that in a natural state all people are born free and equal and that they possess certain rights. These "natural rights," wrote Locke, were life, liberty, and property. For this reason, Locke said, people join together to form governments. The power of government, then, stems from the consent of the governed, who endow the government with responsibility for protecting their lives, liberty, and possessions. Should government fail in this task, Locke continued, it is the right of the people to revolt and institute a new government.

Americans drew three important concepts from Locke's thought. First, Locke's theory of revolution offered the perfect theoretical rationale for the American Revolution. Read the Declaration of Independence reprinted in the appendix of this text to see how closely the founders of the nation followed Locke's theory. Second, Locke (and other social contract theorists such as Thomas Hobbes and Jean-Jacques Rousseau) provided a basis for positive government. **Social contract theory** is the philosophy that government is created through an informal contract, or compact, among the people and a formal contract between the people and the government (a constitution). According to Locke, the role of government is positive—to protect life, liberty, and property from the dangers inherent in a state of nature. Third, Locke's concept of natural rights offered a theoretical foundation for limiting governmental power over the individual. The **doctrine of natural rights** is the belief that individual rights transcend the power of government. People create government to protect their rights, not to abridge them.

Although the nation's founders freely cited the writings of European philosophers such as Locke, they were not passive recipients of European wisdom, simply applying the theories of European thinkers to the United States. Instead, they created a nation and wrote a Constitution based on American

events, experiences, and ideas, citing European writings selectively to reinforce what they already believed. Moreover, the Americans weren't afraid to
disregard the advice of the political theorists when it did not fit their image of
American political reality.[3]

The most important element of American political thought was the
changing conception of the nature of politics and government. At the time of
the Revolution, American political theorists believed that politics was a never-
ending struggle between the people and the government. In their view, the
people were virtuous, with a single, undifferentiated interest. The government, personified by the king, was corrupt and oppressive. After declaring
their independence, the Americans knew they needed a national government
(the alternative was anarchy), but they didn't want a strong one. The Articles
of Confederation fit the bill nicely.

After a few years of independence, however, many Americans recognized
that they had been wrong about the nature of the people and the role of government. Instead of seeing society as an undifferentiated homogeneous mass,
they saw that it is composed of a variety of interests or factions who oppose
one another on a number of policy issues. What's more, practical political experience in the states demonstrated that the people aren't so virtuous after all.
When one faction gained control of the government of a particular state
or locality, it would often use its power to enforce its will over opposing
interests.

By 1787, Americans had decided that a strong national government could
play a positive role in society. First, the national government could reconcile
the divergent concerns of interest groups to produce policies designed to
achieve the public good. A large nation, such as the United States, includes a
wide range of interest groups competing for power. Although a particular
group or faction might be strong enough in one state or local area to control
policymaking there, no single group would be able to dominate nationwide.
Consequently, a strong national government would provide a forum in which
groups would be able to reconcile their differences. The result, the American
political theorists believed, would be policies that would be acceptable to a
broader range of interests.

Second, a strong national government could protect individual liberty
and property from the power of oppressive majorities. At the state or local
level, a dominant faction could adopt policies designed to advance its own religious or economic interests at the expense of other groups. At the national
level, however, no one group or faction would be powerful enough to enforce
its will on the entire nation. Since every group held minority status in one
state or another, it would be in each group's interest to protect minorities
against the power of oppressive local majorities.[4]

For example, the constitutional provision guaranteeing separation of
church and state arose from the American circumstance of a multiplicity of religious sects, each fearing domination by another. Although many of the early
American religious groups would have liked nothing better than to establish

their faith as the official state religion, they lacked the power to do so. Consequently, they preferred an official governmental policy of religious freedom to risking the possibility that another religious group would gain official recognition.[5]

PROFILE OF THE CONSTITUTION

The United States Constitution has its roots in American political experience and American political thought. Turn to the appendix in the back of this text and examine the copy of the Constitution reprinted there as we review its major features.

In Articles I, II, and III, the Constitution outlines the structures of government; names the major public officials; and defines their roles, powers, and responsibilities. Article I establishes a bicameral Congress, with a House of Representatives and a Senate. It specifies the qualifications, methods of selection, powers, and responsibilities of members of Congress and discusses how bills become law. Article I, Section 8 lists the powers of Congress, while Sections 9 and 10 restrict the powers of Congress and the states, respectively.

Article II focuses on the presidency. It describes the method of presidential selection, the requirements of the office, presidential compensation, and the oath of office. In Sections 2 and 3, the Constitution lists powers of the presidency, including that of commander in chief of the armed forces and the power to negotiate treaties and make appointments. The final section of the article deals with impeachment and removal.

In Article III, the Constitution vests judicial power in a Supreme Court and whatever other courts Congress may establish. It lists the types of cases the Supreme Court may hear and discusses treason.

Article IV examines the relationship of the states with one another and with the national government. Section 1 contains the **full faith and credit clause**, which is a constitutional provision requiring that states recognize the official acts of other states. Wills, contracts, deeds, marriages, divorces, and other legal actions taken in one state must be recognized as legitimate by other states. Section 2 deals with privileges and immunities and extradition. The **privileges and immunities clause** is a constitutional measure requiring that the citizens of one state not be discriminated against when traveling in another state. This provision requires that visitors to a state be accorded the same legal protections, travel rights, and property rights as a state's own citizens. The courts have held, however, that states may deny out-of-state residents certain privileges, such as voting and lower tuition at state colleges and universities. **Extradition**, meanwhile, is the return from one state (or nation) to another of a person accused of a crime. Sections 3 and 4 of Article IV discuss the creation of new states, the governance of territories, and the responsibility of the national government to guarantee each state a "Republican Form of Government" and to protect states from invasion.

Howard Chandler Christy's famous painting of the signing of the Constitution in Philadelphia on September 17, 1787.

Articles V, VI, and VII cover a number of miscellaneous subjects. Article V details procedures for amending (or changing) the Constitution. In Article VI, the Constitution states that the new government would assume the debts incurred under the Articles of Confederation and declares that the Constitution is the "supreme Law of the Land." Article VI also prohibits religious tests for officeholders. (A **religious test** is a legal requirement that an individual express belief in a particular religious faith or in a Supreme Being as a requirement for holding public office.) Finally, Article VII specifies the method of ratification for the new Constitution.

Since its ratification in 1789, the Constitution has been amended twenty-six times. (A **constitutional amendment** is a formal, written change or addition to the nation's governing document.) The first ten amendments, known as the Bill of Rights, were added in 1791. Among other rights, these amendments guarantee freedom of religion, speech, press, and assembly. They protect against unreasonable searches and seizures, cruel and unusual punishments, and excessive fines. They guarantee those accused of crimes the right to confront witnesses testifying against them, to obtain counsel for their defense, and to be tried by a jury of their peers.

The Eleventh and Twelfth amendments correct errors in the original document. The Eleventh Amendment prohibits federal lawsuits against states by citizens of other states or other nations. The Twelfth Amendment, meanwhile, revises the operation of the electoral college.

The Thirteenth through Fifteenth amendments record constitutional changes brought about by the Civil War and its aftermath. The Thirteenth Amendment outlaws slavery, while the Fourteenth Amendment grants citizenship to former slaves and guarantees "due process of law" and "equal protection of the laws" to all persons under state law. The Fourteenth Amendment also denies ex-Confederates the right to hold federal office and repudiates the Confederate war debt. The Fifteenth Amendment guarantees African-Americans the right to vote.

Amendments Sixteen through Twenty-six deal with a variety of matters. The Sixteenth Amendment gives Congress the power to assess an income tax, while the Seventeenth Amendment requires the direct election of senators. The Eighteenth Amendment enacts Prohibition; the Twenty-first Amendment repeals the Eighteenth. In the meantime, women won the right to vote with the Nineteenth Amendment, and the Twentieth Amendment changes the timetable for beginning new presidential and congressional terms as well as elaborates on presidential succession. The Twenty-second Amendment limits a president to two terms, while the Twenty-third amendment gives the District of Columbia three electoral votes. The Twenty-fourth Amendment prohibits poll taxes in federal elections. The Twenty-fifth elaborates further on presidential succession and disability. Finally, eighteen-year-olds won the right to vote with the Twenty-sixth Amendment.

CONSTITUTIONAL PRINCIPLES

To understand the American Constitution, we must study the principles it embodies and their application and interpretation. Let's look in detail at some of the document's key features.

Popular Sovereignty and Representative Democracy

To survive and govern effectively, a government must enjoy a measure of political legitimacy in the eyes of its citizens. **Political legitimacy** is the popular acceptance of a government and its officials as rightful authorities in the exercise of power. Citizens who believe that their nation's government is legitimate will be inclined to obey its laws and regulations, pay taxes, participate in election processes, and serve willingly in the nation's armed forces. In contrast, if people think that a government is illegitimate, they will tend to break laws, evade taxes, ignore elections, and avoid military service. Moreover, citizens who believe that their government lacks legitimacy may participate in political demonstrations against the regime and even take up arms to overthrow it.

In America, political legitimacy is based on the principle of **popular sovereignty**, that is, the concept that ultimate political power rests with the people. Do you remember the following famous words from the Declaration of Independence?

> We hold these truths to be self-evident, that all men are created equal, that they are endowed by their Creator with certain unalienable Rights, that among these are life, liberty and the pursuit of happiness. That to secure these rights, governments are instituted among men, *deriving their just powers from the consent of the governed* [italics added].

As you see, the founders believed that government was legitimate insofar as it enjoyed the support of the people.

Nonetheless, the authors of the Constitution were skeptical about the judgment of the common people. Few of the framers favored **direct democracy**, which is a political system in which citizens vote directly on matters of public concern. The framers feared that direct democracy combined with majority rule would produce policies reflecting hasty, emotional decisions rather than well-considered judgments. Moreover, the Constitution's authors worried that under direct democracy a majority of the people would enact policies which would silence, disadvantage, or harm the minority point of view, thus producing a tyranny of the majority. (A **tyranny of the majority** is the abuse of the minority by the majority.) The framers of the Constitution believed that elected representatives were needed to act as a buffer between the people and governmental policies. Instead of a direct democracy, then, the Constitution created a **representative democracy** (or a **republic**), that is, a political system in which citizens elect representatives to make public policy decisions on their behalf.

Rule of Law

The **rule of law** is a political doctrine that holds that the discretion of public officials in dealing with individuals is limited by the law. As the maxim states, we have a government of laws, not of people. The very existence of a written constitution implies the rule of law, but certain constitutional provisions deserve special notice. In Article I, Section 9, the Constitution guarantees the privilege of the writ of habeas corpus except in time of war or civil war. A **writ of habeas corpus** is a court order requiring government authorities either to release a person held in custody or to demonstrate that the person is held in accordance with law. Habeas corpus, then, ensures that the police or military may not simply arrest individuals and hold them without filing charges against them or trying them in a court of law.

Article I, Section 9 also prohibits the passage of bills of attainder and ex post facto laws. A **bill of attainder** is a law declaring a person or group of persons guilty of a crime and providing for punishment without benefit of judicial proceeding. An **ex post facto law** is a retroactive criminal statute which operates to the disadvantage of accused persons. It makes a crime out of an act that was not illegal when it was committed.

In both the Fifth and Fourteenth amendments, the Constitution provides that neither Congress (the Fifth Amendment) nor states (the Fourteenth

Amendment) may deprive any person of "life, liberty, or property, without due process of law." **Due process of law** is a constitutional provision holding that government should follow fair and regular procedures in actions that might lead to an individual's suffering loss of life, liberty, or property. Due process of law generally protects individuals from the arbitrary actions of public officials. Before individuals may be imprisoned, fined, or executed, they must be given their day in court in accordance with law. Among other rights, the Constitution guarantees accused persons the right to a speedy, public trial by an impartial jury, the right to confront witnesses, and the right to legal counsel.

Limited Government

The framers intended that the powers of the government they created be limited. This concept is embodied in the rule of law and reflected in the constitutional principles of separation of powers with checks and balances, federalism, and bicameralism. Perhaps the most important constitutional limitation on the power of government is the Bill of Rights. (A **bill of rights** is a constitutional document guaranteeing individual rights and liberties.)

The Bill of Rights was not part of the original Constitution. A majority of delegates at the Constitutional Convention of 1787 believed that the powers of the new national government were so limited that it would not threaten individual freedom. Moreover, they worried that if they attempted to list individual rights they might leave some out. When the absence of a bill of rights became an issue during the debate over ratification of the Constitution, however, the Constitution's supporters agreed to endorse the addition of a series of amendments to serve as a bill of rights once the new constitution took effect. By December 1791, ten amendments had been adopted and ratified by the required number of states. These amendments came to be known as the Bill of Rights.

The authors of the American Constitution intended that the Bill of Rights apply only to the national government. As the First Amendment states, "Congress shall make no law...." It does not mention state action. Then, at the close of the Civil War, Congress proposed the Fourteenth Amendment in order to place the civil rights of African-Americans on firm footing. It forbade states to take life, liberty, or property without "due process of law," or to deny anyone "equal protection of the laws." States were also prohibited from making laws abridging the "privileges or immunities" of citizens.

The exact intent of this phrasing is unclear. Historians tell us that some of the amendment's authors apparently believed that it provided protection for basic rights in general, while others thought it included all or some of the rights guaranteed in the Bill of Rights. Interpretation has fallen on the shoulders of the Supreme Court. In the twentieth century, the Court has dealt with the issue through a process known as the **selective incorporation of the Bill of Rights**. This is the process through which the United States Supreme

Citizens of Illinois "ratify" a huge copy of the American Constitution as part of the state's celebration of the document's bicentennial in 1987.

Court has interpreted the due process clause of the Fourteenth Amendment of the United States Constitution to apply most of the provisions of the national Bill of Rights to the states. The Supreme Court has never ruled that the Bill of Rights as a whole applies to the states, but it has selectively, one at a time, held that virtually all its key provisions apply to the states through the due process clause of the Fourteenth Amendment.

Separation of Powers with Checks and Balances

The framers of the United States Constitution adopted separation of powers with checks and balances as a means for controlling government. Although the roots of these concepts went back a century, their modern development was the work of the eighteenth-century French political philosopher Baron de Montesquieu. Montesquieu identified three kinds of political power: the power to make laws (**legislative power**), the power to enforce laws (**executive power**), and the power to interpret laws (**judicial power**). If liberty is to be preserved, he said, these three powers should not all be held by one person or one group of persons. Instead, Montesquieu advocated a **separation of powers**, that is, the division of political power among executive, legislative, and judicial branches of government. He called for a system of checks and balances to prevent any one of the three branches from becoming too strong. **Checks and balances** refers to the overlapping of the powers of the branches of government so that public officials limit the authority of one another.

James Madison was the principal architect of America's system of separation of powers with checks and balances. In fact, scholars sometimes refer to the nation's constitutional apparatus as the Madisonian system. James Madison, Alexander Hamilton, and John Jay wrote a series of essays known as the *Federalist Papers* to argue for the new constitution's ratification. In *The Federalist*, no. 51, Madison identifies two threats to liberty: (1) factions (or special interests) who seek their own good at the expense of the common good, and (2) the excessive concentration of political power in the hands of government officials. Madison's remedy for these dangers was the creation of a strong national government with separation of powers and checks and balances.

First, Madison believed that the nation needed a strong national government to balance the power of local interests. In this regard, Madison noted the advantage of a large nation with multiple diverse interests. At the local or state level, he said, one interest group might be powerful enough to dominate. Over the breadth of the entire nation, however, the narrow perspective of that group would be checked by the interests of other groups entrenched in other areas. A strong national government would provide an arena in which narrow local interests would check one another. National policies, therefore, would reflect compromise among a range of interests.

Second, Madison echoed Montesquieu by advocating separation of powers with checks and balances in order to prevent tyranny. As Madison put it, the aim was "to divide and arrange the several offices [of government] in such a manner as that each may be a check on the other...."[6] In this fashion, the selfish, private interests of officeholders would counterbalance each other to the public good. To use Madison's words, "Ambition must be made to counteract ambition."[7]

The American Constitution distributes political power among legislative, executive, and judicial branches and provides for a series of checks and balances among the branches. Although the president appoints members of the Supreme Court, for example, the Senate must confirm those appointments. Congress passes bills, but the president may veto them. Congress in turn can override the veto by a two-thirds vote of each house. Although Congress alone has the authority to declare war, the president is commander in chief.

The framers designed this elaborate network of check and countercheck to prevent any one official or small group of officials from becoming too powerful, but it also guarantees a certain amount of tension in the political system. The authors of the Constitution refused to draw clear lines of demarcation among the powers of the three branches of government. In fact, the phrase *separation of powers* is misleading. What really exists is a system in which separate institutions *share* power.[8] Friction is inevitable.

Federalism

The Americans who gathered in Philadelphia in 1787 for the constitutional convention had lived under both a unitary system and a confederation. The British North American colonies were part of a **unitary government**, which is a governmental system in which political authority is concentrated in a single national government. The local colonial governments were created by Parliament and could constitutionally exercise only those powers specifically granted them by the central authorities. The defenders of unitary government argue that it provides for consistent policy administration throughout a country and allows more efficient handling of nationwide problems. In contrast, the critics of unitary government say that it fails to permit sufficient local variation to accommodate differing local circumstances. As we know, American dissatisfaction with the policies of Britain's centralized administration led to the Revolution.

The Articles of Confederation established a confederal form of government. A **confederation** is a league of nearly independent states, somewhat like the United Nations today. Under the confederal government, individual Americans were citizens of their respective states but not of the national government. As a result, the government under the Articles lacked the authority to deal directly with individuals (to tax them, for example); it could deal only with the governments of the thirteen states. The advantage of a confederation is that it allows states to cooperate without surrendering any of their basic powers. The disadvantage, however, is that it provides for a weak central government. That, of course, proved the undoing of the confederation government.

The framers of the Constitution set out to establish a government that would be capable of effective administration but would not undermine the American tradition of local control. Their solution was to create a federation. A **federation** (or **federal system**) is a political system that divides power between a central government—with authority over the whole nation—and a series of state governments.

A federation is a compromise between unitary and confederal government. In a unitary system, the national government is sovereign. (**Sovereignty** is the authority of a state to exercise its legitimate powers within its boundaries, free from external interference.) The powers of state and local governments (if they exist) are granted to them by the national government. In a confederation, meanwhile, the states are sovereign. The national government's authority flows from the states. In a federal system, however, both the national (or federal) government and the state governments are sovereign. They derive their authority not from one another but from the Constitution. Both levels of government act directly upon the people through their officials and laws; both are supreme within their proper sphere of authority; and both must consent to constitutional change.

A federation offered Americans two distinct advantages. First, it provided a means of political representation that could accommodate the diversity of American society. Individual Americans would be citizens of their states and the nation as well, and would participate in the selection of representatives to both governments. As Madison saw it, the federal system would permit local interests to shape local policy and provide national political institutions in which local interests from different regions would check one another, permitting the national interest to prevail. Second, federalism was a mechanism for protecting individual freedom from governmental interference. Just as the framers created separation of powers with checks and balances to ensure against the concentration of power within the national government, they designed federalism to provide a check and balance on the power of both state and nation.

Nonetheless, a federal system presents certain disadvantages. Local variations confuse citizens and hinder business. Traveling Americans face different traffic laws in each state. People who move from one state to another must usually adapt to different laws regarding marriages, divorces, wills, occupational licensing, and the like. Businesses must adjust to variations in tax laws and regulations. California, for example, imposes tougher automobile emissions standards than the national government or other states, forcing manufacturers to specially equip cars to be sold in that state. Federalism also sets the stage for conflict. American history is filled with examples of disputes between states and the national government. Issues such as the 55-mph speed limit and the twenty-one-year-old minimum drinking age are contemporary examples of conflicts between states and the national government.

Bicameralism

The authors of the Constitution expected the legislative branch to be the dominant institution of American national government (as it was then the dominant branch of state governments). To prevent the national legislature from becoming too powerful, the framers divided Congress into two houses with different sizes, terms of office, responsibilities, and constituencies. The precise organization of America's bicameral (two-house) Congress was the product of a compromise (known as the Connecticut Compromise) between large-state and small-state forces at the convention. Members of the House of Representatives would be chosen by direct popular election to serve two-year terms, with the number of representatives from each state based on population. In the Senate, meanwhile, each state would be represented by two senators chosen by the state legislature to serve six-year terms. Subsequently, the Seventeenth Amendment provided for direct popular election of senators.

The framers expected that a radical, aggressive, elected House would be constrained by a conservative, appointed Senate. With a two-year term, members of the House would be closer to the people, the framers thought, but they would also be more likely to act hastily in accordance with short-term popular sentiment. In contrast, senators, chosen by state legislatures and serving longer terms, would be insulated from popular pressures, thus enabling them to act more cautiously and to put the national interest ahead of short-term political gain.[9]

THE CONSTITUTION TODAY: A LIVING DOCUMENT

The United States Constitution has not just survived for two hundred years but has grown and matured with the nation, serving still as the fundamental framework for policymaking. When the original document was written in 1787, the United States was a nation of farms and small towns. The population was only about four million, and many people—slaves, women, and individuals without property—were denied full rights of participation in the policymaking process. Today, the country is dramatically changed, but the Constitution, with only twenty-six formal amendments, endures as the centerpiece of policymaking in America.

Majestic Vagueness

The genius of the United States Constitution lies in a quality that can be labeled "majestic vagueness." At first, this seems a contradiction in terms. *Majestic* is a lofty adjective, but we seldom consider vagueness a virtue. What is the explanation?

The Constitution is a brief, general document that is frequently non-specific. The Eighth Amendment, for example, prohibits "cruel and unusual punishments." But what does that phrase mean? We presume it forbids staking a criminal to an anthill, but does it outlaw public flogging and locking wrongdoers in the stocks? These last two punishments were used in colonial times. How about the death penalty? It is certainly cruel. And it is somewhat unusual in the United States today.

We can find other examples of vague terms and phrases in the Constitution. Article I, Section 8 gives Congress the power to regulate "commerce." What is commerce? Article II, Section 4 says the president may be impeached and removed from office for "treason, bribery, or other high crimes and misdemeanors." How are these defined? The Fourth Amendment prohibits "unreasonable searches and seizures," but what is unreasonable?

The Constitution is often vague, but the founders intended it to be so. They set down certain basic, fundamental principles, but left out the details in order to allow succeeding generations to supply specifics in light of their own experiences. The basic idea behind "cruel and unusual punishments," for example, is that government may not go too far in punishing criminals. The precise definition of "too far" depends on the times. Punishments acceptable in the 1790s might not be considered appropriate in the 1990s. The prohibition against "unreasonable searches and seizures" places limits on the police. Had the authors of the Constitution decided to spell out everything in detail, they would have produced a document far longer and less satisfactory than the one we have. Eventually, the nation would have outgrown it and either cast it aside or been forced to amend it repeatedly.

Constitutional Change

Because the Constitution is vague—majestically vague—it has grown and matured with the country. It has been able to change as the nation has changed, and not just through the process of amendment.

Change Through Amendment

One means by which the Constitution has changed has been through formal amendment. A major flaw in the Articles of Confederation, you recall, was that the Articles could be amended only by unanimous vote. As a result, correcting weaknesses in the document proved impossible because of the obstinacy of one or only a few states. In 1787, then, the Constitution's framers were careful to include a reasonable method of amendment—difficult enough to preclude hasty, ill-conceived changes, yet not impossible.

They provided two methods for proposing constitutional amendments and two methods for their ratification (see Figure 2.1). An amendment can be

FIGURE 2.1
Amending the Constitution

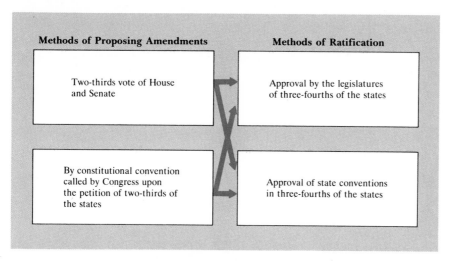

proposed by either a two-thirds vote of each house of Congress or a constitutional convention called by Congress upon application of two-thirds of the
states. The former method of proposal has been used many times: all twenty-
six amendments that have been added to the Constitution were proposed by
Congress.

Although the convention procedure has never been used, conservative
taxpayer groups in recent years made a concerted effort to force a convention
to consider an amendment to require a balanced federal budget. By the mid-
1980s, thirty-two of the required thirty-four states had submitted petitions to
Congress calling for a convention. Since the procedure has never been used,
however, no one knows for sure just how the process would work. Would
Congress *have* to call a convention if the required number of states submitted
petitions? Would the convention be limited to drafting an amendment to balance the budget, or could it set about to rewrite the entire document? These
are questions that cannot be answered, and, largely because of them, many
constitutional scholars are apprehensive about the possibility of a new
convention.

In practice, Congress generally responds to a convention movement by
addressing the issue it raises. In 1986, for example, Congress adopted the
Gramm-Rudman Deficit Control Act to establish a timetable for balancing the
federal budget. Subsequently, the movement to call a constitutional convention stalled.

After an amendment is proposed, either by Congress or by convention, it
must be ratified. Ratification can be accomplished either by vote of the leg-

islatures of three-fourths of the states or by approval of conventions in three-fourths of the states. The former method has been used successfully twenty-five times, the latter only once (to ratify the Twenty-first Amendment, repealing Prohibition).

The road to constitutional amendment may be difficult, but a number of groups believe their cause is worth the effort. In the 1970s and early 1980s, the Equal Rights Amendment (ERA), guaranteeing equality before the law regardless of sex, passed Congress and came within three states of ratification. Congress set, then extended, a time limit for ratification. The revised time limit finally expired in 1982, but women's-rights groups hope to start the process over again in Congress. In 1978, Congress also passed an amendment to grant the District of Columbia voting representation in the House and Senate. Like the ERA, however, the D.C. amendment fell short of ratification.

In 1982, the ERA fell three states short of becoming the Twenty-seventh Amendment to the Constitution.

In recent years, Congress has considered a number of other amendment proposals. Antiabortion groups want an amendment to outlaw abortion. Other groups push for an amendment to permit oral prayers in public schools. In 1990 Congress rejected a proposed constitutional amendment to permit the federal government and the states to outlaw desecration of the American flag. Meanwhile, the effort to amend the Constitution to require a balanced budget continues.

Change Through Custom and Usage

A second means through which the Constitution has changed has been through custom and usage. The role of the presidency, for example, is far broader today than it was in George Washington's time, but not because of formal constitutional amendments. For the most part, the powers of the presidency have grown through the actions of incumbent presidents, especially during wartime. The role of the bureaucracy in supplying the specific details of laws has developed because of the general delegation of that power by Congress. Meanwhile, such important aspects of American government as political parties, the committee system in Congress, and the cabinet have developed even though the Constitution is silent about them.

Change Through Judicial Interpretation

A final means of constitutional change is judicial interpretation. In fact, it may be no exaggeration to say that what counts most in constitutional law is what the courts say, particularly the Supreme Court. As former Chief Justice Charles Evans Hughes once said, "The Constitution is what the judges say it is."[10] Many phrases important to constitutional law aren't even in the Constitution, including "war power," "clear and present danger," "separation of church and state," "right of privacy," and "police power." These famous words appear not in the Constitution but in judicial opinions.

Judicial interpretation of the Constitution is inevitable because of the document's general character. As we have seen, many of the phrases of the Constitution are purposely ambiguous, requiring continuous reinterpretation and adaptation. Indeed, one constitutional scholar says that we have an unwritten constitution, whose history is the history of judicial interpretation.[11]

The power of courts to evaluate the actions of other branches and units of government to determine whether they are consistent with the Constitution and, if they are not, to declare them null and void is known as **judicial review**. Although the Constitution is silent about the power of judicial review, many historians believe that the founders expected the courts to exercise the authority. Ironically, the Supreme Court assumed the power of judicial review through constitutional interpretation, first holding an act of Congress unconstitutional in 1803 in the case of *Marbury* v. *Madison*.[12] (See the Perspective for a discussion of the case.)

PERSPECTIVE

Marbury v. *Madison*

Today, scholars recognize *Marbury* v. *Madison* as the first case in which the Supreme Court exercised the power of judicial review by holding an act of Congress unconstitutional. In its own day, however, the case was better known for its political significance.

The case had its roots in the election of 1800, when President John Adams was defeated for reelection and his party, the Federalists, lost its majority in Congress. In the period between the election and the inauguration of the new president, Thomas Jefferson, Adams proceeded to nominate, and the Senate to confirm, the appointments of a number of loyal Federalists to the federal courts.

One of these judicial appointments went to William Marbury, who was named a justice of the peace for the District of Columbia. President Adams signed and sealed Marbury's official commission on the day before he was to leave office. Unfortunately for Marbury, however, the secretary of state failed to deliver the commission. Then, when President Jefferson took office, he ordered his secretary of state, James Madison, not to deliver the commission. Marbury subsequently sued, asking the Supreme Court to issue a writ of mandamus against Madison ordering him to deliver the commission. (A **writ of mandamus** is a court order directing a public official to perform a specific act or duty.)

The case presented the Supreme Court with a dilemma. Chief Justice John Marshall and the other members of the Court were Federalists. They would have liked nothing better than to blast the Jefferson administration and order Madison to deliver the commission. Had the Court done so, however, it was likely that Jefferson would simply have defied the Court. Marshall knew that defiance by the president would destroy the Court's prestige, but he also wanted to avoid ruling for the administration.

Judicial review provided Marshall and the Court a way out of their dilemma. Marshall used the Court's opinion to scold Jefferson and Madison for refusing to deliver the commission. Marbury was entitled to his commission, said Marshall, and a writ of mandamus was in order. Marshall ruled, however, that the Supreme Court lacked the power to issue the writ. Marshall pointed out that the Constitution lists the types of cases that may be tried before the Supreme Court in Article III, Section 2, and that the list does not include the power to issue writs of mandamus to federal officials. That authority had been granted by Congress in the Judiciary Act of 1789. Marshall held, however, that Congress has no constitutional authority to extend the Court's jurisdiction. Therefore, the section of the Judiciary Act that gave the Court the power to issue writs of mandamus was unconstitutional. By this means, Marshall was able to attack Jefferson while avoiding the risk that Jefferson would defy the Court's power.

The long-term significance of the *Marbury* case is the Supreme Court's claiming the power to hold acts of Congress unconstitutional. In his ruling, Marshall stated that the Constitution is the "fundamental and paramount law of the nation" and that it was the duty of the courts to interpret the law. "Thus," Marshall continued, "the particular phraseology of the Constitution of the United States confirms and strengthens the principle, supposed to be essential to all written constitutions, that a law repugnant to the Constitution is void, and that the courts as well as other departments are bound by that instrument." Marshall concluded that in conflicts between the Constitution and acts of Congress, it was the Court's duty to enforce the Constitution by refusing to uphold the law.*

*Marbury v. Madison, 1 Cranch 137 (1803).

Judicial review requires courts to interpret the Constitution in light of current circumstances and contemporary judicial thinking. The Fourteenth Amendment, for example, says that "No State shall...deny to any person within its jurisdiction the equal protection of the laws." Historians tell us that Congress proposed this phrase (known as the equal protection clause) to safeguard the civil rights of African-Americans by requiring states to treat their residents equally under state law, regardless of their race.

The application of the equal protection clause to specific policy controversies has, of course, fallen to the Supreme Court. In 1896 in the case of *Plessy* v. *Ferguson*, the Court ruled that state laws requiring separate facilities for whites and blacks on rail cars were constitutional as long as accommodations were equal. "Separate but equal" facilities, said the Court, were sufficient to satisfy the requirements of the Fourteenth Amendment.[13] Almost sixty years later, however, in the case of *Brown* v. *Board of Education of Topeka* (1954), the Supreme Court overruled *Plessy*, holding that the equal protection clause of the Fourteenth Amendment prohibits state laws requiring racial segregation in public schools. Separate but equal, ruled the Court, was a contradiction in terms.[14] And so the Constitution was changed, not because of the adoption of a formal amendment (the wording of the equal protection clause remained the same), but because of changing judicial interpretation.

CONCLUSION: THE CONSTITUTION AND PUBLIC POLICY

The United States Constitution is perhaps the most important background element in America's policy process in that most policy decisions must be made through the workings of the constitutional system of separation of powers with checks and balances, bicameralism, and federalism. In short, the Constitution fragments power. The separation-of-powers provision divides power at the national level among legislative, executive, and judicial branches. Bicameralism, in turn, splits the legislative branch in two, dividing power between the House and Senate. Federalism, meanwhile, distributes power among the levels of government—national, state, and local. The phenomenon of divided party control of the executive and legislative branches of government fragments power even further.

Consider the difference in policymaking between Great Britain and the United States. The British have no separation of powers, no checks and balances, no judicial review, no federalism. In Britain, political power is concentrated in the hands of the House of Commons, that is, one chamber of Parliament, the British legislature. Although Parliament is bicameral, the House of Lords has little real power. The House of Commons chooses the prime minister, who, along with the cabinet, administers the government. What's more, British courts lack the power of judicial review and, since the British political system is unitary, local governments have no independent authority. Consequently, the election of a new parliamentary majority can make for dramatic change in the direction of public policy in Britain.

In contrast, the fragmentation of political power in America produces slow, incremental change. Presidents need the cooperation of Congress to have their programs enacted. For its part, Congress has difficulty acting without presidential initiative or at least acquiescence. Both president and Congress need the support of the bureaucracy if their policies are to be faithfully executed, and frequently they need the cooperation of state and local officials as well. The courts, meanwhile, can reverse or delay policies adopted at other levels or by other branches of government. With so many steps and so many power centers involved in the policy process, change is usually slow in coming if it comes at all. What policy changes do occur are generally incremental, gradual changes, reflecting compromise among the various power centers involved in the process.

America's constitutional system is biased in favor of the status quo, but that's because the founders preferred a system that would ensure deliberation and delay rather than precipitous action. They were cautious people, wary of rapid change and none too confident about the judgment of popular majorities. Consequently, they created a constitutional apparatus that would work slowly and be unlikely to produce dramatic upheavals in public policy. The founders feared that rapid, major change would too often produce more harm than good. With the system they established, the framers ensured that nothing bad would happen quickly; with luck, it might not happen at all.

The framers of the Constitution also wanted to ensure that the diversity of political interests in American society would be represented in the policy process. During the debates at the convention of 1787, one of the major issues was how best to protect the small states from large-state domination. In response, the authors of the Constitution established a system that would provide opportunity for the varied groups and interests of American society to have a say in policymaking. Today, many Americans still see this as a virtue.

Nonetheless, America's constitutional arrangements are not without their critics. The oldest complaint, first voiced by the Anti-Federalists who opposed the Constitution's ratification, is that the document benefits special interests at the expense of the majority of the people. The Anti-Federalists charged that the Constitution favored the rich and well-born over the interests of the common people. In the early twentieth century, historian Charles Beard echoed the position of the Anti-Federalists by arguing that the framers of the Constitution had been members of a propertied upper class who set out to preserve and enhance the economic and political opportunities of their class.[15]

Although modern historians have refuted most of Beard's research, a number of contemporary observers nonetheless believe that the Constitution benefits special interests. The constitutional fragmentation of power that presents a range of forums in which different groups may be heard also provides a series of power centers that interest groups can control. Because of the complexity of the constitutional process, entrenched groups can frequently muster the influence to halt policy changes they consider unfavorable, even though the changes may be supported by a sizable majority in Congress and a majority in the nation.

The most basic criticism of the Constitution, however, is that it is a blueprint for political deadlock among the branches and units of government. By dividing government against itself, the founders ensured that all proposals for policy change must pass through a maze of power centers. The complexity of the arrangement not only slows the policymaking process but also gives most of the trump cards to the forces opposing whatever measure is under consideration. It's easier to defeat policy proposals than to pass them.

The critics of the Constitution believe that policymaking stalemate is even more likely in today's political world because of divided party control of the executive and legislative branches. Presidential proposals are defeated by Congress, while congressional initiatives are vetoed by the president. The result is that the elected branches of government are unable or unwilling to govern. Major policy problems remain unresolved or are left to the bureaucracy and the courts to handle.

Professor James Sundquist believes that American history is filled with failures of the system to respond effectively to policy crisis. Consider the dilemma of the Vietnam War. Congress and the president were unable to agree either to withdraw American forces or to do what was necessary to win the war. As a result, the nation was condemned to a half-in, half-out compromise policy that satisfied no one and, in the long run, proved disastrous. Sundquist says the same constitutional paralysis hindered the nation's ability to deal with secession in the 1860s, the Great Depression in the 1930s, and the federal budget deficits of our own day.[16]

In sum, the United States Constitution represents a trade-off between limited government and political efficiency. The framers of the Constitution created a system of checks and balances in order to protect individual liberty against oppressive governmental power. The price for this protection, however, was a governmental apparatus prone to stalemate. What's more, the present-day phenomenon of divided party control of government makes the likelihood of political deadlock greater.

KEY TERMS

bicameral

bill of attainder

bill of rights

checks and balances

confederation

constitution

constitutional amendment

direct democracy

doctrine of natural rights

due process of law

executive power

ex post facto law

extradition

federation (federal system)

full faith and credit clause

judicial power

judicial review

legislative power

political legitimacy

popular sovereignty

power of the purse

privileges and immunities clause

religious test

representative democracy

republic

rule of law

selective incorporation of the Bill of Rights

separation of powers

social contract theory

sovereignty

tyranny of the majority

unicameral

unitary government

writ of habeas corpus

writ of mandamus

NOTES

1. Barbara G. Salmore and Stephen A. Salmore, *Candidates, Parties, and Campaigns: Electoral Politics in America*, 2d ed. (Washington, DC: Congressional Quarterly Press, 1989), p. 247.
2. Gordon S. Wood, *The Creation of the American Republic 1776–1787* (Chapel Hill: University of North Carolina Press, 1969), pp. 131–48.
3. Donald S. Lutz, "The Changing View of the Founding and a New Perspective on American Political Theory," *Social Science Quarterly* 68 (December 1987): 669–86.
4. Wood, pp. 601–14.
5. Lutz, p. 677.
6. *The Federalist*, no. 51.
7. Ibid.
8. Richard Neustadt, *Presidential Power*, rev. ed. (New York: Wiley, 1976), p. 33.
9. Edward C. Carmines and Lawrence C. Dodd, "Bicameralism in Congress: The Changing Partnership," in Dodd and Bruce I. Oppenheimer, eds., *Congress Reconsidered*, 3d ed. (Washington, DC: Congressional Quarterly Press, 1985), pp. 414–36.
10. Charles Evans Hughes, *Addresses*, 2d ed. (New York: Putnam, 1916), p. 185.
11. Leonard Levy, *Judgments: Essays on American Constitutional History* (Chicago: Quadrangle Books, 1972), p. 17.
12. *Marbury* v. *Madison*, 1 Cranch 137 (1803).
13. *Plessy* v. *Ferguson*, 163 U.S. 537 (1896).
14. *Brown* v. *Board of Education of Topeka*, 347 U.S. 483 (1954).
15. Charles A. Beard, *An Economic Interpretation of the Constitution of the United States* (New York: Macmillan, 1913).
16. James L. Sundquist, *Constitutional Reform and Effective Government* (Washington, DC: Brookings Institution, 1986), p. 5.

SUGGESTED READINGS

Currie, David P. *The Constitution of the United States*. Chicago: University of Chicago Press, 1988.

Goldwin, Robert A., and Kaufman, Art, eds. *Separation of Powers—Does It Still Work?* Washington, DC: American Enterprise Institute, 1986.

Kukla, Jon, ed. *The Bill of Rights: A Lively Heritage*. Richmond, VA: Virginia State Library and Archives, 1987.

Manley, John F., and Dolbeare, Kenneth M. *The Case Against the Constitution: From the Anti-Federalists to the Present*. Armonk, NY: M. E. Sharpe, 1987.

Riemer, Neal. *James Madison: Creating the American Constitution*. Washington, DC: Congressional Quarterly Press, 1986.

Sundquist, James L. *Constitutional Reform and Effective Government*. Washington, DC: Brookings Institution, 1986.

Witt, Elder. *The Supreme Court and Individual Rights*, 2d ed. Washington, DC: Congressional Quarterly Press, 1988.

Wood, Gordon S. *The Creation of the American Republic 1776–1787*. Chapel Hill: University of North Carolina Press, 1969.

3

THE FEDERAL SYSTEM

LEARNING OBJECTIVES

1. To describe the division of powers between the national and state governments, considering both constitutional and political issues.
2. To trace the historical development of America's federal system.
3. To outline the process through which the various types of federal programs are created and implemented.
4. To explain how federal programs reflect politics, discussing the role of interest groups, state and local governments, the president, and Congress.

October 1, 1986, was a memorable day for many young Americans. Several states with drinking ages of eighteen, nineteen, or twenty raised the legal minimum to twenty-one. Although the new age limit was set by state law, the impetus for the change came from Washington, D.C. In 1984, Congress passed and President Reagan signed a measure requiring state governments to establish a minimum drinking age of twenty-one by October 1986 or risk losing a portion of their federal highway grant money. The bill provided that states that failed to comply would lose 5 percent of their federal highway funds in 1987 and 10 percent in 1988. In Texas, for example, a state with an extensive highway system, the stakes were high—nearly $35 million in federal funds in 1987, more than $70 million in 1988.[1] Although state legislators around the nation complained about the pressure, eventually every state complied with the federal drinking age limit rather than lose highway money.

Mothers Against Drunk Driving (MADD) and other anti-drunk-driving groups were the primary supporters of the twenty-one-year-old minimum drinking age requirement. They lobbied Congress for the measure, saying it was needed to control drunk driving among young people. They pointed to statistics showing that although teenagers comprise only 10 percent of licensed drivers, they account for 21 percent of alcohol-related traffic deaths.[2] Moreover, MADD argued that a national uniform drinking age would prevent teenagers in states with a drinking age of twenty-one from driving to neighboring states where they could drink legally and, perhaps, drive home drunk.

In contrast, opponents of the measure, including restaurant owners, distillers, and student groups, said that the legislation unfairly singled out young people and would lead to an increase in illegal underage drinking. The bitterest opposition, however, was based on the grounds that the federal requirement infringed on a matter (liquor regulation) that traditionally had been under state control. As one United States senator asked, "Who are we [in Congress] . . . to tell . . . state legislatures . . . how to conduct their business?"[3] Nevertheless, the measure sailed through Congress and the president signed it.

This example illustrates both the operation of federal programs and some of the policy issues they involve. But, before we turn our attention to the policies and politics of federal programs, let's consider the constitutional basis of the federal system and its historical development.

THE CONSTITUTIONAL BASIS OF FEDERALISM

The American Constitution creates a federal system. As we discussed in the last chapter, a **federation**, or **federal system**, is a political system that divides power between a central government, with authority over the whole nation, and a series of state governments. The Constitution outlines the division of power between the national government and the states in broad terms.

National Powers

In Articles I, II, and III, the Constitution grants the national (or federal) government certain powers. The powers of the federal government which are specifically listed in the United States Constitution are known as the **delegated**, or **enumerated**, **powers**. The most extensive list is that of powers delegated to Congress in Article I, Section 8. "The Congress shall have the power," it says, "to lay and collect taxes, duties, imposts, and excises, to pay the debts and provide for the common defense and general welfare...." Among other powers, the Constitution grants Congress the authority to borrow money, regulate commerce, coin money, declare war, create courts, raise and support armies and a navy, govern the District of Columbia, and establish post offices.

The last of the delegated powers is more general than the rest: "[Congress shall have the power] to make all laws which shall be necessary and proper for carrying into execution the foregoing powers, and all other powers vested by this Constitution in the government of the United States, or in any department or office thereof." This passage is known as the **necessary and proper clause** (or **elastic clause**). It is the constitutional provision found in Article I, Section 8 granting Congress the power to make all laws "necessary and proper" for carrying out the delegated powers. Although the Constitution restricts the authority of Congress to the delegated powers, the necessary and proper clause grants Congress the means to exercise its delegated authority.

The necessary and proper clause provides the constitutional basis for the doctrine of implied powers. **Implied powers** are those powers of Congress not specifically mentioned in the Constitution, but derived by implication from the delegated powers. The Constitution, for example, explicitly grants Congress the authority to raise armies and a navy. The power to draft men into the armed forces, then, would be an implied power. Although the authority to draft is not explicitly granted as a delegated power, it can be inferred as an action "necessary and proper" to carrying out one of the delegated powers—raising armies and a navy.

The Constitution also addresses the question of the relative power of the national and state governments in Article IV, in a passage known as the **national supremacy clause**. This is the constitutional provision that declares that the Constitution, the laws made under it, and the treaties of the United States are the supreme law of the land. In short, the national supremacy clause means that the legitimate exercise of national power supersedes state action.

State Powers

Although the national supremacy clause makes the national government the senior partner in the federal union, the Constitution includes a number of guarantees of state sovereignty. (**Sovereignty**, you recall, refers to the authority of a state to exercise its legitimate powers within its boundaries, free from external interference.) In Article IV, the Constitution declares that states may not be divided or consolidated without permission. The Constitution also guarantees states a republican form of government (a **republic** is a representative democracy), defense against invasion, and protection from domestic violence when requested. In Article V, the Constitution pledges that states may not be deprived of equal representation in the United States Senate. The Eleventh Amendment promises that the federal courts will not hear lawsuits brought against a state by individual citizens.

Perhaps the best-known guarantee made to the states is found in the Tenth Amendment: "The powers not delegated to the United States by the Constitution, nor prohibited by it to the States, are reserved to the States, respectively, or to the people." This clause means that the powers of state governments are residual powers. The powers of the national government, you recall, are enumerated in the Constitution; we call them the delegated powers. According to the Tenth Amendment, the powers not delegated to the national government are reserved to the states. **Reserved**, or **residual**, **powers**, then, are the powers of government left to the states. In other words, the national government may exercise only those powers granted to it by the Constitution, while state governments possess all powers not given to the national government, nor prohibited to the states by the Constitution.

On its surface, this description of the federal system implies that the division of powers between the national government and the states resembles a layer cake, with each level of government exercising its own authority in its own sphere without overlap. In practice, however, the authority of the national government and the powers of the states overlap considerably, especially in twentieth-century America. Those powers which are jointly exercised by the national and state governments are known as **concurrent powers**. Both levels of government, for example, have the power to tax, to spend, and to regulate. Instead of a layer cake, then, the federal system today more closely resembles a marble cake with its overlapping textures.

We can identify four broad areas of state authority. First, states have the power to tax and spend. The most important tax sources for state and local governments (which are subunits of states) are sales, property, excise, and income taxes. The major budget items are education, highways, transportation, police and fire protection, and public welfare assistance.

States may exercise the power of eminent domain to obtain land for freeway construction.

Second, states may exercise **police power**. This is the authority of states to promote and safeguard the health, morals, safety, and welfare of the people. States enact and enforce criminal laws. They operate hospitals and schools, and require that children be immunized against disease. Most states also regulate the sale and consumption of alcoholic beverages and prohibit prostitution.

Third, states regulate local commerce. Some states, for example, have Sunday closing laws. Most cities zone areas for particular uses. (**Zoning** is the regulation by law of the uses to which land may be put.) Many states also enforce consumer-protection laws.

Fourth, states exercise the power of **eminent domain**. This is the authority of government to take private property for public use upon just compensation. State and local governments may exercise this power to obtain land to build a freeway or to construct a prison.

The States' Rights/Strong National Government Controversy

The division of political power between the states and the national government has been a continuing source of conflict throughout American history. **States' rights** is an interpretation of the Constitution that would limit the implied powers of the federal government while expanding the reserved powers of the states. Nationalists, meanwhile, favor a strong national government. Proponents of states' rights and advocates of a strong national government debated in the nineteenth century over the power of the federal government to prohibit the extension of slavery. In the twentieth century, issues ranging from school integration to prison reform to the twenty-one-year-old drinking age have been argued in terms of states' rights and national powers.

The supporters of states' rights and the proponents of a strong national government have debated the issue on both constitutional and practical political grounds. The constitutional controversy has centered on the relative position of the state and national governments. The advocates of states' rights argue that the Constitution is a compact among the states that restricts the national government to those powers specifically granted to it by the Constitution, that is, to the delegated powers. Thus, they believe that the scope of the implied powers should be closely limited. In contrast, the supporters of a strong national government contend that the Constitution is a compact among the people rather than the states. After all, they say, the document begins, "We the people . . . ." Consequently, nationalists believe that the implied powers should be construed broadly in order to further the interests of the people.

The states' rights/strong national government controversy has also been argued on a practical political basis. States' rights advocates believe that local control makes for better public policy. Local control, they say, promotes efficient government because it permits a closer match between the services government provides and the policy preferences of constituents. After all, who should know better what public policies citizens prefer—national officials or local officeholders? What's more, the supporters of states' rights believe that local control of public policy enhances the opportunity for citizen participation. State and local governments are closer to the people, they say. If citizens disapprove of policy decisions, they can work to change state policies and policymakers more effectively than they can influence policies and officeholders at the national level.

In contrast, the supporters of a strong national government believe that national control makes for good public policy. A strong national government, they say, can set policy standards for the entire country in such policy areas as poverty relief, racial integration, and environmental protection. State governments may lack the resources to assist the poor. State and local officials may choose to discriminate against racial minorities or they may be indifferent to environmental hazards. According to the proponents of a strong national government, only the federal government can supply the resources and the political will to achieve national goals.

The Court Speaks

The most important judicial ruling on the nature of the federal system came in the famous case of *McCulloch* v. *Maryland*, decided in 1819. The background of this case dates to 1791, when Congress chartered a national bank, the First Bank of the United States, amid great controversy. Thomas Jefferson, who was then secretary of state, opposed the bank, saying the authority to create it was "not among the powers specifically enumerated by the Constitution."[4] In contrast, Alexander Hamilton, who was secretary of the treasury, supported the bank and the power of Congress to establish it. He argued that the action of Congress was justified as an exercise of authority reasonably *implied* by the delegated powers. Despite the debate, no legal challenge to the bank arose, and it operated until its charter expired in 1811.

In 1816, Congress chartered the Second Bank of the United States. It too became the subject of controversy, particularly in the West and South. Accusations of corruption and inefficiency arose, but the most serious charge was that the bank was responsible for an economic depression. In response to the public outcry against the bank, a number of states passed restrictions on it or levied heavy taxes against it. Maryland, for example, required payment of an annual tax of $15,000 on the bank's Baltimore branch, which was a sum large enough to drive the bank out of business in the state. This, of course, was just what the Maryland legislature wanted. McCulloch, the bank's cashier, refused to comply with the law, and Maryland sued. The case presented two important constitutional issues: Does the national government have the authority to charter a bank? And does a state have the power to tax an arm of the national government?

Chief Justice John Marshall wrote the unanimous opinion of the Supreme Court. First, the Court upheld the authority of Congress to charter a bank on the basis of the doctrine of implied powers. Marshall noted that although the Constitution does not specifically grant Congress the power to incorporate a bank, the Constitution does say that Congress may lay and collect taxes, borrow money, and raise and support armies and a navy. What, Marshall asked, if money raised in the North is needed in the South to support the army? The creation of a national bank to transport that money would be a "necessary and proper" step to that end. The power to charter the bank, Marshall held, was *implied* by the necessary and proper clause. Then, in one of the most famous passages in constitutional law, Marshall broadly defined the extent of implied powers:

> Let the end be legitimate, let it be within the scope of the Constitution, and all means which are appropriate, which are plainly adapted to that end, which are not prohibited, but consistent with the letter and spirit of the Constitution, are constitutional.[5]

Second, the Court ruled that Maryland's tax was unconstitutional. The power to tax, said Marshall, is the power to destroy, since a high tax can drive the object of the taxation out of existence. If Maryland or any state has the authority to tax an arm of the national government, it could effectively shut it down. That, concluded Marshall, would be contrary to the nature of the federal union as stated in the national supremacy clause.

In sum, the Supreme Court settled the debate about the constitutional powers of the national government and the position of the national government in the federal system. By giving broad scope to the doctrine of implied powers, the Court provided the national government with a vast source of power. Then, by stressing the importance of the national supremacy clause, the Court denied states the right to interfere in the constitutional operations of the national government.

Although the Supreme Court later had second thoughts about the decision in *McCulloch* v. *Maryland*, the *McCulloch* precedent stands today as good constitutional law. Indeed, it is fair to say that the doctrine of states' rights presents no *constitutional* limitation to the exercise of authority by the national government. In essence, the Supreme Court has left the responsibility of balancing national and state policy interests to the other branches of government. If states believe that their sovereignty has been trampled on by the national government (as with the twenty-one-year-old drinking age), they may ask Congress and the executive branch of the national government for redress through the political process. The Supreme Court, however, will not intervene to settle the dispute on constitutional grounds.[6] Accordingly, in 1987 the Supreme Court upheld the requirement of Congress that states raise their legal minimum drinking age to twenty-one or risk losing federal highway funds.[7]

THE DEVELOPMENT OF THE FEDERAL SYSTEM

The Supreme Court's position on states' rights has by no means ended the debate between the advocates of local policy control and the proponents of a strong national government. It has merely shifted the site of that debate from the courthouse to the halls of Congress and the offices of the executive branch of American national government. Let's examine the development of America's federal system.

The System Established

In the early years of the nation, the division of responsibilities in the federal system was relatively clear-cut. The national government defended the borders, delivered the mail, and promoted westward expansion. State and local governments, meanwhile, provided most domestic public services.

By the end of the nineteenth century, the role of government in American society was growing. Industrialization and urbanization created problems that Americans asked government to solve. Although most of the growth in government in the late nineteenth and early twentieth centuries came at the state and local levels, the activities of the national government increased as well. In 1887, the United States Congress created the Interstate Commerce Commission (ICC) to regulate the railroads nationwide. Congress passed the Sherman Antitrust Act in 1890 and the Clayton Antitrust Act in 1914 in an effort to control monopolies.

Cooperative Federalism and Developmental Federal Programs

A key event in the development of the modern federal system was the ratification in 1913 of the Sixteenth Amendment, the income-tax amendment, because it provided the national government with a substantial source of revenue that could be used to finance federal grant-in-aid programs. **Grant-in-aid programs** are programs through which Congress makes funds available to state and local governments for expenditure in accordance with set standards and conditions. After the ratification of the income-tax amendment, Congress enacted programs giving federal money to the states and, occasionally, local governments for highway construction, vocational education, hospital construction, agricultural development, housing, and aid to the blind. During the 1930s, Congress created numerous federal programs designed to help states and localities recover from the Great Depression. By the end of this decade, the national government was spending as much for domestic programs as the other levels of government combined.[8]

The role of the national government in the provision of domestic public services grew because many Americans perceived it to be a more efficient, effective, and equitable provider of public services than state and local governments. As we have noted, the income tax gave the federal government a substantial, steady source of revenue. State and local governments, meanwhile, were often saddled with less dependable tax sources that fluctuated considerably with the health of the economy. During the 1930s, many states and localities were simply unable to respond adequately to the demands for public services engendered by the Great Depression. When this happened, the national government under the leadership of President Franklin Roosevelt stepped in to attempt to deal with the crisis.[9]

Scholars often refer to the period in the development of the federal system from 1913 until the decade of the 1960s as the era of cooperative federalism. It was a time in which the national government and the states worked together to carry out the functions of government. State and local officials asked Uncle Sam for assistance in accomplishing their goals, and Congress responded by creating federal programs to provide money for highway and hospital construction, vocational education, and the like.[10] One group of political scientists calls the federal programs established in that period **developmental programs** because they were designed to help communities to improve their economic positions.[11]

The Great Society and Redistributive Federal Programs

The size and scope of federal grant-in-aid programs changed dramatically in the 1960s and early 1970s. The most rapid changes took place in the middle 1960s as Congress passed many of the federal programs proposed by President Lyndon Johnson in his legislative program (known as the **Great Society**). Between 1963 and 1968, Congress established 227 grant programs. It added another 150 by 1980,[12] bringing the total number of programs in operation to more than 530. In the meantime, the price tag for federal programs rose to $91.5 billion by 1980. This represented 15.5 percent of the federal budget and 26.3 percent of state and local expenditures. Moreover, the number and variety of grant recipients increased. Federal money went not just to state and local governments, but to universities and nonprofit organizations as well.[13]

Once again, the impetus behind the growing national role in the provision of domestic public services lay with the perceived strength of the national government and the perceived weakness of state and local governments. The 1960s was a decade of unprecedented economic growth that generated steadily increasing tax revenues for the national government. These tax revenues could be put to work solving the nation's problems, and Presidents John Kennedy and Lyndon Johnson offered idealistic visions of how that could be accomplished through federal programs.

President Lyndon Johnson gained support for his "war on poverty" by publicizing the plight of families like this one. Here, he and the First Lady are greeted by a Kentucky couple whose total 1963 income—to provide for themselves and eight children—was $400.

In contrast, state and local governments were at low ebb in effectiveness and public esteem. In 1967, Terry Sanford, a former governor of North Carolina, began a book with these words: "The states are indecisive. The states are antiquated. The states are timid and ineffective. The states are not willing to face their problems."[14] Few disagreed with Sanford's assessment. Many state governments were hamstrung by out-of-date state constitutions that prevented them from dealing effectively with twentieth-century policy problems. State legislatures were often unrepresentative of state populations, with rural voters having more influence than more numerous urban voters. As a result, many state governments were indifferent to the growing problems of major urban areas, including poverty, urban decay, substandard housing, inadequate health care, unemployment, and racial discrimination.[15] It is not surprising, then, that city governments and urban interests turned to the national government for help with their problems rather than to their own state capitals.

Most of the federal grant-in-aid programs established during the Great Society period could be labeled **redistributive programs**. These were programs designed to benefit low-income individuals or other disadvantaged groups, such as the elderly, minorities, and the disabled. Congress enacted the Medicare and Medicaid programs, for example, to provide medical care for the elderly and the poor, respectively. It created the CETA (Comprehensive Employment and Training Act) program to teach job skills to the unemployed. Other federal programs dealt with low-income housing, school integration, special education for disabled youngsters, and community development for blighted neighborhoods. What's more, Congress revised many of the older federal programs to add redistributive features.

The new redistributive federal programs differed from traditional developmental programs in the way they targeted beneficiaries. The older programs were aimed at providing a modest amount of benefits to a large number of recipients, such as all vocational students or all hospital patients in a community. In contrast, the new programs attempted to help a relatively small number of "needy" beneficiaries a great deal. Congress passed the Special Education Act of 1975, for example, to assist schoolchildren with physical handicaps or learning disabilities.

Federal programs also changed in the manner of their initiation. Congress enacted most of the older federal programs, such as the Highway Act, in response to broad public pressure and requests from state officials. In contrast, demands for redistributive federal programs often came from narrowly based interest groups or from within the federal bureaucracy. By the 1960s, interest groups learned that they could frequently have more success lobbying Congress than lobbying their state legislatures or city councils. MADD, for example, turned to Congress to legislate a national minimum drinking age after failing to convince state legislatures to raise the drinking age to twenty-one.

Initiatives for redistributive federal programs also came from within the federal bureaucracy. In many cases, national government employees with scientific or professional expertise identified what they saw as problems and proposed federal programs for their solution. Frequently, the bureaucrats (in alliance with interest groups) had the political power to win congressional approval for their programs, despite the opposition of state and local officials. The old pattern of the national government helping state and local authorities attain state and local objectives was reversed. Now federal programs often represented an effort by Washington to impose national goals on states and localities.[16]

The expansion of federal programs in the 1960s and 1970s proved controversial. The supporters of redistributive federal programs spoke in favor of setting national goals in policy areas such as health care, education, welfare, housing, police protection, conservation, and civil rights. To achieve these goals would require a massive commitment of resources which, they said, only the government in Washington could supply. Moreover, the proponents of redistributive federal programs argued that national power was needed to stamp out discrimination that state and local governments were unable or unwilling to end, and to ensure the equitable treatment of all Americans.

In contrast, many state and local officials saw the new federal programs in a different light. They welcomed the federal money, of course, but resented

"Lobbies"

Reprinted with permission: Tribune Media Services.

the red tape and federally imposed conditions that came with it. They complained about confusion, duplication, overlap, and a breakdown of intergovernmental cooperation.

Moreover, many Americans no longer regarded the national government as an efficient provider of public services. The Vietnam War and Watergate shook the faith of many Americans in the ability and honesty of national political leaders. Meanwhile, some of the federal programs of the 1960s came under attack as wasteful and ineffective. One widely circulated book on the antipoverty programs of the Kennedy-Johnson years was entitled *Maximum Feasible Misunderstanding*.[17] Finally, growing federal budget deficits led many observers to question whether the resources of the national government were sufficient to solve the nation's problems.

Reagan's New Federalism

During the 1980 presidential campaign, Ronald Reagan appealed to public misgivings about the growing national role in the federal system. The national government isn't the solution to America's problems, said Reagan; it's part of the problem. Reagan promised a "new federalism" that would return power to state and local authorities.

Once in office, President Reagan sent his New Federalism program to Congress. The president proposed a realignment of nation-state responsibilities with the elimination of some federal programs and the consolidation of others. Moreover, he asked Congress to reduce funding for many federal programs. As you can see from Figure 3.1, spending for federal programs as a percentage of state/local outlays reached a peak in 1978 and began to fall back in the final years of the Carter administration. Reagan proposed further substantial reductions. Finally, the president asked Congress to give state and local officials greater leeway in deciding how to spend the money they did receive.[18]

Congress adopted some but not all of Reagan's New Federalism package. Although the president's proposal for shifting program responsibilities between the national and state governments never got off the ground, Congress did agree to consolidate some federal programs, reducing their number to around four hundred by 1984.[19] Congress also relaxed some of the restrictions on how states and localities may spend federal aid money.

Reagan's greatest success, however, came on his budget-cut proposals, especially during the early years of his presidency. As Figure 3.1 indicates, Congress sliced billions from the budget for federal aid to states and localities in the early 1980s, reducing the federal contribution to state and local budgets from about 26 percent in 1980 to around 21 percent in 1983. Federal aid programs for cities were particularly hard hit, especially programs to provide low-income housing assistance.

FIGURE 3.1

The Rise and Decline of Federal Aid, 1958–88
(as a percentage of state/local outlays)

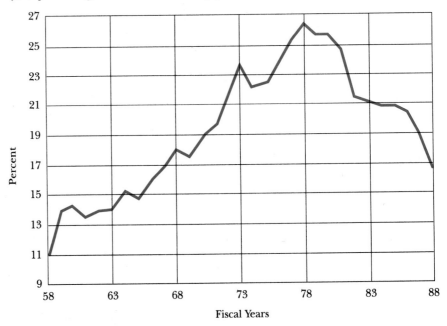

Source: *Intergovernmental Perspective*, Winter 1988, p. 13.

Despite the steep reductions in spending for federal programs, Congress generally refused to cut as deeply as President Reagan asked. Congress also failed to eliminate more than a handful of programs. Over the years, each program had developed sufficient political support to weather the most severe budget-cutting storm. This was true even for the more controversial programs of the Great Society era. In sum, then, the net effect of Reagan's New Federalism was less to restructure the federal system or to eliminate federal programs than it was to reduce funding for programs.

The federal budget cuts left state and local authorities with the difficult choice of deciding whether to reduce services in their communities or to raise local taxes to make up for lost federal funds. By and large, state and local governments were up to the challenge. They responded to the reductions in federal aid with remarkable creativity, far more creativity than anyone would have thought possible in the 1950s and early 1960s. Since the early 1960s, state and local governments had undergone significant reforms. State legislatures had become more representative of state populations, including more women, minorities, and urban residents in their memberships than ever before. Many states had adopted new constitutions or reformed their old ones to increase the power of state governors and to streamline state administration. What's more, state officials, both elected and appointed, were generally better educated, more capable, and better informed than state officials in the past, and they were aided by professional staffs and expert research assistance.[20]

States and localities responded to the federal budget cuts of the early 1980s with tax increases, some service reductions, and a number of program innovations. Between 1980 and 1987, most states and many local governments increased taxes and fees, and a majority of states adopted lotteries to raise money as well. In many cases, the added revenues more than made up for the lost federal dollars. States and localities often used the extra money to finance new programs in economic development and education.[21]

Nonetheless, state and local governments did not move to replace the lost federal grant funds in programs across the board. When the budget ax fell, states and localities generally replaced the federal grant money lost for health, highways, education, and mass transit—that is, developmental programs in areas of traditional concern for state and local governments. In contrast, state and local governments generally failed to cover funding losses in redistributive programs directed toward low-income residents: public assistance, public housing, job training, community antipoverty, and community development programs.[22]

The Federal System in the 1990s

The most important factor affecting the development of the federal system in the 1990s is the federal budget deficit. Because of the deficit, Congress and the executive branch simply haven't the money to launch major new federal programs or to significantly expand established programs. At least for the foreseeable future, then, the supporters of most federal programs will be fighting a defensive action to maintain current funding levels.

Despite the lack of money, federal officials have found creative ways to influence state and local policymaking. In the words of one observer, "The money ran out, but the activism didn't."[23] In recent years, Congress and the White House have attempted to achieve policy goals through legislative mandates on state and local governments. A **mandate** is a legislative requirement placed on a lower level of government by a higher level of government that requires the lower level of government to take certain policy actions. In this fashion, Congress and the president are able to pursue their policy goals without spending many federal dollars.

Federal mandates come in a variety of forms. Some mandates are conditions attached to the receipt of federal funds for programs already in operation. The twenty-one-year-old drinking age requirement is an example of federal legislation that requires states to adopt a federal policy or risk losing federal funds. Other federal mandates simply require state and local actions. Congress, for example, sets minimum environmental standards, as in the Clean Air Act, and requires states to administer them. Still other federal mandates direct states to cover the cost of federal programs. When Congress expanded Medicare to include catastrophic illness, for instance, it specified that states pay premiums, deductibles, and co-insurance premiums for poor, elderly, and disabled persons unable to pay themselves. (The catastrophic illness program has since been repealed.)

In the 1990s, the debate over federalism will most likely center around the use of mandates by Congress to achieve policy goals. In today's world of huge deficits, Congress sees this approach as the only politically and economically feasible method for accomplishing its policy aims. In contrast, state and local officials believe that mandates make them little more than field hands for the federal government.[24]

THE STRUCTURE OF FEDERAL PROGRAMS

Congress and the president create federal programs through the legislative process. Both houses of Congress must agree to establish a program and the president must either sign the legislation or allow it to become law without his signature. If the president should veto a measure, it can only become law if Congress votes to override the veto by a two-thirds margin in each house.

Federal programs must be authorized and funds appropriated for their operation. The **authorization process** is the procedure through which Congress legislatively establishes a program, defines its general purpose, devises procedures for its operation, specifies an agency to implement the program, and indicates an approximate level of funding for the program (but does *not* actually provide money). In 1973, for example, Congress authorized the creation of the Urban Mass Transit Administration (UMTA) to award mass transit grants to local governments and to oversee their implementation. Although Congress authorizes some federal programs on a one-time-only basis, it stipulates that other programs be reauthorized periodically. The **appropriation process**, meanwhile, is the procedure through which Congress legislatively provides money for a particular purpose. The appropriation process takes place annually. Each year, for example, funds for the operation of UMTA must be appropriated as part of the federal budget.

Federal programs come in a variety of forms. A **categorical grant program** is a federal grant-in-aid program that provides funds to state and local governments for fairly narrow, specific purposes. The Interstate Highway Program is an example of a categorical grant program. In this type of program, Congress leaves little discretion to state and local officials as to how the money is spent. During the 1960s, more than 90 percent of all federal aid came through categorical grants. Although they are somewhat less numerous today, categorical grants still provide most federal aid money.[25]

A **block grant program** is a federal grant program that provides money for a program in a broad, general policy area. The Community Development Program is an example of a block grant program. State and local governments have more discretion in spending block grant funds than they do with categorical grant money. Still, they are required to plan how they will use the money and report how the money has been spent. President Reagan preferred block grant over categorical grant programs because, he said, block grants reduce bureaucratic red tape and give local officials more discretion. In response to Reagan's request, Congress consolidated 57 categorical grant programs into 9 block grant programs in 1981. In later years, however, Congress resisted efforts by the White House to fold more categorical grant programs into block grants.[26]

Federal grants differ in the criteria by which funding is awarded. A **project grant program** is a grant program that requires state and local governments to compete for available federal money. State and local governments present detailed grant applications which federal agencies evaluate in order to make funding decisions. UMTA grants, for example, are project grants. Cities and local mass transit authorities make application to the Urban Mass Transit Administration for federal funds to construct subways, bus lanes, and the like. The agency then decides which applications merit funding.

A **formula grant program** is a grant program that awards funding on the basis of a formula established by Congress. In contrast to project grants, formula grants provide money for every state and/or locality that qualifies under the formula. For example, the Interstate Highway Act is a formula grant program. It provides money to states based on a formula that includes a state's geographic size, population, and rural-mail-route mileage.

Both categorical and block grants come with conditions. First, Congress usually requires states and localities to provide **matching funds**. This is the legislative requirement that the national government will provide money for a project or program only on condition that the state or local government in-

volved supply a certain percentage of the total money required for the project
or program. For example, if the total cost of a sewage treatment plant in,
say, Colorado Springs, Colorado, is $5 million, the national government may
supply $4 million (80 percent) while requiring the city to match the federal
money with $1 million of local funds (20 percent). Even federal programs that
don't require financial participation by state and local governments usually require contributions in kind. Although the national government covers the entire cost of food stamps, for instance, it requires that states administer the
program.

Second, federal money for categorical and block grants comes with many
across-the-board requirements. These include provisions in the area of equal
rights, equal access for the disabled, environmental protection, historic preservation, and wage rates for contractors' personnel. Moreover, individual
programs have particular conditions attached. For example, Congress tacked
the twenty-one-year-old minimum drinking age requirement onto the Highway Act.

THE POLITICS OF FEDERAL PROGRAMS

Federal programs reflect politics. **Politics**, you recall, is the process that determines who shall occupy the roles of leadership in government and how the
power of government shall be exercised. The policymaking process for federal programs includes a broad range of individuals and groups, each of
whom has certain political goals. Let's identify some of those political actors
and examine their impact on federal program policymaking. (For a closer
look at the politics of federal programs, see the Perspective on page 78.)

Interest Groups and Federal Programs

Interest groups often see federal programs as useful tools for accomplishing
their goals. The Council for Exceptional Children and the National Association
for Retarded Children, for example, helped shape the Special Education Act of
1975 to conform to their approach to government assistance for children with
disabilities. On many occasions, interest groups pressure Congress to attach
conditions to federal programs. Minority-rights groups support nondiscrimination provisions. Environmental groups demand that federal construction
contracts include environmental impact statements. Labor unions and manufacturers join forces to push for "buy American" requirements on equipment
purchases. Handicapped-rights groups insist on "equal access" for all agencies
and institutions receiving federal aid.

States and Localities and Federal Programs

State and local governments are directly affected by federal programs, so it is not surprising that they try to influence their formulation, adoption, and implementation. A recent study of the allocation of federal grants found that local government demand is an important factor in determining the distribution of federal money.[27] In fact, states and localities often retain professional lobbyists to represent their interests in Washington, D.C. State and local governments also lobby through national associations, including the National League of Cities, the U.S. Congress of Mayors, the National Governors Association, and the National Conference of State Legislatures.

State and local governments often back up their lobbying efforts with cash. In the mid-1980s, Congress announced plans to build a $4.4 billion Superconducting Supercollider, a research tool for high-energy physics. The attraction of the Supercollider project was obvious—it would provide 4,500 construction jobs, 2,500 permanent jobs, and pump $200 million a year into a local economy. State governments around the nation went to work to land the

A minority-rights group demonstrates in support of affirmative action.

PERSPECTIVE

Frostbelt Versus Sunbelt

Some of the sharpest battles over federal funds are fought between the Frostbelt and the Sunbelt. In the early 1970s, members of Congress from the Northeast and Midwest produced statistics showing that their regions generally paid more in tax money than they received in federal aid, while Sunbelt states generally received more money in aid than they paid in taxes. Using these statistics as a rallying point, Frostbelt representatives formed the Northeast-Midwest Congressional Coalition in 1976 to work for more federal grant money for their region.

The Frostbelt coalition succeeded in revising some federal programs to benefit their region. When Congress created the Community Development Program in 1974 to help cities revitalize blighted neighborhoods, for example, it based funding on a formula that included a city's population, its poverty rate, and a measure of overcrowded housing. This formula tended to favor Sunbelt cities because their rapid growth produced housing shortages. In 1977, however, the Frostbelt coalition won a battle when Congress revised the formula to emphasize the percentage of a city's housing built before 1940. Naturally, this change shifted funding away from the young cities of the Sunbelt to the older cities of the Northeast and Midwest. Another example of the Frostbelt coalition's success came in 1979, when Congress en-

acted a program to assist poor families in paying their home heating bills.

Before long, however, members of Congress from the Sunbelt organized and began to fight back. Their computers produced statistics showing that the Sunbelt wasn't really getting more than its fair share of federal money after all. As a region, they noted, the Sunbelt was still poorer than the Frostbelt, and therefore in need of more federal aid than other areas. What's more, they argued, rapid population growth can produce problems nearly as severe as population decline.

The most potent weapon in the Sunbelt arsenal is demography: The Sunbelt's population is growing more rapidly than the population in the Frostbelt, and that translates into more political influence for the South and West. After the 1980 census, Sunbelt states picked up seventeen seats in the U.S. House. As a result, the Sunbelt began to win some victories in Congress. In the early 1980s, for example, Sunbelt forces succeeded in expanding the energy-assistance program to include aid to low-income families in paying home cooling as well as home heating bills. Moreover, the political future looks bright for the Sunbelt, with the Census Bureau predicting a shift of at least another dozen House seats from Frostbelt to Sunbelt states after the 1990 census.

project. More than a dozen states spent at least a million dollars apiece for surveys, environmental reviews, and political lobbying. Texas, the state that eventually won the project, promised to contribute a total of $2.5 billion to the project if Congress voted to locate the Supercollider in the Lone Star State.[28]

The President and Federal Programs

Presidential priorities for federal programs generally reflect the interests of the political forces that put the president in office. Democratic presidents usually receive their strongest electoral support from inner-city residents, minorities, and working-class and lower-middle-class families. In contrast, Republican presidents generally enjoy the support of suburbanites and upper-class and upper-middle-class families. Once in office, both Democratic and Republican presidents endorse federal programs tilted to benefit their particular support groups. Democratic President Johnson, for example, asked Congress to enact scores of redistributive federal programs that provided money to inner cities. After Republican Richard Nixon succeeded to the White House in 1968, he asked Congress to redirect federal funds away from central cities. President Carter proposed federal programs that shifted money back to cities.[29] Then, in the 1980s, Ronald Reagan's New Federalism reversed the direction of federal funds once again.

In fact, a strong case can be made that Reagan's policies demonstrated less a change in the philosophy of government than they reflected different spending priorities. Although Reagan called for a reduction in the role of the federal government, government spending did not fall. In fact, during Reagan's first few years in office, federal government spending as a percentage of gross national product actually increased, jumping from 22.7 percent of GNP in 1981 to 24.3 percent in 1983.[30]

President Reagan's main impact on federal spending was to shift priorities away from domestic social spending toward national defense. In the 1981 federal budget, the last budget proposed by President Carter, the national government allocated 53 percent of its resources to social programs, 23 percent for defense. In contrast, Reagan's 1987 budget reduced social spending's share of the budget to 48 percent while increasing defense's proportion to 29 percent.[31] What difference does this make in terms of who benefits from government policies? Less social spending means less money for inner cities and other economically depressed areas that usually support Democrats. Higher defense spending, meanwhile, favors high-technology industries and technically skilled workers who, it so happens, lean Republican.

Congress and Federal Programs

Congress is the principal architect of federal programs, and politics is an ever-present part of its designs. Professor Morris P. Fiorina believes that Congress formulates federal programs to meet the political needs of its members. Federal programs allow members the opportunity to claim credit for producing benefits for their districts and, since money is appropriated annually, members can claim credit often. Members of Congress even benefit when federal programs work poorly, he says, because it gives them the opportunity to intervene to cut the red tape burdening their constituents.[32]

Although Fiorina's view of federal programs may be a bit cynical, there's no doubt that the policymaking process for federal programs is highly political. Members of Congress are ever vigilant to see that their states or districts receive their fair share of federal money. They generally regard the equitable distribution of federal funds as one in which states share equally (for senators) or in which benefits are distributed on the basis of population (for members of the House). Other considerations such as those involving program needs or demands for services often take a back seat. Consequently, the distribution of law enforcement grants is based primarily on population rather than the incidence of crime. Urban mass transit grants reflect population size and density, but not how many people actually use mass transit.[33] Grant money to fight AIDS (Acquired Immune Deficiency Syndrome) goes to all fifty states, including states with almost no cases.[34]

CONCLUSION: BACKGROUND FACTORS AS BOUNDARIES FOR POLICYMAKING

In the last three chapters, we have studied the factors comprising the background for policymaking in America. We examined the nation's people, economy, and political culture in chapter 1. In the second chapter, we studied the American Constitution. Then, in this chapter, we have discussed the federal system.

Although background factors are important to our study of public policy in America, they don't explain everything. No one background factor or set of factors determines public policy in the United States with specificity. To explain American government on the basis of the nation's frontier heritage or the U.S. Constitution or the Supreme Court's interpretation of the doctrine of implied powers is simplistic. Each background factor gives us insight, but the realities of policymaking are too complex to be explained so easily.

In a sense, each of these factors helps determine the boundaries for policymaking. They set limits on the nature of public policy in the nation and help define its content. Economic and human resources, for example, affect the nation's ability to respond to social needs. Similarly, America's political culture defines, in large part, what public policy alternatives are acceptable to the nation's people. The Constitution and the federal system, meanwhile, establish a set of legal/constitutional boundaries for policymaking.

In the remaining chapters of this text, we study political participation, the institutions of American government, and the content of public policy in a number of major issue areas. As you learn about these aspects of the policy process, keep in mind the role background factors play in shaping policymaking in America.

KEY TERMS

appropriation process	categorical grant program
authorization process	concurrent powers
block grant program	delegated powers

developmental programs

elastic clause

eminent domain

enumerated powers

federation (federal system)

formula grant program

grant-in-aid programs

Great Society

implied powers

mandate

matching funds

national supremacy clause

necessary and proper clause

police power

politics

project grant program

redistributive programs

republic

reserved powers

residual powers

sovereignty

states' rights

zoning

NOTES

1. Stephanie A. McGrath, "Last Call Comes Early for Teens As Drinking Age Raised," *Houston Chronicle*, 1 September 1986, sec. 1, p. 12.
2. Stephen Gettinger, "Congress Clears Drunk Driving Legislation," *Congressional Quarterly*, 30 June 1984, pp. 1557–58.
3. Ibid., p. 1557.
4. Quoted in *Time*, 11 August 1986, pp. 71–72.
5. *McCulloch* v. *Maryland*, 4 Wheaton 316 (1819).
6. James R. Alexander, "State Sovereignty in the Federal System: Constitutional Protections Under the Tenth and Eleventh Amendments," *Publius: The Journal of Federalism* 16 (Spring 1986): 1–15.
7. *South Dakota* v. *Dole*, 107 S. Ct. 2793 (1987).
8. John E. Chubb, "Federalism and the Bias for Centralization," in Chubb and Paul E. Peterson, eds., *The New Direction in American Politics* (Washington, DC: Brookings Institution, 1985), pp. 273–306.
9. Ibid., pp. 275–77.
10. George E. Hale and Marian Lief Palley, *The Politics of Federal Grants* (Washington, DC: Congressional Quarterly Press, 1981), chap. 1.
11. Paul C. Peterson, Barry G. Rabe, and Kenneth K. Wong, *When Federalism Works* (Washington, DC: Brookings Institution, 1986), p. 32.
12. Chubb, pp. 273–306.
13. David B. Walker, "A Perspective on Intergovernmental Relations," in Richard H. Leach, ed., *Intergovernmental Relations in the 1980s* (New York: Marcel Dekker, 1983), pp. 1–13.
14. Terry Sanford, *Storm Over the States* (New York: McGraw-Hill, 1967), p. 1.
15. Denis P. Doyle and Terry W. Hartle, "*De Facto* New Federalism," *State Legislatures*, February 1986, pp. 21–24.
16. Daniel H. Haider, "The Intergovernmental System," *Proceedings of the Academy of Political Science* 34 (1981): 20–30.

17. Daniel P. Moynihan, *Maximum Feasible Misunderstanding* (New York: Free Press, 1970).
18. Albert J. Davis and S. Kenneth Howard, "Perspectives on a 'New Day' for Federalism," *Intergovernmental Perspective* 7 (Spring 1982): 9–21.
19. Chubb, p. 291.
20. Neal R. Peirce, "Reagan's Surprise Legacy to States and Cities," *National Journal,* 21 January 1989, p. 145.
21. John Herbers, "The New Federalism: Unplanned, Innovative and Here to Stay," *Governing,* October 1987, pp. 28–37.
22. Richard P. Nathan and Fred C. Doolittle, "Federal Grants: Giving and Taking Away," *Political Science Quarterly* 100 (Spring 1985): 53–74.
23. Jacqueline Calmes, "Bricks Without Straw: The Complaints Go On but Congress Keeps Mandating," *Governing,* September 1988, pp. 21–26.
24. Ibid.
25. Kenneth K. Wong and Paul E. Peterson, "Urban Response to Federal Program Flexibility: Politics of Community Development Block Grants," *Urban Affairs Quarterly* 21 (March 1986): 293–309.
26. Chubb, pp. 287–91.
27. Michael J. Rich, "Distributive Politics and the Allocation of Federal Grants," *American Political Science Review* 83 (March 1989): 193–213.
28. *Governing,* October 1987, p. 12; Marsha Tanner, "Supercollider Spurs Super State Competition," *State Government News,* June 1987, pp. 18–19.
29. Ann Markusen, Annalee Saxenian, and Marc Weiss, "Who Benefits from Intergovernmental Transfers," *Publius* 11 (Winter 1981): 5–35.
30. Robert A. Rankin, "The Reagan Legacy," *Houston Chronicle,* 21 February 1988, sec. 1, p. 19.
31. *U.S. News & World Report,* 17 February 1986, p. 25.
32. Morris P. Fiorina, *Congress: Keystone of the Washington Establishment* (New Haven, CT: Yale University Press, 1977), p. 48.
33. R. Douglas Arnold, "Local Roots of Domestic Policy," in Thomas E. Mann and Norman J. Ornstein, eds., *The New Congress* (Washington, DC: American Enterprise Institute, 1981), pp. 250–87.
34. "Grants Marked for AIDS Fight," *Houston Post,* 21 May 1986, p. 16A.

SUGGESTED READINGS

Benton, Edwin J., and Morgan, David R., eds. *Intergovernmental Relations and Public Policy.* Westport, CT: Greenwood Press, 1986.

Chubb, John E., and Peterson, Paul E., eds. *The New Direction in American Politics.* Washington, DC: Brookings Institution, 1985.

Dilger, Robert J. *The Sunbelt/Snowbelt Controversy: The War over Federal Funds.* New York: New York University Press, 1982.

Kettl, Donald F. *Government by Proxy: (Mis?)Managing Federal Programs.* Washington, DC: Congressional Quarterly Press, 1988.

Nathan, Richard P., et al. *Reagan and the States*. Princeton, NJ: Princeton University Press, 1987.

Peterson, Paul E., Rabe, Barry G., and Wong, Kenneth K. *When Federalism Works*. Washington, DC: Brookings Institution, 1986.

Reagan, Michael, and Sanzone, John G. *The New Federalism*. Boston: Little, Brown, 1981.

4

PUBLIC OPINION

LEARNING OBJECTIVES

1. To examine the process of political socialization, focusing on the role played by the various agents of political socialization.
2. To explain the theory underlying survey research, evaluating the utility and limitations of the method.
3. To define public opinion and evaluate its scope and depth.
4. To outline what research has learned about each of the following subject areas: political knowledge, support for democracy, political trust, political efficacy, and political philosophy.
5. To analyze the relationship between public opinion and public policy.

The final vote wasn't close. The House of Representatives defeated the proposal by a count of 380 to 48. Earlier, the Senate had turned it down by an even more lopsided margin of 94 to 6. Ironically, the bill was favored by former President Reagan, President Bush, and, privately, by a large majority of the members of Congress. What was this measure that went down to such a resounding defeat in both houses of Congress? A pay-raise proposal that would have increased the salaries of the members of Congress by more than 50 percent, from $89,500 to $135,000 a year.

In late 1988, a special commission established to evaluate the salary levels of roughly twenty-five hundred top government officials recommended substantial pay raises for members of Congress, federal judges, and a number of upper-level officials in the executive branch. Both outgoing President Reagan and incoming President Bush endorsed the commission's report and included money for salary increases in their budget proposals. According to law, the pay raises would take effect unless both houses of Congress voted to reject them within thirty days. The strategy of the congressional leadership, who favored the pay increase, was to let the Senate vote against the raise but to delay a vote in the House until after the deadline. Consequently, the pay raise would become law without members of Congress having to go on record in favor of increasing their own salaries.

Congressional leaders, however, had not counted on an overwhelmingly negative public reaction. Newspaper editorial writers and radio talk-show hosts attacked Congress over the size of the pay raise and the strategy behind its implementation, with much of the criticism directed against Speaker of the House Jim Wright. Thousands of citizens wrote angry letters to their senators and representatives, and a national opinion poll found that 85 percent of the American people opposed the pay increase.[1] Even a number of members of Congress publicly attacked the pay raise (despite, in some cases, privately hoping it would become law). Eventually, Speaker Wright gave in to the pressure. He scheduled a vote in the House and the pay raise was defeated by a huge margin.[2]

The story of Congress' ill-fated pay raise is a good illustration to begin our study of public opinion in America. On this issue, public opinion determined public policy, at least for the short run. The pay-raise question, however, was a highly publicized controversy about a matter that most Americans readily understand. On other issues, less visible and more complex, the relationship between public opinion and public policy is not as clear.

Indeed, six months later Congress got its raise, although not as large as the original proposal. The House voted a 7.9 percent salary increase for 1990, an election year, to be followed by a 25 percent raise in 1991. The Senate, meanwhile, limited itself to a 9.9 percent increase for 1990. The difference between this pay-raise proposal and the one that failed earlier in the year was that this increase was smaller and more straightforward (Congress made no effort to avoid a vote), and the measure was packaged with a number of ethics reforms that included limitations on outside income. What's more, congressional leaders of both parties and President Bush all agreed to support the proposal, promising they would not use the vote as an election issue.

In this chapter, we examine public opinion in America and consider its role in the policymaking process. We begin with the process of opinion formation—political socialization.

POLITICAL SOCIALIZATION

Political socialization is the process whereby individuals acquire political knowledge, attitudes, and beliefs. Although socialization is a learning process, much of what individuals know and believe about politics and government isn't the result of formal teaching. To be sure, some of our knowledge of government was taught to us in the classroom or explained to us by our parents when we were youngsters. Much of what we know and believe about politics, however, we learn informally throughout our entire lives. We are socialized politically when we see our parents go to the polls, hear schoolmates discuss the war on illegal drugs, listen to newscasts, serve on a jury, pay property taxes, or wait for police after we discover that a burglar has broken into our home.

Process of Socialization

Studies have found that young children tend to personalize and idealize the political system. By the age of five or six, most youngsters are able to associate police officers and the president with government. Their attitudes toward these figures are positive. Children regard police officers as friends and helpers, and they tell researchers that the president is someone who is smarter and more honest than most people. Most children can distinguish the American flag from others and they say that it is their favorite.

As children grow older, their knowledge of government increases, but they still recognize people and symbols more readily than they understand procedures and processes. Although grade-school youngsters are able to identify such terms as *Congress*, *political party*, and *democracy*, for instance, their understanding of these concepts is still rudimentary. Most children think of Congress as a group of men and women who help the president. Many youngsters can name the political party their family supports, but they are unable to note differences between the parties. Even though most children declare democracy to be the best form of government, few understand the term's meaning.[3]

In adolescence, young people begin to resemble adults politically. They are able to separate individual roles from institutional roles, recognizing that it is possible to criticize the president, for example, while still supporting the presidency. Procedures and processes such as voting and lawmaking are more visible and important to adolescents, and their general knowledge of the political process is more sophisticated. Moreover, in adolescence, the attitudes of different groups toward the political system begin to diverge. Studies have found that the socialization experiences of young children are similar. In adolescence, though, minority children grow less trustful of authority figures, especially police officers. In contrast, young people from middle-class white families remain supportive of the political system.[4]

Although basic political attitudes and beliefs are often set by the time individuals reach adulthood, political socialization is a lifelong process. As young adults enter the work force, purchase homes, start families, change careers, and, eventually, retire, their political views may change. Let's consider some of the factors that influence the development of political knowledge, attitudes, and beliefs.

Agents of Socialization

Those factors that contribute to political socialization by shaping formal and informal learning are known as **agents of socialization**. These factors affect the level, intensity, and direction of our thoughts and actions about politics. In American society, the agents of socialization include the family, the school, peer groups, religious institutions, the media, and events.

Family

The family's influence on political socialization is important, but it is difficult to assess precisely because the family's power is private, subtle, and ongoing. We know, however, that families filter information about politics for children and transmit signals about political events. Family background, for example, affects interest and involvement in politics. Children whose parents are politically active are more likely to grow into politically active adults than are youngsters from families with little political involvement.[5] Moreover, the influence of family can strengthen or weaken the impact of other socializing forces, such as school or peer groups. One study found that children from lower-class backgrounds experience patterns of political socialization different from those of middle-class children.[6] These differences may help explain class variations in political attitudes among adults.

For years, the accepted wisdom of political science was that families shape the development of political-party loyalties. One study of fourth graders found that 60 percent of the children identified with a party even though the youngsters had virtually no knowledge of party history, issues, or candidates. Instead, they merely adopted the party of their parents in much the way they accepted their parents' religious affiliation. Proclaiming "We're Democrats" was as natural for the children as saying "We're Catholics."[7] A study of high-school students found that most young people shared their parents' party loyalties.[8] Nonetheless, party identification isn't necessarily fixed in childhood and adolescence. By the age of twenty-five, young adults often adjust their partisanship to place it in line with the party they prefer on the issues about which they care.[9]

School

The school is an important agent of political socialization, but not, ironically, because of civics education. Children learn some of the basic mechanics of government in elementary school, but high-school civics classes add little to their knowledge and understanding. Research has found that civics courses have almost no effect on students' knowledge of government, participatory skills, political tolerance, or support for democracy.[10] Perhaps this is an indication of the general weakness of American education; some studies show that high-school civics teachers often know little about their subject.[11]

Schools are effective, however, at teaching patriotism, at molding children into little Americans. In the classroom, students pledge allegiance to the flag, sing patriotic songs, commemorate national holidays, and study the lives of great Americans. Schools also give young people firsthand experience working within a power structure. A school is a self-contained political system, with peers, authorities, rules, rewards, and punishments. Youngsters inevitably develop attitudes about authority and their roles as participants in the system. Schools aren't democracies, of course; principals and teachers are often more interested in discipline than participation. Some scholars believe that the primary focus of schools on compliance hinders the development of political participation skills.[12] Research has found this is particularly true of schools in working-class areas.[13]

The effects of college on political socialization are difficult to measure. Students who attend college differ politically from people who do not, but the college-bound tend to vary from their peers even before they go to college. Studies have found that high-school graduates who go on to college are more knowledgeable and interested in politics and feel more capable of influencing the policy process than young people who are not college-bound.[14]

Nevertheless, college life does appear to loosen family ties as far as political attitudes are concerned. College can be a broadening experience as students are exposed to a greater variety of ideas and people than they were in high school. As a result, collegians are less likely to share their family's political views than people who do not attend college. We should add, though, that the political impact of college depends on the type of institution students attend, their major field of study, and whether or not they work their way through school.

Religious Institutions

For many Americans, churches, synagogues, and other religious institutions are important agents of political socialization. Survey research indicates that Catholics, Protestants, and Jews often hold differing viewpoints on such issues as abortion, capital punishment, school prayer, and liquor regulation. Studies have also found important issue differences among white Protestants based on their frequency of church attendance—with people who attend church regularly holding more conservative views on such social issues as abortion, school prayer, pornography, and the rights of gay people than do people who are less active religiously.[15]

Churches and other religious bodies constitute communities that are often well suited to the transmission and maintenance of group norms. In a recent study of Protestant churches, several political scientists found that churches often promote distinctive political outlooks. Even though people tend to join churches whose political beliefs are similar to their own, churches have an independent effect on political views. What's more, the researchers discovered that, with the exception of some denominations, church attendance and electoral participation are positively related.[16]

Peer Groups

Our peers are the people with whom we associate socially and professionally. Peer-group influence on political socialization is found in many settings: back-fence conversations between neighbors, beauty shop and barbershop visits, union meetings, and boardrooms. Studies have found that peers are more important in shaping the issue positions of young people than are their parents[17] and that when adults change peer groups because of a new job or a move to a different city, their political views may change as well.[18]

The impact of a peer group on an individual's political views depends on the importance of the group to the individual. People are more likely to share the values of a group that is important to them than they are those of a group that is less significant. Nonetheless, many persons remain in groups despite value disagreements because they overlook the conflict. A recent study of conservative Christian churches found that nearly 40 percent of women members held feminist views. The feminist women perceived little or no connection between their religious beliefs and their political views.[19]

The much-publicized confrontation between George Bush and CBS News anchor Dan Rather in front of a national television audience during the 1988 presidential campaign.

Media

Political scientists believe that the media, especially television, determine the relative importance Americans attach to various national problems. In other words, the media help set the policy agenda. One study found, for example, that television news stories influence the priorities Americans assign to various national problems.[20] Another study discovered that a local television investigation of police brutality increased public perceptions of the importance of the issue.[21]

Scholars also think that media coverage of political events draws attention to some aspects of political life at the expense of others. News reports, for example, help define the criteria by which the public evaluates a president's performance. If the media focus on national defense, for example, studies find that citizens judge the president largely by their perception of how well the president has provided for national defense. In 1980, the media's extensive coverage of the Iranian-hostage crisis led voters to cast their ballots against President Carter on the basis of his handling of that issue.[22] (For a discussion of the political content of news media coverage, see the Perspective.)

Scholarly research indicates that the manner in which television news frames political issues for viewers influences individual evaluations of those issues. A recent study found, for example, that when viewers watch news accounts of poverty that deal with poverty rates, hunger, and the homeless, they tend to regard the problem as a national concern requiring a public policy solution. In contrast, when they see news stories that highlight an individual poor person, viewers tend to blame the individual for being poor. Since the individualized approach is indeed the way the media usually cover poverty, news reports may (inadvertently) reduce public support for public policies designed to alleviate hunger and help the homeless.[23]

Nonetheless, Professor Michael J. Robinson, a specialist in the political role of the media, warns against overestimating the importance of the media in shaping political attitudes. Even though the media set the policy agenda, he says, political leaders often set the agenda for the media. If the president travels abroad, for example, it is likely that television network news anchors will go along and the president's visit will be the lead story for every newscast.

Moreover, the public does not necessarily follow the lead of the press. Throughout the 1984 presidential campaign, for example, Democratic vice-presidential candidate Geraldine Ferraro's standing in public-opinion polls fell despite improving press coverage.[24] Similarly, a study of network coverage of the 1988 presidential nomination campaign found that the candidate who received the most positive press coverage was Governor Bruce Babbitt of Arizona, who got nowhere in his campaign for the Democratic nomination. In contrast, George Bush, who won it all, received less favorable coverage than either of his two main Republican opponents, Congressman Jack Kemp and Senator Robert Dole.[25]

Events

Events are not as tangible as parents and schools, but they too are important agents of political socialization. Elections, for example, provide children and adolescents with information about political processes and institutions. During an election campaign, young people become more aware of political authority. Adults are also socialized by political events. Dramatic events attract media attention, prompting discussions among citizens and increasing the likelihood that people's normal understanding of the political world will be challenged and perhaps altered. Moreover, events can be personal as well as distant. An individual's attitude about the criminal justice system, for instance, can be affected by a personal encounter with a police officer or by serving on a jury.

Politics of Socialization

As we have noted, much of our political socialization is the result of incidental experiences. As children, we overhear our parents discussing politics, or a police officer helps us when we become lost. As adults, we watch a television movie about abortion, or we lose our job during a recession. Although we learn about politics and government from each of these experiences, our learning isn't the result of conscious teaching.

At other times, however, political authorities and others consciously attempt to shape our attitudes and beliefs. In the late nineteenth and early twentieth centuries in particular, public schools worked diligently to teach Americanism to the children of a nation of immigrants. Today, political leaders manipulate symbols and images in hopes of influencing public opinion. After American forces landed in Grenada, for example, President Reagan criticized reporters who called the action an "invasion." It was a "rescue mission" for the American medical students there, he said. Similarly, the Bush administration's code name for the invasion of Panama was "Operation Just Cause."

PERSPECTIVE

Are the News Media Biased?

In the late 1960s, the Nixon administration, spearheaded by Vice President Spiro Agnew, attacked the news media for an alleged liberal bias. "Nattering nabobs of negativism," sputtered Agnew in describing the press. In contrast, other, more liberal observers believe that the media act to reinforce society's dominant values. One critic argues that, for economic reasons, the media try not to offend anyone. As a result, radical ideas don't receive a hearing.*

Scholarly research on the subject has provided no clear answer to the question of political bias in the news media. One study of the 1980 election found that Democratic President Jimmy Carter received more negative press coverage than Republican candidate Ronald Reagan.[†] In contrast, a study of the 1988 campaigns for the Democratic and Republican presidential nominations calculated that while 56 percent of all press references to Democratic candidates were favorable, 54 percent of the references to Republicans were favorable as well.[‡]

Political scientists have found, however, that news-media coverage doesn't necessarily mirror real life. A recent study compared American network news coverage of international terrorism with a data set listing reported acts of terrorism gathered from a broad range of worldwide news sources. In some years, the study found, international terrorism increased while coverage decreased, and vice versa. The networks (ABC, CBS, and NBC) tended to overplay hostage seizures, hijacking, attacks against private citizens, and terrorist incidents in the Middle East. In contrast, the networks underplayed bombings, political threats, attacks against U.S. business executives, and terrorism in Latin America. The scholars concluded that network coverage made it difficult for viewers to develop an accurate image of the nature and frequency of terrorism. The networks' picture made the Middle East seem more chaotic than it is while Latin America appeared less important. Moreover, the networks' coverage made terrorism seem irrational, even random, because it obscured the reasons terrorists select their victims.[§]

*Eric Barnow, *The Sponsors: Notes on a Modern Potentate* (New York: Oxford University Press, 1978).
[†]Michael J. Robinson and Margaret Sheehan, *Over the Wire and on TV* (New York: Russell Sage Foundation, 1983).
[‡]S. Robert Lichter, Daniel Amundson, and Richard Noyes, *The Video Campaign: Network Coverage of the 1988 Primaries* (Washington, DC: American Enterprise Institute, 1988), p. 97.
[§]Michael X. Delli Carpini and Bruce A. Williams, "Television and Terrorism: Patterns of Presentation and Occurrence, 1969–1980," *Western Political Quarterly* 40 (March 1987): 45–64.

MEASURING PUBLIC OPINION

Survey research (the measurement of public opinion) is now a familiar part of the American scene. Businesses use market surveys to assess public tastes for their products and services. Political campaigns employ polls to plan strategy. The media use polls to gauge public reaction to political events and to forecast election results. Scholars rely on survey research as a tool for studying political knowledge, attitudes, and beliefs. Measuring public opinion is big business, and major national pollsters—Gallup, Harris, Roper, Yankelovitch—are household names for many Americans. The Center for Political Studies (CPS), formerly the Survey Research Center (SRC), at the University of Michigan is the most prominent center for academic survey research.

Sampling

The theory behind survey research is that one can accurately measure the characteristics of a universe by examining a relatively small sample. In survey research, a **universe** is the population being studied. It may consist of all Americans, all Californians, or all Catholics. A **sample** is a subset of a universe. Statisticians tell us that a sample of only a thousand persons produces results that are accurate within plus-or-minus three percentage points 95 percent of the time (regardless of the size of the universe). If our survey shows that 60 percent of a particular sample of Americans tell interviewers that they favor gun control, for example, then the odds are 95 in 100 that 57 to 63 percent of all Americans (our universe) would say that they favor gun control.

To be an accurate reflection of a universe, a sample must be representative of that universe. If we are interested in the views of all Americans, a sample of one thousand people from Detroit, one thousand women, or one thousand callers to a radio talk program would not likely be representative. Statisticians tell us that an unrepresentative sample is a **biased sample**, that is, a sample that tends to produce results that don't reflect the true characteristics of the universe because it is unrepresentative of the universe.

A biased sample produced one of the most famous polling errors in history. During the 1920s and 1930s, a magazine called the *Literary Digest* conducted presidential polls every four years. In 1936, the magazine mailed ten million ballots to individuals whose names and addresses were drawn from telephone directories and automobile registration lists across the country. About two million people responded. On that basis, *Literary Digest* predicted that Alf Landon, the Republican challenger, would defeat Democratic President Franklin Roosevelt by a resounding 57 to 43 percent. Instead, Roosevelt was reelected by the largest landslide in American history.

What went wrong? *Literary Digest*'s sample included only telephone and automobile owners. In the midst of the Great Depression, these people were generally middle- and upper-income folks, who tended to vote Republican. In contrast, many poor and working-class people who could not afford cars and telephones weren't sampled by the poll. On election day, they voted for Roosevelt.

Although nothing can guarantee a representative sample 100 percent of the time, the ideal approach is to employ a random sample. A **random sample** is a sample in which each member of a universe has an equal likelihood of being included; it is unbiased. If our universe were students at a college, we could select a random sample by picking every fifth or tenth student from a master list. Taking a true random sample of all adult Americans or all Californians, however, is virtually impossible, since no master list is available to researchers. At any rate, a completely random sample of one thousand Americans would likely be so scattered about the country that it would be prohibitively expensive for interviewers to meet with each one. Respondents could be telephoned, of course, but that would omit those without phones. A mail survey is an even less desirable alternative because many people won't reply and those individuals who do may or may not be similar in important respects to those who do not. (In general, scholars believe that middle- and upper-income people are more likely to return a mail questionnaire than working-class individuals.) This was another major weakness of the *Literary Digest* poll.

Today, most reputable survey researchers use a method known as **cluster sampling**, which is a technique for taking a sample in stages. If the universe were all adult Americans, researchers would first divide the country into geographic regions. Within each region, they would select several counties at random. Within each county, then, the researchers would randomly choose a number of census tracts (fairly small areas for which census data are available). Next, they would select several city blocks from each tract. In each block, interviewers would choose particular households on the basis of an established rule—say, the second house from the southeast corner. Finally, an interviewer would question one person of voting age at the house. To save time and expense, many polling firms group people by telephone exchanges instead of neighborhoods and then conduct telephone interviews with individuals called at random. This procedure is somewhat less satisfactory, since it excludes people without telephones. Technically, cluster sampling is random in the sense that every individual in the universe has an equal likelihood of being included, but, for statistical reasons, it is not as efficient a method as a simple random sample. In general, though, a national cluster sample of about fifteen hundred persons is as accurate as a simple random sample of a thousand.

Question Wording

The best sample is worthless if survey questions are invalid. If researchers want to ask respondents whom they prefer in an upcoming election, the question is straightforward and the results are clear. Asking about issues, however,

Drawing by Mort Gerbert; © 1987 The New Yorker Magazine, Inc.

is more complex. Changes in question wording, even subtle changes, can produce dramatic variations in response. In 1980, for example, the *New York Times* commissioned a poll in which interviewers asked individuals if they favored a constitutional amendment prohibiting abortion. Twenty-nine percent said yes, 62 percent no, and 9 percent expressed no opinion. Later in the same poll, interviewers asked the same respondents if they favored an amendment protecting the life of an unborn child. This time, 50 percent favored the amendment, 39 percent opposed it, and another 11 percent did not have an opinion.[26] Did either question accurately measure public opinion on the issue? No one can say for sure. This example also demonstrates the potential for mischief from those who would like to manufacture survey data to support their own points of view. Moral Majority Leader Jerry Falwell once surveyed his followers with this question: "Do you approve of the present laws legalizing abortion on demand that result in the murder of 1.5 million unborn babies every year?" It's easy to see which side Falwell is on, and it's easy to predict the kind of responses he received.

Attitudes and Non-Attitudes

Another troubling problem facing survey researchers involves differentiating between attitudes and "non-attitudes," as one scholar calls them. People tend to make up responses to questions they have thought little about so they won't appear ignorant. These non-attitudes are so weakly tied to the respondents' thinking that interviewees are likely to give opposite answers to the same question within a matter of days or weeks.[27] One study designed to measure the extent of this phenomenon found that 20 to 25 percent of survey respondents expressed opinions on completely fictitious policy issues.[28] Professional pollsters try to filter out uncommitted opinions by offering respondents a relatively painless opportunity to confess they haven't heard of an issue or don't have an opinion. Still, the difficulty of separating real attitudes from non-attitudes is potentially a serious problem for any survey.

Interviewer-Respondent Interaction

Researchers know that the race or gender of an interviewer can sometimes affect poll results as respondents struggle to say the "right thing," based on the race or gender of the interviewer. One poll found, for example, that when interviewers were white, black respondents were considerably more likely to say that white people could be trusted than when the interviews were conducted by fellow blacks.[29] Similarly, a recent survey found differences as great as 20 percentage points when women were asked questions on abortion by a female as opposed to a male interviewer.[30]

Timing

Even the most professionally conducted survey is only a snapshot of public opinion on the day of the poll. Surveys don't make good crystal balls because of the variability of public opinion. In 1980, for example, the final Gallup and Harris surveys taken a week before the election showed the race too close to call, yet Ronald Reagan won by a substantial margin. Were the polls wrong? No, but they proved to be poor prognosticators. Polls conducted for the candidates also showed a close race until the weekend before election day. At that point, polls by both the Carter and Reagan camps indicated that the undecided vote turned dramatically against President Carter. The Gallup and Harris polls apparently had been correct when they were taken, but by election day, the climate of opinion had changed.

THE CONTENT OF PUBLIC OPINION

Public opinion is the combined personal opinions of adults toward issues of relevance to government. Not all Americans, though, hold opinions on all issues. In fact, most Americans are unaware of, or at least uninterested in, many political issues. One scholar divides the public into three groups. At one end of the political interest spectrum, we find a large group of people, about a fifth of the population, who are indifferent to politics; they have no opinions. At the other end are political junkies, a small group, probably less than 5 percent of the population, who are interested in politics and well informed. The great majority of Americans, meanwhile, fit in the middle. Most of the time, they follow political developments halfheartedly. Although they have carefully developed opinions on some issues, on most issues, their opinions are vague and incomplete.[31]

Persons who have an active and continuing interest in a particular political issue are known as the **attentive public** for that issue. Most Americans belong to an attentive public for only one issue or a small number of issues. A physician, for example, might be part of the attentive public on the issue of medical malpractice insurance reform. An accountant would probably be alert to changes in tax laws. On a few issues, such as the Vietnam War during the late 1960s and early 1970s, the attentive public may be relatively large, including, perhaps, a majority of Americans. For most issues, though, the attentive public is small, perhaps minuscule. One scholar estimates that on most issues, only one in five Americans has a stable, firmly held opinion.[32] Probably only a fraction of that number would be interested enough in a particular issue to be considered part of its attentive public.

Individuals hold political views with varying degrees of intensity. Some Americans feel strongly about nuclear energy, for instance, while others hold opinions on the subject without much emotion. Few Americans are neutral about the issue of abortion. The adoption of daylight savings time, though, has provoked few political demonstrations.

Finally, public opinion waxes and wanes as issues grow in importance or recede from view. In the late 1970s, many Americans held strong views about the Panama Canal Treaty that returned sovereignty over the canal to Panama. After the Senate ratified the treaty, however, passions cooled and the issue faded. In contrast, public concern about drug abuse is greater now than it was in the 1970s.

Political Knowledge

Americans in general are poorly informed about politics and government. Surveys have found that a majority cannot name their representative in Congress or even one of the United States senators from their state. Most Americans are unable to identify the Bill of Rights or name the three branches of government. Barely a majority know that *Brown* v. *Board of Education* involved school integration.[33] To be sure, a minority of Americans are knowledgeable about politics, and most people are probably informed on at least a few matters of concern to them. Still, it appears, as one group of scholars puts it, that the American public includes "a hard core of chronic know-nothings."[34]

Who's to blame? One prominent political scientist, the late V. O. Key, Jr., points the finger at the political process. Candidates and officeholders don't explain issues to the voters, he says. We might add that the media often do a poor job of educating the public about politics as well. An additional explanation is that most people are more interested in matters other than politics. Some of us may be political junkies, but most Americans would rather devote their time and energy to earning a living, raising a family, and enjoying life than to learning about government.

Americans' general lack of political sophistication affects the policy process. First, it means that style usually wins out over substance in election campaigns. Candidates focus on images and sloganeering rather than intelligent discussions of issues. Second, a majority of adult Americans probably lack an understanding of public affairs sufficient to participate intelligently in the policy process. In fact, only about half the nation's eligible voters take part in presidential elections. Third, the public's ignorance about politics means that public opinion offers little specific guidance for policymakers. For example, a recent survey found that 42 percent of a national sample of Americans believe that government spends too much on welfare, with just 23 percent saying it spends too little. The same survey also asked about government "assistance to the poor." This time, 68 percent said that government spends too little; only 7 percent said too much.[35] Besides illustrating the problem of question wording, this example tells us something about the public's knowledge of government programs. Many Americans apparently don't know that welfare and government programs to assist the poor are the same. One can see why policymakers are confused about the sort of public policy a majority of Americans prefer. Finally, some observers worry that democracy may be threatened by political ignorance. As one scholar asks, "Will people who do not understand American democracy sufficiently value it so that they will want to preserve it?"[36]

Support for Democracy

Do Americans support the democratic principles of majority rule and minority rights? Political scientists have worked for several decades to answer this question. During the 1950s, Professor Samuel Stouffer conducted a major study to evaluate public opinion toward civil liberties. He found a high level of intolerance toward persons with unpopular views. For example, only 27 percent of the persons interviewed in his sample would allow "an admitted communist" to make a speech.[37]

In 1960, two political scientists, James W. Prothro and C. W. Grigg, published what has become a classic study on the subject of political tolerance. Their sample of Americans overwhelmingly endorsed statements that public officials should be chosen by majority vote and that people whose opinions were in the minority should have the right to convince others of their views. When Prothro and Grigg asked about specific, concrete situations, however, they found dramatically less support for the practice of majority rule and minority rights. Many respondents in their survey said that a communist should not be allowed to take office even if legally elected. Many persons also thought that atheists should not be allowed to speak publicly against religion.[38] In the years since the Prothro and Grigg study first appeared, other research has confirmed that Americans are more likely to endorse democratic principles in the abstract than in specific application. One study even found a majority of Americans opposed to many of the specific provisions of the Bill of Rights.[39]

Then, in the 1970s, a number of studies concluded that Americans were growing more tolerant of political diversity. Using questions almost identical to those asked by Stouffer twenty years earlier, political scientists found significantly larger percentages of Americans willing to tolerate such "nonconformists" as atheists, socialists, and communists. Some scholars concluded that the trend toward greater tolerance reflected a younger, more urbanized, better-educated population.[40]

More recent research, however, contradicts the conclusion that Americans have grown more tolerant of political diversity. These studies have found that while attitudes toward socialists, communists, and atheists have generally become more tolerant, many Americans, including well-educated persons, express intolerant attitudes towards racists and persons advocating military rule in the United States. Apparently, Americans are no more tolerant of persons with unpopular views today than they were in the 1950s. The only difference is that the targets of their intolerance have changed.[41]

A number of political scientists believe that the general public has little understanding or concern for civil liberties. (**Civil liberties** are the protection of the individual from the unrestricted power of government.) "[T]he only time many people consider... [civil liberties]," one scholar says, "is when they are being queried about it in public-opinion surveys."[42] Consequently, people respond to questions about civil liberties based on their perception of a particular group's threat to society. In the 1950s, many Americans feared communism and, as Stouffer discovered, favored limiting free speech for communists. Americans today are not as likely to regard communists as a threat to the nation's well-being as they are groups such as the Ku Klux Klan. When answering survey questions, then, they express more tolerance for communists than for Klansmen.[43]

Americans' apparent indifference to civil liberties, at least as they apply to people with unpopular views, disturbs a number of observers. Many political theorists believe that maintenance of a free society requires a high degree of popular support for civil liberties. How, then, can we explain the stability of democracy in America in the face of research that has often found a lack of support for the fundamental principles of democracy?

Political scientists offer three possible explanations for this paradox. First, attitudes don't necessarily lead to action. Although many Americans may tell interviewers that they think communists or Klansmen or whoever should not be allowed to express their views, this doesn't mean that they are ready to take action to halt free speech.

Second, Americans don't agree on the target groups to be suppressed. Some people believe that communists should be kept from expressing their

The constitutional right of free speech is guaranteed to all citizens—even those who hold unpopular views.

views or holding public office, while others favor silencing Klansmen, anti-abortionists, or pro-abortionists. Since Americans don't agree on which groups should be suppressed, they are unable to unite behind undemocratic public policies.

Finally, a number of political scientists believe that public opinion on this issue isn't nearly so important as the views of political leaders. Studies have found that practical support for democratic principles is stronger among people who are politically active than among individuals who are politically uninvolved. The saving grace for American democracy may be that those who are most directly involved in policymaking—political elites—are the most supportive of the principles of majority rule and minority rights.[44]

Political Trust

Many scholars believe that political trust is essential to the preservation of a healthy democracy. For the most part, democracy depends on the voluntary cooperation of its citizens rather than their coercion. People pay taxes and obey laws essentially because they believe such actions are proper. They work to redress grievances through the political system, and they peacefully accept the outcome of the election process.

If a significant proportion of the population ceases to trust the political system, however, the quality of democracy declines. Tax evasion and disrespect for the rule of law increase. Potential for a revolutionary change in the political order may develop. Political battles may be fought with bullets, not ballots.

The Center for Political Studies (CPS) has attempted to measure political trust by means of a series of questions regularly asked of national samples of Americans. The questions probe the degree to which citizens believe government leaders in Washington, D.C., are honest (or crooked) and competent (or incompetent). One question, for example, is phrased as follows: "How much of the time do you think you can trust the government in Washington to do what is right—just about always, most of the time, or only some of the time?" Another question reads, "Do you think that quite a few of the people running the government are a little crooked, not very many are, or do you think hardly any of them are crooked at all?"[45]

When the CPS first began asking these questions in 1958, about 70 percent of respondents scored medium or high on a political trust index derived from responses to the survey questions. That figure remained fairly constant until the mid-1960s, when the index began to record a sharp decline in trust. By 1980, fewer than 40 percent of respondents in the CPS national survey scored medium or high on the trust index. Although survey data showed that Americans' level of trust in government rose during the first half of the 1980s, it fell again after the Iran-contra scandal (in which it was revealed that the Reagan administration sold arms to Iran and diverted profits to the contra guerrillas in Nicaragua).[46]

The variation in data suggests that the CPS political trust index doesn't so much measure trust in American democracy as it assesses confidence in government institutions and political leaders. One group of scholars argues that the answers Americans give to CPS questions reflect their reaction to political events, such as the Vietnam War and the Iran-contra scandal. What's more, answers to other survey questions indicate that most Americans still have a deep-seated allegiance to the values of democracy. In short, these political scientists say, there is no evidence that the nation is facing a crisis of political legitimacy.[47] (**Political legitimacy**, you recall, is the popular acceptance of a government and its officials as rightful authorities in the exercise of power.)

Political Efficacy

Political efficacy is the extent to which people believe they can affect the policymaking process. Political scientists identify two components to this concept: **internal political efficacy** concerns individuals' evaluations of their own ability to influence policy, while **external political efficacy** refers to individuals' assessment of governmental responsiveness to their demands. The CPS has sought to measure political efficacy by asking respondents if they believe government cares what they think, if they believe they have a say in what government does, and if they think government is too complicated to understand. CPS data show that internal efficacy has risen over the last two decades, especially among young people, while external efficacy has fallen steadily. Ironically, Americans have grown more confident in their ability to understand government and to articulate their political views, but they are less confident that government cares about and will listen to what they have to say. Many political scientists believe that this decline in external efficacy is responsible for much of the drop in voter turnout the nation has experienced over the last twenty years or so.[48]

Political Philosophy

Have Americans grown more conservative? Many political commentators say that they have, and they point to the elections of Ronald Reagan in 1980 and 1984 and George Bush in 1988 as evidence of the nation's turn to the right (the more conservative side). Table 4.1 presents data showing how Americans describe their own political philosophy. As you can see, the proportion of people who call themselves liberal declined between 1976 and 1988, while the proportion of self-described conservatives remained fairly constant. In contrast, the number of people calling themselves moderates grew. (You may want to turn back to chapter 1 to review the definitions/descriptions of liberalism and conservatism.)

Nonetheless, political scientists warn against putting too much stock in self-appraisals of political philosophy. Studies have found that many Americans cannot accurately define liberalism and conservatism. Moreover, research shows that few people structure their thinking along liberal-conservative lines.[49] It is not unusual for individuals who call themselves conservatives to express liberal positions on particular issues, or vice versa. Also, many Americans hold liberal views on some issues and conservative opinions on others.

The survey data presented in Table 4.1 represent the views of a national sample of Americans. National figures, though, obscure variations in opinion among subgroups of the population. Let's look briefly at the political viewpoints associated with a few important subgroups.

Social Class

Studies have found a number of interesting differences of opinion between working-class and middle-income Americans. On one hand, working-class people tend to be more liberal on social-welfare issues than middle-class individuals. People in low-income groups often see themselves as beneficiaries of these programs, while middle-income people think in terms of paying the bills. On the other hand, working-class individuals are often more conservative than other Americans on noneconomic issues. They are less supportive of women's rights and the rights of persons accused of crimes. Working-class whites are less supportive of civil rights for blacks than are middle-income whites.[50] In foreign-policy matters, working-class individuals are more isola-

TABLE 4.1

How Americans Describe Their Own Political Philosophy

Year	Liberal	Moderate	Conservative	Don't Know
1988	21%	41%	33%	5%
1981	18	39	37	6
1976	25	33	33	9

Source: CBS News/*New York Times* survey, January 1988, reported in *Public Opinion*, November/December 1988, p. 30.

tionist than middle-income people but also more supportive of the use of force in dealing with other nations. In contrast, middle- and upper-income people have a more internationalist perspective; they tend to favor free trade, foreign aid, and negotiated settlements of disputes.[51]

Race

Blacks, whites, and Hispanics hold different beliefs and values on many political and social issues. Although middle-class blacks are more conservative than working-class blacks on social-welfare issues (and, perhaps, affirmative action as well), blacks are substantially more liberal than whites at each income level.[52] Perhaps the best explanation for black liberalism is that blacks as a group have frequently benefited from the use of federal power. Hispanic-Americans tend to be more conservative than African-Americans but more liberal than whites on economic issues. On social issues, however, such as the proper role of women and the legalization of small amounts of marijuana, Hispanics are more conservative than either whites or blacks.[53]

Religion

Differences in public opinion are sometimes related to religion. On economic issues, Catholics have generally been more liberal than Protestants, though this may be class-related (historically, a disproportionate number of Catholics held low-income jobs). Jews tend to be liberal across the issue spectrum, although this phenomenon may be a consequence of education (as a group, Jews are better educated than Americans in general). White evangelical Protestants tend to be more conservative than other groups, especially on social and foreign-policy issues.[54]

Generation

Scholars have identified a number of differences in opinion among generations. Traditionally, younger Americans are more liberal than older Americans. Studies have found some interesting variations, however, in the attitudes of the youngest group of voters, ages 18 to 24. They tend to be more conservative than preceding generations on crime, anticommunism, and the role of government in the economy but more liberal on life-style issues, such as the role of women and the rights of gay people.[55]

Region

Differences among people from different geographical regions are fewer now than they once were, but they still exist. In general, people from the East or West coasts are more liberal than those from the southern, midwestern, or Rocky Mountain areas. Most regional differences, however, can be explained by other factors—class, race, religion, education. Nevertheless, some bona fide regional variations based on unique cultural and historical factors may play a role in the political fabric of the nation. The South's lingering identification with the Old Confederacy is perhaps the most notable example of how history can affect the political thinking of a region.

Gender

Through the 1970s, scholars found few differences between the attitudes of men and those of women. Even on so-called women's issues, such as abortion and the Equal Rights Amendment, the views of men and women were similar. Recently, however, survey researchers have discovered a **gender gap**, that is, differences in political opinion and behavior between men and women. Studies have found major differences between men and women on a number of issues, particularly those concerning war and peace. Men are more prone to favor the use of military force in the conduct of foreign affairs, while women are more concerned about the danger of war. In 1986, for example, a poll found that 73 percent of men supported the U.S. bombing raid on Libya, while only 58 percent of women approved.[56] Surveys have also found that women tend to be more liberal than men on social issues. Women, for example, are more often against the death penalty than are men and more frequently opposed to the relaxation of environmental standards.[57]

Political scientist Pamela Johnston Conover believes that women differ from men in their political values depending on the degree to which they identify with the feminist (women's-rights) movement. Her research shows that nonfeminist women and men hold similar views on most issues. In contrast, feminist women are more committed than men to the value of equality, both between the sexes and among races. Feminists are also more liberal than men and nonfeminist women on a broad range of issues.[58]

CONCLUSION: PUBLIC OPINION AND PUBLIC POLICY

Does public opinion affect public policy? High-school civics classes sometimes give the impression that public opinion translates directly and immediately into policy, but that view is naive. In the meantime, some critics of American government believe that public attitudes have no impact on policy. Their position, however, is too cynical. In fact, the truth lies somewhere between those two extreme views.

Several studies have found a relationship between public opinion and policy at least some of the time. One scholarly study finds that national policy corresponds to public attitudes about two-thirds of the time.[59] That research is supported by a study of state policymaking that concludes that public opinion is a major determinant of state public policy.[60] Other research indicates that a politically active community can affect policy at the local level.[61] Nonetheless, political scientists generally agree that public opinion is usually only one of several factors affecting the public policy process.

The relative importance of public opinion in the policymaking process varies from issue to issue. When the attentive public is large and feelings are intense, the impact of public opinion can be considerable. Issues such as abortion, environmental protection, drug abuse, and congressional pay-raise proposals attract large, highly motivated attentive publics. On these types of issues, policymakers ignore public opinion at their peril. Even on some of these issues, however, public officials enjoy considerable policy leeway. On the issue of illegal drugs, for example, polls show general agreement that drugs are a serious problem but indicate no consensus on how best to handle the matter. Americans apparently want action, but they aren't united on what action they prefer.

Even on issues for which a sizable attentive public exists, political decision-makers, especially the president, can often swing majority support behind the policies they wish to pursue. This is particularly true in foreign affairs. In the late 1960s, for example, surveys consistently showed large majorities of Americans opposing United States recognition of the People's Republic of China. Then President Nixon traveled to Beijing and American public opinion turned around overnight, especially among Republicans, who as a group had been adamantly opposed to direct dealings with the Chinese communists.

On many issues, the attentive public may be small and/or relatively uninfluential. When this occurs, public attitudes may be an unimportant part of the policy process. We suspect, for instance, that public opinion plays little role in shaping American policy on the status of Tibet and the Dalai Lama. The Tibetan community in the United States is small, and most Americans probably think that the Dalai Lama is either a painter or a Peruvian beast of burden. Consequently, there is little public opinion on this matter, leaving American foreign policymakers free to set policy on other grounds.

Considering the American public's general ignorance of public affairs, policymakers enjoy considerable leeway in many, perhaps most, policy areas. This does not mean, however, that policymakers can disregard the public. Studies show than many voters hold public officials accountable for perceived policy outcomes.[62] For officeholders, reelection depends on policies that the public considers successful. Public opinion may offer little specific guidance on how to conduct economic policy, for instance, but voters know the difference between a healthy economy and a weak one and vote to reward or punish officeholders accordingly.

KEY TERMS

agents of socialization

attentive public

biased sample

civil liberties

cluster sampling

external political efficacy

gender gap

internal political efficacy

political efficacy

political legitimacy

political socialization

public opinion

random sample

sample

survey research

universe

NOTES

1. *Washington Post* poll, quoted in *National Journal*, 4 February 1989, p. 306.
2. "How the Pay-Raise Strategy Came Unraveled," *Congressional Quarterly Weekly Report*, 11 February 1989, pp. 264–67.
3. Fred I. Greenstein, *Children and Politics* (New Haven, CT: Yale University Press, 1956); Robert D. Hess and Judith V. Torney, *The Development of Political Attitudes in Children* (Chicago: Aldine Press, 1967); and David Easton and Jack Dennis, *Children in the Political System: Origins of Political Legitimacy* (New York: McGraw-Hill, 1969).
4. Edward Greenberg, "Orientations of Black and White Children to Political Activity," *Social Science Quarterly* 5 (December 1970): 561–71; Chris F. Garcia, *Political Socialization of Chicano Children* (New York: Praeger, 1973).
5. Paul Allen Beck and M. Kent Jennings, "Pathways to Participation," *American Political Science Review* 76 (March 1982): 94–108.
6. Robert E. Lane, "Fathers and Sons: Foundations of Political Beliefs," *American Sociological Review* 24 (August 1959): 502–11.
7. Greenstein, pp. 71–75.
8. M. Kent Jennings and Richard G. Niemi, "The Transmission of Political Values from Parent to Child," *American Political Science Review* 62 (March 1968): 169–84.
9. Charles H. Franklin, "Issue Preferences, Socialization, and the Evolution of Party Identification," *American Journal of Political Science* 28 (August 1984): 459–78.
10. Kenneth P. Langton, *Political Socialization* (New York: Oxford University Press, 1969), pp. 84–119.
11. Byron Massialas, *Education and the Political System* (Reading, MA: Addison-Wesley, 1969), p. 172.
12. Robert Cleary, *Political Education in the American Democracy* (Scranton, PA: Intext, 1971), p. 37.
13. Edgar Lott, "Civic Education, Community Norms, and Political Indoctrination," *American Sociological Review* 28 (February 1963): 69–75.
14. Langton, p. 116.
15. John R. Petrocik and Frederick T. Steeper, "The Political Landscape in 1988," *Public Opinion*, September/October 1987, pp. 41–44.

16. Kenneth D. Wald, Dennis E. Owen, and Samuel S. Hill, Jr., "Churches as Political Communities," *American Political Science Review* 82 (June 1988): 531–48.

17. Jennings and Niemi.

18. Herbert P. Hyman, *Political Socialization* (Glencoe, IL: Free Press, 1959), pp. 109–15.

19. Clyde Wilcox, "Feminism and Anti-Feminism Among Evangelical Women," *Western Political Quarterly* 42 (March 1989): 147–60.

20. Shanto Iyengar and Donald R. Kinder, *News That Matters: Television and American Opinion* (Chicago: University of Chicago Press, 1987), pp. 112–13.

21. Donna R. Leff, David L. Protess, and Stephen C. Brooks, "Crusading Journalism: Changing Public Attitudes and Policy-Making Agendas," *Public Opinion Quarterly* 50 (Fall 1986): 300–315.

22. Iyengar and Kinder, pp. 114–16.

23. Shanto Iyengar, "Television News and Citizens' Explanations of National Affairs," *American Political Science Review* 81 (September 1987): 815–31.

24. Michael J. Robinson, "News Media Myths and Realities: What Network News Did and Didn't Do in the 1984 General Campaign," in Kay Lehman Schlozman, ed., *Elections in America* (Boston: Allen and Unwin, 1987), pp. 143–70.

25. S. Robert Lichter, Daniel Amundson, and Richard Noyes, *The Video Campaign: Network Coverage of the 1988 Primaries* (Washington, DC: American Enterprise Institute, 1988), pp. 72, 89.

26. *New York Times*, 18 August 1980, p. A15.

27. Philip Converse, "Attitudes and Non-Attitudes: The Continuation of a Dialogue," in Edward Tufte, ed., *The Quantitative Analysis of Social Problems* (Reading, MA: Addison-Wesley, 1970), pp. 168–69.

28. George F. Bishop, Alfred J. Tuchfarber, and Robert W. Oldendick, "Opinions on Fictitious Issues: The Pressure to Answer Questions," *Public Opinion Quarterly* 50 (Summer 1986): 240–50.

29. Howard Schuman and Jean Converse, "The Effects of Black and White Interviewers on Black Response in 1968," *Public Opinion Quarterly* 35 (Spring 1971): 44–68; and Shirley Hatchett and Howard Schuman, "White Respondents and Race of Interviewer Effects," *Public Opinion Quarterly* 39 (Winter 1975): 523–28.

30. Richard Morin, "Women Asking Women About Men Asking Women About Men," *Washington Post*, National Weekly Edition, 15–21 January 1990, p. 37.

31. W. Russell Neuman, *The Paradox of Mass Politics: Knowledge and Opinion in the American Electorate* (Cambridge, MA: Harvard University Press, 1986).

32. Philip Converse, "Attitudes and Non-Attitudes."

33. Stephen Earl Bennett, "'Know-Nothings' Revisited: The Meaning of Political Ignorance Today," *Social Science Quarterly* 69 (June 1988): 476–90; Robert A. Goldwin, "What Americans Know About the Constitution," *Public Opinion*, October 1987 pp. 9–10; Richard Morin, "They're All Crooks—Whatever Their Names Are," *Washington Post*, National Weekly Edition, 29 May–4 June 1989, p. 39.

34. Angus Campbell, Philip E. Converse, Warren E. Miller, and Donald Stokes, *The American Voter* (New York: Wiley, 1960), p. 186.

35. *Public Opinion*, September/October 1988, p. 21.

36. Bennett, p. 485.

37. Samuel A. Stouffer, *Communism, Conformity, and Civil Liberties: A Cross Section of the Nation Speaks Its Mind* (Garden City, NY: Doubleday, 1955), pp. 28–42.

38. James W. Prothro and C. W. Grigg, "Fundamental Principles of Democracy: Bases of Agreement and Disagreement," *Journal of Politics* 22 (Spring 1960): 276–94.

39. Robert Chandler, *Public Opinion: Changing Attitudes on Contemporary Social and Political Issues*, A CBS News Reference Book (New York: R. R. Bowker, 1972), pp. 6–13.

40. Clyde Z. Nunn, Harry J. Crockett, Jr., and J. Allen Williams, Jr., *Tolerance for Nonconformity: A National Survey of Americans' Changing Commitment to Civil Liberties* (San Francisco: Jossey-Bass, 1978); James A. Davis, "Communism, Conformity, Cohorts, and Categories: American Tolerance in 1954 and 1972–73," *American Journal of Sociology* 81 (November 1975): 491–513.

41. John L. Sullivan, James Piereson, and George E. Marcus, *Political Tolerance and American Democracy* (Chicago: University of Chicago Press, 1982); John Mueller, "Trends in Political Tolerance," *Public Opinion Quarterly* 52 (Spring 1988): 1–25.

42. Mueller.

43. Donald Philip Green and Lisa Michele Waxman, "Direct Threat and Political Tolerance," *Public Opinion Quarterly* 51 (Summer 1987): 149–65.

44. Herbert McCloskey, "Consensus and Ideology in American Politics," *American Political Science Review* 58 (June 1964): 361–82; James L. Gibson, "Political Intolerance and Political Repression During the McCarthy Red Scare," *American Political Science Review* 82 (June 1988): 511–29.

45. Quoted in Arthur H. Miller, "Political Issues and Trust in Government: 1964–70," *American Political Science Review* 68 (September 1974): 951–72.

46. Ralph Erber and Richard R. Lau, "Political Cynicism Revisited: An Information-Processing Reconciliation of Policy-Based and Incumbency-Based Interpretations of Trust in Government," *American Journal of Political Science* 34 (February 1990): 231–53.

47. Seymour Martin Lipset and William Schneider, "The Confidence Gap During the Reagan Years, 1981–1987," *Political Science Quarterly* 102 (Spring 1987): 1–23.

48. Paul R. Abramson, *Political Attitudes in America* (San Francisco: Freeman, 1983), pp. 228–32.

49. William G. Jacoby, "The Sources of Liberal-Conservative Thinking: Education and Conceptualization," *Political Behavior* 10 (Winter 1988): 316–32.

50. Seymour Martin Lipset and Earl Rabb, *The Politics of Unreason* (New York: Harper & Row, 1970).

51. Eugene R. Wittkopf and Michael R. Maggiotto, "Elites and Masses: A Comparative Analysis of Attitudes Toward America's World Role," *Journal of Politics* 45 (May 1983): 303–34.

52. Susan Welch and Lorn Foster, "Class and Conservatism in the Black Community," *American Politics Quarterly* 15 (October 1987): 455–70.

53. Barry Sussman, "Searching for the Views of Ethnic Minorities," *Washington Post*, National Weekly Edition, 8 September 1986, p. 37.

54. Arthur H. Miller and Martin P. Wattenberg, "Politics from the Pulpit: Religiosity and the 1980 Elections," *Public Opinion Quarterly* 48 (Spring 1984): 301–17; Corwin Smidt, "Evangelicals and the 1984 Election: Continuity or Change?" *American Politics Quarterly* 15 (October 1987): 419–44.

55. Norman Ornstein, "What Political Dreams Are Made Of," *Public Opinion*, September/October 1986, pp. 13–14.

56. "Approval for Reagan Matches His Highest," *Houston Post*, 5 May 1986, p. 12D.

57. *Gallup Report*, January-February 1986, p. 13; *Houston Post*, 15 August 1983.

58. Pamela Johnston Conover, "Feminists and the Gender Gap," *Journal of Politics* 50 (November 1988): 985–1010.

59. Alan D. Moore, "Consistency Between Public Preferences and National Policy Decisions," *American Politics Quarterly* 7 (January 1979): 3–19.
60. G. C. Wright, Jr., R. S. Erikson, and J. P. McIver, "Public Opinion and Policy Liberalism in the American States," *American Journal of Political Science* 31 (November 1987): 980–1001.
61. Sidney Verba and Norman H. Nie, *Participation in America* (New York: Harper & Row, 1972), Part III.
62. Morris P. Fiorina, *Retrospective Voting in American National Elections* (New Haven, CT: Yale University Press, 1981).

SUGGESTED READINGS

Abramson, Paul R. *Political Attitudes in America*. San Francisco: Freeman, 1983.

Erikson, Robert S.; Luttbeg, Norman G.; and Tedin, Kent L. *American Public Opinion: Its Origins, Content, and Impact*, 2d ed. New York: Wiley, 1980.

Graber, Doris A. *Media Power in Politics*, 2d ed. Washington, DC: Congressional Quarterly Press, 1990.

Iyengar, Shanto, and Kinder, Donald R. *News That Matters: Television and American Opinion*. Chicago: University of Chicago Press, 1987.

Neuman, W. Russell. *The Paradox of Mass Politics: Knowledge and Opinion in the American Electorate*. Cambridge, MA: Harvard University Press, 1986.

Sullivan, John L.; Piereson, James; and Marcus, George E. *Political Tolerance and American Democracy*. Chicago: University of Chicago Press, 1982.

5

INDIVIDUAL AND GROUP PARTICIPATION

LEARNING OBJECTIVES

1. To list the methods individuals may use to participate in the policy process.
2. To compare the level of political participation in the United States with that in other democracies, identifying reasons political scientists give for the differences in participation rates.
3. To identify the reasons political scientists give to explain the recent decline in American voter turnout.
4. To explain why some people participate in politics while others do not.
5. To describe the relationship between political participation and such factors as age, socioeconomic status, and group identity.
6. To evaluate the effect of individual participation on the policy process.
7. To identify the incentives individuals have for joining groups.
8. To list the factors accounting for group strength or weakness.
9. To explain why the number of interest groups active in American politics has increased in recent years.
10. To identify the various types of groups active in American politics, discuss their political goals, and evaluate their effectiveness at achieving their goals.
11. To describe the various tactics interest groups use to achieve their goals and assess their effectiveness.
12. To evaluate the accuracy of the elitist and pluralist models for explaining American politics.

On January 17, 1989, a drifter named Patrick Edward Purdy walked into a schoolyard in Stockton, California, and began firing an AK-47 assault rifle. Before Purdy finally turned the rifle on himself, committing suicide, he had killed five children and injured thirty others. The nation was in shock.

The Stockton schoolyard massacre focused public attention once again on the issue of gun control. A number of chiefs of police and many ordinary citizens wrote letters to newspapers and their representatives in Congress asking that something be done about the availability of semiautomatic weapons. In the meantime, Handgun Control and other groups advocating strict gun regulation called for a ban on the manufacture, sale, and ownership of assault weapons such as the AK-47. They argued that tough new federal restrictions on gun ownership were necessary to keep military-style weapons out of the hands of criminals such as Purdy, and they pointed to poll data showing that 72 percent of the American people agreed that assault guns ought to be banned.[1]

In contrast, the opponents of gun control, led by the National Rifle Association (NRA), argued that further restrictions on Americans' right to bear arms would only limit the law-abiding, because criminals would obtain

By Schorr for the L.A. Herald.

weapons illegally. It's people, they said, not guns, that are the problem. What's more, they noted, federal law already prohibits convicted felons, such as Purdy, from obtaining weapons. The NRA called upon its members to contact their representatives in Washington, asking them to oppose additional gun-control laws.

The gun-control controversy is a good illustration to introduce our study of individual and group participation in America since it concerns the policy-making role of both individuals and groups. In the first part of this chapter, we examine the ways individuals take part in the policy process, the extent of individual participation in America, and the effect of individual participation on policy. The second section of the chapter focuses on group participation. It considers the types of interest groups active in American politics today, their strategies and tactics, and their role in the policymaking process.

INDIVIDUAL PARTICIPATION

Representative democracy implies citizen participation to elect public officials and to apprise them of citizens' policy preferences. Let's begin our study by discussing how individuals take part in the policy process.

Methods of Participation

Individuals attempt to influence the policy process through various forms of political participation, but the most common political act is voting. Americans have the opportunity to vote for president every four years. Every two years, the entire House of Representatives and a third of the Senate must stand for election as well. Meanwhile, voters periodically go to the polls to elect a host of state and local officials. At times, they must also vote to approve state constitutional amendments and city-charter changes and to cast ballots in bond elections and state and local referenda elections.

Voting is not the only way people participate in politics. Individuals who want to do more for their candidate than just vote participate in election campaigns. They contribute money, stuff envelopes with campaign literature, phone potential voters, put up yard signs, and work at the polls on election day.

Another way to take part in politics is through groups. One person casting a single ballot or working alone for a candidate is not as effective as a group of people working together. Many Americans try to make their voices heard by participating in such political organizations as the League of Women Voters, Mothers Against Drunk Driving (MADD), Handgun Control, and the NRA.

We can also participate in politics by contacting government officials. We may write our senators about clean-air legislation. We may send a telegram to our state legislators asking for more funding for public education. We may telephone our city-council representative about fixing a pothole on a neighborhood street.

Finally, some Americans participate through unconventional political acts, such as protest demonstrations, sit-ins, or even violence. During the 1960s, thousands of people took to the streets on behalf of the civil rights movement or in opposition to the war in Vietnam. In recent years, political activists concerned about AIDS (Acquired Immune Deficiency Syndrome) have conducted noisy demonstrations in favor of more government support for patient services and for research.

The Level of Participation

The most common political act in the United States is voting. Presidential elections attract the highest level of participation proportionally, with more than 91 million Americans casting ballots for president in 1988. Still, that figure represented only about half of those individuals eligible to vote.[2] Turnout for other types of elections is generally less than in presidential contests. The 1986 congressional elections attracted only about a third of the potential electorate to the polls.[3]

The percentage of Americans who report taking part in forms of political participation other than voting is lower than the number who cast ballots on election day. According to survey data compiled by the Center for Political Studies (CPS), 32 percent of a national sample reported trying to persuade others how to vote in 1984, 12 percent gave money to a party or candidate, 9 percent wore political buttons or put bumper stickers on their cars, 8 percent said they attended political meetings, and 4 percent reported working for a party or candidate.[4]

PERSPECTIVE

What If They Gave an Election and Everybody Came?

Democratic party leaders worry more about the declining American electorate than their Republican counterparts. Although the pool of nonvoters in presidential elections is now so large that it includes substantial numbers of people from virtually every socioeconomic category, nonvoters as a group are less educated, poorer, younger, more likely to be single, more likely to be minority, and more likely to have moved recently than are voters as a group. Since less-educated, working-class voters generally cast their ballots for Democrats, some party leaders believe that heavier voter turnouts would help their party. Consequently, they organize voter-registration drives and get-out-the-vote campaigns to increase turnout and, they hope, improve Democratic chances.

Political scientists, however, are skeptical that increasing voter turnout alone would be enough to enable the Democrats to win the White House. First, the number of Democratic-leaning nonvoters hasn't been large enough to close the gap for recent Democratic presidential candidates. In 1988, for example, Democratic candidate Michael Dukakis lost the popular vote to Republican George Bush by a 54 to 46 percent margin. Even if working-class people or blacks and Hispanics had turned out at the same, or even a somewhat higher, rate than nonpoor people and whites, Dukakis would still have lost.

Second, scholarly studies have seldom uncovered any evidence that nonvoters would have chosen a different president from the individual actually selected. In fact, political scientists have found that nonvoters are usually more supportive of the candidate who actually wins the presidency than are voters. In 1988, for example, Bush led Dukakis in the actual popular vote by 8 percentage points. A CBS News/*New York Times* poll of nonvoters, however, showed Bush with a 16 percentage-point lead. Had everyone voted, Bush would have won by an even larger margin.

Sources: Ruy A. Teixeira, "Registration and Turnout," *Public Opinion*, January/February 1989, pp. 12–13, 56–58; Teixeira, "Will the Real Non-Voter Please Stand Up?" *Public Opinion*, July/August 1988, pp. 41–44, 59; E. J. Dionne, Jr., "If Nonvoters Had Voted: Same Winner, but Bigger," *New York Times*, 21 November 1988, p. 10.

Compared with voter turnout in other industrialized democracies, electoral participation in the United States is relatively low. A recent study comparing voter turnout in 28 democratic countries between 1969 and 1986 ranked the United States dead last. American voter turnout averaged 53.6 percent in presidential elections during the period compared with an average participation rate of 77 percent in other countries (not counting those nations that legally require their citizens to vote).[5]

Nevertheless, comparing American voter turnout with data from other countries can be misleading. Studies show that attitudes related to political participation, such as political efficacy and interest in election outcomes, are stronger in the United States than in most other nations. Moreover, Americans rank highly in comparison with the citizens of other democracies in terms of the percentages who say they discuss politics, try to convince others of their political views, and work for candidates.[6]

Professor G. Bingham Powell, Jr., identifies two factors as primarily responsible for America's having a lower voter-turnout rate than other democracies. First, the United States has more cumbersome voter registration procedures than other democracies. Studies show that three-fourths of Americans who are registered to vote do so.[7] The problem is that only about 71 percent of the adult population is registered.[8] In most other democracies, government takes the initiative to register eligible voters. Some nations even use the force of law to require their citizens to register and cast ballots. In contrast, government in America leaves it to citizens to register at their own initiative. What's more, most states in the United States require potential voters to register at least thirty days before an election and to update their registration if they move. Powell estimates that automatic voter registration would increase voter turnout in America by 14 percent.

Second, Powell says that relatively weak political parties inhibit voter participation in the United States. Strong political parties enhance voter turnout by educating citizens about candidates and issues, stimulating interest in election outcomes, and mobilizing citizens to go to the polls. Powell estimates that if American political parties were more centralized and had stronger ties to other social organizations—such as trade unions, religious bodies, and ethnic groups—then voter participation would rise by as much as 10 percent.[9] (For a discussion of the political impact of higher voter turnout, see the Perspective.)

Another point to be made about the level of participation in American politics is that voter turnout has been in a general decline for more than twenty years. As you can see from Table 5.1, participation in presidential elections has fallen every election year since 1964, with the exception of 1984, when turnout edged up slightly before falling again in 1988. Participation in other types of elections has declined as well.

Political scientist Ruy A. Teixeira identifies a number of changes in American society that he believes are responsible for declining voter turnout:

1. The potential electorate has grown younger, and young people are less inclined to vote than older people. As you can see from Table 5.1, the greatest drop in presidential election turnout came between 1968 and 1972. Between those two years (in 1971), the voting age was lowered from twenty-one to eighteen, significantly increasing the number of young people in the pool of potential voters. What's more, the baby-boom generation has come of age, and that too has increased the number of young people in the voting pool.

TABLE 5.1
American Presidential Election Turnout, 1964–84

Year	1964	1968	1972	1976	1980	1984	1988
Turnout	61.9%	60.9	55.2	53.5	52.6	53.3	50.1

Note: Turnout is determined as a percentage of voting-age adults.
Sources: *Statistical Abstract of the United States, 1986* (Washington, DC: U.S. Bureau of the Census, 1985), p. 255; *Congressional Quarterly*, Weekly Report, 21 January 1989.

2. The proportion of adults living in traditional two-adult households has fallen, and studies show that single adults are less likely to vote than adults living in two-adult households.

3. Citizens are more mobile. People who change residences are less likely to vote than people who do not move because they must update their voter registrations. Also, people who are new to an area may lack community ties that lead to increased participation rates.

4. Party identification rates have declined. Studies show that individuals who identify with a political party are more likely to participate than are independents. Consequently, as party identification has fallen, so has voting.

5. Feelings of external political efficacy have fallen. Individuals who believe that government doesn't listen to their views are less likely to participate than those who think that government is responsive.[10]

Why Some People Participate While Others Do Not

Why is it that some of us take part in politics while others do not? A portion of the explanation involves time and convenience. Most American elections take place on Tuesdays, not the most convenient day of the week. In contrast, Europeans hold elections on weekends or declare election day a national holiday so people can vote more easily. Registration is another inconvenience. Both registration and voting require time and effort; other forms of participation can be even more time-consuming. Many Americans are simply too busy earning a living and raising a family to become political activists. Meanwhile, advanced age and ill health prevent other people from taking an active part in the policy process.

Sometimes coincidental factors affect participation. We may stay away from the polls because we work late or experience car trouble or because the weather is bad. Conversely, we may decide to join an election campaign because a friend or relative is involved or because we can get extra credit in a political science class.

The most important factors affecting participation, however, are psychological. As we have noted, both strength of party identification and sense of external political efficacy are closely related to participation. Political trust, meanwhile, is somewhat related.

Another psychological factor affecting political participation is interest. Many Americans find time to be involved in politics because they think it is interesting. Some people enjoy collecting stamps, some like to watch major-league baseball, and others enjoy politics. Many of us like to read about government and follow the course of an election campaign or the struggle to get legislation through Congress. We may be fascinated by the personalities of political leaders and enjoy the camaraderie of a campaign headquarters or a political organization. Writing our senator or state legislator may give us a feeling of influence and importance.

" I THINK VOTER APATHY IS TERRIBLE... EVERYBODY SHOULD COME OUT AND VOTE FOR EITHER WHAT'S-HIS-NAME OR YOU-KNOW-WHO!"

By Stayskal for the Chicago Tribune.

Finally, many of us participate in politics out of a sense of civic duty. When we were children, we listened to our parents discuss public affairs and observed them going to the polls on election day. We learned—we were socialized—to believe that political activity was the duty of an adult. Today, we would feel guilty if we did not vote. We always try to read the newspaper and watch the news on television and, when we can, become involved in the affairs of our community. In contrast, other people feel no such obligation. They can take politics or leave it, but they don't feel guilty either way. They were socialized differently.

Who Participates

Professor W. Russell Neuman divides Americans into three groups according to their level of political interest and involvement. About 20 percent of the population are apolitical. They are apathetic and uninvolved in politics. Another 5 percent are true political activists. They not only vote but also participate in politics beyond voting. The remaining 75 percent are marginally attentive to politics. They accept the duty to vote and do so fairly regularly, but they seldom carry their participation beyond the polling booth.[11]

Who participates in American politics? People who are interested, people who are informed, people who have the time, people with a strong sense of political efficacy, and people who believe that participation is their civic duty. These people are found among all groups of Americans, but some segments of the population are more likely to participate than others.

First, participation is related to age. Young people are less likely to take part in politics than are their elders. As Table 5.2 shows, young people reported voting in the 1984 presidential election in smaller percentages than middle-aged and older Americans. Many young adults are political no-shows because they have matters on their minds other than politics—finishing school, starting a career, beginning a family, buying a home. They are relatively inexperienced politically and probably less informed about public affairs than their parents. Also, since young adults tend to move more frequently than older people, they are less likely to keep their voter registration current.

Participation increases with age until advanced age and ill health force the elderly to slow down. As people approach middle age, they often establish roots in the community. Naturally, they are more concerned about taxes, schools, public services, and regulations than they were in their youth. What's more, they have more experience participating and, probably, more time for political activism than do younger people. Eventually, old age forces people to reduce their level of political activity, particularly for some of the more demanding forms of participation such as campaigning. As you can see from the table, however, the falloff in voting turnout for older people is relatively small.[12]

Labor Unions

Second, political participation is related to socioeconomic status (SES), that is, education, income, and occupational status. Middle-class people are more active politically than lower-income persons; the college-educated participate more than those with high-school educations; professionals and business people are more likely to take part in politics than are clerical workers or laborers. The most important factor in this relationship is education.

TABLE 5.2
Voter Participation in the 1984 Presidential Election

Race		Employment Status	
Whites	61%	Employed	62%
Blacks	56	Unemployed	44
Hispanics	33		
Age		Education	
18–20	37%	Grade school only	43%
21–24	44	1–3 years of high school	45
25–34	55	4 years of high school	59
35–44	64	1–3 years of college	68
45–64	70	4 years of college or more	79
65+	68		
Gender			
Males	59%		
Females	61		

Note: These figures may be inflated since some people may be reluctant to admit not voting.
Source: *Statistical Abstract of the United States, 1986* (Washington, DC: U.S. Bureau of the Census, 1985), p. 256.

Better-educated people are exposed to more information about politics, they better understand how government works, and they feel more confident in their ability to affect the policy process. As you can see from Table 5.2, individuals with higher levels of education reported voting in larger percentages than those with less education.

A final factor affecting participation is group identity. All of us belong to groups in the sense that we are black or white or Asian or female or under thirty or Baptist. Group identity becomes important politically when group members begin to develop a group consciousness and to perceive that certain desired goals can be achieved through collective political action. On the basis of socioeconomic status, for example, we would expect African-American participation rates to be considerably lower than the rate for whites and slightly lower than the rate for Hispanic-Americans. As you can see from Table 5.2, however, black voting turnout is considerably higher than it is for Hispanics and nearly as high as it is for whites. These figures are testimony both to the effectiveness of black political organization and the presence of a sense of group identity among black voters.

The Effect of Individual Participation

How much influence can the average individual have on the policy process in America? The answer depends on the level of government and the issue involved. Although voting is important, it would be naive to suggest that one person's vote will change the outcome of many elections. Occasionally, one vote or a few votes have decided an election contest, but that is rare. To have much effect on elections, individuals need to work actively in campaigns. A good campaign volunteer can be worth dozens, maybe even hundreds, of votes. Although that isn't enough to swing many national or even statewide races, it can have an impact at the local level.

An individual's influence on issues is limited as well. On major, national political issues, the individual is simply outgunned. No one person's arguments, no matter how persuasive, are going to outweigh those of powerful interest groups. Consequently, the effectiveness of individual contacts is generally limited to issues that don't concern the heavyweights of American politics. For the most part, these are local issues, narrow in scope.

In sum, the political effectiveness of the typical individual acting alone is usually limited to local election contests and local issues of narrow focus. Does this mean, then, that political participation for the average American is a sham at worst and a waste of time at best? We think not. Our lives are probably more directly affected by city government, county government, and other units of local government than by events that take place in Washington, D.C., or in state capitals. Also, narrow issues, such as the location of a police substation or the expansion of a local community college, are often important to us. Just because the impact of individual participation is limited doesn't mean it isn't important. Moreover, individuals can increase the weight of their participation significantly by working through groups.

GROUP PARTICIPATION

An **interest group** is an organization of people who join together voluntarily on the basis of some interest they share, for the purpose of influencing policy. Sometimes the interest is economic. Dairy farmers, for example, work through the National Milk Producers Federation to ensure government support for their industry. Coal miners join the United Mine Workers Union to promote their well-being. At other times, however, the interests that unite people involve morals, culture, and values. Individuals concerned about safeguarding the environment may become involved in the Sierra Club. Hunters, meanwhile, may join the NRA to defend the availability of firearms.

Why People Join Groups

George and Inez Martinez are a retired couple living in El Paso, Texas. They recently received a letter from the American Association of Retired Persons (AARP) inviting them to join that organization. Mr. and Mrs. Martinez have heard of the AARP and approve of its lobbying efforts on behalf of the elderly. What's more, AARP dues are relatively low. Still, why should they join? Surely, the few dollars they contribute in dues will be too little to have any appreciable effect on the fortunes of the organization. And, at any rate, as senior citizens, Mr. and Mrs. Martinez stand to benefit from whatever legislative gains the AARP achieves regardless of whether they join the organization or not.

The situation facing the Martinezes illustrates what Professor Mancur Olson calls the free-rider barrier to group membership. The **free-rider barrier to group membership** is the concept that individuals will have little incentive to join a group and contribute resources to it if the group's benefits go to members and nonmembers alike. Olson says that groups attempt to compensate for the free-rider barrier by offering selective benefits that go only to group members.[13] The AARP, for example, provides members with a number of selective benefits, including the opportunity to purchase prescription drugs at a discount.

Political scientists identify three types of incentives individuals have for joining and participating in a group: material, solidary, and purposive incentives. **Material incentives to group membership** are benefits that can be measured in dollars and cents. As we noted, the AARP offers its members discount medicine. **Solidary incentives to group membership** are social benefits arising from associating with other group members. Some people may join and participate in the League of Women Voters, for instance, in order to meet people and make new friends. **Purposive incentives to group membership** are the rewards individuals find in working for a cause in which they believe. Animal lovers may join People for the Ethical Treatment of Animals (PETA) out of their concern for animal welfare. Some scholars believe that an interest group's character is determined by the motivations of its members.[14]

The Strength of Interest Groups

Interest groups are not created equal. Some operate nationwide; others are effective only at the state or local level. Some groups exert a powerful influence on the policy process; others are ineffectual. In general, an interest group's political power depends on the size of its membership, the resources at its disposal, and its reputation in the larger community. First, other factors being equal, larger groups are more influential than smaller groups. They comprise a more substantial voting bloc and offer a larger pool of workers for group activities. The NRA has an advantage over Handgun Control, for example, because it has more members—about 2.8 million for the NRA compared with only 250,000 for Handgun Control.[15] Still, a large membership can be a mixed blessing for a group in that it may create problems of communication and coordination within the group and increase the likelihood of internal divisions.

Second, groups with access to political resources such as money and organizational skills are more influential than groups without such resources. The effectiveness of business groups depends in large part on their access to money. In 1981, for example, the annual budget of the American Petroleum Institute (API), a trade group representing the oil industry, was $50 million. In contrast, the National Low Income Housing Coalition had to scrape by on just $61,000.[16] In general, groups composed of wealthier, better-educated individuals such as doctors and lawyers are more powerful than groups of poorer, less educated people. Higher-status individuals are more likely to possess greater financial resources and personal skills than persons from lower-status groups. Groups can also benefit from the membership and support of well-known and/or highly placed persons. President George Bush, for instance, is a lifetime member of the NRA.

Finally, groups that enjoy a favorable image in society are generally more effective politically than groups that are held in low esteem. Most business groups benefit from a generally positive image. The success of Mothers Against Drunk Driving (MADD) is due primarily to broad support among the general population. In contrast, groups such as NORML, the National Organization for the Reform of Marijuana Laws, face an uphill battle against public opinion.

The Number of Interest Groups

Interest groups have always been important in American politics, but their numbers have proliferated since 1960. Back in the 1950s, business groups, trade associations, and labor unions were the major players in national politics. Today, however, these groups have been joined by an army of new organizations: environmental groups, women's-rights organizations, abortion activists, civil rights associations, peace groups, consumer advocacy groups, antitax groups—the list goes on and on.

Political scientists cite several factors behind the increase in interest-group activity. First, socioeconomic changes have led to the emergence of new groups with new policy perspectives. Advances in biomedical research, for example, have been accompanied by the appearance of new associations of professionals concerned with government grants and regulations. Women joining the work force have formed women's-rights organizations. Second, a better-educated, more affluent middle class with more leisure time has had the interest and resources for group activism. Middle-class activists supply the money and volunteer help needed to maintain social-cause groups involved with environmental issues, consumer matters, neighborhood improvement, animal rights, and the like. Third, new technologies have made it easier for groups to communicate with their members and supporters. Computerized mailing lists, word processors, and WATS lines have significantly improved the ability of groups to raise money and alert their followers for political action. Finally, interest groups have emerged in response to the growth of government. As government has established new programs, organizations of service providers and service recipients have emerged to lobby on behalf of their interests. The AARP, for example, was established *after* Congress created Social Security and other programs designed to benefit the elderly.[17]

Types of Interest Groups

In America, interest groups represent every cause imaginable, from Planned Parenthood to the Casket Manufacturers Association of America; from the Conservative Caucus to the National Gay Task Force; from the American Medical Association to the Hawaiian Golfers for Good Government. Some groups, including many labor unions, have a large number of active members who may attend meetings and work on group projects. These groups have a national office, usually located in Washington, D.C., with local affiliates scattered around the country. Other groups, however, have a "checkbook membership." These groups don't have meetings. They are run by a professional director and paid staff, usually based in Washington, D.C., who mail out newsletters to members and supporters whose only connection to the group is that they contribute money. Let's examine some of the types of groups active in America's policy process, discussing what they want from government and how successful they have been at obtaining it.

Business and Trade Groups

Business and trade groups are the most potent and probably most numerous of America's interest groups. Other groups may be influential at particular levels and at certain points in the policy process, but business groups are powerful everywhere from the White House to the courthouse. Their voices are heard on virtually every major policy issue.

Business and trade groups are effective because they are organized, well financed, and skilled in advocating their positions. Firms in the same general field form associations to present a unified political front. The American Bankers Association speaks for the interests of the banking industry. The National Association of Manufacturers represents larger manufacturing concerns. The Chamber of Commerce, meanwhile, is an advocate for small business.

Business and industry embrace diverse interests, and their concerns reflect that diversity. Auto manufacturers, for example, are interested in laws and regulations affecting pollution controls, exhaust emissions, safety, and the threat of import competition. Corporations such as General Electric and IBM hope to secure government defense contracts. In general, business and trade groups are interested in tax laws, interest rates, environmental regulations, trade policy, labor laws, government contracts, and similar matters.

Business and trade groups don't always achieve their policy goals because, on most issues, they aren't united. Textile manufacturers and other industries hurt by foreign competition favor import restrictions, for example, while major exporters, such as IBM, support free-trade policies. Lawyers' groups and insurance companies oppose one another over limiting the size of damage awards in personal-injury lawsuits. Even firms in the same industry sometimes find themselves on opposite sides in a policy dispute. In the late 1980s, Ford and General Motors lobbied for a relaxation of federal fleet-mileage standards, while Chrysler, which had already achieved the mileage goal, opposed any reduction.

Organized labor is a powerful political force in America, but unlike business groups, labor's influence is not important at all levels across the land. Moreover, labor's strength is perhaps on the decline, its membership decreasing. The largest union federation in the nation is the American Federation of Labor and Congress of Industrial Organizations (AFL-CIO). It is composed of more than one hundred separate unions with nearly 14 million members. All told, about 20 million Americans belong to unions, roughly 20 percent of the total nonagricultural work force. This is down, though, from 1968, when more than 30 percent of the nation's workers belonged to unions.[18]

Organized labor is strongest in the large, industrialized states of the Northeast and Midwest. In Michigan, for example, the United Auto Workers may be the state's most potent political force. In these regions of the country, labor is well organized and skilled at exercising its political muscles at city hall, at the state capitol, and in Washington as well.

In contrast, labor is not so well organized or so politically influential in the Sunbelt, the nation's fastest growing region. In many Sunbelt states, organized labor is hamstrung by antilabor laws and by a diverse and divided work force, many of whose members are anti-union. So far, unionization in the South and Southwest has come in only a few places. As a result, labor's power in most of the Sunbelt is confined to certain localities. In fact, the general political climate is often so anti-union that labor support for a candidate or a cause can be counterproductive.

For many years, Cesar Chavez has led protests against unfair and unsafe farm labor practices.

What does organized labor want politically? Conventional wisdom holds that organized labor and big business counterbalance each other, invariably taking opposing views on public policy issues. At times, that is the case. Management and big labor generally disagree on labor-relations laws, occupational safety and health regulations, and minimum-wage laws. At other times, however, big business and big labor find themselves on the same side in policy disputes. Both labor and business leaders support higher defense spending, for example, because it means more defense contracts and more jobs. The United Auto Workers and automobile manufacturers join forces to push for import restrictions on foreign competition. Both business and labor oppose environmental regulations that could threaten the closing of offending plants and the loss of jobs.

Professional Associations

Auto workers, truck drivers, and coal miners aren't the only American workers who are organized; so are doctors, lawyers, realtors, and other professionals. Their numbers aren't as great as those of blue-collar workers, of course, but professional associations are nonetheless influential because of the relatively high socioeconomic status of their membership. They have the resources to make their voices heard, and they enjoy an added advantage because many elected officials come from the ranks of professionals, especially lawyers.

Professional associations are concerned with public policies that affect their members. The American Medical Association (AMA) would like state legislatures to limit the amount of money judges and juries can award in malpractice lawsuits. Lawyers, meanwhile, oppose doctors on this issue. Realtors are active on issues of development and land-use regulation. Professional associations, in general, are concerned with professional licensing and regulation. Also, professional associations often take stands on policy issues outside the immediate concerns of their membership, such as tax cuts, budget deficits, defense spending, and women's rights.

Farm Groups

Farm groups are among the nation's more politically astute interest groups. They are well organized and know how to exert influence where they are strongest: in state legislatures, in farming regions, and in Washington, D.C. Farmers producing wheat, rice, sugar, tobacco, dairy products, and the like have their own particular associations. The American Farm Bureau and the National Farmers Union, meanwhile, represent farm interests in general. What do farmers want from government? Loan guarantees, crop subsidies, and the promotion of farm exports.

The success of farm organizations can be measured in dollars and cents. In 1989, federal farm subsidies exceeded $20 billion. Still, the outlook for farm groups is troubled. In this day of huge federal budget deficits, a growing number of members of Congress and administration officials see farm programs as an area for budget reduction. Indeed, the federal budget for farm programs has declined considerably since 1986, when it hit a record-high $35 billion.

Racial and Ethnic Groups

The United States is home to innumerable racial and ethnic minority groups: African-Americans, Hispanic-Americans, Native Americans, and Asian-Americans, among others. Minority and ethnic Americans have organized a number of groups to promote their political goals, including the National Association for the Advancement of Colored People (NAACP), the Congress of Racial Equality (CORE), the Urban League, the League of United Latin American Citizens (LULAC), and the American Indian Movement (AIM).

In general, racial and ethnic minority groups in America share certain goals: equality before the law, representation in elective and appointive office, freedom from discrimination, and economic equality. Specifically, minorities are interested in the enforcement of laws against discrimination; the election and appointment of minorities to federal, state, and local offices; and the extension of government programs geared to fighting poverty.

Today, racial and ethnic minority groups are a force to be reckoned with in most big cities and in the South and Southwest, where their numbers translate into political power. In addition, minorities, particularly African-Americans and, to a lesser degree, Hispanic-Americans, remain important in national politics. Nonetheless, the problems facing minority groups in America—subtle discrimination, inadequate housing, substandard health care, malnutrition, poverty, and illiteracy—are particularly obstinate.

Religious Groups

Throughout American history, religious organizations have been actively involved in the policy process. Both the Abolition and Prohibition movements had strong religious overtones, as did the civil rights and antiwar movements of the 1960s and early 1970s. In 1928 and 1960, respectively, the candidacies of Roman Catholics Al Smith and John Kennedy stirred powerful emotions. State aid to parochial schools has long been a cause dear to many members of the Catholic church, and in recent years, Catholic organizations have been heavily involved in the fight against abortion. Jewish groups, meanwhile, have kept close watch over American policy toward Israel.

Today, religiously based groups focus on issues across the political spectrum. Conservative religious organizations, such as the Moral Majority (now disbanded), and conservative Christian leaders, such as Jerry Falwell and Pat Robertson, have campaigned on such issues as abortion, pornography, sex and violence on television, legalized gambling, liquor laws, homosexuality, sex education, prayer in schools, drug abuse, defense spending, and communism. Meanwhile, other religious groups, of a more liberal bent, have become involved with the nuclear-freeze movement (to halt the production of nuclear weapons), the sanctuary movement (to provide shelter for refugees from Latin America), abortion rights, environmental protection, gay rights, aid for

The abortion question has been the subject of much demonstration, with both sides loudly supporting their cause.

the homeless, drug abuse, minority rights, women's rights, hunger relief, and the death penalty.

The ability of religious groups to influence policy depends on the issue. Religiously based groups have the greatest impact on issues when their position enjoys favorable public support and they face relatively little opposition from other organized interests. Jewish groups, for example, have long exerted considerable influence over American policy toward Israel. These groups have been aided by a political climate in which the general public—Jews and non-Jews alike—have sympathized with Israel. What's more, the anti-Israel lobby in the United States is relatively weak. In contrast, Catholic organizations have had a more difficult time winning their battle against abortion. On this issue, public opinion is closely divided, with even a good many Catholics supporting the pro-choice position. Meanwhile, the antiabortion movement faces determined opposition from various abortion-rights groups.

Public-Interest Groups

The last twenty years or so have seen the emergence of a number of groups that claim not to be *special* interest groups but advocates of the *public* interest. They see themselves as spokespersons for the general good, at least as they define it. Common Cause, for example, calls itself "the citizens' lobby." Among other goals, it works for campaign finance reform and tighter rules on interest-group lobbying.

Ralph Nader is probably the best-known spokesperson for public-interest groups. Nader has organized a number of public-interest groups, including Public Citizen, Congress Watch, Tax Reform Research Group, and Public Interest Research Groups (PIRGs), which operate on the campuses of many colleges and universities. Nader and his groups have been involved in such causes as automobile safety, consumer rights, and environmental protection.

Public-interest groups are not generally among the super-heavyweights of American politics, but they have frequently been effective in selling their points of view to the general public, and they have won a number of battles in Congress. As with religious groups, their power varies from issue to issue, depending, for the most part, on the amount of public support they can muster and the extent of opposition they face from other interests.

Single-Issue Groups

A **single-issue group** is an interest group that focuses its efforts on a single issue or a group of related issues. For Right to Life, the cause is opposition to abortion; for the National Organization for Women (NOW), it's women's rights; for the American Civil Liberties Union (ACLU), it's the protection of the rights of individuals as outlined in the Bill of Rights. The NRA and Handgun Control are single-issue groups that concentrate their attention on the issue of gun control.

The influence of single-issue groups is generally limited to their pet causes, and—as with other groups—the success of single-issue groups depends on the political environment surrounding their issues. The NRA, for example, has traditionally held the upper hand in battles over gun control, although incidents such as the shooting in Stockton, California, have put the NRA on the defensive. Also, the supporters of gun control have recently organized anti-gun groups such as Handgun Control to oppose the NRA.

Ideological Cause Groups

In recent years, liberals and conservative political activists have organized groups to promote their particular political points of view. Two relatively new liberal groups are the Progressive Political Action Committee (PROPAC) and the National Committee for an Effective Congress. Americans for Democratic Action (ADA), another liberal organization, has been around for decades. On the conservative side, meanwhile, ideological cause groups include the National Conservative Political Action Committee (NCPAC), Young Americans for Freedom (YAF), and the Congressional Club. Ideological cause groups raise money to support candidates sympathetic to their views and, perhaps more frequently, to oppose candidates they don't like.

As with other groups, the success of ideological cause groups depends on the issue and the political climate. In 1980, for example, NCPAC and other conservative groups raised and spent millions of dollars to defeat President Jimmy Carter and a number of liberal Democratic senators. In subsequent years, however, the conservative groups had trouble raising money and their influence waned.

Neighborhood Groups

Finally, a large number of neighborhood and community organizations across the nation involve themselves in the policy process. Most urban subdivisions have civic clubs or some other sort of neighborhood improvement association. Many schools have active parent teacher associations (PTAs). Although neighborhood groups can be important at the local level, their overall influence on policy is limited. Most of these groups see politics as a secondary activity, and many are not particularly skilled at it.

In recent years, neighborhoods have organized to deal with issues that affect them directly. Here, a group in New York City demonstrates against the problem of illegal drugs in their community.

Interest-Group Strategies and Tactics

The tactics of interest groups vary, ranging from electioneering to lobbying, to public relations, to protest activity, to litigation. In general, the most successful groups in American politics are those groups that form alliances with other interest groups and those that coordinate the use of several political tools. Let's consider the various ways interest groups attempt to influence the policy process.

Electioneering

Interest groups live by the motto: Elect Your Friends; Defeat Your Enemies. Large, influential groups hope to sway election results by endorsing their friends and targeting their enemies. In 1988, for example, the National Rifle Association committed its resources to electing George Bush to the White House and defeating Michael Dukakis. "Defend Firearms, Defeat Dukakis," read NRA bumper stickers. A number of interest groups publish a scorecard showing how legislators voted on issues important to the group. Each congressional election year, for example, an environmental group targets for defeat its "Dirty Dozen," twelve members of Congress who voted consistently against the group's favored legislation. The drawback to these approaches is that group leaders can't always persuade their members to vote for, or against, particular candidates. Moreover, endorsements can sometimes backfire with the general public. In 1985, for example, a poll taken in Virginia found that 51 percent of those surveyed said that they were "less likely" to vote for a candidate endorsed by Moral Majority Leader Jerry Falwell, himself a Virginian.[19]

Perhaps the most effective means that interest groups have for influencing elections is by contributing money through their political action committees. A **political action committee (PAC)** is an organization created to raise and distribute money in election campaigns. Although organized labor created the first PACs in the 1940s, the modern PAC era did not begin until the 1970s, when Congress passed the Federal Election Campaign Act to reform campaign finance. This law limited individual contributions to candidates while permitting PACs to take up much of the slack.[20] Since then, the number of PACs active in American politics has grown to more than forty-eight hundred at the national level, with thousands of others working at the state and local levels.

A PAC's name may or may not connect it with the interest group it represents. Some PAC names are straightforward. Build-PAC, for example, is organized by the National Association of Home Builders. Some names are even clever, such as SixPAC for beer distributors, and Snack-PAC for the Potato Chip/Snack Food Association. In other cases, however, groups apparently prefer to operate incognito. Not many people would guess that the Political Victory Fund is the NRA's PAC or that National PAC, despite its all-embracing name, is organized by supporters of Israel.

During the 1987–88 election cycle, PACs contributed nearly $350 million to candidates for Congress and the presidency. The total included both direct cash contributions to candidates' campaign committees as well as the cost of various in-kind services given by PACs, such as the purchase of television time for campaign advertising.[21] The NRA's PAC, for example, spent more than $1.5 million on behalf of George Bush, mostly on advertising attacking Dukakis.[22] Other big spenders were PACs associated with realtors ($4.1 million), the AMA ($2.9 million), and the Teamsters Union ($2.7 million).[23]

PAC managers consider several factors in determining which candidates to support. When all other considerations are equal, PACs give to candidates who are sympathetic toward their policy preferences. Since corporate and trade PACs generally have more money to contribute than labor PACs, this approach would *seem* to favor Republicans over Democrats. (Republican candidates as a group are generally more sympathetic to the policy preferences of corporations and trade associations than are Democrats, whose policy views are more closely in line with those of organized labor.) In the world of politics, however, other considerations are seldom equal.

PACs also prefer to give money to candidates who they believe have the best chance to win office. Consequently, PAC managers would rather give to a strong candidate who is only somewhat supportive of their group than throw the PAC's money away on an almost certain loser who is completely behind the group's goals. In congressional races, this strategy means that PACs usually contribute to incumbents (an **incumbent** is a current officeholder), because incumbents almost always win reelection. In 1987–88, for example, PACs gave 68 percent of their campaign dollars to incumbents compared to only 21 percent for challengers running against incumbents. (The other 11 percent went to candidates running for open seats.)[24]

Finally, PACs like to give to incumbent officeholders who hold important policymaking positions, such as congressional committee and subcommittee chairs and the members of committees that deal with legislation directly affecting the interest group. In the 1987–88 election cycle, for example, savings and loan association PACs contributed more than a million dollars to candidates for Congress, with most of the money going to members of the House and Senate banking committees and members of the tax-writing committees in each chamber.[25] Both sets of committees were heavily involved in writing legislation to reform the faltering savings and loan industry.

The tendency of PACs to contribute campaign money to incumbents and to officeholders occupying key policymaking positions benefits Democrats over Republicans, at least in races for the United States Congress. Since the Democrats hold a majority of seats in both the House and Senate, they not only have more incumbents but they also chair every committee and subcommittee in both houses of Congress. As a result, Democrats receive the lion's share of PAC money. In 1987–88, for example, PACs gave 37 percent more money to Democratic candidates than they gave to Republicans.[26]

PACs are among the more controversial features of contemporary American politics. Their defenders argue that they are a means whereby thousands of people can participate in politics through financial contributions. In addition, they say, politicians can't be bought for a mere $5,000, the maximum amount a PAC is allowed to give in a campaign to a candidate for Congress. In contrast, critics contend that PAC money plays such a big role in political campaigns that it distorts the traditional relationship between elected officials and their constituents. Why should representatives reach out to a broad base of constituents for support, ask the critics, when they can raise hundreds of thousands of dollars of campaign money from PACs? The result of such a system is that Republicans tend to reflect the interests of giant corporations rather than small business, while Democrats answer to big labor instead of working people.[27]

Common Cause and other good-government groups have proposed reforms in PAC and campaign-funding laws, but change won't come easily because of politics. Campaign reforms are not neutral; they invariably benefit one party at the expense of the other. President Bush, for example, has proposed eliminating PAC contributions in congressional elections, while increasing the amount of money individuals and parties can contribute to election campaigns. That reform would hurt Democrats, because they get most of the PAC money, and help the Republicans, whose candidates are able to raise more money from individual contributors. In contrast, Democrats propose placing a ceiling on campaign expenditures in congressional races. Republicans, however, reject this idea because they believe that spending ceilings would benefit incumbents, most of whom are Democrats.

Do PAC contributions influence public policy? Interest groups obviously think they have some effect or they wouldn't go to such expense. Political scientists, however, have had difficulty establishing a direct link between PAC contributions and votes in Congress. Scholarly studies have found that other factors, such as members' party affiliations and political philosophy, have more influence over congressional votes. PAC contributions make a difference only at the margins, when legislators have no strong policy preferences and PACs have made a major commitment of resources. One scholar concludes that PACs are most effective when the matter at hand is out of the public spotlight, when the issue is specialized and narrowly focused, when PACs work together with other PACs, and when PAC contributions are coordinated with careful lobbying.[28]

Lobbying

A **lobbyist** is a representative for an interest group whose job is to present the group's point of view to political decision-makers. Professional lobbyists are skilled technicians, knowledgeable both in how to approach public officials and in the subject matter vital to their group. Frequently, lobbyists are former congressional staff members or employees of the executive branch who resign their government jobs to earn more money as lobbyists than they could ever make working for Uncle Sam. After he left the White House in 1985, for example, former presidential aide Michael Deaver made more than $400,000 a year lobbying for such clients as TWA, Rockwell International, Armco Steel, CBS, and the governments of Saudi Arabia, South Korea, Canada, and Mexico.[29] Despite Deaver's example, however, most lobbyists work for only a few organizations and represent them on a long-term basis.

Interest groups use different approaches to influence policy. Groups that have a long-range interest in several policy areas generally employ what might be called an insider's approach to achieving influence. The groups give PAC contributions to gain access to officeholders for lobbyists who then work to get to know the public officials on a personal basis. The efforts of interest groups to influence policy are professional and even-tempered. Their lobbyists attempt to persuade with facts and reason rather than threats and emotion. Whatever pressure the interest groups bring to bear on public officials is subtle and unspoken. They believe threats are counterproductive and harmful to the construction of a long-term relationship between the interest group and the officeholder.

In contrast, other groups, whose policy goals are more narrowly focused, follow an outsider's approach to influencing policy. Groups using an outsider's strategy are more heavy-handed in dealing with public officials. They are less willing to compromise on policy issues and more likely to threaten (and attempt to carry out) political reprisals against officeholders who oppose them. For example, after Senator James Exon of Nebraska backed legislation banning nondetectable firearms (because they can easily be smuggled aboard airplanes), the NRA mailed letters to Exon's constituents saying, "Your senator cast a vote against our rights."[30]

Other Tactics

Interest groups employ a number of other tactics to influence public policy. One technique involves public relations. Groups launch campaigns to convince the general public of the correctness of their views and the righteousness of their cause. Utility companies, for example, sometimes include literature with their customers' bills that extols the virtues of nuclear energy or makes the case for a rate increase. The NRA has purchased a series of magazine ads designed to improve the organization's public image. The ads feature hunters, police officers, and business people with the caption, "I am the NRA."

Groups that can't afford public relations experts and advertising costs pursue similar goals by means of protest demonstrations. Civil rights groups used this technique in the 1960s. Today, it is employed by groups pursuing a variety of goals, ranging from organizations opposing construction of a nuclear power plant to antipornography crusaders picketing convenience stores that sell *Playboy* magazine. In general, protest demonstrations are a tactic

Protesting the burning of toxic wastes on an incinerator ship in the North Sea, members of Greenpeace, a group of environmental activists, attempted to board the ship from rubber dinghies to put a stop to the practice. Crew members thwarted the protest by maintaining a wall of water around the ship, and the activists had to give up.

used by groups unable to achieve their goals through other means. Sometimes the protest catches the fancy of the general public, who bring pressure to bear on behalf of the protesting group. In most cases, though, protests have only a marginal impact on public policy.

Occasionally, frustrated groups go beyond peaceful protest to violent, illegal activities. During the 1960s, some groups opposed to the Vietnam War took over college administration buildings or burned ROTC offices on campus. Today, groups such as the Ku Klux Klan and other white supremacist organizations sometimes resort to violence. The difficulty with violence as a political tool is that it often produces a public-opinion backlash against the group and its goals. One can make a case, however, that violence does occasionally succeed in calling attention to an issue that might otherwise be ignored.

Finally, a number of groups have become expert in the use of litigation (that is, lawsuits) to achieve their goals. The NAACP and other African-American groups have often found allies in the federal courts. Other groups that have been frequent litigants include the Sierra Club and the American Civil Liberties Union (ACLU). Litigation has been an important political tool for interest groups, but it has limitations. Court action is both time-consuming and expensive. Also, litigation is reactive. Lawsuits are inevitably filed to overturn public policies that are already in place. Although court action sometimes succeeds in overturning policies, the real political power remains in the hands of those who make the policies in the first place.

CONCLUSION: INTEREST GROUPS, PARTICIPATION, AND PUBLIC POLICY

There are intense debates in American politics about who runs the country. Some observers advance an **elite theory** (or **elitism**). This is the view that political power in America is held by a small group of people who control politics by controlling economic resources. One political scientist believes that American government "represents the privileged few rather than the needy many." Moreover, he says, laws are written "principally to protect the haves against the claims of the have-nots."[31]

Most political scientists are critical of the elite theory. Although they admit that elites are an important element in the policy process, they do not believe that American society is run by a single "ruling elite." Instead, multiple elites are active in American politics. These elites don't all know one another, they don't consult on policy, and they often oppose one another on policy matters.

Some of the critics of elite theory are proponents of the **pluralist theory** (or **pluralism**). This is the view that diverse groups of elites with differing interests compete with one another to control policy in different issue areas. According to this perspective, American society is composed of a wide range of interest groups. On any one policy issue, several groups compete for influence. Business and labor groups, for example, compete over labor laws. The NRA, Handgun Control, police chiefs, associations of police officers, and others contend over gun-control policies. Pluralists believe that different groups are effective on different issues, with no one group dominating on all issues.

Today, most political scientists would probably agree that the reality of American national politics more closely approximates the pluralist approach than elite theory. Because of separation of powers, checks and balances, bicameralism, and federalism, government in America is highly fragmented. Although certain groups may dominate on particular issues or at certain levels of government, most political scientists believe that no one group of elites controls American politics. Moreover, because of the recent explosion in the number of interest groups, especially public-interest and single-issue groups, and the emergence of new political issues, such as abortion and environmental protection, it has now become more difficult for a single, powerful interest group to dominate a particular policy area.[32]

In fact, a number of political scientists use the concept of issue networks to describe policymaking in America. An **issue network** is a group of political actors that is concerned with some aspect of public policy. Issue networks are fluid, with participants moving in and out. They may include technical specialists, journalists, legislators, a variety of interest groups, bureaucrats, academics, and political activists. Powerful interest groups may be involved, but they don't control. Instead, policy in a particular area results from conflicts among a broad range of political actors both in and out of government.[33]

But what does this mean for democracy? Professor E. E. Schattschneider believes that the interests of the disadvantaged and those of broad publics are likely to remain unrepresented in America's political process.[34] First, not all interests are organized. About 52 percent of Americans belong to organizations, including unions.[35] Organizational membership, however, is skewed toward better-educated, higher-income individuals. The interests of the poor are underrepresented in the pressure community. The Census Bureau estimates that 2.5 million Americans are homeless.[36] What interest groups speak for them? Or for persons suffering from mental illness? American politics features group competition, but groups are not equally influential and not all Americans are represented by groups.

Second, broad publics are often slighted in the policy process. Public opinion, even broadly held, may not be represented by a group. The general public often has little impact on policy issues. Most political controversies are not resolved through the will of the people, but as the result of group competition. Except for those few issues on which a sizable chunk of the population is actively informed and interested, the broad public has little clout. Real power is in the hands of groups.

KEY TERMS

elite theory (elitism)

free-rider barrier to group membership

incumbent

interest group

issue network

lobbyist

material incentives to group membership

pluralist theory (pluralism)

political action committee (PAC)

purposive incentives to group membership

single-issue group

solidary incentives to group membership

NOTES

1. *Gallup Report*, March/April 1989, p. 4.
2. "Half of Potential Electorate Voted," *Houston Chronicle*, 11 November 1988, p. 8A.
3. *Congressional Quarterly*, Weekly Report, 21 January 1989.
4. M. Margaret Conway, *Political Participation in the United States* (Washington, DC: Congressional Quarterly Press, 1985), p. 7.
5. "Voters in U.S. Rank Last," *Houston Post*, 8 December 1987, p. 8A.
6. Gabriel A. Almond and Sidney Verba, *The Civic Culture* (Boston: Little, Brown, 1963), pp. 79, 144.
7. "Voters in U.S. Rank Last."
8. "Half of Potential Electorate Voted."

9. G. Bingham Powell, Jr., "American Voter Turnout in Comparative Perspective," *American Political Science Review* 80 (March 1986): 17–43.

10. Ruy A. Teixeira, *Why Americans Don't Vote: Turnout Decline in the United States 1960–1984* (New York: Greenwood Press, 1987), p. 78.

11. W. Russell Neuman, *The Paradox of Mass Politics: Knowledge and Opinion in the American Electorate* (Cambridge, MA: Harvard University Press, 1986).

12. M. Kent Jennings and Gregory B. Markus, "Political Involvement in the Later Years: A Longitudinal Survey," *American Journal of Political Science* 32 (May 1988): 302–16.

13. Mancur Olson, *The Logic of Collective Action* (Cambridge, MA: Harvard University Press, 1971).

14. Peter Clark and James Q. Wilson, "Incentive Systems: A Theory of Organizations," *Administrative Science Quarterly* 6 (September 1961): 126–66.

15. Carol Matlack, "Under Assault," *National Journal*, 22 April 1989, pp. 978–82.

16. Kay Lehman Schlozman and John T. Tierney, *Organized Interests and American Democracy* (New York: Harper & Row, 1986), p. 108.

17. Jack L. Walker, "The Origins and Maintenance of Interest Groups in America," *American Political Science Review* 77 (June 1983): 390–406.

18. Michael Goldfield, *The Decline of Organized Labor in the United States* (Chicago: University of Chicago Press, 1987), p. 11.

19. Dudley Clendinen, "Falwell Falters at Anointing Politicians," *Houston Chronicle*, 1 December 1985, sec. 1, p. 24.

20. Larry J. Sabato, *PAC Power: Inside the World of Political Action Committees* (New York: W. W. Norton, 1984), p. 6.

21. "PAC Spending Record," *Houston Post*, 9 April 1989, p. 8A.

22. Matlack.

23. Richard Morin, "PACking in the Bucks for Incumbents," *Washington Post*, National Weekly Edition, 10–16 April 1989, p. 37.

24. Ibid.

25. *Congressional Quarterly*, Weekly Report, 24 December 1988, pp. 3552–53.

26. Morin.

27. Jack W. Germond and Jules Witcover, "PACs Coming Between Officials and People Who Elected Them," *Houston Post*, 26 January 1983, p. 3B.

28. Sabato, pp. 135–37.

29. Burt Solomon, "Hawking Access," *National Journal*, 3 May 1986, pp. 1048–53; "Cashing In on Top Connections," *Time*, 3 March 1986, p. 28.

30. Joan Biskupic, "Bush Action on Gun Imports Cheers Backers of Curbs," *Congressional Quarterly*, Weekly Report, 18 March 1989, p. 582.

31. Michael Parenti, *Democracy for the Few* (New York: St. Martin's Press, 1974), p. 2.

32. Thomas L. Gais, Mark A. Peterson, and Jack L. Walker, "Interest Groups, Iron Triangles and Representative Institutions in American National Government," *British Journal of Political Science* 14 (April 1984): 161–85.

33. Hugh Heclo, "Issue Networks and the Executive Establishment," in Anthony King, ed., *The New American Political System* (Washington, DC: American Enterprise Institute, 1978), pp. 87–124.

34. E. E. Schattschneider, *The Semisovereign People* (New York: Holt, Rinehart and Winston, 1960).

35. Schlozman and Tierney, p. 60.

36. *Houston Post*, 28 December 1983, p. 12A.

SUGGESTED READINGS

Cigler, Allan J., and Loomis, Burdett A., eds. *Interest Group Politics*, 2d ed. Washington, DC: Congressional Quarterly Press, 1986.

Conway, M. Margaret. *Political Participation in the United States*. Washington, DC: Congressional Quarterly Press, 1985.

Goldfield, Michael. *The Decline of Organized Labor in the United States*. Chicago, IL: University of Chicago Press, 1987.

Matasar, Ann B. *Corporate PACs and Federal Campaign Finance Laws*. New York: Quorum Books, 1986.

Sabato, Larry J. *PAC Power: Inside the World of Political Action Committees*. New York: W. W. Norton, 1984.

Schlozman, Kay Lehman, and Tierney, John T. *Organized Interests and American Democracy*. New York: Harper & Row, 1986.

Teixeira, Ruy A. *Why Americans Don't Vote: Turnout Decline in the United States 1960–1984*. New York: Greenwood Press, 1987.

Wald, Kenneth D. *Religion and Politics in the United States*. New York: St. Martin's Press, 1987.

6

POLITICAL PARTIES

LEARNING OBJECTIVES

1. To describe and evaluate America's two-party system, identifying reasons scholars give for its persistence.
2. To trace the history of political parties in America, briefly describing each of the party eras.
3. To describe the organization of political parties in America and evaluate their organizational strength.
4. To compare and contrast Democratic and Republican party identifiers, voters, and activists.
5. To explain the reasons underlying America's split-level realignment.
6. To evaluate American parties in terms of the strong party/responsible party model.
7. To identify the factors that affect the role of American parties in the policy-making process.

American voters seem intent on electing Republican presidents while choosing Democrats to hold most other offices. In 1988, for example, George Bush's election as president was the third straight triumph for the Republican party and the seventh Republican victory in the last ten presidential elections (dating back to 1952). What's more, during that period, a Democratic presidential candidate won greater than 51 percent of the nationwide popular vote only once (Lyndon Johnson in 1964), while Republican candidates took more than 51 percent five times (Dwight Eisenhower in 1952 and 1956, Richard Nixon in 1972, Ronald Reagan in 1984, and George Bush in 1988).

While the Republican party has been racking up presidential victories, Democrats have done remarkably well in contests for most other offices. When George Bush took office in 1989, for example, he faced a Congress firmly in the control of the opposition party, with Democrats outnumbering Republicans 260 to 175 in the House, and 55 to 45 in the Senate. Democrats also controlled 28 out of 50 state governorships and held roughly 4,500 seats in state legislatures compared with only about 2,900 for the Republicans.

Many political scientists believe that the United States has experienced a split-level realignment.[1] A **realignment** is a change in the underlying party loyalties of voters. A **split-level realignment** is a change in voter allegiances that produces an advantage for one political party in contests for one office or set of offices while another party has the upper hand in other races. In order to study this political phenomenon in more detail, we must examine the background and organization of America's party system.

AMERICA'S TWO-PARTY SYSTEM

A **political party** is a group of individuals who join together voluntarily to seek political office in order to make policy. A party differs from an interest group mainly in its effort to win control of the machinery of government.

Although many democracies have multiparty systems, the American party system seems able to accommodate only two major parties at any one time. Since the Civil War era, those parties have been the Republicans and Democrats. To be sure, there have been others—the Progressives, Populists, Libertarians, American Independents, Socialist Workers, Communists, and more—but the system isn't kind to third parties. In the past, at least, a minor party occasionally got over the hump and became a major party, but minor-party success invariably accompanied the demise of one of the former major parties. In most cases, a minor party flashes onto the political scene, mounts a challenge to the existing party alignment, and then sinks into political oblivion once it becomes apparent that the newcomer will be unable to supplant one of the major parties.

Why does the United States have a two-party system? One explanation is that America's electoral system makes it difficult for minor parties to gain a political foothold. Unlike a number of other democracies, the United States does not have **proportional representation**, which is an election system that awards legislative seats to each party approximately equal to its popular voting strength. In America, only the candidate with the most votes wins. As a result, voters, political activists, and potential financial backers think twice about supporting a party whose chances of winning appear slim. A second problem for minor parties is the adaptability of America's major parties. Both the Republican and Democratic parties are broadly based, mass parties with diverse memberships. Every major economic, racial, ethnic, religious, regional, and ideological group in America can be represented to a greater or lesser degree in one or both of the major parties. Whenever a minor party comes up with an idea that proves popular with the electorate, the major parties are flexible (and opportunistic) enough to adopt it as their own, leaving the minor party without a cause all its own. Finally, election laws penalize minor parties. In many states, minor parties must clear major hurdles just to appear on the ballot.

THE HISTORY OF PARTIES IN AMERICA

Historians have generally divided the history of political parties in America into five periods, or party eras. We will add a sixth party era to the traditional division, reflecting recent changes in the nation's party system.

First Party Era—1790s to Early 1820s

America's first political parties emerged from the policy conflicts personified by Alexander Hamilton and Thomas Jefferson. Hamilton's party, the Federalists, advocated a strong national government that promoted economic growth, a broad interpretation of the Constitution, and close ties with Great Britain. The Federalists reflected the concerns of northern, coastal, and commercial interests. In contrast, Jefferson's party, the Jeffersonians, or Democratic-Republicans, favored states' rights, friendship with France, and a strict interpretation of the Constitution. The Jeffersonians represented southern, interior, and agrarian concerns. Although the Federalists won the first presidential contest between the two parties in 1796 (John Adams edged out Jefferson), the Jeffersonians dominated thereafter. By 1820, the Federalists were no longer a national force in presidential elections.

Second Party Era—1820s to 1860

With the demise of the Federalists, the United States experienced a brief one-party period. In fact, in 1820, during the so-called Era of Good Feelings, President James Monroe was reelected almost unanimously. The Jeffersonians soon split into factions, however, from which emerged the two major parties of the second party era.

The faction led by Andrew Jackson came to be known as the Democrats. Jackson and his party were the favorites of the great mass of common people who had recently won the right to vote, and as a result the Democrats generally enjoyed the upper hand politically. In general, the Democratic party won the support of small farmers, new immigrants, Catholics, and persons living in rural and frontier areas. The party advocated states' rights and opposed the use of national power to assist business expansion. The Democrats were also culturally tolerant of the growing diversity of American society.

The anti-Jacksonians, meanwhile, called themselves the Whigs, after an early English party. The Whigs enjoyed the backing of northeastern business interests, southern planters, Protestants, and native-born Americans. Unlike the Democrats, the Whigs favored a strong national government to help business and promote economic development. The Whigs also appealed to Americans uncomfortable with the different languages and customs of new immigrants.

Third Party Era—1860 to 1896

The slavery issue proved the undoing of the second party era and the basis for a new party alignment. The slavery controversy split both major parties of the second party era, and the Whigs, who were weaker than the Democrats,

The elephant as a symbol of the Republican party made its first appearance in print in this 1874 cartoon by Thomas Nast.

Thomas Nast from *Thomas Nast,* by Albert Bigelow Paine.

failed to survive. Subsequently, the remnants of the northern Whigs and members of a third party called the Know-Nothings organized a new party, the Republicans, to oppose the extension of slavery. The Republican party ran its first presidential candidate in 1856 (John C. Freemont) and elected its first president in 1860 (Abraham Lincoln).

After the Civil War, the Grand Old Party (GOP), as the Republican party was often called, competed with the Democrats as the two major parties of the third party era. The Republicans favored government assistance to business but were reluctant to support government regulation of business. Nevertheless, the GOP endorsed laws to coerce new immigrants to adopt American ways and supported efforts designed to regulate morality, such as Sunday-closing laws and the temperance movement against alcohol. The Republicans won the support of New Englanders, northern Protestants, Union war veterans, African-Americans, and English immigrants. The Democrats, meanwhile, adhered to their traditional principles of states' rights, limited government, and tolerance of cultural diversity. They were supported by southerners, Irish Catholics, farmers, ethnic Americans, labor unions, rural folks, and people opposing the abolition of alcohol.

The party balance during this period was fairly even. The Republican party did best in presidential contests. It captured the White House with Lincoln in 1860 and held it throughout most of the period by waving the flag of Civil War victory and nominating ex-Union generals to the presidency. Many elections were close, however, and the Democratic party did well in other races. The Democrats completely dominated southern politics (where the GOP's association with the Union victory was anathema to most native whites) and enjoyed significant strength in other areas of the country. Although the Republicans held a Senate majority during most of the era, the Democrats frequently controlled the House.

Fourth Party Era—1896 to 1932

The 1896 presidential election between Democrat William Jennings Bryan and Republican William McKinley was a watershed in American political history, changing the party balance to the advantage of the GOP. Although the United States was rapidly industrializing and urbanizing, the Bryan candidacy represented the triumph within the Democratic party of agrarian interests. Bryan carried the rural South and West, but he and his party were crushed in the more urbanized, industrialized, and populous Midwest and Northeast. Bryan lost the election and the Democrats did not soon recover. For the next thirty years, Republicans usually controlled both houses of Congress and elected presidents by landslide margins. Only one Democrat, Woodrow Wilson, was chosen president during the era, winning in 1912, when Teddy Roosevelt and William Howard Taft split the Republican vote, and in 1916, when he ran for reelection.

An 1880 Thomas Nast cartoon helped to popularize the Democratic donkey symbol.

Thomas Nast from *Thomas Nast,* by Albert Bigelow Paine.

The Republican party succeeded in being both antigovernment and progovernment at the same time. On one hand, the party adopted the rhetoric of rugged individualism, opposing social-welfare assistance as getting something for nothing. On the other hand, the GOP endorsed government efforts to aid business, such as the adoption of protective tariffs. As a result, the Republicans were able to appeal to a broad base of voters, including business people, urban workers, northeasterners, and rural Protestants outside the South. The Democrats, meanwhile, dispirited and divided by Bryan's defeat, were confined largely to their bases in the South and their support among Irish Catholics and other ethnic Americans. As the period wore on, however, the party began a comeback, particularly in the cities.

Fifth Party Era—1932 to 1980

The Great Depression set the stage for the fifth party era. When the economy collapsed, many voters blamed President Herbert Hoover and the Republican party, and elected Democrat Franklin Roosevelt president in 1932. FDR's New Deal program demonstrated that the Democratic party had at last adjusted to industrialization and urbanization. The Democrats passed legislation to regulate business and the economy, and they enacted programs to redress the wrongs of industrial society. The GOP, meanwhile, remained the party of business and laissez faire (that is, minimum government involvement in the economy). The Republicans generally opposed government regulation of business and the adoption and expansion of social-welfare programs.

Franklin Roosevelt succeeded in combining the traditional Democratic electoral base with a diverse collection of reformers and groups hard hit by the Depression. Besides white southerners, who were long-standing Democratic party loyalists, the Roosevelt coalition included organized labor; blue-collar workers; poor people; the unemployed; Jews; Catholics; Hispanics; Irish-, Italian-, and Polish-Americans; and blacks, who switched from their traditional Republican loyalties. The Democratic coalition was a varied group, but it was united by support for Franklin Roosevelt the man, and for the programs of the New Deal. Whom did this leave in the camp of the GOP? Primarily middle- and upper-class white Anglo-Saxon Protestants (WASPs) living outside the South.

For years, the Democratic New Deal coalition was a juggernaut, crushing Republicans in its path. It swept Democratic presidential candidates to victory in 1932, 1936, 1940, 1944, 1948, 1960, 1964, and 1976, and kept the party in control of Congress for most of the era. Toward the end of the period, however, Democratic momentum slowed as the GOP captured the White House in 1952, 1956, 1968, and 1972. Even when Democrat Jimmy Carter was able to assemble most of the elements of the Democratic coalition in 1976, he barely won, defeating President Gerald Ford by a narrow 51 to 48 percent popular-vote margin. Then, in 1980 and 1984, Republican Ronald Reagan's substantial election victories swept away whatever remained of the old New Deal voting alignment.

What happened to the once mighty coalition of Franklin Roosevelt? First, the Democratic party was hurt by socioeconomic changes. By the 1970s, many of the working-class groups who in the 1930s cast their lot with FDR and the New Deal for economic reasons had become middle class. Auto assembly-line workers, for example, owned campers, paid mortgages, and sent their kids to college. They may have had working-class jobs, but their incomes were middle class, and so, frequently, were their political concerns: taxes, inflation, and crime—issues emphasized by the GOP.

Second, the Republican party became adept at exploiting issues that divided the Democrats. Republicans appealed to Catholics by stressing opposition to abortion. To attract southern whites, the GOP emphasized support for defense spending, opposition to affirmative action, and adherence to traditional social values. The Republicans lured fundamentalist Protestants by focusing on opposition to abortion and pornography, and support for school prayer.[2] In the meantime, the Vietnam War, which a major segment of the Democratic party opposed, allowed the Republican party to establish itself as the party that was tough-minded on foreign affairs while branding the Democrats as weak on national defense.[3]

Finally, the GOP benefited from the personal popularity and perceived success of Ronald Reagan. Perhaps no American politician since Franklin Roosevelt sustained as high a level of popularity over an extended period. Moreover, the lowered inflation rate and economic recovery after the 1982 recession enabled the GOP to claim credit as the party of prosperity. The contrast with the Carter administration, which many Americans considered a failure, was telling. As a pair of academic observers phrase it, "The Democratic party was seen not as the traditional defender of the middle class but as tax collector for the welfare state, the Republican party not as the tool of Wall Street and the rich but as the instrument to bring about widespread economic growth and opportunity."[4]

Sixth Party Era—Since 1980

The United States has entered a sixth party era, characterized by weakened citizen attachments to parties, changed voting patterns, and split-level realignment. Many political scientists believe that political parties today are a less significant element of the policy process than they were in the early years of the New Deal period. As Table 6.1 shows, the proportion of Americans who call themselves political independents is greater in the 1970s and 1980s than it was in earlier decades. What's more, research shows that party identifiers are now more likely to support the other party's candidates than before, and ticket-splitting is more common. (**Split-ticket voting** refers to citizens voting for candidates of two or more parties for different offices.)

The voting patterns of the current party era have changed from those of the New Deal period. Compared with the earlier voting alignment, African-American voters today are more likely to vote Democratic, while southern whites, who were once loyal Democrats, now support the GOP. Catholics, Jews, and labor union members, three other groups that at one time were closely aligned with the Democratic party, still lean Democratic although they are less supportive of that party than before.

Two researchers, John R. Petrocik and Frederick T. Steeper, identify two important divisions among today's voters, one of which is a continuation from the New Deal era while the other is a recent phenomenon. The older voting division is along socioeconomic lines. Higher-income groups tend to support Republicans while lower-income groups back Democrats. The more recent

TABLE 6.1
Party Identification, 1937–88

Year	Republican	Democrat	Independent
1988	29%	43%	28%
1984	35	38	27
1976	23	48	29
1960	30	47	23
1949	32	48	20
1937	34	50	16

Note: Based on answers to the following question: "In politics, as of today, do you consider yourself a Republican, a Democrat, or an Independent?"
Sources: *The Gallup Report*, September 1988, April 1981.

voting pattern, meanwhile, involves frequency of church attendance among white Christians. For white Protestants and Catholics, the higher the rate of church attendance, the more likely individuals are to vote Republican. (The pattern does not hold true, however, for blacks, who tend to support Democratic candidates regardless of frequency of church attendance.)[5]

Finally, as we discussed in the introduction to this chapter, in America's current party alignment, the Republicans have an advantage in presidential races while Democrats do well in contests for offices below the presidential level. Let's look in more detail at America's party system today.

PARTY ORGANIZATION

Political parties in America are decentralized in a fashion that parallels America's federal system. In a sense, there are fifty-one Republican and fifty-one Democratic parties: the national parties and party organizations in each state. Every four years the national parties assemble in convention to adopt a platform and nominate candidates for president and vice-president. (A **party platform** is a statement of party principles and issue positions.) In addition to picking a presidential–vice-presidential ticket, each national party convention selects a national chairperson and a national committee with members from each state. In practice, the party's presidential nominee handpicks the national chairperson and generally controls the contents of the platform. Between elections, the national chairperson and national committee conduct the work of the national party which, by and large, is geared toward winning the next presidential election. They plan and organize the next convention, raise money, build party support, and attempt to enhance the party's national image.

The main location of party activity in America, however, is the states. Although national party organizations set broad guidelines for choosing delegates to the national party conventions, state parties are fairly independent from national party control. State parties choose their own candidates for state and local office, run their own campaigns, and raise most of their own money.

American political parties are not as strong organizationally as they were in the late nineteenth and early twentieth centuries. In those days, parties controlled virtually every facet of election campaigning, from selecting party candidates to mobilizing voters on election day. Many big-city political party organizations, such as Tammany Hall in New York City, dominated local politics through their control of thousands of patronage jobs. (**Political patronage** refers to the power of an officeholder to award favors, such as government jobs, to political allies.) Since most voters were loyal to one party or the other, campaigns revolved around the efforts of party organizations to get their supporters to the polls. Moreover, because parties played such an important role in their election, officeholders had an incentive to support their party and work for its success.

Over the years, political parties lost much of their power to control campaigns and elections. Most states adopted reforms that took the authority to select party candidates away from party leaders and gave it to party voters participating in primary elections. (A **primary election** is an intraparty election held to determine party nominees for the general-election ballot.) Other reforms eliminated most patronage jobs. Then, as the American electorate grew larger and more mobile, voters' party loyalties weakened and party organizations withered. Modern candidates hired professional campaign consultants to organize their campaigns, and purchased time for television commercials to sell themselves to the voters. Once elected, then, officeholders owed little to party organizations and felt few incentives to support the party.[6]

In the last few years, however, political party organizations have begun to make a comeback, especially the Republican party. Although presidential campaigns are still centered around individual candidates, parties now play a more important role in congressional elections. Both parties have developed mechanisms for raising substantial amounts of money and for organizing campaigns. The national Republican party and, to a lesser degree, the national Democratic party recruit candidates for Congress, train them to develop issues and present themselves to voters, conduct polls to guide campaigns, and provide financial assistance. Many state party organizations are experiencing a revival as well, operating permanent headquarters with full-time directors and staffs. What's more, since the early 1980s, the long-term decline in party voting and party identification has leveled off.[7]

PARTY IDENTIFIERS, PARTY VOTERS, AND PARTY ACTIVISTS

Who are Democrats and who are Republicans? The answer to that question depends on whether you consider party identifiers, party voters, or party activists. Table 6.2 compares Democratic and Republican party identifiers and party voters. Although this table is a bit complicated, it's worth our study. The first three columns of numbers from the left indicate the percentages of respondents in a national survey who call themselves Democrats, Republicans, or Independents. The last two columns, meanwhile, show how members of various groups reported voting in the 1988 presidential election.

Although both parties are broadly based, including large numbers of adherents and voters in most socioeconomic groups, the Republican party is the more homogeneous of the two parties. As you can see from the table, the GOP does best among white, male, middle- and upper-income individuals. By religious affiliation, Republicans are strongest among Protestants, weakest among Jews. By region, the GOP has its largest percentage of party identifiers in the Midwest, historically the strongest region for the party. It is weakest in the South, an area of traditional Democratic dominance. At least in recent presidential voting, however, the South has become a Republican stronghold.

TABLE 6.2
Party Identification and Voting in the 1988 Presidential Election

Group	Affiliation* Democrat	Republican	Independent	Election Day Vote† Dukakis	Bush
National	43%	29%	28%	46%	54%
Race					
White	38	32	30	40	60
Black	75	8	17	89	11
Hispanic	51	23	26	70	30
Income					
<$15,000	51	22	27	63	37
$15–40,000	42	29	29	43	57
>$40,000	34	37	29	39	61
Region					
East	45	30	25	49	51
Midwest	35	31	34	47	53
South	46	27	27	41	59
West	44	30	26	47	53
Religion					
Protestant	41	32	27	40	60
Catholic	46	26	28	47	53
Jewish	na	na	na	65	35
Gender					
Men	40	30	30	42	58
Women	45	29	26	49	51

*Based on answers to the following question: "In politics, as of today, do you consider yourself a Republican, a Democrat, or an Independent?" Source: *The Gallup Report*, September 1988, p. 6.
†Based on interviews with 11,645 voters on election day 1988. Source: CBS News/*New York Times* Survey, quoted in *Public Opinion*, January/February 1989, p. 25.
‡The income categories used by the two surveys are not exactly comparable.
na: Not available

The Democratic party, meanwhile, is strongest among blacks, Hispanic-Americans, women, and lower-income wage earners. The party does better among Jews and Catholics than it does with Protestants. In terms of regional support, Democrats are strongest in the South and East if we consider party identification. If we look at presidential voting patterns, however, Democrats are strongest in the East, weakest in the South.

In addition to party identifiers and voters, each party has a hard core of party activists. Activists volunteer their time and energy to work in political campaigns and do the day-to-day work of the party. Since the proportion of party activists in the population is too small to be measured by national opinion surveys, political scientists identify particular groups of activists for study, such as delegates to the national party conventions of each party.

Table 6.3 profiles the delegates to the 1988 Democratic and Republican conventions. Looking first at the Democrats, we can see that the party's convention delegates resemble party identifiers and voters in their diversity. Blacks, women, Catholics, Jews, and union members are all well represented among Democratic activists, just as they are among party adherents and voters. The major difference between Democratic convention delegates and other groups is in socioeconomic status. Even though the Democratic party receives its strongest voting support from lower-income groups, the annual median income for its convention delegates was a comfortable $52,000. This figure may seem surprisingly high considering the backgrounds of most party identifiers and voters, but keep in mind what we learned in the last chapter, that people who are politically active tend to have relatively high socioeconomic status. Republican convention delegates, meanwhile, were a relatively homogeneous group, similar to GOP identifiers and voters. As you can see from the table, a majority of Republican convention delegates were white male Protestants.

Political philosophy is perhaps the most significant distinction between Democratic and Republican convention delegates. Democratic delegates were evenly divided between those who called themselves liberal and those who said they were moderate, with only 5 percent calling themselves conservative. In contrast, self-proclaimed conservatives dominated the GOP convention, outnumbering moderates 58 to 35 percent. Almost no Republican delegates claimed the liberal label.

TABLE 6.3
Profile of Delegates to the 1988 Party Conventions

	Democratic	Republican
Median annual income	$52,000	$72,000
Median age	46 years	51 years
Women	48%	33%
Blacks	23	4
Lawyers	16	17
Teachers	14	5
Union members	25	3
Protestant	50	69
Catholic	30	22
Jewish	7	2
Liberal	43	0
Moderate	43	35
Conservative	5	58

Sources: Martin Plissner and Warren J. Mitofsky, "The Making of the Delegates, 1968–1988," *Public Opinion*, September/ October 1988, pp. 45–47; Thomas B. Edsall and Richard Morin, "A Convention Taking the Right Path," *Washington Post*, National Weekly Edition, 15–21 August 1988, p. 10.

Table 6.4 compares the views of Democratic and Republican convention delegates with each other and with Democratic and Republican party identifiers. This table is somewhat complex, but rich in detail. The table lists a series of issue questions and then shows the responses of Democratic and Republican convention delegates and party identifiers. Issue A, for example, concerns the percentage of each group that favors a national health-care program. As you can see from the first two columns in the table, more than 80 percent of Democratic convention delegates and party identifiers agreed with the position. Both groups took the liberal position. (You may want to review the discussion of liberalism and conservatism in chapter 1.) From the last two columns, however, you can see that Republican convention delegates not only disagreed with the Democrats on this issue, but were out of step with their own party's identifiers. Even though 61 percent of GOP adherents supported national health care, only 15 percent of the party's convention delegates took that position.

As you study the table you will see, in general, that Democratic activists were more liberal than party supporters. Republican party activists, meanwhile, were more conservative than GOP identifiers. On the issues considered in Table 6.4, Democratic convention delegates, as a group, were as liberal or more liberal than Democratic identifiers, especially on noneconomic questions, such as black civil rights, abortion, and gay rights. In contrast, GOP convention delegates generally took more conservative positions than Republican party identifiers on the issues considered in the table, especially on the questions of a national health-care program, cutting defense spending to fund social programs, and the Equal Rights Amendment.

TABLE 6.4
Major Issues Favored by Convention Delegates, 1988

	Democratic		Republican	
	Delegates	*Voters*	*Delegates*	*Voters*
National health-care program	82%	83%	15%	61%
Cutting defense spending to fund social programs	75	55	13	39
Blacks still lack equal rights	83	60	45	48
Amendment to outlaw abortion	6	35	36	36
Equal Rights Amendment	90	74	29	56
Death penalty	49	64	88	79
Gay rights law	65	43	26	28

Sources: Martin Plissner and Warren J. Mitofsky, "The Making of the Delegates, 1968–1988," *Public Opinion*, September/October 1988, pp. 45–47; Thomas B. Edsall and Richard Morin, "A Convention Taking the Right Path," *Washington Post*, National Weekly Edition, 15–21 August 1988, p. 10.

AMERICA'S SPLIT-LEVEL REALIGNMENT

Political scientists offer a number of explanations for America's split-level re-alignment in which the Republican party generally wins the presidency while Democrats elect majorities to Congress and do well in races for most state and local offices as well. Some observers base their explanations on the belief that split-level realignment is a transitional stage as the party system moves from a period of Democratic majority during the New Deal era to a time in which the GOP becomes the majority party. Democrats maintain majorities in Congress and many state and local offices, the argument goes, because a large number of Democrats enjoy the advantage of incumbency and they have often drawn electoral district lines to their party's advantage.

Although incumbents do enjoy significant electoral advantages and dis-trict lines *may* provide a party with some advantages, it doesn't seem prob-able that the Democrats' success below the level of the presidency primarily reflects these factors. Not only do Democrats hold onto seats in Congress they already occupy, but, since 1980, the Democratic party has actually gained seats, winning more than its share of open seats in which neither candidate is an incumbent. What's more, national opinion poll data still show that more Americans identify with the Democratic than with the Republican party.[8]

The best explanation for split-level realignment involves the different ori-entations voters have toward races for different offices, coupled with the rela-tive diversity of each party. Research shows that voters regard presidential elections as national contests, but see races for Congress as local affairs. (The primary explanation for this is that the national media focus on presidential races while ignoring other elections.)[9] Consequently, voters want different, even contradictory, policies from the president and Congress. Voters believe that protecting the nation's security and promoting economic prosperity are national concerns. It so happens that these are issues on which the GOP seems to have an advantage. In races for Congress, meanwhile, voters are in-terested in more specific policy concerns, such as protecting Social Security, helping farmers or unemployed workers, and promoting local economic de-velopment. Voters think that Democrats do better articulating these concerns.

The second aspect of this explanation involves the relative ethnic and ideological diversity of the two parties. The Democratic party, you recall, is more heterogeneous than the GOP, in terms of both race and political phi-losophy. As a result, the Democrats usually have a more difficult time than the Republicans agreeing on a national leader and finding a message acceptable to all major factions. While the Republicans usually enter presidential cam-paigns united, the Democrats are often divided.

Although the Democrats' ethnic and ideological diversity may be a disad-vantage in nationwide presidential campaigns, it is an advantage when it comes to statewide races for governor and senator and district races for seats in the U.S. House. Because of the party's heterogeneity, the Democrats can usually find liberal candidates to run in liberal districts, conservative candidates for conservative districts, and minority candidates for districts that have large minority populations. In contrast, the Republican party's homogeneity becomes a disadvantage in district campaigns. Since the large majority of Republican party activists are conservative white Protestants, the GOP is often unable to find strong candidates to run in many of the nation's congressional districts.[10]

In sum, the GOP has an advantage in presidential elections because of its ethnic and political homogeneity. The party is able to unite quickly behind its candidate and clearly articulate its position on the national issues of greatest concern to the electorate voting for president—national defense and economic prosperity. In many statewide and congressional district elections, however, the GOP's homogeneity is a disadvantage because the party lacks strong candidates with acceptable messages to compete in many areas. In contrast with the Republicans, diversity among Democrats makes it difficult for the party to unite behind a presidential candidate and to agree on a clear national message. As some say, the party appears to lack vision.[11] In other races, though, the Democratic party's heterogeneity enables the party to offer strong candidates and present messages geared to local voters' concerns.

CONCLUSION: PARTIES, POLICY, AND POLITICS

Political scientists believe that strong political parties perform a positive role in a democracy. Strong parties, they say, organize the concerns of diverse interest groups into a workable program (political scientists call this process **interest aggregation**), recruit candidates for public office, conduct election campaigns, formulate public policies, and, once in office, govern the nation. These last two functions embody the concept of **responsible parties**, that is, parties that clearly spell out issue positions in their platforms and faithfully carry them out in office. Scholars usually describe British parties as responsible parties.

Most political scientists consider American political parties to be neither particularly strong nor responsible. The parties are not always successful at interest aggregation. To be sure, the Democrats under Franklin Roosevelt united an array of groups behind the New Deal. In more recent years, though, the Democratic party has been less effective at bridging the conflicts among groups within its coalition.

As for candidate recruitment, American parties only occasionally recruit candidates for lower office. Most American politicians are self-starters. At the highest levels of government, in particular, the party organizations have little control over who their candidates will be. Both Jimmy Carter and Ronald Reagan, for example, captured their party's presidential nomination running as party outsiders.

American political parties play a secondary role in election campaigns as well. In the first half of this century, parties were the main campaign organizations. They raised money, educated voters, identified supporters, and got out the vote. Subsequently, the parties' campaign machines rusted and candidates organized their own campaigns. Candidates now raise money on their own and hire professional campaign consultants to organize their campaigns, plan strategy, and market the candidate with slick media advertising, especially on television. Only in the last few years have parties begun to make a comeback in terms of fund-raising and providing technical assistance to candidates.

It's also questionable whether American parties actually formulate policy. Instead, they borrow the ideas of others, adopting them as their own. Moreover, the parties' record at implementing policies once in office is only fair.

In sum, American political parties do not live up to the ideal of the responsible party model. In general, political scientists have been critical of the weakness of the nation's parties and have lamented their decline. On occasion, political scientists have even launched scholarly crusades to reform American parties to make them stronger and, presumably, better.[12] The truth, however, is that American political parties are the product of their constitutional, technological, historical/cultural, and political environments.

First, the nation's parties are shaped by the constitutional setting. British parties are strong and responsible in large part because they are centralized. The party with a majority in Parliament (the British legislature) selects the prime minister to run the government. The United Kingdom, though, is a unitary state, without separation of powers and checks and balances. In contrast, the organization of America's decentralized, "weak" parties parallels the federal system and the separation-of-powers system. In America, parties and candidates can make promises to voters but, because of separation of powers and checks and balances, they may be unable to carry them out.

Second, American parties have been weakened by their slowness to adapt to technological change. As we see in the next chapter, television, polling, direct-mail fund-raising, and professional campaign consultants have fundamentally changed the way campaigns are conducted in America. Back in the 1890s, William McKinley campaigned for president from his front porch in Ohio, waving to nearly 750,000 people who were brought into town by the Republican party and paraded past his door.[13] Today, candidates come to voters' living rooms through television, and parties need not be involved. Candidates raise money from individuals and PACs, hire professional campaign consultants, and purchase media time. Only in the last few years have the parties begun to catch up to the new campaign technologies by improving their fund-raising capabilities and developing apparatus to provide technical assistance to their candidates. One observer says that the parties are starting to become super PACs.[14]

Third, parties are affected by historical and cultural developments. During the 1960s and 1970s, for example, many Americans were turned against politics and parties by Vietnam, Watergate, high taxes, and inflation. One study found that young people who were socialized politically during this period developed weaker ties to political parties than their parents' generation.[15] Assorted scandals in the 1980s have no doubt weakened parties as well.

Finally, parties are political institutions. The first goal of parties is to win office; the second goal is to hold office. Policy is a byproduct determined by politics. Parties out of office propose policies aimed at winning majority support. Parties in office adopt the policies demanded by their electoral coalition.[16] In the 1932 election campaign, for example, Franklin Roosevelt called for a balanced budget. Once in office, though, he and his party responded to the policy demands of his constituency by adopting the New Deal. Similarly, the best explanation of President Reagan's economic program was that it benefited the middle- and upper-income white voters at the core of his electoral coalition. American parties make policy, then, but not according to the responsible party model. Instead, they act in response to the politics of their circumstances.

KEY TERMS

interest aggregation
party platform
political party
political patronage
primary election

proportional representation
realignment
responsible parties
split-level realignment
split-ticket voting

NOTES

1. David G. Lawrence and Richard Fleisher, "Puzzles and Confusions: Political Realignment in the 1980s," *Political Science Quarterly* 102 (Spring 1987): 79–92.
2. Christopher Jencks, "Lessons for Liberals," *New York Review of Books*, 22 December 1988, pp. 21–22.
3. Everett Carll Ladd, "The 1988 Elections: Continuation of the Post–New Deal System," *Political Science Quarterly* 104 (Spring 1989): 1–18.
4. Thomas E. Cavanagh and James L. Sundquist, "The New Two-Party System," in John E. Chubb and Paul E. Peterson, eds., *The New Direction in American Politics* (Washington, DC: Brookings Institution, 1985), p. 37.
5. John R. Petrocik and Frederick T. Steeper, "The Political Landscape in 1988," *Public Opinion*, September/October 1987, pp. 41–44.

6. Barbara G. Salmore and Stephen A. Salmore, *Candidates, Parties, and Campaigns: Electoral Politics in America*, 2d ed. (Washington, DC: Congressional Quarterly Press, 1989), pp. 20–44.

7. Xandra Kayden and Eddie Mahe, Jr., *The Party Goes On* (New York: Basic Books, 1985).

8. Gary C. Jacobson, "Congress: A Singular Continuity," in Michael Nelson, ed., *The Elections of 1988* (Washington, DC: Congressional Quarterly Press, 1989), p. 144.

9. Laura L. Vertz, John P. Frendreis, and James L. Gibson, "Nationalization of the Electorate in the United States," *American Political Science Review* 81 (September 1987): 961–66.

10. Michael Nelson, "Constitutional Aspects of the Elections," in Nelson, ed., *The Elections of 1988*, p. 198.

11. William Schneider, "JFK's Children: The Class of '74," *Atlantic Monthly*, March 1989, pp. 35–58.

12. American Political Science Association, *Toward a More Responsible Two-Party System* (New York: American Political Science Association, 1950).

13. Richard L. Kolbe, *American Political Parties: An Uncertain Future* (New York: Harper & Row, 1985), p. 61.

14. David E. Price, *Bringing Back the Parties* (Washington, DC: Congressional Quarterly Press, 1984), p. 299.

15. M. Kent Jennings and Gregory B. Markus, "Partisan Orientations over the Long Haul: Results from the Three-Wave Political Socialization Panel Study," *American Political Science Review* 78 (December 1984): 1000–18.

16. Theodore Lowi, "Party, Policy, and Constitution in America," in William Nesbit Chambers and Walter Dean Burnham, eds. *The American Party System: Stages of Development*, 2d ed. (New York: Oxford University Press, 1975), pp. 238–76.

SUGGESTED READINGS

Chubb John E., and Peterson, Paul E., eds. *The New Direction in American Politics.* Washington, DC: Brookings Institution, 1985.

Kanieniecki, Sheldon. *Party Identification, Political Behavior, and the American Electorate*. Westport, CT: Greenwood Press, 1985.

Kayden, Xandra, and Mahe, Eddie, Jr. *The Party Goes On*. New York: Basic Books, 1985.

Kolbe, Richard L. *American Political Parties: An Uncertain Future*. New York: Harper & Row, 1985.

Price, David E. *Bringing Back the Parties*. Washington, DC: Congressional Quarterly Press, 1984.

Salmore, Barbara G., and Salmore, Stephen A. *Candidates, Parties, and Campaigns: Electoral Politics in America*, 2d ed. Washington, DC: Congressional Quarterly Press, 1989.

Sorauf, Frank J., and Beck, Paul Allen. *Party Politics in America*, 6th ed. Glenview, IL: Scott, Foresman/Little, Brown, 1988.

ELECTIONS

LEARNING OBJECTIVES

1. To identify the types of elections held in the United States.
2. To discuss the practice and politics of legislative redistricting.
3. To describe election campaigns, focusing on the role of money, modern campaign technology, campaign strategy in a television age, and negative advertising.
4. To compare and contrast election campaigns for the U.S. House and the U.S. Senate.
5. To describe presidential elections, focusing on the delegate-selection process, the five stages of the presidential nomination process, and the electoral college.
6. To evaluate the relationship between elections and public policy, considering the various models of voting behavior.

The tone for the 1988 presidential campaign was set in late May in Paramus, New Jersey, a middle-class suburb just across the Hudson River from New York City, where top officials of George Bush's presidential campaign gathered for a strategy session. Although it was still early in the election year, Bush campaign manager Lee Atwater, media consultant Roger Ailes, and pollster Robert Teeter had reason to be worried. A new Gallup Poll found the vice-president trailing Massachusetts Governor Michael Dukakis by 16 percentage points. What's more, the poll showed that while almost as many people had negative images of Bush as had positive impressions, nearly five times as many voters liked Dukakis as disliked him.

The purpose of the meeting in Paramus was to try out some material the Bush people hoped would turn the campaign around. A local marketing company paid thirty people $25 apiece for participating in the study. All of the people were Democrats who had voted for Reagan in 1980 and 1984, but now leaned toward Dukakis.

As the Bush campaign officials watched hidden behind a two-way mirror, a moderator led the New Jerseyites in a discussion of the election. It soon became apparent that the people knew almost nothing about the campaign. Most of them thought that Dukakis was a governor but many did not remember his state. Everyone knew Bush was vice-president but that was about all they could recall about him. Then the moderator asked the people what they would think if they were told that Dukakis had vetoed a bill requiring schoolchildren to recite the Pledge of Allegiance, that he gave weekend prison furloughs to murderers, that he opposed the death penalty, and that he had not cleaned up polluted Boston harbor. Many in the group responded by saying they could not support a candidate with that kind of a record, and by the end of the session half the people said they would not vote for Dukakis.

Armed with these results, the Bush campaign proceeded to launch a series of attacks against Governor Dukakis, focusing on the Pledge of Allegiance, Boston harbor, the death penalty, and prison furloughs. Many Bush television commercials featured the picture of Willie Horton, a black convicted murderer who raped a white woman while on furlough from a Massachusetts prison. The Dukakis campaign, meanwhile, was slow to respond to the onslaught. By the time Dukakis finally fought back, the damage had been done. Polls showed that nearly as many people had a negative image of Dukakis as a positive one, and that Bush had surged into the lead in the race for the White House.[1]

The story of the Paramus meeting and the 1988 presidential campaign introduces a number of important issues concerning American politics and elections. First, the Paramus meeting illustrates the use of modern election technology. Political campaigns today employ tools that were originally developed to market products. Second, the 1988 campaign raises questions about the grounds on which citizens base their voting decisions. Was George Bush elected president *because* of the negative campaign or *in spite* of it? Finally, the 1988 presidential campaign highlights a controversy concerning modern campaigns and their impact on democracy. Much of the campaign dealt with negative issues, many of which were irrelevant to the presidency. In fact, at one point, Vice President Bush told a press conference that he didn't "want to be dragged" into a specific discussion of what he would do as president.[2] Avoiding substantive issues may be a good campaign tactic, of course, but what effect does that strategy have on the quality of democracy in America?

TYPES OF ELECTIONS

Americans have the opportunity to cast ballots in several types of elections held at various times throughout the year. A **general election** is an election to fill state and national offices held in November of even-numbered years. Citizens choose among candidates put forward by the Democratic and Republican parties and, sometimes, minor-party candidates and independent candidates not affiliated with any party. Voters may cast a **split ticket**, in which citizens vote for the candidates of two or more parties for different offices, or a **straight ticket**, in which they vote for all the candidates of a single party for all offices at stake. The winner of a general election is the candidate with the most votes, regardless of whether the candidate has a majority or not; there are no runoffs.

In most states, major parties choose their general-election candidates in primary elections scheduled a month or more before the November general election. A **primary election** is an intraparty election held to determine a party's nominees for the general-election ballot. Democrats compete against other Democrats, Republicans against Republicans. In most states, the candidate with the most votes wins the primary election, regardless of whether the candidate has a majority. Some states, however, including most southern states, require a runoff between the top two candidates if no one receives a majority in the first vote. (A **runoff primary** is an election procedure requiring a second election between the two top finishers should no candidate receive a majority of the vote in the initial primary.)

The runoff primary is controversial. Critics, including civil rights activist Jesse Jackson, argue that the runoff primary system is designed to prevent the election of minority candidates. They say that it is designed to keep a black candidate from winning when several white candidates split the white vote. The defenders of the runoff primary, meanwhile, argue that the underlying issue is democracy: Should public officials be chosen by majority vote? A runoff primary allows for majority rule. The reason the runoff primary is used in the South, they say, is because the South was long a one-party region. Since the winner of the Democratic primary usually won the general election, it was reasonable to require that individual to have the support of a majority of the voters.

In practice, how does the runoff primary affect election outcomes? A recent study examined 215 primary runoff races in Georgia between 1965 and 1982 to test the validity of three conventional views about primary runoffs: (1) that the leader going into the runoff loses; (2) that incumbents forced into runoffs lose; and (3) that the runoff primary hurts minority and women candidates. The study found that each of these three propositions was wrong more often that it was right. Primary front-runners won twice as often as they lost; incumbents forced into runoffs won half the time; and blacks and women who led primaries did as well as white males in similar positions.[3]

In many states, voters also have the opportunity to participate in a variety of non-candidate elections, including bond elections, recall elections, and referendum elections. A **bond election** is a procedure used to obtain voter approval for a state or local government to go into debt. (A **bond** is a certificate of indebtedness, or, in lay terms, an IOU.) **Recall** is a procedure which allows voters to remove elected officials from office before expiration of their terms. If enough signatures can be gathered on petitions, disgruntled citizens can force a recall election to remove the targeted official. Voters then decide whether to keep the officeholder or declare the office vacant. A vacancy would be filled in a special election. (A **special election** is an election called at a time outside the normal election calendar.)

Finally, a number of states and some local governments grant their citizens the right of initiative and referendum. The **initiative** is a procedure whereby citizens can propose legislation by gathering a certain number of signatures (usually 5 to 15 percent of the registered voters) on a petition. The adoption or rejection of the measure depends upon the results of a popular vote, or referendum. A **referendum** is an election in which voters can approve or reject a legislative measure. Referendums can be placed on the ballot either by means of a citizen initiative or by the state legislature. Every election year, for example, California voters cast ballots on a number of propositions that arise through the initiative process.

ELECTION DISTRICTS AND REDISTRICTING

American voters select public officials in a combination of at-large, statewide elections and single-member district elections. An **at-large election** is a method for choosing public officials in which every citizen of a political subdivision, such as a state, votes to select a public official. United States senators, state governors, and other state officeholders are elected at large in statewide elections. Voters select other officials, including members of the U.S. House of Representatives and state legislatures, in single-member district elections. A **single-member district election** is a method for choosing public officials in which a political subdivision, such as a state, is divided into districts and each district elects one official.

The actual task of drawing district lines falls to state legislatures, which must work under certain guidelines. One requirement is that legislative districts must contain roughly the same number of people. For years, many state legislatures neglected to **redistrict**, that is, to redraw boundaries of legislative districts to reflect population movement. As a result, districts in rapidly growing urban areas were often far more heavily populated than districts in rural areas, which had been losing population. In Illinois, for example, one U.S. congressional district in Chicago had a population of 914,053 by the early 1960s, while another district in rural southern Illinois contained only 112,116 people.[4] In the early 1960s, the United States Supreme Court held in its famous one-person, one-vote rulings, *Baker* v. *Carr* (1962) and *Wesberry* v. *Sanders* (1964), that the equal protection clause of the Fourteenth Amendment requires that U.S. House and state legislative districts be nearly equal in population.[5] After each census, state legislatures must now redraw legislative district boundaries to account for population movement within the state.

The Court's one-person, one-vote decisions have affected legislative representation and policy. In the late 1960s, when the rulings were first implemented, rural areas lost representation in Congress and state legislatures while the nation's big cities gained seats. As a result, urban problems, such as housing, education, employment, transportation, race relations, and the like, took center stage on legislative agendas. The initial impact of the Court's rulings was to make Congress and many state legislatures more liberal.[6]

In contrast, the 1980 census showed that during the 1970s, America's population shifted away from generally liberal inner cities to more conservative suburbs and surrounding metropolitan areas. This time, redistricting changes led to fewer representatives from constituencies demanding big government and more representatives from areas where people are wary of government. The result was that Congress and many state legislatures grew more conservative during the 1980s.[7] Many observers expect the 1990 census to show a continuation of the population trends identified in 1980.

In some states, legislatures must also abide by the requirements of the federal Voting Rights Act as they redistrict legislative boundaries. State legisla-

With the passage of the Federal Voting Rights Act in the summer of 1965, black residents of rural Wilcox County, Alabama, came out in force to vote for the first time in a primary election the next May. Wilcox County had previously not had a single registered black voter.

tures in areas with histories of voter discrimination, mostly in the South and Southwest, must follow the guidelines of the Voting Rights Act to safeguard the rights of African-Americans and non-English-speaking minorities, such as Hispanic-Americans. The law prohibits both minority-vote dilution and minority-vote packing. **Minority-vote dilution** is the drawing of election district lines so as to thinly spread minority voters among several districts, thus reducing their electoral influence in any one district. **Minority-vote packing**, meanwhile, is the drawing of election-district lines so as to cluster minority voters into one district or a small number of districts.

The political effect of the Voting Rights Act on southern politics has been to increase legislative representation for black Democrats and, ironically, white Republicans. The law has obliged southern legislatures, which have traditionally been dominated by conservative white Democrats, to create predominantly black congressional districts in regions with substantial black populations, such as the inner-city areas of Atlanta, Houston, Memphis, and New Orleans, and the Mississippi delta country. Black Democrats have been elected to represent each of these districts except the one in New Orleans. In order to construct majority black districts, however, southern legislatures have been forced to redraw district lines to shift African-American voters away from adjacent districts into the new black-majority district. Since black voters are usually Democratic, this has reduced Democratic voting strength in surrounding districts. As a result, white Republicans have picked up some House seats, defeating white Democrats who were stripped of some of their black support by redistricting.[8]

Despite the restrictions of "one person, one vote" and the Voting Rights Act, redistricting remains a highly political process. Legislative districts can be drawn to benefit one political party over another or even to help a particular candidate. **Gerrymandering** is the drawing of legislative district lines for political advantage. It has been used by American politicians for centuries to influence election outcomes. In fact, the word itself dates from early nineteenth-century Massachusetts when Governor Elbridge Gerry signed a bill creating a district that observers said resembled a salamander, hence Gerry-mander.

Political scientists who study redistricting believe that even though it can increase the odds of a party's winning a particular seat, it doesn't guarantee an election outcome because of the power of incumbency and other factors.[9] In general, the politics of redistricting have favored Democrats, because Democrats control more state legislatures and hold more governorships. In California after the 1980 census, for example, a Democratic-controlled legislature and Democratic governor were creative enough to produce a redistricting plan that helped turn a narrow 22-to-21 Democratic edge in the state's congressional delegation to a more substantial 28-to-17 Democratic advantage. Redistricting also tends to produce uncompetitive districts because state legislators, anxious to ensure a particular election outcome, create districts that are safe for one party or the other.[10]

ELECTION CAMPAIGNS

A **political campaign** is an attempt to get information to voters that will persuade them to elect a candidate or not to elect an opponent. Election campaigns are big business in America, featuring professional campaign consultants, well-oiled organizations, and big money. Not all elections fit this description, of course. Many local contests are rather modest affairs. The candidates, their families, and a few friends shake some hands, knock on a few doors, put up some signs, and, perhaps, raise enough money to buy a small ad in the local newspaper. The contest may be hard fought, but the stakes aren't high enough to support a major-league campaign effort. Not so, however, with presidential campaigns, statewide races, local elections in big cities, and many elections for Congress and state legislatures. These contests feature big-time campaign techniques.

The Role of Money

Above all else, big-time political campaigns are expensive. In 1988, for example, winners of U.S. Senate seats spent an average of $4 million apiece. Senator Pete Wilson of California led the way, shelling out nearly $15 million to win reelection.[11] Presidential campaigns are the most expensive American elections because candidates must run nationwide. In 1988, George Bush spent more than $70 million winning the presidency.[12]

Where does the money go? The biggest single item in the big-time campaign budget is media, especially television. In Florida, a state with ten major media markets, a moderate, one-week television buy runs about $250,000, while a heavy buy can exceed $450,000.[13] The cost of television time varies greatly from place to place. In South Dakota, thirty seconds of prime time go for as little as $500. In Los Angeles, a comparable ad would cost about $25,000.[14] Other campaign money goes for campaign literature, office space, postage, telephone banks, polling, travel, and salaries for a professional campaign staff.

Where does the money come from? Candidates who are well-to-do can bankroll their own campaigns or at least provide enough seed money to get started. This is particularly important for challengers, who typically have a more difficult time raising money than incumbents. One study found that serious challengers for seats in Congress average $20,000 apiece on their own campaigns.[15]

Most campaign contributions come from individuals, groups, and parties. Campaigns raise some money in the form of contributions of $50 or less, but big-money campaigns usually depend on big contributions. In 1988, for example, political action committees (PACs) provided about a third of U.S. House candidates' funds and a fifth of the money spent in Senate races.[16] Serious candidates, especially Republicans, may also benefit from contributions of cash or services from their national party organizations. In 1987–88, the GOP spent $257 million on behalf of party candidates while the Democratic party spent $122 million.[17]

Candidates for federal office (Congress and the presidency) must conform with a number of federal campaign-finance regulations concerning public disclosure of campaign funds and contribution limits from individuals and groups. (Candidates for lower office must follow state and local laws that vary from state to state.) Candidates for national office must keep financial records and report to the Federal Election Commission (FEC) the names of contributors giving $200 or more. The law also limits the size of individual and PAC contributions. Individuals may give no more than $1,000 to a single candidate per election (including primary, runoff, and general elections); the limit for PACs is $5,000 per election.[18] (For a discussion of federal laws regulating presidential campaign finance, see the Perspective.)

In practice, federal disclosure requirements and contribution limits have had only a modest impact on campaign finance. There is little evidence that the general public is aware of, or interested in, the names of candidates' financial backers. Moreover, individual contributors who want to maintain at least a degree of anonymity can give money through a PAC. In the meantime, the federal courts have opened a major loophole in the law limiting contributions, by ruling that both individuals and PACs may spend as much money as they like in a campaign as long as their spending is independent and not coordinated with the candidate's organization.

PERSPECTIVE

Presidential Election Finance Regulations

During the Watergate investigation, the nation was shocked by allegations that contributions to President Richard Nixon's 1972 reelection campaign sometimes arrived in suitcases stuffed with hundred-dollar bills and that potential contributors had allegedly been warned to come up with the cash or face a possible tax audit. Congress reacted to the scandal by passing the Campaign Reform Act of 1974. In order to reduce the appearance (and perhaps the reality) that presidents are bought and sold, the law provided for government funding of presidential elections. The money comes from a special fund to which taxpayers may choose to contribute when they complete their income tax returns.

The law allows for partial federal funding of presidential campaigns during the nomination stage. To qualify for money, candidates must prove they are serious contenders by raising at least $5,000 in each of twenty states in individual contributions of $250 or less. The government then matches dollar-for-dollar all contributions of $250 or less up to a certain amount (which is adjusted each election year to account for inflation). Candidates who accept the money (and almost all do) must agree to an overall pre-convention spending ceiling (set at $27.7 million in 1988) and state-by-state limits.

Once the major party nominees are chosen, they are eligible for complete funding for the general-election campaign ($46.1 million in 1988). Candidates accepting the money (and all have) may neither raise nor spend additional funds. Third-party and independent candidates may also receive federal money *if* they win 5 percent or more of the popular vote in November. The catch is that the amount they receive depends on the size of their vote, and they must wait until after election day to collect.

Because of court rulings, decisions by the Federal Election Commission (FEC), amendments to the law, and the resourcefulness of campaign-finance professionals, the Campaign Reform Act has failed to eliminate big money and big-money contributors from presidential politics. The courts have opened a major loophole in the law by ruling that both individuals and PACs may spend as much money as they like in a campaign as long as their spending is independent and uncoordinated with the candidate's campaign. During the 1988 presidential campaign, for example, the NRA spent $1.5 million on behalf of the Bush campaign, mostly on advertising attacking Dukakis.

Congress created another giant loophole when it amended campaign finance laws in 1979 to allow the parties to solicit unlimited contributions from corporations, unions, and individuals as long as they earmark the money for get-out-the-vote drives and other party-building activities. Campaign funds raised by the parties to support their presidential ticket are known as **soft money**. In 1988, the Democratic and Republican parties raised and spent about $50 million each in soft money. What's more, hundreds of individuals, groups, and corporations gave far more money to the parties than the law would allow them to give to individual candidates. For example, film executive Lew Wasserman, Texas businessman Robert M. Bass, and California financier Marvin Davis all gave more than $100,000 to the Democratic party. Big contributors to the GOP, meanwhile, included real estate developer Donald Trump, publisher Walter Annenberg, Atlantic-Richfield Co., and RJR Nabisco.

Sources: David Ignatius, "The Fat Cats Are Back on the Prowl," *Washington Post*, National Weekly Edition, 28 November–4 December 1988, p. 25; Carol Matlack, "Backdoor Spending," *National Journal*, 8 October 1988, pp. 2516–19; and Herbert E. Alexander, "The Price We Pay for Our Presidents," *Public Opinion*, March/April, pp. 46–48.

Money is indispensable to major campaign efforts, but it doesn't guarantee success. Of the top ten fund-raisers among U.S. Senate candidates in 1986, for example, four won but six lost.[19] Political scientists believe that a certain amount of money is necessary to run a competitive campaign, especially for challengers who aren't usually as well known as incumbents. One study finds that candidates challenging incumbent House members must spend at least $250,000 to $300,000 to have a fighting chance.[20] We also suspect that campaign spending is governed by a law of diminishing returns. The marginal difference between spending $7 million and spending $6 million isn't nearly so great as that between $1 million and $2 million. If the average voter in, say, Georgia, has seen a candidate's commercial fifteen times, will it make much difference to see it once or twice more?

Campaign Organization and Strategy

Big-time campaigns are long, drawn-out affairs. Challengers begin planning and organizing their campaigns years before election day. Incumbents, meanwhile, never really quit campaigning. Many observers believe that American politics now features constant election campaigns, as newly elected officeholders start work on their reelections the day they take the oath of office. When Mitchell McConnell of Kentucky won a seat in the Senate in 1984, for example, he promptly created a "McConnell Senate Committee '90" to begin raising money for the next election.[21]

Campaigns start early because much has to be done. Candidates spend the early months of the race raising money, building an organization, seeking group endorsements, and planning strategy. One of the first tasks of a campaign is to prepare the candidate. This often means outfitting the candidate with a new wardrobe, a new hairstyle, and a slimmer waistline. Candidates also memorize a basic speech and rehearse answers to questions reporters might raise.

Many factors shape the course of a campaign and influence strategy, including the type of office at stake, the nature of the constituency, the personalities and images of the candidates, the issues that concern the electorate, and whether one of the candidates is an incumbent. Incumbents seeking reelection, for example, generally employ a different campaign strategy than do challengers seeking to unseat incumbents. Presidents running for reelection often campaign from the White House, trying to appear presidential rather than political. They hold press conferences, meet foreign heads of state, make "nonpolitical" trips to dedicate public-works projects, and control the public announcement of federal grants for projects in closely fought cities and states.

An important goal for many campaigns is to improve the candidate's name recognition, especially if the candidate isn't an incumbent. Citizens generally won't vote for someone with whom they are unfamiliar. Races for less visible offices may never move beyond the name-recognition stage. It helps if voters are already familiar with the candidate. Senator Bill Bradley, for example, was once a professional basketball player. Senator John Glenn was an astronaut. Ronald Reagan, meanwhile, was an actor.

Modern campaigns use the latest in social science research and marketing technology to plan their campaigns. A **focus group**, for example, is a session in which a moderator asks a number of voters a series of political questions or shows them political commercials and asks for their reaction. Campaign consultants use focus groups to test political campaign themes and ads. Bush campaign officials, you recall, employed a focus group to test ammunition they wanted to use against Dukakis.

To an ever-increasing degree, modern election campaigns are fought on television, through paid advertisement and unpaid news coverage. Not only have campaigns become expert at crafting political commercials, but they have grown fairly adept at manipulating news coverage as well. Indeed, the recent presidential campaigns of Reagan and Bush were the prototype of campaign control of news media coverage.

The Reagan-Bush strategy, which has been adopted by other campaigns as well, was based on several principles. First, campaign managers chose a single theme to emphasize each campaign day, such as crime, the environment, or defense. If the candidate and all of the candidate's spokespersons addressed the same issue and that issue only, the news media would likely focus on that issue in their daily campaign reports.

Second, the campaign chose an eye-catching visual backdrop for their candidate that would reemphasize the theme of the day, such as the Statue of Liberty or a defense base. George Bush even staged a campaign event in a factory that makes American flags. Campaign organizers also tried to ensure that everyone in the audience was friendly so television images would convey the impression of popular support.

Third, campaign managers carefully briefed the candidate and directed him to stick to the script. Each speech included one or two carefully worded phrases designed to be used as sound-bites on the evening news. "Read my lips," said Vice President Bush; "no new taxes."

Finally, the Reagan-Bush campaign teams kept their candidates away from reporters and their questions. Not only might the candidate's answers to reporters' questions distract from the theme-of-the-day, but they would provide the candidate with the opportunity to blunder. Ronald Reagan's detractors still joke about an ad-lib remark he made during the 1980 campaign, in which he said that trees and plants were the major cause of pollution in the country.

Modern campaigns commission public-opinion polls to aid in planning strategy. Polls can provide candidates and their campaign managers with invaluable information about the public's perception of the candidates and the issues. Are the candidates well known to the public? What images do potential

By permission of Mike Luckovich and Creators Syndicate.

voters hold of the candidates? Which issues are important to the voters? With this information, the candidate's media consultants and organizers prepare their strategy. In 1988, you recall, the Bush campaign team learned from their polls that even though people had a positive image of Governor Dukakis, they didn't know much about him. The vice-president's campaign took advantage of the situation by defining Dukakis negatively before the governor was able to firmly establish a positive image.

Even though the Bush campaign used modern campaign techniques to plan attacks against Dukakis, negative campaigning is nothing new in American politics. Thomas Jefferson's enemies denounced him as the Antichrist. Rumor had it that Grover Cleveland beat his wife and fathered an illegitimate child. Theodore Roosevelt was supposedly a drunkard and a drug fiend.[22]

Politicians go negative because it often works. Although people say they hate negative advertising, they remember it. Campaign pollster Mark Mellman explains the phenomenon as follows: "One of the fundamental facts of psychology is that negative information is processed more deeply than positive information."[23] Negative campaigning is particularly effective when attacks go unanswered. A seemingly credible charge unanswered is perceived by the public as true. In the 1988 campaign, for example, Dukakis's slowness in responding to Bush's attacks hurt him badly in the polls.

CONGRESSIONAL ELECTIONS

In America's representative democracy, citizens elect Congress. Voters choose members of the House from single-member districts to serve two-year terms. Senators, meanwhile, run at large statewide for six-year terms. Since Senate terms are staggered, voters elect one-third of the Senate every two years.

House Races

The most striking feature of elections for the U.S. House of Representatives is that incumbents are almost always reelected. In 1988, for example, 409 (out of 435) incumbents sought reelection; 402 won. That's a batting average of more than 98 percent. All seven who lost faced charges of serious ethical misconduct. What's more, most races weren't even close, since more than 70 percent of incumbents won with better than 65 percent of the vote.[24]

Incumbency affords sitting members of Congress a number of advantages. The rules of Congress grant members free mailing privileges (known as the **franking privilege**), give them money to staff one or more offices in the district, and fund numerous trips back to the district during congressional sessions. Incumbents can also generate free publicity by sending press releases to local media outlets and making speaking appearances in the district. The result is that incumbent House members are better known than challengers. One study reports that only about 20 percent of the electorate can even recall the challenger's name.[25]

To become known, and hence competitive, challengers need to spend several hundred thousand dollars on their campaigns. Once again, however, all of the advantages lie with incumbents. In 1988, for example, PACs gave $82.8 million to House incumbents, but only $9 million to challengers.[26] Most interest groups and large individual contributors don't want to give money to a challenger who doesn't have a realistic chance of winning, but challengers can't become competitive unless they have money. Consequently, many potential challengers decide not to run.

Political scientists tell us that House races have increasingly become local events, more and more isolated from presidential politics and national issues. House members running for reelection stress personal qualities and the services they provide their districts.[27] Unless the incumbent is involved in a personal scandal or appears to lose touch with the district, this approach often leaves challengers little ground on which to base a successful campaign.

Another reason for the high reelection rate for incumbents is that many congressional districts are safe for one party or the other. State legislators who draw district lines aren't interested in close elections; their primary concern is that their favored party and candidates win. A Democratic-controlled legislature, for example, would try to ensure the reelection of Democratic incumbents by concentrating Democratic voters in their districts. In the process, the legislature would invariably draw a number of districts with heavy concentrations of GOP supporters. Legislators would have no interest in creating a district that was evenly balanced along party lines. As a result, most congressional districts around the country are fairly safe for one party or the other. Incumbents may face serious challengers in their party's primary, but they are unlikely to be unseated in a general election.

Senate Races

Senate races are more competitive than House elections. Incumbency is a factor in Senate contests, but it's not the overwhelming advantage that it is in House races. In 1988, for example, four of the twenty-eight incumbent senators seeking reelection lost. That's an 86 percent reelection rate—good, but less than the 98 percent success rate for House incumbents. What's more, many Senate races were relatively close, with 44 percent of Senate incumbents winning with less than 60 percent of the vote.

Political scientists identify a number of differences between Senate and House races that account for the relatively greater vulnerability of Senate incumbents. First, Senate constituencies are more heterogeneous than House constituencies, and hence more competitive. United States House districts, you recall, are often drawn to the clear electoral advantage of one party or the other. In contrast, senators must run at large statewide, and both parties are now capable of winning statewide races in any state.

Second, incumbent senators more frequently face serious challengers. In contrast to elections for most House seats, state and local media usually cover elections for the U.S. Senate. As Senate challengers become known to many voters, candidates' qualifications and issues grow in significance. Moreover, Senate challengers can generally raise enough money to run at least a minimal campaign. Interest-group and individual contributors know that most Senate challengers have some chance to win. Also, they believe that a senator, as one member out of a hundred, is more important than a U.S. representative, who is one out of 435.

Finally, research has found that voters tend to perceive Senate races as national election contests. As a result, national issues often play a prominent role in Senate campaigns and national trends frequently affect Senate election outcomes.[29] National factors are as likely to hurt incumbents as to help them. In 1980, for example, a number of Democratic senators were swept out of office by Republican challengers who rode to victory on Ronald Reagan's coattails. (The **coattail effect** is a political phenomenon in which a strong candidate for one office gives a boost to fellow party members on the same ballot seeking other offices.) In 1986, however, national tides ran against the GOP and many of the Republican senators who were first elected in 1980 lost to Democratic challengers.

PRESIDENTIAL ELECTIONS

The presidential election process consists of two distinct phases with different rules, requiring candidates to wage two separate campaigns. The first phase is the nomination stage in which candidates compete for their party's nomination, which is awarded at a national party convention. The second phase is the general-election stage in which the two major party candidates and, perhaps, a third-party candidate or an independent compete to win an electoral college majority in the November election.

The Presidential Nomination Stage

In the first stage of the presidential election process, candidates compete for their political party's nomination. In the summer of an election year, the two major parties hold conventions to which the party organizations in each state, the District of Columbia, and the various territories send delegates. The size of each state's delegation depends on a formula set by the party that includes both the state's population and the success of party candidates in the state. The convention's chief task is to select presidential and vice-presidential nominees to run on the party's ticket in the November general election. This selection is done by majority vote of the convention delegates. Until the conventions have done their work, the real contest is not between Democrats and Republicans, but among Democrats for the Democratic presidential nomination and among Republicans for their party's nomination. Since the convention delegates make the actual selection, the candidates focus on the delegate-selection process in each state, hoping to get their supporters selected as delegates to the national convention.

The Delegate-Selection Process

The process of selecting delegates to the national party conventions varies in a crazy-quilt pattern from state to state. In 1988, about two-thirds of the Democratic delegates and three-fourths of the Republican delegates were selected in presidential preference primaries.[30] A **presidential preference primary** is a procedure for selecting national party convention delegates in which party voters cast their ballots for the presidential candidate they prefer or for delegates pledged to support that candidate. In each primary state, Democratic voters choose among the Democratic presidential candidates while Republican voters select from the GOP candidates.

Presidential primary election campaigns are similar to other election campaigns except that the voter pool is different. Since only party voters participate in presidential primaries, candidates must pitch their campaigns toward their own party members and activists. Moreover, turnout in primaries is less than that of a general election and less representative of the population. One study finds, for instance, that well-educated people make up a greater proportion of presidential primary voters than they do of general-election participants.[31]

States that do not conduct presidential preference primaries choose national convention delegates with the caucus method. The **caucus method of delegate selection** is a procedure for choosing national party convention delegates that involves party voters participating in a series of precinct and district or county political meetings. The process begins with party members attending local precinct meetings or caucuses at which they elect delegates to district or county meetings. The district/county meetings, in turn, select delegates for the party state convention. Finally, the state convention chooses national convention delegates.

Candidates must use a different strategy for competing in presidential caucuses than they employ in primary elections. Since caucus meetings require more time and effort than simply voting in a primary, the number of people who participate in them is generally far less than the number of primary participants. The key to success for a presidential candidate, then, is to cultivate committed supporters who will take the time to attend caucus meetings. In 1988, for example, Republican presidential candidate Pat Robertson did well in caucuses, thanks to a small army of highly committed supporters. In primaries, though, Robertson's forces were badly outvoted.

The presidential nomination process has changed a great deal in recent years. For more than a century, the Democratic and Republican parties nominated their presidential candidates at national conventions that were dominated by elected officials and local party leaders. The main concern of party leaders was the selection of a candidate whose popularity would boost local candidates' chances of election and who would cooperate with local party leaders once elected. Only about a dozen states held primaries, and serious candidates might only focus on one or two primaries in order to demonstrate their voter appeal to the party leadership. Critics of this system charged it was undemocratic because it allowed for relatively little input from ordinary party members and voters. In contrast, the system's defenders said that it produced candidates with solid party credentials who were qualified to become president.

After 1968, the Democratic party reformed the delegate-selection process. Party leaders' control over the presidential selection process had already begun to slip because of the long-term decay of party organization in the United States. The process of change was accelerated after 1968 by the efforts of a group of reformers within the Democratic party. The reformers were anti–Vietnam War activists who were outraged with a system that permitted Vice President Hubert Humphrey to win the Democratic presidential nomination in 1968 without entering a single primary. They charged that too much power was in the hands of party bosses such as Mayor Richard Daley of Chicago. Since Humphrey and the party leadership needed the activists' support to win the general election against Republican Richard Nixon (they lost anyway), they granted the reformers a major concession: the formation of a reform commission chaired by antiwar Senator George McGovern of South Dakota.

The McGovern Commission revised the Democratic party delegate-selection process in a fashion consistent with the goals of the antiwar activists. First, the commission opened the process to increased participation for rank-and-file party members and activists, giving no special advantages to party insiders. Second, the commission mandated representation in the process by groups favored by the reformers—African-Americans, women, and young people. Later, the party added Hispanic-Americans, Native Americans, and gays and lesbians to the list. Finally, the commission pushed for a system that would award convention delegates to candidates in rough proportion to their voting strength in a state. This reform replaced the traditional winner-take-all system in which the candidate who won the most votes in a primary or caucus won all of the state's delegates to the national convention.[32]

By the end of the 1970s, a number of Democrats thought that the reforms had gone too far. The attempt to reduce the power of party leaders had worked so well that many Democratic members of Congress and Democratic governors did not attend the 1972 and 1976 conventions. The leaders' power over delegates had been largely lost to candidates and interest-group representatives. Moreover, many Democrats feared that the new process produced weak nominees outside the mainstream of the party, such as George McGovern in 1972 and Jimmy Carter in 1976. After Carter's defeat in 1980, Democratic party regulars counterattacked, pushing through changes in the rules that would reserve more than 10 percent of delegate seats for party officials and elected officeholders. Nonetheless, few observers believed that party leaders had regained their lost power of presidential selection.

While the Democrats struggled over reforming delegate-selection procedures, the GOP was content to leave most delegate-selection decisions to state parties, acting only to ensure more participation by poorly represented groups, especially women. Still, the Republican nomination process has not gone unchanged. As political parties grew weaker, GOP leaders, like their Democratic counterparts, were hard pressed to maintain control over the presidential nomination process. Moreover, many state legislatures responded to the Democratic party reforms by reforming delegate-selection procedures in their states.

The effect of the changes in the presidential nomination process in both parties has been to weaken the authority of party leaders in the presidential nomination process while increasing the power of party voters and party activists. On one hand, the nomination process was opened to millions of ordinary Americans voting in primaries and participating in caucuses. In 1988, for example, more than 35 million people voted in presidential preference primaries. This aspect of the process gives an advantage to well-known politicians who can raise the resources for a long campaign, such as Ronald Reagan, Walter Mondale, and George Bush.

On the other hand, today's nomination process grants a significant role to organized groups of party activists who are willing to devote the time, money, and energy to the difficult and time-consuming task of becoming national convention delegates. In the Democratic party, you recall, most activists are liberal. GOP activists, meanwhile, are conservative. Candidates for the Democratic nomination, therefore, compete for the support of activists who are pro-choice on abortion; against the death penalty; in favor of women's rights, gay rights, and black civil rights; supportive of reducing defense spending; sensitive to environmental protection; and friendly toward organized labor. In contrast, Republican candidates campaign for the backing of activists who are against abortion; in favor of school prayer; against gay rights, affirmative action, and the Equal Rights Amendment; in favor of increasing defense spending; against raising taxes; and sympathetic to big business.[33] The dilemma for each party is that party activists may prefer a candidate whose issue positions are a liability in the general election, where the party must appeal to the full electorate and not just the party faithful.

The Road to Nomination

Political scientist Rhodes Cook identifies five stages in today's presidential nomination process:[34]

1. *The Exhibition Season.* For at least a year before convention delegates are chosen, persons considering a run for the White House begin their campaigns by assembling campaign teams, raising money, gathering group endorsements, establishing campaign organizations in key primary and caucus states, and building name recognition among party voters and activists. As in the exhibition season in major-league baseball, serious presidential candidates use this period to prepare for the long series of primaries and caucuses that decide the nomination.

2. *The Media Fishbowl—Iowa and New Hampshire.* The first caucus, in Iowa, and the first primary, in New Hampshire, held in February of an election year, are the most important contests because they are first and, hence, receive the most media attention. One study of television news coverage of the 1988 campaign found that the three major networks aired 285 stories on the Iowa caucus and 210 stories on the New Hampshire primary. In contrast, the networks presented only 41 stories on the California primary, even though California voters chose nearly three times as many convention delegates as Iowa and New Hampshire voters combined. In fact, the Iowa caucus alone received more television news coverage than the delegate-selection process in every other state west of the Mississippi combined![35]

Because they are relatively small states, Iowa and New Hampshire feature a good deal of personal campaigning—what campaign professionals call "retail politics." Candidates often make dozens of personal appearances, drinking coffee and discussing issues with groups of voters and party activists. Since Iowa and New Hampshire are small and candidates can spend months campaigning, someone who is relatively unknown nationally can become known within the state and do well, as did Jimmy Carter in 1976.

Success or failure in these early contests depends to a significant degree on media interpretation based on expectations. Candidates build momentum by exceeding expectations, lose momentum by falling short of expectations. In 1972, for example, Senator Edmund Muskie, the early front-runner for the Democratic nomination, was expected to do especially well in New Hampshire because he was from the neighboring state of Maine. When the votes were counted, Muskie did win the primary, but his victory margin over runner-up George McGovern was less than anticipated, so the media discounted his victory. Muskie's campaign never recovered and McGovern went on to win the nomination.

The Iowa caucus in February is the first test of a presidential candidate. Here, Jesse Jackson addresses supporters in Iowa prior to the 1988 caucus.

The Iowa caucus and New Hampshire primary serve to narrow the field of candidates for the next round of primaries and caucuses. Candidates who do well in Iowa and New Hampshire become front-runners, or at least major contenders, with name recognition and momentum that can be used to raise money and win votes in later contests. In fact, more often than not, the winner of the New Hampshire primary goes on to win the nomination. In contrast, candidates who do poorly in Iowa and New Hampshire face an uphill battle trying to get their campaigns on track.

3. *Super Tuesday.*   One or two weeks after the New Hampshire primary, several states hold primaries and caucuses on the same day, choosing so many delegates in total that the press refers to the day as Super Tuesday. In 1988, for example, nearly every southern state and several states outside the South selected convention delegates on Tuesday, March 8. The Super Tuesday primaries are too numerous and the states too large for the type of personal campaigning that candidates often use in Iowa and New Hampshire. Except for candidates who are already well known, such as Jesse Jackson, Super Tuesday campaigning requires millions of dollars to purchase time for television commercials.

Super Tuesday either settles the nomination or reduces the field to two or three contenders. Super Tuesday is particularly likely to be the decisive battle for the Republican nomination because the GOP generally awards convention delegates to candidates on a winner-take-all basis, enabling a front-runner to build a substantial lead in delegates. In 1988, for example, Bush won nearly every delegate at stake on Super Tuesday, essentially wrapping up the nomination in the process.

In contrast, the Democrats generally award convention delegates on a modified proportional basis, allowing candidates to win delegates with as little as 15 percent of a state's primary vote. This procedure prevents front-runners from pulling too far ahead, while keeping also-rans in the race longer.

A number of observers believe that Democratic nominees are hurt by their inability to wrap up the nomination quickly. While Democrats are still fighting each other, Republicans are preparing for the fall election. When the Bush campaign people were preparing their media blitz in Paramus, New Jersey, for example, Dukakis was still worrying about uniting his party behind his candidacy.

In 1990, the California legislature considered a measure to move the California primary from June, late in the primary season, to the first Tuesday in March, one week after the New Hampshire primary and one week before Super Tuesday. National democratic party leaders supported the move, hoping that the change would enable one candidate to wrap up the nomination early so the party could unite for the November election. Analysts disagreed, however, about the political impact of holding the California primary early in the election season. Although some observers predicted the change would help well-known candidates able to raise the substantial amounts of money needed for a campaign in a state with several major media markets, other analysts warned that predictions about the effects of changes in the primary elections schedule have been wrong in the past.

4. *The Mop-up Stage.*   From Super Tuesday until the end of the primary season in June, the remaining candidates fight it out from one state to the next, on almost a weekly basis. A front-runner emerges (if Super Tuesday hasn't produced one already) and eventually begins to pull ahead in the delegate

count. By the end of the primaries, one candidate has the nomination either locked up or close at hand. Most of the other candidates, meanwhile, have dropped out of the race.

5. *The National Party Conventions.* The national party conventions are great shows, of course, but they also have some serious business to transact. One of the first chores is to seat the various state delegations. Normally, the seating of a delegation is a mere formality, but occasionally a delegation's credentials are challenged on the grounds that its selection violates party rules. Sometimes these challenges can be politically significant. In 1952, for example, a delegate-certification dispute at the Republican convention turned into a showdown between the forces supporting Robert Taft for the nomination and those backing General Dwight Eisenhower.

Another task for the convention is to adopt a **party platform**, which is a statement of party principles and issue positions. Traditional wisdom holds that platforms are both bland and meaningless, forgotten by Labor Day, but that's overstating the case. At times, platforms do include rather general language, but that's because they often represent compromises among different factions within the party. Sometimes compromises on the platform are used to help unite a party divided by a bruising nomination fight.

Nonetheless, the Democratic and Republican platforms often differ clearly, as you can see from Table 7.1. Republican platforms generally emphasize defense and government-management issues, such as a balanced budget, while Democratic platforms stress labor and social-welfare issues. Also, there is evidence that platform promises aren't so meaningless after all. One study finds a close connection between federal spending priorities and prior platform promises.[36] At any rate, convention delegates don't consider platforms irrelevant. In 1948, for instance, a Democratic fight over civil rights led to a southern walkout and the formation of a splinter Dixiecrat party.

The most important business of a convention is to select a presidential nominee. Traditionally, this takes place during prime time on the third evening of the convention. Festivities begin as speakers place the names of prospective nominees before the convention and their supporters respond with exuberant (and planned) demonstrations. Eventually, the time comes to call the roll of the states, and the delegates vote. A majority must agree on a nominee. At every convention for nearly forty years, delegates have selected a winner on the first ballot. At most conventions, there hasn't even been suspense; the eventual winner has come to town with a majority of delegates already pledging their support. If no one wins on the first ballot, the delegates vote again, and then again, until a nominee is chosen. When this happens, it is an occasion for high political drama as old candidates drop out, new ones enter the field, and party leaders wheel and deal behind the scenes. Unfortunately for those who like political drama, however, today's delegate-selection process makes multiple ballots unlikely.

The final business of the convention is to pick a vice-presidential candidate. The selection process is formally identical to the method for choosing a

TABLE 7.1

Party Platform Positions on Selected Issues, 1988

Issue	Platform Planks	
	Democratic	*Republican*
National defense	Criticizes expenditures on questionable weapons systems	Supports military buildup
Taxes	Says that wealthy and corporations should pay their fair share	Opposes any tax increases
Crime	Supports increased federal assistance for local law enforcement	Favors death penalty
Abortion	Supports freedom of reproductive choice	Favors amendment to outlaw abortion
Housing	Calls for an increase in public housing and subsidized housing	Supports enforcing child-support laws; cutting red tape for housing rehabilitation
AIDS	Promises more research, education, and prevention efforts	Supports research and promises "to protect those who do not have the disease"
Drugs	Opposes legalizing illicit drugs	Supports use of military to fight drugs

Sources: *Houston Chronicle*, 17 August 1988, p. 12A; 20 July 1988, sec. 1, p. 13; *Houston Post*, 17 July 1988, p. 15A, 14 August 1988, p. 5B.

presidential nominee, but, in practice, the presidential candidate makes the choice and the convention ratifies it. Above all else, presidential nominees look for running mates who will help them win in November. Frequently, this means trying to balance the ticket by selecting a vice-presidential candidate from a different region, a different political background, or, perhaps, a different wing of the party from that of the presidential candidate. Vice-presidential selections can sometimes be used to help unify a divided party. Also, it's helpful if the vice-presidential candidate comes from a populous state.

By these criteria, Senator Lloyd Bentsen made an excellent running mate for Michael Dukakis. Dukakis was from the Northeast; Bentsen from the Southwest. Dukakis was seen as a liberal; Bentsen, a conservative. Dukakis lacked Washington experience, while Bentsen was a Washington insider. Also, Bentsen came from a large state, Texas.

In contrast, most observers believe that Senator Dan Quayle added little to the Bush campaign. Although Quayle came from a different region than Bush, he was from a small state, Indiana, that is reliably Republican in presidential elections. Moreover, Quayle was regarded by many voters as poorly qualified for the office of vice-president.

The General-Election Stage

After the party conventions, the presidential election process enters its second and decisive phase. The field has now been narrowed to one Democrat, one Republican, and, perhaps, another candidate or two running on third-party tickets or as independents. What's more, the rules of the political game have changed as each campaign considers what it must do to win an electoral college majority.

The **electoral college** is the system established in the Constitution for indirect selection of the president and vice-president. The authors of the Constitution lacked confidence in the wisdom of the common people to elect a president directly, so they devised an indirect method. Instead of citizens picking a president and vice-president themselves, the voters would choose electors to do it for them. The framers intended that these electors be community leaders, people of stature, who could be trusted to act prudently.

Under the electoral college system, each state is entitled to as many electors as the sum of its representatives in the U.S. House and Senate. Texas, for example, with twenty-seven representatives (as of the 1988 election) and two senators, is able to choose twenty-nine presidential electors; California, with forty-five representatives and two senators, picks forty-seven. Altogether, the number of electors is 538, based on 435 members of the House, 100 senators, and 3 electors for the District of Columbia. It takes a majority (270 electoral votes) to elect a president.

In practice, the electoral college does not operate quite the way the framers planned. Political parties put forward slates of potential electors pledged to cast their electoral ballots for party nominees. Consequently, when citizens vote for president and vice-president in November, they are actually voting for a slate of electors pledged to support the candidates for whom they are voting. The slate of electors backing the candidate winning the most popular votes in a state (a majority is not required) wins the right to cast *all* that state's electoral votes. Come December, the electors gather in the state capital officially to mark their ballots for president and vice-president. Theoretically (and constitutionally), they can vote for whomever they like, but almost all honor their promise and vote for their party's candidate. In January, Congress convenes, opens the ballots, and formally confirms that the individual everyone thought was elected president in November has indeed been constitutionally chosen.

What happens if no one receives a majority of electoral votes? Then Congress picks the president and vice-president. The Constitution states that the House chooses the president from among the three presidential candidates with the most electoral votes. Each state delegation has one vote, and a majority is needed for election. The Senate, meanwhile, names the vice-president from the top two vice-presidential candidates. Each senator has one vote, and a majority is required for election.

Handicapped citizens casting their ballots at a polling site in Chicago, Illinois.

Few features of America's electoral system come under more criticism than the electoral college. In the eyes of many, it is a constitutional crisis waiting to happen—something that should be fixed before disaster strikes. One problem might be called the danger of the faithless elector. Since electors can constitutionally vote for whomever they wish, some electors may break their pledges and vote contrary to the popular vote in their state. In 1988, for example, one Democratic elector from West Virginia cast her official presidential ballot for Lloyd Bentsen instead of Michael Dukakis as a protest against the electoral college. Nonetheless, most academic observers downplay the seriousness of this problem because most electoral-vote outcomes are substantial enough that dozens of electors would have to change their votes to affect an election's outcome.

A second potential problem with the electoral college is that Congress picks the president and vice-president should no candidate receive a majority of the electoral vote. This procedure would be in accord with the Constitution, of course, but many Americans would likely be disturbed by the prospect of a chief executive chosen through behind-the-scenes maneuvering. In 1824, the last time Congress named the president, the selection of John Quincy Adams over Andrew Jackson was marred by dark rumors of back-room deals. In recent years, the closest the nation has come to seeing an election go to Congress was in 1968, when independent candidate George Wallace won forty-six electoral votes.

A third problem with the electoral college is the most likely to happen: The candidate who wins the popular vote could lose the electoral vote and thus the White House. The electoral college system awards a candidate all of a state's electoral votes whether he or she has a victory margin of one vote or a million votes. If Candidate A wins several states by large margins while Candidate B carries other states by small margins, Candidate A could garner more popular votes than Candidate B, but fewer electoral votes. It happened to Samuel Tilden in 1876, when he lost to Rutherford B. Hayes, despite getting a larger popular vote. In 1888, it happened again: Grover Cleveland won a majority of the popular vote but lost the electoral college—and the presidency—to Benjamin Harrison. It almost happened in 1976. Gerald Ford would have returned to the White House if only 9,245 voters in Ohio and Hawaii had voted for him instead of Jimmy Carter, even though Carter would still have enjoyed a 1.7-million-vote lead nationwide.

What can be done about the electoral college to head off these potential crises? There are nearly as many reform proposals as there are critics, but the simplest and most popular idea is to abolish the system altogether and choose the president by direct popular vote. Besides being simple, direct popular vote is more democratic—the candidate with the most votes nationwide wins.

Nonetheless, direct popular election has its detractors. Some critics complain that candidates would make fewer public appearances, concentrating even more on television than they do now. Other opponents fear that parties would be weakened further by a proliferation of independent and minor-party candidates. Spokespersons from small states worry that their regions would be totally ignored if direct popular election were adopted.

What's more, some groups fear a loss of political influence if the electoral college were eliminated. The present system forces candidates to concentrate on the most populous states: in particular, California, New York, Texas, Illinois, Ohio, Pennsylvania, Michigan, Florida, and New Jersey. Presidential races in these states are often close, so groups that are powerful in each of the states have their influence magnified. For example, 14 percent of the population of New York State is Jewish, compared with only about 3 percent of the population nationwide. Is it surprising, then, that major-party candidates usually go out of their way to emphasize American support for Israel? And, of course, it's not just Jewish groups that benefit indirectly from the electoral college. Large states also tend to be areas where organized labor is strong and racial and ethnic minority groups are relatively well organized. Thus, these groups have a political stake in the preservation of the electoral college.[37]

Perhaps the greatest barrier to reforming the electoral college is public apathy. Americans don't believe in fixing something that's not broken, and many people aren't convinced the electoral college system is broken. The general public probably won't be concerned about the electoral college until it

© 1987 Washington Post Writers Group, reprinted with permission.

produces a constitutional crisis. In the middle 1970s, a constitutional amendment to replace the electoral college with direct popular election came to a
vote in the Senate. It received fifty votes, well short of the required two-thirds.
Notably, no public outcry arose, one way or the other.

CONCLUSION: ELECTIONS AND PUBLIC POLICY

What role do elections play in the public policy process? Scholars offer three
general models to explain American elections. One model is that of the policy-
oriented voter. In this view, voters evaluate the policy alternatives presented
to them by candidates and then vote for the candidate whose policy views
most closely parallel those of the voter.

Political scientists disagree about the accuracy of this model. Some
scholars have conducted research showing that voters consider at least some
issues some of the time. A recent study, for example, finds that the public per-
ceives clear differences between candidates on foreign-policy issues and that
the issues affect voter choice.[38] In contrast, other political scientists are skeptical about the frequency of issue voting. They argue that candidates often
avoid issues, instead taking ambiguous positions that can appeal to a broad

range of voters. Moreover, research shows that most voters know too little about issues and candidates to be issue voters. In 1980, for example, survey data showed that only 36 percent of voters could associate at least one *general* issue with each presidential candidate, while only 6 percent were able to connect one *specific* position with each candidate.[39]

A second approach to voting and elections can be called the Michigan model, because of its association with scholars at the University of Michigan. In this model of voting behavior, citizens respond to a number of factors—candidates' style, party loyalty, voters' perceptions of candidates' leadership abilities, and others. One recent study of presidential voting concludes that voters evaluate candidates on the basis on their image of what a president should be like. This study found that citizens see competence, integrity, and reliability as qualities they desire in a president. Come election day, voters pick the candidate they believe best matches the qualities the office requires.[40] Another study concludes that voters respond to candidates on the basis of their emotional evaluation of candidates' moral leadership and competence rather than a rational assessment of public policies. Issues and policy considerations have only an indirect effect on voting by influencing voters' feelings toward candidates.[41]

The retrospective voter model is a third approach to voter behavior. **Retrospective voting** refers to citizens choosing candidates based on their

Presidential debates, which are intended as forums where issues are discussed, have only an indirect effect on election outcomes. Here, candidates George Bush and Michael Dukakis debate in September 1988.

perception of an incumbent candidate's past performance in office or the performance of the incumbent party. Instead of voting for promises, they vote for performance, at least as they perceive it. Voters may be ignorant of specific policies and policy proposals, but they do have a sense about the direction of the city, state, or nation. If voters believe that things are going well, incumbent officeholders and their party usually get the credit. They get the blame, though, if voters think the situation is going poorly.[42]

Political scientists point to the 1980 and 1984 presidential contests as examples of retrospective voting. Studies of the 1980 race indicate that Reagan did not win because of his positions on the issues. In fact, many of the people who voted for Reagan disagreed with many of his issue positions. Instead of Reagan *winning* the election, it appears that President Carter *lost* because of widespread dissatisfaction with his performance in office and uncertainty over his competence as a political leader.[43] Similarly, in 1984, Reagan won reelection handily despite polls showing that many Americans disagreed with him on many issues. A majority of voters felt they were better off economically in 1984 than in 1980; consequently, they voted for Reagan.[44]

George Bush's 1988 election victory can be explained on the basis of retrospective voting as well. President Reagan, the incumbent Republican, was still held in high esteem. (A *Los Angeles Times* poll in November of 1988 showed the president with a 60 percent approval rating.)[45] Moreover, most Americans felt they were personally better off than they had been before Reagan came to office. One scholar summarizes the election as follows: "Voters ignored Quayle, the Iran-contra issue, the negative campaigning, and the positive aspects of the Dukakis campaign. Instead, they focused on their personal economic situation."[46]

Which of the three models, then, most closely approximates the reality of voting in America: the policy-oriented voter model, the Michigan model, or the retrospective voter model? Professors Kay Lehman Schlozman and Sidney Verba suggest that all three models may contain some elements of truth. They offer a theory of dual accountability, that is, that candidates/officeholders must appeal to two distinct groups—party activists and ordinary voters.[47]

On one hand, party activists are issue-oriented voters. Activists are concerned about issues, knowledgeable about candidates' stands on issues, and attentive to see that officeholders keep their promises. Otherwise, they support someone else next time around. To be sure, party activists are a relatively small segment of the population, but, as we have seen, they play a disproportionately important role in the presidential nomination process and as workers in political campaigns. Candidates and officeholders cannot afford to write off their support.

On the other hand, the general public evaluates candidates based on both retrospective voting and some of the elements of the Michigan voting model. Average voters evaluate candidates/parties based on their perceptions of the state of the nation, particularly the nation's economy, and their judgment about the candidates' leadership and competence. One recent study, for example, finds that both voters' perceptions of the state of the economy and their evaluations of the candidates determine presidential election outcomes.[48]

In sum, America's democracy demands that officeholders play before two audiences: party activists and the general public. The activists are the most demanding. They insist that candidates make specific promises and they watch to see that the promises are fulfilled. In contrast, the demands of ordinary voters are less specific. For the most part, they are unaware of the policy debates that fascinate the party activists. The general public does, however, form judgments about the competence and leadership abilities of candidates and parties, and about the state of the economy and its effect on their personal well-being.

KEY TERMS

at-large election

bond

bond election

caucus method of delegate selection

coattail effect

electoral college

focus group

franking privilege

general election

gerrymandering

initiative

minority-vote dilution

minority-vote packing

party platform

political campaign

presidential preference primary

primary election

recall

redistrict

referendum

retrospective voting

runoff primary

single-member district election

soft money

special election

split ticket

straight ticket

NOTES

1. Paul Taylor and David S. Broder, "How the Presidential Campaign Got Stuck on the Low Road," *Washington Post*, National Weekly Edition, 7–13 November 1988, p. 14; *Washington Post*/ABC News Poll, cited in *Washington Post*, National Weekly Edition, 26 September–2 October 1988, p. 37; and *Time*, 21 November 1988, p. 49.
2. David Hoffman, "Bush Takes a Stand," *Washington Post*, National Weekly Edition, 24–30 October 1988, p. 13.
3. Charles S. Bullock III and Loch K. Johnson, "Runoff Elections in Georgia," *Journal of Politics* 47 (August 1985): 937–47.
4. Robert E. Cushman and Robert F. Cushman, *Cases in Constitutional Law*, 3d ed. (New York: Appleton-Century-Crofts, 1968), p. 42.

5. *Baker* v. *Carr*, 369 U.S. 186 (1962), and *Wesberry* v. *Sanders*, 376 U.S. 1 (1964).
6. Matthew D. McCubbins and Thomas Schwartz, "Congress, the Courts, and Public Policy: Consequences of the One Man, One Vote Rule," *American Journal of Political Science* 32 (May 1988): 388–415.
7. Michael Barone and Grant Ujifusa, *The Almanac of American Politics 1984* (Washington, DC: National Journal, 1983), Preface.
8. Kimball Brace, Bernard Grofman, and Lisa Handley, "Does Redistricting Aimed to Help Blacks Necessarily Help Republicans?" *Journal of Politics* 49 (February 1987): 169–85.
9. Richard Born, "Partisan Intentions and Election Day Realities in the Congressional Redistricting Process," *American Political Science Review* 79 (June 1985): 320–33.
10. Harry Basehart, "The Seats/Votes Relationship and the Identification of Partisan Gerrymandering in State Legislatures," *American Politics Quarterly* 15 (October 1987): 484–98.
11. "'88 Senate Campaigns Costlier," *Houston Post*, 24 February 1989, p. A-25.
12. "Primary Candidates for President in '88 Triple Spending of '76," *Houston Post*, 26 August 1989, p. A-12.
13. Bill Peterson, "Running for the Senate Is Like Giving a Giant Tupperware Party," *Washington Post*, National Weekly Edition, 11 August 1986, pp. 12–13.
14. "Negative Ads Spur Efforts to Curb Campaign Spending," *Houston Post*, 10 November 1986, p. 8-B.
15. Clyde Wilcox, "I Owe It All to Me—Candidates' Investments in Their Own Campaigns," *American Politics Quarterly* 16 (July 1988): 266–79.
16. Jack W. Germond and Jules Witcover, "Fund-Raising Imperative Drives Campaigning," *National Journal*, 18 March 1989, p. 694.
17. "GOP Whips Democrats in Donations, Spending," *Houston Post*, 27 March 1989, p. A-1.
18. Candice J. Nelson and David B. Magleby, "Congress and Campaign Money," *Brookings Review*, Spring 1989, p. 38.
19. Thomas B. Edsall, "The Republicans Found Out That Money Can't Buy You Love," *Washington Post*, National Weekly Edition, 17 November 1986, p. 8.
20. Gary C. Jacobson, "Parties and PACs in Congressional Elections," in Lawrence C. Dodd and Bruce I. Oppenheimer, eds., *Congress Reconsidered*, 4th ed. (Washington, DC: Congressional Quarterly Press, 1989), p. 143.
21. *Wall Street Journal*, 18 July 1986, p. 10.
22. Charles Paul Freund, "But Then, Truth Has Never Been Important," *Washington Post*, National Weekly Edition, 7–13 November 1988, pp. 29–30.
23. Quoted in Taylor, p. 6.
24. Stuart Rothenberg, "The House and the Senate," *Public Opinion*, January/February 1989, pp. 8–11, 59.
25. Robert S. Erikson and Gerald C. Wright, "Voters, Candidates, and Issues in Congressional Elections," in Dodd and Oppenheimer, eds., *Congress Reconsidered*, p. 100.
26. Quoted in Jack Germond and Jules Witcover, "Bush's Campaign Reform Largely Wishful Thinking," *Houston Post*, 3 July 1989, p. A-23.
27. Benjamin Radcliff, "Solving a Puzzle: Aggregate Analysis and Economic Voting Revisited," *Journal of Politics* 50 (May 1988): 440–55.
28. Gary C. Jacobson, "Congress: A Singular Continuity," in Michael Nelson, ed., *The Elections of 1988* (Washington, DC: Congressional Quarterly Press, 1989), p. 136.

29. Alan I. Abramowitz, "Explaining Senate Election Outcomes," *American Political Science Review* 82 (June 1988): 385–403.

30. Rhodes Cook, "The Nominating Process," in Nelson, ed., *The Elections of 1988*, p. 28.

31. Lawrence S. Rothenberg and Richard A. Brody, "Participation in Presidential Primaries," *Western Political Quarterly* 41 (June 1988): 253–71.

32. Austin Ranney, "Farewell to Reform—Almost," in Kay Lehman Schlozman, ed., *Elections in America* (Boston: Allen and Unwin, 1987), pp. 87–111.

33. Thomas B. Edsall and Richard Morin, "The Democrats: Delegates and Voters," *Washington Post*, National Weekly Edition, 18–24 July 1988, p. 10.

34. Cook.

35. S. Robert Lichter, Daniel Amundson, and Richard Noyes, *The Video Campaign: Network Coverage of the 1988 Primaries* (Washington, DC: American Enterprise Institute, 1988), pp. 10–14.

36. Ian Budge and Richard I. Hofferbert, "Mandates and Policy Outputs: U.S. Party Platforms and Federal Expenditures," *American Political Science Review* 84 (March 1990), pp. 111–31.

37. Lawrence D. Longley and James D. Dana, Jr., "New Empirical Estimates of the Biases of the Electoral College for the 1980s," *Western Political Quarterly* 27 (March 1984): 157–75.

38. John H. Aldrich, John L. Sullivan, and Eugene Borgida, "Foreign Affairs and Issue Voting: Do Presidential Candidates 'Waltz Before a Blind Audience?'" *American Political Science Review* 83 (March 1989): 123–41.

39. W. Russell Neuman, *The Paradox of Mass Politics: Knowledge and Opinion in the American Electorate* (Cambridge: Harvard University Press, 1986), p. 26.

40. Arthur H. Miller, Martin P. Wattenberg, and Oksana Malachuk, "Schematic Assessments of Presidential Candidates," *American Political Science Review* 80 (June 1986): 521–40.

41. George E. Marcus, "The Structure of Emotional Response: 1984 Presidential Candidates," *American Political Science Review* 82 (September 1988): 737–61.

42. Morris P. Fiorina, *Retrospective Voting in American National Elections* (New Haven, CT: Yale University Press, 1981).

43. Gregory B. Markus, "Political Attitudes During an Election Year: A Report on the 1980 NES Panel Study," *American Political Science Review* 76 (September 1982): 530–60.

44. Larry M. Schwab, "The Myth of the Conservative Shift in American Politics: A Research Note," *Western Political Quarterly* 41 (December 1988): 817–23.

45. Quoted in Everett Carll Ladd, "The 1988 Elections: Continuation of the Post–New Deal System," *Political Science Quarterly* 104 (Spring 1989): 2.

46. James Dyer, "Pundits Overlooked Reasons for Bush's Win," *Texas Poll*, Fall 1988, p. 10.

47. Kay Lehman Schlozman and Sidney Verba, "Sending Them a Message—Getting a Reply: Presidential Elections and Democratic Accountability," in Schlozman, ed., *Elections in America*, pp. 3–25.

48. Robert S. Erikson, "Economic Conditions and the Presidential Vote," *American Political Science Review* 83 (June 1989): 567–73.

SUGGESTED READINGS

Brady, David W. *Critical Elections and Congressional Policymaking*. Stanford, CA: Stanford University Press, 1988.

Herrnson, Paul S. *Party Campaigning in the 1980s*. Cambridge, MA: Harvard University Press, 1988.

Lichter, S. Robert; Amundson, Daniel; and Noyes, Richard. *The Video Campaign: Network Coverage of the 1988 Primaries*. Washington, DC: American Enterprise Institute, 1988.

Nelson, Michael, ed. *The Elections of 1988*. Washington, DC: Congressional Quarterly Press, 1989.

Orren, Gary R., and Polsby, Nelson W. *Media and Momentum: The New Hampshire Primary and Nomination Politics*. Chatham, NJ: Chatham House, 1987.

Salmore, Barbara G., and Salmore, Stephen A. *Candidates, Parties, and Campaigns: Electoral Politics in America*, 2d ed. Washington, DC: Congressional Quarterly Press, 1989.

Schlozman, Kay Lehman, ed. *Elections in America*. Boston, MA: Allen and Unwin, 1987.

Watson, Richard A. *The Presidential Contest*, 3d ed. Washington, DC: Congressional Quarterly Press, 1988.

8

CONGRESS

LEARNING OBJECTIVES

1. To compare and contrast the structures, responsibilities, and characteristics of the two houses of Congress.
2. To profile the membership of Congress, assessing members' compensation and evaluating turnover rates.
3. To describe the organization of Congress on the floor of the House and Senate, focusing on the role of the party leadership in each chamber.
4. To outline the organization of congressional committees and subcommittees.
5. To evaluate the impact of larger staffs on congressional policymaking.
6. To identify the various tasks of Congress other than making laws.
7. To trace the steps of the legislative process.
8. To evaluate the impact of the following factors on the legislative process: political parties, leadership, committees and subcommittees, interest groups, ideology, constituency, congressional norms, personalities, and the White House.
9. To trace the policymaking history of Congress and evaluate the factors accounting for its role in the policymaking process.

Henry Waxman represents California's Twenty-fourth Congressional District, which includes Hollywood, West Hollywood, and part of Los Angeles. Although Waxman isn't well known nationally, he is influential on certain policy matters of particular interest to him, mainly health issues. In the last decade, Congressman Waxman has succeeded in expanding health care for the poor, elderly, and children. He has helped to reduce the cost of prescription medicine, improve the availability of drugs for treating rare diseases, and increase funding for AIDS research. What's more, Waxman accomplished these goals at a time when the federal budget was tight and the White House generally opposed his efforts.[1]

Several factors account for Congressman Waxman's ability to affect health policy. To some degree, Waxman's influence can be attributed to his position in the legislative process. Having served in the House since 1975, Waxman has accumulated a good deal of seniority, chairing the Health and the Environment Subcommittee of the House Energy and Commerce Committee. This position enables Waxman to participate in health policymaking, giving him the opportunity to have an impact.

Nonetheless, position doesn't guarantee influence. In America's political system, with bicameralism and separation of powers with checks and balances, no one person—not even the president—has the power to dictate policy. Waxman has been effective because he has skillfully used the political resources at his disposal. He has set attainable policy goals and waited for the right opportunity to act. Although Waxman hasn't always gotten everything he has wanted, he has had influence.

Finally, Waxman's success has depended on the presence of a number of favorable contextual factors. For the most part, Waxman's policy goals have enjoyed support in and out of Congress. Democrats have long held a majority of seats in the House and, since 1987, they have had a majority in the Senate as well. Since Democrats as a group are more supportive of federal health-care spending than are Republicans, Waxman, a Democrat, has often been able to find allies among fellow party members. Congressman Waxman has also won the support of attentive publics and organized health-care interests outside Congress who have worked with him, lobbying on behalf of the policies he favors. At the same time, President Reagan, who generally opposed increases in federal spending on health programs, suffered a significant loss of influence in Congress toward the end of his second term. In short, Waxman has been influential not just because of his position and political skills, but because of a political context that was ripe for his success.

This profile of Congressman Waxman is a useful introduction to our study of Congress. To be sure, explaining congressional policymaking is more complicated than accounting for the influence of one member of the House. Nonetheless, just as Congressman Waxman's role in the policymaking process stems from his position in the House, his political skills, and the policy context, so does policymaking in Congress reflect the dynamics of the legislative process, the political skills of various political actors, and the configuration of contextual factors.

BICAMERALISM

Congressional policymaking takes place within the context of bicameralism. Article I of the Constitution declares that the legislative powers of the United States be vested in a **bicameral** (two-house) Congress, consisting of a Senate and a House of Representatives. The original Constitution stipulated that each state be represented by two senators chosen by its state legislature. Members of the House, meanwhile, were to be elected by direct popular vote, with the size of a state's delegation dependent on the state's population (with the exception that each state, no matter how small, would have at least one representative).

Through the years, the formula has remained unchanged except that senators are now chosen by direct popular vote, as a result of the ratification of the Seventeenth Amendment in 1913. Today, fifty states elect one hundred senators, running at large to serve six-year staggered terms. One-third of the Senate must stand for reelection every other year.

By law, House membership is fixed at 435 representatives plus nonvoting delegates from the District of Columbia, American Samoa, the Virgin Islands, Guam, and one resident commissioner from Puerto Rico. The members from

Members of the House of Representatives take the oath of office in January 1989 at the opening ceremonies for the 101st Congress.

the District and the territories may, however, participate in floor debate and serve on committees where they may vote. Members of the House run from single-member districts for two-year terms, so the entire House is up for reelection every other year.

The Constitution assigns certain responsibilities to the Senate alone. The Senate ratifies treaties (by two-thirds vote) and confirms most presidential appointments of federal judges, ambassadors, and executive department heads (all by majority vote). The only major appointment requiring House approval as well involves the president's filling a vacancy in the office of vice-president. This action requires a majority vote of both chambers.

The Senate and House share other duties. Both houses must vote by a two-thirds margin to propose constitutional amendments and both must agree by majority vote to declare war. No money can be raised or spent without majority approval of both chambers, although the Constitution specifies that all tax bills originate in the House. Other legislation may begin in either chamber, but must pass the House and Senate in identical form before going to the president. As for impeachment, the Constitution specifies that proceedings begin in the House with a majority vote. The Senate, then, must vote by a two-thirds margin to remove a president or other executive or judicial officeholder.

Because of their different constitutional structures and responsibilities, the House and Senate have developed into distinct legislative bodies. The Senate is often likened to a great debating society, where senators discuss the grand design of national policy. In contrast, the House is a less prestigious body, whose members have a reputation for devotion to technical expertise, personalized constituency service, and responsiveness to local political interests.

Why the difference? Although the Senate's relatively small size permits it the luxury of freewheeling debate, senators are too few in number to delve into the details of a wide range of policy issues. Instead, senators focus on the big picture. Moreover, the Senate's special constitutional responsibilities ensure that its agenda includes major issues of foreign policy, because it debates treaties.

The House, meanwhile, is too large to function with rules of debate as relaxed as those of the Senate. Unlike the Senate, however, the House has sufficient personnel to concentrate on the details of policy. Committee and subcommittee work are more important in the House than the Senate. Because of the small size and relative homogeneity of House districts as well as the frequency of elections, House members tend to stress local concerns and constituency service more than national policy issues.[2]

MEMBERSHIP

The United States Constitution requires that members of the House be no less than twenty-five years of age, American citizens for at least seven years, and residents of the state in which their district is located. Senators must be thirty years old, citizens for nine years, and residents of the state they represent. If disputes arise about qualifications or election results, each chamber of Congress determines the eligibility of its own members. After the 1984 election, for example, the House conducted a ballot recount to decide a closely contested race in Indiana.

Profile of the Membership

The profile of Congress indicates that a number of informal qualifications influence the membership of Congress. By and large, voters choose people who are white, middle-class, middle-aged, Protestant, small-town in origin, and male. Most members come from legal or business backgrounds. Because of the Voting Rights Act, the Supreme Court's one-person, one-vote decisions, and changing social mores, however, today's Congress is more diverse than ever before.

The 101st Congress, which took office in 1989, included more African-Americans, Hispanic-Americans, and women than ever before, although white males still easily dominated both chambers. The Black Congressional

Caucus in the House numbered twenty-five members, including the nonvoting delegate from the District of Columbia. Twenty-seven women, twelve Hispanics, one Native American, and five Asian-Americans also sat in the House. Although no African-Americans or Hispanic-Americans served in the Senate, two women (Nancy Landon Kassebaum of Kansas and Barbara Mikulski from Maryland) and two Asian-Americans (Daniel Inouye and Spark Matsunaga, both of Hawaii) sat in that chamber. Nonetheless, despite the influx of women and nonwhite members, more than three-fourths of the total membership of the 101st Congress were white males.

Demographic data for the 101st Congress showed diversity in terms of occupation and religious affiliation. Although law, business, and banking were the most common occupations for members of Congress, a number of representatives and senators had backgrounds in public service, education, journalism, agriculture, and other fields. The most commonly cited religious affiliations were Roman Catholic, Methodist, Episcopalian, Baptist, Presbyterian, Jewish, and Lutheran. The average age was 52.8 years.[3]

Republican Senator Nancy Landon Kassebaum of Kansas, one of only two women in the U.S. Senate in 1990.

Compensation

Congressional compensation is controversial. Many observers (including most members of Congress) believe that high pay is needed to attract the best people. Although congressional salaries are more than adequate by most standards, the advocates of higher pay point out that senators and representatives earn less money than corporate executives and probably less than they could make in private business, law practice, or lobbying. Also, most members of Congress must maintain two residences—one in Washington, D.C., and the other in their district or state. In contrast, the opponents of higher congressional pay argue that high salaries are elitist. How can Congress be a representative institution, they ask, if its members earn several times more money than average Americans?

Interest-group honoraria are another controversial aspect of congressional compensation. Besides their salaries, members of Congress have traditionally been allowed to accept thousands of dollars in earned outside income (in addition to whatever investment income they may have). Some extra money comes from legal fees and business income. In practice, though, most outside income takes the form of honoraria paid to members of Congress by interest groups as fees for giving speeches and making personal appearances. Critics charge that honoraria enable well-to-do special interests to buy legislative favors not available to ordinary citizens. As evidence, they note that the largest honoraria go to the most influential members of Congress, such as party leaders, committee chairs, and members of key committees. In 1988, for example, Congressman Dan Rostenkowski, who chairs the tax-writing House Ways and Means Committee, received $222,500 in honoraria, including thirty-two paid trips, five of which were to golf tournaments. Congressman Waxman, meanwhile, accepted $71,750 in honoraria, much of it for appearances before health-care groups affected by legislation considered by his sub-committee.[4] Since both Rostenkowski and Waxman received honoraria exceeding the legal maximum for outside income, they gave the additional cash to charity.

Congress attempted to deal with the compensation issue in 1989. After Congress rejected a controversial 50 percent salary increase early in the year, congressional leaders prepared a compromise proposal, packaging a smaller pay raise with the elimination of honoraria. The proposal would limit earned outside income other than honoraria to 15 percent of a member's salary. The House adopted the leadership's plan, banning honoraria while increasing annual pay for its members from $89,500 in 1989 to $125,000 in 1991. The Senate, meanwhile, balked at so large a salary increase, choosing to limit pay raises for senators to $98,400. The Senate also refused to follow the House's lead on banning honoraria, instead deciding to allow senators to accept as much as $26,568.

In addition to their salaries (and, for senators, honoraria), members of Congress have provided themselves with a number of perks. Benefits include enough money to take at least thirty-two trips home every year; free travel abroad on official business; half-price life insurance; free medical care; free postage for official business (**franking privilege**); access to cut-rate barber-shops, beauty salons, and restaurants; free use of a fitness center and gymnasium; free parking at Capitol Hill and at Washington airports; and free WATS lines to make long-distance telephone calls from home or office. One observer estimates the value of congressional perks at $37,000 a year.[5]

Being a member of Congress has other benefits, too. The experience can lead to higher office within government, as representatives run for the Senate and members of both chambers eye the White House. Occasionally, presidents appoint former members of Congress to the cabinet, the federal courts, or an ambassadorship. What's more, members of Congress can often look forward to lucrative careers in the private sector after they leave office, as consultants and lobbyists. For example, former Senator John Tower, who chaired the Senate Armed Services Committee from 1981 to 1985, earned $750,000 in consulting fees from defense contractors over a three-year period after he retired from the Senate.[6]

Congressional Ethics and Reform

Several recent scandals have given impetus to efforts to reform congressional ethics rules. In 1989, Speaker of the House Jim Wright resigned while under investigation for charges that he used a book-royalty scheme to circumvent House limits on outside income. At about the same time, Congressman Tony Coelho, the third-ranking Democrat in the House, resigned over allegations concerning his purchase of investment bonds with money loaned him by individuals with a financial stake in legislation pending before the House. On the Senate side, meanwhile, several senators faced accusations that they had exerted improper influence on behalf of big-money campaign contributors.

Reformers propose changing congressional ethics rules in two broad areas. First, they want to limit financial ties between interest groups and sitting members of Congress by abolishing honoraria in the Senate as in the House and limiting the role of interest-group money in congressional elections. Second, reformers want to increase competition for seats in Congress, especially in the House. Besides limiting (or eliminating) PAC contributions in congressional races, they advocate reducing members' franking privileges to include only letters addressed to individuals by name (rather than mass mailings that go to every residence in a district).

Membership Turnover

As we discussed in chapter 7, members of Congress seeking reelection usually win, especially members of the House. In 1988, for example, 402 of 409 House incumbents and 24 of 28 senators seeking reelection won. In light of these figures, some observers have attacked what they call the "permanent Congress," insulated from the winds of political change. Congress has "less turnover...than...the Supreme Soviet [the Russian Congress]," complained former President Reagan.[7]

In fact, however, Congress experienced more than a 50 percent turnover during the decade of the 1980s. By 1989, only 190 of 435 House members and 56 of 100 senators serving in 1980 were still in office. That's a turnover rate of

Reprinted with permission, Copley News Service.

By Kelley for The San Diego Union

56 percent in the House and 44 percent in the Senate.[8] Although a number of departed members were ballot-box casualties, many others simply chose not to seek reelection. Some members quit out of frustration with life in Congress, burned out or broke, while others left to seek higher office.

ORGANIZATION

The House and Senate choose leaders, establish committees, and hire staff assistants in order to facilitate their work. Let's consider each of these organizational aspects of the United States Congress.

Organization of the Floor

The phrases "floor of the House" and "floor of the Senate" refer physically to the large rooms in which members of each chamber assemble to do business. As a practical matter, however, "the floor" refers to the full House or full Senate taking official action.

The organization of the floor is based on party strength in each chamber. After the 1988 election, the Democratic party held majorities in both houses, by a 261 to 174 margin in the House, and 55 to 45 in the Senate. We say that the Democrats controlled the House and Senate. They were the majority party in each chamber; the Republicans, the minority party.

The Constitution designates the vice-president as the Senate's presiding officer, but, in practice, the role of the vice-president is relatively unimportant. The vice-president may not address the Senate without permission of the body and only votes in case of a tie, something George Bush was able to do only six times during his eight years as vice-president. More often than not, the vice-president attends to other tasks, leaving the chore of presiding in the Senate to others.

According to the Constitution, the Senate president pro tempore presides in the vice-president's absence. The Senate as a whole selects the president pro tempore, but customarily members elect from the majority party the senator with the longest tenure, or **seniority**, in the chamber. In practice, the post of Senate president pro tempore is more honorary than substantive, and the rather tedious chore of presiding in the Senate is usually left to junior members of the majority party.

Real power on the floor of the Senate (and the House) is in the hands of the political-party organizations. At the beginning of each session of Congress, the Republican and Democratic members of each chamber caucus, or meet separately, to elect leaders. In the Senate, the head of the majority party is called the **majority leader**. The majority leader's first assistant is the **majority whip**. The minority party, meanwhile, is led by the **minority leader** and a **minority whip**. Both the majority whip and the minority whip coordinate the work of a number of assistant whips. Each party also selects a policy committee to consider party positions on legislation, a committee to appoint party members to standing committees, and a campaign committee to plan for the next election.

The Speaker is the presiding officer in the House of Representatives. The full House membership selects the Speaker, but since members always vote for their party's candidate, the Speaker is invariably the leader of the majority party. As in the Senate, the Democratic and Republican members of the House caucus separately at the beginning of each session to choose leaders. The majority party selects a Speaker, a majority leader (who, ironically, is actually the second-ranking party leader in the House), and a majority whip. In the meantime, the minority party elects a minority leader and a minority whip. As in the Senate, the House whips head extensive networks of assistant whips, numbering, in the larger House, dozens of members.

The Senate majority leader and the Speaker of the House exercise a number of formal powers that make them the single most important legislators in their respective chambers. The Senate majority leader and the Speaker appoint members to special committees and influence assignments to standing committees. They refer legislation to committee and control the flow of business to the floor. These last two powers are especially important for the Speaker, who is often able to use them to control the timing of legislation and to determine the policy options available to House members voting on the floor. Moreover, the Speaker's role as presiding officer is a source of power because presiding is more important in the larger House, which has more restrictive rules of debate than the Senate.

The Senate majority leader and the Speaker hold positions of high visibility and great prestige, in both Congress and the nation. As party leaders, they work with fellow party members in Congress to set policy goals and to assemble winning coalitions. They consult widely with various party factions, working to compromise differences among party members and maintain party harmony. As national political leaders, the majority leader and Speaker publicize the achievements of Congress, promote their party's positions in the media, and react to presidential initiatives.

Since party-leadership posts are elective, the Senate majority leader and Speaker maintain their power by helping members achieve their goals: reelection, influence in Washington politics, policy enactment, and election to higher office. The majority leader and Speaker can help members win reelection or election to higher office by assisting with fund-raising and sharing the media spotlight. In fact, congressional leaders have even formed their own PACs, which they fund with money contributed to them by interest-group PACs. The leaders then funnel money from their PACs to the reelection campaigns of fellow party members. In 1987–88, the House Leadership PAC, run by the Speaker and House majority leader, gave more than a million dollars to Democratic congressional candidates. Similarly, Congressman Waxman, who was the first member of Congress to establish his own PAC, gave several hundred thousand dollars to Democrats on the House Energy and Commerce Committee.[9]

Speaker of the House Thomas Foley, with Democratic Rep. William Gray of Pennsylvania.

Congressional leaders help fellow party members achieve more goals than just reelection. The majority leader and Speaker can promote members' status in Washington politics by naming them to important special committees and by pushing for their selection to prestigious standing committees. Party leaders can assist with policy goals by supporting members' favored legislation.[10]

The leadership in Congress is both collegial and collective. It is collegial in the sense that the Senate majority leader and the Speaker of the House base their power on tact and persuasion rather than threats or criticism of other members. The two leaders generally do their best to satisfy the needs of rank-and-file party members, gathering IOUs that can be cashed in later. For example, the majority leader and the Speaker may adapt the legislative schedule to accommodate members' trips home.

In the meantime, leadership is collective in that the top party leadership consults regularly with a broad range of party members, attempting to involve every party faction in setting party policy in the chamber. The whip networks, in particular, work to transmit information between party leaders and members. What's more, on specific pieces of legislation, the Speaker of the House often appoints a group of rank-and-file party members to task forces to plan strategy for the passage of the party's program.[11]

The role of the minority-party leadership in the House and Senate is similar to that of the majority-party leadership, with some important exceptions. The minority leaders and the minority whips work to determine a party program in their chamber, plan strategy, and unite party members behind party positions. As with the Senate majority leader and the Speaker, the Senate and House minority leaders may become media spokespersons for their party.

Nonetheless, because of their party's minority status, the minority leaders simply don't have the power of their majority-party counterparts. Although the majority leader in the Senate and the Speaker of the House may consult with the minority-party leadership on bill scheduling, the authority to control the flow of business to the floor lies with the majority-party leadership. Moreover, the minority leaders' ability to influence legislative policy is limited by their party's minority status. Although the Senate majority leader and the Speaker need hold only the votes of their own party members to pass most measures, the minority leadership must win over a number of legislators from the other party in addition to holding the votes of their own members.

The style of party leadership in Congress depends to a large degree on the occupant of the White House. Congressional leaders feel obliged to support the agenda of a president from their own party. In 1977, for example, Democratic Speaker Thomas P. "Tip" O'Neill used his skill and resources to pass Democratic President Carter's energy program.[12] Similarly, in 1981, Howard Baker, the Republican majority leader in the Senate, described his relationship with GOP President Reagan as follows: "I am the president's spear carrier in the Senate."[13]

When the other party controls the presidency, however, congressional leaders have more options. They may work for compromise, try to defeat the president's program, or push legislation of their own. In 1987, for example, when the Democrats regained a majority in the Senate, the new majority leader, Robert Byrd, let it be known that President Reagan would face a more difficult time getting his way in the chamber: "The Senate will no longer be an agent of the White House. The people wanted checks and balances, and they're going to get them."[14] In the House, meanwhile, Speaker Jim Wright pushed a Democratic legislative agenda on catastrophic health insurance, aid to the homeless, trade, highways, and increased funding for education, most of which became law.[15]

Committee and Subcommittee Organization

The detailed work of Congress takes place in committee. The advantage of the committee system is that it allows Congress to divide legislative work among a number of subgroups while giving individual members the opportunity to specialize, developing expertise in particular policy areas. The disadvantage of the committee system is that the division of broad issues into smaller subissues impedes the development of comprehensive and coordinated national policy. Because Congress deals with policy problems on a piecemeal basis, it tends to offer piecemeal solutions.[16]

As you can see from Table 8.1, the House has twenty-two standing committees; the Senate, sixteen. A **standing committee** is a permanent committee. Each house has special, or select, committees as well. A **special**, or **select, committee** is a committee established for a limited time only. In 1987, for example, Congress created the Select Committee on Secret Military Assistance to Iran and the Nicaraguan Opposition to investigate the Iran-contra scandal. This special committee was also an example of a joint committee in that it included both senators and members of the House. A **joint committee** is a committee that includes members from both houses of Congress.

Committees are divided into subcommittees. Not all committees have subcommittees, and not all bills are referred to subcommittee, but in the House, in particular, subcommittees have become the center of legislative work. The House Energy and Commerce Committee, for instance, has six subcommittees, including the Health and the Environment Subcommittee that Congressman Waxman chairs. As of 1988, the House had 140 subcommittees, the Senate, 85.

With this many committees and subcommittees, individual senators and representatives have several committee assignments. In 1989, senators averaged eleven committee and subcommittee positions, while the average member of the House served on nearly seven committees and subcommittees.[17]

TABLE 8.1

Standing Committees in the House and Senate, 1989

House	Senate
Agriculture	Agriculture, Nutrition, and Forestry
Appropriations	Appropriations
Armed Services	Armed Services
Banking, Finance, and Urban Affairs	Banking, Housing, and Urban Affairs
Budget	Budget
District of Columbia	Commerce, Science, and
Education and Labor	Transportation
Energy and Commerce	Energy and Natural Resources
Foreign Affairs	Environment and Public Works
Government Operations	Finance
House Administration	Foreign Relations
Interior and Insular Affairs	Governmental Affairs
Judiciary	Judiciary
Merchant Marine and Fisheries	Labor and Human Resources
Post Office and Civil Service	Rules and Administration
Public Works and Transportation	Small Business
Rules	Veterans' Affairs
Science, Space, and Technology	
Small Business	
Standards of Official Conduct	
Veterans' Affairs	
Ways and Means	

Source: Phil Duncan, ed., *Politics in America 1990* (Washington, DC: Congressional Quarterly Press, 1989).

Congressman Waxman, for example, was a member of two standing committees, one select committee, and five subcommittees.

When senators and representatives first reach Congress, they request assignment to particular standing committees that they believe will help them win reelection, gain influence in the capital, and/or affect policy. Committees dealing with money fit the bill on all three counts and, accordingly, are in great demand. The money committees are Appropriations, Budget, and Finance in the Senate; and Appropriations, Budget, and Ways and Means in the House. First-year lawmakers probably won't rate such coveted assignments, but other committees can be attractive as well because of their relevance to constituency interests. A representative from farm-belt Iowa, for example, would probably be interested in a seat on the Agriculture Committee.

Party committees in each chamber make committee assignments for members of their party. For the most part, these committees are controlled by the party leadership, who, theoretically, could use them to reward friends and punish enemies. In practice, though, the party committees try to accommodate members' preferences, usually giving members either their first or second choices of committee assignments. Once members are named to particular committees, they generally keep that assignment unless they request a change. Members are not subject to regular reappointment.

An important policy consequence of the self-selection nature of committee assignment is that committees tend to be composed of members whose constituencies are directly affected by the committee's work. Agricultural committees are populated by members from farm areas, while representatives from coastal districts flock to the Merchant Marine and Fisheries Committee. As a result, policy tends to reflect the concerns of particularized interests, such as farmers or shipbuilders, rather than national perspectives.

If members are unhappy with a committee assignment, they may request a transfer when openings occur on other, more desirable committees. Switching committees, however, has a drawback. Influence on a committee is related to seniority on that committee. When members change committees, they must start over on the seniority ladder of the new committee. This works to prevent much committee-assignment reshuffling, although it's not unusual for members to request transfer to one of the really choice committees.

Power on congressional committees is determined in large part by party affiliation and seniority. At the beginning of each session of Congress, the members of each chamber vote to set the number of members and the party ratio on each committee. The majority party, of course, has the votes to ensure itself a majority of seats on each committee and subcommittee. Each committee and subcommittee chair will be a member of the majority party as well. The House Energy and Commerce Committee, for example, includes 25 Democrats and 17 Republicans, with Democrat John Dingell of Michigan as its chair. Should the GOP win a majority of House seats in a future election, the party ratio on the committee would be reversed and a Republican would become chair.

Although seniority alone no longer determines power on congressional committees, it remains a major factor. Before the 1970s, the rules of Congress awarded committee chairs to the majority-party member with the most seniority on the committee. The chair would then appoint subcommittee chairs. Today, however, committee and subcommittee chairs are elected. The Democrats select their standing-committee chairs and Appropriations subcommittee chairs by secret-ballot vote of the full party caucus. On standing committees other than Appropriations party members on each committee select subcommittee chairs. Republican party procedures, meanwhile, allow party members on each committee to choose both committee and subcommittee chairs, when the GOP controls a chamber. Nonetheless, seniority remains an important factor as party members usually elect the most senior members to chair committees and subcommittees. Moreover, committee members volunteer for subcommittee assignments in order of their seniority.

Staff

No legislative body in the world has a larger staff than the United States Congress. More than 15,000 people staff individual congressional offices or work for committees and subcommittees. Members of the House may hire as many as twenty-two staffers, while senators employ seventy to eighty, depending on the size of their states. Staff members may work in Washington, D.C., or manage offices back in members' home states and districts.[18]

Congressional staffs have grown substantially in the last two decades, tripling since 1970. Political scientists say that staff size increased because the workload of Congress grew, policy problems became more complex, and members of Congress wanted to place their branch of government on more equal footing with the executive branch. Some observers believe that staffs have grown so large that they distance members from the policymaking process.[19]

THE CONGRESSIONAL TASKS

Every schoolchild knows that Congress makes laws, but the role of Congress in the policymaking process extends beyond legislating. As we noted earlier in the chapter, the Constitution empowers Congress (or one house thereof) to ratify treaties, confirm presidential appointments, propose constitutional amendments, declare war, adopt a budget, and impeach and remove officials in the other two branches of government.

Two other areas of congressional authority are administrative oversight and constituency service. Congress has the power to oversee the implementation of public policy, investigating problem areas. In recent years, for example, committees in both houses of Congress have conducted investigations into alleged fraud and other wrongdoing in the Department of Housing and Urban Development (HUD).

Constituency service concerns members of Congress and their staffs attending to the individual, particular needs of constituents. Citizens sometimes ask senators or representatives to resolve problems with federal agencies, such as the Social Security Administration or the Immigration and Naturalization Service. Constituents may ask members and their staffs to supply information about federal laws or regulations. Also, local civic clubs and other organizations frequently invite members of Congress to make public appearances at functions in their districts or states and to meet with various groups of constituents about problems of local concern.

Political scientists disagree about the political impact of constituency service. Some scholars believe that constituency service is a major reason why members of Congress, especially House members, usually win reelection.[20] In contrast, other political scientists say that their research shows little evidence that constituency service has much effect on vote totals. Although incumbents may *think* that constituency service is important to their reelection, most recipients either do not vote or they already support the incumbent.[21]

THE LEGISLATIVE PROCESS

Congress conducts much of its work through the legislative process, which is outlined in Figure 8.1. Let's examine the steps of the legislative process in detail.

Origin and Introduction

Bill introduction is a fairly straightforward process. Any member of either chamber may introduce any measure, with the sole exception that revenue-raising bills must originate in the House. Only members of Congress may formally introduce bills, but the thinking and initiative behind legislation can come from many sources, including individual constituents, interest groups, state and local officials, federal agencies, academic reports, congressional committee investigations, or the White House.

Members of Congress don't always introduce legislation with the expectation that it will become law, at least not in the short run. Members sometimes introduce bills as symbolic gestures. In the early 1950s, for example, legislators introduced civil rights measures, knowing full well they would not pass. Instead, they wanted to raise civil rights issues to the public agenda in hopes of seeing their proposals become law in the future. Members may also introduce bills that are unlikely to pass in order to placate constituents or score political points. Sometimes the bills' sponsors themselves secretly hope the legislation fails.

Committee and Subcommittee Action

Once a bill is introduced, the presiding officer of the chamber assigns it a number (H.B. 235, for House Bill 235, for example; S.B. 58, for Senate Bill 58) and refers it to one or, sometimes, more than one committee for consideration. Committee referral decisions are frequently routine. A tax bill, for example, clearly fits under the jurisdiction of the Ways and Means Committee in the House and the Finance Committee in the Senate.

In today's increasingly complex world, however, proposed legislation sometimes addresses issues that are within the jurisdictions of two or more standing committees. Congress has attempted to resolve this dilemma through **multiple referral of legislation**, a practice that allows bills to be considered jointly, sequentially, or partially by more than one committee.

FIGURE 8.1

How a Bill Becomes a Law

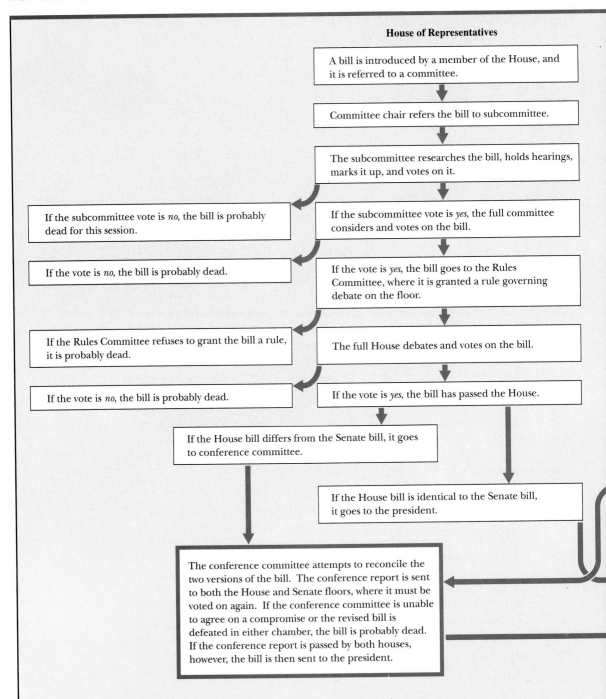

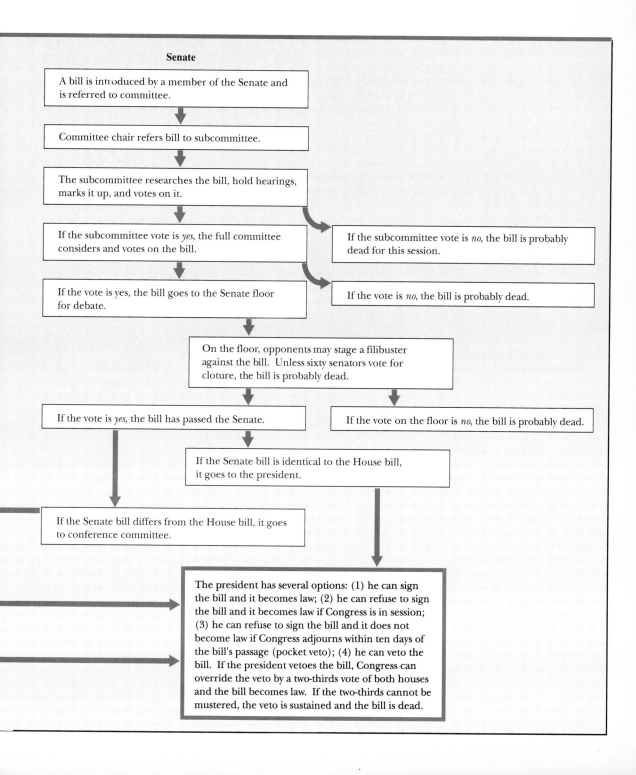

Senate

A bill is introduced by a member of the Senate and is referred to committee.

Committee chair refers bill to subcommittee.

The subcommittee researches the bill, hold hearings, marks it up, and votes on it.

If the subcommittee vote is *yes*, the full committee considers and votes on the bill.

If the subcommittee vote is *no*, the bill is probably dead for this session.

If the vote is yes, the bill goes to the Senate floor for debate.

If the vote is *no*, the bill is probably dead.

On the floor, opponents may stage a filibuster against the bill. Unless sixty senators vote for cloture, the bill is probably dead.

If the vote is *yes*, the bill has passed the Senate.

If the vote on the floor is *no*, the bill is probably dead.

If the Senate bill is identical to the House bill, it goes to the president.

If the Senate bill differs from the House bill, it goes to conference committee.

The president has several options: (1) he can sign the bill and it becomes law; (2) he can refuse to sign the bill and it becomes law if Congress is in session; (3) he can refuse to sign the bill and it does not become law if Congress adjourns within ten days of the bill's passage (pocket veto); (4) he can veto the bill. If the president vetoes the bill, Congress can override the veto by a two-thirds vote of both houses and the bill becomes law. If the two-thirds cannot be mustered, the veto is sustained and the bill is dead.

About a fourth of committee workloads in the House now consist of measures shared with other committees. Although Senate rules permit multiple referrals, the practice is fairly infrequent in that chamber.

In the House, multiple referrals have weakened committees, but strengthened the Speaker. The power of a committee is diminished in that a multiple referral deprives it of exclusive jurisdiction over a bill. In the meantime, multiple referral has enhanced the Speaker's authority in that the process allows the Speaker to impose time limits on consideration of multiply referred bills. Moreover, when committees produce differing legislation, the Speaker can play a role in compromising differences before the bill goes to the floor.[22]

Committees are gatekeepers in the lawmaking process, killing about 85 percent of bills sent to them. Because so many bills are introduced (more than nine thousand in a session), committees have time to consider only a fraction in any detail.[23] In practice, bills that receive the most attention are those that committee and subcommittee chairs personally favor, those that enjoy broad support in Congress as a whole, and those that are pushed by the White House. Bills that lack support or that are opposed by the committee leadership usually lose out.

Committees and subcommittees do the detailed work of Congress. Once a bill is sent to committee or subcommittee, the chair asks the staff to prepare a report on the bill's merits. For major legislation, the committee or subcommittee chair schedules hearings to allow the measure's supporters and opponents the chance to make their case. Full committees generally conduct Senate hearings; subcommittees hold most hearings in the House.

The next step is **mark-up**. This is the process in which legislators go over a bill line by line, revising, amending, or rewriting it. In most cases, the final product reflects compromise. Mark-up may take place in committee, subcommittee, or both.

Once mark-up is complete, first the subcommittee and then the full committee votes on whether to recommend passage. If the bill is voted down at either stage or members vote to **table** it (that is, postpone consideration), the bill is probably dead, at least for the session. If the bill is approved in subcommittee and committee, however, the next step is the floor of the full House or Senate.

Floor Action

The process of moving bills from committee to the floor is more complicated in the House than the Senate. In the House, bills that pass standing committees go to the Rules Committee, which must grant a rule before a bill can go to the floor. Since more bills clear committee than the full House has time to consider, the Rules Committee determines which bills go forward. What's more, the Rules Committee sets time limits for debate and specifies whether amendments may be considered on the floor and, if so, which amendments.

The Rules Committee, for example, might grant a rule restricting debate to twenty hours: ten for proponents, ten for opponents, with an additional two hours for amendments. The Rules Committee might limit amendments to those initially proposed in the standing committee that originally considered the bill. Once a bill has been granted a rule, the Speaker schedules a time for floor debate.

In today's House of Representatives, the Rules Committee is an important element of the Speaker's power. The majority-party members of the Rules Committee, unlike other House committees, are personally appointed by the Speaker, thereby ensuring control. The Speaker cannot only use the Rules Committee to determine which bills reach the floor, but can also use the committee to structure the policy choices available to members on the floor. When Jim Wright was Speaker, for example, he employed the Rules Committee to restrict amendments to legislation he favored, in order to further his policy goals.[24] In fact, since the early 1980s, few major controversial bills have been considered on the House floor without rules limiting amendments.[25]

Moving a bill from standing committee to the floor is a simpler process in the Senate. Once a bill passes committee, the majority leader, usually in consultation with the minority leader, schedules the measure for debate. Even if the majority leader fails to act, the bill's supporters can propose the measure as an amendment to legislation already on the floor and ensure its consideration anyway.

Congress has a reputation as one of the great debating bodies of the world, but it's unusual for debates to sway many votes. Tourists are often shocked at how poorly attended floor debates sometimes are and at the inattentiveness of many of the members who are present. The real work of Congress, however, doesn't take place on the floor, but in committee and subcommittee, in congressional offices, in the cloakroom, and elsewhere around the Capitol. Debates allow members to read into the record the case for and against a bill and to justify their own positions to their constituents. Debates serve to inform the world outside Congress rather than sway opinion within.

Floor proceedings are relatively more structured in the House than in the Senate. Though disgruntled House members can sometimes delay action through parliamentary maneuvers, the Rules Committee system generally ensures that House proceedings move forward in a predictable fashion. Such is not the case in the Senate. The rules of the Senate are designed to maximize the rights of expression of individual senators and, in practice, action on the Senate floor often takes place under unanimous agreements that require the approval of every member of the chamber. Consequently, one senator, or a small group of senators, is often able to produce chaos on the Senate floor.

Indeed, senators sometimes take advantage of Senate rules to defeat legislation they oppose. Because Senate rules do not limit the amount of time a senator or the chamber as a whole can spend discussing a measure, a bill's opponents may **filibuster**, that is, attempt to defeat the bill through prolonged

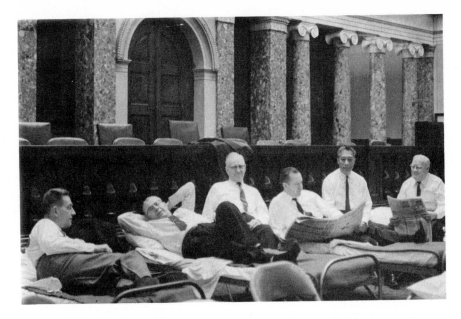

Senators prepare for a long filibuster against a civil rights bill in 1960. Party minorities in the Senate have traditionally used the filibuster to delay or scuttle legislation supported by the majority.

debate. Since no vote can be taken until debate is concluded, opponents hope to extend debate until the bill's supporters give up and agree to go on to other business.

The procedure for ending a filibuster is known as **cloture**. Senators wanting to halt a filibuster must announce their intentions and gather the signatures of one-sixth of the Senate to force a vote on cloture, which, in turn, requires a three-fifths vote of the Senate membership (sixty votes) to succeed. Although Senate rules limit post-cloture debate to thirty hours, a bill's opponents often delay action even longer through parliamentary maneuvering.

The filibuster is a powerful weapon. With it, a minority of senators can almost surely delay a bill, possibly defeat it, and probably force a compromise with its backers, who may eventually agree to policy concessions in order to win over enough votes to invoke cloture. It's not surprising, then, that the filibuster has more critics than defenders, but the same people aren't always on the same sides on the filibuster issue. During the 1950s and 1960s, conservatives sometimes employed the filibuster to defeat civil rights bills, and liberals deplored the action. In the early 1980s, however, the sides reversed, as liberals sometimes filibustered against conservative legislation, such as measures against abortion.

What's more, filibusters have grown more common. Thirty years ago, the Senate had more the atmosphere of an exclusive social club than it does today. Members understood that the filibuster was to be reserved for issues of great import and emotion. From 1955 to 1960, the Senate experienced only two filibusters. In contrast, between 1971 and 1980, the Senate averaged 11.4

filibusters per session. Almost every issue is now fair game for a filibuster. Moreover, groups of senators sometimes use the filibuster to force concessions on other, perhaps unrelated issues.[26]

Conference Committee Action

A bill doesn't pass Congress until it passes both the House and Senate in identical form. Should legislation pass each chamber in different form, one house could simply agree to accept the changes made by the other. For major legislation, however, such as the annual appropriations bill, the House and Senate are seldom able to settle their differences so easily. Then, the two chambers create a conference committee to negotiate a compromise.

A **conference committee** is a special, joint committee created to negotiate differences on similar pieces of legislation passed by the House and Senate. Once the two chambers agree to go to conference, the leadership of each house appoints a group of negotiators, called conferees, to represent their chamber. Each house's conferees usually include the chair and senior members of the standing committee that originally considered the legislation. Once a majority of each chamber's conferees (voting separately) agree upon a compromise, the revised bill, called the conference report, goes back to the floor of the House and Senate, where it can be accepted, rejected, or returned to conference for more negotiations. If both chambers accept the conference report, the bill has passed Congress and goes to the president.

Presidential Action

The Constitution gives the president several options for dealing with legislation passed by Congress. If the president signs a bill, it becomes law. If the president doesn't sign the measure, it becomes law anyway after ten days unless Congress is adjourned, in which case the bill dies. (The action of a president allowing a bill to die without signature after Congress has adjourned is known as a **pocket veto**.) Congress stays in session nearly year-round now, so presidents have few opportunities for pocket vetoes. Moreover, image-conscious presidents believe it appears more decisive either to sign a bill or veto it outright.

The president must accept or reject a measure in its entirety. Congress takes advantage of the situation by passing megabills, hundreds or even thousands of pages long, that intermix provisions the president wants with measures the president would veto were they standing alone. Congressman Waxman, for example, succeeded in getting his measures to expand health-care coverage past President Reagan's veto pen by attaching them to appropriations bills as riders. (A **rider** is a provision, unlikely to become law on its own merits, that is attached to an important bill so that it will "ride" through the legislative process.)

Both Presidents Reagan and Bush have complained about this practice, asking for a constitutional amendment to give the president a line-item veto, a power enjoyed by most state governors. The **line-item veto** is the power of an executive to veto sections, or items, of an appropriation bill while signing the remainder of the bill into law. (An **appropriation bill** is a legislative authorization to spend money for particular purposes.) It seems unlikely, though, that Congress would agree to surrender power to the president, especially when one party controls Congress while the other holds the White House.

A president vetoes a bill by returning it to Congress with a statement of objections. If Congress overrides the veto by a two-thirds vote of each house, the bill becomes law anyway. Should either house fall short of two-thirds, however, the veto is sustained and the measure has failed. All told, fewer than 10 percent of the bills introduced in Congress eventually become law.[27]

ANALYZING THE LEGISLATIVE PROCESS

Step by step, that's how a bill becomes a law, but it's not the whole story. Let's consider some of the factors influencing the legislative process.

Political Parties

Political scientists believe that strong, disciplined parties can play an important role in the legislative process. They can join with a president of their own party to formulate policies and see them enacted. They can present alternatives to the policies of a president from the other party.

The strength of political parties in Congress has paralleled the strength of American parties in general. One study asserts that parties were the basic determinant of the vote in Congress in the early decades of this century. In the 1930s, 65 percent of congressional votes were party votes (defined as a vote in which a majority of each party's members were on opposite sides). By the 1970s, however, the strength of American parties had declined and the percentage of party votes in Congress had fallen to about 40 percent. Weaker parties meant that members of Congress were apt to push their own issues, rather than the issues of the party. Forming legislative coalitions became more difficult, and less work was accomplished.[28]

Today, political parties are making a comeback in Congress, as the percentage of party votes has again risen above the 60 percent mark and party caucuses in Congress have begun meeting regularly to set policy and plan strategy.[29] In part, this development reflects the recent strengthening of American parties, as both the Democrats and Republicans have improved their resources to help party candidates to win election. The resurgence of congressional parties also results from America's split-level realignment in which Democrats control Congress while a Republican occupies the White House. Unable to win the presidency, Democrats in Congress have coalesced to develop and promote their own policy initiatives. Congressional Republicans, meanwhile, have united in support of presidential programs.

In terms of policy, Democrats and Republicans in Congress divide over labor legislation, business regulation, social-welfare measures, and military/defense initiatives. In each case, Democrats as a group tend to be more liberal; Republicans, more conservative.[30] Another difference between Democrats and Republicans in Congress involves support for the president's program. The members of each party tend to back the initiatives of a president of their own party but oppose those of a president from the other party. In 1985–86, for example, Senate Republicans voted to support Reagan more than 75 percent of the time; Senate Democrats, less than 40 percent.[31]

Leadership

The power of congressional leaders to shape policy reached its zenith in the late nineteenth and early twentieth centuries, particularly in the House under the leadership of Speakers Thomas B. Reed and Joseph "Uncle Joe" Cannon. In those days, House speakers controlled the floor by chairing the Rules Committee. They controlled standing committees by appointing committee members and committee chairs. In 1910, however, House members revolted against Cannon's autocratic leadership, removing the Speaker from the Rules Committee and providing for the selection of committee chairs by seniority rather than appointment.

Having lost many of their formal powers, congressional leaders subsequently resorted to political bargaining and persuasion to gain influence. Two Texans, Sam Rayburn, who was Speaker of the House for all but four years between 1941 and 1961, and Lyndon Johnson, who was Senate majority leader from 1955 to 1961, epitomized this style of leadership. Rayburn built his power on persuasion and coalition; Johnson was a renowned arm-twister. Both men were consummate Washington insiders. They understood Congress—its rules, procedures, and personalities—and their impact on public policy was considerable.[32]

Because of a changed policy environment, leadership in Congress today involves more than the back-room political bargaining for which Rayburn and Johnson were famous. As we discussed in earlier chapters, the number and diversity of groups active in Washington politics has expanded rapidly since the early 1960s, and new issues such as abortion, energy, and the environment have appeared on the policy agenda. The importance of the media has grown. Consequently, today's legislative battles are frequently fought outside the halls of Congress via television, among the larger political community. President Reagan set the model for use of the media in 1981, when he pushed his economic program through the Democratic-controlled House, not with behind-the-scenes bargaining but by taking his case directly to the voters through television. Since then, congressional leaders have planned their own media strategies, including televised floor speeches and television news/interview program appearances.

Political scientist Barbara Sinclair believes that today's congressional leadership, especially in the House, is stronger than any leadership of modern times. Because of GOP control of the executive branch, Democrats in Congress have developed their own policy agenda on trade, civil rights, aid to the homeless, the environment, health, Central American policy, child care, and other issues; and they have given the leadership, especially the Speaker of the House, more power to promote that agenda. In the meantime, congressional leaders in both chambers have become adept at using the media to achieve policy goals.[33]

Committees and Subcommittees

One result of the revolt against Speaker Cannon's leadership was to strengthen the hand of committee chairs. For decades, committee chairs, especially in the House, had the power to run their committees as personal fiefdoms, and some did just that. They decided which bills would get a hearing, who would testify at the hearing, when it would be held, and whether it would be open to the public. What's more, committee chairs dominated subcommittees in much the way the Speaker once controlled committees. They appointed subcommittee chairs and members, and decided which bills to refer to them. In sum, committee chairs had the power to push along bills they favored but act as one-person logjams to block bills they opposed.

The power of committee chairs was controversial. Critics charged that the system was undemocratic because it gave too much authority to members whose sole qualification was an ability to be continually reelected, thus building up seniority. Moreover, many committee chairs were conservatives from the (then) one-party South who used their influence to bottle up civil rights legislation. In contrast, the system's defenders argued that strong committee chairs furthered the policy process because they had the authority to broker compromises among competing interests, thus producing legislation.

In the 1970s, Congress reformed its procedures to reduce the power of committee chairs. The method for choosing committee chairs was changed to provide for secret-ballot election rather than automatic selection based on seniority. Also, Congress increased the number and authority of subcommittees. To be sure, committee chairs remained influential, but a good deal of their power was now dispersed to elected subcommittee chairs and subcommittee members.

The reforms of the 1970s had a number of effects on the legislative process. On the positive side, subcommittees with enlarged staffs enabled Congress to give more specialized investigation to the complex policy problems of the day. Subcommittees also gave a broader range of members than before the opportunity to influence the legislative process. The disadvantage of the reforms was that they shifted legislative work away from full committees to subcommittees, which have a more narrow focus. Consequently, subcommittees were less successful at achieving satisfactory policy compromises among competing interests than were full committees. Moreover, subcommittee chairs weren't generally able to provide the strong policy leadership committee chairs once exercised.

In the past decade, the federal budget deficit has been the single most important factor affecting the development of the committee system. As the deficit mounted, the money committees (Finance, Appropriations, and Budget in the Senate; Ways and Means, Appropriations, and Budget in the House) became the policymaking centers of Congress. Members with ideas for new policy initiatives knew they had to deal with these committees to find the money. Congressman Waxman, for example, lobbied the House Budget Committee to fund his health-care proposals. In the meantime, most other standing committees were left with little to do.[34]

Interest Groups

Washington is awash with interest groups trying to influence the legislative process. Arms manufacturers work to ensure that their weapons are included in the defense budget. Child-nutrition advocates push for the adoption of nutrition standards for children's cereals. Business groups press for legislation to limit their liability for defective products. Although business and trade groups are the most numerous and best financed, the entire range of interest groups active in American politics is involved in legislative policymaking.

Interest groups employ a number of tactics to influence legislation. Lobbying is probably the most familiar and widely used tool. Many groups augment their Washington lobbying by promoting contacts from the constituents of a senator or representative. A number of groups, including many labor unions and single-issue groups such as the National Rifle Association, also try to practice a bit of legislative intimidation by keeping a legislative scorecard, showing how members of Congress have voted on issues of importance to the group.

The most controversial aspect of interest-group participation in the legislative process involves money, because groups contribute campaign funds through their political action committees (PACs) or give honoraria to senators for speeches, breakfast seminars, and factory tours. What's more, interest-group money flows in the greatest amounts to members holding key positions in the leadership or in committees. In the 1987–88 election cycle, for example, Congressmen Thomas Foley, Richard Gephardt, and Robert Michel, all members of the Democratic (Foley and Gephardt) or Republican (Michel) leadership, each received more than $500,000 in PAC contributions, despite facing weak election-day opposition. Altogether, candidates for the House and Senate received more than $150 million in PAC support.[35]

Do interest groups buy favorable treatment from Congress? Groups obviously think they receive some return for their investment, but PAC managers argue that they are merely purchasing access, that is, the opportunity to present their side of complex policy issues to lawmakers. The right to "petition the government" is constitutionally guaranteed, they note, and members of Congress benefit from the information that groups provide. Moreover, so many groups are involved in Washington politics that they tend to counterbalance one another.

Political scientists have had difficulty establishing a direct link between PAC contributions and votes in Congress. Scholarly studies have found that other factors, such as members' party affiliations and political philosophy, have more influence over congressional votes. PAC contributions make a difference only at the margins, when legislators have no strong policy preferences and PACs have made a major commitment of resources. One scholar concludes that PACs are most effective when the matter at hand is out of the public spotlight, when the issue is specialized and narrowly focused, when PACs work together with other PACs, and when PAC contributions are coordinated with careful lobbying.[36] Perhaps the best assessment of the relationship between interest-group contributions and congressional policymaking is that contributions are a factor but by no means the only, or necessarily the most important, factor.

Ideology

Historically, the political ideology (liberalism/conservatism) of individual members of Congress has had an important effect on the legislative process. For years, the dominant voting bloc in Congress was the **conservative coalition**, an informal alliance between conservative Democrats, mostly from the

Distributed by King Features Syndicate, Inc.

South, and Republicans. As recently as 1981, many conservative southern Democrats joined Republicans in passing President Reagan's tax-cut and budget proposals in the House, despite the overall numerical advantage of the Democrats.

Today, however, the conservative coalition is less likely to form because southern Democrats are less conservative. Part of the explanation for this development is that many conservative southern voters have defected to the GOP. In the meantime, Democratic members of Congress from the South now depend heavily on the electoral support of African-American voters, who tend to be liberal.[37]

Although each party in Congress has its liberal and conservative elements, the two parties are ideologically polarized. Based on an analysis of roll-call votes in Congress in 1989, the *National Journal* counted 37 liberal senators and 175 liberal House members. All of the liberal senators and all but two of the liberal representatives were Democrats. In contrast, Republicans outnumbered Democrats among conservative senators by 36 to 3, and accounted for 147 out of 177 conservative members of the House. The *Journal* reported that Democrats from the East and West coasts were the most liberal, while Republicans from the West and the South were the most conservative. Southern Democrats and East Coast Republicans tended to be moderates.[38]

Constituency

Constituency pressures are an important influence on policymaking in Congress, but it's often difficult to separate the overlapping effects of party, ideology, and constituency. How, for example, can we explain Congressman Waxman's interest in tighter regulation of nursing-home care and increased government funding for AIDS research? Waxman is a Democrat, and these are issues that the Democrats often support. Waxman is also liberal: "I believe that government has a responsibility to help those people who are otherwise going to be unprotected," he says.[39] What's more, these issues are good politics in Waxman's Los Angeles district, which has a heavy concentration of elderly voters and Jews, and a sizable gay population.

Political scientists tell us that members of Congress have grown increasingly attentive to constituency interests in the last few decades. As political parties declined in importance, members not only felt more vulnerable to electoral challenge but recognized that their political fortunes depended more heavily on their own efforts. Moreover, the growing size and scope of federal-government activities led to an increase in communications from constituents to their elected representatives in Congress.

To deal with constituent demands and, perhaps, also help ensure reelection, Congress has provided its members with resources for tending to constituent needs and staying in touch with the folks back home. In addition to franking privileges and the use of WATS lines, members now have larger staffs, many of whom can be assigned to district offices. What's more, House and Senate leaders have adapted legislative scheduling to allow members more time to spend at home. The Senate, for example, stands in recess one week out of every four to allow members to attend to the home front.

In terms of policy, members of Congress are most responsive to constituents who make their views known. Interest-group spokespersons say that their groups' most effective tool for influencing votes in Congress is to generate a grass-roots lobbying effort in a member's district or state.[40] What's more, a study of Congress' adoption of President Reagan's economic program in 1981 found that those Democrats who voted to support Reagan received a significant amount of mail from constituents backing the president. The study also found, however, that the activists who contacted their legislators, asking them to vote for the president's program, did not represent the views of the general public in the Democrats' districts, many of whom opposed the president's economic policies.[41]

Congressional Norms

Congress is an organization in which men and women work together on a regular basis. It has formal rules of procedure, of course, but it also has informal rules, or norms. **Norms** are unwritten, but expected modes of behavior. They exist in any social group—a university sorority, a softball team, and the United States Congress.

Writing in 1960, one political scientist identified the norms of Congress as specialization, courtesy, reciprocity, institutional loyalty, and apprenticeship.[42] Several of these terms require some definition or explanation. The norm of specialization is that new legislators should focus on a particular policy area, learning it well, so they can contribute to the legislative process. Reciprocity is the expectation that members will cooperate with one another, exchanging favors. The norm of institutional loyalty holds that the ideal lawmaker is someone who sees the House or Senate as a career, rather than a stepping stone to higher office. Apprenticeship, meanwhile, is the norm that new members of Congress should work to learn the ropes from some of the more experienced members before speaking out on policy matters.

Norms are informal rules and so must be enforced informally, by group disapproval. Members who bend the norms may be told by more experienced members that they need to conform. As Speaker Sam Rayburn put it, members get along by going along. If members go too far, flouting the norms of the institution, they may discover that their favorite legislation never seems to get anywhere.

Today, the norms of Congress are similar to what they were in 1960, except that presidential ambition and the ability to attract press attention are now seen as positive attributes.[43] To be sure, members whose primary goal is to achieve influence in Congress may find it advantageous to adhere to the institution's traditional norms. Congressman Waxman probably fits in this category. Many members, however, want to enhance their political standing outside of Congress, in order to ensure reelection or to build a following for a run at higher office. They know that learning the details of policy issues and working behind the scenes to get legislation passed are not usually effective strategies for building statewide or nationwide name recognition. Consequently, a good number of senators and representatives, including some first-termers, have become media entrepreneurs, making speeches and issuing press releases on a broad range of policy matters.

Personalities

Personalities can also affect the legislative process. Some members of Congress are bright; others, slow. Some are capable; others, inept. Some are broad-minded; others, petty.

One study of House leadership attributes at least some of the changes in congressional policymaking to differences in the approaches of Speaker O'Neill, who retired in 1986, and Speaker Wright, who succeeded him. O'Neill was a consensus builder who worked to fashion legislation that could command broad support. In contrast, Wright wasn't particularly interested in building consensus as long as he had sufficient votes to pass legislation. He focused on policymaking, pushing (and passing) major legislation in a number of policy areas.

The White House

The president is often a key player in the congressional policymaking process. Presidents present legislative programs to Congress and push for passage during committee and subcommittee proceedings, sending cabinet officers to testify at hearings. Presidents use their influence to round up votes on the floor. If Congress seems likely to include provisions the president opposes, the president can threaten a veto, thus forcing a compromise. Moreover, in today's media-centered politics, presidents often attempt to get what they want from Congress by going public, asking the voters to contact their legislators to urge them to support presidential programs. We consider the role of the chief executive in the legislative process in more detail in chapter 9.

CONCLUSION: CONGRESS AND PUBLIC POLICY

The founders of American government expected Congress to be the dominant branch, and throughout most of the nineteenth and early twentieth centuries, their expectations were fulfilled. Congress was active, assertive. Writing in the 1880s, Woodrow Wilson, a political-science graduate student who later made good, argued in his doctoral thesis that Congress was the dominant branch of government.[44]

In the middle decades of the twentieth century, however, the impetus for legislation came more frequently from the White House than from Congress, as presidents such as Woodrow Wilson, Franklin Roosevelt, Harry Truman, and Lyndon Johnson presented legislative programs to Congress and lobbied for their passage. To be sure, many of the presidential initiatives were for ideas that had been knocking around Congress for years, but the necessary momentum for their passage came from the White House.

The low point for Congress as an institution came in the late 1960s and early 1970s. On one hand, Congress found itself under fire for its internal operations. Critics charged that Congress had become a fundamentally undemocratic body, operating for the most part behind closed doors. Too frequently, they said, elderly committee chairs, chosen solely on the basis of seniority, used their considerable influence to block legislation that enjoyed broad support among the general public and in Congress as well. What's more, the critics said, much of the business of Congress took place out of public view, either in closed committee sessions or in unrecorded votes on the floor.

On the other hand, much of the constitutional role of Congress in the policy process had seemingly been taken over by the White House. For all practical purposes, Congress had lost two of its most important powers: the power to declare war and control of the budget. The Korean War and then the war in Vietnam were waged without congressional declarations of war, fought instead under the president's authority as commander in chief. Moreover, certain aspects of the Vietnam War were kept secret, from both the people and Congress. Similarly, in the early 1970s, President Nixon, claiming extraordinary executive powers, began impounding funds, refusing to spend money duly appropriated by Congress. (**Impoundment** is the refusal of the president to spend funds already appropriated by Congress.)

In the mid-1970s, the unpopularity of the Vietnam War and President Nixon's resignation over the Watergate scandal presented Congress with the opportunity to regain lost power. First, Congress passed legislation to reassert itself in relation to the president. In 1973, for example, it enacted the War Powers Act (over Nixon's veto) restricting the president's authority to wage undeclared war without authorization by Congress. (See the Perspective for a discussion of the War Powers Act.) A year later, Congress passed the Budget and Impoundment Control Act to limit the president's ability to impound appropriated funds and to give Congress more control over the budgetary process. Second, Congress moved to improve its ability to function as an active part of the policymaking process, by increasing staff sizes and upgrading congressional research and information services. Finally, Congress reformed its internal procedures to make the legislative process more open and democratic.

The reforms of the 1970s made Congress more open, more democratic, and more representative, but less efficient. Because of the reforms, most subcommittee, committee, and conference-committee proceedings were opened to the public, and most votes were recorded. Consequently, citizens (and lobbyists) were better able to follow the legislative process. Congress was also more decentralized. By weakening committee chairs and strengthening subcommittees, Congress allowed more members input into the legislative process. Stronger subcommittees, however, increased legislative fragmentation by including an additional step in the legislative process. One scholar summarizes the impact of the reforms of the 1970s as follows: "On balance, Congress has become more democratized, more responsive to a multitude of forces inside and outside its halls, and as a result more hard-pressed to formulate and enact coherent, responsive public policies."[45]

During the 1980s, however, power in Congress became more centralized. Democrats in the House of Representatives responded to Republican control

PERSPECTIVE

The War Powers Act

Congress passed the War Powers Act in 1973 in response to what it regarded as presidential infringement on its constitutional power to declare war. First, the act required the president to consult with Congress "in every possible instance" before introducing American forces into situations where hostilities would be likely. Second, the law obliged the president to make detailed, periodic reports on the necessity and scope of the operation. Third, the act declared that American forces must be withdrawn after sixty days of the first reports of fighting (with a thirty-day grace period to ensure safe withdrawal) unless Congress declared war or voted to authorize the presence of the American forces. Finally, the War Powers Act gave Congress the power to order the withdrawal of American forces by majority vote of both houses at any time, even before the sixty-day period had expired. This last provision was apparently invalidated, however, by a 1983 Supreme Court decision that found similar measures unconstitutional.

Since its inception, presidents have been critical of the War Powers Act and sought ways to circumvent it. Instead of consulting with Congress, asking for advice about possible U.S. military action, presidents have generally only informed congressional leaders in advance of actions they already planned to take. President Reagan, for example, notified congressional leaders about his decision to invade Grenada, but he did not ask for their advice. Chief executives have also tried to avoid application of the War Powers Act by denying that military actions they order fall under the scope of the law. President Carter failed to consult congressional leaders before ordering the ill-fated hostage-rescue mission in Iran, arguing that rescue missions aren't combat situations.

In practice, the War Powers Act is probably a less effective check on the president's war-making power than public opinion. If a president's actions enjoy broad public support, as was the case with President Reagan's bombing raid on Libya or the Grenada invasion, Congress is unlikely to order a pull-out of U.S. forces. In contrast, the risk of adverse public reaction may deter some military initiatives or cut short others. In 1983, for example, President Reagan ordered American forces withdrawn from Beirut well in advance of a War Powers Act cut-off date after several hundred marines were killed in a terrorist bombing. Perhaps more significant, the ordered withdrawal was also well in advance of the 1984 presidential election.

of the White House and, until 1987, the Senate as well, by strengthening the authority of the Speaker to manage the legislative process. In the meantime, the preoccupation of Congress with budgetary matters (because of record-setting federal deficits) has placed standing committees dealing with the budget, appropriations, and taxes at the center of the legislative process.

We began our study of Congress with a profile of Congressman Henry Waxman, identifying and evaluating the factors accounting for his influence on health policy: his position in the legislative process, his personal political skills, and the contextual factors surrounding his efforts. We can explain the policymaking role of Congress as an institution using a similar approach, by focusing on legislative processes, the personalities and skills of congressional leaders, and the policymaking context.

Consider the policy accomplishments of the 100th Congress (1987–88), which passed major legislation dealing with water quality, illegal drugs, catastrophic health care, civil rights, fair housing, highways, aid for the homeless, hunger, trade, plant-closing notification, and farm-credit reform. No session of Congress since the 89th Congress of 1965 and 1966 enacted more landmark legislation. What's more, the 100th Congress, unlike the 89th, was not generally acting in response to presidential leadership. In fact, the 100th Congress passed several major bills over President Reagan's veto, including measures dealing with civil rights, highway construction, and water quality.[46]

We can explain this Congress' burst of legislative activity on the basis of the legislative process, the personal styles of legislative leaders, and the policymaking context. First, the centralization of power in the House in the hands of the Speaker and committees dealing with the budget enhanced that chamber's ability to legislate. In particular, control of the Rules Committee gave the Speaker considerable power over the legislative options available to the floor of the House.

Second, the top legislative leadership, Speaker Jim Wright and Senate Majority Leader Robert Byrd, were determined to pass their party's legislative agenda and willing to use all their powers to achieve those ends. In 1987, for example, when a House vote on an important bill stood 205 to 206 against the Speaker's position, Wright held the vote open until he convinced a Democratic congressman from East Texas who owed the Speaker a favor to change his vote so the measure would pass, 206 to 205.[47]

Finally, the 100th Congress' burst of legislative action reflected the presence of a number of favorable contextual factors. After the 1986 congressional elections, Democrats held comfortable majorities in both the House and Senate, and party members in Congress were relatively united behind the party's basic legislative agenda. Indeed, many of the measures Congress passed enjoyed strong bipartisan (two-party) support both inside and outside Congress, including the backing of President Reagan. Nonetheless, the Democrats' legislative successes could also be attributed to the president's being at a low point in interest and influence. A more vigorous, more influential president could have demanded and received a greater role in the legislative process.

KEY TERMS

appropriation bill

bicameral

cloture

conference committee

conservative coalition

constituency service

filibuster

franking privilege

impoundment

joint committee

line-item veto

majority leader

majority whip

mark-up

minority leader

minority whip

multiple referral of legislation

norms

pocket veto

rider

select committee

seniority

special committee

standing committee

table

NOTES

1. Julie Kosterlitz, "Watch Out for Waxman," *National Journal*, 11 March 1989, pp. 577–81.
2. Edward G. Carmines and Lawrence C. Dodd, "Bicameralism in Congress: The Changing Partnership," in Lawrence C. Dodd and Bruce I. Oppenheimer, eds., *Congress Reconsidered*, 3d ed. (Washington, DC: Congressional Quarterly Press, 1985), pp. 414–36.
3. *Houston Post*, 4 January 1989, p. A-9.
4. "Top Giver," *Houston Chronicle*, 11 July 1989, p. 4A.
5. David Keating of National Taxpayers Union, quoted in Thomas J. Brazaitis, "Congressional Perks Add Up to an Estimated $37,000 per Year," *Houston Chronicle*, 8 January 1989, p. 22A.
6. *Time*, 20 February 1989, p. 30.
7. Quoted in Michael Kinsley, "In Defense of Congress," *Time*, 17 April 1989, p. 84.
8. Al Swift, "The 'Permanent Congress' Is a Myth," *Washington Post*, National Weekly Edition, 26 June–2 July 1989, p. 29.
9. James A. Barnes, "Growing Clout of 'Leadership PACs,'" *National Journal*, 6 May 1989, p. 1120.
10. Barbara Sinclair, "Party Leadership and Policy Change," in Gerald C. Wright, Jr., Leroy N. Rieselbach, and Lawrence C. Dodd, eds., *Congress and Policy Change* (New York: Agathon Press, 1986), pp. 175–200.
11. Walter J. Oleszek, *Congressional Procedures and the Policy Process*, 3d ed. (Washington, DC: Congressional Quarterly Press, 1989), pp. 30–34.
12. Barbara Sinclair, "House Majority Party Leadership in the Late 1980s," in Lawrence C. Dodd and Bruce I. Oppenheimer, eds., *Congress Reconsidered*, 4th ed. (Washington, DC: Congressional Quarterly Press, 1989), p. 312.

13. Quoted in *Congressional Quarterly*, Daily Edition, 28 July 1983, S11029.
14. Quoted in *New York Times*, 5 January 1987, p. A13.
15. Sinclair, "House Majority Party Leadership."
16. Oleszek, p. 15.
17. Richard L. Hall, "Committee Decision Making in the Post-Reform Congress," in Dodd and Oppenheimer, eds., *Congress Reconsidered*, 4th ed., p. 203.
18. "Big Congressional Staffs Still Growing," *Houston Post*, 9 July 1989, p. A-9.
19. Norman J. Ornstein, Robert L. Peabody, and David W. Rohde, "Change in the Senate: Toward the 1990s," in Dodd and Oppenheimer, eds., *Congress Reconsidered*, 4th ed., pp. 32–33.
20. David R. Mayhew, *Congress: The Electoral Connection* (New Haven: Yale University Press, 1974), chapter 2.
21. John C. McAdams and John R. Johannes, "Congressmen, Perquisites, and Elections," *Journal of Politics* 50 (May 1988): 412–39.
22. Melissa P. Collie and Joseph Cooper, "Multiple Referral and the 'New' Committee System in the House of Representatives," in Dodd and Oppenheimer, eds., *Congress Reconsidered*, 4th ed., pp. 245–72; Sinclair, "House Majority Party Leadership," p. 314.
23. Oleszek, p. 81.
24. Sinclair, "House Majority Party Leadership," pp. 318–21.
25. Steven S. Smith, "Taking It to the Floor," in Dodd and Oppenheimer, eds., *Congress Reconsidered*, 4th ed., p. 347.
26. Christopher J. Deering, "Leadership in the Slow Lane," *PS: Political Science and Politics*, Winter 1986, pp. 37–42; Bruce I. Oppenheimer, "Changing Time Constraints on Congress: Historical Perspectives on the Use of Cloture," in Dodd and Oppenheimer, eds., *Congress Reconsidered*, 3d ed., pp. 393–413.
27. Oleszek, p. 81.
28. Melissa P. Collie and David W. Brady, "The Decline of Partisan Voting Coalitions in the House of Representatives," in Dodd and Oppenheimer, eds., *Congress Reconsidered*, 3d ed., pp. 272–87.
29. Lawrence C. Dodd and Bruce I. Oppenheimer, "Consolidating Power in the House: The Rise of a New Oligarchy," in Dodd and Oppenheimer, eds., *Congress Reconsidered*, 4th ed., p. 42.
30. Richard L. Kolbe, *American Political Parties: An Uncertain Future* (New York: Harper & Row, 1985), pp. 101–2.
31. David S. Broder, "Reagan's Next-to-Last Hurrah," *Washington Post*, National Weekly Edition, 17 November 1986, p. 4.
32. Joseph Cooper and David Brady, "Institutional Context and Leadership Style: The House from Cannon to Rayburn," *American Political Science Review* 75 (June 1981): 411–25.
33. Sinclair, "House Majority Party Leadership."
34. Dodd and Oppenheimer, "Consolidating Power in the House."
35. "The 1988 PAC Scorecard: Who Got What in the Campaign," *Washington Post*, National Weekly Edition, 22–28 May 1989, p. 14.
36. Larry J. Sabato, *PAC Power: Inside the World of Political Action Committees* (New York: W. W. Norton, 1984), pp. 135–37.
37. William R. Shaffer, "Ideological Trends Among Southern U.S. Democratic Senators," *American Politics Quarterly* 15 (July 1987): 299–324.
38. *National Journal*, 27 January 1990, pp. 195–221.

39. Quoted in Kosterlitz, p. 578.

40. Janet M. Grenzke, "PACs and the Congressional Supermarket: The Currency Is Complex," *American Journal of Political Science* 33 (February 1989): 1–24.

41. Darrell M. West, "Activists and Economic Policymaking in Congress," *American Journal of Political Science* 32 (August 1988): 667–80.

42. Donald R. Matthews, *U.S. Senators and Their World* (New York: Vintage Books, 1960), pp. 116–17.

43. John R. Hibbing and Sue Thomas, "The Modern United States Senate: What Is Accorded Respect?" *Journal of Politics* 52 (February 1990), pp. 126–45

44. Woodrow Wilson, *Congressional Government* (New York: Meridian Books, 1956).

45. Leroy N. Rieselbach, "Assessing Congressional Change, or What Hath Reform Wrought (or Wreaked)?" in Dennis Hales, ed., *The United States Congress* (New Brunswick, NJ: Transaction Books, 1983), pp. 203–4.

46. "Kings of the Hill," *Time*, 3 October 1988, p. 26.

47. Sinclair, "House Majority Party Leadership," p. 321.

SUGGESTED READINGS

Cain, Bruce; Ferejohn, John; and Fiorina, Morris. *The Personal Vote: Constituency Service and Electoral Independence*. Cambridge, MA: Harvard University Press, 1987.

Dodd, Lawrence C., and Oppenheimer, Bruce I., eds. *Congress Reconsidered*, 4th ed. Washington, DC: Congressional Quarterly Press, 1989.

Duncan, Phil, ed. *Politics in America 1990*. Washington, DC: Congressional Quarterly Press, 1989.

Oleszek, Walter J. *Congressional Procedures and the Policy Process*, 3d ed. Washington, DC: Congressional Quarterly Press, 1989.

Parker, Glenn R. *Homeward Bound: Explaining Changes in Congressional Behavior*. Pittsburgh, PA: University of Pittsburgh Press, 1986.

Rieselbach, Leroy N. *Congressional Reform*. Washington, DC: Congressional Quarterly Press, 1986.

Smith, Steven S., and Deering, Christopher J. *Committees in Congress*. Washington, DC: Congressional Quarterly Press, 1984.

Wright, Gerald C., Jr.; Rieselbach, Leroy N.; and Dodd, Lawrence C., eds. *Congress and Policy Change*. New York: Agathon Press, 1986.

9

THE PRESIDENCY

LEARNING OBJECTIVES

1. To outline the constitutional presidency, considering qualifications, term of office, impeachment and removal, succession, and disability.
2. To trace the evolution of the vice-presidency.
3. To describe the constitutional powers and duties of the office of president, focusing on legislative, diplomatic, military, judicial, and executive powers.
4. To trace the development of the modern presidency.
5. To evaluate the two-presidencies thesis.
6. To describe the relationship between the presidency and the media.
7. To outline the organization of the presidential bureaucracy, describe its role in presidential decision making, consider reasons for its growth, and identify the problems it may present to the president.
8. To compare and contrast Neustadt's and Kernell's approaches for explaining presidential influence.
9. To evaluate Barber's approach to presidential personality.
10. To describe the relationship between presidential popularity and presidential influence.
11. To assess the role of the presidency in America's policy process.

One of the first actions of the Bush administration upon assuming office in 1989 was to negotiate a compromise with Congress over aid to the contras, a guerrilla force attempting to overthrow the government of Nicaragua. By terms of the agreement, Congress would provide humanitarian (nonmilitary) assistance to the contras. In return, the administration would pursue a peaceful solution to the conflict in Central America. Congress would reserve the right, however, to halt aid if it decided that the administration was not sincere about negotiating a peaceful settlement in the region.

The agreement not only ended a long-running battle between the White House and Congress over contra aid, but it reversed what had been a cornerstone of President Reagan's foreign policy. Reagan supported the contras because he believed that the Sandinistas, the political faction controlling the Nicaraguan government, were allowing their country to be used by the Russians and Cubans as a staging ground for communist aggression. If communist influence in Central America is not checked, the president warned, then El Salvador, Honduras, Mexico, and eventually the United States itself would be threatened.

In contrast, critics of Reagan's Central American policy argued that the United States' interests in the region could best be protected through negotiations rather than military force. Although Reagan called the contras "freedom fighters" and "the moral equivalent of the Founding Fathers," opponents of military aid charged that the contras were a ragtag army of bandits led by corrupt followers of former Nicaraguan dictator Anastasio Somoza. Moreover, the critics warned, American support for the contras could well lead the United States into a protracted regional war in Central America similar to the one in Vietnam.

The removal of the Sandinista government was the centerpiece of President Reagan's global strategy for rolling back communism. When Reagan took office in 1981, he ordered the Central Intelligence Agency (CIA) to fund and direct the contra guerrilla force in Nicaragua. From the beginning, the White House informed appropriate congressional committees of administration policy in Central America and in 1982 Congress adopted a resolution permitting the administration to support the rebels. In 1983, Congress voted to fund the contras openly. Congress cut off military aid to the contras in 1984, however, after learning that the CIA had mined Nicaraguan harbors in apparent violation of international law. Although Congress appropriated money for nonmilitary, humanitarian aid, it specifically prohibited the transfer of U.S. funds for military purposes. Congress voted to resume military aid to the contras in 1987, but refused to appropriate more money in 1988 after the Iran-contra scandal became public.

The Iran-contra scandal involved a conspiracy by a number of White House staff members, including Marine Lieutenant Colonel Oliver North and Naval Vice Admiral John Poindexter, to circumvent Congress' prohibition against supplying military aid to the contras. North, Poindexter, and other National Security Council officials sold arms to Iran and then diverted profits from the sale to Central America to help the contras. Although the transfer of money to the contras allegedly took place without the knowledge of either President Reagan or Vice President Bush, the affair stiffened opposition against further American military assistance to the contras.

The Bush administration's decision to compromise with Congress over Central American policy illustrates the nature of presidential power. Presidential influence depends on environmental factors, political coalitions, and, probably to a lesser extent, the personal skills of the incumbent.[1] Reagan was most successful implementing his Central American policy in the early years of his presidency when his party held a majority in the Senate and tensions between the United States and USSR were relatively high. By the end of the Reagan presidency, however, the situation had changed. Democrats controlled both the House and the Senate, East-West tensions had eased, and the Iran-contra scandal undermined the president's position. As a result, Reagan, despite his best lobbying efforts, was unable to convince Congress to supply military aid to the contras. When George Bush became president, he accepted political realities and struck the best deal he could get. As it turned out, American efforts to remove the Sandinista government succeeded. After years of economic and military pressure from the United States, the Sandinistas agreed to a peace plan proposed by the leaders of other Central American governments. The plan called for elections in Nicaragua. The election was held in December 1989 and the citizens of Nicaragua voted the Sandinistas out of office.

THE CONSTITUTIONAL PRESIDENCY

The president works within the broad outlines of the office established by the Constitution, primarily in Article II.

Qualifications

The formal qualifications for president are broadly enough defined to include most Americans. The Constitution requires a president to be thirty-five years old, a natural-born American citizen, and a resident of the United States for at least fourteen years. Nonetheless, presidents have come from fairly narrow social circles. Two presidents were father and son (John and John Quincy Adams); two, grandfather and grandson (William Henry and Benjamin Harrison); and two, cousins (Theodore and Franklin Roosevelt). All the nation's presidents have been white males of Western European ancestry. All but one, John Kennedy, have been Protestants. Most have been fairly well-to-do, and the majority have been experienced politicians. In recent years, though, social barriers have begun to fall as the nation has elected a Catholic (Kennedy), a southerner (Jimmy Carter), and a divorced person (Reagan) to the White House.

Term of Office

The president's constitutional term of office is four years. The framers of the Constitution placed no limit on the number of terms presidents could serve, believing that the desire to remain in office would compel presidents to do their best. George Washington, however, established the custom of retiring after two terms.

When Democrat Franklin Roosevelt broke tradition by successfully seeking third and fourth terms in 1940 and 1944, unhappy Republicans launched a drive to amend the Constitution to limit the president to two terms. They succeeded with the ratification of the Twenty-second Amendment in 1951. The proponents of the two-term limit argued that it prevents a president from becoming too powerful. In contrast, critics of the limit believed that it not only weakens the presidency but denies voters the right to reelect a president they admire.

Although some reformers support a repeal of the Twenty-second Amendment, others favor the adoption of a single six-year term for the president. They believe that a single six-year term would relieve the president of the political pressures of running for reelection while allowing the chief executive to concentrate on shaping sound public policy. In response, opponents argue that a single six-year term would weaken the president's political bargaining power. Moreover, they say, six years is too short a term for a good president, too long for a bad one.

Impeachment and Removal

The Constitution states that the president may be impeached for "treason, bribery, or other high crimes and misdemeanors." Scholars tell us that the founders foresaw two broad, general grounds on which a president could be impeached and removed from office. First, impeachment could be used against a president who abused the powers of office, thereby threatening to become a tyrant. Second, it could be employed against a president who simply refused to carry out the duties of the office.[2]

The actual process of impeachment and removal involves both houses of Congress. The House initiates the process by drawing up articles of impeachment. Technically, the word *impeach* means to accuse, so when the House impeaches the president by majority vote, it is accusing the president of committing offenses that may warrant removal from office. The Senate then tries the president, with the chief justice presiding. The Senate must vote by a two-thirds margin to remove the president from office.

The impeachment and removal process has twice been initiated against presidents. In the 1860s, the House impeached Andrew Johnson, Lincoln's successor in the White House, but the Senate fell one vote short of removing him from office. In the 1970s, the House began impeachment proceedings against President Nixon during the Watergate scandal. Nixon resigned, however, before the full House could vote. (For an overview of the Watergate scandal, see the Perspective.)

Presidential Succession and Disability

The vice-president succeeds a president who is removed, resigns, or dies in office. After the vice-president, the line of succession goes to the Speaker of the House, the president pro tempore of the Senate, the secretary of state, and on through the cabinet. In American history, nine vice-presidents have succeeded to the presidency but no Speakers or Senate presidents. Because of the Twenty-fifth Amendment, it is unlikely that the order of succession will need to extend beyond the office of vice-president.

The Twenty-fifth Amendment was ratified in 1967, after President Eisenhower's heart attack and President Kennedy's assassination focused attention on the problems of presidential succession and disability. The amendment empowers the president to fill a vacancy in the office of vice-president subject to majority confirmation of both houses of Congress. This procedure was first used in 1973, when President Nixon nominated Gerald Ford to replace Vice President Spiro Agnew, who resigned under accusation of criminal wrongdoing. When Nixon himself resigned in 1974, Ford moved up to the presidency and appointed Nelson Rockefeller to be the new vice-president.

PERSPECTIVE

Watergate

Other than the Vietnam War, no recent event has had a greater impact on the presidency in particular and American politics in general than the Watergate scandal. Since Watergate, the press has become more aggressive, less willing to take presidential pronouncements at face value. The public has grown more cynical about government and officeholders. Congress, meanwhile, has become more assertive.

The Watergate affair began on 12 June 1972, when five men were arrested breaking into the Democratic National Committee's headquarters in the Watergate office complex in Washington, D.C. The burglars were employed by the Committee to Reelect the President, hired to plant electronic eavesdropping devices in the opposition's headquarters. Their mission was part of a conspiracy formed by aides of President Nixon to manipulate the Democratic party nomination campaign to assist in nominating the weakest Democratic candidate and to defeat any potential nominee strong enough to beat Nixon. It was many months, however, before these facts were generally known.

Once the burglars were arrested, President Nixon and his aides launched a second conspiracy, one to conceal the nature of the first conspiracy. They paid more than $300,000 in hush money to the burglars and their supervisors to keep them quiet. The White House, meanwhile, played down the significance of the break-in. "A third-rate burglary," said Nixon.

The coverup did not begin to unravel until early 1973, when the burglars stood trial. Although they remained silent, Judge John Sirica voiced the opinion that the truth had not come out. In the meantime, two investigative reporters for the *Washington Post*, Carl Bernstein and Bob Woodward, began to uncover facts and ask questions about the affair.

By early summer 1973, the investigation was proceeding on several fronts. In the Senate, a select committee chaired by Senator Sam Ervin conducted televised hearings at which presidential aides told startling tales of political dirty tricks and coverups in the White House. "What did the president know, and when did he know it?" asked Senator Howard Baker. While the hearings continued, Special Prosecutor Archibald Cox conducted an investigation on behalf of the Justice Department. In October, however, Nixon decided that Cox's probe was coming too close to the truth, and he fired Cox in what came to be known as the Saturday Night Massacre. For the first time, congressional leaders publicly considered impeachment.

Nixon clung to his presidency for another nine and a half months. Although he called upon the nation "to put Watergate behind us," that was not to be. Each week brought new accusations and revelations. In 1974, the House Judiciary Committee held hearings on proposed articles of impeachment against the president, eventually recommending impeachment to the full House. Meanwhile, a new special prosecutor, Leon Jaworski, pursued the investigation, aided immeasurably by tape recordings the president had secretly made of his conversations with his aides.

Watergate came to a climax in midsummer 1974, when the Supreme Court ordered Nixon to hand over a key group of tapes to the special prosecutor. One tape, containing a conversation between the president and Chief of Staff H. R. Haldeman, proved to be the "smoking gun" that linked Nixon directly to the coverup. Whatever support Nixon still had in Congress and the Republican party crumbled. In August, he resigned the presidency.

Other provisions of the Twenty-fifth Amendment establish procedures for the vice-president to become acting president should the president become disabled and incapable of performing the duties of office. The president may declare disability by written notice to the Senate president pro tempore and to the Speaker of the House. The vice-president then becomes acting president until the president declares in writing an ability to resume the responsibilities of office. If the president is unable or unwilling to declare disability, such a declaration can be made by the vice-president in conjunction with a majority of the cabinet. Should the vice-president/cabinet and president disagree on the question of the president's disability, Congress may declare the president disabled by a two-thirds vote of each house.

The Vice-Presidency

President George Bush and Vice President Dan Quayle.

The vice-presidency has always been an office with potential, but until recent administrations, the vice-president had been the forgotten person of Washington. In 1848, Daniel Webster, a prominent political figure of the time, rejected the Whig vice-presidential nomination, saying, "I do not propose to be buried until I am dead."[3] John Nance Garner, one of Franklin Roosevelt's vice-presidents, once declared the job wasn't worth a "bucket of warm spit." As the importance of the presidency has grown, however, so has the significance of the vice-presidency, and men and women of stature are more willing to accept the position.

Recent presidents have actively involved their vice-presidents in their administrations. President Carter, for example, used Vice President Walter Mondale as an adviser, trouble-shooter, and emissary to interest groups and to Congress. President Reagan named George Bush to chair the Task Force on Regulatory Relief and placed the vice-president in charge of the administration's war on drugs. Both Mondale and Bush enjoyed an open invitation to attend all presidential meetings.[4]

Constitutional Powers and Duties

The Constitution outlines the powers and duties of the president, primarily in Article II, Sections 2 and 3. The sections aren't long, but they give the president important powers in certain key policy areas.

Legislative Powers

The Constitution grants the president certain tools for shaping the legislative agenda. From time to time, it says, the president shall "give to Congress Information of the State of the Union, and recommend to their Consideration such Measures as he shall judge necessary and expedient." Traditionally, the president makes a State of the Union address each January before a joint session of Congress and a national television audience. The president may send legislative recommendations to Congress at any time. President Reagan, for example, argued for contra aid both in annual State of the Union addresses and in special messages he sent to Congress.

The veto, meanwhile, gives the president an instrument for influencing the final content of legislation. Presidents can veto measures they oppose. Moreover, by threatening veto, the president can often force Congress to compromise.

The Constitution gives the president sufficient legislative authority to participate in the legislative process but not enough legislative tools to dictate policy. Although President Reagan kept the issue of contra aid before Congress throughout his administration, he wasn't able to convince Congress to commit as many resources to the contras as he would have liked. In practice, presidents are policy dramatists. They present proposals to Congress, highlighting certain problems and solutions while ignoring others. Their policy successes or failures depend on a number of factors, including the issue, the party balance in Congress, presidential leadership skills, and the president's popularity.[5]

Diplomatic Powers

The Constitution gives the president, as **head of state** (the official head of government), broad diplomatic authority to conduct foreign relations. The president has the power to grant diplomatic recognition to other nations and to receive and appoint ambassadors. President Nixon, for example, began the process of normalizing relations with the People's Republic of China, a country the United States had never officially recognized. President Carter completed the process and the two nations exchanged ambassadors. The only constitutional limitation on the president's power of diplomatic recognition is that ambassadorial appointments must be approved by majority vote of the Senate. They usually are.

The president also has the power to negotiate treaties with other nations, subject to a two-thirds vote of ratification by the Senate. Although the Senate approves most treaties, it has issued a number of history-making rejections, including the defeat of the Treaty of Versailles negotiated by President Woodrow Wilson at the end of World War I. In most cases, however, presidents withdraw treaties from Senate consideration rather than see them go down to defeat, as did President Carter with the Strategic Arms Limitation Treaty (SALT II), negotiated by Presidents Ford and Carter with the Soviet Union.

The use of executive agreements has enhanced the president's diplomatic powers. **Executive agreements** are international understandings between the president and foreign nations that do not require Senate ratification. Although the Constitution says nothing about executive agreements, the Supreme Court has upheld their use based on the president's diplomatic and military powers.

Executive agreements are more numerous than treaties. Between 1940 and 1977, presidents negotiated 420 treaties while concluding 7,715 executive

Soviet President Mikhail Gorbachev and U.S. President George Bush clasp hands at their December 1989 meeting aboard a Soviet ship docked in Malta. Soviet Foreign Minister Eduard Shevardnadze and U.S. Secretary of State James Baker join in the congenial mood.

agreements.[6] Many executive agreements involve relatively trivial matters, such as the exchange of postal service between nations. Some agreements, though, deal with important policy issues, such as the agreement between America and Japan to limit the number of Japanese automobiles imported into the United States.

Historically, executive agreements have been a source of conflict between the president and Congress. Although most members of Congress would prefer not having to vote on every issue contained in executive agreements, they believe that presidents sometimes use executive agreements to cut Congress out of the policy process. As a result, Congress requires the secretary of state to submit to Congress the final text of all executive agreements within sixty days of their negotiation.

Military Powers

The Constitution names the president commander in chief of the armed forces. This constitutional provision embodies the doctrine of **civilian supremacy of the armed forces**. This is the concept that the armed forces should be under the direct control of civilian authorities. The doctrine of civilian supremacy is based on the belief that war is too important to be left to the military; political considerations frequently outweigh military ones. It also reflects the view that the preservation of representative democracy depends on keeping the military out of politics. In many nations, political power grows out of the barrels of the guns of the armed forces. Soldiers rule.

In the United States, however, the president, a civilian, stands at the apex of the armed forces' command structure. As commander in chief, the president has the authority to make final military decisions. President Franklin Roosevelt, for instance, chose the time and place of the Normandy invasion in World War II. Truman decided to drop the atomic bomb on Japan. President Carter dispatched an expedition to attempt to rescue the American hostages held in Iran. Reagan ordered the invasion of the Caribbean island of Grenada and directed air strikes against Libya.

Judicial Powers

The president also has a role in judicial policymaking. The president nominates all federal judges pending majority-vote confirmation by the Senate. The Senate usually approves nominees, but not without scrutiny, especially for Supreme Court selections. President Nixon saw two consecutive Supreme Court appointments rejected before nominating a candidate the Senate would approve.

The Constitution also gives the president the power to grant pardons and reprieves. A **pardon** is an executive action that frees an accused or convicted person from all penalty for an offense. A **reprieve**, meanwhile, is an executive action that delays punishment. With some exceptions, such as President Ford's pardon of former President Nixon, most presidential pardons and reprieves are noncontroversial.

Executive Powers

Finally, the Constitution gives the president powers of administration. The president is the nation's **chief executive**, that is, the head of the executive branch of government. The Constitution grants the president authority to require written reports of department heads. It also enjoins the president to "take Care that Laws be faithfully executed."

As head of the executive branch of government, presidents sometimes issue executive orders to manage the federal bureaucracy. An **executive order** is a rule or regulation issued by an executive official to an administrative agency or executive department. During the early days of World War II, for example, President Franklin Roosevelt used an executive order to direct the internment of Japanese-Americans living on the West Coast. In 1957, President Eisenhower issued an executive order to send the National Guard into Little Rock, Arkansas, to protect black youngsters attempting to attend a whites-only public high school. As with executive agreements, the Constitution says nothing about executive orders. The courts, however, have upheld their use based on law, custom, and the Constitution.

THE MODERN PRESIDENCY

Although the Constitution grants the president important powers, the full scope of presidential authority has evolved through the practice of American government over the last two hundred years.

The Development of the Modern Presidency

In the early days of the nation, presidents generally confined their initiatives to foreign affairs. President Thomas Jefferson, for example, engineered the Louisiana Purchase, and President James Monroe proclaimed the Monroe Doctrine. In contrast with foreign policymaking, the president's role in domestic politics was minimal. Early presidents did not negotiate with Congress over policy and they used the veto only when they considered legislation unconstitutional. Three of the first six presidents vetoed no legislation at all. (By comparison, President Ford cast sixty-six vetoes; Carter, thirty-one.[7])

Presidents Andrew Jackson and Abraham Lincoln broadened the powers of the presidency. Jackson built upon a strong base of political party support outside Washington, D.C., to expand the president's role in legislative policymaking. Unlike his predecessors, Jackson vetoed legislation on policy grounds, issuing more vetoes than the first six presidents combined. During the Civil War, Lincoln used his authority as commander in chief to take actions without congressional authorization. He declared martial law, ordered the blockade of southern ports, freed slaves in rebelling territories, stationed troops in the South, and spent money not appropriated by Congress.

After the impeachment of Andrew Johnson in 1868, Congress reasserted its policymaking dominance. One study found that from 1870 to 1900, congressional initiative lay behind the passage of 78 percent of major legislation, while the president initiated only 8 percent.[8] Many of the individuals elected president during this era showed little interest in legislative politics. In contrast, strong legislative leadership backed by disciplined political parties enhanced the policymaking capabilities of Congress.

Presidents in the early twentieth century were more active than most of their nineteenth-century counterparts, especially Theodore Roosevelt and Woodrow Wilson. In foreign affairs, Roosevelt sent the navy halfway around the globe and schemed to acquire the Panama Canal. Domestically, Roosevelt attacked monopolies, crusaded for conservation, and lobbied legislation through Congress. Wilson, meanwhile, was the first president to recommend a comprehensive legislative program to Congress. He was also the first president to conduct face-to-face diplomacy with foreign leaders as he negotiated the League of Nations Treaty.

The era of the modern presidency began with the administration of Franklin Roosevelt. FDR was first elected during the Great Depression and held office through most of World War II. Both of these events served to increase the scope of federal governmental activities and to centralize policymaking in the executive branch. The Depression generated considerable public pressure for the national government to act to revive the nation's economy, to help those hardest hit by the collapse, and to regulate business and industry in an effort to prevent recurrence of the disaster. President Roosevelt responded to public demands for action by proposing the New Deal, a legislative package of reform measures that involved the federal government more deeply in the nation's economy than ever before.

World War II also served to increase presidential power. Wars in general enhance presidential power as presidents exercise their authority as commanders in chief and Congress delegates extraordinary powers to the chief executive to expedite the war effort. Indeed, during World War II, Congress ceded so many powers to the presidency that scholars often refer to FDR during the war years as a constitutional dictator. It was President Roosevelt, you recall, who ordered the internment of American citizens of Japanese descent living on the West Coast.

By and large, the changes in the presidency that took place during the 1930s and 1940s remained after the Depression and World War II were over. The size and scope of federal governmental activities continued to grow, especially during the 1960s and early 1970s. In foreign affairs, meanwhile, the United States assumed leadership of the Western alliance against the spread of international communism, fighting wars in Korea and Vietnam. Both of these developments served to maintain and enhance presidential power in the postwar years. What's more, the presidency had now become the focus of growing public expectations about the responsibility of government to solve the nation's problems.[9]

Scholars, too, looked to the presidency for positive policy leadership. Historian Arthur Schlesinger, Jr., for example, wrote admiringly of Franklin Roosevelt and his use of presidential power. His image of the chief executive was that of the **heroic president**, a larger-than-life president who personifies the best in American government. In this view, the nation needed a strong president to deal with the complex policy problems of the twentieth century.[10]

By the 1970s, however, scholars began to rethink their conception of the presidency as Presidents Johnson and Nixon committed American forces to combat in Southeast Asia without declaration of war, and Nixon became entangled in the Watergate controversy. Observers now warned that the presidency had grown too powerful. This time Schlesinger wrote of an **imperial president**, a president who uses the considerable power of the office in a harmful fashion.[11]

After Vietnam and Watergate, Congress reasserted itself, acting to restrict presidential authority in foreign and budgetary policymaking with such measures as the War Powers Act and the Budget Control Act. With the Ford and Carter administrations, scholars worried about a **tethered president**, a president whose powers are too constrained to provide necessary policy leadership. Some political scientists warned that political parties had grown too weak to assist presidential leadership, Congress had become too decentralized to bargain with, the bureaucracy had grown too large to direct, and the media had become too adversarial to give the president a chance. What's more, many observers believed that Congress had overreacted to Vietnam and Watergate, placing too many limitations on presidential power.[12]

Ronald Reagan restored luster to the presidency. Not only was Reagan the first president since Eisenhower to serve two complete terms, but, in his first year in office, he persuaded Congress to cut taxes and enact a major change in budgetary priorities, shifting funds from domestic programs to the military. Nonetheless, after the initial burst of success, President Reagan's initiatives often failed. Reagan was unable to convince Congress to adopt his social agenda on issues such as abortion, school prayer, and tuition tax credits for parents sending their children to private school. After 1981, Congress frequently rewrote Reagan budgets to cut money from defense to support social programs. On Reagan's pet foreign-policy issues, such as aid to the contras, the president generally achieved only partial successes. What's more, by the end of the Reagan administration, Congress had ended the defense buildup and enacted into law its own policy approaches in a number of issue areas, including civil rights, plant-closing notification, trade, and pollution control.[13]

Today, the presidency is an important participant in America's policymaking process, but not necessarily the dominant participant. As the long-running battle between the White House and Congress over aid to the contras demonstrated, the presidency must share power with other political actors and institutions. Moreover, the relative influence of the presidency varies depending on the issue, the political climate, and the political resources of the incumbent.

The Two-Presidencies Thesis

The **two-presidencies thesis** is the hypothesis that presidents have more influence over foreign affairs than domestic policymaking. The proponents of the two-presidencies thesis offer several theoretical explanations for the phenomenon. As commander in chief of the armed forces and as head of state, they say, the president possesses clearer constitutional authority in foreign and defense policy than in most other policy areas. Members of Congress, meanwhile, often have less interest in, and knowledge about, foreign policymaking than domestic politics. Also, fewer interest groups pressure Congress on foreign-policy matters than on domestic policy.

Research shows that presidents do indeed enjoy a higher level of support on international issues, but for only a limited period of time and only under special circumstances. Looking at congressional votes taken between 1946 and 1982, one political scientist discovered congressional backing for presidential initiatives in international affairs increased for a thirty-day period after the visible use of military force. At other times and under other circumstances, however, the study found no significant difference in the level of congressional support between domestic and foreign-policy issues. The researcher explained this phenomenon as a result of the short-term psychological tendency of the public (and members of Congress, as well) to rally round the president in times of international crisis.[14]

Perhaps the best assessment of the debate over the two-presidencies thesis comes from political scientists Gary King and Lyn Ragsdale. They believe that the concept of one presidency for foreign policy and another for domestic policy is simplistic. Instead of two presidencies, King and Ragsdale argue that there are multiple presidencies. In their view, presidential influence in policy-making varies among a broad range of issues.[15]

The Modern Presidency and the Media

The modern president has become a media figure. Television in particular is "up close and personal," focusing on the national level of government and the person of the president. One study of TV coverage of the presidency and Congress in 1977 found that the three major networks ran 3,556 news stories on the presidency, compared to only 2,080 stories about Congress.[16]

Research indicates that television news coverage can shape the standard by which citizens evaluate presidential performance, by focusing on one set of issues while ignoring others. One study found, for example, that if people are shown news stories that focus on national defense, they then tend to judge the president on the basis of defense issues. The authors of the study conclude that television's extensive coverage of the Iranian hostage crisis in 1980 probably hurt President Carter because it led voters to cast their ballots for, or against, the president on the basis of his handling of that issue.[17]

Knowing the importance of the media, presidents and their staffs go to extraordinary lengths to influence news coverage. No recent presidency was more attuned to public-relations than the Reagan administration. "This was a PR outfit that became president and took over the country," said Leslie Janka, a former deputy press secretary for President Reagan. "The Constitution forced them to do things like make a budget, run foreign policy, and all that.... But their first, last, and overarching activity was public relations."[18]

Some observers believe that public relations concerns often guided Reagan administration policy decisions. Before the Reagan administration decided to bomb Qaddafi's Libya in 1986 for allegedly supporting international terrorism, presidential pollster Richard Wirthlin conducted opinion surveys to gauge public reaction to American military action. Wirthlin's polls found that public opinion favored military action, as long as the strike was seen as a quick, reluctant response to Libyan provocation. Reagan ordered the bombing raid and, sure enough, polls taken after the attack showed the president's popularity soared to 68 percent approval, the high point of his presidency.[19]

THE ORGANIZATION OF THE PRESIDENCY

The development of the modern presidency has been accompanied by a significant growth in both the size and power of the presidential bureaucracy, that is, the White House staff and the Executive Office of the President. Early chief executives wrote their own speeches and even answered their own mail. They had only a few aides, whom they paid from their own funds. Congress subsequently authorized the president to employ aides and advisers using government funds. In the late 1920s, President Herbert Hoover had four aides and a support staff of forty. Franklin Roosevelt increased the number of White House assistants to a dozen with a support staff of fifty. By the 1950s, the number of White House assistants had jumped to 320. Today, well over fifteen hundred people work for either the White House or the Executive Office of the President.[20]

The White House Staff

The White House staff consists of personal aides, assistants, and advisers to the president, including a press secretary, several speech writers, an appointments secretary, a national security adviser, a legislative liaison, a counselor to the president, a host of special assistants, and a chief of staff. Each of these individuals has at least one deputy, secretarial assistance, and a support staff. The president selects the White House staff without need of Senate confirmation. As with most presidential appointees (the exceptions are federal judges and regulatory commissioners), White House staff members serve at the president's pleasure (meaning the president can fire them at will).

Political loyalty is usually the foremost criterion the president uses in selecting a staff. When Jimmy Carter became president, for example, he brought in Hamilton Jordan, Jody Powell, and other people from his campaign team to run the White House. Although these individuals had little experience in Washington politics, Carter knew he could count on their loyalty. George Bush, meanwhile, named New Hampshire Governor John Sununu to head his White House staff. Sununu, another Washington outsider, played an indispensable role in helping Bush win the New Hampshire Republican primary.

The White House staff is involved in both policy and politics. They guide the cabinet, screen key appointments, advise the president on policy, and act to see that the president's wishes are carried out. The staff also tries to make the president look good politically. In 1986, for example, the Reagan White House faced an embarrassing situation over a summit conference held between President Reagan and Soviet leader Mikhail Gorbachev in Reykjavik, Iceland, at which the two leaders discussed arms control. After the meeting, Reagan apparently could not remember whether or not he had agreed to a Gorbachev proposal for each country to eliminate all of its nuclear weapons.

The White House staff acted quickly to put a good face on the situation, issuing press releases and holding briefings designed to emphasize the positive aspects of the conference. Subsequently, White House Chief of Staff Donald Regan described his work to make the president look good in the following words: "Some of us are like a shovel brigade that follows a parade down Main Street cleaning up. We took Reykjavik and turned what was really a sour situation into something that turned out pretty well."[21]

The Executive Office of the President

Congress established the Executive Office of the President in 1939 after a special investigative commission concluded that the responsibilities of the presidency were too great for any one individual. "The president needs help," the committee said. Congress established the Executive Office, allowing the president to create and disband components without further congressional authorization. Today, the major agencies of the Executive Office are the Office of Management and Budget (OMB), National Security Council (NSC), Council of Economic Advisers (CEA), Council on Environmental Quality, Office of Science and Technology Policy, Office of the Special Representative for Trade Negotiations, and Intelligence Oversight Board. Of these agencies, the first two agencies are the most prominent.

The OMB is an important instrument for presidential control of the executive branch. It assists the president in preparing the annual federal budget to be submitted to Congress, screens bills drawn up by executive departments to ensure that they don't conflict with the president's policy goals, monitors expenditures by executive-branch departments, and evaluates regulations proposed by executive agencies. As with other federal agencies, most OMB personnel below the level of executive management are career employees chosen through a merit hiring system. The president appoints the director of the OMB and other top-level agency officials pending Senate confirmation.

The National Security Council (NSC) is composed of the president, vice-president, secretaries of state and defense, and others the president may choose to include, such as the national security adviser, the head of the Joint Chiefs of Staff, and the director of the Central Intelligence Agency (CIA). Although the NSC was created primarily as an advisory body, it has increasingly become involved in policy formulation and implementation. During the Nixon years, National Security Adviser Henry Kissinger became the guiding force behind American foreign policy. In the Reagan presidency, the NSC staff planned and directed the Grenada invasion, the air raid against Libya, the arms sales to Iran, and the transfer of profits from those sales to the contras. The last, you recall, was reportedly accomplished without presidential knowledge or consent.

The Growing White House Bureaucracy

The size and policymaking importance of the White House staff and the Executive Office of the President have grown for a number of reasons. First, the role of the president in the policymaking process has expanded significantly. The job is now too big for one person, and today's complex policy problems require expertise that most presidents don't have, especially after spending four to ten years on the campaign trail.

Second, the presidential bureaucracy has been augmented by the addition of public relations and media experts, whose job is to sell and resell the president. It's as if the campaign for reelection begins on inauguration day. In the Carter administration, for example, the White House staff included an assistant to the president for public liaison with the American Jewish community, a liaison for minority affairs, and a media aide (whom Carter's more irreverent critics referred to as a presidential assistant in charge of symbolism).

Third, growth has a way of feeding on itself. Every new council needs a staff; every new adviser requires a deputy. Moreover, people hired to deal with a crisis seldom depart once the crisis is over. Instead, they find new work for themselves and stay on as part of the permanent White House bureaucracy.[22]

Finally, the White House is generally uncomfortable with the federal bureaucracy. Bureaucracies are slow and often intractable, and those conditions make activist presidents impatient. Bureaucrats also have interests of their own: They are loyal to their jobs, their departments, and the programs they administer, but not necessarily to the president, especially if the president wants to reorganize the bureaucracy or cut back programs. This trait makes reform-minded presidents distrustful. Executive department heads (that is, the cabinet) are appointed by the president, but they are often chosen for political reasons rather than their loyalty to the president and administration programs. Also, over time, department heads tend to adopt the perspectives of the bureaucracies they head—it's a phenomenon Nixon aide John Ehrlichman once referred to as "marrying the natives." Consequently, presidents turn to people whose loyalty is more certain, the White House staff.

The Presidential Bureaucracy and Presidential Decision Making

Presidential decision-making styles differ. Some presidents, such as Kennedy, Nixon, and Carter, are reluctant to delegate authority to their aides, preferring to do everything themselves. Kennedy, for example, was known to read long reports from cover to cover and to plan menus for state dinners. Carter, meanwhile, immersed himself in the minutiae of the office. He checked the

President George Bush meets with his cabinet.

arithmetic in budget tables and corrected the grammar of staff memos. He even reviewed requests to use the White House tennis courts. Carter recognized that such activities were a ridiculous waste of his time, of course, but he still preferred to do things himself.[23]

Other presidents, such as Eisenhower, Ford, and Reagan, prefer to delegate considerable authority to their subordinates. President Reagan, for example, came to office with certain overriding policy goals, but he was notorious for his lack of knowledge and interest in the details of public policy. One of Reagan's former advisers described the president's understanding of policy issues as follows: "In my experience, he fails the essay questions but gets the multiple choices."[24] Reagan chose to focus his attention on the big picture and leave the details to his aides, in the process giving them considerable power.

President Bush's approach to leadership combines aspects of a hands-on managerial style with those of a chief executive who delegates a good deal of authority to subordinates. On one hand, Bush enjoys being at the center of the decision-making process, particularly on foreign-policy matters (about which he has more background and expertise). After the United States invaded Panama, for example, Bush personally telephoned the leaders of several Latin American countries to explain the action. On the other hand, Bush has delegated considerable policymaking authority to cabinet members and advisers, especially to trusted old friends, such as Secretary of State James Baker, Secretary of Commerce Robert Mosbacher, Secretary of the Treasury Nicholas Brady, and Secretary of Defense Richard Cheney. Baker, for instance, negotiated the contra-aid deal with Congress.[25]

Problems of the Presidential Bureaucracy

The presidential bureaucracy is essential to the effective operation of the modern presidency, but it can also present problems. First, the White House staff may isolate the president. Richard Nixon, for example, permitted his chief of staff, H. R. Haldeman, to build a wall around the president. This isolation forced Nixon to depend on a few staff members—Haldeman in particular—to present him with a variety of ideas.

Second, presidential aides may not be up to the task of advising the president on policy issues and helping the president manage the executive branch. Members of the White House staff, in particular, are chosen primarily for their loyalty. Frequently, they are former campaign managers, given the task of running the country whether they have the background or not. Jimmy Carter, for example, named Frank Moore his liaison with Congress. Moore had been liaison to the Georgia legislature when Carter was governor, but, like Carter, Moore had no experience in Washington politics. He failed to return calls, ignored consultations, and generally appeared indifferent to the political needs of members of Congress. As a result, Carter's influence with Congress waned.[26]

Third, presidential advisers may go into business for themselves, becoming, in effect, assistant presidents. In the Iran-contra scandal, for instance, Colonel North and Admiral Poindexter apparently made major policy decisions in the basement of the White House with neither the president's knowledge nor his consent. As a result of their actions, United States foreign policy was left in shambles, and the president was weakened.

Finally, presidential advisers tend to compete with one another for influence with their boss. Some disputes center on policy, but others involve petty rivalries and jealousies. A certain amount of competition within an administration can be healthy if it enables the president to be presented with alternative policy proposals. Taken to an extreme, however, political infighting dissipates energy and gives the appearance that the White House is divided over policy. In the Reagan administration, bitter and often public disputes arose among cabinet officers and members of the White House staff over various policy matters, including Iran.

THE PERSONAL PRESIDENCY

The presidency more than any other position in American government is a personal office. Although environmental factors and the nature of political coalitions probably have more to do with presidential success, the skills, abilities, and personality of the incumbent officeholder play a role as well. Indeed, one political scientist argues that presidential influence depends on the compatibility between the personality and skills of the president and the circumstances under which the president must exercise leadership.[27]

The Power to Persuade

Political scientist Richard Neustadt believes that presidents succeed or fail based upon their skills as political bargainers. The power of the presidency, says Neustadt, is the power to persuade others in political life to cooperate voluntarily. Presidents must resort to persuasion because they lack authority to command public officials, other than the staff, cabinet, and armed forces. Because of separation of powers, the president has no authority to order compliance from Congress or the federal judiciary. Federalism ensures that presidents cannot command state officials.[28]

Moreover, the interests of other political actors don't always coincide with the concerns of the president. While presidents worry about their reelection by voters nationwide, members of Congress focus on winning reelection from their districts or states, whose voters are often more concerned about local problems than national issues. Farm-belt representatives, for example, oppose reductions in farm-price supports that the president may favor in order to reduce the budget deficit.

The president cannot necessarily count on the cooperation of the federal bureaucracy. While presidents and their programs come and go, the bureaucracy stays. Except for the White House staff, the Executive Office, and the cabinet—all of whom serve at the pleasure of the president—the loyalty of federal employees lies with their jobs in their own little niches in the bureaucracy, not with the president's program. A chief executive who wants to reorganize the bureaucracy or cut federal programs invariably meets resistance from within the executive branch.

Consequently, Neustadt says, presidents must bargain with other political actors and groups to try to win their cooperation. Presidents are brokers, consensus builders. In this task, presidents have several assets: they have a number of appointments to make; they prepare a budget; they can help supporters raise money for reelection; and they can appeal to others on the basis of the national interest or party loyalty.

To use these assets to their fullest, presidents must understand the dynamics of political power. Lyndon Johnson, for example, learned as majority leader in the Senate how to build a political coalition to get legislation passed. In the White House, he put those skills to work and won passage for his legislative program (known as the Great Society). In contrast, Jimmy Carter never mastered the mechanics of political power. He ran for president as an outsider, someone who would ride into Washington and clean up the town. Once in office, Carter appeared standoffish. He had won the Democratic nomination and been elected president without having to bargain with the Washington establishment, and he thought he could govern without bargaining. He was wrong. Politics involves negotiation, give-and-take, compromise. Carter never understood that and consequently was frustrated in many of his goals.

Going Public

Professor Samuel Kernell believes that contemporary presidents frequently use the strategy of appealing to the general public to enhance their position in Washington politics. While political bargaining involves an exchange of favors, "going public," as Kernell calls it, is more akin to force than negotiation. By going public, the president appeals to voters to pressure other political actors to support the president's goals. In 1981, for example, President Reagan went on television to ask citizens to contact their representatives in Congress to support his economic program. The public responded, and Congress approved the president's budget proposals.

Going public isn't new—Franklin Roosevelt was famous for his fireside chats—but the strategy has now become more common. Modern communications and transportation technologies make going public relatively easy. Moreover, today's presidential selection process tends to favor people who are better at public appeals than political bargaining. Perhaps most important, going public has become an easier and more efficient method for achieving political goals than bargaining. In the 1950s, a president pushing a policy agenda had to bargain with a handful of party leaders and committee chairs in Congress. The reforms of the 1970s, however, fragmented power in Congress, increasing the number of members of Congress with whom a president must negotiate. What's more, the number of interest groups active in Washington politics has increased as well. As a result, it has become easier for presidents to go public than to engage in political bargaining.[29]

In practice, contemporary presidents use both political bargaining and going public, depending on the issue. In general, presidential appeals to the public are most effective on high-profile issues, such as bottom-line budget priorities or tax reform. Going public is less effective, however, when it comes to the arcane details of fairly obscure policies, such as cargo-preference requirements for United States flag shipping vessels or soybean price supports. The public is too ill-informed and uninterested in such issues to respond to presidential appeals. Instead, the best strategy for presidential influence is for the president to negotiate with key members of Congress and the various interest groups involved.

The Presidential Character

Political scientist James David Barber believes that a president's performance in office depends on personality traits formed primarily during childhood but also in adolescence and early adulthood. Barber classifies personality along two dimensions. The first dimension involves the amount of energy an indi-

A high point of Jimmy Carter's presidency came in 1978 when he brought together Egypt's Anwar Sadat (left) and Israel's Menachem Begin at Camp David to negotiate a peace treaty between their countries.

vidual brings to the office. Active presidents throw themselves into their work, immersing themselves in the details of the office. Barber says that Presidents Franklin Roosevelt, Truman, Kennedy, Lyndon Johnson, Nixon, Ford, and Carter were active presidents. In contrast, passive presidents devote relatively little energy and effort to the job. According to Barber, Presidents Warren G. Harding, William Howard Taft, Calvin Coolidge, Eisenhower, and Reagan were passive presidents.

The second dimension to Barber's personality classification scheme involves presidents' attitudes toward their job. Positive presidents enjoy their work. They have an optimistic, positive attitude. In contrast, negative presidents feel burdened by the weight of the office. They tend to be pessimists.

Barber uses these two dimensions to create four general types of presidential personalities. According to Barber, the best type of personality for a president is active-positive. This president is self-confident, optimistic, flexible, and enjoys the job. Franklin Roosevelt, for example, was a supremely self-confident man who set out to master the intricacies of his office. He was a flexible, skillful politician who truly enjoyed being president. Barber also classifies Truman, Kennedy, Ford, Carter, and Bush as active-positive presidents.

Barber believes that the most dangerous chief executive is the active-negative president. This type of president puts great energy into work, but derives little pleasure from it. Barber says that active-negative presidents suffer from low self-esteem and tend to view political disputes in terms of personal success or failure. They are pessimistic, driven, and compulsive. Richard Nixon is an example of a president Barber classifies as active-negative. He was personally insecure, combative, tough, and vindictive. He was a loner who saw himself as a righteous leader besieged by enemies. Other examples of active-negative presidents include Herbert Hoover and Lyndon Johnson.

Barber lists two other categories of presidential personalities, passive-positive and passive-negative. Barber identifies Eisenhower as an example of a passive-negative president, that is, one who is involved in politics out of a sense of duty. The passive-negative president avoids conflict and uncertainty and just plain dislikes politics. Finally, the passive-positive president is indecisive and superficially optimistic. This president tends to react rather than initiate. Barber classifies Reagan as passive-positive.[30]

Scholars identify a number of weaknesses in Barber's classification scheme. It isn't always clear, for example, in which category a president should be placed. President Reagan can be labeled *passive*, for example, because of his inattentiveness and willingness to allow aides to carry a good deal of his workload. Nonetheless, the Reagan administration had a substantial impact on public policy, taking important initiatives in a wide range of policy areas. Is that the record of a passive president? Moreover, some critics complain that Barber's categories are so broad as to be little help in differentiating among presidents. Barber puts Presidents Franklin Roosevelt and Jimmy Carter in the same category—active-positive. How helpful is Barber's classification scheme if two such different presidents fit in the same category?

PRESIDENTIAL POPULARITY

Many political scientists believe that popular support influences presidential power. Personal popularity affects the position of the president as a political broker and the ability of the president to appeal to the public for policy support. A president who is politically popular can offer more benefits and inducements to other political actors for their cooperation than can an unpopular chief executive. Campaign help from a popular president is more valuable and support for legislative proposals is more effective. Similarly, a popular president can claim to speak for the national interest with greater credibility. Lyndon Johnson enjoyed considerably more political influence after his landslide reelection victory in 1964, for example, than did Richard Nixon in the midst of the Watergate scandal in early 1974.

A popular chief executive is also better positioned to ask the public to pressure members of Congress on behalf of presidential programs. In 1981, for instance, President Reagan, whose popularity peaked after a failed assassination attempt, was able to generate broad public support for his economic program. By 1982, however, Reagan's standing in the polls had slipped because of a serious economic downturn. This time, when Reagan went public over budget issues, the strategy failed.

Political scientists have a good deal of data on presidential popularity. For more than forty years, the Gallup Poll has asked national samples of Americans the following question every month or so: "Do you approve or disapprove of the way _____ is handling his job as president?" Figure 9.1 shows the course of presidential popularity for the full eight years of the Reagan presidency.

As you can see from the figure, a president's popularity responds to events. Reagan's standing in the polls rose early in his first term after a failed assassination attempt but then fell in 1982 as the economy soured. The president's popular approval rating picked up in 1983 as the economy improved, and then jumped after the Grenada invasion. Reagan's popularity rose again in 1986 after the bombing raid on Libya. In late 1986, however, the president's poll standing plummeted as talk of the Iran-contra scandal filled the news.

In domestic policy matters, presidential popularity rises with good news, falls with bad news. Although Reagan was called the "Teflon President" (regardless of what he did wrong, no blame stuck to him), he was an unpopular president during the recession of 1982. Only when the economy began to recover did Reagan's popular standing again exceed the 50 percent approval mark.

In times of international crisis, however, a president's standing in the polls almost always rises, at least in the short run, regardless of whether the news is good or bad. As you can see from the figure, President Reagan's popularity increased not only after the Grenada invasion, which most observers considered a success, but also after the tragic events of the terrorist bombing of the American embassy in Beirut and the Iraqi missile attack against the USS *Stark*.

One scholar explains this phenomenon on the basis of public response to cues from political leaders and the press. In times of domestic crisis, such as an economic downturn or severe inflation, the president is usually the target of considerable criticism from political opponents and the press. When the nation appears threatened from abroad, however, the political criticism that generally accompanies presidential action is muted. Consequently, the White House is able to get its interpretation of events before the public, while opposition political leaders react cautiously to avoid being perceived as undermining the president during a crisis. Hearing only one side, the public tends to support the president.

This doesn't mean, of course, that presidents can't be damaged by unfavorable international developments. In the long run, criticism builds if events develop poorly, and the president's popularity falls. This happened to Presi-

FIGURE 9.1
Presidential Popularity

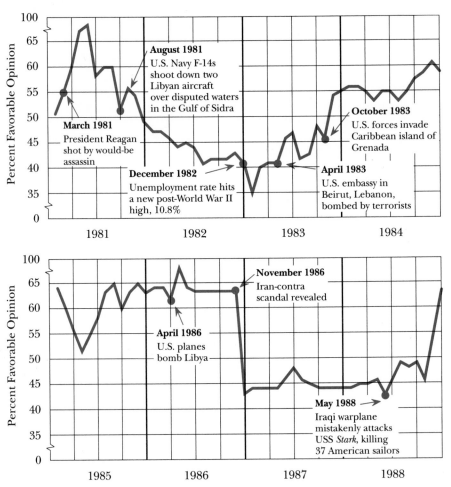

dent Truman with the Korean War, Lyndon Johnson with Vietnam, and Carter with the hostage crisis.[31]

Although popular presidents are more influential than unpopular presidents, the Reagan presidency demonstrates that personal popularity alone isn't sufficient to guarantee a president policy success. In 1981, when Reagan's poll standing was high, the president succeeded in convincing Congress to cut taxes and adopt his budget priorities. As we would expect, Reagan's influence waned in 1982 as his popularity fell. Although the president's popularity regained lost ground and even hit a new high in 1986, Reagan's political influence never fully recovered. Even in 1986, when President Reagan's approval rating soared above the 60 percent mark, Congress rewrote Reagan's budget and refused to approve military aid to the contras.

These developments illustrate that presidents need more than just public approval to influence policy. The difference between 1981 and 1986 lay with the political balance in Congress. In 1981, the Republican party controlled the Senate and held enough seats in the House to win most major votes with the support of a number of conservative southern Democrats. By 1986, though, the GOP majority in the Senate had shrunk and the Democrats had added enough seats in the House so that the Republican–conservative Democrat coalition was no longer a majority. Then, after 1986, President Reagan's influence declined even further as Democrats won control of the Senate.

CONCLUSION: THE PRESIDENCY AND PUBLIC POLICY

What role does the presidency play in America's policymaking process? That is a complex question which can't be answered easily. Nonetheless, we can make a few points.

First, presidential influence depends on a number of factors, including the president's constitutional position, the make-up of political coalitions, the role of the presidential bureaucracy, the political skills and personality of the incumbent, the president's popular standing, and a range of environmental factors too numerous to mention. One important environmental factor for President Bush, and probably his successor as well, is the federal budget deficit. Presidents can't propose policy initiatives without first considering how to pay for them.

Second, presidential influence varies, depending on the issue and the time. As we have seen, President Reagan was most influential in the first year of his first term, and on budget matters. Reagan was less successful on social issues, such as abortion, and less influential later in his administration.

Finally, a president's overall impact on government is generally limited to the margins of public policy. To be sure, the presidency is a major element in American government and the president is an important political actor. Nonetheless, the president's power is limited by constitutional and environmental factors. Separation of powers with checks and balances and the federal system ensure that the president must share authority with other political actors and governmental institutions. In the meantime, environmental factors, such as the deficit, reduce the president's policy options. In sum, then, we can say about the presidency what we can say about each of the other institutions of American government—it influences public policy but it doesn't control.

KEY TERMS

chief executive	heroic president
civilian supremacy of the armed forces	imperial president
	pardon
executive agreements	reprieve
executive order	tethered president
head of state	two-presidencies thesis

NOTES

1. Bert A. Rockman, "Reforming the Presidency: Nonproblems and Problems," *PS: Political Science and Politics*, Summer 1987, pp. 643–49.
2. Raoul Berger, *Impeachment: The Constitutional Problems* (Cambridge, MA: Harvard University Press, 1973).
3. Quoted in Michael Nelson, "Choosing the Vice President," *PS: Political Science and Politics*, Fall 1988, p. 859.
4. Paul C. Light, *Vice-Presidential Power* (Baltimore: Johns Hopkins University Press, 1984).
5. Gary King and Lyn Ragsdale, *The Elusive Executive: Discovering Statistical Patterns in the Presidency* (Washington, DC: Congressional Quarterly Press, 1988), pp. 59–60.
6. Louis Fisher, *Presidents and Congress* (New York: Macmillan, 1972); and Thomas E. Cronin, *The State of the Presidency*, 2d ed. (Boston: Little, Brown, 1980).
7. George C. Edwards III and Stephen J. Wayne, *Presidential Leadership: Politics and Policy Making* (New York: St. Martin's Press, 1985), p. 344.
8. Lawrence C. Chamberlain, *The President, Congress, and Legislation* (New York: Columbia University Press, 1984).
9. Sidney M. Milkis, "The Presidency, Democratic Reform, and Constitutional Change," *PS: Political Science and Politics*, Summer 1987, pp. 628–29.
10. Arthur M. Schlesinger, Jr., *The Age of Roosevelt—The Coming of the New Deal*, vol. II (Boston: Houghton Mifflin, 1958).
11. Arthur M. Schlesinger, Jr., *The Imperial Presidency* (Boston: Houghton Mifflin, 1973).
12. Thomas Franck, ed., *The Tethered Presidency* (New York: New York University Press, 1981).
13. "Reagan Added Luster but Little Clout to Office," *CQ Weekly Report*, 7 January 1989, pp. 3–12.
14. Richard J. Stoll, "The Sound of the Guns," *American Politics Quarterly* 15 (April 1987): 223–37.
15. King and Ragsdale, p. 53.
16. Michael J. Robinson, "Three Faces of Congressional Media," in Thomas E. Mann and Norman J. Ornstein, eds., *The New Congress* (Washington, DC: American Enterprise Institute, 1981), p. 91n.
17. Shanto Iyengar and Donald R. Kinder, *News That Matters: Television and American Opinion* (Chicago: University of Chicago Press, 1987), pp. 114–15.

18. Quoted in Mark Hertsgaard, "How Ronald Reagan Turned News Hounds into Lap Dogs," *Washington Post*, National Weekly Edition, 29 August–4 September 1988, p. 25.
19. Jane Mayer and Doyle McManus, *Landslide: The Unmaking of the President, 1984–88* (Boston: Houghton Mifflin, 1988), p. 221.
20. Robert E. DiClerico, *The American President* (Englewood Cliffs, NJ: Prentice-Hall, 1979), p. 210.
21. Quoted in James Reston, "Reagan Needs Help, Not Blame," *Houston Chronicle*, 25 November 1986, sec. 1, p. 14.
22. Thomas E. Cronin, *The State of the Presidency*, 2d ed. (Boston: Little, Brown, 1980), pp. 229–81.
23. Harold M. Barger, *The Impossible Presidency: Illusions and Realities of Executive Power* (Glenview, IL: Scott, Foresman, 1984), pp. 215–16.
24. Quoted in Leslie H. Gelb, "The Mind of the President," *New York Times Magazine*, 6 October 1985, p. 112.
25. David Hoffman and Ann Devroy, "The Open Oval Office Door," *Washington Post*, National Weekly Edition, 14–20 August 1989, pp. 6–7; Michael Duffy, "Mr. Consensus," *Time*, 21 August 1989, pp. 16–22.
26. Barger, p. 129.
27. Dean Keith Simonton, *Why Presidents Succeed: A Political Psychology of Leadership* (New Haven: Yale University Press, 1987), p. 235.
28. Richard E. Neustadt, *Presidential Power: The Politics of Leadership* (New York: Wiley, 1960).
29. Samuel Kernell, *Going Public: New Strategies of Presidential Leadership* (Washington, DC: Congressional Quarterly Press, 1986).
30. James David Barber, *The Presidential Character*, 3d ed. (Englewood Cliffs, NJ: Prentice-Hall, 1985); "Carter and Reagan: Clues to Their Character," *U.S. News & World Report*, 27 October 1980, pp. 30–33.
31. Richard Brody, "International Crises: A Rallying Point for the President?" *Public Opinion*, December/January 1984, pp. 41–43, 60.

SUGGESTED READINGS

Edwards, George C. III, and Wayne, Stephen J. *Presidential Leadership*. 2d ed. New York: St. Martin's Press, 1990.
Greenstein, Fred I. *Leadership in the Modern Presidency*. Cambridge, MA: Harvard University Press, 1988.
Hart, John. *The Presidential Branch*. New York: Pergamon, 1987.
Kernell, Samuel. *Going Public: New Strategies of Presidential Leadership*. Washington, DC: Congressional Quarterly Press, 1986.
King, Gary, and Ragsdale, Lyn. *The Elusive Executive: Discovering Statistical Patterns in the Presidency*. Washington, DC: Congressional Quarterly Press, 1988.
Light, Paul C. *Vice-Presidential Power*. Baltimore, MD: Johns Hopkins University Press, 1984.
Mayer, Jane, and McManus, Doyle. *Landslide: The Unmaking of the President, 1984–88*. Boston, MA: Houghton Mifflin, 1988.
Simonton, Dean Keith. *Why Presidents Succeed: A Political Psychology of Leadership*. New Haven, CT: Yale University Press, 1987.

10

THE FEDERAL BUREAUCRACY

ORGANIZATION OF THE BUREAUCRACY
PERSONNEL
RULEMAKING
POLITICS AND ADMINISTRATION
CONCLUSION: ADMINISTRATIVE POLICYMAKING

LEARNING OBJECTIVES

1. To outline the organization of the federal bureaucracy.
2. To describe the relationship between the organization of the federal bureaucracy and politics.
3. To trace the history of federal personnel policies from the spoils system to recent civil service reforms.
4. To explain how the professional backgrounds of federal bureaucratic managers can affect administrative policymaking.
5. To describe the steps in the rulemaking process.
6. To identify the perspectives and political resources each of the following has in the administrative process: the president, Congress, interest groups, and bureaucrats themselves.
7. To compare and contrast the concepts of subgovernments and issue networks.

TED stands for turtle-excluder device. Sewn into a fishing net, a TED works like a trapdoor to allow sea turtles to escape. Otherwise, they drown. Environmentalists insist that shrimpers use TEDs to protect the Kemp's ridley turtle and other endangered sea turtles. Shrimpers, however, maintain that TEDs endanger their livelihood because they permit shrimp to escape, thus reducing the size of their catch. The two sides have been fighting over the use of TEDs for more than a decade.

In 1973, Congress passed, and the president signed into law, the Endangered Species Act. The measure's goal was to protect threatened wildlife from extinction by making it illegal to buy, sell, possess, export, or import any endangered or threatened species or any product made from an endangered species.[1] Congress empowered the National Marine Fisheries Service, a division of the National Oceanic and Atmospheric Administration (NOAA), to administer the program by drafting rules to protect animals on the list of endangered and threatened species.

The Kemp's ridley sea turtle has been on the endangered species list since the early 1970s. After the government of Mexico took steps to protect the turtle's nesting areas, scientists estimated the most serious remaining threat to the survival of the Kemp's ridley was trawling nets pulled by shrimp boats. The National Marine Fisheries Service developed the turtle-excluder device to protect the turtles and, in 1980, the agency asked shrimpers to use TEDs voluntarily. For the most part, though, shrimpers refused to cooperate, arguing that TEDs reduced the size of their catch.

By 1986, environmental interest groups lost patience with the government and the shrimpers. The Center for Marine Conservation, an environmentalist organization, threatened to file suit against the government to ask a federal court to order the National Marine Fisheries Service to make TEDs mandatory. To head off the lawsuit, the agency drafted rules to require the use of TEDs, but delayed their imposition to allow conservationists and shrimpers an opportunity to negotiate their differences.

When the two sides failed to reach agreement, Congress intervened to require shrimpers to phase in the use of TEDs. Shrimpers trawling offshore would have to begin using TEDs in May 1989, while shrimpers working inland waters, such as bays and sounds, could wait until the spring of 1990. Although shrimpers filed suit to block the law's enforcement, a federal court rejected their challenge.

Nonetheless, the imposition of turtle-excluder devices did not go smoothly, at least not on the Gulf Coast. Angry shrimpers responded by burning their TEDs and blockading ports. After several days of confrontation between shrimpers and the Coast Guard, Secretary of Commerce Robert Mosbacher announced he was suspending enforcement of the TED rules for several months for further study.

This time it was the environmentalists' turn to go to court. The National Wildlife Federation filed suit against Mosbacher, saying he had no legal justification to suspend use of turtle-excluder devices and that his action violated the Endangered Species Act.[2] A federal judge agreed that Mosbacher lacked authority to halt enforcement of the act, but allowed him time to present an alternative plan to using TEDs. Mosbacher responded with a proposal to permit shrimpers to trawl without TEDs provided they limited tow times to 105 minutes between checking nets for trapped turtles. Shrimpers using TEDs could trawl without limits. Mosbacher's rationale for limiting tow times was that turtles can survive trapped in a net for as long as 105 minutes. Many conservationists, however, disagreed with that assessment. They also charged that the Coast Guard would be unable to enforce the tow-time limit.

As environmental groups prepared a lawsuit, the Commerce Department reversed itself one more time, again requiring turtle-excluder devices. Shrimpers not using TEDs could be fined as much as $8,000 for a first offense and $15,000 for a second offense. After a third offense, shrimpers could also suffer the confiscation of their boats. Shrimpers complained bitterly about the new TEDs rule, but most began using the apparatus rather than risk fine and loss of their boats.

The dispute over TEDs illustrates a number of important points about the role of the federal bureaucracy in America's policy process. First, federal agencies make important policy decisions. Congress typically writes legislation in broad terms, leaving room for bureaucrats to supply details. In the TEDs controversy, federal agencies determined that sea turtles are endangered, decided that shrimpers are a major threat to their survival, developed TEDs to protect the turtles, drafted rules for their use, and then changed the rules.

Second, bureaucratic decisions are political. Shrimpers, environmental interest groups, local officials from coastal areas, and members of Congress all pressured the bureaucracy to adopt and enforce rules favorable to their interests. Secretary of Commerce Mosbacher's decision to forgo enforcement of TEDs rules can only be described as a concession to political pressures from the shrimping industry and elected officials representing coastal areas. Ultimately, political pressures from environmentalists coupled with the threat of a lawsuit convinced Mosbacher and the Bush administration to require TEDs after all.

Finally, federal agencies function within America's system of checks and balances. The bureaucracy has power but, as with other elements of American government, bureaucratic power is not unchecked. In our example, both Congress and the federal courts intervened to redefine the ground rules under which federal agencies functioned.

ORGANIZATION OF THE BUREAUCRACY

Figure 10.1 diagrams the government of the United States. As you can see, the Constitution establishes the three branches of American government. The federal bureaucracy is contained within the executive branch.

The Constitution says little about the organization of the federal bureaucracy. It refers briefly to executive departments, but gives few details about their organization and responsibilities. Instead, Congress has created the executive departments, commissions, agencies, and bureaus of the federal bureaucracy on a piecemeal basis over the last two hundred years. As a result, the structures of the bureaucracy often reflect political compromise and historical accident rather than any conscious organizational philosophy or scheme. Let's consider the various types of structures in the executive branch.

Cabinet-Level Executive Departments

Cabinet-level executive departments administer a significant share of the activities of the federal government. In George Washington's day, the executive branch included five departments: State, Treasury, War, Navy, and the Office of the Attorney General. Subsequently, the War and Navy departments merged to form the Department of Defense, the Office of the Attorney General became the Justice Department, and Congress created ten additional departments: Interior, Agriculture, Commerce, Labor, Housing and Urban Development (HUD), Transportation, Energy, Health and Human Services, Education, and Veterans' Affairs. The two largest cabinet-level executive departments are Defense, and Health and Human Services. The Department of Defense has more than a million civilian employees, while Health and Human Services employs about 145,000 workers. Each department's budget exceeds $300 billion.

FIGURE 10.1
The Government of the United States

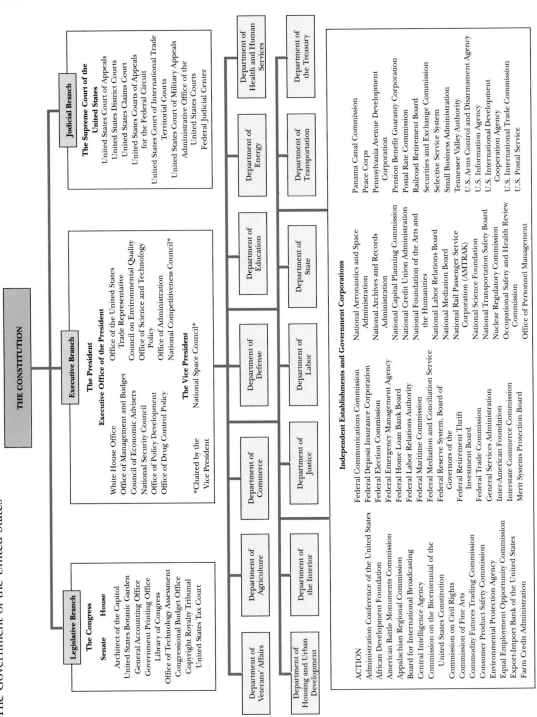

Each cabinet-level executive department includes a number of smaller administrative units. The National Oceanic and Atmospheric Administration (NOAA), for example, is a subdivision of the Commerce Department. The Coast Guard is part of the Department of Transportation. The Social Security Administration, Food and Drug Administration, and Center for Disease Control are among the many subunits of the Department of Health and Human Services.

Each of the cabinet-level executive departments is headed by a secretary, such as the secretary of state or secretary of defense. The exception is the Justice Department, which is headed by the attorney general. The president appoints department secretaries and the attorney general pending Senate approval. Senate rejections of presidential nominees for these posts are rare because senators generally believe that presidents should be allowed to choose their own people to head executive departments. Also, presidents usually withdraw the names of individuals who prove too controversial. The most recent rejection of a nominee came in 1989 when the Senate defeated John Tower, President Bush's selection to be secretary of defense. Tower suffered from charges of heavy drinking, womanizing, and too close ties to defense contractors. Department secretaries and the attorney general serve at the president's pleasure, meaning the president can remove them at will.

Presidents employ a number of criteria in selecting executive department heads. They look for knowledge, administrative ability, experience, loyalty, and congeniality. Presidents try to include women and minorities in the cabinet, and they like to have a geographical balance. Some cabinet posts may be given to reward campaign assistance. What's more, presidents often seek individuals who fit the style and image of their department and who will be acceptable to the interest groups with which their department works most closely. The secretary of the treasury, for example, is always a conservative individual who dresses like a banker. The secretary of agriculture is a farmer, usually from the Midwest. The secretary of the interior, meanwhile, is a rugged outdoors type from a western state who organizes hikes and goes mountain climbing.

The **cabinet** is an advisory group composed of the executive department heads and other officials the president may choose to include, such as the ambassador to the United Nations and the national security adviser. The policy-making role of the cabinet varies from president to president. President Eisenhower, for example, delegated considerable responsibilities to cabinet members. Most presidents, however, rely more heavily on the White House staff, the Executive Office of the President, and individual cabinet members than they do the cabinet as a whole. The cabinet includes too many people working from too many different perspectives to be an effective policymaking body. Moreover, the White House usually grows to distrust the cabinet. Eventually, members of the White House staff begin to suspect that department heads are growing too attached to the programs their departments administer and to the clientele groups they represent. Remember John

Ehrlichman's line about "marrying the natives"? Charles O. Dawes, who was Calvin Coolidge's vice-president, put it like this: "Cabinet members are vice-presidents in charge of spending, and as such they are natural enemies of the president."[3]

The traditional image of the cabinet is that its members' primary responsibilities are, first, counseling the president on policy formulation and, second, leading their departments in implementing policy. In practice, most executive department heads don't do much of either. For policymaking assistance, presidents usually turn to smaller groups of aides, advisers, and selected department heads, often including the secretaries of state, defense, and the treasury, and the attorney general. In fact, these four officials—the secretaries of state, defense, and the treasury, and the attorney general—are known as the **inner cabinet** because of their traditional close association to the president. Full cabinet meetings tend to become forums for presidential pep talks or show-and-tell sessions for cabinet members to discuss the latest developments in their departments. As for leading their departments, many secretaries soon learn that their departments are not easily led. Also, most department heads haven't time to concentrate on the details of administration. They are too busy dealing with Congress, doing public relations work with their department's constituents, selling the president's program, and campaigning for the president's reelection.

Independent Executive Agencies

Congress has created a number of executive-branch agencies that are not part of any of the fourteen cabinet-level departments, hence the designation independent executive agencies. Individual administrators head some of these agencies, such as the Peace Corps, National Aeronautics and Space Administration (NASA), Central Intelligence Agency (CIA), and Environmental Protection Agency (EPA). (In 1990, Congress debated legislation to elevate the EPA to a cabinet-level executive department.) Multimember boards administer other agencies, including the Federal Election Commission (FEC) and National Traffic Safety Board (NTSB). The president appoints both individual agency heads and board members, pending Senate confirmation. In some cases (as with the Small Business Administration), Congress has stipulated detailed qualifications for appointees.

Government Corporations

Government corporations are organized much like private corporations except that they are owned by the government instead of stockholders. Their organizational rationale is that an agency which makes a product or provides a service can be run by methods similar to those used in the private sector. The Postal Service, for example, is run by an eleven-member board of governors

Launch of NASA's space shuttle Columbia *at the Kennedy Space Center, June 27, 1982.*

appointed by the president to serve nine-year, overlapping terms. The board names a postmaster general, who is in charge of the day-to-day operation of the service. In addition to the Postal Service, the list of government corporations includes the National Rail Passenger Service Corporation (AMTRAK), Corporation for Public Broadcasting, Federal Deposit Insurance Corporation (FDIC), Commodity Credit Corporation, and Tennessee Valley Authority (TVA).

An important principle behind government corporations is that they be self-financing, at least to a large degree. In the case of the Postal Service, users pay most of the cost of operation through service charges. Not all government corporations, however, are financially self-sufficient. AMTRAK, for example, still requires a substantial subsidy from Congress to keep its trains rolling.

Foundations and Institutes

Foundations and institutes administer grant programs to local governments, universities, nonprofit institutions, and individuals for research in the natural and social sciences or for artistic endeavors. These agencies include the National Science Foundation and the National Foundation on the Arts and Humanities. Foundations and institutes are governed by multimember boards appointed by the president (with Senate concurrence) from lists of nominees submitted by various scientific and educational institutions.

Independent Regulatory Commissions

Since 1887, when the Interstate Commerce Commission was established to regulate railroads, Congress has created a number of independent commissions with the authority to regulate significant portions of economic life. The Federal Trade Commission (FTC) enforces antitrust laws against monopolies and protects consumers against deceptive advertising. The Federal Communications Commission (FCC) licenses and regulates radio and television stations. The Securities and Exchange Commission (SEC), meanwhile, regulates the sale of stocks and bonds.

One of Congress' motivations in creating independent regulatory agencies has been to insulate them from direct political pressure, especially from the White House. These agencies are headed by boards of three to seven members who are appointed by the president with Senate approval. Unlike cabinet members and the heads of other executive departments, however, commissioners cannot be removed by the president. Instead, they serve fixed, staggered terms ranging from three to fourteen years. As a result, a new president must usually wait several years before having much impact on the composition of the boards. Congress also generally requires that no more than a bare majority of board members be from the same political party.

A second motivation behind the establishment of independent regulatory commissions is to provide closer, more flexible regulation than Congress itself can offer through **statutory law**, that is, law that emerges from the legislative process. Consequently, Congress has delegated authority to these agencies to control various business practices using broad, general language. Congress authorized the FTC, for instance, to regulate advertising in the "public convenience, interest, or necessity." In the meantime, Congress empowered the Equal Employment Opportunity Commission (EEOC) "to prevent any person from engaging in any unlawful employment practice."

The New York Stock Exchange operates under the regulation of the Securities and Exchange Commission (SEC).

Private, Nonprofit Corporations

Finally, several dozen organizations, including the Rand Corporation, Institute for Defense Analysis, Aerospace Corporation, and Institute for Urban Studies, exist in a twilight zone between the public and private sectors. These organizations technically are not part of the federal bureaucracy; they are private, not-for-profit corporations. In general, however, they have been created at government initiative. Virtually their entire workload involves providing technical and advisory assistance on a contract basis to such governmental agencies as the Departments of Defense, Energy, Labor, and State, and to NASA.

The Politics of Organization

Traditional organization theory holds that the ideal bureaucratic model resembles a pyramid. A number of functional units, each responsible for a particular activity, sit at the bottom of the organizational pyramid. Each of these units is headed by an executive officer, who reports to a middle-level executive, who, in turn, oversees the activities of several functional units. A chief executive with final authority over the whole organization sits at the top of the organizational pyramid.

In contrast to the ideal bureaucratic model, the organization of the federal bureaucracy often seems haphazard or even eccentric. Sometimes, agencies share responsibilities for a single activity. For example, the Army Corps of Engineers in the Defense Department, the Soil Conservation Service in the Department of Agriculture, and the Bureau of Reclamation in the Interior Department are all involved in water-resource management. The system developed incrementally, and each step was logical in itself. The resulting arrangement, however, includes overlapping responsibilities, duplication of effort, and competition among agencies—features that seldom make for organizational efficiency. Nonetheless, Congress is unlikely to make any significant modifications in the system. Each of the agencies involved is under the jurisdiction of a different set of congressional committees and subcommittees, each of which jealously guards its prerogatives. The creation of a single agency in the bureaucracy to oversee water-resource development and conservation would require a reshuffling of committee and subcommittee jurisdictions in Congress, and that could not be achieved without a fierce political struggle.[4]

The bureaucracy is disorganized, and Congress, interest groups, and the bureaucracy itself like it that way. Committee and subcommittee chairs want to protect the jurisdictions of their own committees/subcommittees. Interest groups, meanwhile, often develop working relationships with committee and agency staffs, and they don't want to see those arrangements disturbed. Bureaucrats oppose reorganizations that might threaten their positions. In short, political forces supporting the organizational status quo are usually stronger than those favoring reorganization.

Examples of the politics of organization abound. In 1966, Congress created two separate agencies to administer the highway-safety program and authorized the president to appoint a single administrator to head both agencies. In that way, two Senate committees could have a voice in confirming the agency head.[5]

The structure of independent regulatory commissions reflects politics, too. Experts in organizational efficiency believe that administration by a single executive officer is more efficient than administration by plural executives. With the latter, no one is in charge; it's government by committee. Nevertheless, Congress has prescribed plural executives for the independent regulatory

Reprinted by permission of Newspaper Enterprise Association, Inc.

commissions. Why? Because Congress is concerned that a single executive could be controlled too easily by the president. Plural executives may be less efficient, but, Congress hopes, they will also be independent of the White House and more responsive to the legislative branch.[6] When politics and organizational theory clash, politics wins.

Then there's the case of the nonprofit corporations. The rationale for the use of nonprofits is that they can do certain activities faster and more efficiently than government. But there are political reasons for their existence as well. The bureaucracy is frequently too inflexible to undertake new and complex tasks. Agencies have personnel ceilings that can't be easily raised. After all, no one in Congress wants to be accused of voting to enlarge the federal bureaucracy. Moreover, reorganizing existing agencies can't be accomplished without a political dogfight. Consequently, Congress assigns activities to private nonprofit corporations. It's simply easier to spend money than it is to hire more personnel or reorganize the bureaucracy. The result is a political shell game. The federal government's activities and expenditures expand, while its work force remains surprisingly stable.[7]

PERSONNEL

The size of the federal bureaucracy has grown dramatically since the early days of the nation. In 1800, only about 3,000 persons worked for Uncle Sam. The number grew to 95,000 by 1881 and half a million in 1925. Today, the federal bureaucracy is the largest civilian work force in the noncommunist world, with more than 3 million employees stationed in every state and city in the country and almost every nation in the world.

In the last few decades, however, the number of federal employees has leveled off, despite a dramatic increase in federal spending. Congress has developed ways to increase federal government activities and federal spending without enlarging the federal bureaucracy. One technique is to use contract workers and consultants. Their salaries come from the federal government, but their names don't appear on federal personnel rosters. One study estimates that for every worker on the federal payroll, four others work indirectly for the government.[8] Another method Congress has used to keep the size of the federal bureaucracy in check has been to rely upon state and local bureaucrats to administer federal programs. Between 1960 and 1986, the size of the federal work force went from 2.4 to 3 million, while the number of state and local employees rose from 6.2 to 13.9 million.[9] Much (but certainly not all) of the increase in the size of state and local bureaucracies was the result of the growth in federal programs.

Employment Practices

Employment practices in the early days of the nation emphasized character, professional qualifications, and political compatibility with the administration in office. Under President Andrew Jackson (1829–37), however, political considerations became paramount. A new president would fire old government workers and replace them with friends and supporters. To the victors belong the spoils, they said, and federal jobs were the spoils. The method of hiring government employees from among the friends and supporters of elected officeholders was known as the **spoils system**.

For years, the spoils system was a prime target for reformers. Their efforts were unsuccessful, however, until 1881, when President James Garfield's assassination at the hands of a disgruntled office seeker provided the impetus the reformers needed. Congress reacted with the Pendleton Act (the Civil Service Act), creating a Civil Service Commission. Congress empowered the commission to establish a hiring system based on competitive examinations and to protect federal workers from dismissal for political reasons. Initially, the civil service system covered only about 10.5 percent of federal jobs, but Congress gradually expanded coverage to include most career federal workers. In 1939, Congress enacted another reform, the Hatch Act, to restrict the political activities of federal employees to voting and the private expression of views. The rationale behind the law was to protect government workers from being forced by their superiors to work for particular candidates.

Although civil service ended the spoils system, it too became the target of criticism. Many observers charged that the civil service system was too inflexible to reward merit, punish sloth, or transfer civil servants from one agency to another without having to scale a mountain of red tape. It was frequently easier to promote incompetent employees than to fire them. Other critics attacked **veterans' preference**, the system that awarded extra points on civil service exams to veterans of the armed forces. Opponents of veterans' preference charged that it violated the principle of merit selection and discriminated against nonveterans, particularly women.

Congress responded to complaints against the civil service system by passing a package of reforms in 1978. First, Congress established a Senior Executive Service (SES) composed of approximately eight thousand top civil servants who would be eligible for substantial merit bonuses but who could be transferred, demoted, or fired more easily than other federal employees. Second, Congress replaced the old Civil Service Commission with two new agencies: an Office of Personnel Management to manage the federal work force and a Merit Systems Protection Board to hear employee grievances. Third, Congress provided greater protection for whistle-blowers—that is, workers who report wrongdoing or mismanagement. Fourth, Congress granted federal workers the legal right to join unions and bargain collectively on matters other than wages. Congress did not, however, give federal employees the right to strike. (President Reagan dramatized this point in 1981 when he fired several thousand air traffic controllers for engaging in an illegal strike.) Finally, Congress streamlined procedures for dismissing incompetent employees.

Despite the reforms, many observers had concluded by the mid-1980s that the Civil Service Reform Act of 1978 had not gone far enough. Critics charged that the system was still too inflexible, with some workers paid too much and others too little. In response, Congress began considering proposals to revise the system of pay scales and to give supervisors more authority.

The Impact of Professional Perspectives on Policymaking

As government has become more complex and its tasks more technically oriented, the people staffing the bureaucracy have assumed more substantive roles in the policy process. This is especially true for the men and women who serve in the Senior Executive Service (SES) and individuals with the highest Government Service (GS) grades. They are the executives and technical managers of government. They have substantive knowledge, technical skills, and an understanding of the workings of the executive branch.

Although government managers and technicians represent a broad range of professional fields, such as law, medicine, and engineering, individuals with particular professional backgrounds tend to concentrate within particular agencies. Consequently, the character of an agency is often shaped by the professional perspectives of its personnel. The Federal Housing Administration (FHA), for example, the agency that insures home mortgages, has long reflected the professional values and prejudices of the real estate people and mortgage bankers who staff it. Their primary concern is that the loans they insure be safe. Accordingly, they avoid high-risk clients, such as poor inner-city residents. Although this approach produces a remarkably low default rate on FHA loans, critics question whether default rates should be the sole criterion for judging the effectiveness of the program.

We can cite innumerable examples of professional perspectives affecting agency behavior. The Army Corps of Engineers, which constructs dams, levees, harbors, waterways, and the like, is dominated by engineers who evaluate projects primarily on the basis of engineering design. Independent regulatory commissions are the domain of lawyers, who see problems as cases and use trial-like procedures to produce solutions.[10]

Finally, consider the case of government policy toward tobacco products. Observers frequently note the inconsistency of the federal government's subsidizing tobacco farming while at the same time warning consumers about the health hazards of smoking. There's a logic to the inconsistency, however— a bureaucratic logic. Tobacco-subsidy programs are formulated by the agriculture committees of the House and Senate and are administered by the Department of Agriculture. Both the congressional committees and the Department of Agriculture are populated by individuals with agricultural backgrounds, and all are vigorously lobbied by tobacco interests. In their perspective, tobacco is simply another crop whose growers should be supported and whose sales promoted. It's the natural order of things. In contrast, the Public Health Service is the turf of medical professionals. Naturally enough, their primary concern is health. Consequently, while the Agriculture Department subsidizes tobacco farmers, the Surgeon General's office cranks out scientific reports on the health dangers of smoking.

RULEMAKING

Independent regulatory commissions and other regulatory agencies in the executive branch do much of their work through the rulemaking process. When Congress passes regulatory legislation, it frequently delegates authority to an independent regulatory commission or to an executive branch agency to make rules implementing the legislation. A **rule** is a legally binding regulation. **Rulemaking** is the regulatory process used by government agencies to enact legally binding regulations. The requirement that shrimpers use TEDs, for example, was a rule adopted by the National Marine Fisheries Service under authority granted them by Congress in the Endangered Species Act.

The rulemaking process begins with an agency giving advance notice that it is considering issuing a rule in a particular policy area. The agency publishes the text of the proposed rule, and interested parties have the opportunity to comment on the rule. When the agency officially adopts the rule, it is published in the Code of Federal Regulations.

In 1981, President Reagan added another step to the rulemaking process for executive branch agencies. He issued an executive order requiring that any executive branch agency issuing a new rule with an economic impact of

$100 million or more must prepare a regulatory impact statement of costs and benefits and submit it to the Office of Management and Budget (OMB) for approval. Reagan's order applied to executive branch agencies such as the Environmental Protection Agency (EPA), but not to independent regulatory commissions, such as the FCC, which are independent of direct presidential control.

Federal courts also play a role in the rulemaking process. As the TEDs controversy illustrates, parties unhappy with agency decisions sometimes turn to the federal courts for relief. In recent years, courts have heard challenges not just from business groups who believed that federal regulations had gone too far, but also from consumer and environmental groups who argued that regulations were not strict enough. In general, the courts have ruled that agency decisions must be supported by evidence and reasoned explanations and that agencies must follow statutory requirements to give notice, hold hearings, and consult with parties outside the affected industry.[11]

Although federal judges almost always base their decisions on whether agencies followed procedural guidelines, one study finds evidence that, in fact, judges often decide cases on a policy basis. The study discovered that conservative judges are most likely to uphold agency decisions supporting business interests and utility companies. In contrast, liberal jurists more frequently support agency decisions favoring consumer and environmental groups.[12]

POLITICS AND ADMINISTRATION

Bureaucratic policymaking is a complex process involving the president, Congress, interest groups, and the bureaucracy itself. Each of the participants has its own particular perspectives and its own set of political resources for achieving its goals. Let's consider the role each of the various political actors plays in administrative policymaking.

The President

Presidents have an important stake in the faithful and efficient implementation of federal programs, but they must work to influence the administrative process and even then their success is not assured. Being chief executive does not entitle a president to command the federal bureaucracy so much as it offers the opportunity to attempt to influence implementation. In 1977, for example, President Carter ordered relevant federal agencies to develop guidelines to implement the administration's policy of discouraging industrial and commercial development in areas subject to repeated flooding. More than two year later, however, only 15 of the 37 agencies most directly involved had done so. Another 13 agencies were working on guidelines, while 12 others had done nothing at all![13]

Presidents have several tools for influencing the bureaucracy. The first is the power of appointment. The president has the authority to name most of the top administrators in the bureaucracy, including department secretaries and undersecretaries, agency heads, and regulatory commissioners. The Reagan White House carefully screened potential appointees to ensure they were conservative Republicans, loyal to the president. Moreover, Reagan used the SES to transfer or demote career civil servants the White House deemed uncooperative with the president's policy goals.[14] Reagan's appointees had their greatest impact in the regulatory commissions and agencies, such as the Occupational Safety and Health Administration (OSHA) and the Federal Trade Commission (FTC), which adopted more conservative, business-oriented postures. Nonetheless, many presidents have been troubled by independent-minded appointees. Moreover, department heads and agency chiefs are often unable to command their agencies. Usually the best they can do is to bargain with their departments over policies and procedures.

A second instrument for White House control of the bureaucracy is the White House staff. In practice, agency heads and most cabinet members deal far more frequently with staff members than they do with the president. Staff members are loyal to the president and can oversee agency actions to see that they conform to presidential policies. Still, most White House staffers have little experience or expertise in most areas of administrative policymaking. As a result, their ability to control the bureaucracy on the president's behalf is limited.

Third, presidents may propose a reorganization of the executive branch. President Franklin Roosevelt, for example, asked Congress to create new agencies to overcome the inertia of the old. President Reagan proposed the elimination of the Departments of Energy and Education. In general, however, getting Congress to agree to a reorganization is easier said than done. The Departments of Energy and Education remained after Reagan had retired.

A final and perhaps most important tool a president has to influence the bureaucracy is the Office of Management and Budget. The OMB evaluates agency performance and scrutinizes budget requests for the president, who, in turn, submits a budget to Congress. The president's role in the budgetary process provides an attractive carrot and an imposing stick for keeping the bureaucracy in line, but it's not without limitations. Congress has the final say on the budget, and agencies can sometimes make end runs around the White House to protect their particular slices of the budgetary pie. On numerous occasions, Congress appropriated more money for agencies than the Reagan administration requested. The National Institutes of Health, for example, regularly saw its budget request trimmed by Reagan's OMB and then restored or even increased by Congress.

The OMB has also become a clearinghouse for federal regulations made by executive branch agencies. Under Reagan, the OMB generally used its power to relax regulations it considered burdensome to industry. In 1984, for example, the OMB forced the EPA to ease proposed pollution regulations for diesel vehicles.[15] One study found that between 1981 and 1985, the OMB forced agencies to modify or withdraw 19 percent of proposed rules. What's more, that figure underestimated the real impact of the OMB, because agencies often revised rules to make them acceptable to the White House before submitting them for OMB review.[16]

By and large, presidents face a continuous struggle to have a major impact on bureaucratic policymaking. The federal bureaucracy is too large and too spread out for easy oversight from the White House, and many federal programs are administered by state and local officials and private contractors over whom the president has little direct authority. Moreover, presidents often haven't the time to manage the bureaucracy and may be uninterested in trying. It's more glamorous and politically rewarding, at least in the short run, to propose new policy initiatives than to supervise the implementation of programs already in place.

Congress

The powers of Congress to manage the federal bureaucracy are considerably greater than those of the president. After all, Congress created the various bureaucratic agencies and delegated authority to them. What Congress gives, Congress can take away. Specifically, Congress can abolish an agency, reorganize its structure, change its jurisdiction, cut its budget, investigate its performance, and overrule its decisions. (See the Perspective for a discussion on the legislative veto.)

On occasion, Congress has seen fit to clamp down on particular agencies. In the late 1970s, for example, Congress overrode the Food and Drug Administration's ban on over-the-counter sales of saccharin after laboratory tests discovered a link between it and cancer in rats. In the late 1980s, Congress summoned officials of the Department of Housing and Urban Development (HUD) to explain revelations that some of the money appropriated to build low-income housing had been used to build luxurious condominiums and golf courses.

Then there's the case of the Architectural and Transportation Barriers Compliance Board. Congress created the agency to set guidelines to allow disabled persons access to federal facilities. In January 1981, however, the board announced standards that would have required the remodeling of entrances, corridors, elevators, toilets, and meeting rooms in all federal buildings. Many observers argued that the board's guidelines were unreasonably restrictive. One rule, for example, would have required every federal office with as many as two telephones to purchase an expensive teleprinter for use by the deaf. After the board announced its new rules, other federal agencies began to voice opposition and Congress began to pressure the board. A number of congressional leaders dropped hints that the board just might become a casualty

PERSPECTIVE

The Legislative Veto

The **legislative veto** is a provision in a bill giving one, or both, houses of Congress, or a congressional committee, the authority to invalidate an action by the executive branch. (Note the distinction between the legislative veto and the veto exercised by the president in the legislative process. The presidential veto allows the chief executive to block legislation passed by Congress unless each legislative chamber is able to override the president's veto by a two-thirds margin. In contrast, the legislative veto enables Congress to override a decision made by an executive branch agency.)

Legislative-veto provisions can come in a variety of forms. Some measures allowed Congress to disapprove agency decisions before they went into effect. Others required the advance approval of Congress. Still other provisions established a waiting period in which Congress could act to overturn bureaucratic decisions through the legislative process.

Through 1983, Congress had enacted roughly four hundred legislative-veto provisions. Although use of the veto dates from the 1930s, Congress adopted more than two hundred veto provisions during the Nixon, Ford, and Carter administrations. As government grew in size and complexity, Congress delegated more and more authority to the bureaucracy. It used the legislative veto to maintain control, enacting provisions that affected a broad range of administrative actions.

In practice, Congress used the legislative veto more as a bargaining lever than as a weapon. Through 1983, Congress had used the veto to nullify agency rules only nineteen times. Instead, Congress employed the veto as a threat to force agencies to modify or withdraw proposed rules.

The legislative veto was controversial. Critics attacked the veto because it allowed Congress to interject "political" influences into the administrative process (which supposedly should be neutral). Proponents believe, however, that agency decisions are inherently political. The legislative veto, they say, serves a positive function by forcing an additional round of political bargaining among competing interests.

The Supreme Court dealt a serious blow to the legislative veto in 1983 in the *Chadha* case. The Court held one-house legislative-veto provisions unconstitutional as a violation of bicameralism. It also invalidated veto measures allowing Congress to disapprove agency actions without presidential involvement on the basis that such legislative-veto provisions violate separation of powers.* The Court's decision effectively knocked out most legislative-veto provisions then on the books, although it left intact measures requiring a waiting period before agency rules go into effect and veto provisions that require the explicit approval by Congress of agency decisions.

Since the *Chadha* ruling, Congress has found numerous means to accomplish what the legislative veto previously achieved. It has rewritten some veto restrictions to make them compatible with the Court's requirements. It has tied other restrictions on the executive branch to appropriations bills. One observer makes the following statement about the ability of Congress to cope with the loss of the legislative veto: "Congress can be a very creative animal. When you slap it down, a hundred new powers, like flowers, will bloom."†

Immigration and Naturalization Service v. *Chadha*, 462 U.S. 919 (1983).
†Quoted in Stephen Labaton, "Wrong Again, Supreme Court," *Washington Post*, National Weekly Edition, 19 August 1985, p. 10.

of budget cuts. By December 1981, the board was in full retreat, and it scaled back the guidelines.[17]

Although Congress has the power to manage the bureaucracy, it does so only on a piecemeal basis through the committee and subcommittee system. For the most part, the interest of members of Congress in the administration of federal programs is limited to programs most directly affecting their districts and states. Representatives from farm-belt Iowa are concerned about agricultural programs. Senators from Nevada worry about federal land management. Consequently, members of Congress volunteer for committees that supervise the programs closest to their hearts, where they can oversee the administration of the programs most important to their constituents. One scholar reports, for example, that three-fourths of the members of the House Agriculture Committee represent districts in which the percentage of people employed in agriculture is more than twice the national average.[18]

Congress supervises the parts of the bureaucracy but not the whole. Power in Congress is fragmented and uncoordinated, and that's how Congress oversees the bureaucracy. Each committee and subcommittee is concerned with the agencies within its jurisdiction but lacks incentive for overall supervision. Ironically, Congress has the power to coordinate control of the bureaucracy, but it doesn't have the incentive; the president has the incentive, but not the power.[19]

Interest Groups

Every agency has several or perhaps dozens of interest groups vitally concerned about the programs it administers. The airline industry, aircraft manufacturers, airline employees' associations, and consumer groups have an interest in the Federal Aviation Administration (FAA). Western land interests and environmentalists monitor the activities of the Interior Department. Postal workers' unions, direct-mail advertisers, publishers, and consumer groups worry about the Postal Service.

How do interest groups influence the bureaucracy? One approach is lobbying bureaucratic agencies. Department heads devote a significant portion of their time to dealing with interest groups concerned with their agency's activities. The secretary of commerce, for example, meets with various business groups. The secretary of defense deals with veterans' groups and manufacturers doing contract work for the Department of Defense. At times, the relationship between agency heads and interest groups is so close that the White House begins to regard cabinet secretaries and other agency heads as spokespersons for the interests rather than for the president.

Second, groups lobby Congress to pressure the bureaucracy on their behalf. In 1986, for example, the House Appropriations Committee voted to overrule the United States Army's $75 million contract with the Italian-owned Beretta Company at the behest of the American manufacturer Smith and Wesson. The Army awarded the contract to Beretta after tests showed their

Robots on an auto assembly line in a Chrysler plant. Facing financial collapse in 1979, Chrysler Corporation executives lobbied Congress for help and received $1.5 billion in federal loan guarantees—money the company was later able to pay back in full.

weapon to be superior to its competition. Once the Army turned them down, however, Smith and Wesson asked members of Congress from Massachusetts (where the Smith and Wesson handgun is manufactured) to lead the fight to force the Army to reopen competition.[20]

Finally, groups can file suit to block or reverse an agency's decisions. In the TEDs controversy, for example, both environmental groups and shrimpers filed lawsuits against the government. Studies show that federal courts support agency decisions about two-thirds of the time.[21] Nonetheless, lawsuits often delay the implementation of agency rules. A case between the DuPont Chemical Company and the Environmental Protection Agency (EPA), for instance, dragged on for five years before the Supreme Court issued a final ruling.

Critics of the federal agencies charge that they often become **captured agencies**, that is, agencies that work to benefit the economic interests they regulate rather than serving the public interest. The Federal Maritime Commission, for example, historically has worked closely with shippers. The Federal Power Commission has been accused of working for the electric-utility industry. Proponents of the captured-agencies thesis point to what they describe as a revolving door between industry and the bureaucracy as evidence of the cozy relationship between the regulatory commissions and industry. Presidents appoint corporate lawyers and industry executives to serve as commissioners. When the commissioners eventually leave government, then, they often take jobs in the industries they once regulated.

Today, many political scientists believe that the captured-agencies thesis is too simplistic. Studies have found that capture is not the norm, and when it does occur, it doesn't always last.[22] Instead, agency decisions are affected by a range of factors, including presidential appointments, congressional committees and subcommittees, judicial actions, economic conditions, and agency staffs.[23]

Bureaucrats

Bureaucrats have goals of their own. As one scholar puts it, "Within the professional bureaucracy, primary loyalty is given to the profession, program, bureau, and department, probably in that order."[24] The president's program falls somewhere further down the list. Consequently, bureaucrats rally to protect their departments and programs against proposed budget cuts or reorganizations.

Bureaucrats have resources for defending their turf. Sometimes career employees resort to subtle, behind-the-scenes resistance to policy changes they oppose—sort of a bureaucratic guerrilla warfare. In an organization as large as the federal bureaucracy, presidential initiatives can be opposed in a number of quiet ways. Changes can be delayed. Bureaucrats may follow the letter but not the spirit of directives. Officials may "forget" to pass along orders to subordinates. News of mistakes or internal bickering can be leaked to the press.

At other times, bureaucrats roll out the heavy artillery to fight their policy battles. Expertise is an important weapon. Today's public policy problems are so complex that technical expertise and experience are virtually indispensable. Therein lies power. Professor Samuel Beer goes so far as to argue that government specialists with in-depth training and expertise have taken the policymaking lead in many important policy areas:

> In the fields of health, housing, urban renewal, transportation, welfare, education, poverty, and energy, it has been, in very great measure, people in government service, or closely associated with it, acting on the basis of their specialized and technical knowledge, who first perceived the problem, conceived the program, initially urged it on the president and Congress, went on to help lobby it through to enactment, and then saw to its administration.[25]

Bureaucracy also finds power in alliances with important members of Congress and with interest groups. Executive-branch agencies are some of the most vigorous and effective lobbyists. By assisting key members of Congress with problems involving constituent complaints, agencies build friendships. Moreover, most agencies have interest-group constituencies that are willing to use their political resources on behalf of the agency. Teachers' groups lobby for the Department of Education; defense contractors fight for the defense budget. Medical professionals, meanwhile, support the Public Health Service.

CONCLUSION: ADMINISTRATIVE POLICYMAKING

Political scientists use different concepts to explain administrative policymaking. One approach to understanding the administrative process is the concept of subgovernments or iron triangles. A *subgovernment*, or *iron triangle*, is a cozy, three-sided relationship among government agencies, interest groups, and key members of Congress in which all parties benefit. On one side of the subgovernmental triangle, the bureaucracy and interest groups enjoy a special relationship. Agencies enhance the economic status of their interest-group clientele through favorable regulation or the awarding of government contracts. Interest groups return the favor by lobbying Congress on behalf of the agency.

On the second side of the triangle, interest groups and members of Congress enjoy a mutually beneficial relationship as well. Interest groups assist senators and members of the House by contributing to their election campaigns. In the meantime, members of Congress vote to appropriate money for programs the interest groups support.

Finally, there's the relationship between agencies and members of Congress. Politically wise bureaucrats know that it is important to keep key members of Congress happy by providing all the information they request, solving problems members of Congress bring to their attention, and paying special notice to the needs of home districts of key senators and representatives.

Take, for example, the highway subgovernment. On one side are interest groups that benefit from highway construction: auto manufacturers, autoworkers' unions, tire companies, asphalt and cement dealers, road contractors, and oil companies. The second side of the triangle is the Federal Highway Administration, which, of course, is interested in the preservation of the programs it administers. On the third side of the triangle are the congressional committees and subcommittees that consider highway-construction bills: the Transportation Subcommittee of the Environment and Public Works Committee in the Senate, the Surface Transportation Subcommittee of the Public Works and Transportation Committee in the House. Senators and representatives from states with extensive interstate highway systems, such as Texas, California, and Oklahoma, are also involved.

Each part of the subgovernment serves, and is served by, the other two. The members of Congress involved work to maintain federal support for highway construction and maintenance. This keeps the interest groups and the bureaucrats happy. The interest groups lobby Congress on behalf of highway programs, and their PACs contribute campaign money to members of Congress on key committees and subcommittees. The agency, meanwhile, makes sure that the districts and states of the members of Congress involved get more than their share of new highways and bridges. Also, if some town in the district wants a special favor, local officials call their representative or senator, who passes the request along to the agency. The agency is eager to please and just as eager to give the member of Congress the credit. The people back home are happy, and the representative or senator gets the credit.

Scholars who study subgovernments say that a great deal of public policy is made just this way: through cozy, behind-the-scenes understandings among interest groups, key members of Congress, and the federal bureaucracy. When issues arise, the participants in the subgovernment settle the matter, with little input from political actors outside the triangle, including the president. The result is that public policy is tailored to the wishes of those groups most closely associated with the policy itself. Energy policy, they say, reflects the interests of the oil and gas industry. Highway programs are geared to match the concerns of the highway lobby.

In recent years, however, many political scientists have concluded that although subgovernments exist in American politics, their influence is less than it was during the 1940s and 1950s. Subgovernments prospered in a time when public policy was the work of a relatively small number of fairly autonomous participants: a handful of powerful committee chairs, a small number of interest groups, and a few agency administrators. Moreover, most policy decisions were made outside the public's eye.

Today's policy environment has changed. Power in Congress is more decentralized, as subcommittees and subcommittee chairs have gained power at the expense of committee chairs. In the meantime, a better-educated population and better communications have produced larger attentive publics, which have led to an explosion of interest groups, particularly public-interest and single-issue groups. What's more, new issues have arisen—abortion, energy, consumer protection, the environment, and the like—for which it is all but impossible to identify clearly who the dominant actors are.[26]

Political scientist Hugh Heclo says that policymaking today is characterized by issue networks. An **issue network** is a group of political actors that is concerned with some aspect of public policy. Issue networks are fluid, with participants moving in and out. They include technical specialists, journalists, members of Congress, a variety of interest groups, bureaucrats, academics, and political activists. Powerful interest groups may be involved, but they do not control. Instead, policy in a particular area results from conflicts among a broad range of political actors both in and out of government.[27]

Consider what has happened with the Highway Trust Fund. A subgovernment once dominated federal highway policy, but that is no longer the case. During the 1970s, the number of interest groups concerned with highway construction grew. Environmentalists worried about the effect of highway construction on the environment. Minority-rights groups became alarmed about the impact of freeway construction on minority neighborhoods. Groups advocating energy conservation argued that government should divert money from highways to mass transit. In the meantime, congressional committees and subcommittees with jurisdiction over highway programs began to include members of Congress allied with groups opposed to highway spending. As a result, federal highway policy is now made in a more conflictual, uncertain environment than it once was.[28]

We can conclude with another look at the TEDs controversy illustration with which we began this chapter. The TEDs policy was hardly the result of a quiet agreement between participants in a subgovernment. Instead, policy in this area reflected conflict among numerous parties, including several segments of the federal bureaucracy, shrimpers, environmental groups, environmentally minded members of Congress, and members of Congress from coastal areas.

As the TEDs controversy suggests, administrative policymaking is probably more frequently characterized by conflict than by cooperation. The White House distrusts the bureaucracy; the bureaucracy distrusts the White House. Career bureaucrats have one set of priorities; appointed administrators have another. Competing sets of interest groups fight for influence in the bureaucracy and control over policy implementation. Rival power centers in Congress contend for influence. The courts are often called upon to mediate disputes, and so they become participants in the administrative process as well. In sum, the administrative policymaking process is complex, involving a broad range of political actors, none of whom dominates more than a narrow range of policy decisions.

KEY TERMS

cabinet	rule
captured agencies	rulemaking
inner cabinet	spoils system
iron triangle	statutory law
issue network	subgovernment
legislative veto	veterans' preference

NOTES

1. Public Law 93–205.
2. Bill Dawson, "Years of Talks Led to Turtle Protection Mandate," *Houston Chronicle*, 26 July 1989, pp. 1A, 10A.
3. Quoted in Kermit Gordon, *Reflections on Spending* (Washington, DC: Brookings Institution, 1967), p. 15.
4. Harold Seidman, *Politics, Position, and Power*, 3d ed. (New York: Oxford University Press, 1980), pp. 47–51.
5. Ibid., p. 47.
6. Ibid., p. 66.

7. Martha Derthick, "The Government's Use of Nonprofit Organizations for Social Demonstrations," in Harold Orlans, ed., *Nonprofit Organizations: A Government Management Tool* (New York: Praeger, 1980), p. 3.

8. Judith Havemann, "Reagan's Redistribution of Federal Employment," *Washington Post*, National Weekly Edition, 15–21 February 1988, p. 35.

9. Advisory Commission on Intergovernmental Relations, *Significant Features of Fiscal Federalism 1988 Edition*, Washington, DC, July 1988, p. 10.

10. Seidman, pp. 154–56.

11. Alan B. Morrison, "Close Reins on the Bureaucracy: Overseeing the Administrative Agencies," in Herman Schwartz, ed., *The Burger Years* (New York: Viking, 1987), pp. 191–205.

12. Donald W. Crowley, "Judicial Review of Administrative Agencies: Does the Type of Agency Matter?" *Western Political Quarterly* 40 (June 1987): 265–83.

13. Ron Duhl, "Carter Issues an Order, but Is Anybody Listening?" *National Journal*, 14 June 1979, pp. 1156–58.

14. Marshall R. Goodman and Margaret T. Wrightson, *Managing Regulatory Reform: The Reagan Strategy and Its Impact* (New York: Praeger, 1987), pp. 39–40.

15. Kay Lehman Schlozman and John T. Tierney, *Organized Interests and American Democracy* (New York: Harper & Row, 1986), p. 353.

16. Joseph Cooper and William F. West, "Presidential Power and Republican Government: The Theory and Practice of OMB Review of Agency Rules," *Journal of Politics* 50 (November 1988): 864–95.

17. Timothy B. Clark, "Here's One 'Midnight Regulation' That's Slipped Through Reagan's Net," *National Journal*, 7 February 1981, pp. 221–24; *New York Times*, 21 September 1981, p. 17.

18. Dennis D. Riley, *Controlling the Federal Bureaucracy* (Philadelphia, PA: Temple University Press, 1987), p. 62.

19. Morris P. Fiorina, "Congressional Control of the Bureaucracy: A Mismatch of Incentives and Capabilities," in Lawrence C. Dodd and Bruce I. Oppenheimer, eds., *Congress Reconsidered*, 2d ed. (Washington, DC: Congressional Quarterly Press, 1981), pp. 332–48.

20. Michael Isikoff, "Gunfight at the O.K. Committee," *Washington Post*, National Weekly Edition, 1 September 1986, p. 32.

21. David H. Willison, "Judicial Review of Administrative Decisions," *American Politics Quarterly* 14 (October 1986): 317–27.

22. Schlozman and Tierney, pp. 341–46.

23. Terry M. Moe, "Control and Feedback in Economic Regulation: The Case of the NLRB," *American Political Science Review* 79 (December 1985): 1094–1116; Jeffrey E. Cohen, "The Dynamics of the 'Revolving Door' on the FCC," *American Journal of Political Science* 30 (November 1986): 689–708.

24. Seidman, p. 144.

25. Samuel H. Beer, "Federalism, Nationalism, and Democracy in America," *American Political Science Review* 72 (March 1978): 17.

26. Thomas L. Gais, Mark A. Peterson, and Jack L. Walker, "Interest Groups, Iron Triangles and Representative Institutions in American National Government," *British Journal of Political Science* 14 (April 1984): 161–85.

27. Hugh Heclo, "Issue Networks and the Executive Establishment," in Anthony King, ed., *The New American Political System* (Washington, DC: American Enterprise Institute, 1978), pp. 87–124.

28. John R. Provan, "The Highway Trust Fund: Its Birth, Growth, and Survival," in Theodore W. Taylor, ed., *Federal Public Policy* (Mt. Airy, MD: Lomond Publications, 1984), pp. 221–58.

SUGGESTED READINGS

Bryner, Gary C. *Bureaucratic Discretion: Law and Policy in Federal Regulatory Agencies*. New York: Pergamon Press, 1987.

Goodman, Marshall R., and Wrightson, Margaret T. *Managing Regulatory Reform: The Reagan Strategy and Its Impact*. New York: Praeger, 1987.

Hasin, Bernice Rothman. *Consumers, Commissions, and Congress: Law, Theory, and the Federal Trade Commission, 1968–1985*. New Brunswick, NJ: Transaction, 1987.

Kettl, Donald F. *Government by Proxy: (Mis?)Managing Federal Programs*. Washington, DC: Congressional Quarterly Press, 1988.

Radin, Beryl A., and Hawley, Willis D. *The Politics of Federal Reorganization: Creating the U.S. Department of Education*. New York: Pergamon, 1988.

Riley, Dennis D. *Controlling the Federal Bureaucracy*. Philadelphia, PA: Temple University Press, 1987.

11

THE FEDERAL COURTS

LEARNING OBJECTIVES

1. To distinguish among the various kinds of court cases and identify the various forms of law.
2. To describe typical court procedures used in resolving disputes.
3. To explain how everyday judicial disputes can sometimes lead to major policy decisions by the courts.
4. To evaluate approaches to judicial interpretation of the Constitution and the proper role of judges.
5. To trace the history of the Supreme Court as a policymaking body, explaining the legal and political significance of the following landmark cases: *Marbury* v. *Madison*, *McCulloch* v. *Maryland*, *Plessy* v. *Ferguson*, *Brown* v. *Board of Education of Topeka*, *Miranda* v. *Arizona*, *Roe* v. *Wade*, and *Webster* v. *Reproductive Health Services*.
6. To outline the organization of the judicial branch of American government, considering judicial selection and court jurisdiction for U.S. district courts, the courts of appeals, and the Supreme Court of the United States.
7. To describe the decision-making process of the Supreme Court, focusing on the selection of cases to decide, opinion assignment and opinion writing, and implementation.
8. To evaluate the role of the federal courts in the policy process.

In the summer of 1987, Lewis Powell gave Ronald Reagan the opportunity to make what was perhaps the most significant appointment of his presidency. Powell, an associate justice on the United States Supreme Court, resigned, allowing Reagan to name his successor. The importance of the appointment derived from the political balance on the Supreme Court. On many issues, the Court was evenly split between liberal and conservative justices, with Powell, a political moderate, casting the deciding vote. Powell's successor would be in a position to tip the Court's political balance one way or the other.

Reagan's first choice for the job was Robert Bork, an appeals court justice, a legal scholar, and a conservative on such issues as abortion, affirmative action, separation of church and state, and the rights of persons accused of crimes. While the president praised Bork's qualifications, critics, both inside and outside the Senate, charged that Bork was an aggressive conservative who would tip the court's balance toward an extreme position. Groups such as the National Organization for Women (NOW), the National Association for the Advancement of Colored People (NAACP), and the American Civil Liberties Union (ACLU) led the fight against the Bork nomination, running television commercials to sway public opinion and organizing letter-writing campaigns directed at wavering senators. Although President Reagan and conservative groups lobbied hard for Bork, the Senate ultimately rejected him, with most Democratic senators and a number of Republicans voting against the nominee.

Douglas Ginsburg, another appeals court justice and a former law school professor, was Reagan's second choice to fill Powell's seat on the Court. Ginsburg was younger than Bork and had not written as extensively. Although Ginsburg's inexperience led some observers to question his credentials to serve on the high court, it relieved the nominee from having to defend controversial positions. Nonetheless, the nomination never came to a vote in the Senate. Ginsburg withdrew from consideration after it was revealed that he had smoked marijuana at parties while on the law faculty at Yale University.

President Reagan's third and final choice to succeed Powell was Anthony Kennedy, yet another appeals court justice. Kennedy was more experienced than Ginsburg and less controversial than Bork. Although Kennedy's record on the court of appeals was conservative, his writing and demeanor indicated an open mind. Moreover, on a number of controversial issues, such as abortion, Kennedy had no written record that opponents could attack. The Senate approved Kennedy's nomination.

Courts in America are political institutions operating in a legal setting. Although the debates over the nominations of Bork, Ginsburg, and Kennedy were framed in terms of qualifications and legal credentials, the participants in those debates—the president, members of Congress, and a range of interest groups—were primarily concerned with the Supreme Court's policy decisions and their political implications. And, as we shall see, the Kennedy appointment did indeed have a major impact on the Court's policy direction.

THE ROLE OF THE COURTS

The courts are political participants in the policymaking process, but they work in a judicial setting under legal ground rules. Let's examine the work of the courts and see how it fits into the policy process.

Settling Disputes

The everyday task of courts in the United States is to settle disputes. In America's legal system, disputes are classified as either criminal or civil.

Criminal Disputes

A **criminal case** is a legal dispute dealing with an alleged violation of a penal law. The **defendant** is the party charged with a criminal offense. The **prosecutor** is the attorney who tries a criminal case on behalf of the government. The role of the court in a criminal case is to guide and referee the dispute. Ultimately, a judge and/or jury rule on the defendant's guilt or innocence and, if the verdict is guilty, assess punishment.

Criminal cases are classified according to their severity. A **misdemeanor** is a relatively less serious offense, such as a minor traffic violation. Misdemeanors are punishable by a relatively small fine and/or a brief time in jail, usually no more than a year. In contrast, a **felony** is a more serious crime, such as murder, assault, or burglary. Convicted felons may be fined heavily and sentenced to long prison terms. In thirty-four states, convicted capital murderers may be sentenced to death. The death penalty is known as **capital punishment**.

Civil Disputes

Courts also settle civil disputes. A **civil case** is a legal dispute concerning a private conflict between two parties—individuals, corporations, or government agencies. In a civil case, the party initiating the lawsuit is called the **plaintiff**, while the **defendant** is the responding party. The plaintiff feels wronged by the defendant and files suit to ask a court to award monetary damages or to order the defendant to remedy the wrong.

Civil disputes include property, probate, domestic-relations, contract, and tort cases. A **property case** is a civil suit over the ownership of real estate or personal possessions, such as land, jewelry, or an automobile. A **probate case** is a civil suit dealing with the disposition of the property of a deceased individual. A **domestic-relations case** is a civil suit based on the law involving the relationships between husband and wife, and between parents and children, such as divorce and child custody cases. A **contract case** is a civil suit dealing with disputes over written or implied legal agreements, such as a suit over a faulty roof-repair job. Finally, a **tort case** is a civil suit involving personal injury or damage to property, such as a lawsuit stemming from an airplane crash.

Forms of Law

A **law** is a rule of conduct prescribed by or accepted by the governing authority of a state or nation and enforced by courts. The oldest form of law in America is the common law. The **common law** is law that was made centuries ago by English judges who decided cases on the basis of local custom and precedent. (A **precedent** is a court ruling that sets a basis for deciding similar cases.) Those decisions and legal principles that came to be accepted nationwide were the common law—common, that is, to all England.

The principles of equity and *stare decisis* are important elements of the common law. **Equity** is a branch of law that allows a judge to do what is fair in a particular case regardless of the common law. Equity is an inheritance from an old English tradition that allowed an injured party to petition the king to redress a wrong for which the law provided no remedy. ***Stare decisis***, meanwhile, is the legal principle that court decisions stand as precedents for future cases involving the same issues.

The American colonists brought the common law to the New World, where it still forms the basis of legal procedures in every state except Louisiana, where the law is built on the French civil law tradition. American legal disputes, for example, often center on the application of precedents as lawyers try to convince judges that the facts of a particular case most closely fit precedents favorable to their clients. In turn, judges make decisions by deciding among competing precedents.

Other forms of law in America are statutory law, administrative law, and constitutional law. **Statutory law** is law written by the legislature. Although it supersedes the common law, many statutes are based on the common law and judges interpret statutes according to the common law tradition. Administrative rules adopted by regulatory agencies are known as **administrative law**. The highest form of law in America, meanwhile, is constitutional law. **Constitutional law** is law that involves the interpretation and application of the Constitution.

The Courts and the Federal System

Because of the federal system, America's judicial structure is divided into a national court system and court systems for each of the states. In practice, most legal disputes are settled in state courts rather than in the federal court system. Federal criminal cases are confined to those matters that have some direct or indirect connection with federal activity, federal authority under the United States Constitution, or federal statutes, and include such offenses as postal theft, bank robbery, counterfeiting, or threatening the president. Because of the interstate commerce clause of the American Constitution, criminal activity that transcends state borders can also become a federal offense. Nevertheless, the great bulk of criminal cases, including most murders, robberies, thefts, and misdemeanor offenses, involve state laws only and are handled by state courts. The overwhelming majority of civil cases are also decided in state courts. Federal civil cases are limited to such matters as bankruptcy petitions, customs, some tax disputes, patents, and certain civil cases involving parties from different states and at least $10,000.

Court Procedures

The typical image of a court at work is that of a trial with judge, jury, witnesses, and evidence. The parties in the case, the **litigants**, are represented by counsel engaging in an adversary proceeding. An **adversary proceeding** is a legal procedure in which each side in a lawsuit presents evidence and arguments to bolster its position, while rebutting evidence that might support the other side. Theoretically, it's a process that helps the judge and/or jury determine the real facts in a case.

In practice, most legal disputes are settled not by trials but through a process of negotiation and compromise between the parties involved. In civil cases, litigants usually decide that it's quicker and less costly to settle out of court than to go through the trial process. Most criminal cases, meanwhile, are resolved through a plea-bargain agreement between the prosecutor and the defendant. **Plea bargaining** is a procedure in which a defendant agrees

A trial court in session in Newport, Rhode Island.

to plead guilty in order to receive punishment less than the maximum for an offense. On occasion, defendants may plead guilty to lesser offenses than those with which they were originally charged.

Moreover, some of the most important judicial decisions aren't made at the original trial but rather on appeal. A **trial** is the formal examination of a civil or criminal action in accordance with law before a single judge who has jurisdiction to hear the dispute. Trials involve witnesses, testimony, evidence, judges, juries, and attorneys. In civil cases, the verdict determines which party in the lawsuit prevails. A criminal verdict, meanwhile, decides whether the defendant is guilty or not guilty as charged. In general, the outcome of a trial can be submitted to an appellate court for review.

An **appeal** is the taking of a case from a lower court to a higher court by the losing party in a lower court decision. The procedures of appeals courts differ notably from those of trial courts. In general, trial courts are concerned with questions of fact and the law as it applies to those facts. In contrast, appeals are based on issues of law and procedure. Appellate courts do not retry cases appealed to them. Instead, they make decisions based upon the law and the Constitution, the written and oral arguments presented by the attorneys for the litigants in the lawsuit, and the written record of the lower court proceedings. Also, appellate court justices usually make decisions collectively in groups of three or more rather than singly, as trial court judges do.

Judicial Policymaking

Every time a court acts it makes policy, although most judicial decisions are quite mundane. After all, the course of history doesn't hinge on the adjudication of the typical traffic ticket, divorce proceeding, or personal-injury lawsuit. Still, some scholars believe that when trial judges make consistent decisions on the same subjects over an extended period of time, they engage in cumulative policymaking.[1] Family law judges, for example, usually award custody of young children to their mothers, even when the law treats parents in an evenhanded fashion.[2] Moreover, as the public outcry against drunken driving has grown, judges have begun sentencing DWI (driving while intoxicated) offenders more severely.

On occasion, seemingly ordinary cases become instruments for policy decisions whose importance far transcends the particulars of the case involved. In 1963, for example, the United States Supreme Court ruled that states must provide attorneys for criminal defendants who cannot afford to hire a lawyer on their own. The particular case involved Clarence Earl Gideon, a Florida man who was sentenced to prison for breaking and entering. Although the circumstances of the *Gideon* case were unremarkable, the dispute provided a vehicle for the Court to make a major policy decision.[3]

The courts' most important policymaking power stems from their authority to interpret and apply the law and the Constitution. As interpreters of the Constitution, courts exercise the power of judicial review. **Judicial review** is the power of courts to evaluate the actions of other branches and units of government to determine whether they are consistent with the Constitution and, if they are not, to declare them null and void. As we discussed in chapter 2, the Constitution does not specifically grant courts the power of judicial review. Instead, the Supreme Court simply assumed the authority in the case of *Marbury* v. *Madison* in 1803.[4]

Altogether, the Supreme Court has overturned at least one provision in more than three hundred federal laws (counting the two hundred or so laws affected by the legislative-veto decision) and about a thousand state laws and local ordinances. In *Marbury*, for example, the Court reviewed and invalidated an act of Congress. In the *Gideon* case, meanwhile, the Supreme Court ruled on trial procedures in the state of Florida.

Most scholars and jurists agree that the courts are obliged to interpret the Constitution. After all, the American Constitution is often vaguely worded.

The precise meaning of such phrases as "unreasonable searches and seizures" and "equal protection of the laws" is not readily apparent to even the careful reader. Moreover, some modern policy issues, such as wiretapping, drug testing, and nuclear-waste disposal were unknown to the framers and could not have been addressed directly.

Controversy rages, however, over the leeway courts should exercise in interpreting the Constitution. It's a debate that dates from the days of Thomas Jefferson and Alexander Hamilton. The Jeffersonians, you recall, favored a narrow construction of national powers, while Hamilton's Federalist party stood for a broad interpretation. In the case of *McCulloch* v. *Maryland* (1819), the Supreme Court resolved the issue in favor of a loose construction of the Constitution.[5] Although this position has generally prevailed as the dominant basis for constitutional interpretation in America, the debate has not ended.

Strict construction is a doctrine of constitutional interpretation holding that the document should be interpreted narrowly. Advocates of strict construction believe that judges should stick close to the literal meaning of the words in the Constitution and place themselves in harmony with the framers' purpose. Otherwise, they argue, judges become law *makers* rather than law *interpreters*.

In contrast, **loose construction** is a doctrine of constitutional interpretation holding that the document should be interpreted broadly. Loose constructionists argue that strict construction is neither possible nor desirable. They point out that it is often difficult to ascertain the framers' original intent, since no complete and accurate record exists to tell us what the Constitution's authors had in mind. Moreover, we know from records that do exist that the nation's founders often disagreed with one another about the Constitution's basic meaning. (Witness the debate between Hamilton and Jefferson, two of the nation's more prominent founders.) Another question concerns whose intent judges should follow—the framers at the Philadelphia convention? the members of Congress who drafted amendments? or state legislators who ratified amendments? Perhaps the best argument for loose constructionists is that the framers themselves never intended that future generations be bound by the exact language of the Constitution. Former Federal Judge Irving R. Kaufman makes the argument as follows:

> The open-textured nature of most of the vital clauses of the Constitution signifies that the drafters expected future generations to adapt the language to modern circumstances, not to conduct judicial autopsies into the minds of the framers. When the founding fathers talked about due process, equal protection, and freedom of speech and religion, they were embracing general principles, not specific solutions....The framers' legacy to modern times is the language and spirit of the Constitution, not the conflicting and dated conceptions that may lie beneath the language.[6]

Although the controversy over constitutional interpretation raises some important legal/constitutional issues, the essence of the debate over constitutional interpretation is political. In general, proponents of strict construction oppose the policy direction of Court rulings, while loose constructionists favor the Court's decisions. (See the Perspective for another angle to this debate.)

THE SUPREME COURT AND POLICYMAKING

Throughout most of its history, the United States Supreme Court has been an active participant in some of the nation's most significant public policy debates. In its first decade, however, the Court was relatively unimportant. It decided only fifty cases from 1789 to 1800, and some of its members even resigned to take other, more prestigious jobs.[7]

After John Marshall was named chief justice, the Supreme Court's role in the policy process began to take shape. Chief Justice Marshall (1801–35) built the Court's prestige through his intellect and personality. Under his leadership, the Court claimed the power of judicial review (*Marbury* v. *Madison*, 1803)[8] and assumed the authority to review the decisions of state courts on questions of federal law (*Martin* v. *Hunter's Lessee*, 1816).[9]

The Marshall Court also decided a number of landmark cases on commercial law and the nature of the federal system. In the *Dartmouth College* case (1819), the Court held that the Constitution protects private contracts from legislative infringement.[10] The Court ruled in favor of a strong national government in the cases of *McCulloch* v. *Maryland* (1819) and *Gibbons* v. *Ogden* (1824). In *McCulloch*, the Court struck down a Maryland tax on the national bank and gave broad scope to federal authority under the Constitution.[11] In *Gibbons*, meanwhile, the Court overturned a New York law establishing a steamboat monopoly as an infringement on the federal government's power to regulate interstate commerce.[12]

The Supreme Court initially continued the policies of the Marshall years during the tenure of Chief Justice Roger Taney (1836–64). Eventually, however, the Court, like the rest of the nation, became embroiled in the slavery controversy. The Court's involvement culminated in the infamous *Dred Scott* decision (1857), in which it declared the Missouri Compromise unconstitutional and held that the federal government had no power to prohibit slavery in the territories.[13]

After the Civil War and Reconstruction, the Supreme Court focused its attention on government efforts to regulate business activity. Initially, the Court's positions were mixed, but by the 1920s and early 1930s, the Court had grown increasingly hostile to government regulation of business. It scrutinized state and federal taxing and regulatory policies and found many of them unconstitutional under the due process clause of the Fourteenth Amendment.

PERSPECTIVE

Judicial Restraint Versus Judicial Activism

An important aspect of the debate between strict and loose construction is the controversy over judicial restraint and judicial activism. Although the issues in the two debates are similar, they are not identical. The former dispute involves constitutional interpretation, while the latter deals with the proper role of judges.

Judicial restraint is the principle that judges, who aren't elected, should avoid substituting their policy judgments for those of legislators and executives, who are elected. The late Supreme Court Justice Felix Frankfurter articulated the philosophy of judicial restraint as follows:

> As a member of this Court I am not justified in writing my private notions of policy into the Constitution.... [O]ne's own opinion about the wisdom or evil of a law should be excluded altogether when one is doing one's duty on the bench.*

Judicial activism, meanwhile, is the principle that judges should use their position and authority to promote desirable social ends. The proponents of judicial activism note that lawmakers, either unable or unwilling to draft detailed legislation, often write statutes broadly with the expectation that bureaucrats and judges will flesh out the vague language of the law. What's more, they say, the framers of the Constitution expected the courts to protect constitutional rights against infringements by legislatures and executives. By granting life tenure to federal judges, the Constitution's authors made it clear they expected judges to make unpopular decisions from time to time.

Frequently, the philosophical issues raised in the debate between judicial activism and judicial restraint are overshadowed by political concerns. Advocates of judicial activism typically support only those activist decisions that happen to coincide with their own policy judgments. In contrast, spokespersons for judicial restraint usually limit their opposition to judicial activism to cases with which they disagree on policy grounds. From the mid-1950s through the late 1980s, for example, conservatives, uncomfortable with judicial rulings on issues such as abortion and affirmative action, called for judicial restraint, while liberals endorsed judicial activism.

Today, as the Supreme Court takes more conservative policy positions, the sides sometimes flip-flop. Consider the case of *City of Richmond* v. *Croson Co.*, which dealt with a Richmond, Virginia, city council ordinance setting aside 30 percent of city construction contracts for businesses owned or controlled by minorities. Even though Richmond is 50 percent black, less than 1 percent of city contracts had gone to minority contractors in the five years preceding the adoption of the ordinance. Nonetheless, the United States Supreme Court ruled by a 5-to-4 vote that the ordinance was unconstitutional because the city government had not proved a history of discrimination in Richmond's construction industry. Ironically, the Court's conservative justices made up the activist majority in the case, striking down the city ordinance. The Court's outnumbered liberal wing, meanwhile, stood in dissent, arguing that the majority should have shown greater respect for the wisdom of the local officials.[†]

West Virginia State Board of Education v. *Barnette*, 319 U.S. 624 (1943), dissenting opinion.
[†]*City of Richmond* v. *Croson Co.*, 109 S. Ct. 706 (1989).

Among the measures the Court struck down were child-labor laws and several bills passed during the early days of the **New Deal** (the legislative program proposed by President Franklin Roosevelt).

While the Supreme Court protected the property rights of business corporations, it ignored the civil rights of African-Americans. Around the turn of the century, a number of states, primarily in the South, enacted **Jim Crow laws**, which were legal provisions requiring the social segregation of blacks in separate and generally unequal facilities. In the meantime, many states, again mostly in the South, adopted fiendishly clever devices to prevent blacks from voting. The Supreme Court responded to this situation by legitimizing segregation in *Plessy* v. *Ferguson* (1896)[14] and essentially overlooking voting-rights violations.

In 1937, the Supreme Court changed its tune and its agenda. In a remarkable turn of events, the Court began to uphold the constitutionality of New Deal legislation. No longer would the Court protect business against government regulation. Although the modern Supreme Court has generally required that government agencies follow proper procedures in their regulatory activities, it has broadly and consistently endorsed the right of government to regulate business and the nation's economy.

Since 1937, the agenda of the U.S. Supreme Court has dealt primarily with civil liberties and civil rights. **Civil liberties** refer to the protection of the individual from the unrestricted power of government. **Civil rights**, meanwhile, concern the protection of the individual from arbitrary or discriminatory acts by government or by individuals.

Under the leadership of Chief Justice Earl Warren (1953–69), the Supreme Court adopted liberal policy positions on a number of civil-liberties and civil-rights issues. The Court strengthened the First Amendment rights of freedom of expression and freedom of religion, broadened the procedural rights of persons accused of crimes, and ruled decisively for civil rights of blacks and other minorities. In *Brown* v. *Board of Education of Topeka* (1954), for example, the Court struck down laws requiring school segregation, overturning the *Plessy* decision.[15] In *Mapp* v. *Ohio* (1961), the Court extended the exclusionary rule to the states.[16] (The **exclusionary rule** is the judicial doctrine stating that when the police violate an individual's constitutional rights, the evidence obtained as a result of police misconduct or error cannot be used against the defendant.) In *Miranda* v. *Arizona* (1966), meanwhile, the Court held that persons arrested for crimes must be apprised of their constitutional rights before being interrogated by police officers.[17]

During Warren Burger's tenure as chief justice (1969–86), the Supreme Court continued to focus primarily on civil liberties and civil rights, but its policy preferences were neither consistently liberal nor conservative. In some issue areas, such as abortion rights, capital punishment, education for the children of illegal aliens, affirmative action, school busing, and sex discrimination, the Burger Court broke new ground. In *Swann* v. *Charlotte-Mecklenburg*

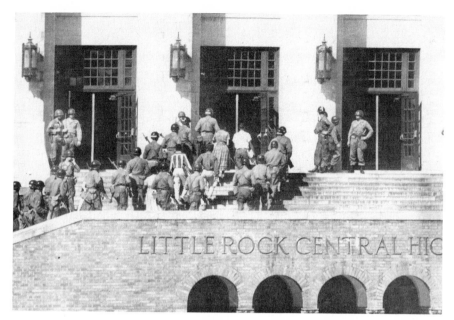

Though the Warren Court struck down laws requiring segregation in Brown v. Board of Education, *there was widespread resistance to the ruling, particularly in the South. In September 1957 President Eisenhower sent federal troops to Little Rock, Arkansas, to enable nine black students to attend a previously all-white school.*

Board of Education (1971), for example, the Court ruled that busing was a constitutionally acceptable means to achieve racial integration.[18] In *Roe* v. *Wade* (1973), the Court held that states could not prohibit abortion in the first two trimesters of pregnancy.[19] In other policy areas, however, particularly on issues involving the rights of persons charged with crimes, the Burger Court limited or qualified Warren Court positions without directly reversing any of the major precedents set during the Warren years.

Under the leadership of Chief Justice William Rehnquist (since 1986), the Supreme Court has taken a decidedly more conservative turn, particularly since the addition of Anthony Kennedy. With Justice Kennedy casting the deciding vote, the Court has issued a number of conservative rulings by 5-to-4 votes. The Court weakened civil rights laws, for example, by making it more difficult for women and minorities to prove discrimination but easier for white males to bring reverse discrimination suits. (**Reverse discrimination** is the allegation that affirmative-action efforts on behalf of women and minority group members effectively discriminate against white males.) In the area of criminal justice, the Court permitted states to execute convicted murderers who are mentally retarded or who were as young as the age of sixteen at the time of the crime.[20] Finally, in the case of *Webster* v. *Reproductive Health Services* (1989), the Court gave state governments greater power to regulate abortion.[21] Many observers predicted that it was only a matter of time before the Court overturned *Roe* v. *Wade* in its entirety.

THE FEDERAL COURT SYSTEM

The Constitution says little about the organization of the federal courts. It mentions a chief justice and a Supreme Court but leaves most of the details to the discretion of Congress. "The judicial power of the United States," it says in Article III, Section 1, "shall be vested in one supreme Court, and in such inferior Courts as the Congress may from time to time ordain and establish." For the most part, then, the present organization of the judicial branch of American national government is the work of Congress, which has frequently acted at the initiative of the president and the urging of the judiciary itself.

Figure 11.1 diagrams the federal court system. The courts at the bottom of the judicial pyramid are trial courts, conducting initial hearings in civil and criminal disputes. The Court of Claims, the Court of International Trade, and the Tax Court are specialized trial courts, created by Congress to deal with some of the more complex areas of federal law. The most important federal trial courts, however, are the United States district courts. They, along with the United States courts of appeals and the United States Supreme Court, are the primary courts in the federal judicial system.

District Courts

Congress has created ninety-five district courts, with at least one court in every state and one each in the District of Columbia, Guam, Puerto Rico, and the Virgin Islands. Although only one judge presides in each courtroom, most of the districts have enough business to warrant several courtrooms, each with its own judge. The number of judges per district ranges from one to twenty-seven. Altogether, nearly six hundred full-time judges plus more than a hundred semi-retired senior judges staff the district courts. In addition, each district court has attached to it a clerk's office, a United States marshal's office, and one or more bankruptcy judges, probation officers, court reporters, and magistrates. The magistrates are attorneys appointed by federal district-court judges under a merit selection system to serve eight-year terms. They conduct preliminary hearings, set bail, issue arrest warrants, and, if litigants consent, conduct trials in civil disputes and misdemeanor criminal cases. In practice, magistrates handle from 15 to 20 percent of civil cases in full or in part.[22]

Jurisdiction

Jurisdiction refers to the authority of a court to hear and decide a case. The jurisdiction of district courts includes both civil and criminal matters, with civil disputes outnumbering criminal cases by a nearly 7-to-1 margin.[23] In sheer volume, the district courts' main chores are naturalizing aliens and granting passport applications. District courts also have jurisdiction over bankruptcy cases filed under federal law, civil cases involving more than

FIGURE 11.1
The Federal Court System

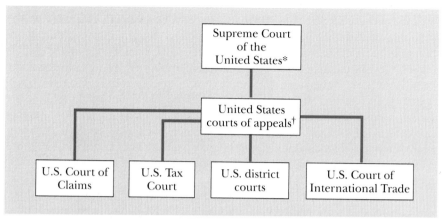

Connecting lines indicate the path of appeals.

*The United States Supreme Court may also hear appeals from the highest court in each of the states, from the Court of Military Appeals, and from three-judge district courts.
†The United States courts of appeals may also hear appeals concerning decisions of federal regulatory agencies.

$10,000 in which the U.S. government is a party, and, if either litigant requests it, lawsuits in which the parties live in different states and more than $10,000 is at stake. In these last types of cases, federal judges apply the laws of the applicable state rather than federal law.

As for criminal matters, district courts try all cases involving violations of federal law as well as criminal offenses occurring on federal territory, federal reservations, or the high seas. District judges must also handle a good many habeas corpus petitions filed by inmates in both state and federal prisons. A **writ of habeas corpus** is a court order requiring government authorities either to release a person held in custody or to demonstrate that the person is detained in accordance with law. Habeas corpus petitions allege that a prisoner is being held contrary to law and ask a court to inquire into the matter. An inmate's attorney may charge, for example, that a state trial court erred in admitting certain evidence, thereby violating the Fourth and Fourteenth amendments to the United States Constitution. If the judge sees merit in the petitioner's complaint, the judge can direct the jailer to reply, and a suit will be joined. Habeas corpus petitions are often used by prisoners on death row hoping to avoid, or at least delay, execution.

Litigants who lose their district-court cases may appeal to a United States court of appeals. In practice, about 12 percent of district-court cases are appealed.

Selection of Judges

The president appoints federal judges subject to Senate confirmation by majority vote. In most instances, the selection of district-court judges is determined by the practice of senatorial courtesy. **Senatorial courtesy** is the custom that senators from the president's party have a veto on judicial appointments from their states. In practice, the appointment power for district judges has shifted from the president to members of the Senate from the president's party. When district-court vacancies occur, senators from the president's party submit names to the president, who, in turn, makes the formal nomination to the Senate. The president can reject a senator's recommendation, of course, but rarely does. When vacancies develop in states where neither senator shares the president's party affiliation, the White House usually consults state party leaders and/or members of the House for their recommendations.

The Senate Judiciary Committee evaluates district-court nominees. After the committee staff conducts a background check, the committee chair schedules a hearing to allow the nominee and interested parties an opportunity to be heard. The confirmation of district-court judges is usually a fairly quiet affair, with few nominees ever rejected.

What type of individual reaches the district-court bench through this process? The foremost answer seems to be that presidents and senators favor judges from their own political party. The overwhelming majority of President Jimmy Carter's judicial appointments were Democrats, while President Reagan preferred Republicans. Second, presidents tend to appoint white, Anglo-Saxon, middle-aged men, from middle- and upper-class families. Most appointees have legal training and political experience. The major exception to this pattern was President Carter, who insisted that senators consider women and minorities in making district-court recommendations. As a result, Carter appointed more women, African-Americans, and Hispanic-Americans to the federal bench than any president in history. Of Carter's 258 appointments to district and appellate courts, 16 percent were women, 14 percent were black, and 6 percent were Hispanic. President Reagan, however, dropped Carter's affirmative-action requirements. During his two terms in office, Reagan appointed 379 judges. Only 8 percent were women, 2 percent were black, and 3 percent Hispanic.[24]

Research shows that judges' rulings sometimes reflect the political philosophy of the president who appointed them. One study found that judges appointed by President Reagan were less supportive of the claims of disadvantaged minorities and plaintiffs charging violations of civil rights and civil liberties than were judges appointed by President Carter or other recent presidents.[25] Reagan judges agreed with plaintiffs claiming racial discrimination only 13 percent of the time, for example, compared with judges appointed by President Carter, who sided with plaintiffs charging discrimination at a rate of 59 percent.

Indeed, one result of the large number of Reagan appointees on the federal bench is that groups and individuals are reluctant to file civil rights cases in federal courts because they think their chances of winning are slim. In 1976, the federal courts heard more than a thousand employment-discrimination suits. By the end of the 1980s, though, the number of discrimination cases filed had fallen to fewer than fifty a year.[26]

District judges (and federal judges in general) hold lifetime appointments, pending "good behavior," as the Constitution puts it. Although federal judges may not be retired involuntarily or removed for political reasons, they are subject to impeachment by the House and removal by the Senate. Historically, only a handful of judges have been impeached and removed from office, as most judges who get in trouble resign rather than face the humiliation of impeachment.

Courts of Appeals

The United States courts of appeals (also known as circuit courts of appeals) are the primary intermediate appellate courts in the federal system. There are thirteen of them, one for each of the eleven judicial circuits, or regions, one for the District of Columbia, and a thirteenth court called the United States Court of Appeals for the Federal Circuit, which specializes in customs and patent appeals from the district courts. Figure 11.2 shows how the United States is divided among the circuits. The number of judges for each of the circuits ranges from three to twenty-four. Altogether, 168 justices staff the courts of appeals, plus an additional forty or so senior justices.

Jurisdiction

The courts of appeals are exclusively appellate courts, usually hearing cases in panels of three judges each. Cases are appealed to the courts of appeals from the Tax Court, the Court of Claims, and the Court of International Trade, but their largest source of business is the United States district courts. The courts of appeals also hear appeals on the decisions of the regulatory commissions. Of these, the decisions of the National Labor Relations Board (NLRB) produce the most appeals.

The courts of appeals are generally not required to hold hearings in every case. After reading the legal briefs in a case (a **legal brief** is a written legal argument) and reviewing the trial-court record, appeals-court justices may decide not to hear formal arguments. In this instance, the lower court ruling stands.

When an appeals court decides to accept an appeal, the court generally schedules a hearing at which the attorneys for the two sides in the dispute present oral arguments and answer the justices' questions. Appeals courts, you recall, do not retry cases. Instead, they review the trial-court record and consider legal arguments. After hearing oral arguments and studying legal

FIGURE 11.2

United States Courts of Appeals and United States District Courts

Courts of appeal boundaries
State boundaries
District boundaries

Source: Congressional Research Service, The Library of Congress

briefs, appeals-court justices discuss the case among themselves and eventually vote on a decision, with a majority vote of the justices required to decide a case. The court may affirm (uphold) the lower court decision, reverse it, modify it, or affirm part of the lower court ruling while reversing or modifying the rest. Frequently, an appeals court remands (sends back) a case to the trial court for reconsideration in light of the appeals-court decision.

Selection of Justices

The White House generally takes more care with nominations to the courts of appeals than it does with district-court selections. Since the judicial circuits usually include several states, senatorial courtesy doesn't dictate the selection of justices on the courts of appeals. When a vacancy occurs, a deputy attorney general gathers names of potential nominees, consulting party leaders, senators, and members of the House for their advice. The American Bar Association (ABA) Committee on the Federal Judiciary may offer its advice on the qualifications of nominees. Eventually, the deputy attorney general suggests a name or perhaps a short list of names for the president's consideration. Although the Senate examines appellate-court nominees more closely than it does district-court selections, rejections are rare.

The Supreme Court

The Supreme Court of the United States is the highest court in the land. Its rulings take precedence over the decisions of other federal courts and, on matters involving federal law and the United States Constitution, over state courts as well.

The Constitution says nothing about the size of the Supreme Court, leaving the number of justices to Congress. Through the years, Congress has varied the size of the Court from as few as five justices to as many as ten, but its present membership of nine justices has been in effect for more than a century. In the 1930s, Franklin Roosevelt's attempt to enlarge the Court so he could add justices friendly to the New Deal was popularly attacked as a court-packing plan and defeated by Congress. Since then, no serious efforts have been made to change the Court's size.

Today's Court includes a chief justice and eight associate justices. The justices are equal and independent, like nine separate law firms, but the chief justice is first among them. The chief presides over the Court's public sessions and private conferences. The chief justice can call special sessions of the Court and helps administer the federal court system. The chief also assigns justices the responsibility of writing the Court's opinions in cases.

The chief justice is a political leader who, to be successful, must deal effectively with political pressures both inside and outside the Court. Internally, the chief attempts to influence the other members of the Court. Externally, the chief justice lobbies Congress, responding and/or reacting to attacks against the Court. One scholar rates John Marshall, Charles Evans Hughes, and Earl Warren as the nation's best chief justices, not because they were the best legal philosophers—they weren't—but because they were the best political leaders.[27]

Regular sessions of the Supreme Court run from the first Monday in October until the end of June or early July. The summer months are a time for vacation and individual study by the Court's members, although the chief justice can call a special session to consider particularly pressing matters.

Jurisdiction

Technically, the Supreme Court can be both a trial court and an appellate court. The Constitution says the Court's **original jurisdiction** (that is, the set of cases a court may hear as a trial court) extends to "Cases affecting Ambassadors, other public Ministers and Consuls, and those in which a State shall be a Party," provided the state has initiated the case. In practice, however, the Court never conducts trials. The Court shares jurisdiction with the federal district courts on the matters included in its original jurisdiction and leaves most of the cases for the district courts to handle. Even for the few cases of original jurisdiction that the justices consider worth their while, the Supreme Court doesn't hold a trial. Instead, the Court appoints a special master to conduct a hearing to determine the facts before it decides the legal issues.

The Court's appellate jurisdiction is set by law, and, through the years, Congress has made the Supreme Court of the United States the nation's highest appellate court for both the federal and the state judicial systems. In the federal system, the most important sources of appeals by far are the courts of appeals. Cases may also come from the Court of Military Appeals and the special three-judge district courts. From the state court systems, appeals can be made to the Supreme Court of the United States from the highest court in each state, usually the state supreme court.

The justices of the Supreme Court in a 1989 photo. Standing, left to right: Antonin Scalia, John Paul Stevens, Sandra Day O'Connor, and Anthony Kennedy. Seated: Thurgood Marshall, William Brennan, William Rehnquist (chief justice), Byron White, and Harry Blackmun.

Congress can reduce the jurisdiction of the Supreme Court if it chooses. After the Civil War, for example, Congress removed the authority of the Court to review the constitutionality of Reconstruction legislation. Since then, however, Congress has been reluctant to tamper with the jurisdiction of the federal courts on grounds that it would interfere with the independence of the judicial branch. In recent years, attempts to limit the federal courts' jurisdiction in cases involving such controversial issues as abortion, school prayer, busing, and the rights of criminal defendants have all failed.

Selection of Justices

Nominating individuals to the Supreme Court is one of the president's most important responsibilities. Certainly it's an opportunity that may not come often. President Richard Nixon was able to appoint four justices in less than six years in office, but President Carter was unable to make any appointments during his four-year term. Moreover, each appointment has the potential to affect public policy for years to come, particularly if the Court is closely divided or the president has the chance to name a new chief justice.

The formal procedures of appointment and confirmation of Supreme Court justices are similar to those for appellate-court justices except they are generally performed more carefully and receive more publicity. The attorney general begins the task by compiling a list of possible nominees. The president narrows the list to a few names and the FBI conducts background checks on each.

In selecting individuals to serve on the Supreme Court, presidents employ a number of criteria. First, they look for competence and ethics. Most Supreme Court justices have been scholarly and honorable. Some justices, such as Justices Benjamin Cardozo and Oliver Wendell Holmes, have been brilliant. Others, including Chief Justice Burger, were criticized for a lack of scholarly acumen. On occasion, ethical questions have arisen. In 1969, for example, Associate Justice Abe Fortas was forced to resign in the face of accusations of conflict of interest.

Second, presidents prefer nominees who share their own political philosophy: Conservative presidents seek conservative justices; liberals look for liberals. When President Franklin Roosevelt finally had the chance to make appointments to the Supreme Court, he was careful to select nominees sympathetic to the New Deal. In contrast, President Reagan carefully screened nominees to ensure their political conservatism.

Nevertheless, presidents are sometimes surprised and disappointed by the performance of their nominees on the Court. Liberal President Woodrow Wilson, for example, appointed James MacReynolds, one of the crustiest conservatives ever to sit on the Court. Similarly, conservative President Eisenhower chose Chief Justice Warren and Associate Justice William Brennan, two of the more liberal justices ever to serve. What was Ike's reaction? Asked if he had made any mistakes as president, Eisenhower replied, "Yes, two, and they are both sitting on the Supreme Court."[28]

Third, presidents occasionally hand out Supreme Court appointments as rewards for political support or personal friendship. In 1952, Earl Warren, who was then governor of California, helped Eisenhower win the Republican presidential nomination. Ike owed Warren a favor and paid it back when he named him chief justice. In the 1960s, both John Kennedy and Lyndon Johnson appointed old friends and political allies to the Court. Kennedy named Byron White and LBJ picked Abe Fortas.

Finally, presidents sometimes make appointments in hopes of scoring political points. Eisenhower's selection of Catholic William Brennan before the 1956 election, for example, may have been timed to influence the Catholic vote. Certainly Lyndon Johnson was aware of the political significance of nominating Thurgood Marshall as the Court's first black member. President Reagan's appointment of Sandra Day O'Connor, the first woman to serve on the Court, was done to fulfill a campaign promise.

The Senate scrutinizes Supreme Court nominations more closely than it does the president's lower court appointments. The Judiciary Committee staff and individual senators' staffs carefully examine the nominee's background and past statements on policy issues. The committee conducts hearings at which the nominee, interest-group spokespersons, and other interested parties testify. The Senate as a whole then debates the nomination on the floor before voting to confirm or reject.

The entire process is highly political because the administration and interest groups of various stripes roll out their heaviest lobbying artillery to try to sway the vote. In 1987, you recall, President Reagan's nomination of Robert Bork turned into a political tug of war between civil-rights and civil-liberties groups and the White House. Reagan lost that battle, of course, but he may have won the war when the Senate confirmed Anthony Kennedy, a younger man than Bork whose voting record on the Court has proved at least as conservative as Bork's record would have been.

In the end, the Senate confirms most Supreme Court nominees. Bork's rejection was the exception, not the rule. Overall, the scorecard reads 116 confirmations out of 144 nominations. In the twentieth century, it's 48 out of 58.[29]

Supreme Court justices come to the bench from a variety of backgrounds, but most are no strangers to politics. Chief Justice William Rehnquist, for example, was assistant attorney general in the Nixon administration before his nomination as associate justice. (Reagan elevated Rehnquist to chief justice in 1986.) Earl Warren had been governor of California. Other justices have backgrounds that are less specifically political. Thurgood Marshall was chief counsel for the NAACP. Justices Antonin Scalia and Anthony Kennedy were both federal judges. Justice John Paul Stevens was a law school professor.

Do the backgrounds of justices affect judicial decisions? Political scientists have compared the backgrounds of judges with court rulings on a number of federal and state courts. They have found that judicial backgrounds are related to decisions in certain types of cases. In general, younger judges,

Robert Bork appears before the Senate Judiciary Committee in September 1987. Nominated by President Reagan to serve on the Supreme Court, Bork was rejected by the Senate after his highly publicized confirmation hearings.

judges who are Democrats, and judges who are Catholic or Jewish tend to support the claims of "underdog" litigants (such as women, minorities, aliens, atheists, indigent persons, and criminal defendants) more frequently than do judges who are older, Republican, and Protestant.[30]

As with other federal judges, members of the Supreme Court enjoy the ultimate in job security. With "good behavior," they can serve for life, and many have continued on the bench well past traditional retirement age. Associate Justice Hugo Black, for example, served until age eighty-five; William O. Douglas stayed on the Court until he was seventy-seven. Justices can be impeached and removed from office, but Congress is unlikely to act without clear evidence of misconduct. Politics or old age and ill health probably aren't reason enough for Congress to initiate impeachment proceedings. During the Warren years, some of the Court's conservative critics launched a billboard campaign to "Impeach Earl Warren," but the effort never got far.

Deciding to Decide

Supreme Court justices themselves decide which cases they will hear and decide. Each year, litigants appeal four or five thousand cases to the Supreme Court, far more than the one or two hundred cases the Court can reasonably handle. As a result, the justices screen the cases brought to them to decide which ones merit their attention.

Cases are the raw material from which the Supreme Court makes policy. An important judicial ground rule is that the Court must wait for a case to be appealed to it before it can rule. The Supreme Court does not issue advisory opinions. Although the members of the Court essentially decide themselves what cases they will hear, their choices are limited to those cases that come to them on appeal. During the Civil War, for example, Chief Justice Roger Taney and perhaps a majority of the members of the Supreme Court believed the draft law unconstitutional. They never had the opportunity to rule, however, since no case challenging the law ever reached the Court. Today, questions have been raised about the constitutionality of the limitations of the War Powers Act on the president's prerogatives as commander in chief, but the issue remains undecided, since a case has yet to arise under the law.

The legal requirement that the Supreme Court can only rule when presented a case gives interest groups an incentive to promote and finance test cases. A **test case** is a lawsuit initiated to assess the constitutionality of a legislative or executive act. *Brown* v. *Board of Education of Topeka*, the school desegregation case, was a test case initiated by the NAACP. Linda Brown was an actual student who was prohibited by law from attending a whites-only school nearest her home. The NAACP recruited the Brown family to file suit and then provided the legal and financial resources for carrying the case through the long and expensive process of trial and appeals.

Lawyers for losing parties in lower courts begin the process of appeal to the Supreme Court by filing petitions with the Court and submitting briefs explaining why their clients' cases merit review. Appellants must pay a filing fee and submit multiple copies of the paperwork, but the Court will waive these requirements when a litigant is too poor to hire an attorney and cover the expenses of an appeal. The Court allows indigent appellants to file ***in forma pauperis***, as the procedure is called. Frequently, pauper petitions come from prison inmates who study lawbooks and prepare their own appeals. The Court rejects most of these petitions, but a few, including the *Gideon* case, make the Court's docket for full examination. In these instances, the Court appoints an attorney to prepare and argue the case for the indigent petitioner. During a recent Court term, for example, about half the roughly four thousand petitions the Court received were filed *in forma pauperis*. The rest were paid. The Court agreed to hear 10 of the pauper petitions and 169 of the paid cases.[31]

With the help of clerks, the chief justice prepares and circulates a discuss list of cases worth consideration. Any of the justices may add to the list, but only about 30 percent of the cases make it this far. The justices then select the cases to be granted **certiorari**, or **appeals**, the technical terms for the Court's decision to hear arguments and make a ruling in a case. The Court rejects the appeals of the other cases without a hearing, upholding the decision of the lower court.

The actual selection process takes place in **conference**, a closed meeting attended only by the justices. The Court decides which cases to hear based on the **Rule of Four**, a decision process used by the Supreme Court to determine which cases to consider on appeal, holding that the Court will hear a case if four of the nine justices agree to the review. In practice, the Supreme Court grants certiorari, or appeals, to fewer than 5 percent of all cases appealed it. Once the Court accepts a case, however, the appellant usually wins. The Court reverses lower court decisions 75 to 90 percent of the time in cases it agrees to decide. Apparently, the Court accepts cases when it disagrees with a lower court.[32]

What kinds of cases does the Supreme Court accept? Important ones, of course. These include cases with legal issues of national importance that the Court has not already decided; cases involving conflicts among courts of appeals or between a lower court and the Supreme Court; and cases in which the constitutionality of a state or federal law is under attack. Congress requires the Court to hear cases in which a state supreme court has found a federal law unconstitutional and cases in which a federal appeals court has declared a state law unconstitutional. The Court rejects cases it considers trivial or local in scope, and cases that raise issues already decided by earlier Court rulings. The Court won't accept appeals from state courts, unless the appellant can demonstrate that a substantial national constitutional question is involved.

All of this is sufficiently vague to leave considerable discretion to the justices. They set their own rules for deciding which cases to accept, and they follow or violate the rules as they see fit. For years, the Supreme Court refused to consider whether legislative districts that varied considerably in population size violated the Constitution. It was a political question, the Court said, that should be resolved by the legislative and executive branches of government. In 1962, however, in *Baker* v. *Carr*, the Court chose to overlook its political-questions doctrine and rule on the dispute, issuing its famous one-person, one-vote decision.[33]

Political scientists search for clues as to which cases the Court will agree to decide. In general, studies have found that the justices are more likely to agree to hear a case when the United States government is the appellant, when civil-liberties or race-related issues are involved, when a number of interest groups file supporting briefs in a case, and when lower courts disagree with one another. The members of the Supreme Court also choose cases that enable them to express their policy preferences with maximum impact. During the 1950s and 1960s, the Warren Court accepted cases to extend the guarantees of the Bill of Rights to the poor and other underdog litigants in both federal and state courts. In contrast, today's more conservative Supreme Court often selects cases in order to cut back, if not reverse, the policy directions of the Warren Court. "Upperdogs," such as the government and business corporations, are more successful in having their appeals heard.[34]

Deciding the Case

The Supreme Court usually deals with the cases it chooses to hear in one of two ways. It decides about three-quarters of them without oral arguments. The Court issues a ruling accompanied by an unsigned written opinion called a **per curiam opinion** that briefly explains the Court's decision. The justices may use this approach, for example, to reverse a lower court ruling that is contrary to an earlier decision of the Court.

The Court gives full treatment to the remainder of the cases it accepts. The attorneys for the litigants submit briefs arguing the merits of the case, and the Court schedules oral arguments. The Court may also receive **amicus curiae**, or **friend-of-the-court**, **briefs**, which are written legal arguments presented by parties not directly involved in the case, including interest groups and units of government. Amicus briefs offer the justices more input than they would otherwise receive, and they provide interest groups an opportunity to lobby the Court.

Attorneys for the litigants present oral arguments publicly to the nine justices in the courtroom of the Supreme Court building. The Court usually allows each side half an hour to present its case and answer any questions the justices may ask. A few days after oral arguments, the justices meet in closed conference to discuss the case and take a tentative vote. If the chief justice sides with the Court's majority on the initial vote, the chief either writes the majority opinion or assigns another justice the task. The **majority opinion** is the official voice of the Court, serving as a guideline for lower courts when similar legal issues arise in the future. If the chief justice is not with the majority, the responsibility for opinion assignment falls to the most senior justice in the majority.

When the initial opinion assignment is made, everything is still tentative. A great deal of negotiating and haggling usually takes place before the Court is ready to hand down its ruling. Over the next several months, some justices may switch sides on the vote, and others may threaten to switch if the majority opinion isn't written to their liking. The justice drafting the majority opinion searches for language to satisfy a majority of the Court's members. Inevitably, the opinion will be a negotiated document, reflecting compromise among the justices.

In the meantime, other justices may be preparing and circulating concurring or dissenting opinions. A **concurring opinion** is a judicial statement that agrees with the majority opinion's ruling but disagrees with its reasoning. A **dissenting opinion** is a judicial statement that disagrees with the decision of the court's majority. Only the majority opinion of the Court has legal force.

The Decision

Eventually, the justices' positions harden or coalesce, and the Supreme Court is ready to announce its decision. The announcement takes place in open court, and the final versions of the justices' opinions—majority, concurring, and dissenting—are published in the *United States Reports*. Majority rules on the Court. Cases can be decided 9 to 0, 5 to 4, or anything in between (assuming, of course, that the Court is fully staffed and every justice participates).

Many observers believe that the strength of a Supreme Court decision depends at least in part on its unanimity. Take the case of *Brown* v. *Board of Education of Topeka*. The Court's decision was unanimous; the death or resignation of one or two justices wasn't going to reverse the majority on the issue should a similar case come before the Court in the near future. What's more, the Court issued only one opinion, the majority opinion written by Chief Justice Warren. The decision offered no comfort to anyone looking for a weakness of will on the Court.

In contrast, the Court's decision in *Furman* v. *Georgia* (1972) was muddled. In this case, the Court ruled that the death penalty as then practiced was discriminatory and hence unconstitutional. The Court did not say, however, that the death penalty as such was unconstitutional. The ruling's weakness, perhaps fragility, came from the closeness of the vote (5 to 4) and the number of opinions (4 concurrences and 4 dissents besides the majority opinion). The justices could not agree on which facts were important in the case or what goals the Court should pursue.[35]

Implementation

Political scientists Charles Johnson and Bradley Canon divide the judicial policymaking process into three stages. First, higher courts, especially the Supreme Court of the United States, develop policies. Although major policy cases, such as *Brown* v. *Board of Education*, make headlines, the Supreme Court frequently clarifies and elaborates on an initial decision with subsequent rulings on related issues. In the years after the *Brown* case, for example, the Court issued other rulings that defined constitutionally appropriate means for achieving racial integration. The *Swann* case, you recall, held that busing could be used as an integration tool.

Second, lower courts interpret the higher court rulings. In theory, lower federal courts apply policies formulated by the United States Supreme Court without modification. In practice, however, Supreme Court rulings are often general, leaving room for lower courts to adapt them to the circumstances of specific cases. What's more, studies have found that lower court judges don't always follow the Supreme Court's lead.[36]

The third stage of Johnson and Canon's model of judicial policymaking is the implementation of court decisions by relevant government agencies and private businesses.[37] State legislatures had to rewrite death-penalty statutes to comply with the *Furman* ruling. State courts had to provide attorneys for indigent defendants after the *Gideon* decision. The implementation of the *Miranda* case fell to local law-enforcement authorities. Local school boards had the task of developing integration plans to comply with the *Brown* decision. After the Court's decision in *Roe* v. *Wade*, the availability of abortion services depended primarily on the willingness of private hospitals and clinics to offer them.

Although the implementation of Supreme Court rulings is not automatic, direct disobedience is rare because Court actions enjoy considerable symbolic legitimacy. When the Supreme Court ordered President Nixon to deliver key Watergate tapes to the special prosecutor, for example, Nixon complied. Had the president made a bonfire of them, as some suggested, he probably would have been impeached for that reason. Instead of defiance, unpopular Supreme Court decisions are often met with delay and subtle evasion. One study reports that ten years after the *Brown* ruling, there wasn't a single state in the deep South where as many as 10 percent of black students attended school with any white youngsters.[38] Another study found widespread evasion of the Supreme Court's rulings against government-sponsored school prayer.[39]

CONCLUSION: POLICYMAKING AND THE COURTS

How much influence do federal courts have in the policymaking process? How responsive are they to public concerns? On different occasions in American history, various groups and individuals have attacked the federal courts as both too powerful and undemocratic. In the early 1930s, for example, liberals said the members of the Supreme Court were "nine unelected old men" who abused their power to unravel the New Deal despite strong popular support for President Roosevelt's program. In the 1960s and 1970s, conservatives complained about court rulings that gave rights to accused criminals, atheists, and political protesters, while preventing state and local governments from outlawing abortion or controlling the racial balance of local schools.

Political scientists who study the judicial branch identify a number of restrictions on the power of the federal courts. The Constitution and the law place a number of checks on judicial power. The president appoints federal judges, and the Senate must confirm their appointments. In the long run, Franklin Roosevelt won his battle with the Supreme Court by waiting for justices to die or retire and then replacing them with individuals friendly to New Deal policies. It helped, of course, that Roosevelt was elected to four terms. Similarly, today's Supreme Court has grown more conservative with the addition of several conservative justices appointed by President Reagan. When voters select a president, they also choose a Supreme Court.

If Congress and the president believe that judicial rulings are wrong, they can undo the court's work by changing the law or the Constitution. In 1978, for example, the Supreme Court ruled that the completion of a dam on the Little Tennessee River would violate the Endangered Species Act because it threatened a tiny fish called the snail darter.[40] The following year, Congress legislated to reverse the Court. Amending the Constitution to overturn court rulings is a more difficult procedure, of course, but it has been done. The Twenty-sixth Amendment, giving eighteen-year-olds the right to vote, was passed and ratified after the Supreme Court held that Congress could not legislatively lower the voting age because of constitutional restrictions.[41]

The power of the federal courts is also limited by the practical nature of the judicial process. As we have seen, courts are reactive institutions. They respond to policies adopted in other branches and at other levels of government, and then only when presented a case to decide.

What's more, the courts cannot enforce their own rulings. They must depend on the cooperation and compliance of other units of government and private parties to implement their decisions. Consider, for example, the difficulty in enforcing the Court's school-prayer rulings. For years, a public high school in a suburb of Houston, Texas, used a school song that was essentially a prayer set to music. It asked God's blessing and guidance and ended with the phrase, "In Jesus' name we pray. Amen." Despite the Supreme Court's longstanding decision against government-prescribed official prayers in public school classrooms,[42] the school was still using the song in the early 1980s. Who was to enforce the Court's rulings? Federal marshals are not assigned to review school songs. Eventually, a federal judge ordered the use of the song discontinued, but the ruling came only after several offended parents brought a lawsuit to federal court. Had no one objected to the song and, just as important, had no one been willing to go to the expense and to endure the public pressure involved with a lawsuit, the students in that school would be singing that prayer/song at official school functions today.

Political scientist Robert Dahl believes that the courts are not out of step with Congress and the executive branch for long. Dahl conducted a study in which he traced the fate of twenty-three "important" laws which had been struck down by the Supreme Court. Three-fourths of the time, Dahl found that Congress' original policy position ultimately prevailed. In most instances, Congress simply passed legislation similar to the measure that had been initially invalidated. The second time around, however, the Court ruled the legislation constitutional. The role of the courts, Dahl said, is to legitimize the policy decisions made by the elected branches of government rather than to make policy on their own.[43]

Nonetheless, other political scientists believe that Dahl underestimated the policy influence of the courts. Other scholars note that while Dahl examined issues that he considered important, many so-called unimportant decisions may not be unimportant at all, particularly to the groups most directly affected. Even on important matters, Dahl admits that court rulings affect the timing, effectiveness, and details of policy.[44]

The federal courts are important participants in America's policy process, but their relative influence depends on the political environment, the issue, and the political skills and values of the judges. One study concludes that the power of the federal courts, particularly the Supreme Court, hinges on the capacity to forge alliances with other political forces, including interest groups and the executive branch. In the 1960s, for example, the Supreme Court joined forces with civil rights groups and the White House under Presidents Kennedy and Johnson to promote the cause of black civil rights.[45] Another study finds that federal judges are more likely to rule against presidential policy when the chief executive has lost popularity than when the president enjoys strong public support.[46]

The role of the courts varies from issue to issue. In today's policy process, the courts are most likely to defer to the other branches of government on issues involving foreign and defense policy, and economic policy. The courts are least likely to follow the lead of other branches and units of government on matters dealing with civil rights and civil liberties.

Judicial policymaking also depends on the skills and values of judges. One scholar concludes, for instance, that the nation's most effective chief justices have been those who were best at unifying the members of the Supreme Court and building political alliances with forces outside the Court.[47] Another study finds that the votes of Supreme Court justices generally conform to the justices' personal policy preferences.[48]

In many respects, then, the role of the federal courts in the policymaking process resembles that of the other institutions of American government—Congress and the president. As with the other branches, the courts are important participants in the policy process. Their relative influence depends, however, on the political environment, the issue, and the political skills and values of the individual political actors.

KEY TERMS

administrative law
adversary proceeding
amicus curiae brief
appeal
appeals
capital punishment
certiorari
civil case
civil liberties
civil rights
common law
concurring opinion
conference

constitutional law
contract case
criminal case
defendant
dissenting opinion
domestic-relations case
equity
exclusionary rule
felony
friend-of-the-court brief
in forma pauperis
Jim Crow laws
judicial activism

judicial restraint	probate case
judicial review	property case
jurisdiction	prosecutor
law	reverse discrimination
legal brief	Rule of Four
litigants	senatorial courtesy
loose construction	*stare decisis*
majority opinion	statutory law
misdemeanor	strict construction
New Deal	test case
original jurisdiction	tort case
per curiam opinion	trial
plaintiff	writ of habeas corpus
plea bargaining	
precedent	

NOTES

1. Henry R. Glick, *Courts, Politics, and Justice* (New York: McGraw-Hill, 1983), pp. 278–81.
2. Norma Juliet Wikler, "Equal Treatment for Men and Women in the Courts," *Judicature* 64 (November 1980): 202–9.
3. *Gideon* v. *Wainwright*, 372 U.S. 335 (1963).
4. *Marbury* v. *Madison*, 1 Cranch 137 (1803).
5. *McCulloch* v. *Maryland*, 4 Wheaton 316 (1819).
6. Irving R. Kaufman, "Don't Stop at 'Original Intent,'" *Houston Chronicle*, 8 January 1987, sec. 3, p. 11.
7. Robert A. Carp and Ronald Stidham, *The Federal Courts* (Washington, DC: Congressional Quarterly Press, 1985), p. 5.
8. *Marbury* v. *Madison*, 1 Cranch 137 (1803).
9. *Martin* v. *Hunter's Lessee*, 1 Wheaton 304 (1816).
10. *Dartmouth College* v. *Woodward*, 4 Wheaton 518 (1819).
11. *McCulloch* v. *Maryland*, 4 Wheaton 316 (1819).
12. *Gibbons* v. *Ogden*, 9 Wheaton 1 (1824).
13. *Dred Scott* v. *Sandford*, 19 Howard 393 (1857).
14. *Plessy* v. *Ferguson*, 163 U.S. 537 (1896).
15. *Brown* v. *Board of Education of Topeka*, 347 U.S. 483 (1954).
16. *Mapp* v. *Ohio*, 367 U.S. 643 (1961).
17. *Miranda* v. *Arizona*, 377 U.S. 201 (1966).
18. *Swann* v. *Charlotte-Mecklenburg Board of Education*, 402 U.S. 1 (1971).
19. *Roe* v. *Wade*, 410 U.S. 208 (1973).

20. Al Kamen, "The Reagan Revolution Takes a Seat on the Supreme Court," *Washington Post*, National Weekly Edition, 10–16 July 1989, p. 31.
21. *Webster* v. *Reproductive Health Services*, 109 S. Ct. 3040 (1989).
22. Carp and Stidham, *The Federal Courts*, p. 79.
23. Ibid., pp. 38–39.
24. Al Kamen and Ruth Marcus, "The Next Species for the Endangered List: Liberal Judges," *Washington Post*, National Weekly Edition, 6–12 February 1989, p. 31.
25. Ronald Stidham and Robert A. Carp, "Judges, Presidents, and Policy Choices: Exploring the Linkage," *Social Science Quarterly* 68 (June 1987): 395–404.
26. Kamen and Marcus, "The Next Species."
27. Robert J. Steamer, *Chief Justice: Leadership and the Supreme Court* (Columbia, SC: University of South Carolina Press, 1986), pp. 296–97.
28. Quoted in Henry J. Abraham, *Justices and Presidents: A Political History of Appointments to the Supreme Court* (New York: Oxford University Press, 1974), p. 246.
29. Lawrence Baum, *The Supreme Court* (Washington, DC: Congressional Quarterly Press, 1981), p. 25.
30. Glick, chap. 9.
31. *Houston Chronicle*, 3 January 1984, sec. 1, p. 8.
32. Glick, p. 214.
33. *Baker* v. *Carr*, 369 U.S. 186 (1962).
34. Gregory A. Caldeira and John R. Wright, "Organized Interests and Agenda Setting in the U.S. Supreme Court," *American Political Science Review* 82 (December 1988): 1109–27.
35. *Furman* v. *Georgia*, 408 U.S. 238 (1972).
36. Traciel V. Reid, "Judicial Policy-Making and Implementation: An Empirical Examination," *Western Political Quarterly* 41 (September 1988): 509–27.
37. Charles A. Johnson and Bradley C. Canon, *Judicial Policies: Implementation and Impact* (Washington, DC: Congressional Quarterly Press, 1984).
38. Harrell R. Rodgers, Jr., and Charles S. Bullock III, *Law and Social Change* (New York: McGraw-Hill, 1977), p. 75.
39. H. Frank Way, Jr., "Survey Research on Judicial Decisions: The Prayer and Bible Reading Cases," *Western Political Quarterly* 21 (June 1968): 189–205.
40. *Tennessee Valley Authority* v. *Hill*, 437 U.S. 153 (1978).
41. *Oregon* v. *Mitchell*, 400 U.S. 112 (1970).
42. *Engel* v. *Vitale*, 370 U.S. 421 (1962).
43. Robert Dahl, "Decision-Making in a Democracy: The Supreme Court as a National Policy-Maker," *Journal of Public Law* 6 (Fall 1957): 279–95.
44. Johnson and Canon, pp. 231–32.
45. Mark Silverstein and Benjamin Ginsberg, "The Supreme Court and the New Politics of Judicial Power," *Political Science Quarterly* 102 (Fall 1987): 371–88.
46. Craig R. Ducat and Robert L. Dudley, "Federal District Judges and Presidential Power During the Postwar Era," *Journal of Politics* 51 (February 1989): 98–118.
47. Steamer.
48. Jeffrey A. Segal and Albert D. Cover, "Ideological Values and the Votes of U.S. Supreme Court Justices," *American Political Science Review* 83 (June 1989): 557–65.

SUGGESTED READINGS

Brigham, John. *The Cult of the Court*. Philadelphia, PA: Temple University Press, 1987.

Calvi, James V., and Coleman, Susan. *American Law and Legal Systems*. Englewood Cliffs, NJ: Prentice-Hall, 1989.

Carp, Robert A., and Stidham, Ronald. *Judicial Process in America*. Washington, DC: Congressional Quarterly Press, 1990.

Fisher, Louis. *Constitutional Dialogues: Interpretation as Political Process*. Princeton, NJ: Princeton University Press, 1988.

Schwartz, Herman, ed. *The Burger Years*. New York: Viking, 1987.

Steamer, Robert J. *Chief Justice: Leadership and the Supreme Court*. Columbia, SC: University of South Carolina Press, 1986.

The Supreme Court at Work. Washington, DC: Congressional Quarterly Press, 1990.

Witt, Elder. *The Supreme Court and Individual Rights*, 2d ed. Washington, DC: Congressional Quarterly Press, 1988.

12

ECONOMIC POLICYMAKING

LEARNING OBJECTIVES

1. To describe the Gramm-Rudman deficit-reduction act and evaluate its effectiveness.
2. To evaluate the size of the federal budget.
3. To identify the major items in the federal budget.
4. To evaluate the federal tax system in terms of tax incidence, tax burden, and tax fairness.
5. To analyze the nature of today's budget dilemma.
6. To identify and evaluate the major goals of economic policy.
7. To describe the major approaches to economic policy.
8. To trace the policymaking process for economic policymaking.
9. To describe the relationship between economic policymaking and politics.

> Congress and the president have handcuffed themselves to one another and jumped off the cliff without knowing whether they will land on a plump mattress or a bed of nails.
>
> Political Scientist
> Norman Ornstein[1]

Thus did one observer describe the Balanced Budget and Emergency Deficit Control Act of 1985, better known as Gramm-Rudman (after two of its principal sponsors, Senators Phil Gramm of Texas and Warren Rudman of New Hampshire). The aim of Gramm-Rudman was to reduce the federal budget deficit and, eventually, produce a balanced budget. (A **budget deficit** is the amount by which budget expenditures exceed budget receipts.) Budget deficits aren't new in Washington politics, but in the early 1980s, the deficit hit record-high levels, even surpassing the $200 billion mark. Many economists believed that the deficit had become so large that it threatened the long-term health of the nation's economy.

Gramm-Rudman reflected both the determination of Congress and the president to reduce the deficit and their inability to agree on an approach. Although President Reagan and congressional leaders of both parties called for deficit reduction, they deadlocked on how best to achieve it. Reagan's plan centered on making deep cuts in domestic spending other than Social Security, which he pledged during his 1984 reelection campaign not to touch. The president opposed cuts in defense spending and promised to veto any tax-increase measure that reached his desk. In contrast, the Democratic leadership in the House, led by Speaker Tip O'Neill, favored reductions in defense spending but opposed cutting Social Security or other domestic programs. Although House Democrats would accept a tax increase, maybe even welcome one, they wanted the president to propose it. Otherwise, they feared giving Republicans an election issue. The Senate leadership, meanwhile, led by Republican Majority Leader Robert Dole, adopted a more comprehensive approach to the deficit problem. They called for cuts in both defense and domestic spending, some tax increases, and a reduction in the automatic cost-of-living adjustment (COLA) for Social Security. (A **cost-of-living adjustment (COLA)** is a mechanism designed to regularly increase the size of a payment, such as a Social Security pension check, to compensate for the effects of inflation.)

Gramm-Rudman was a gimmick pushed forward by the Senate leadership to break the deadlock between the president and the House over deficit reduction. The measure set a step-by-step timetable for eliminating the deficit, requiring Congress and the president to shave roughly $30 billion from the deficit each year until **fiscal year** (budget year) 1991, when the deficit would reach zero and the budget would be balanced. If Congress and the president missed meeting any of the annual deficit-reduction goals by more than $10 billion, the law required automatic across-the-board percentage-spending reductions to bring the deficit into line with the Gramm-Rudman timetable. (Congress and the president subsequently agreed to revise the Gramm-Rudman timetable to postpone the elimination of the budget deficit from fiscal year (FY) 1991 until later in the decade.)

Gramm-Rudman soon developed tremendous political momentum. President Reagan hesitated, then announced his support. In the meantime, Majority Leader Dole rushed the measure through the Senate without committee consideration as an amendment to another bill. Gramm-Rudman then went to a conference committee with the House, where Democratic House leaders forced a number of changes. The final bill that emerged from conference exempted more than half of all federal spending from the automatic cuts, including Social Security and several antipoverty programs. What's more, the measure stipulated that any automatic spending reductions be evenly divided between defense and nondefense spending.

Congress and the president eagerly embraced Gramm-Rudman because each side saw the measure as a weapon to force political opponents to compromise on the budget. Made without regard to priorities, automatic formula budget reductions would disrupt government, harming civilian programs, defense, and, perhaps, the economy as well. Consequently, Congress and the president would have a strong incentive to agree on budget reductions to keep automatic cuts from kicking in. Senate Republicans hoped the measure would force President Reagan and Speaker O'Neill to compromise their budget differences. House Democrats, meanwhile, wanted the president to have to choose between his goal of higher defense spending and his pledge not to raise taxes. For his part, Reagan hoped Gramm-Rudman would force Congress to cut nondefense spending. Perhaps the most fundamental appeal of Gramm-Rudman, however, was that it offered members of Congress and the president the opportunity to cast a politically popular vote against budget deficits without having to vote to cut spending or raise taxes. These unpopular decisions could be made another day, when, perhaps, someone else would have to make them.

Despite Gramm-Rudman, the budget deadlock between Congress and the White House continued into the 1990s, even though both President Reagan and Speaker O'Neill had retired and Robert Dole was no longer Senate majority leader (Democrats having won a Senate majority in the 1986 elections). As president, George Bush was apparently no more willing than his predecessor to consider a tax increase to reduce the deficit, at least during the first two years of his administration. "Read my lips," said the president; "no new taxes." In the meantime, Democratic leaders in both houses of Congress were just as determined not to cut spending for programs they favored.

Consequently, the federal government has continued running sizable budget deficits into the 1990s. Even though the revised Gramm-Rudman law called for an official deficit below $80 billion in 1991, many observers said the reductions were more cosmetic than real. Unable to agree on significant spending reductions or meaningful tax hikes, Congress and the president resorted to a series of small budget cuts, minor tax increases (labeled revenue enhancements), and creative bookkeeping to meet the Gramm-Rudman goals. In 1989, for example, Congress and the White House conspired to keep billions of dollars in federal spending needed to bail out the financially troubled savings and loan industry "off-budget" so it would not add to the official budget deficit. What's more, Congress and the president decided to count large surpluses of more than $50 billion a year in the Social Security trust funds as general revenues, even though these funds were supposed to be kept as reserves to finance Social Security benefits to retirees in the next century. Because of these practices, many economists estimate that the real budget deficit was almost $200 billion higher than the official figure.[2]

Senators Phil Gramm of Texas and Warren Rudman of New Hampshire, principal sponsors of the Balanced Budget and Emergency Deficit Control Act of 1985.

Nonetheless, it would be inaccurate to say that Gramm-Rudman has had no effect on the federal budget process. If nothing else, the measure forced Congress and the president to weigh the budget implications of spending proposals. Moreover, a number of observers agree that Gramm-Rudman reinforced a broad consensus among policymakers that the growth in government spending should be slowed, if not halted. Gramm-Rudman restrictions played a major role, for example, in curtailing President Reagan's defense buildup and in heading off proposals to expand domestic programs.[3]

The Gramm-Rudman Deficit Control Act illustrates the dilemma of American economic policy. Democrats in Congress and Republicans in the White House do not agree on how best to resolve the deficit problem, and neither side sees a political interest in meaningful compromise. While Gramm-Rudman provides political shelter for both Congress and the president by at least giving the appearance that the deficit is being reduced, the measure hasn't succeeded in forcing a grand compromise that would put the government's budgetary house in order. As a result, budgetary concerns dominate Washington policymaking, overshadowing all other issues.

PROFILE OF THE FEDERAL BUDGET

A **budget** is an estimate of the receipts and expenditures needed by government to carry out its programs in some future period, usually a fiscal year. Let's consider the size of the federal budget and examine its major components.

Size of the Budget

In actual dollars, the federal budget is enormous, exceeding $1.2 trillion in FY 1991. That's a significant amount of money, of course, but we must place the figure in context to understand its true size. Economists tell us that the best way to evaluate the size of the budget is to consider it in proportion to the nation's **gross national product (GNP)**, which is a standard measure of the size of a nation's economy.

Figure 12.1 graphs federal expenditures as a percentage of GNP. Before the 1930s, the federal budget accounted for less than 10 percent of GNP. During the New Deal era (the 1930s) and World War II (1941–45), federal spending increased dramatically, exceeding 45 percent of GNP during the war

FIGURE 12.1
Federal Expenditures as a Percentage of GNP, 1920–90

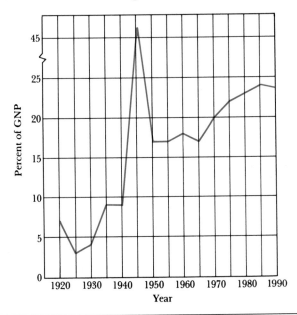

Data sources: *Historical Statistics of the U.S.*, U.S. Department of Commerce, Bureau of the Census (Washington, DC: U.S. Government Printing Office, 1975), pp. 224, 1114; Robert A. Rankin, "The Reagan Legacy," *Houston Chronicle*, 21 February 1988, sec. 1, p. 19; *Statistical Abstract of the United States, 1989* (Washington, DC: U.S. Government Printing Office, 1989), pp. 304, 421.

TABLE 12.1
Federal Expenditures in Fiscal 1981, 1984, and 1990

Category	1981	1984	1990
		$ Billions (%)	
Social Security and Medicare	179 (27)	240 (27)	345 (29)
National defense	160 (24)	238 (27)	296 (25)
Interest on the debt	69 (10)	108 (12)	176 (15)
Income security	86 (13)	96 (11)	147 (12)
Health	27 (4)	31 (4)	58 (5)
Education and training	31 (5)	29 (3)	38 (3)
Veterans' benefits	23 (3)	26 (3)	29 (2)
Transportation	23 (3)	26 (3)	29 (2)
Commerce and housing	4 (1)	4 (−1)	23 (2)
Natural resources, environment	14 (2)	12 (1)	18 (2)
Agriculture	6 (1)	11 (1)	15 (1)
State department and foreign affairs	11 (2)	14 (2)	15 (1)
Science, space, and technology	6 (1)	8 (1)	14 (1)
Law enforcement	5 (1)	6 (1)	11 (1)
General government	4 (1)	6 (1)	11 (1)
Community development	9 (1)	8 (1)	9 (1)
Energy	10 (1)	4 (−1)	3 (−1)

Note: Percentages (shown in parentheses) may not add up to 100 percent because of rounding. Figures for 1990 are estimated.
Source: Office of Management and Budget, *1981, 1984, 1990 Budget.*

years. After World War II, federal expenditures declined to about 17 percent of GNP and held steady until the mid-1960s, when they began to rise, peaking at roughly 24 percent of GNP in the mid-1980s. Federal spending in proportion to GNP slowly declined throughout the rest of the 1980s.

Budget Expenditures

The actual budget document runs over two thousand pages in small type, so it's necessary to group items together into broad categories in order to describe it briefly. Table 12.1 divides the federal budget into seventeen categories and compares spending for these items in three years: 1981, the last budget of the Carter years; 1984, the mid-point of the Reagan administration; and 1990, the first full budget of the Bush presidency. As you can see from the table, Social Security and Medicare, national defense, interest on the debt, and income security are the budget's big-ticket items.

Social Security and Medicare

Social Security and Medicare are entitlement programs designed to assist retired and disabled workers and their dependents. An **entitlement program** is a government program providing benefits to all persons qualified to receive them under law. Together, Social Security and Medicare now make up the single largest category in the federal budget.

Congress created the Social Security program in the 1930s to provide limited coverage to workers in industry and commerce upon retirement at age sixty-five. Through the years, Congress has extended the program's scope and increased its benefits. Even before the first benefit checks were mailed, Congress expanded coverage to include the aged spouse and children of a retired worker as well as the young children and spouse of a covered worker upon the worker's death. Congress added disability insurance to the package in 1956 and Medicare in 1965.

Congress has also increased Social Security benefits, especially over the last two decades. Congress raised benefits 15 percent in 1970, 10 percent in 1971, and 20 percent in 1972. Beginning in 1975, Congress indexed benefits to the **consumer price index (CPI)**, a measure of inflation. If the CPI indicates a 5 percent annual inflation rate, for example, Social Security beneficiaries receive a 5 percent cost-of-living adjustment (COLA) in their benefit checks.

Social Security and Medicare are financed by payroll taxes established by the Federal Insurance Contribution Act (FICA). Tax receipts go into the three Social Security and Medicare trust funds—Old Age and Survivors Insurance, Disability Insurance, and Health Insurance. Although wage earners and employers contribute equally to the funds, economists generally consider the entire amount to be a tax on workers since employers regard their share as part of their compensation package to employees.

For years, FICA payroll taxes were relatively modest. Initially, an employee's annual share was one percent of the first $3,000 in wages earned. The most a worker could pay in a year was only $30, with the combined employee/employer contribution limited to $60.

Despite relatively low payroll tax rates, the trust funds maintained healthy surpluses into the early 1970s. With the baby-boom generation coming of age and more women entering the work force than ever before, the pool of workers paying taxes into the system grew more rapidly than did the number of retirees collecting benefits. What's more, the system benefited from a healthy economy and rising wages.

Eventually, demographic and economic changes combined with political decisions to drive the Social Security system into near bankruptcy. Increased longevity and falling birthrates served to swell the ranks of Social Security beneficiaries while slowing the increase in the number of employees paying taxes. In the meantime, Congress and the president increased benefits and pegged future increases in Social Security payments to the inflation rate. When the economy slumped and inflation soared in the late 1970s, the Social Security system faced a financial crisis.

Congress and the president responded to the situation by adopting a Social Security bailout plan that increased payroll taxes significantly while somewhat limiting future benefit payments. By 1990, payroll taxes had risen to 7.65 percent on wages up to $51,300. A worker earning $25,000 a year, for example, would pay $1,912.50 in FICA taxes, with a combined employee/

employer cost of $3,825. In order to reduce benefit payments, the plan provided for an increase in the retirement age by small annual increments after the year 2000 until age sixty-seven. Also, the bailout legislation provided that half the benefits of upper-income recipients be counted as taxable income for income tax purposes.

The goal of the Social Security bailout plan was not only to keep the program solvent for the short-term but to ensure long-range stability despite unfavorable demographic trends. In 1945, fifty workers paid taxes for every person drawing benefits. In 1980, the ratio was 5 to 1. By the year 2020, however, when much of the baby-boom generation will have retired, the ratio of workers to retirees will be only 2 to 1. The architects of the bailout plan hoped that the payroll tax increases would be sufficient to allow the Social Security trust funds to build up sizable surpluses that could be used to pay benefits in the twenty-first century.

In practice, the Social Security bailout plan has put the system in the black. By the end of the 1980s, the Social Security trust funds were no longer near bankruptcy. Instead, they had built up surpluses totalling more than $160 billion and growing at the rate of more than $50 billion a year. Officials project that the surplus will climb to a peak of $12 trillion in the year 2030 before shrinking as baby-boom retirement benefits begin to exceed tax receipts.

Nonetheless, a number of observers worry about the future of Social Security. Federal law requires that Social Security trust fund balances be invested in U.S. Treasury securities. Since the overall budget is in deficit, each year's Social Security surplus reduces the amount of money the Treasury Department must borrow from other sources. Consequently, instead of building up cash reserves, the Social Security trust funds are accumulating IOUs. In the twenty-first century when the Social Security system begins drawing upon its reserves to pay retirement benefits, Congress and the president will either have to raise taxes dramatically or allow the federal budget to go deeply into a deficit. Since neither course of action is politically attractive, political pressures may mount to reduce Social Security benefits.[4]

Medicare, meanwhile, is a government insurance program for elderly retired workers. Part A of Medicare is compulsory health insurance, financed from premiums deducted from retirees' Social Security checks as well as payroll taxes. Medicare Part B is a voluntary medical insurance plan to cover physicians' fees, paid for by premiums deducted from the Social Security checks of participating retired persons. Since payroll taxes and insurance premiums do not cover the full cost of the Medicare program, it is subsidized from general tax revenues. In 1990, for example, more than a fourth of the cost of Medicare came from general revenues.[5]

National Defense

The defense budget is the second largest item in the federal budget, accounting for a fourth of total spending. At the height of the Vietnam War in the late 1960s, defense spending made up more than 40 percent of the budget. Thereafter, it declined proportionally as the war wound down and social programs claimed an ever larger slice of the federal pie. By the late 1970s, the defense budget had declined proportionally to less than 23 percent of the total. A consensus developed, however, that the nation's military machine needed an overhaul. President Carter proposed and Congress passed significant increases in the defense budget. In the early 1980s, President Reagan asked for (and received) even more substantial increases than his predecessor, pushing the defense share of the budget as high as 28 percent in FY 1988. Subsequently, the pressures of the deficit and Gramm-Rudman combined to halt the defense buildup. Then, by 1990, Congress and the administration were debating how deeply defense spending could be cut in light of political developments in Eastern Europe and the Soviet Union.

Interest on the Debt

A **budget surplus** is the amount by which budget receipts exceed expenditures. In contrast, a budget deficit is the amount by which budget expenditures exceed receipts. Before the 1930s, the national budget was usually balanced or in slight surplus. Deficits were primarily a wartime phenomenon as the government went into debt to finance the war effort. Since the New Deal era, however, budget deficits have become commonplace. Indeed, the last federal budget surplus was in FY 1969, a tidy $4.2 billion.

The 1980s, in particular, was a decade of record-setting deficits. As you can see from Figure 12.2, the deficits of the 1980s dwarfed those of earlier years. In 1981, President Reagan proposed, and Congress enacted, a major tax cut coupled with an increase in spending for defense. Although Congress reduced nondefense spending (at the president's request), the cuts were insufficient to prevent the deficit from soaring above the $200 billion mark in 1983, 1985, and 1986. In fact, the deficits were so high during the 1980s that the national debt more than doubled, to roughly $3 trillion by 1990. The **national debt** is the accumulated indebtedness of the federal government. While a budget deficit is the annual budget shortfall, the national debt is the cumulative deficit less the cumulative surplus.

Few subjects are more misunderstood than the national debt. A debt so large doesn't mean the nation is bankrupt any more than a family's $50,000 home-equity mortgage means that it is bankrupt. As long as government has the power to tax and the will to pay interest on the debt, it remains solvent. Moreover, about a fifth of the debt is owed to government accounts, such as the Social Security trust funds. The rest is held by banks, insurance companies, brokers, state and local governments, nonprofit institutions, and individuals, mostly Americans. In recent years, however, foreigners who have earned dollars from selling goods to Americans have invested much of that money in United States government securities.

Nevertheless, many economists are troubled by the record-high deficits of recent years because the deficits enable government to provide goods and services to Americans without their paying their full cost in taxes. Govern-

FIGURE 12.2

Federal Budget Deficits, 1966–89

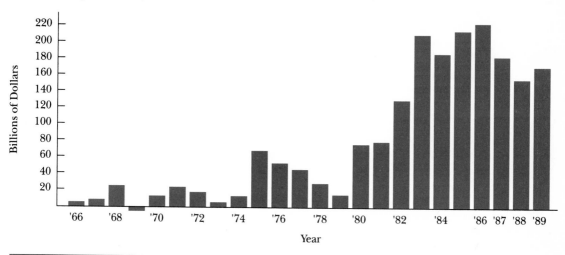

Data sources: *Houston Post*, 16 April 1989, p. A-28 (for 1988–89); *Washington Post*, National Weekly Edition, 20 October 1986, p. 20 (for 1980–87); Roy J. Ruffin and Paul R. Gregory, *Principles of Economics* (Glenview, IL: Scott, Foresman, 1978), p. 224 (for 1970–79); *Houston Chronicle*, 24 October 1986, sec. 1, p. 1 (for 1966–69).

ment covers the shortfall by borrowing. Although most observers doubt the debt will ever be paid off, it must be serviced through interest payments. Consequently, deficits force future generations to pay the bills for this generation's public services.

Income Security

The last of the four big-ticket items in the federal budget is income security. This category includes many public assistance programs, such as unemployment insurance, housing assistance, food stamps, Aid to Families with Dependent Children (AFDC), Medicaid, and Supplemental Security Income (SSI). Many of these programs were targets of President Reagan's budget-cutting knife in the early 1980s. As you can see from Table 12.1, spending for income-security programs proportionally declined from 13 to 11 percent of the budget between the 1981 and 1984 budgets. After the early 1980s, however, Reagan had little success in convincing Congress to trim social programs further. By the end of the 1980s, income security's share of the budget had stabilized at roughly 12 percent.

Other Expenditures

The other budget categories in Table 12.1 are relatively smaller than our big four, but they add up. To paraphrase the late Senator Everett Dirksen, a billion dollars here, a billion dollars there, and pretty soon we're talking about real money. Many of these items were also targets of Reagan budget cuts in the early 1980s, including various programs in the areas of health, education and social services, transportation, natural resources, and community development.

Other federal financial activities merit our attention, but they aren't part of the formal budget. These **off-budget operations** are loans and loan guarantees made available by the federal government to a broad array of individuals and institutions, great and small. (A loan involves an actual exchange of cash, while a loan guarantee involves the government promising to repay a third-party loan should the borrower default.) Each year, the federal government loans money or guarantees loans for thousands of college students, small business owners, farmers, and home-buyers, with 60 percent of the loans going to farmers. The total amount of money involved is substantial, more than $250 billion in loans at the end of 1986, with another $450 billion in outstanding loans backed by government guarantees.[6] Uncle Sam invariably loses money on loans because the government charges interest rates that are usually well below what the government pays to borrow. In 1985, for example, the Office of Management and Budget estimated that the government lost $10 billion in loan subsidies.[7]

Revenues

The major sources of federal revenue are individual income taxes, Social Security payroll taxes, borrowing, corporate income taxes, and excise taxes. (An **excise tax** is a tax levied on the manufacture, transportation, sale, or consumption of a particular item or set of related items.) As Table 12.2 shows, the relative importance of each of these revenue sources has varied over the years. Although the figures have fluctuated, the relative proportion of total revenues generated by individual and corporate income taxes and excise taxes has fallen since 1970. In contrast, the relative importance of Social Security payroll taxes and borrowing has grown.

Tax Incidence

Although all Americans pay taxes to one degree or another, the burden of taxation falls more heavily on some groups than others. The term **tax incidence** refers to the point at which the actual cost of a tax falls. Using this concept, economists identify three general types of taxes: progressive, proportional, and regressive.

A **progressive tax** is a levy that taxes persons earning higher incomes at a greater rate than it does individuals making less money. The advocates of progressive taxation often defend the concept on the basis of the ability-to-pay theory of taxation. The **ability-to-pay theory of taxation** is the approach to government finance that holds that taxes should be based on individuals' ability to pay. Well-to-do persons can better afford taxes than

TABLE 12.2

Federal Revenue Sources in Selected Years, 1970–89

Source	1970	1975	1980	1985	1989
Individual income tax	46	37	41	34	38
Social Security payroll taxes	23	25	27	28	32
Borrowing	1	16	12	23	12
Corporate income tax	17	12	11	7	11
Excise taxes	8	5	4	4	3
Other revenue	5	5	5	4	4

Sources: *Statistical Abstract of the United States, 1986* (Washington, DC: U.S. Government Printing Office, 1985), p. 306; Office of Management and Budget, *1991 Budget.*

lower-income individuals. Moreover, the supporters of progressive taxation point out that a progressive tax helps to reduce the income differential between the poor and the affluent.

In contrast, the opponents of progressive taxation believe that the progressive income tax discourages middle- and upper-income persons from working harder to earn more money, since much of it would only go to the government. In their view, the only fair tax is a proportional tax. A **proportional tax** is a levy that taxes all persons at the same percentage rate, regardless of income. The biblical tithe, in which everyone pays 10 percent of income, is a proportional tax. Even though people making more money pay more than the poor, everyone contributes the same percentage of income.

The income tax is the only major federal tax that is clearly progressive. The income-tax system divides taxable income into segments, or brackets, and applies a different tax rate to the portion of income falling into each bracket, with higher income brackets generally taxed at higher rates than lower brackets. Before passage of the Tax Reform Act of 1986, the federal income tax had fourteen tax brackets, with rates ranging from 11 to 50 percent. In 1986, tax reform legislation reduced the number of tax brackets to four, with rates of 15, 28, 33, and 28 percent. In 1990, for example, a married couple filing a joint return paid a tax rate of 15 percent on their first $31,000 in taxable earnings; 28 percent on income between $31,000 and $75,000; 33 percent on earnings from $75,000 to $155,000; and 28 percent on taxable income above $155,000. Even though the top income-tax rate isn't the highest tax rate, the federal income tax is still generally progressive overall.

No other federal tax is clearly progressive. The corporate income tax has a top rate of 34 percent and two lower rates on corporate incomes below $75,000. Although this *appears* progressive, it may not be, since economists disagree on just who pays corporate income taxes, stockholders or consumers.

In the meantime, Social Security payroll taxes and excise taxes are both regressive. A **regressive tax** is a levy whose burden falls relatively more heavily upon low-income groups than upon wealthy taxpayers. Payroll taxes are regressive because they are collected on salaries and wages, but not on income generated from investments. Middle- and upper-income people are more likely to earn investment income than lower-income individuals. Moreover, the law limits the total amount of money an individual must pay in Social Security taxes in any one year, regardless of income. In the meantime, excise taxes levied on tires, gasoline, tobacco, and other products are regressive because lower-income persons pay a greater proportion of their earnings for these items than upper-income persons.

Economists tell us that the federal tax system is either slightly progressive or slightly regressive, depending on the set of assumptions one accepts (involving, for example, the incidence of corporate income taxes). Since state and local tax systems tend to be regressive, it's probably fair to say that taxes in America as a whole are either roughly proportional or somewhat regressive.[8]

Nonetheless, recent changes in federal tax policy have made America's tax system more regressive, less progressive. During the 1980s, Congress and the president cut income-tax rates, especially for persons at the upper end of the income scale. In the meantime, they dramatically increased Social Security payroll tax rates, which fall more heavily on low- and middle-income persons. Since Social Security trust fund surpluses are now used to finance general government services and not just Social Security beneficiary checks, the result of tax changes adopted in the 1980s was to shift the burden of taxation away from persons earning high incomes to lower- and middle-income wage earners.

Tax Burden

How high are taxes in America? According to data comparing national, state, and local tax rates in twenty democracies, the tax rate in the United States is relatively low, at 30 percent of GNP. Only Japan (27 percent) and Spain (25 percent) are lower. In contrast, the tax rate in West Germany equals 37 percent of that nation's GNP; Great Britain, 40 percent; and Sweden, 50 percent.[9]

During the 1970s, the pain of paying taxes grew sharper for Americans as Social Security payroll taxes and individual income taxes both rose. Ironically, the income-tax increase came without Congress and the president enacting a tax hike. In 1965, the average taxpayer's **marginal tax rate**, the rate of tax imposed on the last dollar earned, was 21 percent. In 1981, without a major tax increase, it had jumped to 32 percent. The culprit was **bracket creep**, that is, the phenomenon of inflation pushing taxpayers into higher and higher brackets while their real earnings did not increase. Ronald Reagan made rising taxes a major issue in the 1980 presidential election, proposing a 30 percent income-tax cut spread over three years. In 1981, Congress gave President Reagan most of what he requested, reducing income taxes by 25 percent over three years. Congress also indexed tax rates to inflation to prevent bracket creep from increasing taxes all over again. Unfortunately for taxpayers, most of the savings from the individual income-tax cut were wiped out by higher state and local taxes and by increases in other federal taxes. In 1982, 1983, 1984, and 1987, Congress passed and President Reagan signed major increases in federal excise taxes and Social Security payroll taxes.

Tax Fairness

Another controversial aspect of the income tax is tax preferences. A **tax preference** is a tax deduction or exclusion that allows individuals to pay less tax than they would otherwise. Because of a variety of exclusions and deductions, two persons earning the same income may pay significantly different tax bills. A **tax exemption** is the exclusion of some types of income from taxation. Social Security and veterans' benefits, pension contributions and earnings, and interest earned on state and local government bonds are all exempt from the income tax. A **tax deduction** is an expenditure that can be subtracted from a taxpayer's gross income before computing the tax owed. These deductions include home-mortgage interest payments, charitable contributions, and state and local property taxes paid.

Tax preferences have both critics and defenders. Their opponents say that tax preferences erode taxpayer confidence in the income tax. The tax code has become so intricate that professional tax preparation has become a major industry. Tax preferences also reduce tax receipts. Mortgage-interest deductions alone cost the treasury $35 billion in 1990.[10] Moreover, critics charge that tax loopholes frequently allow the wealthy to pay little or no tax, making the income tax less progressive.

Still, every tax preference has its defenders. One person's loophole is another's sacred right. Homeowners, wage earners, the elderly, churches, schools, businesses, and many others benefit from one tax preference or another. What's more, the defenders of tax preferences point out that they are a mechanism that government can use to promote certain activities or to assist particular groups of taxpayers. By allowing taxpayers to deduct contributions to charitable institutions, government promotes private efforts to assist the poor, further the arts, care for the disabled, and the like. Government encourages business expansion by giving tax credits for investment expenditures. It helps the elderly by granting an additional tax deduction to people over age sixty-five.

The Budget Dilemma

These aren't happy days for American budget-makers, at least not in comparison with the 1960s and early 1970s. During the earlier period, federal revenues grew rapidly enough to allow policymakers to finance new programs and pass out tax cuts every few years. From 1960 to 1973, the economy grew at the relatively robust pace of 4 percent a year (after inflation). Individual incomes rose and, with them, so did tax collections. Because of bracket creep, even inflation helped increase tax revenues by pushing taxpayers into higher tax brackets. Every 10 percent rise in inflation produced a 16 percent increase in taxes. What's more, if Congress and the president needed a quick shot of extra revenue, they could close a few loopholes in the tax code without adversely affecting average taxpayers. Policymakers also gained budget leverage as the Vietnam War wound down, freeing defense dollars for other uses.

Today, circumstances are less favorable for budget-makers. With the economy growing at a relatively slower pace, personal incomes and tax collections have risen more slowly. Raising taxes has also become more difficult politically. Because tax brackets are now indexed to inflation, policymakers can no longer count on bracket creep to produce hidden tax increases. Moreover, recent tax reforms have eliminated all the easy-to-close loopholes and used the money to lower individual tax rates.

The legacy of the Reagan years was a set of spending priorities no one likes, frozen into place. Ronald Reagan came to the White House with three budgetary goals in mind: a tax cut, an increase in defense spending, and a balanced budget, in that order. In 1981, Congress generally accepted Reagan's tax-cut proposal, slashing income-tax rates by 25 percent over three years. It also agreed to a significant acceleration of the defense buildup begun under President Carter, increasing military spending at an annual rate of 7.5 percent after inflation from 1981 to 1986. The president and Congress failed, however, to cut nondefense spending sufficiently to compensate for the loss in tax revenue and to finance the defense buildup. Although Reagan succeeded in convincing Congress to reduce domestic spending, Congress eliminated few domestic programs entirely. The result was a series of record-high budget deficits. In effect, Reagan sacrificed his third goal, a balanced budget, in exchange for the tax cut and increased military spending. Then, the deficit and Gramm-Rudman halted the defense buildup. It was a state of affairs that left both liberals and conservatives unhappy: liberals because there wasn't more money for social programs, conservatives because there wasn't more for defense. But as long as Congress and the White House were unable to agree on economic policy, it was a state of affairs unlikely to change.[11]

THE GOALS OF ECONOMIC POLICY

Congress and the president disagree on economic policy because they don't agree on the goals of that policy. Let's examine some of the aims of economic policy and consider the political debates that surround them.

Financing Government Services

The most obvious goal of economic policy is to finance government services. Nonetheless, Americans disagree over spending priorities and over the appropriate level of funding for federal government activity. Liberals generally favor relatively high levels of federal spending for social programs because they believe that society's needs are great and only the national government has the resources to adequately address major social problems. Because of the deficit and an unwillingness by political leaders to enact necessary tax increases, liberals complain that government has no resources to fight the war on drugs, provide affordable housing for the homeless, reform the nation's educational system, or take advantage of a historic opportunity to advance the cause of democracy in Eastern Europe.

In contrast, conservatives contend that the federal government is too large. They argue that state and local governments and private enterprise can often deal more efficiently with social problems than the national government. What's more, they say, government activity, financed by either taxes or borrowing, crowds out private investment and consumption, thus retarding economic growth.

Incentives and Disincentives for Private Action

Another aim of economic policy is to offer incentives or disincentives for private action. Government promotes certain activities by means of a variety of direct and indirect subsidies. A **subsidy** is a financial incentive bestowed by government upon private individuals, companies, or groups to improve their economic position and accomplish some public objective.

Consider the case of government subsidies for logging in the Tongass National Forest. The Tongass is a seventeen-million-acre virgin forest in Southeastern Alaska that includes the largest remaining rain forest in North America. Each year the U.S. Forest Service spends $40 million there building roads and taking other measures to help lumber companies harvest trees which are ground into pulp and sold to Japan and other Asian countries. Although loggers pay the government for the timber, the government loses money on the deal. In fact, a congressional study estimates that the federal government lost more than $350 million during the 1980s helping lumber companies cut down the Tongass rain forest. This policy, of course, is controversial. Conservationists charge that loggers are destroying a unique natural resource that cannot be replaced. In contrast, timber interests argue that the government subsidy preserves timber-industry jobs essential to the health of the local economy.[12] (See the Perspective for a discussion of government farm subsidies.)

Government subsidies also support America's merchant marine. America's shipbuilding and shipping industries are not competitive in the world market, primarily because of high labor costs. The federal government has kept the industry afloat, however, by funneling government contracts through American shipyards and subsidizing the salaries of American crews. In 1986, for example, Uncle Sam shelled out $370 million in direct subsidies to U.S. shippers. The rationale for the subsidy is national security. American

PERSPECTIVE

Farm Subsidies

Government subsidizes farmers with three types of programs. The first involves government price-support loans. Farmers borrow money from the government, using their crops as collateral. The value of the crops and hence the amount a farmer can borrow is determined by a target commodity price set by the U.S. Department of Agriculture (USDA). If the market price rises above the target price, the farmer sells the crop and repays the loan. Should the market price stay below the target price, however, the farmer is allowed to forfeit the crop to the government as repayment for the loan.

Each year, the government effectively purchases a significant portion of America's agricultural production. In 1985, for example, Uncle Sam bought more than half the nation's 8.9-billion-bushel corn crop. The government gives away some of its commodity surplus through the Food for Peace program or to the poor in this country, but, since the law prevents the government from selling commodities at less than their purchase price, much of the surplus is stored, eventually to spoil.

In a second type of farm program, the government subsidizes farmers directly. If the market price falls below a target price, the government pays farmers the difference between the two prices, either in cash or in certificates for government-stored commodities. Finally, the government subsidizes farmers by intervening to limit commodity production, thus driving up market prices. In the mid-1980s, for example, the USDA paid dairy farmers $1.8 billion to slaughter dairy cattle to reduce the surplus of milk.[*]

Who benefits and who pays the bill for farm programs? Farmers benefit, of course, but most financial aid goes to those least in need of assistance. A USDA analysis of subsidies found that only 17 percent of government aid money makes it to financially distressed farmers, while 32 percent goes to

agribusiness. In 1986, for example, the government paid nearly $20 million in subsidies to J. G. Boswell Company, one of the nation's largest cotton producers.[†]

Foreign suppliers also benefit from government farm subsidies. In many instances, commodity target prices are far enough above the world market price that foreign suppliers can ship their produce here, sell it just below the target support price, and still make a profit. Consider the honey market in America. The government support price for honey is considerably higher than the world price. American producers sell most of their honey to the government rather than accept the lower market price, while foreign suppliers satisfy most of the American consumer demand for honey.[‡]

Consumers and taxpayers foot the bill for farm subsidies. Consumers pay in the form of higher prices for agricultural products. One study estimates, for example, that peanut price supports increase consumer costs by about 13 cents a pound.[§] The bill for taxpayers isn't exactly peanuts either; it was $20 billion in 1988.

As political scientists, how can we explain the persistence of programs that provide benefits to a small number of individuals at the expense of a large number? The explanation lies in the distribution of costs and benefits and in the nature of the attentive publics involved. The costs of farm programs are widely spread among millions of unorganized consumers and taxpayers. Since no one pays a large amount and the costs are hidden, consumers and taxpayers have little incentive to educate themselves about the details of farm-subsidy programs. In contrast, the beneficiaries of farm programs are relatively few and their benefits are large and apparent. Farm producers are organized and attentive to policy in this area. As a result, they enjoy more influence than does the general public.

Time, 21 July 1986, p. 46.
[†]*Time*, 18 August 1986, p. 38.
[‡]Jonathan Rauch, "A Federal Honey Program Drones On," *National Journal*, 1 April 1989, p. 807.
[§]"Goober Madness at the USDA," *Regulation*, January/February 1985, pp. 6–8.

shipbuilders and ship crews, the argument goes, are vital to the nation's defense. Politics plays a role, too, of course. The merchant-marine lobby is one of the most powerful in Washington.[13]

The list of subsidy recipients goes on and on. The Postal Service subsidizes publishers and bulk-rate advertisers with low rates and then makes up the losses by charging more for first-class mail. Beekeepers benefit, too, and not just from honey price supports. During the 1970s, the federal government gave beekeepers $30 million as compensation for bees killed by federally registered pesticides.[14]

Government promotes a variety of private activities through tax incentives. Tax exemptions and credits for business are aimed at encouraging investment, thereby enhancing economic growth. Tax exemptions for home-mortgage interest and state and local property taxes promote home ownership. Similarly, exemptions for charitable contributions help a broad range of educational, religious, and charitable institutions.

Taxes can also be used to discourage certain activities. An increase in the federal gasoline tax in 1982 was designed not just to raise money but also to promote energy conservation by making fuel more expensive. Moreover, at least part of the rationale behind taxes on alcohol and tobacco is to discourage their use.

Income Redistribution

Another goal of federal economic policy is the redistribution of income. Since the New Deal, the federal government has become a mammoth instrument for redistributing wealth, that is, taking items of value (especially money) from some groups of Americans and giving them to others. While some programs help the poor, other policies assist those at the other end of the income spectrum.

A number of federal programs are geared toward assisting low-income families and individuals. Supplemental Security Income (SSI) and Aid to Families with Dependent Children (AFDC) are examples of cash-transfer programs. A **cash-transfer program** is a public assistance program that gives money directly to eligible recipients. Food stamps, the school lunch program, subsidized housing, and Medicaid are federal programs that provide in-kind benefits to individuals on the basis of need. An **in-kind benefits program** is a public assistance program that distributes goods and services directly to eligible recipients.

Most public assistance programs are federal programs in that they involve state and local governments in addition to the national government. Congress creates the programs, setting guidelines for their implementation, while states administer them. Most of the money for welfare programs comes from Washington, with states supplementing the federal contribution with funds of their own.

Public assistance programs are quite important to poor Americans. People in the lowest fifth of the income spectrum receive more than half their incomes from government.[15] Moreover, a Census Bureau study estimates that without public assistance programs the poverty rate would be twice as high as it is.[16]

The poor, however, are not the only beneficiaries of federal largess. The largest and most expensive federal benefit programs—Social Security, Medicare, civil service pensions, military pensions, and unemployment compensation—go to persons without regard for need. These programs help many poor persons, of course, but they also put dollars in the pockets of millions of middle- and upper-income individuals. In fact, former Secretary of Commerce Peter Peterson says that federal programs end up "subsidizing the middle class far more than the poor."[17]

Consider the distribution of federal housing assistance. The federal government subsidizes housing for both the poor and the well-to-do, with the largest subsidies going to persons who need them least. While the poor benefit from low-income housing assistance, middle- and upper-income families enjoy federal income tax deductions for mortgage interest payments and property taxes, and a deferment of capital gains taxes on the sale of their principal residences. (A **capital gains tax** is a levy assessed on income from investments.) One study estimates that families earning less than $10,000 a year receive less than 16 percent of government housing subsidies. In contrast, families making more than $50,000 a year receive 52 percent of subsidies.[18]

Taxes are another tool for redistributing income. Historically, the progressive income tax has been credited with narrowing the gap between rich and poor. Those in lower income brackets pay almost no income tax, while upper-income groups pay a sizable proportion of their earnings in taxes. Other federal taxes tend to be regressive, however, falling more heavily on lower-income persons.

Income redistribution is controversial. Liberals believe that society has a moral duty to aid the poor. The job is too great for private charity and state and local governments, they say; the federal government must intervene. Some liberals distrust great wealth and argue that significant differences of income are unhealthy for society.

In contrast, conservatives believe that differences in ability and initiative are natural; some persons inevitably do better and grow wealthier than others. The poor will always be with us. Is it fair, they ask, for government to tax away the wealth of the successful to give to non-achievers? To be sure, government should establish a safety net of aid programs for the truly needy, they say, but it doesn't help the poor to make them dependent on the federal government. What's more, the high taxes necessary to support federal programs dampen the economy and, in the long run, hurt everyone.

In recent years, American economic policy has more closely reflected conservative values than liberal views. While Congress and the president have reduced income-tax rates, especially for persons at the upper end of the income spectrum, they have increased Social Security payroll taxes, which fall more heavily on the poor and middle class. Moreover, recent budget reduc-

The Orchard Park Housing Project in Roxbury, Massachusetts, stands in disrepair. Recent federal budget cuts have sapped programs established to assist people with low incomes.

tions have cut more deeply into programs that award benefits on the basis of need, such as food stamps, school lunches, subsidized housing, Medicaid, AFDC, and SSI. The larger programs that provide benefits regardless of need—programs Peter Peterson says subsidize the middle class—have escaped almost untouched by recent budget cuts.

Recent economic policies have helped to further tilt America's distribution of income toward the well-to-do. The Census Bureau reports that in 1988 the poorest fifth of Americans received only 4.6 percent of total national family income, the lowest percentage since 1954. In contrast, the wealthiest fifth of the nation's families received 44 percent of national income, the highest figure ever recorded.[19]

Economic Stabilization

A further goal of economic policy is to stabilize the economy. Americans want steady economic growth, a stable dollar, moderate interest rates, and low unemployment. Nonetheless, neither policymakers nor economists agree on how these goals can best be achieved.

Classical Economics

Classical economic theory is built on the principles of laissez faire, which is a French phrase that means to leave alone. **Laissez faire** is an economic philosophy holding that government intervention impedes the free-market forces that drive a healthy economy. It is based on the principles of capitalism outlined by Adam Smith in his classic study, *The Wealth of Nations*, published in

1776. Smith described the **business cycle**, which is the rhythmic fluctuation of a free economy, involving movements from prosperity to recession, followed by economic recovery and a return to prosperity. According to Smith, the economic ups and downs of the business cycle correct themselves naturally, without government intervention.

Suppose, for example, that the economy is in **recession** (an economic slowdown characterized by declining economic output and rising unemployment) or, more severely, a **depression** (a severe and prolonged economic slump). As sales of goods and services fall, manufacturing plants reduce output and lay off employees in order to cut costs. Without paychecks coming in, unemployed workers and their families cut back on their purchases, forcing other companies to reduce output and lay off employees as well. Consequently, the economy spirals deeper into recession or depression.

At some point, however, market forces intervene to reverse the process. As demand for goods and services fall, prices drop as well, eventually luring consumers to resume their purchases. Similarly, the falling demand for labor drives down wage rates. Eventually, wages fall to the point where employers begin rehiring. The economy starts to recover.

At the apex of the business cycle, the economy works at full capacity with full employment. Since everyone who wants a job has one, employers must offer higher and higher wages to compete for workers. With higher incomes, workers and their families are willing to increase their purchases of goods and services, but supply cannot be readily increased, since the economy is already at full throttle. Instead, prices rise. This general increase in prices produces a decline in the purchasing power of the currency, called **inflation**.

Once again, the "invisible hand" of the market comes to the rescue. Sooner or later, prices rise so high that consumers reduce their purchases. Consequently, some producers can no longer sell all of their output. With sales falling, they can no longer afford as many employees at the current high wage level, so they lay off a few workers, further reducing demand for goods and services. Both wages and prices stabilize as the economy cools.

According to laissez-faire economics, good economic times follow bad times in a natural cycle. Since the market is self-correcting, government need not play a role in the economy. Indeed, laissez-faire economists believe that government intervention invariably does more harm than good.

Laissez faire was the accepted economic model throughout most of the nineteenth and early twentieth centuries, but American economic policy did not necessarily reflect the theory. In practice, the pure capitalism of the laissez-faire model never really existed. Although the national government did not adopt a comprehensive policy of economic stabilization, Congress and the president did respond to the demands of major economic groups who urged government to intervene on their behalf through promotion and regulation. For example, the federal government adopted tariffs to protect some industries while enacting regulations to control others. Also, state and local governments consistently intervened on the side of management in labor disputes.

The Great Depression forced American policymakers to rethink both the theory and practice of economic policy as the economy collapsed and did not rebound. The theory of laissez-faire economics counseled patience, but, as the depression deepened, the patience of many Americans grew thin. As a result, policymakers looked elsewhere for solutions to the nation's economic problems.

Keynesian Economics

Onto the scene stepped John Maynard Keynes (pronounced kanes), a British economist with a new theory that offered a solution to the depression. He said that recessions and depressions result from a lack of demand in the economy, or too little spending. Even though prices fall during a recession, Keynes noted, spending may not increase much because consumers have little money. Moreover, businesses will hesitate to expand because they know that consumers can't afford to purchase additional goods and services. The only sure way out of the depression, Keynes said, was for government to bolster purchasing power to increase demand.

Keynes believed that government can increase consumers' purchasing power by running a budget deficit and financing it by creating new money. When government taxes, it takes money out of the economy. It returns money through expenditures, by either giving cash to individuals, such as Social Security recipients, or purchasing goods and services, such as tanks for the military or medical care for the elderly. When the budget is balanced, the process of taking and returning money roughly evens out. When government runs a deficit, however, it puts more money into the economy than it withdraws. The latter, said Keynes, is precisely what government should do to combat depression/recession. By cutting taxes and/or increasing expenditures, government can pump income into the economy. People will then have more money to spend, causing demand for goods and services to rise. Manufacturers will begin rehiring workers to make goods to meet increased demand. The economy will recover.

We can define **Keynesian economics** as an economic theory that utilizes the machinery of government to guide and direct a free enterprise economy. While classic laissez-faire economics says that the economy should be left alone to correct itself, the Keynesians believe that government can successfully intervene to correct the imbalances of recession and inflation by careful manipulation of fiscal and monetary policy. **Fiscal policy** is the use of government spending and taxation for the purpose of achieving economic goals. **Monetary policy** is the control of the money supply for the purpose of achieving economic goals. Although Keynes himself initially developed Keynesian economic theories dealing with fiscal policy, his successors defined the role of monetary policy.

Monetary policy concerns the amount of money in circulation in the economy. Fluctuations in the money supply affect interest rates. **Interest**, you recall, is money paid for the use of money. The law of supply and demand

Selling apples on street corners became a symbol of the Great Depression, when many millions of Americans were unable to find jobs.

stipulates that interest rates will rise and fall with the money supply. If money is "tight" (that is, in short supply), interest rates rise. If money is "easy" (that is, plentiful), they fall.

Interest rates have an important effect on the economy. Low interest rates encourage investment and discourage savings; high interest rates do the opposite. Suppose a corporation is considering borrowing money to finance a major expansion. The higher the interest rates, the less incentive corporate managers have to undertake the expansion. Instead, they may choose to wait until interest rates fall, thus reducing the costs of expansion.

Keynesian economists believe that policymakers can use fiscal and monetary policy to manage the economy. During times of recession, government can stimulate the economy by spending more or taxing less (thus running a budget deficit) and/or by increasing the money supply to reduce interest rates (thus increasing overall demand). If the problem is inflation, government can slow the economy by reducing spending or increasing taxes (thus running a budget surplus) and/or by reducing interest rates (thus reducing excess demand).

In 1958, economist Alban W. H. Phillips introduced his famous Phillips curve as a corollary to the Keynesian thinking. The **Phillips curve** is an economic model holding that unemployment goes up as the rate of inflation goes down. Phillips, who studied unemployment and inflation rates in Great Britain between the years 1861 and 1913, found that inflation went up when unemployment went down, and vice versa. The price we pay for full employment, said Phillips, is inflation. It can be reduced, but only at the cost of more unemployment. Consequently, policymakers must accept a trade-off. The challenge for policymakers is to balance an acceptable level of inflation with moderate unemployment.

Through the end of the 1960s, the Keynesian explanation of economic reality seemed accurate. With inflation and unemployment rates both under 5 percent, it appeared the economy could be managed. The fluctuations of the business cycle seemed under control.

In the 1970s, however, changing economic conditions shattered the consensus over Keynesian economics and the Phillips curve. Huge increases in the price of petroleum initiated by the Organization of Petroleum Exporting Countries (OPEC) fueled inflation in the United States and Western Europe. By the late 1970s, American inflation rates approached and sometimes exceeded 10 percent. In the meantime, unemployment topped the 8 percent mark as economic growth lagged. The trade-off between inflation and unemployment no longer seemed to be working. Instead, the United States suffered from **stagflation**, an economic condition in which high unemployment, reduced output, and high rates of inflation exist at the same time. What had happened to the government's ability to manage the economy?

Contemporary Economic Models

The key feature of the American economy of the 1990s is its increasing level of integration with the world economy. Because of international trade and investment, decisions made in Tokyo, Japan, or Riyadh, Saudi Arabia, may have as great an impact on the American economy as decisions made in Washington or New York. In the face of the complexity of the global economy, professional economists disagree on how the economy works and what policies government officials should pursue to promote stable economic growth. While some economists warn about the dangers of the federal budget deficit, for example, others point out that the official deficit has shrunk as a percentage of GNP and, as such, is quite manageable.[20]

Policymakers seeking advice on the economy can turn to a number of schools of economic thought for guidance. Although each of these approaches has its supporters, no one school of thought dominates economic theory as did Keynesian economics after World War II.

Keynesian economics.   Despite the stagflation of the late 1970s, Keynesian economics is by no means extinct. Keynesian economists may not be as confident of their ability to explain and predict economic developments today as they were twenty years ago, but they nonetheless believe that the basic principles of Keynesian analysis are sound. The challenge, as they see it, is to adapt Keynesian theories to contemporary conditions.

Monetarist school.   **Monetarism** is the economic theory holding that stable economic growth can best be assured through management of the money supply. Monetarists, led by economist Milton Friedman, challenge the Keynesian idea that government can effectively use fiscal and monetary policy to manage the economy. In the long run, monetarists believe that government efforts to manage the economy will do harm, hence the stagflation of the late 1970s and deep recession of the early 1980s. Monetarists think that government can only assure economic stability by holding the rate of growth in the money supply to the potential growth rate of the economy. Increasing the supply of money faster than output produces inflation. If the money supply grows more slowly than the economy, the result is recession.[21]

Supply-side economics.   **Supply-side economics** is the economic theory that focuses on factors, such as tax rates, that affect the supply of goods and services in the economy. Supply-side economists believe that high tax rates discourage investment and worker productivity. Why work harder to earn more money if government is going to tax away much of it? Supply-side economists advocate tax reductions in order to stimulate investment and economic growth. In fact, supply-siders believe that economic growth generated by tax reductions will be sufficient to actually produce an increase in tax receipts.

Rational-expectations school.   The **rational-expectations school of economics** is an approach to economic theory holding that people closely observe government policies and then react in accordance with their own self-interest, which may run counter to policy objectives. If union and corpo-

*"...First I was a
Keynesian...
Next I was a
monetarist...
Then a supply-sider...
Now I'm a bum..."*

Reprinted with permission: Tribune Media Services.

rate leaders believe that the government may impose wage and price controls in order to control inflation, for example, they will act to protect their own interests by pushing for wage and price increases now before government acts. As a result, inflation grows worse. Members of the rational-expectations school believe that the market works best without government intervention.

Neoclassical international theory. **Neoclassical international economic theory** (also known as **New Wave economics**) is an approach to economic theory holding that the openness of the American economy makes it immune to economy-wide recessions, although slumps may strike certain weak industries. New Wave economists believe that the close interconnections among the economies of the world have changed the nature of the business cycle. In the global economy, American business executives can overcome high interest rates in the United States, for example, by borrowing from abroad. Similarly, American manufacturers can avoid high domestic labor costs by opening plants in other countries. Individual industries may suffer recessions, but not the whole economy.

Each of these approaches to economic theory has its adherents among professional economists, with no one school of thought dominating. Indeed, each approach has its shortcomings. Supply-side economics, for example, was the theoretical rationale for the 25 percent reduction in income-tax rates President Reagan pushed through Congress in 1981. The result was somewhat less than the economic boom and balanced budget that the supply-siders predicted, because the nation slipped into a deep recession and the budget deficit soared.

Many economic forecasters don't rely on any one economic theory. Instead, they blend in ideas that appear useful.[22] Economist Michael Boskin, who was appointed by President Bush to head the Council of Economic Advisers, says this about economic forecasting: "We have learned that the various schools of thought all have important elements of truth in them. But none of them is by itself a sufficient explanation of what goes on in the economy."[23]

ECONOMIC POLICYMAKING

Do you recall the five stages of the policymaking process that we outlined in the introduction to this textbook? **Agenda building**, the first stage, is the process through which issues become matters of public concern and governmental action. The second stage, **policy formulation**, involves the development of courses of action for dealing with problems on the official agenda. **Policy adoption**, the third stage of the process, refers to the official decision of a governmental body to accept a particular policy and put it into effect. The fourth stage, **policy implementation**, is the stage of the process in which policies are carried out. Finally, **policy evaluation** is concerned with the assessment of policy. Let's use the policy process as a tool for analyzing federal economic policymaking.

Agenda Building

Nearly everyone has a stake in economic policy, and many make their voices heard. The general public prefers good times, of course, meaning low unemployment and stable prices. People tend to vote their pocketbooks. Presidents and parties that preside over hard economic times usually pay an electoral price, as did Herbert Hoover and the Republican party during the Great Depression.

In terms of specific policy preferences, the general public often offers contradictory guidance to policymakers. Although Americans favor most spending programs, they often oppose the taxes necessary to pay for them. A recent poll, for example, found that 86 percent of respondents agreed that all Americans should "have access to the same quality of health care regardless of ability to pay." Only 26 percent of the sample, however, were willing to pay as much as $50 a year in additional taxes "to cover the cost of health care for those who cannot afford it."[24]

Attentive publics with specific policy demands press their concerns on policymakers. (An **attentive public** is a group of people who have an active and continuing interest in a particular political issue.) The elderly, for example, focus on Social Security and Medicare. Farmers worry about farm programs. Veterans' groups are concerned with veterans' programs.

In the meantime, thousands of interest groups lobby for particular causes. Industries hard pressed to meet foreign competition call for import restrictions. Defense contractors support the defense programs on which they work. Real estate interests work to maintain favorable tax treatment.

Some of the most active lobbying on economic issues comes from the public sector, that is, from government itself. State and local officials lobby Washington over federal programs. When federal grants-in-aid are cut back, as they were in the early 1980s, state and local governments must either raise taxes or cut revenues. Neither is a pleasant prospect politically. Pressure also comes from within the federal bureaucracy. Program managers and bureau chiefs see their current expenditure levels (including an increment for inflation) as their base. They press for more money and strongly resist any effort to give them less.

Policy Formulation and Adoption

Since the 1930s, the president has taken the initiative in economic policymaking. The primary instrument of presidential influence in economic policy is the budget. It outlines presidential priorities for spending and taxation. Also, it is a tool for presidential control of the executive branch. Because of the president's power to propose budget increases or decreases, agencies have an incentive to cooperate with the chief executive's program. Finally, the president can use the budget as an instrument for economic stabilization.

Economic Advisers

Economic policy is complex, so the president frequently turns to others for assistance and advice. The Council of Economic Advisers (CEA) provides the president with information on the state of the economy and suggests policies to promote stable economic growth. The Office of Management and Budget (OMB) coordinates preparation of the budget. The president also receives input on economic policy from the cabinet, particularly the secretary of the treasury. Frequently, however, the president's most influential economic advisers are members of the White House staff. Although their economic expertise may be slight, staff members have an eye for politics. After all, economic decisions are also political decisions. Economists worry about the long run, but the president stands for reelection in the short run.

Constraints on Budgeting

The president must operate under a number of restraints in preparing the budget. First, economic data may be faulty. Estimates of current economic conditions are frequently proven incorrect. Also, there are lags in compiling statistics. The nation may be in or out of a recession for months before the data reveal it. Moreover, economic indicators may be unreliable. Many experts believe that the consumer price index (CPI) is a poor indicator of inflation. Another measure, the GNP deflator, is probably superior, but it comes out only every three months. Meanwhile, many economists criticize the unemployment index because it doesn't count workers who have given up finding a job.

Second, economic predictions are often less accurate than long-range weather forecasts. The complexity of the economy makes prediction a chancy business. Moreover, events, such as droughts, strikes, or international crises, can intervene to wreak havoc with the most careful prognostication. Few economists predicted the OPEC-initiated oil price increases of the 1970s with their dramatic impact on the American inflation rate. A further problem is that administrations are notorious for making rosy predictions. The traditional political defense for a weak economy, of course, is to announce that prosperity is just around the corner.

Third, fiscal policy at best is a clumsy tool for stabilizing the economy. Preparation of the annual budget begins eighteen to twenty months before the start of the fiscal year. Who can foresee accurately what the economy will then be like? Also, Congress is slow. If the president asks for a tax cut to counter today's recession, it may not be passed and in place until recovery is well under way, just in time, perhaps, to fuel inflation.

Finally, more than three-fourths of the expenditures in the budget are **uncontrollable expenditures**; that is, they are funds that must be included in the budget because of existing contracts or laws. This category includes interest on the national debt, expenditures for weapons systems ordered in previous years, and money for entitlement programs, such as Social Security, Medicare, and federal pensions. Spending in these areas cannot be changed without legislative action.

These circumstances leave little room for maneuver. The part of the budget that is controllable can't be changed easily for political reasons. Every dollar has its defenders. Balance the budget, they say, but leave my pet programs alone. Also, the system is biased toward rising expenditures. Entitlements grow because the number of eligible recipients increases and because benefits are often indexed to inflation. Then there's the camel's nose phenomenon. Many programs start small and then grow. To cut back means to risk wasting money already spent. In other words, once the camel has poked his nose under the tent, it's hard to get him out. Before long, the little program is a big one and the entire camel is in the tent. Perhaps the best description of the budget, then, is that it is less an economic plan than an estimate of what is likely to happen.

The Budget Process

The actual process of formulating a budget begins in the spring, a year and a half before the start of the fiscal year. The president consults advisers, setting economic goals and establishing overall revenue and expenditure levels. The president may map plans for spending initiatives in some areas, retrenchments in others.

Around March, the OMB sends spending-level guidelines to the various agencies of the executive branch. In the early summer, agencies submit their budget proposals to the OMB, proposals which are invariably over the ceiling. The OMB cuts their requests, and the agencies react with horror. A period of negotiations follows, after which agencies may appeal to the deputy director of the OMB, the director, and, eventually, the president. The whole process isn't complete until early January. The president then submits the budget to Congress. Gramm-Rudman requires the president's proposed budget to be within the deficit goals for the year.

The budget process in Congress begins in November, eleven months before the start of the next fiscal year, when the president submits a current services budget to the Joint Economic Committee (JEC). The **current services budget** is an estimate of the cost of continuing present government programs at current levels. Using economic data and economic forecasts prepared by the Congressional Budget Office (CBO), the JEC, which is composed of members of the tax-writing and appropriations committees of each house, prepares overall budget recommendations to submit to the budget committees of each chamber by year's end. In practice, the recommendations of the JEC represent a starting point for negotiations between congressional leaders and the White House over budget priorities.

When the president sends the budget to Congress in January, it is chopped up, never to be reassembled. Tax measures go to the Ways and Means Committee in the House and the Finance Committee in the Senate. Because the Constitution stipulates that revenue-raising bills must originate in the House, Ways and Means gets the first shot. Spending bills are referred to the appropriation committees in each chamber.

The spending side of the budget requires the enactment of both authorization and appropriation bills. **Authorization** is the process through which Congress legislatively establishes a program, defines its general purpose, devises procedures for its operation, specifies an agency to implement the program, and indicates an approximate level of funding for the program (but does *not* actually provide money). Authorization bills are considered by the standing legislative committees in each chamber, such as Agriculture and Armed Services. Congress may authorize a program for one year only or for several years. The **appropriation process**, meanwhile, is the procedure through which Congress legislatively provides money for a particular purpose. Appropriations bills begin in the appropriations committees in each house although, by tradition, the House committee considers spending bills first. Congress appropriates money annually.

The traditional view of the budget process was that the president was an advocate of spending while the House played the role of guardian of the treasury. The Senate then acted as an appeals court for interest groups and government agencies that felt shortchanged by the House. In the 1980s, however, the roles changed as President Reagan advocated major increases in defense spending and major reductions in domestic spending. Although the

Republican-controlled Senate generally supported the president, at least in the early years of the decade, the Democratically controlled House opposed Reagan, favoring more modest changes in budget priorities than the president. As these developments showed, presidential and congressional budgetary roles are not fixed, but change in response to political circumstances.[25]

The traditional approach political scientists have used for studying budgeting is the incrementalist model. The **incrementalist model of budgeting** is a theoretical effort to explain the budget process on the basis of small (incremental) changes in budget categories from one budget to the next. Scholars following this approach believe that agency heads, members of Congress, and the president all see an agency's current budget share as its base, evaluating each year's budget in comparison with the prior year's. As a result, changes in individual budget items tend to be small. Another explanation for incremental budget making is that an agency's current budget reflects its political strength relative to the political strength of other agencies competing for money. Since the relative political influence of various claimants for budget dollars is unlikely to change dramatically from one budget period to the next, budget figures are unlikely to change dramatically either.[26]

In recent years, a number of political scientists have concluded that incrementalism doesn't explain the budget process in every instance. Budgets are not always stable. As Table 12.1 shows, spending for national defense increased substantially between 1981 and 1984, both in actual dollar amount and as a percentage of the total budget. Scholars have learned that executives and members of Congress do more than just consider year-to-year changes in individual budget items. They also compare budget shares among items across time. In the 1980s, for example, budget debates often centered on setting priorities between spending for defense and domestic programs. What's more, environmental factors, such as wars and depressions, and changes in political coalitions can often have a major impact on the budget process.[27]

In general, the appropriation committees and Congress as a whole follow the president's lead, at least in terms of overall expenditures. One study found that from 1947 to 1984, Congress appropriated an average of $0.8 billion a year less than the president requested. With a Republican president, Congress appropriated an average $1.9 billion a year more than asked; for Democratic presidents, Congress spent $3.4 billion less. On average, Congress appropriated more for defense and less for domestic programs than Democratic presidents requested, but just the opposite when a Republican was in the White House.[28]

While the authorization and appropriation processes are in progress, the budget committees in each house are at work to establish bottom-line spending and revenue targets for the budget year. Using information from the CBO, the JEC, and standing committees, the budget committees prepare a budget resolution by April 15, which meets Gramm-Rudman guidelines. For the next few months, the appropriation and authorization committees work to get the various segments of the budget in line with overall targets.

Congressional budget-makers must also conform to Gramm-Rudman guidelines. On August 15, the CBO and OMB estimate the deficit for the coming year. If the projected deficit exceeds the Gramm-Rudman limit, Congress has until October 1, when the fiscal year begins, to make necessary spending cuts or tax increases to meet the limit. Should Congress fail to reach the deficit goal, Gramm-Rudman requires the president to order across-the-board spending cuts, evenly divided between defense expenditures and domestic programs (exempting Social Security and a number of other programs).

Although the budget process requires Congress and the president to complete work on the budget by the beginning of the fiscal year on October 1, they seldom meet the deadline. In practice, Congress eventually lumps together several spending bills into a single telephone-book-size piece of legislation at the last minute. The president must either sign the catchall bill or risk having the government shut down as a new budget year begins without a budget in place.

Although Congress' budget procedures hardly seem a model of governmental efficiency, they reflect the politics of budget making in an era when different parties control the legislative and executive branches. The rules of the legislative process, you recall, require the president to either veto appropriation bills or allow them to become law. By giving the president a single catchall spending bill instead of a series of shorter appropriation measures, Democratic leaders in Congress hope to force Republican presidents to accept measures which they oppose and would veto were they standing on their own. What's more, by waiting until the last minute, Democrats in Congress raise the political price for a presidential veto, since a veto would likely mean that the government would literally have to shut down because it lacked legal authority to spend money.

Both President Reagan and President Bush responded to Democratic budget tactics by calling for a constitutional amendment to allow the president a line-item veto on appropriation bills. The **line-item veto** is the power of an executive to veto sections or items of an appropriation bill while signing the remainder of the bill into law. Reagan and Bush point out that most state governors enjoy the power of the line-item veto on appropriation bills and argue that the item veto would enable the president to eliminate "wasteful spending." In contrast, opponents of the line-item veto fear that it would give the president too much power, upsetting the constitutional balance between the executive and legislative branches. At this point, it seems unlikely that Congress would agree to give the president the item veto, especially since one party controls Congress while the other holds the White House.

Monetary Policy

Monetary policy is the domain of the Federal Reserve Board. The Fed, as the board is called, is an independent regulatory commission, headed by a seven-member board of governors appointed by the president with Senate confirmation to serve fixed, overlapping terms of fourteen years. The president also names a board chair with Senate approval to serve a four-year term. In 1987, for example, President Reagan appointed economist Alan Greenspan to chair the Fed.

The idea behind this arrangement is that the Fed should be independent of presidential and congressional control. In theory, the board sets monetary policy on the basis of economic considerations, not political ones. The problem with independence, however, is that fiscal and monetary policy may not always mesh. They may even cancel each other. In 1981, for example, President Reagan and Congress launched their great experiment in supply-side economics by enacting a tax cut that they hoped would stimulate an economic boom. Meanwhile, the Federal Reserve tightened the money supply to get a handle on inflation. The resultant higher interest rates slowed the economy, helping to produce a severe recession.

In practice, the Fed is far from an apolitical body. It lobbies Congress and the executive and, in turn, receives pressure from Congress, the White House, and the banking community, among other interests. What's more, a number of studies have uncovered evidence that the Federal Reserve bends with the political winds, adopting monetary policies that accommodate the incumbent president's fiscal policies.[29] For example, one scholar finds that since 1960, the Fed has almost always increased the money supply more rapidly in the two years preceding a presidential election than in the two years following, thereby stimulating the economy and presumably enhancing the president's reelection prospects.[30]

Alan Greenspan, chairman of the Federal Reserve, with former chairman Paul Volcker at the rear.

Policy Implementation and Evaluation

The implementation of economic policy involves nearly the whole of government in America. For the most part, the Treasury Department is responsible for tax collection and borrowing. The Federal Reserve and its member banks implement monetary policy. Money is spent by the agencies of the executive branch and, through federal programs, by an array of state and local governments.

Impoundment has sometimes been a major issue in economic policy implementation. **Impoundment** is the power of the president to impound, or refuse to spend, money appropriated by Congress. President Nixon claimed broader powers of impoundment than any of his predecessors, and Congress responded legislatively to limit the chief executive's ability to impound funds. Under present law, the president can propose that an appropriation be rescinded. The rescission doesn't hold, however, unless Congress votes to accept the president's proposal.

Both the executive and legislative branch of American government have mechanisms for evaluating economic policy. The OMB assesses the operation of programs within the executive branch for the president while the General Accounting Office (GAO) performs a similar role for Congress, investigating agency activities and auditing expenditures. Outside of the GAO, however, efforts at oversight are haphazard and unsystematic. Moreover, when they do occur, they tend to focus on nickel-and-dime matters, such as expense accounts and limousine use, or on well-publicized abuses, such as cost overruns on weapons systems purchased by the Pentagon.

CONCLUSION: ECONOMIC POLICY AND POLITICS

The best explanation for economic policy lies not in economic theory but in political reality. Members of Congress of both parties support programs that most benefit their districts. Presidents endorse policies that favor their political support bases. Democratic administrations generally endorse policies designed to assist their traditional support groups: organized labor, inner-city voters, the lower and lower-middle classes. Republicans, meanwhile, steer economic policy to benefit their support groups: business people and professionals, suburban voters, the upper- and upper-middle-income groups. One study finds that the income gap between the richest and poorest Americans increases by 4 to 5 percent under the typical two-term Republican administration, but falls by around 12 points during eight years of Democratic control of the White House.[31]

A strong case can be made that political leaders embrace particular economic theories for their political appeal, not their economic merit. In the 1988 presidential campaign, for example, Republican George Bush advocated a reduction in the federal capital gains tax. (Capital gains are profits earned from the sale of stocks and other investments.) Bush supported his position with an argument drawn from supply-side economics: a capital gains tax cut will encourage investment, stimulating economic growth. Although economists disagreed about whether a reduction in capital gains taxes would have much effect on investment, no one disagreed about the tax cut's prime beneficiaries—taxpayers with incomes greater than $200,000 a year, a group which, incidentally, happens to be an important constituency for the Republican party.

Finally, let's consider the politics behind the federal budget deficit. Although no one in Washington really *likes* the deficit, a good many political leaders prefer it to the alternative. Conservatives see the alternative to the deficit as bigger government. They believe that Congress would use any additional tax moneys to fund more programs. Many conservatives also fear that higher taxes could hurt the economy. In contrast, liberals see the alternative to the deficit as smaller government. They believe that government should be spending more money for education, housing, drug treatment, health care, and the environment, not less. Moreover, liberals worry that deficit reduction could bring on a recession.[32] In sum, the deficit persists because policymakers, and Americans in general, do not agree on who should pay the cost of its reduction, either in higher taxes or in reduced services.

KEY TERMS

ability-to-pay theory of taxation

agenda building

appropriation process

attentive public

authorization

bracket creep

budget

budget deficit

budget surplus

business cycle

capital gains tax

cash-transfer program

consumer price index (CPI)

cost-of-living adjustment (COLA)

current services budget

depression

entitlement program

excise tax

fiscal policy

fiscal year

gross national product (GNP)

impoundment

incrementalist model of budgeting

inflation

in-kind benefits program

interest

Keynesian economics

laissez faire

line-item veto

marginal tax rate

monetarism

monetary policy

national debt

neoclassical international economic theory

New Wave economics

off-budget operations

Phillips curve

policy adoption

policy evaluation

policy formulation

policy implementation

progressive tax

proportional tax

rational-expectations school of economics

recession

regressive tax

stagflation

subsidy

supply-side economics

tax deduction

tax exemption

tax incidence

tax preference

uncontrollable expenditures

NOTES

1. Quoted in *Washington Monthly*, December 1986, p. 34.
2. Richard Locayo, "Dirty Little Secret," *Time*, 19 February 1990, pp. 48–49.
3. Elizabeth Wehr, "Gramm-Rudman Legislation Proves Blessing and Curse," *Houston Chronicle*, 28 December 1986, sec. 1, p. 14.
4. Jai P. Bajaj, "Predicted Social Security Surpluses, Savings Revival Could Erase U.S. Deficit," *Houston Post*, 30 July 1989, D-3.

5. Jodie T. Allen, "Now That We've Got a Big Social Security Surplus, Let's Not Blow It," *Washington Post*, National Weekly Edition, 13–19 June 1988, p. 23.

6. John Crawford, *Budgeting for America*, 2d ed. (Washington, DC: Congressional Quarterly Press, 1989), p. 72.

7. *National Journal*, 9 August 1986, p. 1946.

8. Joseph A. Pechman, *Federal Tax Policy*, 5th ed. (Washington, DC: Brookings Institution, 1987), p. 5.

9. *Statistical Abstract of the United States, 1985* (Washington, DC: U.S. Government Printing Office, 1984), p. 850.

10. *CQ Weekly Report*, 28 January 1989, pp. 155–60.

11. Jonathan Rauch, "The Fiscal Ice Age," *National Journal*, 10 January 1987, pp. 58–64.

12. John Lancaster, "The Amazon Isn't the Only Rain Forest That's Disappearing," *Washington Post*, National Weekly Edition, 11–17 September 1989, p. 33.

13. Michael Isikoff and Howard Kurtz, "Down to the Sea in Federal Subsidy Rights," *Washington Post*, National Weekly Edition, 20 May 1985, p. 32.

14. Carl P. Chelf, *Public Policymaking in America* (Glenview, IL: Scott, Foresman, 1981), pp. 159–62.

15. Joel Havemann, "Sharing the Wealth: The Gap Between Rich and Poor Grows Wider," *National Journal*, 23 October 1982, pp. 1788–95.

16. "Census Study: 10.3% Poverty Would Soar If Not for Benefits," *Houston Chronicle*, 28 December 1988, sec. 1, p. 1.

17. Peter G. Peterson, "No More Free Lunch for the Middle Class," *New York Times Magazine*, 17 January 1982, pp. 40–41, 56–63.

18. *CQ Weekly Report*, 28 January 1989, pp. 155–60.

19. "U.S. Economic Expansion Fails to Improve Poverty Rate in 1988," *Houston Chronicle*, 19 October 1989, p. 4A.

20. John Greenwald, "Knitting New Notions," *Time*, 30 January 1989, p. 46.

21. Crawford, p. 38.

22. Alfred L. Malabre, Jr., and Lindley H. Clark, Jr., "Changes in Economy Cause Much Confusion Among Economists," *Wall Street Journal*, 27 March 1989, pp. A1, A4.

23. Quoted in Greenwald, p. 46.

24. *Washington Post*, National Weekly Edition, 6–12 November 1989, p. 38.

25. James Malachowski, Samuel Bookheimer, and David Lowery, "The Theory of the Budgetary Process in an Era of Changing Budgetary Roles, FY48–FY84," *American Politics Quarterly* 15 (July 1987): 325–54.

26. Aaron Wildavsky, *The Politics of the Budgetary Process* (Boston, MA: Little, Brown, 1964).

27. Irene S. Rubin, ed., *New Directions in Budget Theory* (Albany, NY: State University of New York Press, 1988), p. 4.

28. Paul E. Peterson, "The New Politics of Deficits," *Political Science Quarterly* 100 (Winter 1985–86): 575–601.

29. Nathaniel Beck, "Elections and the Fed: Is There a Political Monetary Cycle?" *American Journal of Political Science* 31 (February 1987): 194–216.

30. Robert J. Shapiro, "Politics and the Federal Reserve," *Public Interest* 66 (Winter 1982): 119–39.

31. Douglas A. Hibbs, Jr., and Christopher Dennis, "Income Distribution in the United States," *American Political Science Review* 82 (June 1988): 467–90.

32. Jonathan Rauch, "Is the Deficit Really So Bad?" *Atlantic Monthly*, February 1989, pp. 36–42.

SUGGESTED READINGS

Crawford, John. *Budgeting for America*, 2d ed. Washington, DC: Congressional Quarterly Press, 1989.

Danziger, Sheldon H., and Weinberg, Daniel H. *Fighting Poverty: What Works and What Doesn't*. Cambridge, MA: Harvard University Press, 1986.

Lynch, Thomas D. *Public Budgeting in America*, 3d ed. Englewood Cliffs, NJ: Prentice-Hall, 1990.

Pechman, Joseph A. *Federal Tax Policy*, 5th ed. Washington, DC: Brookings Institution, 1987.

Pechman, Joseph A. *Who Paid the Taxes, 1966–85?* Washington, DC: Brookings Institution, 1985.

Peterson, Peter G., and Howe, Neil. *On Borrowed Time: How the Growth in Entitlement Spending Threatens America's Future*. San Francisco, CA: ICS Press, 1988.

Rapp, David. *How the U.S. Got into Agriculture*. Washington, DC: Congressional Quarterly Press, 1988.

Wildavsky, Aaron. *The New Politics of the Budgetary Process*. Glenview, IL: Scott, Foresman, 1988.

13

REGULATORY
POLICYMAKING

THE HISTORY OF REGULATION IN AMERICA
REGULATORY FEDERALISM
THE PROS AND CONS OF REGULATION
REGULATORY POLICYMAKING
CONCLUSION: REGULATORY POLICY AND POLITICS

LEARNING OBJECTIVES

1. To trace the history of federal regulatory policy, distinguishing between older and newer regulatory agencies and describing the scope of federal regulation today.
2. To describe the roles played by state and local governments in the regulatory process.
3. To identify arguments for and against government regulation.
4. To trace the steps of the regulatory policymaking process.
5. To describe the politics of regulation.

What do National, Western, People Express, Republic, Ozark Air, Pacific, Southwest, Frontier, Muse Air, Jet America, and Empire have in common? They are airlines that are no longer in business. Since 1978, when Congress passed, and President Carter signed, legislation deregulating the airline industry, more than two hundred air carriers have gone out of business or merged with stronger competitors.[1]

The airline business was once stable and predictable. From 1938 until 1978, the Civil Aeronautics Board (CAB), an independent regulatory commission, closely monitored the industry. The CAB licensed air carriers, set fares, designated routes, and even specified the size of sandwiches airlines could serve their passengers.

Economists agreed that the chief impact of CAB regulation was to protect existing airlines from competition. During forty years of regulation, the CAB refused to license a single new carrier, turning down seventy-nine applications. Critics charged that the lack of competition meant high fares and poor service for consumers. They called for deregulation.

The primary opposition to deregulation came from the airlines themselves. They argued that deregulation would initially produce competition but that competition would lead to business failures. Eventually, only a few giant companies would survive, resulting in less competition than before deregulation. The only other significant opposition to deregulation came from smaller cities, which feared that deregulation would lead to a loss of service.

By the mid-1970s, political momentum had swung to the side of those favoring deregulation. Several academic and Department of Transportation studies documented the costs of regulation, and well-publicized scandals in the airline industry undercut its position. Both Presidents Ford and Carter endorsed an end to airline regulation, appointing proponents of deregulation to serve on the CAB. Then, in 1978, Congress passed legislation phasing in deregulation over a period of six years. At the end of 1984, the CAB would go out of business.[2]

Deregulation opened the airline industry to competition as dozens of new carriers took to the skies. By 1984, the number of airlines had grown from thirty-six to well over a hundred. As they competed for passengers, both new companies and the established firms slashed fares and offered new services.[3]

Competition produced winners and losers. While some airlines increased their profits and their share of the market, more than a hundred other carriers filed for bankruptcy or merged with other companies. Many airline workers were among the losers as well. To cut costs to meet competition, air carriers reduced salaries and benefits, often substantially. What's more, despite the addition of new airlines, total employment in the industry remained about the same.

Observers disagree, however, on the long-term impact of regulation on consumers. Initially, consumers in major population centers reaped a windfall in lower fares and supersaver discounts. They also benefited from a wider variety of flight options. In recent years, as the number of air carriers has shrunk because of business failures and takeovers, airline ticket prices have risen, although not as rapidly as the inflation rate. What's more, the industry is beset by congestion, complaints over service quality, and concerns about safety.[4]

The story of airline deregulation introduces the policies and politics of government regulation in America. Regulatory policymaking is controversial, the stakes are high, and the number of participants, both inside and outside of government, is substantial. In the end, regulatory policy results from the workings of the political process.

THE HISTORY OF REGULATION IN AMERICA

The modern era of federal government regulation began in 1887 with the enactment of the Interstate Commerce Act. Before the late nineteenth century, the national government's relationship with business was relatively modest and aimed generally at promoting economic growth. Congress levied tariffs on imports to protect American manufacturers and gave land grants to railroads to further westward expansion.

By the late nineteenth century, the Industrial Revolution was well under way and many Americans, wary of the growing power of big business, called for government regulation. Small business owners, for example, worried about being gobbled up by giant corporations. Farmers, meanwhile, denounced railroads for charging discriminatory rates for hauling grain and livestock to market.

State efforts to regulate business proved ineffective. Because large enterprises, such as railroads, were interstate operations, state-by-state regulation was too piecemeal to work well. Then, after the Supreme Court ruled state regulation of interstate railroads unconstitutional in 1886, reformers had nowhere else to turn but the national government.[5] Congress responded with the Interstate Commerce Act.

The ICC and Other Independent Regulatory Commissions

The Interstate Commerce Act created the Interstate Commerce Commission (ICC) to regulate railroads. The ICC was an independent regulatory commission whose stated objective was to protect consumers by keeping prices low and preventing unfair acts or rates. To achieve this, Congress authorized the ICC to set rates, grant routes, regulate service, and control entry into the industry.

Congress followed the creation of the ICC with other ventures in regulatory policymaking. In 1890, Congress passed the Sherman Antitrust Act, outlawing monopolies or attempts to monopolize a market. The measure gave enforcement authority to the Justice Department. Congress passed the Clayton Act in 1914 to plug loopholes in the Sherman Act, empowering the Justice Department to block mergers that might prove monopolistic. Congress also enacted the Federal Trade Commission Act in 1914, creating the Federal Trade Commission (FTC) and empowering it to safeguard against "unfair competition" and "deceptive trade practices."

Congress subsequently extended the scope of federal regulation, particularly during the New Deal era in the 1930s. Congress expanded the ICC's jurisdiction to include interstate trucking in addition to rail transportation. It created the CAB to regulate the airline industry; the Federal Maritime Commission (FMC) to control the commercial shipping industry; the Securities and Exchange Commission (SEC) to regulate the sale of stocks and bonds; the Federal Energy Regulatory Commission (formerly the Federal Power Commission) to oversee the production, sale, and interstate transmission of electrical power and natural gas; and the Federal Communications Commission (FCC) to have authority over interstate communications services, including television and radio broadcasting and interstate telecommunications services.

Before the 1960s, Congress' regulatory efforts usually involved the creation of independent regulatory commissions empowered to control competition and prices in a particular industry. As you recall from our discussion in chapter 10, independent regulatory commissions are agencies headed by multimember boards appointed by the president with Senate confirmation to serve fixed, overlapping terms. Congress generally assigns authority to these boards in broad terms, to set rates that are "just and reasonable" and to regulate "in the public interest." The CAB, for example, was to license air carriers that were "fit, willing, and able" to provide service.

Congress' regulatory actions before the 1960s often came at the request of affected industries. Air carriers, for example, lobbied for the creation of the

CAB, arguing that regulation was necessary to control "destructive competition." Once in place, regulatory agencies often worked in cooperation with the industries they regulated. Consequently, spokespersons for public-interest groups, such as Ralph Nader, charged that the CAB and other regulatory agencies were **captured agencies**, that is, agencies that work to benefit the economic interests they regulate rather than serving the public interest.

Newer Regulatory Agencies

The emergence of politically powerful public-interest groups in the early 1960s led to a new wave of federal regulatory activity. Groups such as the Sierra Club, Friends of the Earth, and the various organizations founded by consumer activist Ralph Nader mobilized public support for federal action to protect consumers, the environment, workers, and the disabled. These groups lobbied Congress to create a number of new regulatory agencies, structured to reduce the likelihood that they would be captured by the industries they were established to regulate.

Congress responded in the 1960s and 1970s by creating a series of new regulatory agencies that varied in several important respects from most of the older regulatory commissions. First, most of the new agencies differed structurally from their older counterparts. With the exception of the Consumer Product Safety Commission (CPSC), which was created as an independent regulatory commission, most of the new agencies, including the Environmental Protection Agency (EPA), National Highway Traffic Safety Administration (NHTSA), and Occupational Safety and Health Administration (OSHA), were independent executive agencies, part of the executive branch of government but not part of one of the cabinet-level departments. Agency heads would be appointed by the president with Senate approval to serve at the president's pleasure (that is, the president could remove them at will). This sort of structure gave the president considerably more control over these agencies' operations than was the case with independent regulatory commissions. The public-interest groups and their friends in Congress hoped that a president sympathetic to the goals of consumer safety, environmental protection, and the like would use the authority of office to ensure against industry capture of new agencies.

Second, Congress established broader goals for the new agencies than it set for the older commissions. The stated aims of the traditional regulatory agencies were primarily economic, such as ensuring reasonable rates and fair competition. In contrast, regulatory efforts launched in the 1960s and 1970s embraced social goals, such as clean air, a safe workplace, pure water, and safe and effective products.

Third, the new agencies differed from most of their older counterparts in that Congress gave them authority to regulate certain aspects of production across industry lines. Congress established most of the older agencies to oversee a single industry or a small number of related industries. Congress created the SEC, for example, to regulate the stock and bond markets. In contrast, the regulatory activities of the more recently established agencies affected a broader range of industries. Congress empowered OSHA, for instance, to regulate working conditions across industry lines. As a result, the regulatory impact of the new agencies was felt more broadly than that of the older commissions.

Fourth, Congress gave the newer agencies more specific, more rigid instructions than it had given the older commissions. The legislation authorizing the regulatory work of the older agencies, you recall, had been cast in broad, flexible language. Congress left a good deal of discretion to the expertise of administrators. In the 1960s, however, many members of Congress believed that agency flexibility can frequently lead to industry influence. Consequently, in creating the new regulatory agencies, Congress often mandated specific goals and set deadlines for their fulfillment.

Finally, Congress empowered the newer regulatory agencies to regulate the conditions under which goods and services are generated as well as the physical characteristics of the products made. The older commissions were generally limited to setting rates and controlling entry into an industry. The FCC, for example, was established to license radio and television broadcasters. In contrast, Congress authorized the newer agencies to set performance standards for products and production. Congress gave the EPA authority to set pollution-emission standards for industry. It empowered the CPSC to draft mandatory safety standards for consumer goods, such as cribs and children's sleepwear.

Warning labels on cigarette packages represent a political compromise between public health advocates and the tobacco industry.

Deregulation

By the mid-1970s, political momentum had built for deregulation, at least in some areas. Liberals pushed for reform of the older agencies, many of whose regulatory efforts, the liberals argued, only kept prices high and service poor because they protected industry from competition. The liberals were joined in their efforts by some conservatives who were philosophically opposed to regulation in general as unwarranted interference with the marketplace. Moreover, Presidents Ford and Carter both called for deregulation of certain segments of the economy. In the late 1970s, Congress responded by approving the phased deregulation of the trucking, airline, and financial industries.

In 1981, Ronald Reagan took office promising to step up the pace of deregulation. President Reagan believed that many government regulations, especially the social regulations adopted in the 1960s, harm business and make the economy less efficient. One of Reagan's first acts as president was to issue an executive order requiring that all regulations adopted by executive-branch agencies be cleared by the Office of Management and Budget (OMB). The president stipulated that OMB should base its review on **cost-benefit analysis**, which is an evaluation of a proposed policy or regulation based on a comparison between its expected benefits and anticipated costs. In 1985, for example, the OMB reviewed 2,221 agency rules, rejecting or forcing changes in 29 percent. Moreover, the 29 percent figure probably underestimates the real impact of OMB review because many agencies likely chose not to put forward rules that the OMB could be expected to reject.[6]

OMB review proved controversial. Although the White House claimed that OMB review was directed at saving money, critics charged that the OMB was a political filter to strain out rules the administration opposed. What's more, a number of observers argued that cost-benefit analysis is biased against factors that are difficult to measure, such as scenic beauty, historic preservation, and the value of human lives saved by regulations.

President Reagan used his appointive powers and influence over the budget to weaken regulatory agencies that he considered most obnoxious. Between 1981 and 1983, for example, Reagan succeeded in persuading Congress to trim the EPA's budget for enforcing air-pollution regulations from $11.4 to $2.3 million and reduce the number of personnel authorized for enforcement by 31 percent.[7] In the meantime, Reagan appointed an individual to head OSHA whose family's construction company had been cited forty-eight times by OSHA for safety violations. James Watt, Reagan's choice as secretary of the interior, had headed a private group that fought against interior-department restrictions on oil drilling on federal lands.[8]

President Reagan's campaign to lighten the burden of regulation met with mixed success. On one hand, Reagan and his appointees succeeded in ebbing the flow of new regulations and relaxing enforcement of old ones. OMB review served to screen out many new regulations that were inconsistent with the administration's business-oriented perspective. Moreover, budget and personnel cuts forced agencies to reduce the enforcement of existing rules. OSHA, for example, limited the number of workplaces subject to routine inspection and cancelled most follow-up inspections. As a result, OSHA fines fell by 40 percent during the Reagan years.[9]

On the other hand, Reagan failed to achieve all of his regulatory goals because of resistance from Congress, the courts, the public, and agencies themselves. In 1984, for example, Congress, concerned that the ICC was allowing trucking companies to expand operations in violation of federal safety standards, passed legislation requiring the ICC to deny new routes to trucking firms that failed to pass safety inspection.[10] Meanwhile, federal court rulings prevented the Reagan administration from rescinding regulations already in place without following the process established by law for enacting regulations in the first place.

By mid-1990, the political momentum behind deregulation had dissipated and Congress was considering the enactment of new regulations. In a number of areas—airlines, telecommunications, and trucking—the benefits of deregulation had apparently fallen short of initial expectations. Meanwhile, serious scandals in the EPA and the savings and loan industry led to calls for tougher environmental controls and tighter government regulation of financial institutions. (See the Perspective for a closer look at the scandal in the savings and loan industry.) The federal budget deficit also contributed to an increase in regulatory activity as members of Congress, anxious to influence policy but short of money, relied on legislative mandates to require states and localities to implement federal policies. (A **mandate** is a legislative requirement placed on a lower level of government by a higher level of government.)

The Scope of Regulation Today

Despite a decade of deregulation, the regulatory hand of the federal government remains pervasive. In several industries, new firms must obtain government permission before they can begin doing business. The FCC, for example, licenses radio and television stations. The Nuclear Regulatory Commission (NRC) licenses nuclear power plants. In other industries, new products must meet government standards. The Consumer Product Safety Commission sets safety standards for a long list of products ranging from lawn mowers to toys. New drugs must be approved by the Food and Drug Administration (FDA). Importers, meanwhile, sometimes face restrictions such as tariffs and quotas designed to shelter American producers from foreign competition. (A **tariff** is a tax levied on imported goods, while an **import quota** is a limit placed on the amount of a given product that may be imported in a year.)

PERSPECTIVE

Bailing Out the S&Ls

The savings and loan (S&L) crisis produced the most expensive failure of deregulation. By the end of the 1980s, hundreds of S&Ls were insolvent, with liabilities exceeding assets by billions of dollars. Although savings and loan institutions are private businesses, their deposits were insured by the Federal Savings and Loan Insurance Corporation (FSLIC), a government agency. As a result, taxpayers were on the hook for much of the shortfall. In 1989, Congress and President Bush agreed on a savings and loan bailout plan to close insolvent S&Ls and pay off depositors. It was estimated that the cost to taxpayers would be at least $60 billion out of nearly $150 billion.

Deregulation set the stage for the S&L crisis. Ini-tially, savings and loans were exclusively home-mortgage lenders, turning small savings accounts into home-mortgage loans. In the 1970s, Congress permitted S&Ls to offer savers higher interest rates in order to compete for funds. In the early 1980s, Congress allowed thrift institutions more leeway in making investments. A number of S&Ls responded by investing in everything from strip shopping centers to racehorses. Some of these investments violated sound financial principles; others, allegedly, involved fraud. Failed investments coupled with falling real estate values, particularly in Texas, pushed more than 350 savings and loans (out of 3,100) over the brink to insolvency.

Sources: "Bush's Thrift Plan Greeted With Caution on Hill," *Congressional Quarterly Weekly Report*, 11 February 1989, pp. 255–58; Margaret E. Kriz, "Saving the S&Ls," *National Journal*, 14 January 1989, pp. 60–66.

Reprinted with permission: Tribune Media Services.

Government regulations also affect a wide range of business operating procedures. OSHA regulates conditions in the workplace. The EPA establishes and enforces regulations regarding air pollution, water pollution, and solid-waste disposal. The government requires most employers to adhere to wage and hour laws and to provide their employees with Social Security coverage, workers' compensation, and unemployment insurance. The Equal Employment Opportunity Commission (EEOC), meanwhile, enforces laws prohibiting discrimination on the basis of race, color, religion, sex, or national origin.

Finally, the government enforces an extensive series of regulations through its status as a major purchaser of goods and services. Some firms—defense contractors, for example—do nearly all of their business with the government; others do a significant share. Any company signing a contract of any significance with the federal government must conform to a host of stipulations. The Davis-Bacon Act, for example, requires that contractors pay prevailing wages (read *union* wages) on any project that is financed or subsidized by the federal government. Other regulations require government contractors to prefer American-made products in their purchases, to hire the disabled, to refrain from polluting, and to implement affirmative-action programs for hiring minorities.

REGULATORY FEDERALISM

Regulatory policymaking in America reflects the contours of the federal system, with governmental units at the national, state, and local levels all involved in the regulatory process. The national government has enacted extensive regulations governing such matters as labor/management relations, product safety, environmental protection, communications, banking and finance, airline safety, advertising, bankruptcy, shipping, nuclear power transmission, interstate commerce, workplace safety, pure food and drug standards, and international trade. The states, meanwhile, regulate utilities, deal with industrial safety, control access to professions, regulate the sale and consumption of alcoholic beverages, struggle with environmental issues, and charter corporations. Local governments (which constitutionally are subunits of the states) control land use, enforce building codes, and regulate local commerce.

As you can see, the regulatory activities of the national government and those of states and localities overlap. The federal courts have held that states may legislate in those fields where the national government has not acted, even though the national government has the power to do so. Even in subject areas in which the national government has acted, Congress may permit state regulation as well.

The courts have ruled, however, that states may not adopt regulations of their own in subject areas where Congress has adopted national regulations with the intent of achieving national uniformity. An act of Congress adopting regulatory policies that overrule state policies in a particular regulatory area is known as a **federal preemption of state authority**. The proponents of preemption argue that uniform national regulatory standards are preferable to state-by-state regulation. In contrast, critics of preemption contend that congressional efforts to override state authority violate states' rights principles that hold that state legislators know best what policies are most appropriate for their states.

In general, the extent of federal preemption increased during the late 1960s and early 1970s, then decreased during the late 1970s and early 1980s. During the earlier period, Congress passed a series of laws specifically overruling whatever state laws might be in effect in a given area. One law, for example, set a national standard on flammable children's pajamas while preempting state regulations in the area.

Beginning in the middle 1970s, the federal regulatory tide turned and Congress relaxed or repealed federal regulations affecting the trucking, airline, and financial industries, among others. In the 1980s, the Reagan administration significantly reduced federal enforcement of antitrust, consumer-protection, and environmental regulations. A number of states responded to federal inaction by increasing their own regulatory efforts. Ironically, many business interests which once complained about federal regulation have asked Congress to reenact regulations in a number of areas in order to preempt tough regulatory action at the state level. As one state official put it, "A lot of...companies feel it is easier to work with Congress than fifty state legislatures."[11]

THE PROS AND CONS OF REGULATION

Regulation is controversial. For society, it offers the promise of safe products, a safe working place, a healthy environment, and fair prices. For the regulated, however, it may involve great expense and inconvenience. Let's examine some of the arguments for and against regulation.

The Case for Regulation

The proponents of regulation justify it as necessary to compensate for free-market failures and imperfections, such as monopoly and oligopoly. A **monopoly** is a market condition in which a single firm is the sole supplier of a good or service. An **oligopoly**, meanwhile, is a market condition in which only a few firms control the supply of a good or a service, and the firms do not compete vigorously with one another. Instead, they may formally or informally agree to a prearranged division of the market and/or a minimum price level.

Consumers are hurt by both monopoly and oligopoly. Because firms don't compete with one another, consumers have little or no choice in the price and quality of goods and services. Quality is likely to be lower and prices higher than would be the case in a competitive market.

The proponents of regulation believe that government should intervene to break up monopolies and oligopolies, and to prevent their formation. This was the rationale behind the passage of the Sherman Act and the Clayton Act, outlawing monopolies. Later, Congress amended the Clayton Act to authorize the FTC to police mergers of major corporations in order to prevent excessive concentrations of industry in large corporate entities.

A recent example of antitrust enforcement concerned American Telephone and Telegraph (AT&T, also known as Ma Bell). In 1974, the Justice Department filed suit against the phone company for violating antitrust laws, accusing it of unfair competitive practices. The case was eventually settled in 1982, with the company agreeing to divest itself of local telephone-service operating companies. In the past, AT&T (the long-distance phone company) and the local phone companies (Southwestern Bell, Pacific Bell, and so on) were all part of the same company. Today, they are separate.

Economists tells us that monopoly is sometimes inevitable, even desirable. Consider the case of a **natural monopoly**, which is a monopoly bestowed by nature on a geographical area, or one that, because of the nature of an enterprise, would make competition wasteful. Electricity, natural gas, and local telephone service (as opposed to long-distance service) are examples of natural monopolies. Start-up costs and operating expenses are so high in these industries that competition is unlikely to develop. Indeed, electric, natural gas, and telephone companies may find it uneconomical to do business at all in remote or sparsely populated areas. Each of these concerns is also a **public utility**, that is, a privately owned business that performs an essential service for the community.

The advocates of regulation say that government should establish service standards and set rates for public utilities that are natural monopolies. The government can require these companies to provide service to all residents in a region at reasonable rates. In return, government can guarantee a firm's profitability, making it easier for such companies to raise investment capital.

On the national level, the FCC sets interstate telephone rates, while the Federal Energy Regulatory Commission regulates interstate gas and electric utilities. Intrastate regulation, meanwhile, is the responsibility of state and local agencies, frequently state public utility commissions.

Another type of market imperfection the proponents of regulation wish to correct involves something economists call externalities. An **externality** is a cost or benefit not taken into account by private decision-makers. Suppose a chemical plant pollutes a river. In this example, the harm caused by the pollution is an external cost of production, not included in the selling price of the chemicals. Instead, the cost of pollution is borne by people living downstream, who can no longer use the river for drinking, irrigation, commercial fishing, or recreation. The advocates of regulation argue that this is an instance in which government should intervene to shift the external cost of pollution to the price of the product. Let those who purchase the chemicals pay all of the costs of production, they say. Government can do this either by fining the plant's owners an amount equal to the cost of cleaning the river or by requiring the plant to reduce dumping harmful wastes into the river.

The proponents of regulation also believe that government should act to protect those who are economically weak. Child-labor laws, for instance, are written to shelter children from exploitation. Minimum-wage laws are aimed at protecting unskilled workers. Import restrictions protect American manufacturers (and their workers) from foreign competition. Truth-in-packaging requirements are designed to provide customers with information necessary for protecting themselves. The FTC tries to shield credulous consumers from false and deceptive advertising.

The Case Against Regulation

The opponents of regulation argue that government intervention in the economy disrupts market forces. First, they point out that regulations are expensive to implement and consumers pay the bill. A government report, for example, concluded that federal regulations add more than $650 to the sticker price of an average car and between $1,500 and $2,000 to the cost of a home.[12] Another study estimated that limitations on Japanese auto imports have cost American consumers $5.8 billion in higher car prices, or about $105,000 per job saved in the U.S. auto industry.[13]

Second, opponents of regulation argue that federal regulations are inevitably tangled in confusion and red tape. Take, for example, OSHA's well-known regulation for wooden ladders (since repealed): "The general slope of grain shall not be steeper than one in fifteen rungs and cleats. For all ladders cross-grain not steeper than one in twelve are permitted."[14] Other OSHA regulations (since repealed) have specified the diameter of toilet seats and how high above the floor a fire extinguisher must be placed. Bureaucratic red tape can also mean delay. The Food and Drug Administration (FDA) spent ten years trying to set standards governing the percentage of peanuts in peanut butter. It took the NHTSA seven years to establish automobile brake standards.

A third argument against regulation is that it sometimes produces unintended and unwanted side effects. One study found, for example, that tougher auto emissions standards adopted in 1981 actually made the air *dirtier*, at least in the short run. The study estimated that the addition of new antipollution equipment added $475 to the cost of a new car. This additional expense reduced new car sales by almost 4 percent. Because fewer new cars were sold (leaving older cars on the road), the air was actually dirtier after the new standard was in effect than it was under the less stringent standard. Over the long run, the air grew cleaner, of course, but probably not before 1985.[15]

Finally, critics believe that regulation short-circuits the law of supply and demand. Minimum-wage laws, they say, drive up the cost of labor, thereby decreasing the number of jobs available for unskilled workers. Similarly, rent-control laws (that limit the amount landlords can increase rents) produce housing shortages because developers have little incentive to build new rental units.

REGULATORY POLICYMAKING

Regulatory policymaking in America is a complex process involving a broad array of interest groups and political actors. Let's examine the process step by step.

Setting the Agenda

Who sets the agenda for regulatory policymaking in America? Public opinion plays a role. The creation of the ICC in the 1880s and the passage of the Sherman Antitrust Act in 1890 took place in an atmosphere of general public distrust of big business and outright animosity toward the railroads. In the 1930s, public opinion again supported an extension of the federal regulatory role, this time to counter the Great Depression. Similarly, the expansion of federal regulatory activities in the 1960s and 1970s was spurred by strong public support for the environmental and consumer movements. In recent years, public concerns about airline safety, hazardous-waste disposal, environmental protection, corporate mergers, and the savings and loan crisis have produced widespread support for increased regulation in these areas.

Opinion leaders often play an important role in shaping and organizing public opinion in support of government regulation. (An **opinion leader** is someone who shapes public attitudes about an issue.) In the 1930s, for example, Franklin Roosevelt articulated remedies for the Depression that involved large doses of government regulation. In the 1960s, Rachel Carson's

A group of citizens attend a hearing of the Chicago Transit Authority board to urge improved bus service for disabled riders.

book *Silent Spring* helped stimulate public concern about the environment, while Ralph Nader's *Unsafe at Any Speed* called attention to consumer issues.[16]

Interest groups are also involved in setting the agenda for regulatory policymaking. Some of the most active groups are business groups. The popular image is that business opposes regulation. Business groups lobbied against the creation of OSHA and the EPA, for example, and regularly complain about government paperwork requirements. Nonetheless, business groups don't always oppose regulation. The airline industry, you recall, lobbied Congress in the 1930s to create the CAB and then led the fight against deregulation in the 1970s. Moreover, the business community is sometimes divided over particular regulatory policies because of the differential impact of regulation. One study notes, for example, that FTC requirements that advertisers substantiate the accuracy of their claims gives large advertising firms an advantage over their smaller competitors because they have the resources to fulfill this requirement.[17]

Business groups aren't the only voices heard in regulatory policymaking. Farmers supported the creation of the ICC, and organized labor backed the establishment of OSHA. In recent decades, public-interest groups have been vocal advocates of government regulation to protect the environment, consumers, and public health and safety.

Another force involved in regulatory policymaking is the bureaucracy it-self. The people who head the regulatory agencies and staff their offices have policy perspectives of their own and are frequently successful in promoting them. One of the major criticisms of the older regulatory agencies—the CAB, SEC, ICC, FDA—was that they were captured by the industries they regulated. For years, these regulatory agencies were generally staffed by lackluster com-missioners whose main qualification was friendship with powerful members of Congress. Agency heads were often former employees of the industries they regulated, and they frequently returned to executive positions in those industries after leaving government service.

In contrast, most of the newer regulatory agencies developed close ties to the public-interest groups that lobbied for their creation. One study found, for example, that the initial response of the EPA to the inauguration of Ronald Reagan, an ardent critic of the agency, was to increase pollution-control activi-ties. The EPA did not cut back its work until Congress reduced its budget. Even then, disgruntled career employees in the EPA fought back by leaking evidence of wrongdoing by Reagan appointees to Congress and the press.[18]

Policy Formulation and Adoption

Federal regulatory policy formulation and adoption are fragmented, involving Congress, the president, courts, and dozens of boards, agencies, and commis-sions. Congress creates agencies and delegates authority to them. At times, Congress drafts regulatory legislation in specific detail because it wants laws that bureaucrats cannot subvert. The 1970 Clean Air Act amendments, for ex-ample, mandated the elimination of pollution, regardless of cost.[19] At other times, though, Congress can't agree on the details of regulatory policy, so it adopts vague, general language, leaving the policy specifics to the bureau-cracy and, frequently, to the courts. In 1972, Congress voted to outlaw dis-crimination based on gender in college and university programs receiving federal funds. Congress left the difficult job of interpretation and enforce-ment to the bureaucracy.

The courts also participate actively in the federal regulatory process. The Administrative Procedures Act makes agency actions subject to court review, and recent years have seen a flurry of lawsuits over such regulatory policies as strip mining, efficiency standards for household appliances, content labeling for alcoholic beverages, and the relaxation of crash-worthiness standards for car bumpers.

In general, the policy impact of the federal courts has been to expand the scope and effect of regulation. As one observer phrases it, "[T]he judicial branch has given the 'green light' to many types of rules and regulations, and sometimes has prodded agencies and Congress into more forceful action, adding considerably to the sum total of regulation on its own."[20] Even during the early Reagan years, when the political climate in Washington favored

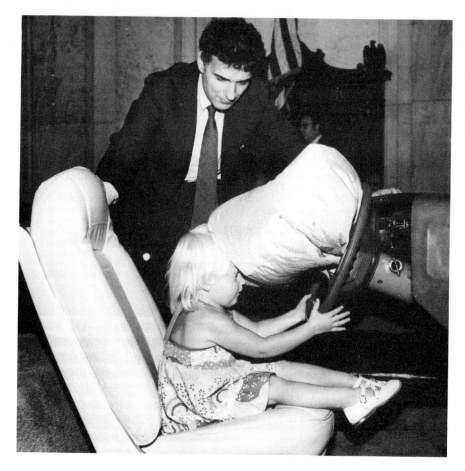

deregulation, the federal judiciary continued to rule in favor of the expansion of regulatory activity and to erect legal barricades against attempts to repeal regulations.[21]

Presidents are also actively involved in regulatory policy formulation and adoption. They appoint agency heads and submit budget requests to Congress. By establishing the requirement for OMB clearance for executive-branch agency rules, President Reagan added an important tool presidents can use for controlling regulatory policy.

Policy Implementation and Evaluation

Congress delegates authority to enforce and implement regulatory policies to the federal bureaucracy. Agencies have the authority, for example, to order the recall of defective products and even to ban hazardous ones. Advertisers can be forced to warn consumers about potential dangers or to retract misleading statements about their products. Agencies may file civil suits against violators, and the Justice Department may initiate criminal proceedings that could result in fines and prison sentences for offenders.

The sheer size of the regulatory task makes enforcement haphazard. In America there are 12,000 potentially hazardous waste sites to be monitored, 15,000 sewage treatment plants to be upgraded, nearly 300 endangered species of plants and animals to be protected, and more than 3.5 million workplaces to be inspected.[22]

Another problem for agencies is that Congress has often written regulatory statutes without sufficient concern for implementation and enforcement. Congress passed the Clean Air Act amendments of 1970 without regard to whether national air-quality standards could be met under even the best of circumstances. Moreover, many waste-water treatment plants built to meet national standards established by Congress haven't worked as expected because of technical problems.

Implementation is also hindered by scarce resources. Few agencies have the funds or the personnel to carry out their regulatory tasks efficiently. This problem was compounded by reductions in agency budgets and staffs during the early 1980s.

Finally, implementation of regulatory policy faces political roadblocks. Agencies often have the power to withhold federal funds from state and local government programs or to shut down industrial plants that fail to comply with federal regulatory standards. Politically, however, such sanctions are dif-

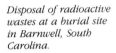
Disposal of radioactive wastes at a burial site in Barnwell, South Carolina.

ficult to impose. Members of Congress don't take kindly to reports that their communities are about to lose federal grant money or that a major manufacturing plant employing many people in their state or district is about to be closed.

Who evaluates regulatory policy? The president, for one. Recent chief executives have been particularly concerned about the effects of regulation on the economy. One of President Reagan's first acts in office was to name Vice President Bush to head a presidential task force on regulatory reform. The job of the task force was to evaluate federal regulatory policy and to recommend which existing regulations should be eliminated.

Congress is also involved in evaluation, sometimes changing laws to reverse regulatory policies. Take the case of the automobile interlock seat-belt system. The NHTSA required this device on all new cars sold in the United States, beginning with 1974 models. In 1975, however, Congress responded to adverse public reaction by legislating its end.

Then there's the example of saccharin. After laboratory tests discovered a link between saccharin and the incidence of cancer in white rats, the FDA, following the letter of the law, moved to ban its nonprescription use. Congress changed the law, however, permitting the continued use of saccharin but with a health warning.

The courts play a part in evaluation as well. In the early 1980s, federal district and appellate courts took much of the steam out of the Reagan administration's efforts at reducing the federal regulatory burden. They held that agencies cannot repeal rules without thorough, in-depth documentation on the grounds for the change.[23] In so doing, the courts served notice that they were not just an arena for appealing agency rules, but they would also hear challenges to agency efforts to repeal regulations already in place. For example, the U.S. Court of Appeals for the District of Columbia rejected EPA efforts to relax regulations enforcing the Clean Air Act.[24]

Finally, many groups and individuals outside the federal government are involved in the evaluation of regulatory policy. Evaluation comes from state and local governments directly affected by federal regulations. The press is involved, albeit in a sporadic and haphazard fashion. Also, academic experts have produced a growing number of scholarly evaluations on the effects of regulatory policy on the nation's economy and society.

CONCLUSION: REGULATORY POLICY AND POLITICS

Regulatory policymaking is political. Individuals and groups favor regulations that benefit them, while opposing regulations that do them harm. The airlines supported the CAB, for example, because they believed that regulation was to their economic benefit. In contrast, consumer groups favored deregulation because they thought it was in their interest.

Smog settles over New York City.

Political leaders support regulatory policies favored by the support groups that put them in office. Even though Ronald Reagan was a philosophical advocate of less regulation, he favored increased regulation when that course advanced the cause of conservative groups or business interests than helped put him in office. The Reagan administration, for example, attempted to force local family planning centers receiving federal aid to report minors seeking birth-control assistance to their parents.[25]

Regulatory policy, as with economic policy, reflects the political environment. For decades, civil aviation policy was controlled by what political scientists call a **subgovernment**, that is, a cozy, mutually beneficial, three-sided relationship among government agencies, interest groups, and key members of Congress. The airline industry profited from high fares and guaranteed routes. CAB commissioners often left service in the agency to take lucrative jobs in the airline industry. The chairs of key congressional committees, meanwhile, could depend on the airlines to provide good service to communities in their states and districts.

By the 1970s, however, the power of the airline subgovernment was broken. A number of other interest groups arose to challenge the established airlines for control of aviation policy. As the popularity of air travel grew, potential competitors began to push for entry into the field. Consumer groups, armed with academic studies on the effect of airline regulation, called for deregulation. Congress, meanwhile, had grown more decentralized, giving more members an opportunity to participate in regulatory policymaking. Some members of Congress, allied with consumer interests, took the lead in publicizing the issue (as did the news media), setting the agenda for eventual deregulation. Moreover, both Presidents Ford and Carter, who favored airline deregulation, appointed individuals to the CAB who shared their view. Airline deregulation was the result of a changed political landscape, with forces favoring deregulation gaining the upper hand over those supporting the old system.

In short, the subgovernment that once controlled federal aviation regulatory policymaking was replaced by an issue network. An **issue network** is a group of political actors that is concerned with some aspect of public policy. Unlike subgovernments, issue networks are fluid, with participants moving in and out. They may include technical specialists, journalists, members of Congress, a variety of interest groups, bureaucrats, academics, and political activists. Powerful interest groups may be involved, but they do not control. Instead, policy in a particular area results from conflict among a broad range of political actors, both in and out of government.[26]

To a considerable degree, the evolution of aviation regulatory policymaking resembles that of regulatory policymaking in general. For years, many, if not most, areas of regulatory policymaking were under the influence of subgovernments. In recent years, however, changes in the political environment (such as an increase in the number of interest groups, changes in the power structure of Congress, and an enlargement in the political role of the media) have undermined the power of subgovernments. As a result, the regulatory policymaking process today generally involves a wide range of political actors, inside and outside government, no one of whom dominates.

KEY TERMS

captured agencies

cost-benefit analysis

externality

federal preemption of state authority

import quota

issue network

mandate

monopoly

natural monopoly

oligopoly

opinion leader

public utility

subgovernment

tariff

NOTES

1. Janice Castro, "The Sky Kings Rule the Routes," *Time*, 15 May 1989, pp. 52–54.
2. Ann Cooper, "Free-Wheeling Airline Competition Is Apparently Here to Stay," *National Journal*, 2 June 1984, pp. 1086–90.
3. George C. Eads and Michael Fix, *Relief or Reform? Reagan's Regulatory Dilemma* (Washington, DC: Urban Institute Press, 1984), pp. 70–73.

4. Hobart Rowen, "Deregulation Revisited," *Washington Post*, National Weekly Edition, 24–30 October 1988, p. 5.
5. *Wabash, St. Louis & Pacific Railroad Co.* v. *Illinois*, 118 U.S. 557 (1986).
6. Joseph Cooper and William F. West, "Presidential Power and Republican Governent: The Theory and Practice of OMB Review of Agency Rules," *Journal of Politics* 50 (November 1988): 864–95.
7. B. Dan Wood, "Principals, Bureaucrats, and Responsiveness in Clean Air Enforcement," *American Political Science Review* 82 (March 1988): 219.
8. Eads and Fix, p. 144.
9. Edward Paul Fuchs, *Presidents, Management, and Regulation* (Englewood Cliffs, NJ: Prentice-Hall, 1988), p. 95.
10. Larry N. Gerston, Cynthia Fraleigh, and Robert Schwab, *The Deregulated Society* (Pacific Grove, CA: Brooks/Cole Publishing, 1988), p. 16.
11. Idaho Attorney General Jim Jones, quoted in Martha M. Hamilton, "On Second Thought, We'd Prefer the Feds on Our Backs," *Washington Post*, National Weekly Edition, 14 December 1987, p. 32.
12. Quoted in Carl P. Chelf, *Public Policymaking in America* (Glenview, IL: Scott, Foresman, 1981), p. 246.
13. William A. Niskanen, "U.S. Trade Policy," *Regulation* (1988), pp. 34–42.
14. *U.S. Code of Regulations*, Title 29, Section 1910.25(b)(3)(ii).
15. Howard K. Gruenspecht, "Differentiated Regulation: The Case of Auto Emission Standards," *American Economic Review*, May 1982, pp. 328–30.
16. Rachel Carson, *Silent Spring* (Boston, MA: Houghton Mifflin, 1962); Ralph Nader, *Unsafe at Any Speed* (New York: Grossman, 1965).
17. Richard S. Higgins and Fred S. McChesney, "Truth and Consequences: The Federal Trade Commission's Ad Substantiation Program," in Robert J. Mackay, James C. Miller III, and Bruce Yandle, eds., *Public Choice and Regulation: A View from Inside the Federal Trade Commission* (Stanford, CA: Hoover Institution, 1987), pp. 181–204.
18. Wood.
19. Advisory Commission on Intergovernmental Relations, *Protecting the Environment: Politics, Pollution, and Federal Policy*, Report A-83 (Washington, DC: U.S. Government Printing Office, 1981), pp. 23–25, 52.
20. David R. Beam, "From Law to Rule: Exploring the Maze of Intergovernmental Relations," *Intergovernmental Perspective* 9 (Spring 1983): 7–22, 15.
21. Thomas J. Madden and David H. Remes, "The Courts and the Administration: Marching to Different Drummers," *Intergovernmental Perspective* 9 (Spring 1983): 23–29.
22. Beam, p. 17.
23. *State Farm Mutual Automobile Insurance Co. et al.* v. *NHTSA*, 680 F. 2d 206 (1982).
24. *Natural Resources Defense Council* v. *Gorsuch*, 685 F. 2d 718 (1982).
25. Marshall R. Goodman and Margaret T. Wrightson, *Managing Regulatory Reform: The Reagan Strategy and Its Impact* (New York: Praeger, 1987), pp. 108–9.
26. Hugh Heclo, "Issue Networks and the Executive Establishment," in Anthony King, ed., *The New American Political System* (Washington, DC: American Enterprise Institute, 1978), pp. 87–124.

SUGGESTED READINGS

Brown, Anthony E. *The Politics of Airline Deregulation*. Knoxville, TN: University of Tennessee, 1987.

Fuchs, Edward Paul. *Presidents, Management, and Regulation*. Englewood Cliffs, NJ: Prentice-Hall, 1988.

Gerston, Larry N.; Fraleigh, Cynthia; and Schwab, Robert. *The Deregulated Society*. Pacific Grove, CA: Brooks/Cole, 1988.

Goodman, Marshall R., and Wrightson, Margaret T. *Managing Regulatory Reform: The Reagan Strategy and Its Impact*. New York: Praeger, 1987.

Leone, Robert A. *Who Profits? Winners, Losers, and Governmental Regulation*. New York: Basic Books, 1986.

Mackay, Robert J.; Miller, James C. III; and Yandle, Bruce, eds. *Public Choice and Regulation: A View from Inside the Federal Trade Commission*. Stanford, CA: Hoover Institution, 1987.

14

CIVIL-LIBERTIES
POLICYMAKING

LEARNING OBJECTIVES

1. To define the philosophical issues involved in civil-liberties controversies.
2. To trace the history of the Bill of Rights from its inception through selective incorporation.
3. To outline the contours of civil-liberties policy in the areas of religious liberty, freedom of expression, and due process of law.
4. To outline the policymaking process for civil liberties.
5. To recognize that civil-liberties policymaking is affected by politics.
6. To identify the significance of the following landmark Supreme Court decisions: *Roe* v. *Wade, Webster* v. *Reproductive Health Services, Barron* v. *Baltimore, Palko* v. *Connecticut, Everson* v. *Board of Ewing Township, Lemon* v. *Kurtzman, Engel* v. *Vitale, West Virginia State Board of Education* v. *Barnette, Schenck* v. *United States, New York Times* v. *Sullivan, Near* v. *Minnesota, Miranda* v. *Arizona, Gideon* v. *Wainwright, Furman* v. *Georgia*, and *Gregg* v. *Georgia*.

Abortion. Perhaps no issue in American politics is so controversial, or difficult to resolve. Pro-choice supporters argue that the issue is a woman's right to control her own body. The decision to terminate a pregnancy should be made by a woman and her doctor, they say, not the government. In contrast, pro-life advocates contend that the issue is the life of an unborn child. They believe that government should protect unborn life by prohibiting abortion, unless the mother's life is at risk.

In *Roe* v. *Wade* (1973), the Supreme Court adopted an abortion policy that was a compromise between pro-choice and pro-life positions. The case dealt with a challenge by an anonymous Dallas woman, "Jane Roe," to a Texas law prohibiting abortion except to save the life of the mother. The Court found the Texas statute unconstitutional, saying that a woman's right to personal privacy under the United States Constitution includes her decision to terminate a pregnancy so long as state government does not have a rational basis for regulation. To this extent, the Court said, a woman's right to privacy is not absolute and must be balanced against the state's interest in protecting health, medical standards, and prenatal life.

The Supreme Court balanced these competing interests by dividing a pregnancy into three trimesters. During the first trimester, state governments may not interfere with a physician's decision, reached in consultation with a pregnant woman patient, to terminate a pregnancy. In the second trimester, the Court held that the state may regulate abortion but only to protect the health of the mother. In the third trimester, after the fetus has achieved viability, the Court ruled that states may choose to prohibit abortion, except when necessary to preserve the life or health of the mother.[1]

Instead of resolving the debate over abortion, the Supreme Court's decision made the controversy more intense. Both pro-choice and pro-life groups continued to fight for their respective positions, but, because *Roe* was perceived as a victory for the pro-choice side, antiabortion forces had greater incentive to organize. While pro-choice advocates considered their battle won, pro-life groups launched a political drive either to amend the Constitution to outlaw abortion or to influence the selection of Supreme Court justices who would vote to overturn the *Roe* decision.

By the end of the 1980s, the antiabortionists' political efforts had borne fruit. The appointment of Anthony Kennedy to the Supreme Court by President Reagan in 1988 created a majority on the Court that was willing to allow greater state restrictions on abortion. In *Webster* v. *Reproductive Health Services* (1989), the Supreme Court upheld a Missouri law prohibiting the use of public employees or facilities to perform or assist an abortion except to save the mother's life, and making it a crime to use public funds, employees, or facilities to encourage or counsel a woman to have an abortion not necessary to save her life. Citing recent medical advances, the Court abandoned the trimester system adopted in *Roe* by allowing Missouri to require physicians to perform medical tests to determine whether a fetus is viable beginning at twenty weeks.[2]

The effect of the *Webster* decision was to move the battle over abortion from the courts to the legislative and executive branches of national and state government. Several states considered adopting legislation restricting abortions. Moreover, abortion became a major issue in a number of election campaigns.

Just as *Roe* v. *Wade* served as an impetus for antiabortion groups to mobilize politically, the *Webster* case energized the pro-choice movement. Abortion-rights groups increased their membership substantially and organized to oppose state legislative efforts to pass antiabortion laws. What's more, candidates supporting the pro-choice position enjoyed the upper hand in a number of state and local elections. Nonetheless, the debate over abortion seemed certain to continue, with each side enjoying a substantial base of committed supporters.

The controversy over abortion illustrates well the nature of civil-liberties policymaking in America. Civil-liberties issues are often controversial, pitting the rights of individuals against one another or against the interests of society as a whole. As with abortion, legislatures and executives at the state and national levels of government initially adopt civil-liberties policies in the form of laws and regulations. Individuals and groups losing in those branches then appeal to the courts, which may modify or limit the original policies. Consequently, civil-liberties policies are frequently set by the courts in response to initiatives made by other branches and levels of government.

PHILOSOPHICAL ISSUES

Civil liberties concern the protection of the individual from the unrestricted power of government. Abortion is a civil-liberties issue, for example, because it involves the power of government to compel a woman to carry a pregnancy to term. Although civil liberties are an essential element of democracy, Americans disagree about how best to balance individual freedom with the interests of society.

The Case for Civil Liberties

One of the best-known appeals for individual liberty comes from the nineteenth-century English philosopher John Stuart Mill. In his essay *On Liberty*, Mill argues forcefully for an absolute freedom of expression:

> If all mankind minus one, were of one opinion, and only one person were of the contrary opinion, mankind would be no more justified in silencing that one person, than he, if he had the power, would be justified in silencing mankind. Were an opinion a personal possession of no value except to the owner, ... it would make some difference whether the injury was inflicted only on a few persons or on many. But the peculiar evil of silencing the expression of an opinion is, that it is robbing the human race. ... If the opinion is right, they are deprived of the opportunity of exchanging error for truth: if wrong, they lose, what is almost as great a benefit, the clearer perception and livelier impression of truth, produced by its collision with error.[3]

In the United States, individual liberty is so firmly entrenched in the nation's political culture that Americans have had less need to defend freedom than to praise it. Consider the eloquent words of the late Supreme Court Justice Robert H. Jackson:

> If there is any fixed star in our constitutional constellation, it is that no official, high or petty, can prescribe what shall be orthodox in politics, nationalism, religion, or other matters of opinion or force citizens to confess by word or act their faith therein. ... The very purpose of a Bill of Rights was to withdraw certain subjects from the vicissitudes of political controversy, to place them beyond the reach of majorities and officials and to establish them as legal principles to be applied by the courts. One's right to life, liberty, and property, to free speech, a free press, freedom of worship and assembly, and other fundamental rights may not be submitted to vote; they depend on the outcome of no election.[4]

The Case for Limiting Civil Liberties

Although few Americans philosophically oppose individual freedom, many believe that the rights of individuals must be balanced against the interests of society as a whole. As the late Supreme Court Justice Felix Frankfurter phrased it, "The choice is not between order and liberty. It is between liberty with order and anarchy without either."[5] Does freedom of speech entitle an individual to advocate the violent overthrow of the government? During wartime, should individuals be permitted to counsel avoidance of the draft? Many Americans would say no, including the late Supreme Court Justice Oliver Wendell Holmes, Jr. "When a nation is at war," said Holmes, "many things that might be said in time of peace are such a hindrance to its effort that their utterance will not be endured."[6]

At other times, tension exists between individual rights and the right of the majority to have the kind of society it wants. Consider the issue of pornography. Many people believe that sexually explicit material undermines the moral fabric of society and degrades women. They argue that government's interest in regulating pornography transcends the right of the individual to produce it, promote it, sell it, and purchase it.

Finally, the rights of different groups of individuals may come in conflict. Various religious groups claim the right to proselytize their faith by passing out pamphlets door-to-door and in public places such as airports. Many people on the other side of the issue believe that they have a right not to be disturbed at home or to be confronted with someone else's religion unless they desire it. The abortion issue pits the rights of women to terminate a pregnancy against the rights of the unborn.

Members of the Hare Krishna cult giving a musical performance on the street to attract interest in their faith.

CIVIL LIBERTIES AND THE CONSTITUTION

The framers of the Constitution included a number of civil-liberties guarantees in the original document. Article I, Section 9 prohibits bills of attainder and ex post facto laws. It also provides for the writ of habeas corpus except in the extraordinary circumstances of rebellion or invasion. A **bill of attainder** is a law that declares someone guilty of a crime and inflicts punishment without benefit of a trial. An **ex post facto law** is a retroactive criminal statute which operates to the disadvantage of accused persons. A **writ of habeas corpus**, meanwhile, is a court order requiring government authorities either to release a person held in custody or to demonstrate that the person is detained in accordance with law. In Article III, Section 3, the Constitution defines treason, setting standards for proof and establishing penalties. Article IV, Section 2 provides for the extradition of criminal fugitives from one state to another. Finally, Article VI forbids the use of religious tests as a qualification for national office. (A **religious test** is a legal requirement that an individual express belief in a particular religious faith or in a Supreme Being as a requirement for holding public office.)

The Bill of Rights

The original Constitution did not include a **bill of rights**, that is, a list of constitutionally guaranteed individual rights and liberties. The Constitution's framers debated adding a bill of rights, but decided against it. Some of the delegates to the constitutional convention argued that a bill of rights was unnecessary because the powers of the national government were so limited that it would pose no threat to individual freedom. Other delegates opposed writing a bill of rights because they feared that some rights might inadvertently be omitted.

The debate over a bill of rights continued as the states considered ratifying the Constitution. The opponents of the Constitution, the Anti-Federalists, warned that the absence of a bill of rights in the national constitution would open the door to encroachments upon the liberties of the people. In response, the Constitution's supporters, the Federalists, offered a compromise. They pledged to add a bill of rights by amendment once the new government was established.

The Federalists proved true to their word. With James Madison taking the lead, Congress proposed twelve constitutional amendments and submitted them to the states for ratification. By November 1791, three-fourths of the state legislatures had ratified ten of the amendments. Of the two losing amendments, one would have postponed any congressional pay raise from taking effect until after an election. The other rejected amendment would have provided for a representative in the U.S. House for every fifty thousand persons. The ten amendments that were ratified were added to the Constitution as the Bill of Rights.

Although the historical significance of the adoption of the Bill of Rights cannot be underestimated, its early impact on public policy in America was slight. Initially, it did not apply to the states (whose state constitutions included their own bills of rights). Congress intended the national Bill of Rights to apply only to the national government, and the Supreme Court so ruled in the case of *Barron* v. *Baltimore* in 1833.[7] What's more, the Bill of Rights proved unable to prevent a serious abuse of individual rights. In 1798, a Federalist-party majority in Congress passed, and President John Adams signed, the Sedition Act, a law against writing, printing, or publishing any criticism of the government, Congress, or the president, even if the criticism were true. The Adams administration enforced the Sedition Act vigorously, prosecuting a number of opposition newspaper editors who dared criticize the Federalists. Even though the Sedition Act clearly violated the First Amendment's guarantees of freedom of speech and press, the federal courts, staffed by Federalist judges, refused to find the measure unconstitutional. The Sedition Act remained in effect until after the election of 1800, when the voters turned Adams and the Federalists out of office and a new Congress repealed the law.

The Fourteenth Amendment

The ratification of the Fourteenth Amendment in 1868 and its subsequent interpretation by the Supreme Court changed the constitutional basis for civil liberties in America. Section 1 of the amendment contains this well-known passage:

> No State shall make or enforce any law which shall abridge the privileges or immunities of citizens of the United States; nor shall any State deprive any person of life, liberty, or property, without due process of law; nor deny to any person within its jurisdiction the equal protection of the laws.

The historical intent of this section is one of the most hotly debated topics in constitutional history. Historians tell us that the amendment's framers wanted to protect the civil rights of African-Americans. Moreover, the phrase "life, liberty, or property, without due process of law" is quoted verbatim from the Fifth Amendment. Beyond these facts, however, the framers' goals are unclear. Did Congress intend to apply only the guarantees of the Fifth Amendment to the states? Did it want to apply the entire Bill of Rights to the states? Or did it intend to apply a larger body of rights and privileges, including—but not limited to—those found in the first ten amendments?

Regardless of the framers' intent, the Supreme Court initially interpreted the provisions of the Fourteenth Amendment narrowly. In the Slaughterhouse cases (1873), for example, the Court ruled that the privileges and immunities of United States citizenship were a brief list, not even including the right to vote.[8] Then, in *Hurtado* v. *California* (1884), the Court held that the due process clause of the Fourteenth Amendment did not extend the specific protections of the Bill of Rights to the states.[9] In the view of a majority of the Supreme Court in the late nineteenth century, the Fourteenth Amendment hadn't really changed anything as far as civil liberties were concerned; the *Barron* precedent stood.

Selective Incorporation

In 1925, in the case of *Gitlow* v. *New York*, the Supreme Court began the selective incorporation of the Bill of Rights against the states. The **selective incorporation of the Bill of Rights** is the process through which the United States Supreme Court interpreted the due process clause of the Fourteenth Amendment of the United States Constitution to apply most of the provisions of the national Bill of Rights to the states. The *Gitlow* case concerned the validity of a New York law making it illegal to advocate the violent overthrow

Opponents of an ordinance outlawing handguns in Morton Grove, Illinois, based their arguments on the Second Amendment right to "keep and bear arms."

of the government. Although the Court upheld the law, the majority opinion stated specifically that the First Amendment guarantees of free speech and press "are among the fundamental personal rights and 'liberties' protected by the Due Process Clause of the Fourteenth Amendment from impairment by the states."[10]

The Supreme Court developed a rationale for selective incorporation in 1937 in *Palko* v. *Connecticut*. The case involved a Connecticut law that allowed the state to appeal lower court decisions in criminal cases, thus placing defendants in double jeopardy. (**Double jeopardy** involves the government trying a criminal defendant twice for the same offense.) Did the due process clause of the Fourteenth Amendment embrace the guarantee against double jeopardy found in the Fifth Amendment? The Court ruled in this case that it did not. The Fourteenth Amendment did not include all the rights guaranteed in the first ten amendments, just those rights "implicit in the concept of ordered liberty" and those principles of justice "so rooted in the traditions and conscience of our people as to be ranked as fundamental." Freedom of speech, the Court said, was a fundamental right; immunity from double jeopardy was not.[11]

Although the Court's interpretation of selective incorporation in the *Palko* case seemed limited, it opened the door for judicial development of a whole series of constitutional rights which the Court might one day find to be "implicit in the concept of ordered liberty" in a modern democracy. As one commentary puts it, selective incorporation allowed the Supreme Court, particularly the liberal Warren Court, "to 'modernize' the Bill of Rights, formulating new constitutional guarantees to protect labor unions in strikes and picketing and championing the rights of racial and religious minorities."[12]

Over the next several decades, the Supreme Court proceeded to broaden the range of fundamental rights guaranteed by the Fourteenth Amendment to encompass the most important provisions of the Bill of Rights. These included separation of church and state, the right to a speedy public trial by an impartial jury, protection against unreasonable searches and seizures, the prohibition against cruel and unusual punishments, the right to competent counsel, protection against self-incrimination, and the right to confront witnesses in a criminal trial. The Court even reversed its position in the *Palko* case, applying the Fifth Amendment protection against double jeopardy to the states.

The Supreme Court has also interpreted the due process clause of the Fourteenth Amendment to include rights beyond those specifically mentioned in the Bill of Rights. In *Griswold* v. *Connecticut* (1965), the Court struck down a seldom-enforced state law that prohibited the use of contraceptives and the dispensing of birth-control information on the grounds that its enforcement would involve government's prying into "the privacy of the bedroom." Although the Constitution includes no specific right of privacy, the majority opinion noted that several provisions in the Bill of Rights (such as the Third Amendment's prohibition against quartering soldiers in private homes and the Fourth Amendment's protection against unreasonable searches and seizures) imply a right to privacy.[13] As you recall, the Court recognized a right to privacy in *Roe* v. *Wade* as well.

The practical effect of selective incorporation has been to set a national minimum standard for individual rights and establish the federal courts as interpreters of that standard. States and localities must grant their residents at least the constitutional rights incorporated by the Supreme Court through the due process clause. Moreover, if state and local governments so choose, they may grant their residents *greater* protections than provided in the national constitution. A number of states, for example, have added equal-rights amendments to their state constitutions, outlawing discrimination on account of gender. At least two states (Wisconsin and Massachusetts) and dozens of cities have adopted laws prohibiting discrimination against gays and lesbians in employment and housing.

In recent years, as the U.S. Supreme Court has begun to interpret the individual-rights guarantees of the United States Constitution more restrictively, state courts, as interpreters of state constitutions, have begun to play a more prominent role as defenders of individual rights. During the 1980s, state courts declared their state constitutions more protective of individual rights than the U.S. Constitution in more than 350 cases.[14] The policy areas in which state courts were the most active were abortion funding, criminal procedure, church/state relations, and gender discrimination.[15]

The Double Standard

Since 1937, the Supreme Court has made protection of individual rights and liberties the foremost item on its policy agenda. In so doing, the Court has adopted a double standard for judging the constitutionality of legislation in the economic/regulatory arena as opposed to legislation dealing with civil rights and liberties. The **double standard** is the judicial doctrine that the Supreme Court will accept economic legislation as constitutional unless proven otherwise, while assuming governmental restrictions on the basic freedoms guaranteed by the Bill of Rights to be unconstitutional. In effect, the double standard means that the executive and legislative branches of government must demonstrate a compelling governmental interest in limiting civil liberties before the Court will uphold the constitutionality of any restriction. In contrast, the Court will bend over backwards to uphold the constitutionality of economic regulations.

The Court's rationale for the double standard is that certain rights, such as freedom of speech and assembly, are fundamental to individual liberty because they make the exercise of other rights possible. Justice Jackson explained the Court's position in this manner:

> Ordinarily, legislation whose basis in economic wisdom is uncertain can be redressed by the processes of the ballot box or the pressure of public opinion. But when the channels of opinion or of peaceful persuasion are corrupted or clogged, these political correctives can no longer be relied on, and the democratic system is threatened at its most vital point. In that event the Court, by intervening, restores the processes of democratic government; it does not disrupt them.[16]

The Court's point is this: If public policy harms your business or threatens your income, you can act to change the policy through the political process. If government actions restrict your freedom of expression or your access to the political process, however, you are stymied. Without freedom of expression and the right to vote, you have no way to complain, no means to redress the grievance. Thus the Court's double standard. The result is that economic and regulatory policymaking in America primarily involves the executive and legislative branches of government, while the courts are major participants in civil-liberties policymaking.

CIVIL-LIBERTIES POLICIES

Civil-liberties policies reflect judicial response to policy initiatives taken by legislatures and executives at the state and national levels of government.

Religious Liberty

The First Amendment addresses the relationship between church and state with these well-known words: "Congress shall make no law respecting an establishment of religion, or prohibiting the free exercise thereof." This somewhat vague language has been the object of considerable controversy as the branches of government have struggled to draw lines of distinction between competing interests and to balance divergent philosophies about the relationship between government and religion.

The Free Exercise Clause

Despite the literal wording of the First Amendment ("Congress shall make no law ..."), the Supreme Court has permitted legislative restrictions on the free exercise of religion in those instances when the national or state governments have been able to demonstrate a compelling interest to intervene. The criminal law is one area in which the Court has accepted governmental limitations on the free exercise of religion. In the late 1870s, for example, the Court ruled that Mormon religious beliefs did not justify the practice of polygamy in violation of federal law.[17] Moreover, religious faith did not shelter television evangelist Jim Bakker from going to prison for fraud in 1989.

Second, the Supreme Court has upheld the application of certain regulations aimed at maintaining or improving public health and welfare despite individual claims of religious liberty. In 1905, for instance, the Court sustained a state law requiring smallpox vaccinations against a challenge by Seventh-Day Adventists who opposed it on religious grounds.[18] The Court has also upheld the right of a state to deny unemployment benefits to state employees who were fired because they used peyote, a hallucinogenic drug, in Native American religious practices.[19]

In other circumstances, however, the Supreme Court has ruled that an individual's right to free exercise of religion outweighs the government's interest in restricting religious activity. In the Flag Salute cases, for instance, the Court held that school districts may not force Jehovah's Witnesses children to recite the pledge of allegiance in violation of their religious beliefs.[20] (See the Perspective for a discussion of the Flag Salute controversy.) The Court has also ruled that Jehovah's Witnesses may distribute religious literature door-to-door and in public places without the permission of local authorities and without paying license taxes.[21]

The Amish are another religious sect that has participated in litigation involving the free exercise of religion. The Amish fear that too much exposure to education will undermine their children's faith in their traditional religion. On religious grounds, the Amish withdraw their children from school after completion of the eighth grade. This action has brought them into conflict with school-attendance laws and into court to argue the First Amendment, where they have won.[22]

PERSPECTIVE

The Flag Salute Cases

During the 1988 presidential campaign, George Bush criticized Massachusetts Governor Michael Dukakis for vetoing a bill as governor that would have required Massachusetts teachers to begin each school day by leading their students in the pledge of allegiance to the American flag. Bush implied that Dukakis's veto showed a lack of patriotism. Although Dukakis explained that he vetoed the bill because he thought it unconstitutional, the issue hurt his candidacy.

Lost in all the flag waving and political posturing were the history of the Flag Salute cases and the constitutional issues they raised. The controversy dates from the 1930s, when a number of school districts adopted policies requiring students to recite the pledge of allegiance each school day. Members of the Jehovah's Witnesses religious faith refused to allow their children to participate, saying that flag salutes violate the biblical commandment against worshiping graven images. Several Witnesses children were expelled over the issue and their parents filed suit. The dispute initially reached the Supreme Court in 1940 in the case of *Minersville School District* v. *Gobitis*. In an 8-to-1 vote, the Court ruled against the Witnesses, holding that the school district's interest in promoting patriotism and national unity outweighed constitutional concerns over religious liberty.*

The Court's ruling proved controversial. Newspapers and law journals wrote editorials and essays criticizing the Supreme Court's decision. Several states responded to the Court's decision by enacting laws requiring flag salutes and stipulating that children who refused to participate would be expelled and their parents prosecuted. As a result, more Jehovah's Witnesses suffered expulsions. In some places, angry mobs attacked Witnesses.

In 1943, in *West Virginia State Board of Education* v. *Barnette*, the Supreme Court voted 6 to 3 to reverse *Gobitis*. The Court's six-person majority included the dissenter from the *Gobitis* ruling, three justices who had changed their minds, and two newly appointed members of the Court. Announcing its decision on Flag Day (June 14, 1943), the Court ruled that the issues in the case went beyond freedom of religion to fundamental questions of personal liberty. Justice Robert H. Jackson, the author of the majority opinion, explained the Court's ruling in one of the more eloquent passages of constitutional law:

> The case is made difficult not because the principles of its decision are obscure but because the flag involved is our own. Nevertheless, we apply the limitations of the Constitution with no fear that freedom to be intellectually and spiritually diverse or even contrary will disintegrate the social organization. To believe that patriotism will not flourish if patriotic ceremonies are voluntary and spontaneous instead of a compulsory routine is to make an unflattering estimate of the appeal of our institutions to free minds. We can have intellectual individualism and the rich cultural diversities that we owe to exceptional minds only at the price of occasional eccentricity and abnormal attitudes. When they are so harmless to others or to the state as those we deal with here, the price is not too great. But freedom to differ is not limited to things that do not matter much. That would be a mere shadow of freedom. The test of its substance is the right to differ as to things that touch the heart of the existing order.†

Minersville School District v. Gobitis, 310 U.S. 586 (1940).
†*West Virginia State Board of Education v. Barnette*, 319 U.S. 624 (1943).

The Establishment of Religion Clause

The Constitution prevents government from making laws "respecting an establishment of religion." From the history of the adoption of the First Amendment, we know that this provision prohibited the naming of an official state church. Scholars disagree, however, as to what other forms of church/state involvement constitute establishment. Some experts believe the framers intended to build a wall of separation between church and state. In contrast, other scholars argue that the nation's founders never envisioned so extreme an interpretation of the establishment clause.

In practice, the Supreme Court has adopted a middle ground on the issue of establishment of religion, attempting to balance the concerns of those groups favoring a strict separation of church and state and the values of those interests calling for accommodation between government and religion. Consider the controversy over state aid to parochial schools. Parents who send their children to private, church-related schools frequently complain that they pay twice for education, once when they pay school taxes and a second time when they pay parochial-school tuition. Why can't government help out a bit, they ask. The parochial school systems save taxpayers millions of dollars. Besides, many church-related schools desperately need financial aid. On the opposite side of the issue are those individuals and groups who contend that taxpayers' money should not be used to support religious education.

The battle over public assistance to parochial schools generally begins in state legislatures and school boards but winds up in the federal courts. In 1941, the New Jersey legislature authorized school districts to subsidize the transportation of students to and from school and, if districts chose, to extend the aid to parochial-school students as well. When Ewing Township did just that, a taxpayer named Everson sued, challenging the constitutionality of the action.

The Supreme Court's decision in *Everson* v. *Board of Ewing Township* set an important precedent on the meaning of the establishment clause. The Court firmly upheld the principle of separation of church and state: "Neither a state nor the federal government can set up a church. Neither can pass laws which aid one religion, aid all religions, or prefer one religion over another." Nevertheless, by a 5-to-4 margin, the Court ruled that New Jersey's transportation plan was constitutional because it had a "secular legislative purpose" (safe transportation for schoolchildren) and "neither advance[d] nor inhibit[ed] religion." Thus the Court created a test for determining the constitutionality of state aid to parochial schools: Aid that serves a nonreligious purpose is constitutional; aid that serves a religious purpose is not.[23]

In *Lemon* v. *Kurtzman* (1971), the Court elaborated on its standard for evaluating the constitutionality of government actions toward religion. To pass constitutional muster, the action must meet three requirements: (1) the purpose of the government action must not be to advance religion; (2) the effect of the action must not be to advance or inhibit religion; (3) the action must not lead to an impermissible entanglement between church and state.

Over the years, the Court has used this three-point test to approve some forms of government aid to parochial schools but reject others. The Court has allowed state income tax deductions for parents sending their children to private schools, including religious schools,[24] and upheld state laws providing textbooks[25] and therapeutic, remedial, and counseling services to students attending parochial schools.[26] The Court has reasoned that each of these actions served the nonreligious purpose of helping students to learn. In contrast, the Court has invalidated state laws providing church-related schools with instructional resource materials such as wall charts, laboratory equipment, films, and slide projectors,[27] and refused to allow New York City to use federal grant money to send teachers into church schools to provide remedial and special education to disadvantaged students.[28] In the eyes of the Court, all of these provisions unconstitutionally advanced religion by assisting religious schools.

The Supreme Court's position on state aid to parochial schools illustrates the type of balancing act the Court frequently performs on tough civil-liberties issues. Critics charge that the Court's test for judging the constitutionality of school-aid plans is highly subjective. It isn't obvious, for example, that textbooks promote education while wall charts assist the school. In fact, say the critics, the Court's promotion-of-good-education standard could be used to justify almost any type of aid. Perhaps the best way to interpret the Court's overall approach is to see it as an attempt to mediate a thorny political/constitutional issue in a pragmatic manner. Does that mean that constitutional law reflects political compromise? Yes, sometimes it does.

The Supreme Court's efforts to balance divergent points of view and competing interests can be seen in other controversies involving the establishment of religion clause. The Court, for example, struck down a state program for providing voluntary religious instruction for public-school children on school grounds,[29] but upheld a similar program in which religious instruction took place off school property.[30] In other cases, the Court allowed Pawtucket, Rhode Island, to include a nativity scene in its annual holiday display that included nonreligious Christmas symbols as well,[31] but struck down a Louisiana law requiring equal time for Creation science in public-school biology classes.[32]

School prayer is perhaps the most controversial issue involving the establishment of religion clause. In *Engel* v. *Vitale* (1962), the Supreme Court considered the constitutionality of the voluntary recitation of a prayer composed by New York's state board of regents. The brief prayer read as follows: "Almighty God, we acknowledge our dependence upon Thee, and we beg thy blessings upon us, our parents, our teachers, and our country." By a 6-to-1 vote, the Court ruled that the prayer's use was "wholly inconsistent with the establishment clause." Justice Hugo Black explained the majority's view:

> The constitutional prohibition against laws respecting an establishment of religion must mean that . . . it is no part of the business of government to compose official prayers for any group of the American people to recite as part of a religious program carried on by the government.

Students observing a moment of silence in a public-school classroom.

Moreover, the voluntary nature of the prayer did not make it acceptable. "When the power, prestige, and financial support of government is placed behind a particular religious belief," wrote Black, "the indirect coercive pressure upon religious minorities to conform to the prevailing officially approved religion is plain."[33]

The Supreme Court subsequently affirmed its position on the school-prayer controversy in the cases of *School District of Abington Township* v. *Schempp* and *Murray* v. *Curlett* (1963). The *Schempp* case concerned a Pennsylvania law that required the classroom reading of at least ten verses from the King James Bible each day, followed by recitation of the Lord's Prayer. The other case involved a suit by Madalyn Murray O'Hair, the well-known atheist, and her son William. They attacked a similar Bible-reading and prayer requirement in the city schools of Baltimore. In each case, the Court ruled 8 to 1 that the Bible readings and prayers were unconstitutional.[34]

In 1985, the Court returned to the school-prayer controversy by considering the constitutionality of an Alabama law setting aside a minute of silence each morning for meditation or prayer. Although the Court ruled that some moment-of-silence laws could be constitutional, it struck down the Alabama statute, calling it a subterfuge for returning prescribed prayer to the classroom. Government's role in the relationship between people and religion, said the Court, should be one of strict neutrality.[35]

Freedom of Expression

The First Amendment guarantees freedom of expression. "Congress shall make no law . . . abridging the freedom of speech, or of the press, or the right of the people peaceably to assemble, and to petition the Government for a redress of grievances." The Supreme Court has incorporated these provisions against the states through the due process clause of the Fourteenth Amendment. Nevertheless, freedom of expression is not absolute in America. Some jurists, including Justice Black, believe that the First Amendment should be taken literally: " 'No law' . . . means . . . no law."[36] The prevailing view, however, has been that compelling governmental interests can justify limits on free expression. As Justice Oliver Wendell Holmes phrased it: "The . . . protection of free speech would not protect a man in falsely shouting fire in a theatre, and causing a panic."[37] The difficulty, of course, comes in applying this philosophy to the concrete circumstances of everyday events.

Free Expression and National Security

Consider the problem of national security. What steps can government take to protect itself from internal disorder and subversion? The Supreme Court directly confronted this issue for the first time in a series of cases arising from the era of World War I and the postwar anticommunist Red scare period. The most important of these cases was *Schenck* v. *United States* (1919), in which the Court affirmed the espionage conviction of the secretary of the American Socialist party for circulating anti-draft leaflets among newly inducted soldiers. In the majority opinion, Justice Holmes articulated the clear-and-present-danger rule:

> The question in every case is whether the words are used in such circumstances and are of such a nature as to create a clear and present danger that they will bring about the substantive evils Congress has a right to prevent. It is a question of proximity and degree. When a nation is at war many things that might be said in time of peace are such a hindrance to its effort that their utterance will not be endured.[38]

The **clear-and-present-danger rule**, then, can be defined as the test used by the Supreme Court to measure the permissible bounds of free speech, holding that government may suppress expression that is of such a nature as to create a clear and present danger of a substantive evil that Congress has a right to prevent.

Although the clear-and-present-danger rule seemed to offer broad protection for expression except in time of national crisis, the Court's majority initially refused to apply it to protect critics of the government. Instead, the Court used the **bad-tendency test**, which is a standard used by the Supreme Court to determine the permissible bounds of free speech, holding that any expression that has a tendency to lead to substantial evil can be banned by the government. In the *Abrams* case, for example, the Court reviewed the conviction of a Russian-born immigrant under the Espionage Act for distributing two pamphlets critical of America's intervention in the Russian Civil War. The pamphlets were poorly produced and not widely circulated; one was even in Yiddish. Nonetheless, the Court voted 7 to 2 to uphold Abrams' conviction and twenty-year prison sentence on the grounds that the pamphlets had a tendency to threaten government. In a forceful dissent, Justice Holmes, joined by Justice Louis Brandeis, argued that the Court should have used the clear-and-present-danger rule to overturn the conviction. "[N]obody can suppose," said Holmes, "that the surreptitious publishing of a silly leaflet by an unknown man" would present a threat to the government of the United States.[39]

Another group of cases involving the issue of free expression and national security arose in the years after World War II, especially during the 1950s, when communist subversion was a major national concern. In *Dennis* v. *United States* (1951), the Supreme Court upheld the conviction of eleven officials of the American Communist party for conspiring to teach and advocate overthrow of the government and for organizing the Communist party with that purpose in mind. Even though the likelihood of communist revolution was slight, the Court used the bad-tendency test to uphold government's limiting free speech. The "gravity of the evil" presented by communism was so great, said the Court, that it justified government's repression of political expression that would tend toward communist revolution, regardless of the probability of that event.[40]

In *Yates* v. *United States* (1957), however, the Supreme Court significantly softened the impact of the *Dennis* ruling by reversing the convictions of a group of second-tier Communist party leaders and party members. In this case, the Court drew a distinction between the advocacy of ideas, or abstract action, which the First Amendment protects, and the advocacy of unlawful action, which the amendment does not protect. Before the government could convict the communists, the Court ruled, it would have to prove that each defendant had specifically urged illegal action.[41]

The Supreme Court's position on free expression and national security reached its modern maturity in *Brandenburg* v. *Ohio*, decided in 1969. Clarence Brandenburg, an Ohio Ku Klux Klan leader, was convicted under state law for threatening "vengeance" against the president, Congress, and the Supreme Court. The Court overturned Brandenburg's conviction, saying that mere advocacy of lawless action was not sufficient to sustain a conviction. Instead, the state must prove that the "advocacy is directed to inciting or producing imminent lawless action and is likely to incite or produce such action."[42] Thus, the Court not only reinstated the old clear-and-present-danger doctrine but carried it one step further by adding the incitement requirement. And, indeed, the Court's position in the *Brandenburg* case stands today as the test for determining the constitutionality of laws restricting political speech. As one scholar summarizes it, neither Congress nor the states may enact a "law abridging anti-government speech, except for that which is directed to inciting or producing imminent lawless action and is likely to incite or produce such action."[43]

Free Expression and Threats to Public Order

Can government constitutionally prohibit expression that may lead to a disruption of public order? Consider the controversy generated by Paul Cohen and his jacket. In 1968, during the midst of the Vietnam War, Cohen wore a jacket into the Los Angeles County Courthouse upon which the words "F—— the Draft" were clearly visible. Cohen was arrested and subsequently convicted by a local court for disturbing the peace. The local court reasoned that the jacket might provoke others to commit acts of violence and sentenced Cohen to thirty days in jail. Cohen appealed, and the case eventually reached the Supreme Court. Before we discuss the Court's ruling in the *Cohen* case, however, let's trace the background of the Court's efforts to resolve such controversies.

The Supreme Court first dealt with the issue of free expression and public order in 1942 in *Chaplinsky* v. *New Hampshire*, in which the Court upheld the conviction of Walter Chaplinsky for calling a city marshal a "G—— d—— racketeer" and a d—— fascist." The Court noted that the First Amendment does not protect certain types of speech—"the lewd and obscene, the profane, the libelous, and . . . insulting or 'fighting' words . . . which by their very utterance tend to incite an immediate breach of the peace." The Court held that there was a clear and present danger that Chaplinsky's "fighting words" would provoke the average person to retaliate, and thereby cause a disturbance of public order.[44]

Since *Chaplinsky*, however, the Supreme Court has gradually narrowed the scope of the fighting-words doctrine. In 1949, the Court overturned the conviction of Arthur Terminiello, a rabble-rousing defrocked priest whose anti-Jewish speech provoked a riot among demonstrators outside the meeting hall. The Court said that the Chicago city ordinance under which Terminiello was convicted was overly broad. It punished Terminiello not for causing a breach of the peace but for giving a speech that stirred people to anger. This, the Court ruled, is one of the functions of free speech under our form of government, and thus it is protected by the Constitution.[45]

Then, in 1971, the Court overturned Paul Cohen's conviction for disturbing the peace. The Court held that government cannot legally forbid shocking language that is not legally obscene and that is not directed at an individual listener (or reader) in such a way as to provoke violence. Otherwise, government risks the unconstitutional suppression of ideas.[46]

Finally, in *Gooding* v. *Wilson* (1972), the Supreme Court upheld the appeals-court reversal of the conviction of an antiwar demonstrator who called a police officer an SOB. The Court ruled that the fighting-words doctrine must be restricted to words that are plainly intended to incite violence from the person to whom they are addressed.[47]

The result of the *Terminiello, Cohen*, and *Gooding* cases has been to limit the scope of the fighting-words doctrine in favor of a standard highly protective of free speech. Simply put, the Court has held that the only type of objectionable language that can be constitutionally prohibited is language spoken in a face-to-face confrontation in a threatening or inciting manner likely to lead to an immediate breach of the peace.

Symbolic Speech

Not all expression is spoken, such as Chaplinsky's fighting words, or written, such as Cohen's jacket. Some expression is symbolic, such as flying the flag, or burning it. In general, the Supreme Court has recognized display as a form of symbolic speech entitled to First Amendment protection. In the *Tinker* case, for example, the Court upheld the right of some high-school students to wear black armbands to school to protest the war in Vietnam.[48] Similarly, in the *Schacht* case, the Court overturned the conviction of a man for wearing a military uniform while acting in an antiwar skit.[49]

In contrast, the Supreme Court has been reluctant to recognize desecration as constitutionally protected free speech. In a case decided in 1972, the Court affirmed the flag-desecration conviction of a New York man whose sculptures displayed the United States flag in the form of a male sex organ.[50] Nonetheless, the Court has been willing to grant First Amendment protection to less offensive forms of desecration, such as wearing the flag as a trousers patch or attaching a peace symbol to the flag.[51]

The most controversial symbolic speech issue is flag burning. In 1989, the Supreme Court overturned a Texas flag-desecration law under which

Gregory Lee Johnson was convicted for burning an American flag at the 1984 Republican convention in Dallas. By a 5-to-4 vote, the Court ruled that Johnson's action was a form of symbolic speech. "If there is any bedrock principle underlying the First Amendment," wrote Justice William Brennan in the majority opinion, "it is that the government may not prohibit the expression of an idea simply because society finds the idea itself offensive or disagreeable."[52] Congress responded to the uproar over the Court's decision by passing a federal anti-flag-burning statute, which, a year later, the Court also ruled unconstitutional. This time, opponents proposed a constitutional amendment to allow states and the federal government to enact legislation to prohibit the physical desecration of the flag, but the amendment fell short of the two-thirds majorities needed to pass the House and Senate.

Gregory Lee Johnson, whose conviction for burning a flag at the 1984 Republican convention was overturned by the U.S. Supreme Court.

Defamation of Character

Defamation involves false written statements (**libel**) or false oral statements (**slander**) that lower a person's reputation or expose a person to hatred, contempt, or ridicule. The United States Supreme Court has always held that defamatory expression is not protected by the First Amendment. In recent decades, however, the Court had adopted a relatively free approach toward the defamation of public figures. (The Court defines public figures as individuals who thrust themselves to the forefront of a particular public controversy in order to influence the resolution of the issues involved.)

The most important case in this area of the law is *New York Times* v. *Sullivan* (1964). In 1960, a group of civil rights activists published a full-page advertisement in the *Times* charging that civil rights demonstrators in Alabama "were being met by an unprecedented wave of terror," some of which came from the police. Subsequently, L. B. Sullivan, a former Alabama commissioner of public affairs, filed a libel suit against the paper, charging that the ad included "defamatory falsehoods" that harmed his reputation. An Alabama state court awarded Sullivan $500,000 in damages, but the Supreme Court overturned the award. The Court held that the Constitution "prohibits a public official from recovering damages for a defamatory falsehood relating to his official conduct unless he proves that the statement was made with 'actual malice'—that is, with knowledge that it was false or with reckless disregard of whether it was false or not."[53]

The practical effect of this decision was to create a double standard for ordinary citizens and public figures in regard to defamation suits. Ordinary citizens can win defamation suits merely by demonstrating that a statement is false and that it lowers their reputation or exposes them to hatred, contempt, or ridicule. Public figures, however, must also show that the statement was made with malice or reckless disregard for truth. The justification for this approach is that public figures, unlike private individuals, have access to channels of effective communication to combat allegations about their conduct. What's more, public figures have voluntarily subjected themselves to public scrutiny.

Obscenity

The regulation of pornography is a controversial and difficult civil-liberties question. Some observers agree with President Johnson's Commission on Obscenity and Pornography, which reported in 1970 that it could find no evidence that exposure to sexually explicit materials caused criminal behavior. The commission recommended lifting all restrictions on adults wishing to see books, pictures, or films.

Critics of the Johnson Commission (and there were many) found solace in the 1986 report of another commission. During the Reagan administration, Attorney General Edwin Meese appointed his own pornography commission, staffing it with well-known anti-smut crusaders. To no one's surprise, this commission concluded that pornography is directly linked to rape and other types of criminal behavior. It recommended tougher laws to rid society of sexually explicit materials.

Although the U.S. Supreme Court has long held that obscenity is not protected by the Constitution, it has had a problem defining obscenity. As Justice John Marshall Harlan once phrased it, "One man's vulgarity is another man's lyric."[54] And so it is. In the 1950s, Maryland's official movie censors found *The Moon Is Blue* to be lewd and lascivious because it contained the terms *pregnant* and *virginity*.[55]

The Court's first effort to establish a yardstick came in 1957 in a pair of cases, *Roth* v. *United States* and *Alberts* v. *California*. In these cases, the Court outlined its prurient-interest test for obscenity: "Whether to the average person, applying contemporary standards, the dominant theme of the material taken as a whole appeals to prurient interest."[56] (The word *prurient* means appealing to unwholesome sexual desire.)

In subsequent years, the Court modified, refined, and in some ways revised its rule. The Court added "patently offensive" to its definition of obscenity in 1962,[57] and in 1964 ruled that the material must be found "utterly without redeeming social importance."[58] In 1966, the Court held that a work's advertising could be considered in judging whether or not it appeals to prurient interest,[59] and in 1968, the Court said it would not invalidate carefully drawn obscenity statutes aimed at protecting minors.[60] The Court has extended this precedent, upholding a New York law in 1982 that banned the distribution of material depicting sexual activity by children.[61]

For a time, all of this qualification and equivocation left the Court in the position of having to act as a national censorship board. The justices spent a good deal of time in the film room, watching movies one lower court or another had ruled obscene. "I don't know how to define hardcore pornography," wrote Justice Potter Stewart, "but I know it when I see it."[62]

In 1973 in *Miller* v. *California*, the Court took another stab at setting guidelines for obscenity. First, the material must depict or describe sexual conduct in a patently offensive manner. Second, it must be such that the "average person, applying contemporary community standards, would find that the work taken as a whole appeals to prurient interest." Finally, the work taken as a whole must lack serious literary, artistic, political, or scientific value.[63]

Subsequently, the Court qualified the *Miller* standard. In 1974, the Court overturned the decision of a local jury in Georgia that the movie *Carnal Knowledge* was obscene, ruling that local juries do not have unlimited discretion to determine obscenity.[64] The Court has also held that national standards, not community standards, should be used to determine whether an allegedly obscene book or film has scientific, literary, or artistic value.[65]

Prior Restraint

In early 1979, *Progressive* magazine announced plans to publish a how-to article on building an H-bomb. The magazine's editors explained that their purpose in printing the article was to inform the public about nuclear weapons. All the information in the article was gleaned from unclassified sources, they said. The article would divulge no real secrets. Nonetheless, the federal government asked a federal judge to block publication of the article on national security grounds.

This example introduces the issue of **prior restraint**, that is, government action to prevent the publication of objectionable materials. As we have seen, expressions involving sedition, defamation, or obscenity can be held punishable after their utterance or publication. The issue of prior restraint considers whether government can block the expression of objectionable materials *before* the fact.

Years of debate on what constitutes obscenity—and whether obscenity is protected by the Constitution—have failed to reach consensus.

The most important judicial ruling on this subject is *Near* v. *Minnesota* (1931). In this case, the U.S. Supreme Court struck down a Minnesota law that permitted prior restraint against materials that were defamatory or obscene. The Court said that the proper recourse against such material was to bring suit or file charges after publication. Prior restraint is such an extreme limitation on expression, the Court declared, that it can be used only in exceptional circumstances, such as time of war.[66] Subsequently, the Court relied on the *Near* precedent to invalidate laws against printing and distributing leaflets and to make the work of state film licensing/movie censorship boards difficult (so difficult, in fact, that none still exist).[67]

The Supreme Court has had more difficulty deciding prior-restraint cases involving national security. In the Pentagon Papers case in 1971, the Court refused to block newspaper publication of government documents detailing the history of American involvement in Vietnam. Although the Nixon administration claimed the documents included military secrets, the newspaper said the government's only real concerns were political; no national security issues were at stake. The Court was deeply divided, however, and its opinion gave little guidance as to how similar disputes might be resolved in the future.[68]

Nor did the *Progressive* controversy enable the Court to clarify the law in this area. After several newspapers published H-bomb articles of their own, the government dropped its case against the magazine; so the issue never reached the Supreme Court. Consequently, the Court has yet to clarify what test it will use in determining when prior restraint is justified to deter a threat to national security.

Due Process of Law and the Rights of the Accused

Several provisions of the Bill of Rights are devoted to protecting the rights of persons under investigation for, or accused of, crimes, including the better part of the Fourth, Fifth, and Eighth amendments. The key constitutional phrase, however, is found in the Fifth Amendment: "No person shall . . . be deprived of life, liberty, or property, without due process of law. . . ." This phrase is used again—in the same words—in the Fourteenth Amendment, so it applies to the states as well as to the national government. But just what does it mean?

Due process of law is the constitutional provision holding that government should follow fair and regular procedures in actions that might lead to an individual's suffering loss of life, liberty, or property. In practice, due process has two faces—substantive due process and procedural due process. **Substantive due process** is the constitutional principle that legislative and executive actions should be neither arbitrary nor unreasonable, nor should they cover subject matter beyond the reach of government. In the late nineteenth and early twentieth centuries, the Supreme Court relied on the doctrine of substantive due process to invalidate many government efforts to regulate business. Since 1937, though, the Court has used the concept sparingly and primarily in civil-liberties matters. For example, federal courts have sometimes relied on the principle of substantive due process to knock down vagrancy, loitering, and public-nuisance statutes for being unconstitutionally vague and arbitrary.

Procedural due process is the constitutional principle that laws should be executed, administered, and interpreted in accordance with accepted standards of justice. As we have noted, the Supreme Court has held on a case-by-case basis that due process incorporates most of the guarantees found in the Bill of Rights. Consequently, neither the federal government nor the states may resort to stacked juries, coerced confessions, self-incrimination, denial of counsel, cruel and unusual punishments, or unreasonable searches and seizures.

These constitutional guarantees were written to protect everyone in America from the arbitrary power of government, but, in practice, they most frequently arise in connection with criminal prosecutions. Some of those who benefit from their application are among the most unsavory individuals in society—accused murderers, rapists, and child molesters. As Justice Felix Frankfurter once put it, "It is a fair summary of history to say that the safeguards of liberty have been forged in controversies involving not very nice people."[69] Consequently, the interpretation and application of the principles of due process have been controversial.

Searches and Seizures

The Fourth Amendment guarantees "[t]he right of the people to be secure in their persons, houses, papers, and effects, against unreasonable searches and seizures...and no Warrants shall issue, but upon probable cause...and particularly describing the place to be searched, and the persons or things to be seized." In general, this means that the police need a **warrant** (that is, an official authorization for some action) for most searches of persons or property. Warrants are issued by judges or other magistrates after the authorities have shown probable cause that certain items will be found.

Through the years the Supreme Court has permitted a number of exceptions to the basic warrant requirement. The police don't need a warrant, for example, to search suspects who consent to searches or to search suspects after valid arrests. They can conduct searches of suspects in the field in circumstances they deem suspicious (based on experience and expertise). The authorities can also search luggage in airports for firearms or explosives and may fingerprint suspects after arrests.

The Court has also permitted warrantless searches when they are justified by probable cause. Consider the *Ross* case. An informant tipped off the District of Columbia police about a narcotics dealer known as Bandit who sold drugs from the trunk of his purplish maroon Chevrolet Malibu. When the police spotted a car fitting the description, they pulled it over and searched the trunk, even though they did not have a warrant. Sure enough, they found heroin and cash in the trunk. The car's driver, Albert Ross, Jr., was subsequently tried and convicted of possession of narcotics with intent to distribute. He appealed, and in 1982 his case reached the Supreme Court. Did the police search of Ross's car trunk without a warrant violate his constitutional rights? The Court said that it did not because the police had legitimately stopped the car and had probable cause to believe it contained contraband. As a result, the police could search the vehicle as thoroughly as if they had a warrant. The Court added, though, that a search "must be limited by its object," that is, the police cannot conduct a general search to see what might turn up. If authorities have probable cause to believe that illegal aliens are being transported in a van, for example, they may search the van, but they have no justification for searching the glove compartment or luggage (where no illegal aliens could possibly be hiding).[70]

In recent years, the Supreme Court has broadened the authority of officials to conduct searches and seizures by defining the term *search* more narrowly and by allowing certain types of searches directed against categories or groups of persons rather than specific individuals. The Court has ruled, for example, that the police do not need a warrant to search garbage bags left at the curb[71] and that police examinations of bank records do not constitute a search.[72] The Supreme Court has also allowed administrative searches of high-school students[73] and approved random drug testing for railway workers.[74] One observer believes that the Court is moving away from requiring government officials to have a specific reason (probable cause) for searching a particular individual to approving categories of searches for certain classes of individuals, such as officers carrying firearms, employees who pose safety risks, and high-school students.[75]

The Exclusionary Rule

The **exclusionary rule** is the judicial doctrine stating that when the police violate an individual's constitutional rights, the evidence obtained as a result of police misconduct or error cannot be used against the defendant. In 1914, the Supreme Court established the exclusionary rule in federal prosecutions in the *Weeks* case. The police arrested Weeks at his place of business and then searched his home. Both of these actions were taken without a warrant. Papers and articles seized in the search were used in federal court against Weeks, and he was convicted. He appealed, arguing that the judge should not have admitted illegally seized materials into evidence. The Supreme Court agreed:

> The tendency of those who execute the criminal laws of the country to obtain convictions by means of unlawful seizures and enforced confessions...should find no sanction in the judgment of the courts.... If letters and private documents can thus be seized and held and used in evidence against a citizen accused of an offense, the protection of the Fourth Amendment...might as well be stricken from the Constitution.[76]

In 1961, the Supreme Court extended the exclusionary rule to the states in the case of *Mapp* v. *Ohio*.[77]

As the crime rate in America soared in the late 1960s and 1970s, criticism of the exclusionary rule increased. Why should the criminal go free, opponents asked, just because a police officer erred? Among the sharpest critics of the rule was Chief Justice Warren Burger, and during his tenure the Court modified the rule's application. In 1974, the Court refused to apply the rule to grand-jury proceedings.[78] Then, in 1984, the Court adopted a "good faith" exception to the exclusionary rule requirement, allowing the use of illegally seized evidence in criminal prosecutions as long as the police acted in good faith.[79]

The *Miranda* Warnings

Other due-process issues concern the right to counsel and the Fifth Amendment privilege against self-incrimination. In the *Gideon* case in 1963, the Supreme Court held that states must provide attorneys for defendants too poor to hire defense attorneys.[80] One year later, the Court ruled that persons have the right to consult an attorney as soon as they become the object of police investigation.[81]

The most controversial case in this area is *Miranda* v. *Arizona* (1966). Arizona police arrested Ernesto Miranda in connection with the kidnapping and rape of a young woman. Under questioning, Miranda confessed, but the police did not inform him of his constitutional rights to remain silent and consult an attorney. On appeal, Miranda challenged the use of his confession as a violation of the Fifth Amendment's guarantee against self-incrimination.

In a 5-to-4 vote, the Supreme Court reversed Miranda's conviction. The Court's majority held that the prosecution may not use a statement against an accused person in a court of law unless the authorities observe adequate procedural safeguards to ensure that the statement is obtained "voluntarily, knowingly, and intelligently." Before questioning, accused persons must be warned that they have a right to remain silent, that any statements they make may be used against them, and that they are entitled to the presence of an attorney, either retained or appointed.[82]

The Court's *Miranda* ruling has sparked fiery debate. Its critics say that it is merely another device for releasing criminals on the basis of technicalities. During the Reagan administration, Attorney General Edwin Meese asked the Court to abandon the rule because it "only helps the guilty." In contrast, *Miranda*'s defenders call it the "poor person's Fifth Amendment." Educated, middle-class defendants don't need the *Miranda* warnings—they know their rights. Instead, it's the poor, uneducated, first-time offender that *Miranda* protects from police coercion. One commentator makes the argument this way:

> [I]n the absence of *Miranda*, a lot of police coercion will return. Poor, uneducated people will say a lot of dumb things that prosecutors desperate for convictions will construe to be powerful circumstantial evidence. *Miranda* gone, every prosecutor in the land will have a better chance of making his record look good by sending some talkative and often innocent "little guy" up the river.[83]

As with the exclusionary rule, the Supreme Court in recent years has weakened the *Miranda* ruling without reversing it. The Court has held that in cross-examining defendants, prosecutors can use statements that don't meet the *Miranda* standard[84] and that the *Miranda* rule does not apply to grand-jury proceedings.[85] The Court even upheld a conviction when the police refused to allow an attorney hired by a suspect's relatives from seeing him since the suspect had not asked to see a lawyer.[86]

Grand-Jury Indictment

The Fifth Amendment provides for a grand-jury indictment for serious criminal offenses. A **grand jury** is a body of citizens who hear evidence against persons accused of serious crimes and determine whether the evidence is sufficient to bring the person to trial. The principle behind the use of the grand jury is to protect individuals from frivolous prosecutions. Theoretically, it is a check on the prosecutor. Nevertheless, grand juries have their critics, who contend that grand juries merely rubber-stamp the prosecutor's recommendations. Moreover, grand-jury proceedings are both time-consuming and expensive. In practice, many states do not use grand juries. (This is one of the few provisions of the Bill of Rights that the Supreme Court has not incorporated against the states.) Instead, they have substituted the **information**, which is a formal accusation made under oath by a prosecuting attorney, charging a person with a crime.

Double Jeopardy

The Fifth Amendment prohibits double jeopardy: No person shall be "twice put in jeopardy of life and limb" for the same criminal offense. Essentially, this statement means that the government cannot appeal acquittals even though defendants can appeal guilty verdicts. The principle behind this provision is to protect individuals from the harassment of repeated prosecutions for the same offense. Nevertheless, the Supreme Court has held that a defendant can be tried multiple times for multiple offenses committed in a single incident.[87] An individual charged with killing a gas-station attendant during a holdup, for example, could be tried first for murder and then for robbery. Also, the Court has ruled that separate prosecutions by different levels of government do not constitute double jeopardy, even for the same offense.[88] An individual arrested for bank robbery, for instance, could legally be tried twice for the same offense, once by the federal government, and once by the state government where the offense occurred.

Self-Incrimination and Immunity

Although the Fifth Amendment protects individuals from having to testify against themselves in criminal proceedings, it does not grant an absolute right of silence. The Supreme Court has held that individuals can be compelled to testify under threat of being held in contempt of court if they are first granted immunity.[89] (**Immunity from prosecution** is an exemption from prosecution for self-incriminating testimony given to a witness in a judicial proceeding or congressional hearing.) In the Iran-contra hearings, for example, Congress forced a number of participants in the scandal to testify by granting them immunity. Another, more limited type of immunity is use immunity. **Use immunity** is an exemption from prosecution that protects individuals from having their actual testimony used against them, but does not shelter them from a prosecution based on evidence gained by other means. Use immunity was also employed in the Iran-contra hearings.

Fair Trial

A number of provisions in the Sixth Amendment are aimed at guaranteeing defendants a fair trial. First, the amendment promises a speedy and public trial. Although the Supreme Court has been reluctant to set timetables for trials, the federal government and many states have adopted "speedy trial laws" to ensure that justice not be long delayed. As for the public-trial requirement, the Supreme Court has held that the public (and the press) may not be excluded from the courtroom except in rare circumstances.[90] Moreover, the Court has said that states may permit the unobtrusive use of television in the courtroom if they wish.[91]

Second, the Sixth Amendment guarantees trial by an impartial jury. Although juries are traditionally twelve persons, the Supreme Court has said that juries with as few as six people are acceptable.[92] The Court has also held that jury-selection processes must ensure that the jury pool represent a cross section of the community. The Court has ruled, for example, that prosecutors may not systematically exclude minorities from jury service.[93]

Third, the Sixth Amendment grants defendants the right to legal counsel. In *Gideon* v. *Wainwright*, the Supreme Court ruled that states must provide attorneys for indigent defendants charged with serious crimes.[94] The Court has also held that assigned counsel must meet a standard of reasonable competence.[95]

Cruel and Unusual Punishments

The Eighth Amendment prohibits "cruel and unusual punishments." In general, the Supreme Court has interpreted this provision to mean that punishment must fit the crime. The Court, for example, has held that a life sentence without possibility of parole for a series of nonviolent petty offenses is cruel and unusual.[96] The Court has also ruled that capital punishment for rape is unconstitutionally severe.[97]

No issue has generated more controversy under the Eighth Amendment than the death penalty (**capital punishment**). The supporters of capital punishment quote the Bible, "an eye for an eye, a tooth for a tooth," and declare that the death penalty is an effective deterrent to serious crime. In contrast, opponents call the death penalty barbaric and say that it is little less than legalized murder.

A strong line of attack against the death penalty is the argument that it is applied in an arbitrary and capricious fashion, falling disproportionately upon the poor and racial minorities. In 1972, the opponents of capital punishment won a temporary victory in the case of *Furman* v. *Georgia*. By a 5-to-4 vote, the Supreme Court declared the death penalty, *as then applied*, to be unconstitutional because of the arbitrary manner in which it was assigned. Pointedly, the Court did not find capital punishment as such to be unconstitutional.[98]

After *Furman*, many states adopted new capital-punishment laws designed to satisfy the Court's requirement that death-penalty statutes be clearly drawn and that judges and juries carefully consider mitigating circumstances before imposing the death penalty. In 1976, a case challenging Georgia's new death-penalty law reached the Supreme Court. This time, in the case of *Gregg* v. *Georgia*, the Court upheld the law, ruling that the death penalty is not inherently unconstitutional.[99]

Since 1976, the Supreme Court has rejected one challenge to the death penalty after another, and states have carried out more than a hundred executions. In 1987, for example, the Court rejected a claim that the death penalty was racially discriminatory despite evidence that persons convicted of killing whites are several times more likely to be given the death penalty than individuals convicted of murdering blacks.[100] The Court has also ruled that states may execute convicted murderers who are mentally retarded[101] or who were as young as sixteen years of age when they committed their crimes.[102]

CIVIL-LIBERTIES POLICYMAKING

As we study the case law and the philosophical controversies of civil liberties, it is important to remember that we are also studying the policymaking process. Let's discuss the civil-liberties policy process in terms of the public policy approach.

Agenda Setting

A number of political actors help set the agenda for civil-liberties policymaking. Interest groups are particularly important. Conservative groups call on the government to get tough on pornography and crime and to limit access to abortion. Groups with unpopular views, such as Nazis and the Ku Klux Klan, stimulate debate on the First Amendment by attempting to march and demonstrate. In the meantime, many of the civil-liberties disputes reaching the Supreme Court are test cases initiated by groups such as the American Civil Liberties Union (ACLU) or the Jehovah's Witnesses. The latter have been responsible for more than fifty cases involving religious liberty, winning 90 percent of them.[103] What's more, interest groups ranging from the Chamber of Commerce to B'nai B'rith join other civil-liberties cases by means of the amicus brief. (A **test case**, you recall, is a lawsuit initiated to assess the constitutionality of a legislative or executive act. An **amicus curiae brief**, or **friend-of-the-court brief**, is a written legal argument presented by parties not directly involved in a case.)

Individuals can also raise civil-liberties issues to the public agenda. Many due-process/criminal justice disputes arise from appeals filed by convicted felons, such as Ernesto Miranda, who aren't so much interested in the great principles of civil liberties as they are in saving their own hides. One individual who apparently does act on the basis of principle, however, is Madalyn Murray O'Hair, who has become famous (or infamous, depending on the point of view) for initiating test cases to challenge what she regards as unconstitutional government support of religion.

Madalyn Murray O'Hair and her sons on the steps of the Supreme Court building in February 1963, when she was pressing a test case against the use of the Lord's Prayer in the Baltimore public schools. Her challenge was successful; on June 17, the Court ruled that the prayer requirement was unconstitutional, thereby setting off a national debate that continues to this day.

For the most part, the views of the general public are too unfocused to set the agenda on civil liberties in any specific sense. Public opinion, though, can provide some guidelines, especially on high-profile issues, such as the death penalty and abortion. Perhaps it is no coincidence that the Supreme Court's more conservative approach toward the death penalty coincides with public-opinion poll data showing large majorities of Americans supporting capital punishment.

Political elites, such as lawyers, editorial writers, and scholars, generally have a greater impact on civil-liberties policymaking than does the general public.[104] Recall the Flag Salute cases which were discussed in the Perspective. Although these cases were decided before the advent of modern public-opinion polling, it seems likely that the general public strongly supported the Court's original flag-salute ruling that school districts could force Jehovah's Witnesses children to pledge allegiance to the flag regardless of their religious beliefs. After all, the flag is a positive symbol for most Americans, and many people are suspicious of persons with nontraditional religious beliefs. Historians tell us, however, that newspaper editorials and law journal articles strongly condemned the Court's original decision.[105] By reversing its position on the flag-salute issue in *West Virginia State Board of Education* v. *Barnette*, the Court responded to elite concerns rather than those of the general public.

Government officials play an important role in setting the civil-liberties agenda. The flag-salute cases came about because a school board in West Virginia decided to require students to recite the pledge of allegiance and refused to make exceptions for Jehovah's Witnesses. Police-officer associations have lobbied Congress and state legislatures to eliminate legal "technicalities," such as the exclusionary rule.

The government officials with the most influence in civil-liberties agenda setting, however, are judges, particularly justices on the Supreme Court. As we discussed in chapter 11, the members of the Court essentially set their own agenda, picking and choosing from among the thousands of cases appealed to them. Civil liberties have become the primary agenda items of the modern Supreme Court, in large part because the Court's justices have wanted it that way.

Policy Formulation and Adoption

Many civil-liberties policies are formulated and adopted in the courts, ultimately the Supreme Court, but the courts aren't the only political institutions involved. After all, the Supreme Court is a reactive institution. It rules on the validity of the actions of other governmental bodies only when a lawsuit comes before it. The *Miranda* case, for example, concerned law-enforcement procedures and state courts in Arizona. Similar procedures had been fairly standard practice around the nation for decades. Public policy concerning police interrogations and confessions and the use of those confessions in state courts had been set at the state and local levels until the *Miranda* case reached the Supreme Court and a majority of the justices decided to establish a national policy. When we study civil liberties, we devote much of our time to examining Supreme Court decisions, but these are important only insofar as they serve as guidelines for other institutions of government. If we are to understand civil-liberties policy formulation and adoption, we must also study the president, state governors, mayors, Congress, state legislatures, city councils, school boards, chiefs of police, the lower federal courts, and state courts.

Policy Implementation and Evaluation

A broad range of governmental entities participate in the implementation of civil-liberties policy. As we discussed in the introduction to this chapter, the Supreme Court's willingness to allow states to enact greater restrictions on abortion may not necessarily lead to more restrictive abortion policies, at least not in all states. Although some state legislatures may limit access to abortion, other legislatures may not act. What's more, regardless of the legal status of abortion, its availability depends on the willingness of doctors, hospitals, and clinics to provide the service.

Scholars have completed a number of studies evaluating certain aspects of civil-liberties policy. One study concludes that the *Zorach* decision, which involved the issue of religious instruction during school time but off school grounds, had a major effect on attitudes concerning church-state relations.[106] A number of studies suggest that the primary impact of the *Miranda* decision may have been psychological. One scholar finds that the ruling had little appreciable effect on confessions and convictions.[107] Another observer concludes that the ruling has had no measurable impact on reducing police misconduct.[108]

CONCLUSION: CIVIL LIBERTIES AND POLITICS

Civil-liberties policymaking is political. Many of us entertain the notion that civil-liberties questions are somehow above politics because they involve constitutional law and the courts. That, however, is not the case. First, civil-liberties policymaking involves political actors who operate much as political actors do in economic and regulatory policymaking. Interest groups lobby for

Anti-Japanese sentiment reached such a pitch during World War II that hundreds of thousands of American citizens of Japanese descent were evacuated from their homes and sent to internment camps.

their causes. Congress and state legislatures consider civil-liberties legislation as part of their regular legislative processes. Executives at the various levels of the federal system participate as well.

Second, the courts are not apolitical. In chapter 11, you recall, we made the point that federal courts are political institutions operating within a legal setting. Judges are chosen through the political process of presidential selection and Senate confirmation. The internal decision-making processes of courts at the appellate level reflect bargaining and compromise. The implementation of judicial decisions involves political processes as well.

Finally, the substance of civil-liberties policies reflects politics. In the early nineteenth century, the Federalist-controlled Congress passed the Sedition Act as a weapon against political opponents, and the Federalist-dominated judiciary upheld it, despite the Bill of Rights. In the 1930s, the Supreme Court shifted its agenda to focus on civil liberties only after the electoral triumph of New Deal liberalism. Even so, the Supreme Court took time out from its defense of civil liberties to legitimize the government's internment of 120,000 American citizens of Japanese descent in the early days of World War II.[109] The Court said that the Japanese-Americans presented a "clear and present danger," but history indicates that the motivations for the internment included greed, racism, mass hysteria, and politics, not primarily a desire to protect national security.

Civil liberties aren't above politics. They depend very much on political factors, specifically the support of government officials and the politically active segment of the population, and, at the least, the acquiescence of the general public. When these factors are absent, as they were in the days of the Sedition Act or the Japanese-American internment, the civil liberties enumerated in the Bill of Rights don't mean much. Civil-liberties policy in America today is shaped by the Constitution and a political culture that values individual freedom. But it is also the product of contemporary politics.

KEY TERMS

amicus curiae brief

bad-tendency test

bill of attainder

bill of rights

capital punishment

civil liberties

clear-and-present-danger rule

double jeopardy

double standard

due process of law

ex post facto law

exclusionary rule

friend-of-the-court brief

grand jury

immunity from prosecution

information

libel

prior restraint

procedural due process

religious test

selective incorporation of the Bill of Rights

slander

substantive due process

test case

use immunity

warrant

writ of habeas corpus

NOTES

1. *Roe* v. *Wade*, 410 U.S. 113 (1973).
2. *Webster* v. *Reproductive Health Services*, 109 S. Ct. 3040 (1989).
3. John Stuart Mill, *On Liberty* (New York: Appleton-Century-Crofts, 1947), originally published 1859.
4. *West Virginia State Board of Education* v. *Barnette*, 319 U.S. 624 (1943).
5. *Terminiello* v. *Chicago*, 337 U.S. 1 (1949).
6. *Schenck* v. *United States*, 249 U.S. 47 (1919).
7. *Barron* v. *Baltimore*, 7 Peters 243 (1833).
8. Slaughterhouse cases, 16 Wallace 36 (1873).
9. *Hurtado* v. *California*, 110 U.S. 516 (1884).
10. *Gitlow* v. *New York*, 268 U.S. 652 (1925).
11. *Palko* v. *Connecticut*, 302 U.S. 319 (1937).
12. Alfred H. Kelly and Winfred A. Harbison, *The American Constitution: Its Origins and Development*, 5th ed. (New York: W. W. Norton, 1976), p. 752.
13. *Griswold* v. *Connecticut*, 381 U.S. 479 (1965).
14. Elder Witt, "Hans A. Linde: The Unassuming Architect of an Emerging Role for State Supreme Courts," *Governing*, July 1989, p. 56.
15. Paul Marcotte, "Federalism and the Rise of State Courts," *ABA Journal*, 1 April 1987, pp. 60–64.
16. Robert H. Jackson, *The Struggle for Judicial Supremacy* (New York: Random House, 1941), pp. 284–85.
17. *Reynolds* v. *United States*, 98 U.S. 145 (1879).
18. *Jacobson* v. *Massachusetts*, 197 U.S. 11 (1905).
19. *Department of Human Resources of Oregon* v. *Smith*, 58 U.S.L.W. 4433 (1990).
20. *West Virginia State Board of Education* v. *Barnette*, 319 U.S. 624 (1943).
21. *Cantwell* v. *Connecticut*, 310 U.S. 296 (1940); *Martin* v. *Struthers*, 319 U.S. 141 (1943).
22. *Wisconsin* v. *Yoder*, 406 U.S. 205 (1972).
23. *Everson* v. *Board of Ewing Township*, 330 U.S. 1 (1947).
24. *Mueller* v. *Allen*, 463 U.S. 388 (1983).
25. *Board of Education* v. *Allen*, 392 U.S. 236 (1968).
26. *Wolman* v. *Walter*, 433 U.S. 229 (1977).
27. Ibid.; *Meek* v. *Pittenger*, 421 U.S. 349 (1975).
28. *Aguilar* v. *Felton*, 473 U.S. 402 (1985).
29. *Illinois ex rel. McCollum* v. *Board of Education*, 333 U.S. 203 (1948).

30. *Zorach* v. *Clausen*, 343 U.S. 306 (1952).

31. *Lynch* v. *Donnelly*, 465 U.S. 668 (1984).

32. *Edwards* v. *Aguillard*, 107 S. Ct. 2573 (1987).

33. *Engel* v. *Vitale*, 370 U.S. 421 (1962).

34. *School District of Abington Township* v. *Schempp* and *Murray* v. *Curlett*, 374 U.S. 203 (1963).

35. *Wallace* v. *Jaffree*, 472 U.S. 38 (1985).

36. *Smith* v. *California*, 361 U.S. 147 (1959).

37. *Schenck* v. *United States*, 249 U.S. 47 (1919).

38. Ibid.

39. *Abrams* v. *United States*, 250 U.S. 616 (1919).

40. *Dennis* v. *United States*, 341 U.S. 494 (1951).

41. *Yates* v. *United States*, 354 U.S. 298 (1957).

42. *Brandenburg* v. *Ohio*, 395 U.S. 444 (1969).

43. Thomas L. Tedford, *Freedom of Speech in the United States* (New York: Random House, 1985), p. 96.

44. *Chaplinsky* v. *New Hampshire*, 315 U.S. 568 (1942).

45. *Terminiello* v. *Chicago*, 337 U.S. 1 (1949).

46. *Cohen* v. *California*, 403 U.S. 15 (1971).

47. *Gooding* v. *Wilson*, 405 U.S. 518 (1972).

48. *Tinker* v. *Des Moines Independent Community School District*, 393 U.S. 503 (1969).

49. *Schacht* v. *United States*, 398 U.S. 58 (1970).

50. *Ross* v. *Radich*, 92 S. Ct. 2415 (1972).

51. *Smith* v. *Goguen*, 94 S. Ct. 1242 (1974); *Spence* v. *Washington*, 94 S. Ct. 2727 (1974).

52. *Texas* v. *Johnson*, 109 S. Ct. 2533 (1989).

53. *New York Times* v. *Sullivan*, 376 U.S. 254 (1964).

54. *Cohen* v. *California*, 403 U.S. 15 (1971).

55. Henry J. Abraham, *Freedom and the Court: Civil Rights and Liberties in the United States*, 5th ed. (New York: Oxford University Press, 1988), p. 253.

56. *Roth* v. *United States* and *Alberts* v. *California*, 354 U.S. 476 (1957).

57. *Manual Enterprise* v. *Day*, 370 U.S. 478 (1962).

58. *Jacobellis* v. *Ohio*, 378 U.S. 184 (1964).

59. *Ginzburg* v. *United States*, 383 U.S. 463 (1966).

60. *Ginsburg* v. *New York*, 390 U.S. 629 (1968).

61. *New York* v. *Ferber*, 458 U.S. 747 (1982).

62. *Jacobellis* v. *Ohio*, 378 U.S. 184 (1964).

63. *Miller* v. *California*, 413 U.S. 15 (1973).

64. *Jenkins* v. *Georgia*, 418 U.S. 153 (1974).

65. *Pope* v. *Illinois*, 107 S. Ct. 1918 (1987).

66. *Near* v. *Minnesota*, 283 U.S. 697 (1931).

67. *Schneider* v. *State*, 308 U.S. 147 (1939); *Freedman* v. *Maryland*, 308 U.S. 51 (1965).

68. *New York Times* v. *United States*, 403 U.S. 713 (1971).

69. *United States* v. *Rabinowitz*, 339 U.S. 56 (1950).

70. *United States* v. *Ross*, 456 U.S. 798 (1982).

71. *California* v. *Greenwood*, 108 S. Ct. 1635 (1988).

72. *United States* v. *Miller*, 425 U.S. 435 (1976).

73. *New Jersey* v. *T.L.O.*, 469 U.S. 325 (1985).

74. *Skinner* v. *Railway Labor Executive's Association*, 109 S. Ct. 1402 (1989).

75. David O. Stewart, "Slouching Toward Orwell," *ABA Journal* (June 1989), pp. 44–50.

76. *Weeks* v. *United States*, 232 U.S. 383 (1914).

77. *Mapp* v. *Ohio*, 367 U.S. 643 (1961).

78. *United States* v. *Calandra*, 414 U.S. 338 (1974).

79. *United States* v. *Leon*, 468 U.S. 897 (1984).

80. *Gideon* v. *Wainwright*, 372 U.S. 335 (1963).

81. *Escobedo* v. *Illinois*, 378 U.S. 478 (1964).

82. *Miranda* v. *Arizona*, 384 U.S. 436 (1966).

83. Carl T. Rowan, "Meese's Ideas About Constitutional Rights Worrisome," *Houston Post*, 30 January 1987, p. 2B.

84. *Harris* v. *New York*, 401 U.S. 222 (1971).

85. *United States* v. *Mandujano*, 425 U.S. 564 (1976).

86. *Moran* v. *Burdine*, 54 L.W. 4265 (1986).

87. *Cucci* v. *Illinois*, 356 U.S. 571 (1958).

88. *United States* v. *Lanza*, 260 U.S. 377 (1922).

89. *Murphy* v. *Waterfront Commission*, 378 U.S. 52 (1964).

90. *Globe Newspaper Co.* v. *Superior Court*, 457 U.S. 596 (1982).

91. *Chancler* v. *Florida*, 449 U.S. 560 (1981).

92. *Williams* v. *Florida*, 399 U.S. 78 (1970).

93. *Batson* v. *Kentucky*, 476 U.S. 79 (1986).

94. *Gideon* v. *Wainwright*, 372 U.S. 335 (1963).

95. *Tollett* v. *Henderson*, 411 U.S. 258 (1973).

96. *Solem* v. *Helm*, 463 U.S. 277 (1983).

97. *Coker* v. *Georgia*, 433 U.S. 584 (1977).

98. *Furman* v. *Georgia*, 408 U.S. 238 (1972).

99. *Gregg* v. *Georgia*, 428 U.S. 153 (1976).

100. *McCleskey* v. *Kemp*, 107 S. Ct. 1756 (1987).

101. *Penry* v. *Lynaugh*, 109 S. Ct. 2934 (1989).

102. *Stanford* v. *Kentucky*, 109 S. Ct. 2969 (1989).

103. Abraham, p. 296.

104. James L. Gibson, "Political Intolerance and Political Repression During the McCarthy Red Scare," *American Political Science Review*, 82 (June 1988): 511–29.

105. David B. Manwaring, *Render Unto Caesar: The Flag-Salute Controversy* (Chicago: University of Chicago Press, 1962).

106. Frank J. Sorauf, "*Zorach* v. *Clausen*: The Impact of a Supreme Court Decision," *American Political Science Review*, 53 (September 1959): 777–91.

107. Otis H. Stephens, Jr., *The Supreme Court and Confessions of Guilt* (Knoxville, TN: University of Tennessee Press, 1973).

108. Donald L. Horowitz, *The Courts and Social Policy* (Washington, DC: Brookings Institution, 1977), p. 223.

109. *Korematsu* v. *United States*, 323 U.S. 214 (1944).

SUGGESTED READINGS

Abraham, Henry J. *Freedom and the Court: Civil Rights and Liberties in the United States*, 5th ed. New York: Oxford University Press, 1988.

Berger, Raoul. *The Fourteenth Amendment and the Bill of Rights*. Norman, OK: University of Oklahoma Press, 1989.

Cushman, Robert F. *Cases in Civil Liberties*, 5th ed. Englewood Cliffs, NJ: Prentice-Hall, 1989.

Mickelson, Sig, and Teran, Elena Mier Y. *The First Amendment—The Challenge of New Technology*. New York: Praeger, 1989.

Schwartz, Herman, ed. *The Burger Years*. New York: Viking, 1987.

Witt, Elder. *The Supreme Court and Individual Rights*, 2d ed. Washington, DC: Congressional Quarterly Press, 1988.

15

CIVIL RIGHTS
POLICYMAKING

LEARNING OBJECTIVES

1. To trace the history of the more prominent civil rights movements in America.
2. To describe civil rights policy as it relates to equality before the law.
3. To describe civil rights policy concerning voting rights.
4. To describe civil rights policy involving freedom from private discrimination.
5. To describe civil rights policy concerning remedial racial and gender preferences.
6. To outline the policymaking process for civil rights policymaking.
7. To describe the political nature of civil rights policymaking.
8. To identify the significance of the following landmark Supreme Court rulings: *Plessy* v. *Ferguson, Brown* v. *Board of Education of Topeka, Swann* v. *Charlotte-Mecklenburg Board of Education, Civil Rights* cases, *Shelly* v. *Kraemer, Heart of Atlanta Motel* v. *United States* and *Katzenbach* v. *McClung*, and *City of Richmond* v. *J. A. Croson Co.*

A **minority business set-aside** is a legal requirement that firms receiving government grants or contracts allocate a certain percentage of their purchases of supplies and services to businesses owned or controlled by members of minority groups. Proponents of set-aside programs believe they are necessary to remedy the effects of years of racial discrimination. In contrast, critics of minority set-aside provisions argue that they themselves discriminate, against white-owned businesses.

In 1983, the city council of Richmond, Virginia, established a minority business set-aside program for municipal construction contracts. Even though blacks constituted half of Richmond's population, less than 1 percent of city government construction dollars had gone to minority-owned firms over the last several years. In light of this history, the city council passed an ordinance requiring that prime contractors awarded city construction contracts over the next five years subcontract at least 30 percent of the dollar amount of their contracts to one or more minority business enterprises. The ordinance identified a minority business enterprise as a firm at least 51 percent owned and controlled by minority group members, defined as "[c]itizens of the United States who are Blacks, Spanish-speaking, Orientals, Indians, Eskimos, or Aleuts." The ordinance allowed waivers when contractors could prove that the requirements of the ordinance could not be achieved.

Richmond's minority business set-aside program soon became embroiled in litigation. J. A. Croson Company, a contractor whose bid for a city project was rejected for failing to meet the 30 percent minority set-aside, filed suit, charging that the ordinance was unconstitutional. In 1989, the United States

Supreme Court ruled by a 6-to-3 vote that Richmond's set-aside ordinance unconstitutionally violated the equal protection clause of the Fourteenth Amendment because it denied certain citizens the opportunity to compete for a fixed percentage of city contracts based solely upon their race.

The most significant aspect of the *Croson* decision was that the Court, for the first time, applied "strict judicial scrutiny" to race-conscious efforts to remedy the effects of past discrimination. **Strict judicial scrutiny** is the decision-rule holding that the Supreme Court will find a governmental policy unconstitutional unless government can demonstrate a compelling governmental interest justifying the action. For years, the Court had applied the standard of strict judicial scrutiny to governmental restrictions on civil liberties and measures that disadvantaged individuals based on their race or citizenship status. In *Croson*, however, the Court served notice that it would now apply strict scrutiny to programs designed to correct the effects of past discrimination.

The Court's six-justice majority (Chief Justice William Rehnquist along with Justices Sandra O'Connor, Byron White, John Paul Stevens, Anthony Kennedy, and Antonin Scalia) ruled that although minority set-aside programs can be constitutionally justified as a remedy for discrimination in some instances, the Richmond city council failed to demonstrate a specific history of discrimination in the city's construction industry sufficient to justify a race-based program of relief. The mere fact that few city construction contracts had gone to minority firms did not prove discrimination either by city government or in the city's construction industry. Instead of comparing the number of city contracts going to minority businesses with the proportion of minority citizens in Richmond, the Court's majority ruled that the city council should have compared contracts with the proportion of minority-owned enterprises in the city's construction industry. Perhaps Richmond has few minority-owned construction companies. Instead of racial discrimination, the lack of minority-owned businesses may reflect differences in educational opportunities or career choices by members of minority groups. Certainly, the Court said, the city council had no evidence of discrimination against Spanish-speaking, Oriental, Indian, Eskimo, or Aleut persons in the Richmond construction industry.

The Court also held that Richmond's set-aside program was constitutionally unacceptable because it was not narrowly tailored to achieve any goal except "outright racial balancing." The plan gave absolute preference to minority entrepreneurs from anywhere in the country, not just the Richmond area. Moreover, the Court said, the program made no effort to determine whether particular minority business persons seeking a racial preference had themselves suffered the effects of discrimination.

In dissent, Justices Thurgood Marshall, William Brennan, and Harry Blackmun branded the Court's decision "a deliberate and giant step backward.... A profound difference separates governmental actions that themselves are racist," said the dissenters, "and governmental actions that seek to remedy the effects of prior racism or to prevent neutral governmental activity from perpetuating the effects of such racism."

The Court's dissenters argued that the Richmond city council was indeed justified in adopting a minority set-aside program. Not only did the council have ample evidence of discrimination in the construction industry nation-wide, they said, but no one who testified before the council on the issue denied that discrimination in Richmond's construction industry had been widespread. Consequently, the city council had two powerful interests in establishing the set-aside program: (1) to remedy the effects of past discrimination, and (2) to prevent the city government's own spending decisions from reinforcing the effects of past discrimination.

The dissenters also argued that the Richmond set-aside plan was indeed narrowly drafted to achieve its goals, as to both time and scope. The city council limited the program to five years' duration. Moreover, the 30 percent set-aside for city contracts affected only 3 percent of Richmond's contracting, including both private and governmental construction work.[1]

Civil rights refers to the protection of the individual from arbitrary or discriminatory acts by government or by other individuals. As the story of Richmond's minority business set-aside program illustrates, the federal courts, especially the Supreme Court, play a major role in modern civil rights policy-making. Keep in mind, however, that a broad range of political actors and groups participate in civil rights policymaking, including private businesses, universities, interest groups, executive-branch agencies, and legislatures at the state and national levels of government. The Richmond set-aside program, for example, began in a city council and then was challenged in the federal courts by a privately owned construction company.

Civil rights policies are also political. The city councils, state legislatures, and executive-branch agencies that initiate civil rights policies, such as Richmond's minority set-aside program, act in response to political pressures from interest groups and public opinion. It is probably no coincidence that the Richmond city council that adopted the set-aside ordinance was majority black. The Supreme Court, meanwhile, is a political institution as well. It is no coincidence that the six Supreme Court justices who voted to invalidate Richmond's set-aside program included all three justices appointed by Ronald Reagan, a president elected with strong support from conservative white males.

CIVIL RIGHTS MOVEMENTS IN AMERICA

America's history is laced with accounts of ethnic, racial, and social groups struggling for civil rights. The black (African-American) civil rights movement has been the most prominent. Women, although not a numerical minority, have organized to fight for equal status. Two other groups, American Indians (or Native Americans) and Mexican-Americans, have a long history in America, but their campaigns for civil rights have only recently been discovered by the news media. In recent years, several other groups have begun rights campaigns, including Asian-Americans, the elderly, the disabled, and gays and lesbians.

Each rights movement is unique, but we can identify four broad, general stages of development that seem to apply to the various movements. The first stage is one of acceptance and adaptation to unequal treatment. Instead of working to improve their status, group members appear resigned to their fate and concentrate on adapting to the status quo. In the second stage, members of the group become increasingly sensitive to their second-class status and begin organizing to promote group goals. Leadership and the existence of a communications network among group members are key factors in the development of a rights movement. The third stage is marked by an active, aggressive movement, emphasizing group unity and pride. Tactics may range from litigation, to traditional election-oriented politics, to militant protest, perhaps including violence. In the fourth stage of development, the group has won general recognition as a legitimate participant in social, economic, and political life. Although the group has not achieved all of its aims, it has achieved sufficient status so that it can pursue its goals through conventional interest-group politics.[2] Let's trace the development of a number of the nation's more prominent civil rights movements.

Blacks

Until the middle of the nineteenth century, the fate of blacks in America was determined by others—slave traders, slave owners, abolitionists, state governments, and the federal government. During Reconstruction, however, Congress and the states abolished slavery and took steps to elevate African-Americans to full citizenship. The Thirteenth Amendment ended slavery; the Fourteenth Amendment granted citizenship to blacks and guaranteed equal protection under state laws. The Fifteenth Amendment gave blacks the right to vote.

African-Americans responded to freedom by participating actively in Reconstruction-era politics. The records are sketchy, but as many as 700,000 blacks may have registered to vote during the period. What's more, dozens of African-Americans were also elected to office, especially in the South, where most blacks lived.

In 1877, however, the federal government withdrew its troops from the states of the old Confederacy, ending Reconstruction, and white southerners regained control of the region's political, economic, and social affairs. By the end of the century, southern blacks had been effectively deprived of the right to vote and to participate meaningfully in the political process, despite the Fourteenth and Fifteenth amendments. Southern legislatures also passed **Jim Crow laws**, which were legal provisions requiring the social segregation of blacks in separate and generally unequal facilities, ranging from restaurants to cemeteries. New Orleans segregated prostitutes. Birmingham even made it

A segregated bus terminal in Jackson, Mississippi, in 1961.

illegal for blacks and whites to play dominoes together. Every southern state outlawed interracial marriage.

Booker T. Washington, the well-known black educator, offered one kind of response to the situation facing African-Americans in the late nineteenth and early twentieth centuries. He counseled blacks to accept segregation and disfranchisement, at least for the short run. (**Disfranchisement** is the act of depriving someone of the right to vote.) After all, he asked, what other choice did blacks have? Washington urged blacks to concentrate on vocational training to learn skills necessary for the jobs open to them.

Not all blacks accepted Washington's conciliatory and gradualist philosophy. W. E. B. DuBois, another black educator, spoke out against disfranchisement and segregation. He advocated a liberal arts education for bright young blacks, the "talented tenth," as he put it, who could then uplift their brethren. In 1910, DuBois and a group of other black leaders and liberal whites formed the National Association for the Advancement of Colored People (NAACP) to further black interests. (In 1910, *colored* was the politically correct term for individuals of the Negro race, just as black and African-American are terms used today.) Meanwhile, Marcus Garvey, a black businessman, emphasized black pride and initiative. He founded a number of businesses and even proposed a back-to-Africa movement.

Two important demographic/sociological developments in the first half of the twentieth century profoundly influenced the black civil rights movement. The first was the migration of many blacks from the rural South to the big cities of the North, where they found relatively better educational and job opportunities, and the right to vote. With voting rights came political influence. The second important development was the experience of millions of African-Americans in the armed forces during World Wars I and II. In the military, blacks gained skills, confidence, and pride. They came home less willing to accept discrimination than when they left.

The black civil rights movement reached its zenith during the late 1950s and the early 1960s as hundreds of thousands of blacks and sympathetic whites united to attack discrimination on a number of fronts. The NAACP and other civil rights groups organized mass demonstrations, sit-ins, and boycotts to protest discrimination. Black leaders, especially Dr. Martin Luther King, Jr., spoke eloquently of shared dreams of brotherhood and justice, and stirred the conscience of many Americans.

By the late 1960s, blacks had achieved many of their political goals, but millions of blacks still lived in poverty. For them, it seemed that the promise of racial equality was a mirage. Black frustrations sometimes turned violent as riots erupted in several cities during the middle and late 1960s. Some black leaders, such as H. Rap Brown, went beyond talk of black pride to embrace the militant rhetoric of black power. Groups such as the Black Panthers promoted black separatism.

Today, the status report on the black civil rights movement presents a mixed, even contradictory picture. On one hand, a growing black middle class has emerged whose incomes are approaching those of middle-class whites.

Dr. Martin Luther King, Jr. (seventh from right), leads the March on Washington for black rights on August 28, 1963.

Black men and women are more visible than ever before in the media, sports, and entertainment. Many blacks now hold executive or administrative positions in business, government, and education. Black voting turnout has risen, and the number of black elected officials is at an all-time high, increasing from 1,479 in 1970 to 7,226 in 1989. Moreover, a small but growing number of African-Americans have won office in areas that are majority white, including the state of Virginia, where L. Douglas Wilder was elected governor in 1989.[3]

On the other hand, many observers believe that the status of African-Americans is little better now than it was two decades ago. They note that economic conditions for blacks as a group have actually deteriorated since the 1960s. The income gap between whites and blacks has widened, and the percentage of blacks below the poverty line has risen. What's more, despite recent gains, African-Americans remain underrepresented among the nation's elected officials, holding just 2 percent of positions while making up 12 percent of the nation's population.[4]

Women

Women in early America were to be seen and not heard. Under the common-law tradition of Britain and then America, women were accorded few legal rights and were classified with children and imbeciles. A married woman surrendered what rights she did possess to her husband. In the eyes of the law, she was little more than personal property.

The women's movement began as a byproduct of the abolitionist movement. It was socially acceptable for women in early America to become involved in religious and moral issues, so it was natural for many women to enlist in the struggle to abolish slavery. While working against slavery, women such as Lucretia Mott and Susan B. Anthony began to recognize the inferiority of their own status. The catalyst was the World Anti-Slavery Convention, convened in London in 1840, which voted to exclude women as delegates. The American women delegates were forced to sit in the balcony behind a partition.

The American women's-rights movement officially began in 1848 with the convocation of the Women's Rights Convention in Seneca Falls, New York. The delegates adopted a Declaration of Rights and Sentiments, which proclaimed women's right to own property, to obtain a divorce, to enjoy access to education and professional opportunities, and to vote. Initially, the movement focused almost exclusively on the last of these goals. When women's suffrage was achieved in 1920 with the ratification of the Nineteenth Amendment, many women believed that the struggle had been won.

But not all agreed. Some women's-rights advocates pointed out that discriminatory legislation remained in force in many states, covering such areas as employment, divorce, juror qualifications, property ownership, and inheritance. In 1923, they proposed an equal-rights amendment to the Constitution, one that would wipe out discriminatory legislation, making men and women equal in the eyes of the law.

Nonetheless, the women's movement did not become a serious political force again until the early 1960s. Why did the women's movement reemerge when it did? First, technological changes, such as the invention of labor-saving household devices and advances in contraception, freed women from traditional household tasks. Between 1947 and 1978, the percentage of adult women working outside the home rose from 32 to 50 percent.[5] Second, changing lifestyles, including increased divorce rates and more single-parent households, helped dispel the myth that a working woman's earnings merely supplement a man's salary. Working women trying to earn a living for themselves and their families grew increasingly restive over inferior wages and second-class status. Third, the emergence of the black civil rights movement and other social-reform groups served as a model for the formation of women's-rights organizations.

The contemporary women's movement began in 1963 when Betty Friedan published *The Feminine Mystique*. Millions of women identified with Friedan's description of the lack of fulfillment experienced by contemporary women, and they found in the book's pages the incentive to change their own lives and work to transform the society in which they lived.[6] In 1966, Friedan founded the National Organization for Women (NOW) to work for political changes that would benefit women.

Although the goals of the modern women's movement included political, economic, and social equality for women, it was the Equal Rights Amendment (ERA) that became its central focus. The **Equal Rights Amendment (ERA)** was a proposed amendment to the Constitution declaring that "[e]quality of rights under the law shall not be denied or abridged by the United States or any state on account of sex." Congress proposed the ERA in 1972, sending it to the states for ratification, where it won quick approval in many areas. Momentum slowed, though, as opposition mounted, led, ironically, by many women, most notably conservative political activist Phyllis Schlafly. Women's groups were forced to return to Congress for an extension of the original seven-year deadline for ratification. Congress agreed to add three more years to the time limit, but to no avail. The deadline passed and the ERA failed, three states short of the three-fourths majority needed for ratification.

As with the black civil rights movement, the balance sheet for the women's movement today includes both credits and debits. Although the ERA is apparently dead, many of the political changes it was designed to secure have been won through legislation or court decisions, and women's-rights activists are focusing on other issues, such as abortion rights. In addition, the number of women running for, and winning, public office has risen dramatically since the 1960s.

In contrast, the place of women is hardly equivalent to that of men. Men still hold most of the important decision-making positions in government, business, education, religion, and, indeed, most areas of life, while working women often hold relatively low-paying clerical, sales, and service jobs. Consequently, although women have closed the salary gap in recent years, the average working woman still earns only 72 percent of the median earnings of men.[7]

Mexican-Americans

Mexican-Americans have long had a problem gaining recognition as a disadvantaged minority group. In 1969, a bill was introduced in the House of Representatives with the heading: "Establish an Inter-Agency Committee on Mexican-American Affairs." Several months later, the bill's sponsors thought it had vanished. They finally located it, in the Foreign Affairs Committee, to which it had been mistakenly referred by Speaker John McCormack of Massachusetts.[8]

Many people living outside the southwestern United States may not be particularly aware of them, but large numbers of Mexican-Americans have lived in this country since the annexation of Texas and the Treaty of Guadalupe Hidalgo, which ended the Mexican War. As a group, Mexican-Americans have never been as poor as blacks, although their status was usually inferior to that of the white majority. In most areas of the Southwest, Mexican-Americans were informally segregated and accorded inferior educational and employment opportunities. They were denied the opportunity to participate effectively in politics everywhere except in New Mexico.

The initial response of Mexican-Americans to their second-rate status was to prove themselves good Americans. Their attitude was symbolized in the name of one of the earliest Mexican-American organizations, the League of United Latin American Citizens (LULAC), founded in 1929. Its organizers used the term *Latin American* instead of *Mexican-American* because of the perceived negative connotations of the latter name. Also, note the inclusion of the word *citizens*.

World War II played an important role in politicizing the Mexican-American community. The war meant better jobs and better opportunities. After the war, Mexican-Americans who had fought for their country were unwilling again to be relegated to an inferior status. They formed a number of organizations to promote their cause, including the American GI Forum and the Political Association of Spanish-Speaking Organizations (PASO). These organizations supported sympathetic candidates in elections and filed lawsuits to further their cause.

In the 1960s, the Mexican-American rights movement turned more militant with the emergence of the Chicano movement. Chicanos emphasized ethnic unity and pride, reaching out to make common cause with other Hispanic-Americans, such as Cubans in South Florida and Puerto Ricans in the cities of the Northeast. The Chicano movement's leaders included Cesar Chavez, who organized farm workers in California, and Jose Angel Gutierrez, who founded a third-party political movement, La Raza Unida ("The Race United"). By the late 1970s, however, the more militant aspects of the Chicano movement had passed. Chavez was out of the headlines and La Raza Unida was moribund.

Today, Mexican-Americans remain underrepresented in both elective and appointive governmental positions in the Southwest, and despite the emergence of a growing Mexican-American middle class, their economic status remains inferior to that of the Anglo majority in the region. Nonetheless, Mexican-Americans are establishing themselves as legitimate, influential participants in the policy process, especially in California, Texas, New Mexico, and Arizona. Because of their strength in California and Texas, states rich in electoral votes, presidential candidates must compete for Mexican-American support.

American Indians

Since their defeat by the United States Cavalry, American Indians have been at the mercy of the national government. At times, federal policy has been well-meaning, albeit paternalistic; at other times, it has been indifferent or avaricious. Treaties granted Indians reservation land, but it was invariably barren land no white settlers would want. When valuable minerals were discovered on reservations, government policies were sometimes changed to deprive Indians of their resources. The General Allotment Act of 1887, for example, provided for the division of reservation land into individual parcels. Many Native Americans sold their shares or were swindled out of them. Vast amounts of Indian land were lost forever, including most reservation property in oil-rich Oklahoma. Between 1887 and 1934, when the program ended, Indian

In 1969, members of the militant American Indian Movement (AIM) seized control of the abandoned prison on Alcatraz Island in San Francisco Bay to publicize their demand for property rights.

lands shrank from 138 million acres to 48 million. More than a third of the remaining land was semiarid, and thus poorly suited for agriculture.[9]

Although Native Americans living on reservations have benefited from federal government assistance, they have paid a considerable price. The federal government provides social services, welfare, education, and health care to reservation Indians and gives direct subsidies to tribal governments. Historically, however, Indians have had little say in the administration of these services. Indian children were often sent to boarding school hundreds of miles from their homes and forbidden to speak their native language. Tribal governments weren't even allowed to manage their own lands.

Today, many Native Americans live in poverty. Suicide, alcoholism, and unemployment rates are higher for Indians than for other ethnic groups in America. Unemployment on the reservation ranges between 40 and 80 percent, and the average per capita income is well below the national average. Indians who have left the reservation are little better off, crowded into substandard housing in Minneapolis, Chicago, Los Angeles, and other cities.

During the 1960s and 1970s, Indians began to organize to assert their rights. To publicize their demands, militant groups such as AIM (the American Indian Movement) occupied the offices of the Bureau of Indian Affairs (BIA) in Washington, D.C., and provoked a confrontation with federal marshals at Wounded Knee, South Dakota. These events gained attention, but, on the whole, Indians have been more successful at achieving their goals in the courtroom. In 1974, for example, a federal judge ruled that an old treaty entitled Indians to half the West Coast salmon catch. In 1975, federal courts upheld tribal claims to a large area of land in the state of Maine.

In general, however, Indian efforts have been hampered by political weakness and internal divisions. Native Americans are too few and too disorganized to be influential politically, except perhaps in Arizona. Moreover, Indians are divided by ancient tribal rivalries and disagreements about the basic goals of the Indian-rights movement. Some Indians believe that the future lies in the development of the coal, uranium, and oil deposits located on reservation land. Groups such as CERT (the Council of Energy Resources Tribes) want to turn these resources into economic power. Other Indians, however, are more concerned with preserving their traditional way of life. They believe that plans for developing reservation mineral resources would lead to the death of Indian culture.

CIVIL RIGHTS ISSUES AND POLICY

By and large, American civil rights policy takes the form of judicial response to policies initiated by other units of government or the actions of private individuals, groups, or corporations. We will trace the development of civil rights policy in four areas: equality before the law, voting rights, freedom from discrimination, and remedial racial and gender preferences. The last category, which includes affirmative-action programs and minority business set-aside plans, is the most controversial area of civil rights policy. In contrast, American policymakers have reached a consensus at least on the principles of equality before the law, voting rights, and freedom from discrimination.

Equality Before the Law

The Fourteenth Amendment guarantees individuals equal protection under state laws. "No State," it says, "shall...deny to any person within its jurisdiction the equal protection of the laws." Despite the wording of the amendment, the United States Supreme Court has never interpreted the equal protection clause to require that laws deal with everyone and everything in precisely the same fashion. By their nature, laws distinguish among groups of people, types of property, and kinds of actions. The Court has recognized that most distinctions are necessary and desirable, and hence permissible under the Constitution. Only certain types of classifications that the Court considers arbitrary and discriminatory violate the equal protection clause.

The modern Supreme Court uses the doctrine of suspect classification to evaluate equal-protection issues. The **suspect classification doctrine** is the judicial principle that certain types of distinctions among persons violate the equal protection clause of the Fourteenth Amendment unless government can demonstrate that it has a "compelling governmental interest" for making the challenged classification and that it can achieve that interest in no other way. The Court has ruled that classifications based on race and alienage (lack of American citizenship) are suspect classifications. Consequently, the Supreme Court applies strict judicial scrutiny to any state law that distinguishes among persons based on their race or citizenship status.

The Supreme Court has chosen not to look so closely at state laws that discriminate against persons on grounds other than race or alienage. The Court has held that state governments need only demonstrate some "reasonable basis" in order to justify laws that distinguish among persons on the basis of such factors as relative wealth, physical disability, or sexual orientation. As for gender, meanwhile, the Court has ruled that state governments must prove that sex-based distinctions are necessary to achieve some "important governmental objective." Commentators see this standard as somewhere between "compelling governmental interest" and "reasonable basis."[10]

Racial Equality

Historians tell us that the Fourteenth Amendment, which was enacted during the Reconstruction era after the Civil War, was intended to protect the civil rights of freed blacks. Nevertheless, the amendment initially did little to shelter African-Americans from discrimination. Consider the Supreme Court's response to the enactment of Jim Crow laws in the South. *Plessy* v. *Ferguson*, decided in 1896, involved a challenge to a Louisiana law requiring segregated accommodations for black and white railway passengers. By an 8-to-1 vote, the Court ruled that the law was a reasonable exercise of the state's power. States can require separate facilities for whites and blacks as long as the facilities are equal. Thus, the Court adopted the policy known as **separate-but-equal**, that is, the judicial doctrine holding that separate facilities for whites and blacks satisfy the equal-protection requirement of the Fourteenth Amendment. Justice John Marshall Harlan, the Court's lone dissenter in *Plessy*, eloquently called the decision "a compound of bad logic, bad history, bad sociology, and bad constitutional law.... Our Constitution is color-blind," he said, "and neither knows nor tolerates classes among citizens."[11]

Unfortunately for blacks, the Supreme Court allowed state and local governments to judge whether racially segregated facilities were actually equal. In 1899, for example, the Court held that a Georgia school district's decision to close the county's only black high school did not violate the equal protection clause even though two white high schools remained open.[12] In another case, the Court allowed a Mississippi school district to require a girl of Chinese descent to attend a black school in a neighboring district rather than a nearby whites-only school. As far as the Supreme Court was concerned, state and local officials could determine school assignments without interference from federal courts.[13]

After the Supreme Court shifted its focus from guarding property rights to protecting individual rights in the late 1930s, it began to reassess the constitutional status of racial segregation. The Court started chipping away at the *Plessy* precedent in 1938 in *Missouri ex rel. Gaines* v. *Canada*, one of a long line of test cases argued by the NAACP. (A **test case**, you recall, is a lawsuit initiated to assess the constitutionality of a legislative or executive act.) Gaines, a black citizen of Missouri, applied to attend the University of Missouri law school. The state denied him admission, but offered to pay his tuition at a law school in a neighboring state where he could be accepted. Gaines sued, charging that this arrangement violated the equal protection clause, and the Court agreed. Separate-but-equal had to be in the same state.[14]

The Supreme Court further undermined *Plessy* in two cases decided in 1950. In *Sweatt* v. *Painter*, the Court ruled that the hasty creation of a black law school by the state of Texas did not satisfy the constitutional criterion of equal protection.[15] Then in *McLaurin* v. *Oklahoma State Regents*, the Court ruled against segregation within an institution. The University of Oklahoma admitted McLaurin, a black, but forced him to sit in a particular seat, study in a particular carrel, and eat at a particular table in the cafeteria. All of these facilities were labeled "Reserved for Colored." The Supreme Court ordered that McLaurin be treated like other students.[16]

In 1954, the Court took the final step, unanimously overturning *Plessy* in the famous case of *Brown* v. *Board of Education of Topeka*. The Court ruled that racial segregation denied African-American students equal educational opportunity. "Segregation of white and colored children in public schools has a detrimental effect upon the colored children," wrote Chief Justice Earl

Warren in the Court's majority opinion. "A sense of inferiority affects the motivation of the child to learn." In essence, the Court declared separate-but-equal a contradiction in terms. Once the law requires racial separation, it stamps the badge of inferiority on the minority race; separate, therefore, is inherently unequal.[17]

The *Brown* decision may have been the most important judicial ruling of this century, but it left two important questions unanswered. One concerned the distinction between de jure and de facto segregation. **De jure segregation** means racial separation established by law, while **de facto segregation** is racial separation resulting from factors other than law, such as housing patterns. In *Brown*, the Court ruled that de jure segregation was unconstitutional, but it left the question of de facto segregation undecided.

The other problem left unsettled by *Brown* was implementation. How was desegregation to be achieved and at what pace? The Court delayed its implementation decision until 1955. Then it ordered the lower federal courts to oversee the transition to a nondiscriminatory system "with all deliberate speed."[18]

In practice, implementation proved more deliberate than speedy. Although states in the upper South made some progress toward desegregation, public officials in the Deep South responded to the *Brown* decision with delay, evasion, defiance, and massive resistance. Alabama Governor George Wallace spoke for many white southerners: "I say segregation now, segregation tomorrow, segregation forever."[19]

For years, *Brown* was but a hollow victory for civil rights forces. Congress did nothing. President Eisenhower stood silent. Only in 1957 did the president act, ordering federal troops into Little Rock, Arkansas, to enforce a school desegregation order against a stubborn Governor Orval Faubus and an angry mob. Nonetheless, as late as 1964, only 68,650 African-American students out of 2,988,264 (2.1 percent) were enrolled in public schools with any whites in the eleven states of the old Confederacy.[20]

The civil rights movement of the 1960s succeeded in rallying support for the cause of black civil rights. Black protest demonstrations, vividly displayed on the television evening news, moved public opinion to support the cause. Presidents Kennedy and Johnson called for action, and Congress responded with the Civil Rights Act of 1964. One section of this measure authorized the Department of Health, Education, and Welfare (which has since been divided to form the Department of Health and Human Services and the Department of Education) to cut off federal money to school districts practicing segregation. The department set guidelines and some progress took place. What's more, the Supreme Court lost patience with the slow pace of school desegregation, declaring an end to "all deliberate speed" and ordering immediate desegregation.[21]

The Court's decision to order an end to racial segregation forced the justices to deal with the questions left unresolved by the original *Brown* case.

How could integration be achieved? In *Swann* v. *Charlotte-Mecklenburg Board of Education* (1971), the Court unanimously held that busing, racial quotas, pairing or grouping schools, and gerrymandering attendance zones could all be used to eliminate the vestiges of state-supported segregation.[22] Moreover, in 1990 the Court went so far as to rule that federal judges could order school officials to raise local taxes to pay for desegregation remedies.[23]

In 1973 the Supreme Court dealt with the issue of de jure segregation in *Keyes* v. *School District #1, Denver, Colorado*. The Court ordered the integration of Denver schools not because they had been segregated by law, but because the local board had manipulated attendance zones to create one-race schools.[24] After the *Swann* and *Keyes* decisions, integration proceeded at a hasty rate, especially in the South.

Today, both the force of law and the weight of public opinion support racial integration, at least in principle. Many African-American youngsters now attend school with whites, and official opposition to integration has ended. Even Governor Wallace mellowed, crowning a black homecoming queen at the University of Alabama in 1973.

Nonetheless, America's schools remain heavily segregated on an informal basis with nearly two-thirds of the nation's black youngsters attending schools that are predominantly nonwhite.[25] In many areas, housing patterns make integration difficult to achieve without busing, and busing is controversial. It often leads to white flight to more distant suburbs and to private schools. One study reports that whites now make up only 3 percent of public-school students in the nation's 25 largest cities.[26]

Residential segregation is perhaps the most important factor underlying segregation in America today. Using 1980 census data, Professor Reynolds Farley created a residential integration index, ranging from zero (complete integration) to 100 (complete segregation). Farley found that the average metropolitan area scored 79 for blacks, 51 for Hispanics, and 45 for Asians. Chicago and Detroit were the most segregated; Washington, D.C., the most integrated. Residential segregation leads not only to racially segregated schools but to segregation in other areas of life as well. Because of residential segregation, Farley says, "shopping areas, parks, hospitals, restaurants, and transit lines are thoroughly coded by color."[27]

Other Equal-Protection Issues

Not all equal-protection claims involve blacks. The Supreme Court, you recall, has declared that citizenship status, like race, is a suspect classification justifiable only by a compelling government interest. The Court has struck down state laws, for example, that prohibited aliens from becoming lawyers, engineers, or notary publics, and ruled that states may not deny aliens the opportunity to apply for financial aid for higher education.[28] Nonetheless, the Court has ruled that states may legitimately exclude aliens from playing a role in government, either by voting, holding elective office, or working as police officers.

Over the years, the Supreme Court has considered a number of equal-protection issues raised on account of gender. For nearly a century after the adoption of the Fourteenth Amendment, the Court refused to apply the equal protection clause to gender discrimination. Instead, the Court accepted discrimination against women as necessary protection for the weaker sex. In 1873, for example, the Supreme Court upheld an Illinois law denying women the opportunity to practice law with the following explanation: "The natural and proper timidity and delicacy which belongs to the female sex evidently unfits it for many of the occupations of civil life."[29]

Within the past twenty years, the Court has begun to look more closely at claims of gender discrimination. Although the Court has not added gender to its list of suspect classifications, it has required state governments to prove that sex-based distinctions are necessary to achieve some "important governmental objective." In one case, for example, the Court knocked down an Oklahoma law that permitted the sale of 3.2 beer to women at age eighteen but not to men until age twenty-one.[30] Nonetheless, the Court still upholds some laws—such as the decision of Congress to exclude women from the draft—on the basis of traditional attitudes about the respective roles of men and women in society.[31]

Voting Rights

Although the right to vote is a fundamental civil right, universal adult suffrage (**suffrage** refers to the right to vote) is a relatively recent development in the United States. The original Constitution (Article I, Section 2) allowed the states to establish voter qualifications. In the early days of the Republic, states limited the right to vote to adult white males who owned property. Popular pressures forced states to drop the property qualification in the early decades of the nineteenth century. Women won the right to vote with the ratification of the Nineteenth Amendment in 1920.

The struggle for voting rights for African-Americans and other racial minority group members was particularly difficult. The Fifteenth Amendment, ratified in 1870, declared that the right to vote "shall not be denied or abridged by the United States or by any State on account of race, color, or previous condition of servitude." Nonetheless, after Reconstruction, southern white authorities adopted an array of fiendishly clever devices for preventing blacks from exercising meaningful voting rights. Disfranchisement methods included the white primary, literacy tests, tests of understanding, grandfather clauses, and poll taxes.

The **white primary** was an electoral system used in the South to prevent the participation of blacks in the Democratic primary. (A **primary election**, you recall, is an intraparty election held to select party candidates for the general-election ballot.) Since Democrats dominated southern politics from Reconstruction through the 1950s, the Democratic party primary was by far the most important election in the state. By excluding blacks from the

Democratic primary, southern officials effectively excluded them from meaningful participation in state politics. The Supreme Court invalidated the white primary in the case of *Smith* v. *Allwright*, decided in 1944.[32]

Literacy tests, tests of understanding, and poll taxes were often used in combination with a grandfather clause. A **literacy test** was a legal requirement that citizens demonstrate an ability to read and write before they can register to vote. A **test of understanding** was a legal requirement that citizens must accurately explain a passage in the U.S. Constitution or the state constitution before they can register to vote. A **poll tax** was a tax levied on the right to vote. A **grandfather clause**, meanwhile, was a requirement that all prospective voters pay a tax or pass a test, except those whose grandfathers had been eligible to vote at some earlier date. The effect of grandfather clauses was to allow prospective white voters to escape voter requirements used to discourage or disqualify prospective African-American voters.

Although the Supreme Court invalidated grandfather clauses in 1915,[33] tests of understanding, literacy tests, and poll taxes survived constitutional challenge for decades. The Court finally knocked down the use of tests of understanding in 1965, holding that they were often used to deny blacks the right to vote.[34] In the same year, Congress passed the Voting Rights Act, which suspended the use of literacy tests throughout the South. Five years later Congress extended the ban on literacy tests to the entire nation. The poll tax, meanwhile, lasted until the mid-1960s. The Twenty-fourth Amendment, ratified in 1964, eliminated the use of poll taxes for elections to federal office. In 1966, the Supreme Court held the poll tax an unconstitutional requirement for voting in state and local elections as well.[35]

Even after the demise of the white primary, the poll tax, and other methods used to keep African-Americans from the polling box, the opponents of minority voting rights continued to devise methods to reduce the political influence of blacks and other minority group members in American politics. One such technique was the **at-large election**, which is a method for choosing public officials in which every citizen of a political subdivision, such as a city or county, votes to select a public official. Even if a substantial minority of an area's voters were black or Hispanic, at-large elections could result in the election of white officials if the white majority votes as a block for white candidates. In general, the election of minority candidates is more likely in a **single-member district election**, which is a method for choosing public officials in which a political subdivision, such as a state, is divided into districts and each district elects one official. The division of an area into several districts increases the likelihood that one or more districts will have a majority of minority-race voters who could elect black or Hispanic officials.

Nevertheless, single-member election districts are no guarantee against voter discrimination. The opponents of minority voting rights sometimes gerrymander election districts to reduce the political influence of minority voters in single-member district election systems. (**Gerrymandering** is the drawing of legislative district lines for political advantage.) Two gerrymandering techniques are minority-vote dilution and minority-vote packing. **Minority-vote dilution** involves the drawing of election district lines to thinly spread minority voters among several districts, thus reducing their electoral influence in any one district. **Minority-vote packing**, meanwhile, involves drawing electoral district lines to cluster minority voters into one district or a small number of districts. Although minority voters could control a handful of districts, their political influence would be restricted to those few districts.

The 1965 Voting Rights Act has been the most important weapon for fighting such subtle forms of voting discrimination. In states and counties with histories of low voter participation (primarily in the South), the act prohibited all qualifications for voting except age, residence, and criminal record. It provided for the appointment of federal voting registrars who added hundreds of thousands of blacks to the voting rolls in the South in the late 1960s. Subsequently, Congress amended the Voting Rights Act to extend its protections to language minorities, including Mexican-Americans, American Indians, Puerto Ricans, Cubans, and Alaskan Natives. The amendment also mandated bilingual ballots and bilingual election materials in covered areas.

In the long run, the most important section of the Voting Rights Act may have been Section Five. It allows minority-rights groups to file suit in federal court against election laws and procedures in areas covered by the act. Once a procedure is challenged, local authorities bear the burden of proof to demonstrate that the practice is not discriminatory. Moreover, any change in election laws and procedures a covered unit of government wishes to make (such as a redrawing of district boundaries or modification of registration procedures) must be submitted to the United States Department of Justice or to the United States District Court for the District of Columbia for approval before going into effect. (In practice, most submissions have been made to the Justice Department.)

Opportunities for minority participation are greater now than at any time in the history of the nation. The Voting Rights Act has been instrumental in eliminating a number of at-large election systems and invalidating other electoral procedures that discriminated against minority voters. As a result, more minorities are registered to vote than ever before and a good many minority group members have won elective office. In early 1989, a Census Bureau study found that 2 percent of the nation's 500,000 elected officials were black and 1 percent were Hispanic. Both of these figures reflected substantial increases over the previous decade.[36]

Nevertheless, the political impact of minorities in American politics is not proportionate to their numbers. Hundreds of thousands of minority citizens are not registered to vote; thousands of others fail to go to the polls. Another Census Bureau study found that in the 1984 presidential election, 55.5 percent of voting-age whites cast ballots, compared with 51.2 percent of the black population and 32.7 percent of Hispanics.[37] Moreover, the proportion of minority officeholders remains disproportionate to their representation in the

In 1989, L. Douglas Wilder of Virginia became the first black to be elected governor in the United States.

total population. Blacks and Hispanics make up 12 and 6 percent of the population, respectively.

Freedom from Discrimination

Civil rights concerns the protection of the individual not just against government action but also against discrimination by *private* parties, such as hotels, restaurants, theaters, and business firms. During Reconstruction, Congress enacted two important laws designed to ensure the civil rights of freed blacks. The Civil Rights Act of 1866 declared that citizens "of every race and color" were entitled "to make and enforce contracts, to sue, . . . give evidence, to inherit, purchase, lease, sell, hold, and convey real and personal property."[38] Then, the Civil Rights Act of 1875 declared that "all persons within the jurisdiction of the United States shall be entitled to the full and equal enjoyment of the accommodations . . . of inns, public conveyances on land or water, theaters, and other places of public amusement. . . ."[39]

In the *Civil Rights* cases of 1883, however, the U.S. Supreme Court found the Civil Rights Act of 1875 unconstitutional. These cases involved disputes over theaters that would not seat blacks, hotels and restaurants that would not serve blacks, and a train that refused to seat a black woman in the "ladies" car. The Court held that the Fourteenth Amendment protected individuals from discrimination by government but not by private parties.[40] The Court's decision in the *Civil Rights* cases opened the door for private individuals, businesses, and organizations to discriminate in housing, employment, and a broad range of public accommodations.

It took civil rights forces more than eighty years to overcome the precedent set in the *Civil Rights* cases. Consider the issue of housing discrimination. Although the Supreme Court ruled in 1917 that cities could not establish exclusive residential zones for whites and blacks,[41] private deed restrictions called restrictive covenants often achieved the same result. **Racially restrictive covenants** were private deed restrictions that prohibited property owners from selling or leasing property to African-Americans or other minorities. The NAACP finally succeeded in undercutting restrictive covenants in 1948 in the test case of *Shelly* v. *Kraemer*. The Supreme Court held that private contracts calling for discrimination could be written, but state courts could not constitutionally enforce them because enforcement would make the state a party to discrimination.[42]

The battle against housing discrimination extended to the executive and legislative branches of government as well. In 1962, President Kennedy issued an executive order banning discrimination in property owned, sold, or leased by the federal government. Subsequently, Title IV of the 1964 Civil Rights Act extended nondiscrimination provisions to all public-housing and urban-renewal developments receiving federal assistance. The most important legislative move against housing discrimination, however, was the Fair Housing Act, enacted in 1968. It prohibited discrimination in all transactions involving realtors.

A few weeks after the passage of the Fair Housing Act, the Supreme Court ruled that the Civil Rights Act of 1866 prohibited discrimination in all real estate transactions, including those among private individuals. By a 7-to-2 vote, the Court held that Congress in 1866 intended to ban all discrimination in the purchase or lease of property, including discrimination by private sellers. What's more, the Court ruled that the action of Congress in prohibiting private housing discrimination was a constitutional exercise of authority granted by the Thirteenth Amendment, which prohibits slavery. "[W]hen racial discrimination herds men into ghettoes and makes their ability to buy property turn on the color of their skin, then it...is a relic of slavery."[43]

Civil rights forces used litigation and legislation to attack other forms of private discrimination as well. In the late 1950s and early 1960s, for example, black activists would sit at segregated dime-store lunch counters and refuse to leave until served. Local police would then arrest the protesters, charging them with disturbing the peace or breaking a local Jim Crow ordinance. With NAACP legal assistance, the black demonstrators would appeal their convictions to the federal courts, where they would be reversed and the local segregation ordinance overturned. This case-by-case approach served to desegregate many public facilities, but it was slow and expensive.

The 1964 Civil Rights Act was a more efficient tool for fighting discrimination. Title II of the act outlawed discrimination based on race, religion, color, sex, or national origin in hotels, restaurants, gas stations, and other public accommodations. To overcome the precedent of the *Civil Rights* cases that the Fourteenth Amendment prohibits governmental discrimination but not discrimination by private individuals and firms, Congress based Title II on its constitutional authority to regulate interstate commerce. Because hotels, restaurants, gas stations, and the like serve individuals traveling from state to state and purchase products that have been shipped in interstate commerce, Congress reasoned that these facilities are part of interstate commerce and, consequently, subject to regulation by Congress. In *Heart of Atlanta Motel* v. *United States* and *Katzenbach* v. *McClung* (1964), the Supreme Court upheld the constitutionality of Congress' action.[44]

Remedial Racial and Gender Preferences

Economic equality is perhaps the most difficult and controversial contemporary civil rights issue. To be sure, the economic status of women and minorities is hardly comparable with that of white males. In 1986, for example, annual household income for whites was $24,570, compared with $16,400 for blacks, and $18,820 for Hispanics. The average income for households headed by women was $13,130.[45]

Sociological and psychological reasons account in part for these disparities. Minority families tend to be larger, they are more likely to be headed by women, and minority parents are more likely to have children at an early age than are white parents. All of these factors are associated with low-income status. Moreover, minority Americans as a group are generally less well educated than whites. School dropout rates are higher, and proportionally fewer minority youngsters go to college, graduate school, or professional school. Women, meanwhile, traditionally have pursued careers in fields that pay relatively less than male-dominated professions. Also, many women take time out from their careers to raise families, thus reducing their opportunities for professional advancement.

The economic disparities between minorities, women, and white males also result from discrimination and its legacy. Segregated school systems relegated African-Americans and, to a lesser extent, Hispanics to an inferior education. Some observers believe that so-called women's professions, such as teaching and nursing, pay poorly *because* they have been dominated by women, leading reformers to call for salary structures based on the principle of **comparable worth**, which is the concept that wages should be based on the value of a job to an employer. (See the Perspective for more discussion of comparable worth.) Furthermore, minorities and women have suffered discrimination in employment.

Even if all educational and employment barriers were eliminated, great disparities in the socioeconomic status of women, minorities, and white males would still exist and probably persist for years to come. This is the legacy of discrimination. What is government's role in properly compensating for these disparities? Many Americans believe that government should have little or no role in promoting economic equality. They note that the American creed calls for equality of *opportunity*, not equality of status. In contrast, other observers think that government has an obligation to enact policies to compensate disadvantaged groups for errors of the past. Simply ending discrimination isn't enough to ensure equality, they say, at least not in the short run.

Consider the issues raised by the *Bakke* case. Allan Bakke, who is white, sued the University of California at Davis after he was denied admission to medical school. The university had a minority-admissions program, setting aside sixteen of its hundred admissions each year for minority applicants. Since he was not allowed to compete for any of these sixteen positions, Bakke charged that he was the victim of illegal racial discrimination. In defense of its procedures, the university pointed out that minority communities face a serious shortage of doctors. Training minority physicians, the school argued, is a legitimate, justifiable goal for a state university.

In 1978, the United States Supreme Court ordered the university to admit Bakke. By a 5-to-4 vote, the Court held that hard-and-fast numerical quotas for minority admissions violate the equal protection clause of the Fourteenth

PERSPECTIVE

Comparable Worth

Most Americans agree with the concept of equal pay for equal work, at least in principle. The controversy arises in application. Consider the issue of comparable worth. Many women's-rights advocates believe that wage rates are low in professions traditionally dominated by women *because* they have been defined as women's occupations. Secretaries, for example, are sometimes paid less than janitors, even though secretarial work generally requires more specialized training. The proponents of comparable worth believe that this sort of salary differential reflects sex discrimination. They argue that wage rates should be based on a job's value to an employer and/or the skills needed to do the work required.

In contrast, the opponents of comparable worth argue that the forces of supply and demand, not gender distinctions, determine wage scales. Basing wage levels on a concept as fuzzy as that of comparable worth, they say, would produce labor-market distortions. Moreover, comparable worth would be expensive for employers to implement, forcing private business to increase prices and government to raise taxes.

The proponents of comparable worth initially pressed their claims in the courts. The most important case concerned a lawsuit brought by the American Federation of State, County, and Municipal Employees (AFSCME) against the state of Washington. Although a state-hired consultant concluded that the state systematically paid lower wages for predominantly female jobs than for predominantly male jobs with comparable evaluations, the state did nothing to equalize the pay disparity. The union charged that the state's failure to act in light of its own data constituted sex discrimination in violation of the 1964 Civil Rights Act. In 1983, a federal district court ruled in favor of the union. Two years later, however, the Ninth Circuit Court of Appeals reversed the district-court ruling and the parties agreed to a settlement rather than continue their court battle. Because of this and other legal setbacks, the proponents of comparable worth have turned their attention to state legislatures, city and county councils, and union negotiations.

Amendment. The Court added, though, that race could be considered as one of several factors in a university's admissions decisions.[46]

The debate over government's role in reducing the impact of past discrimination raises the issues of affirmative action, racial quotas, and reverse discrimination. **Affirmative action** refers to the legal requirement that companies and other organizations take positive steps to remedy the effects of past discrimination. A **racial quota** is a legal requirement that businesses and other organizations include within their membership or employment a certain percentage of minority group members. **Reverse discrimination**, meanwhile, is the allegation that governmental efforts in behalf of women and minority group members effectively discriminate against white males.

Federal government efforts to remedy the effects of discrimination began in the early 1960s. Presidents Kennedy and Johnson ordered affirmative action in federal employment and hiring by government contractors, but their orders had little practical effect until the late 1960s. Then, Nixon appointees in the Department of Labor began requiring government contractors to employ certain percentages of women and minorities.

For the next ten years, affirmative action took on a momentum all its own. For some, affirmative action meant nondiscrimination. For others, it required seeking out qualified women and minorities. For still others, affirmative action stood for hiring set percentages of women and minorities regardless of their qualifications—a quota system. All the while, employers carefully kept records of how many women and minority group members were part of their operations.

In the 1980s, the Reagan administration moved to dismantle affirmative-action programs and anything that smacked of a quota system for women and minorities. In President Reagan's view, civil rights laws should offer relief not to whole groups of people but only to specific individuals who could prove that they themselves were victims of discrimination. Hiring goals, timetables, and racial quotas, the administration argued, were reverse discrimination against whites.

President Reagan's most lasting impact on affirmative action came in the judicial branch of government. The appointment and confirmation of Justice Anthony Kennedy in 1988 gave the United States Supreme Court a solid five-vote majority (which included two other Reagan appointees—Sandra Day O'Connor and Antonin Scalia) who shared Reagan's conservative philosophy on affirmative-action issues. As we saw in the *Croson* case, dealing with Richmond's minority business set-aside program, the Court has made it clear that it will give strict judicial scrutiny to affirmative-action and set-aside programs to ensure that they do not disadvantage nonminority groups.

The Supreme Court has held that states and localities may adopt race-conscious programs to remedy the effects of past discrimination only when a clear history of specific discrimination can be demonstrated. Statistics showing racial disparities in hiring and promotion aren't sufficient to prove discrimination as long as an employer can produce evidence that employment practices resulting in a racial imbalance are justified by legitimate business necessity, such as the absence of qualified minority workers. Then, the burden of proof is on the worker to disprove the employer's assertion.[47]

The Supreme Court has also made it more difficult for women and minorities to bring discrimination lawsuits. In 1989, for example, the Court reversed a thirteen-year-old precedent that interpreted the Civil Rights Act of 1866 to allow workers to sue employers for job discrimination.[48] The Court ruled that the law only prohibited hiring discrimination, not racial harassment in the workplace and discrimination in promotions.[49] The NAACP Legal Defense Fund estimated that this decision led to lower court dismissals of fifty cases of racial discrimination in less than five months.[50]

While the Court has made it more difficult for minorities to bring discrimination suits, it has made it easier for white male employees to challenge affirmative-action plans already in place. During the 1970s and early 1980s, many private employers and local governments settled discrimination lawsuits out of court by agreeing to the implementation of affirmative-action plans. In 1989, however, the Supreme Court ruled that white male workers who had not participated in an earlier discrimination settlement could now file suit if they believed they were denied promotions on account of race.[51]

The cumulative impact of the Supreme Court's recent decisions has been to shift federal judicial policy away from support for affirmative action to concern for the rights of white males. The Court's rulings ensured that minority-rights groups would not only have a more difficult time bringing their claims to court but would also face a tougher task in proving their cases. In contrast, the Court made it easier for white male employees to challenge affirmative action plans they believe work to their disadvantage.

CIVIL RIGHTS POLICYMAKING

The civil rights policymaking process involves a wide variety of groups and a broad range of political institutions in America. Let's consider the various stages of the policy process.

Setting the Agenda

Public opinion has played an important role in setting the agenda for civil rights policy in America. Unlike some other policy areas, civil rights issues often command large attentive publics. (An **attentive public**, you recall, is those persons who have an active and continuing interest in a particular political issue.) Public policy in this area affects the lives of millions of Americans in ways the average person recognizes. Moreover, many civil rights issues are emotionally charged.

Public-opinion studies show that Americans in general have grown more tolerant of racial and cultural diversity. As recently as the 1940s, a majority of white Americans supported racial segregation and discrimination in both principle and practice. By the 1970s, however, support for overt discrimination had virtually vanished. Today, surveys find that large majorities of Americans of all races and both genders oppose discrimination.

Nonetheless, black and white Americans do not see eye to eye on the rate of minority progress and the extent to which discrimination remains part of the nation's culture. Surveys show that African-Americans believe that economic progress for blacks has been slow and that they still face a good deal of discrimination. One recent poll, for example, found that only 28 percent of blacks surveyed (compared with 57 percent of white respondents) agreed that blacks and other minorities had the same opportunities as whites.[52] In contrast, public-opinion studies find that a majority of white Americans believe that blacks have made considerable progress in achieving equality and that discrimination is no longer the problem it once was. Indeed, one poll found that 56 percent of whites questioned agreed than many of the problems facing blacks today "are brought on by blacks themselves."[53]

Interest groups and civil rights leaders also play an important role in setting the agenda for civil rights policymaking. Groups such as the NAACP, LULAC, and NOW have worked at all levels of government to push for their causes, lobbying legislatures and executive agencies, filing lawsuits as test cases, and organizing protest demonstrations. Rights leaders such as Martin Luther King, Jr., and Betty Friedan raised the consciousness of group members and publicized civil rights issues to the general public. Business groups sometimes oppose affirmative-action plans, arguing that they add to the cost of doing business.

Policy Formulation and Adoption

Civil rights policy formulation and adoption often involve action by the president, Congress, the bureaucracy, local governments, private individuals and corporations, and the courts. To be sure, any study of civil rights policy involves an examination of a good many Supreme Court rulings. Along with civil liberties, civil rights issues make up the better part of the agenda for the modern Supreme Court. By no means, however, are the courts the only political actors involved in civil rights policy formulation and adoption.

First, the civil rights policy issues considered by the courts initially arise in other forums. The minority business set-aside program that the Supreme Court struck down in the *Croson* case, for example, began with the city council of Richmond, Virginia. The minority-admissions plan the Court considered in *Bakke* was originally formulated and adopted by a state university. School desegregation plans are usually formulated and adopted by local school boards.

Second, court rulings set the boundaries for civil rights policymaking for other branches of government. Consider the issue of comparable worth, which we discussed in the Perspective. The federal courts have ruled that neither the Constitution nor federal law requires governmental and private employers to adopt comparable-worth salary schedules for their employees. Employers are free, however, to use comparable-worth guidelines if they so choose. In contrast, the Supreme Court has issued restrictive guidelines for the adoption

The rights of the elderly, now the most rapidly growing segment of our population, are promoted by groups like the Gray Panthers.

of minority business set-aside programs. According to the precedent set in the *Croson* case, state and local governments considering set-asides must formulate the program along the guidelines set out by the Supreme Court if the plan is to be upheld.

Finally, judicial decisions aren't necessarily the last word in civil rights policymaking, especially when the court bases its rulings on interpretations of statutory law. (**Statutory law**, you recall, is law that emerges from the legislative process.) Congress, after all, can rewrite laws to overcome judicial objections. In 1984, for example, the Supreme Court severely restricted the impact of federal laws prohibiting discrimination on the basis of sex, race, age, or disability by institutions receiving federal funds. The Court ruled that the law prohibited discrimination only by the *direct* recipient of the money.[54] Thus, if a university's math department received federal funds but its English department did not, the latter would not be covered. Congress responded to the Court's decision by rewriting the law (and overriding President Reagan's veto in the process).

Policy Implementation and Evaluation

The implementation of civil rights policy falls to the executive branch of the national government, lower federal courts, state and local governments, and even private businesses. Under the provisions of the Voting Rights Act, for example, the Justice Department reviews changes in election laws and procedures proposed by state and local governments in covered jurisdictions. The implementation of school desegregation, meanwhile, took place under the supervision of federal district judges. Employers, both public and private, implement affirmative-action plans.

Political scientists have conducted a number of studies to evaluate the impact of civil rights policies. One study found, for example, that in white-majority congressional districts in the rural South, greater proportions of black voters were associated with more conservative voting patterns in Congress. In southern urban districts, however, greater proportions of black voters were associated with more *liberal* voting patterns in Congress. Apparently, increases in African-American voter participation in the South have helped make the urban South more like the urban North, since inner-city blacks support moderate-to-liberal Democrats for Congress while suburban white voters tend to elect conservative Republicans. In contrast, voting patterns in rural areas have developed along racial lines, with whites voting as a bloc to elect conservatives of either party.[55]

Other research assesses the effects of minority representation on school boards and city councils. One study discovered that the dropout rate for black youngsters was lower in school districts with black school board members. Also, the percentage of African-American students enrolled in classes for gifted children and in enrichment classes was greater than it was in districts with all-white boards.[56] Another study found that black and Hispanic representation on city councils increased minority success in obtaining government jobs.[57]

CONCLUSION: POLITICS AND CIVIL RIGHTS

In general, policymaking in America combines both idealistic and selfish qualities. On one hand, there is the search for good public policy, fairness, and justice. On the other hand, there is the struggle for personal or group advantage of one sort or another. Civil rights policymaking is no exception to this rule.

Civil rights policymaking has always involved a heavy component of group politics. Minorities and women have demanded a larger share of the political and economic pie; white males often haven't wanted to share. Political leaders on all sides have found a personal interest in fanning controversy rather than resolving it.

In the 1950s and 1960s, it was easier to make judgment calls about the merits of civil rights issues than it is today. It was not difficult to see the injustice in laws that kept blacks in the back of the bus and away from the ballot box. How fair was a system that kept women and minorities out of better-paying occupations? Who could support policies that effectively cheated Native Americans of their traditional homelands?

Today, however, the issues are more complex and more difficult to evaluate. In the 1960s, civil rights controversies often dealt with school integration and equal employment opportunities. Today, the issues are affirmative action and minority business set-asides.

Consequently, civil rights politics today more than ever resembles the politics of group interests. In the eyes of many Americans, women and minorities aren't so much "masses yearning to be free" as they are competitors for scarce resources. To be sure, there are still injustices to be corrected and worthy gains to be preserved, but in many cases, civil rights politics has become politics as usual. Right and wrong are on both sides, and there's a good deal of scrambling to protect self-interest. That doesn't make such issues any less controversial, though, nor does it make them any easier to resolve.

KEY TERMS

affirmative action	minority-vote packing
at-large election	poll tax
attentive public	primary election
civil rights	racial quota
comparable worth	racially restrictive covenants
de facto segregation	reverse discrimination
de jure segregation	separate-but-equal
disfranchisement	single-member district election
Equal Rights Amendment (ERA)	statutory law
gerrymandering	strict judicial scrutiny
grandfather clause	suffrage
Jim Crow laws	suspect classification doctrine
literacy test	test case
minority business set-aside	test of understanding
minority-vote dilution	white primary

NOTES

1. *City of Richmond* v. *J. A. Croson Co.*, 109 S. Ct. 706 (1989).
2. Charles Tilley, *From Mobilization to Revolution* (New York: Addison-Wesley, 1978).
3. *Washington Post*, National Weekly Edition, 30 October–5 November 1989, p. 37; and *Washington Post*, National Weekly Edition, 13–19 November 1989, p. 4.
4. "U.S. Elected Officials Top 500,000—and Most Are Men, Statistics Say," *Houston Post*, 25 January 1989, p. A-14.
5. Cynthia B. Lloyd and Beth T. Niemi, *The Economics of Sex Differentials* (New York: Columbia University Press, 1979).
6. Betty Friedan, *The Feminine Mystique* (New York: Norton, 1963).
7. Frank Swoboda, "Closing the Economic Gender Gap," *Washington Post*, National Weekly Edition, 4–10 December 1989, p. 22.
8. Jerry Rankin, "Mexican Americans and National Policy-Making: An Aborted Relationship," in Rudolph O. de la Garza, A. Anthony Kruszewsky, and Tomas A.

Arciniega, eds., *Chicanos and Native Americans* (Englewood Cliffs, NJ: Prentice-Hall, 1973), p. 146.

9. Vine Deloria, Jr., and Clifford M. Lytle, *American Indians, American Justice* (Austin, TX: University of Texas Press, 1983), pp. 14–15.

10. Elder Witt, *The Supreme Court and Individual Rights*, 2d ed. (Washington, DC: Congressional Quarterly Press, 1988), pp. 223–26.

11. *Plessy* v. *Ferguson*, 163 U.S. 537 (1896).

12. *Cumming* v. *Richmond County Board of Education*, 175 U.S. 528 (1899).

13. *Gong Lum* v. *Rice*, 275 U.S. 78 (1927).

14. *Missouri ex rel. Gaines* v. *Canada*, 305 U.S. 337 (1938).

15. *Sweatt* v. *Painter*, 399 U.S. 629 (1950).

16. *McLaurin* v. *Oklahoma State Regents*, 339 U.S. 637 (1950).

17. *Brown* v. *Board of Education of Topeka*, 347 U.S. 483 (1954).

18. *Brown* v. *Board of Education of Topeka*, 349 U.S. 294 (1955).

19. Quoted in Harrell R. Rodgers, Jr., and Charles S. Bullock III, *Law and Social Change* (New York: McGraw-Hill, 1972), p. 71.

20. Carl P. Chelf, *Public Policymaking in America* (Santa Monica, CA: Goodyear, 1981), p. 340.

21. *Alexander* v. *Holmes County Board of Education*, 396 U.S. 19 (1969).

22. *Swann* v. *Charlotte-Mecklenburg Board of Education*, 402 U.S. 1 (1971).

23. *Missouri* v. *Jenkins*, 110 S. Ct. 1651 (1990).

24. *Keyes* v. *School District #1, Denver, Colorado*, 413 U.S. 189 (1973).

25. D. Garth Taylor, *Public Opinion and Collective Action: The Boston Desegregation Conflict* (Chicago: Chicago University Press, 1986), p. 41.

26. University of Chicago study quoted in Juan Williams, "How Reagan and Jackson Managed to Isolate Blacks," *Washington Post*, National Weekly Edition, 28 November–4 December 1988, pp. 23–24.

27. "Northern Cities Most Segregated, Study Claims," *Houston Chronicle*, 29 October 1986, sec. 1, p. 6.

28. *In re Griffiths*, 413 U.S. 717 (1973); *Examining Board of Engineers, Architects and Surveyors* v. *de Otero*, 426 U.S. 572 (1976); *Bernal* v. *Fainter*, 467 U.S. 216 (1984).

29. *Bradwell* v. *Illinois*, 16 Wallace 130 (1873).

30. *Craig* v. *Boren*, 429 U.S. 190 (1976).

31. *Rostker* v. *Goldberg*, 453 U.S. 57 (1981).

32. *Smith* v. *Allwright*, 321 U.S. 649 (1944).

33. *Guinn* v. *United States*, 238 U.S. 347 (1915).

34. *Louisiana* v. *United States*, 380 U.S. 145 (1965).

35. *Harper* v. *State Board of Elections*, 383 U.S. 663 (1966).

36. "U.S. Elected Officials Top 500,000."

37. Quoted in *Houston Chronicle*, 3 February 1985, sec. 3, p. 7.

38. Quoted in Alfred H. Kelley and Winfred A. Harbison, *The American Constitution: Its Origins and Development* (New York: Norton, 1970), p. 460.

39. Quoted in Witt, p. 247.

40. *Civil Rights* cases, 109 U.S. 3 (1883).

41. *Buchanan* v. *Warley*, 245 U.S. 60 (1917).

42. *Shelly* v. *Kraemer*, 334 U.S. 1 (1948).

43. *Jones* v. *Alfred H. Meyer Co.*, 392 U.S. 409 (1968).

44. *Heart of Atlanta Motel* v. *United States*, 379 U.S. 241, and *Katzenbach* v. *McClung*, 379 U.S. 294 (1964).

45. Bob Rast, "Income Inequality Grew During Reagan's Tenure," *Houston Chronicle*, 21 July 1988, sec. 1, p. 10.

46. *Regents of the University of California* v. *Bakke*, 438 U.S. 265 (1978).

47. *Wards Cove Packing Co.* v. *Antonio*, 109 S. Ct. 2115 (1989).

48. *Runyon* v. *McCrary*, 427 U.S. 160 (1976).

49. *Patterson* v. *McLean Credit Union*, 109 S. Ct. 2363 (1989).

50. Aaron Epstein, "Ruling Devastating to Racial Bias Suits," *Houston Chronicle*, 20 November 1989, p. 4A.

51. *Martin* v. *Wilks*, 87–1614 (1989).

52. Gary Langer, "Surveys Indicate Prejudice Declining Steadily for Years," *Houston Chronicle*, 23 April 1989, p. 11A.

53. Richard Morin, "Racial Bias in U.S. Continues to Tumble," *Houston Chronicle*, 29 October 1989, p. 8A.

54. *Grove City College* v. *Bell*, 465 U.S. 555 (1984).

55. Michael W. Combs, John R. Hibbing, and Susan Welch, "Black Constituents and Congressional Roll Call Votes," *Western Political Quarterly* 37 (September 1984): 424–34.

56. Kenneth J. Meier and Robert E. England, "Black Representational and Educational Policy: Are They Related?" *American Political Science Review* 78 (June 1984): 392–403.

57. Kenneth R. Mladenka, "Blacks and Hispanics in Urban Politics," *American Political Science Review* 83 (March 1989): 165–91.

SUGGESTED READINGS

Beckwith, Karen. *American Women and Political Participation: The Impact of Work, Generation, and Feminism*. Westport, CT: Greenwood, 1986.

Combs, Michael W., and Gruhl, John, eds. *Affirmative Action: Theory, Analysis, and Prospects*. Jefferson, NC: McFarland, 1986.

Preston, Michael B.; Henderson, Lenneal J., Jr.; and Puryear, Paul L., eds. *The New Black Politics: The Search for Political Power*, 2d ed. New York: Longman, 1987.

Taylor, D. Garth. *Public Opinion and Collective Action: The Boston Desegregation Conflict*. Chicago: Chicago University Press, 1986.

Virgil, Maurilio E. *Hispanics in American Politics: The Search for Political Power*. Lanham, MD: University Press of America, 1987.

Walton, Hanes, Jr. *When the Marching Stopped: The Politics of Civil Rights Regulatory Agencies*. Albany, NY: State University of New York Press, 1988.

16

FOREIGN AND DEFENSE
POLICYMAKING

AMERICA AND THE WORLD POLITICAL SYSTEM
THE ENDS AND MEANS OF FOREIGN POLICY
AMERICAN FOREIGN POLICY
AMERICAN DEFENSE POLICY
FOREIGN AND DEFENSE POLICYMAKING
CONCLUSION: POLITICS AND FOREIGN POLICY

LEARNING OBJECTIVES

1. To describe the reforms initiated by Soviet leader Mikhail Gorbachev and explain their impact on American foreign and defense policymaking.
2. To identify the goals and means of American foreign policy.
3. To trace the development of American foreign policy from the 1790s to the beginning of the 1990s.
4. To describe the structure of America's strategic and conventional forces and evaluate their adequacy in light of the nation's defense goals and the international environment.
5. To outline the policymaking process for foreign and defense policy.
6. To recognize that politics is involved in foreign and defense policymaking.

Historical changes are taking place in the Soviet Union and Eastern Europe. In the late 1980s, a new Soviet leader, Mikhail Gorbachev, recognized that the Soviet system was failing. Although the USSR was a military superpower, its relative influence in world affairs was in decline; its economy was a shambles. Gorbachev responded to the crisis with a bold series of economic and political reforms that have dramatically changed the Soviet Union and the international political environment as well.

In order to increase production and improve the supply of consumer goods, Gorbachev launched a series of economic reforms known as ***perestroika***, the Russian word for "economic restructuring." Some of Gorbachev's programs, such as his campaigns against excessive alcohol consumption and in favor of better workplace discipline, were traditional Soviet approaches for improving economic productivity. Other aspects of *perestroika*, however, represented real innovations, at least by Soviet standards. Most notably, Gorbachev reduced central planning and added a number of free-market features to the nation's socialist economy. Gorbachev also changed Soviet law to permit the establishment of privately owned, profit-oriented businesses.[1]

In addition to economic reforms, Gorbachev initiated a series of domestic political reforms known as ***glasnost***, the Russian word for "openness." He introduced reforms allowing Soviet citizens unprecedented freedom of political expression and ordered that free, competitive elections be held to choose a Congress of People's Deputies, an elected legislature that would actually play a role in the governing process. Perhaps most significant, Gorbachev pushed through changes in the Soviet constitution to allow opposition political parties to compete against the Communist party.

Western observers disagree about the motivation behind *glasnost*. Some scholars believe that Gorbachev decided to open the political system to participation by ordinary Russian citizens in hopes of generating public support that would help him overcome the opposition of entrenched party and state bureaucrats to *perestroika*.[2] In contrast, other observers believe that Gorbachev initiated *glasnost* because he decided that in today's information age it is unrealistic to expect that the economy can be made more competitive without opening the political system to more competition as well.

Perestroika and *glasnost* led to changes in Soviet foreign and defense policies. Gorbachev reasoned that economic reforms would not succeed unless some of the enormous human and material resources devoted to the Soviet military could be diverted to the domestic economy. In order to make this shift in priorities possible, Gorbachev proposed "New Thinking" in foreign and defense policy to ease tensions with the West and reduce Soviet commitments abroad. Gorbachev declared that the Soviet Union would not intervene militarily in the internal affairs of other nations and ordered the withdrawal of Soviet military units from Afghanistan, where they had been fighting a protracted guerrilla war against anticommunist rebels. Gorbachev also announced significant reductions in Soviet defense spending and called for the negotiation of arms-control and arms-reduction treaties with the United States.

"New Thinking" led to major changes in the status of Eastern Europe. For decades after the end of World War II, the Soviet Union held the nations of Eastern Europe as political satellites, intervening politically and militarily to ensure Communist-party rule. The primary purpose of the policy was to maintain a buffer between the USSR and Western Europe, which in modern times has been the main source of invasion against Russia. Now, however, Gorbachev decided that the Soviet Union could no longer afford to maintain satellites. He ordered the withdrawal of 50,000 Soviet soldiers from Eastern Europe and encouraged the nations of Eastern Europe to adopt political and economic reforms similar to *perestroika* and *glasnost*.

Although the opening of the Berlin Wall may have been the single most dramatic development, nearly every nation in the region underwent major change. In one country after another, one-party communist regimes collapsed under popular pressure to be replaced by reform governments promising democratic elections, individual freedom, and fewer economic controls. In fact, most of the nations of Eastern Europe adopted more extensive economic and political reforms than those in place in the Soviet Union.[3]

Although most Western observers welcomed the developments in the Soviet Union and Eastern Europe, they recognized that the changes might present certain problems. By 1990, for example, East Germany and West Germany were on the verge of merging into a single country. Considering Germany's role in World Wars I and II, many people feared that a reunited Germany would be a threat to world peace. What's more, a number of observers worried that Gorbachev might not survive politically. Although the Soviet leader enjoyed enormous international prestige, his popularity within the Soviet Union was shaky because *perestroika* had not yet produced a better standard of living for most Soviet citizens. Observers worried that

In November 1989 the Berlin Wall, which long symbolized the separation between East and West, was opened.

Gorbachev's overthrow could be followed by civil war, anarchy, or a military takeover. None of those possibilities would likely prove positive for Western democratic interests.

The revolutionary changes that have taken place in the Soviet Union and Eastern Europe have forced American policymakers to rethink the basic premises of the nation's foreign and defense policies. Since the late 1940s, the primary goal of United States foreign policy has been **containment**, which is the policy of keeping the Soviet Union from expanding its sphere of control. The most important aspect of American defense policy, meanwhile, has been to deter Soviet nuclear assault and defend against an invasion of Western Europe by the USSR and its Eastern European allies. Today, however, the threat of nuclear war has receded and the prospects of a Soviet invasion of Western Europe seem remote.

American policymakers are faced with a series of fundamental policy questions: Is containment still a relevant basis for American foreign policy? How should the United States respond to German reunification? Should American troops remain in Western Europe? Can the United States reduce defense spending? Should the United States respond to the developments in the

Soviet Union by helping Gorbachev or by managing the decline of the Soviet empire?

How the United States responds to the developments in the Soviet Union and Eastern Europe is the major foreign policy challenge of the 1990s. We begin our study of American foreign and defense policy by placing the United States in the context of the world political system.

AMERICA AND THE WORLD POLITICAL SYSTEM

The world political system includes more than 160 independent nations, and the United States maintains diplomatic relations with most of them. The term **diplomatic relations** refers to a system of official contacts between two nations in which the countries exchange ambassadors and other diplomatic personnel and operate embassies in each other's country. Cuba, Iran, Libya, Vietnam, and North Korea are among the few nations with whom America does not have formal diplomatic relations.

In addition to the governments of the world, more than one hundred transnational (multinational) organizations are active on the international scene. The best known of these is the **United Nations (UN)**, which is an international organization founded in 1945 as a diplomatic forum to resolve conflicts among the world's nations. The UN hasn't always been able to prevent war, but it has occasionally been a positive force in mediating disputes. In recent decades, UN peace-keeping forces have played a role in settling conflicts in the Congo (now Zaire), Cyprus, and the Middle East. Some of the UN's most important accomplishments have come in other areas, however, including disaster relief, refugee relocation, agricultural development, loan assistance to developing nations, and health programs. In particular, the World Health Organization (WHO), a UN agency, can be credited with the eradication of smallpox worldwide.

Other transnational organizations are important to American foreign and defense policies as well. The **North Atlantic Treaty Organization (NATO)** is a regional defense alliance consisting of the United States, Canada, and their Western European allies, formed after World War II to defend against a Soviet attack in Western Europe. Similarly, the **Warsaw Pact** is a military alliance joining the Soviet Union and most of the countries of Eastern Europe. The USSR formed the Warsaw Pact as a response to NATO. Not all transnational organizations are military alliances. The **Organization of Petroleum Exporting Countries (OPEC)**, for example, is a thirteen-nation oil cartel that attempts to set world oil prices.

Finally, a number of nongovernmental organizations act on the world stage. Thousands of multinational corporations, some of which have considerable resources and influence, play an important international role. Citibank, for example, operates in ninety-five countries and has made substantial loans to a number of governments. International Telephone and Telegraph (ITT) has holdings in more than eighty countries, while the United Fruit Company is a major enterprise in a number of Latin American nations. Both Exxon and General Motors have sales exceeding the GNP of all but twenty or so countries. Other organizations capable of exerting influence internationally are the International Red Cross, the Roman Catholic Church, Amnesty International, a number of international unions, the Palestinian Liberation Organization (PLO), international terrorist groups, and criminal organizations, such as narcotics traffickers.

THE ENDS AND MEANS OF FOREIGN POLICY

Stating the goals of American foreign policy is difficult. First, goals change over time. For years, the United States tried to isolate the People's Republic of China (Communist China), treating it as an outlaw state. The approach changed, however, after President Nixon visited Beijing and began the process of establishing formal diplomatic relations between the two countries. Second, publicly stated goals may not be the real goals. In the early twentieth century, the United States justified its intervention in Panama (then part of Columbia) as assistance to freedom fighters. In fact, though, America's actions were a power play to acquire land to build a canal. Third, policymakers often disagree among themselves about the goals of foreign policy. In recent years, the president and a majority of members of Congress have debated American policy in Central America. Finally, foreign-policy goals are sometimes in conflict. Although peace and national security are both frequently enunciated aims of American foreign policy, they aren't always compatible in the real world.

Nevertheless, we can identify three broad, general goals of American foreign policy that have been pursued consistently throughout the nation's history. The first is national security. A basic aim of American foreign policy is to preserve the nation's sovereignty and protect the country's territorial integrity. During World War II, this goal entailed defeating the Axis powers. In the postwar years, American policymakers pursued the goal through the policy of containment.

Economic prosperity is a second goal of American foreign policy. This goal includes the promotion of capitalist markets, international free trade, and the protection of American economic interests and investments abroad. One reason behind the United States invasion of Panama to overthrow the government of General Manuel Noriega, for example, was to ensure the security of the Panama Canal.

A final general policy goal is the promotion of American ideas and ideals abroad. Historically, American military interventions—whether in World Wars I and II, in Korea, in Vietnam, or in Panama—have been justified as efforts to protect freedom and promote democracy. An important aspect of American policy toward Eastern Europe involves the steps the United States can take to assist in the development of democracy and capitalism in those nations.

America pursues its foreign-policy goals through a variety of means. Military force is one means of achieving foreign-policy goals. Since the end of World War II, the United States has conducted large-scale troop interventions in Korea, Lebanon, the Dominican Republic, Indochina, Grenada, and Panama. Not all American military interventions actually involve U.S. armed forces. During the 1980s, for example, the United States funded and supplied contra forces attempting to overthrow the government of Nicaragua, which President Reagan labeled communist.

Besides the actual use of military force, the United States has pursued its policy goals through defense alliances and the transfer of military hardware to other nations. Since the end of World War II, the United States has participated in a number of defense alliances, including NATO and SEATO (the Southeast Asia Treaty Organization). America is also the world's major distributor of weapons. (The Soviet Union is a close second.) Some international arms sales are private transactions between American firms and foreign governments. Most sales, however, are government-to-government transactions in which the U.S. Department of Defense acts as a purchasing agent for a foreign government wanting to buy American-made weapons.[4]

A second way to achieve foreign-policy goals is through economic means. These may include the promotion or discouragement of trade. Trade can be used to improve international relations. One method the United States employed to build relations with the People's Republic of China was to open the door to trade. In contrast, America has used trade barriers against foreign governments it wished to pressure or punish. Before the American invasion of Panama, the United States imposed economic sanctions in hopes of forcing General Noriega out of office.

Foreign aid is another economic tool America uses to achieve its foreign-policy goals. In 1989, for example, the United States foreign aid budget was nearly $10.8 billion, with about half the money going to Israel and Egypt. Although America ranks second only to Japan in total foreign-aid expenditures, the United States is near the bottom among industrialized nations in foreign aid as a percentage of national wealth.[5]

Third, foreign-policy goals can be achieved by cultural means, including tourism, student exchanges, goodwill tours, and international athletic events. The process of improving relations between the United States and the People's Republic of China, for example, was facilitated by cultural exchanges. In fact, one of the first contacts between the two nations was the visit of an American table-tennis team to China—"ping-pong diplomacy," the pundits called it. The Olympic games, meanwhile, are less a sporting event than a forum for nations to make political statements. The United States boycotted the 1980 Moscow Olympics in protest against the Soviet invasion of Afghanistan. In 1984, the Russians returned the favor by staying home when the games were held in Los Angeles.

U.S. Secretary of State James Baker (left) greets Soviet Foreign Minister Eduard Shevardnadze, as Canadian Prime Minister Brian Mulroney looks on.

Finally, foreign-policy goals can be achieved through diplomacy. **Diplomacy** is the process by which nations carry on political relations with each other. Ambassadors and other embassy officials stationed in other countries provide an ongoing link between governments. The United Nations offers a forum in which the world's nations can make diplomatic contacts, including countries that may not have diplomatic relations with one another. Diplomacy can also be pursued through special negotiations or summit meetings among national leaders.

AMERICAN FOREIGN POLICY

American foreign policy today is best understood within the context of its historical development.

From Isolationism to Internationalism

In his farewell address, retiring President George Washington warned the nation to avoid "entangling alliances." For nearly a century, **isolationism**, that is, noninvolvement in the affairs of other nations, served as the watchword for American foreign policy toward Europe. President James Monroe articulated the policy in his Monroe Doctrine of 1823. We would stay out of European affairs; the Europeans must stay out of ours. Isolationism had its practical side. The United States was far from a world power in the early nineteenth century. Americans devoted their energies to subduing and developing North America and did not welcome European interference. America's policy of isolationism also had an aspect of arrogance in that the country wanted to avoid soiling itself by making alliances with colonial powers. Instead, the United States would serve as a moral example for them. Finally, American isolationism contained an element of hypocrisy since it did not apply to U.S. actions in the Western Hemisphere. The United States reserved for itself the right to interfere in the affairs of the nations of the Americas.

And interfere it did. America fought a war with Mexico in order to annex Mexico's northern provinces (the land that is now California, Arizona, and New Mexico). President Theodore Roosevelt intervened in Colombia to create the nation of Panama so the United States could build a canal. In the twentieth century, America has directly intervened militarily in several Latin American nations, including Cuba, El Salvador, Nicaragua, the Dominican Republic, Grenada, and Panama. The United States has been involved indirectly in the political affairs of many other countries in the hemisphere, including Chile, Honduras, Venezuela, Guatemala, Ecuador, Brazil, and British Guiana. American economic influence, meanwhile, is felt everywhere in Latin America.

America began to break out of its isolationism toward nations outside the Western Hemisphere in the 1890s. The treaty ending the Spanish-American War awarded the United States a colonial empire extending beyond this hemisphere to Guam and the Philippines. Moreover, America had developed trading interests around the world that it wanted to protect. Eventually, World War I thrust the United States to the forefront of world affairs.

Between World Wars I and II, the United States once again turned inward, toward isolationism. Part of the explanation for this is that President Woodrow Wilson had oversold World War I as "the war to end all wars" and "the war to make the world safe for democracy." Idealism faded as casualties mounted, and the international political haggling after the war disillusioned many Americans. Another reason for the return to isolationism was the Great Depression. Americans looked inward as they sought to cope with economic collapse.

By 1945, America's romance with isolationism had ended. Because of improved technology, isolationism was more difficult, if not impossible, to achieve. Modern communications and transportation had shrunk the world. More important, the United States emerged from World War II a great power, militarily and economically. It was the only nation with nuclear weapons and the only major industrial country whose economic foundations had not been battered by war. With important military, political, and economic interests all over the globe, the United States could no longer afford isolationism.

The Cold War and the Policy of Containment

United States–Soviet relations was the dominant element of American foreign policy after World War II. Even though the United States and the Soviet Union had been wartime allies, by the late 1940s, the two nations were locked in a bitter struggle for dominance in the international arena. This period of global tensions between the United States and the Soviet Union was known as the **Cold War**. In the eyes of most Americans, the Soviets were determined to expand their control beyond the Russian borders into Eastern Europe and Southeast Asia. The Soviets, meanwhile, regarded American actions, particularly the Central Intelligence Agency (CIA) activities in Eastern Europe, as a threat to their national security.

The Cold War was both an ideological and a political struggle. On one hand, the Cold War pitted communism against capitalism, dictatorship against democracy. The leaders of both the United States and the USSR pictured the international competition as a contest between different ways of life, one representing good, the other, evil. The Cold War was also a bipolar (two-sided) struggle between the world's remaining military superpowers. The other great powers of the prewar era—Germany, France, Great Britain, Japan—had

The arrival of the millionth ton of Marshall Plan goods in Greece was celebrated by a parade through the streets of Athens in 1949.

been either destroyed or weakened by the war. That left a political vacuum which the war's survivors, the United States and the Soviet Union, sought to enter. As one observer phrased it, they were like two scorpions trapped in a jar. Tension and conflict were probably inevitable.

President Harry Truman first articulated America's response to the Soviet Union and the spread of communism. The **Truman Doctrine** was the foreign policy put forward by President Truman calling for American support for all free peoples resisting communist aggression by internal or outside forces. In particular, Truman asked Congress to appropriate money for military and economic aid to Greece and Turkey to strengthen them against communist insurgencies. Congress complied with the president's request.

The Truman Doctrine was part of the broader American policy of containment, which, you recall, was aimed at keeping the Soviets from expanding their sphere of control. America adopted the policy of containment for essentially the same reason it entered World Wars I and II—to preserve the political balance of power in Europe and Asia. (A **balance of power** is a system of political alignments in which peace and security may be maintained through an equilibrium of forces between rival groups of nations.) As Professor George F. Kennan notes, America's leaders recognized that any nation controlling the whole of Europe and Asia would command more industrial power than the

United States.[6] (Incidentally, the same political/economic circumstances prevail today. Altogether, the nations of Europe and Asia produce 63 percent of the gross world product, whereas America produces only about 22 percent.[7])

America's policy of containment included a number of features. First, the United States gave economic assistance to nations threatened by communist subversion. The **Marshall Plan**, for example, was an American program that provided billions of dollars to the countries of Western Europe to rebuild their economies after World War II. The United States also adopted programs giving technical and economic aid to developing nations. A second feature of America's policy of containment was to maintain defense preparedness. The United States maintained a substantial peacetime army equipped with the latest in weaponry, including nuclear weapons. Finally, America offered military assistance to nations threatened by communism. Not only did the United States send weapons and financial aid to foreign countries, such as Greece and Turkey, but, at times, also committed American fighting forces abroad in countries such as Korea and Vietnam.

In the early 1950s, the Cold War entered a new phase. Before that time, the struggle between the United States and the USSR had been waged on the perimeters of Soviet influence—Eastern Europe, Berlin, China, Indochina, and Korea. In the 1950s, Nikita Khrushchev, an imaginative new Soviet leader, adopted a different tactic. The Soviets leapfrogged the old lines to push their cause well behind the American wall of containment—in Cuba, Egypt, the Congo, Indonesia, and elsewhere in the developing world. What's more, the Soviets had developed nuclear weapons and, with the launch of the Sputnik satellite in 1957, demonstrated that they were ahead of the United States in space technology.

The Cuban missile crisis of 1962 was the climactic event of the Cold War. Despite Sputnik, the Soviet Union remained clearly inferior to the United States in nuclear weaponry. To close the gap, Khrushchev decided to install missiles in Cuba, just ninety miles from American soil. When the United States discovered the Soviet move, President John Kennedy responded with a naval blockade. The stage was set for a nuclear confrontation, but the Soviets backed down, withdrawing their missiles. The two nations were eyeball-to-eyeball, said Secretary of State Dean Rusk, and the Soviets blinked.

Détente

The Cuban missile crisis may have had a sobering effect on the leaders of America and the Soviet Union. In the latter 1960s and early 1970s, the two superpowers embarked on a period of improved relations known as **détente**. To be sure, the two nations still experienced periods of conflict (such as the war in Vietnam), but détente was a time of better communications and visible efforts to relieve tensions. The United States and the Soviet Union increased trade and cultural relations, and they exchanged scientific information in such fields as cancer research, weather forecasting, and space exploration. Some observers promoted a **convergence theory**, the view that communism and capitalism were evolving in similar ways, or converging. As communism and capitalism become more alike, the theory explained, they will no longer be a threat to one another.

Perhaps the most important aspect of détente was arms control. Both the United States and the Soviet Union found advantage in slowing the arms race. Arms control saves money and, perhaps, reduces the probability of nuclear war. It is also good domestic politics, certainly in the United States and probably in the Soviet Union as well.

During the 1960s and 1970s, the United States and the Soviet Union agreed on a number of important arms-control measures. In 1963, the two superpowers and Great Britain signed a treaty banning aboveground testing of nuclear weapons. Subsequently, America and the Soviet Union agreed to ban nuclear weapons from the ocean floor. In 1968, they agreed on a nonproliferation treaty, in an attempt to prevent the spread of nuclear weapons to other countries.

Probably the most important arms-control agreement was the Strategic Arms Limitation Talks (SALT) treaties, signed by President Richard Nixon and Soviet Premier Leonid Brezhnev in 1972 and then ratified by the Senate. The first SALT treaty limited the deployment of antiballistic missile (ABM) systems designed to destroy enemy missiles carrying nuclear weapons. The treaty also established a five-year moratorium on the placement of additional land- and sea-based missiles.

American and Soviet negotiators produced a second arms agreement in 1979, the SALT II treaty, signed by Brezhnev and President Carter. It set limits on weapons, missiles, and long-range bombers. SALT II, however, never came to a vote in the Senate. Many treaty opponents, including then presidential candidate Ronald Reagan, argued that the United States had given up too much. Moreover, détente was ending as a result of the Soviet invasion of Afghanistan and the beginning of a substantial American military buildup.

In retrospect, détente was probably overrated by a world eager to find signs of peace in a nuclear age. Similarly, the convergence theory was more wishful thinking than it was an accurate assessment of reality. The United States and the Soviet Union have vastly different historical, cultural, political, and economic backgrounds. Each nation has interests around the globe, and those interests sometimes clash. Détente was a period of better communications between the superpowers and somewhat eased tensions, but it was naive to expect détente to bring an end to international conflicts.

The Changing World

The international political environment today is considerably different from the environment of the late 1940s and 1950s. First, military capabilities are now more widely spread. To be sure, the United States and the Soviet Union remain the only superpowers; no other nation even approaches their military strength. Nonetheless, the United States and the USSR no longer enjoy a nuclear monopoly. Six nations have openly tested nuclear weapons—the United States (1945), the Soviet Union (1949), Great Britain (1952), France (1960), and India (1974). Several other countries may have the bomb or be on the verge of developing it, including Israel, South Africa, Pakistan, Brazil, and Argentina.

Nor have the United States and the Soviet Union cornered the market on armaments. In 1960, American military spending alone accounted for 51 percent of the world's defense spending. By 1980, the figure had slipped to 28 percent. Although precise data on Soviet defense expenditures aren't available, the best estimate is that the Soviet Union spent about as much for defense in 1980 as did the United States. Consequently, about 40 percent of the world's military spending was distributed among the world's nonsuperpowers.[8]

Moreover, there is evidence that many nations have received considerable bang for their bucks. During the Falklands war between Great Britain and Argentina, an Argentine plane sank a modern British warship, the *Sheffield*, with a relatively inexpensive French-made Exocet missile fired a distance of forty miles. Similarly, in 1987 an Iraqi plane used an Exocet missile to disable the USS *Stark*, an American naval vessel sailing in the Persian Gulf. (Supposedly, the Iraqi pilot mistook the *Stark* for an Iranian ship.) What's more, both the United States (in Vietnam) and the Soviet Union (in Afghanistan) have discovered that small nations waging total war can hold their own militarily against a superpower fighting a limited war.

Second, economic power has shifted since the immediate postwar period. Although the United States still has the world's largest economy, it is hardly unchallenged. In 1945, America commanded a 40 percent share of the world's economy; by 1980, the figure had fallen to 21.5 percent.[9] The economies of Japan, several nations in Western Europe, and a number of newly industrialized countries have grown more rapidly than that of the United States in recent years, and in many fields, American goods are no longer competitive on the world market.

Third, both the communist and noncommunist blocs are far less united than they were in the 1950s. We no longer live in a bipolar world. The nations of Eastern Europe are breaking free from the Soviet orbit to chart their own economic and political course. In Asia, meanwhile, the communist nations of China and Vietnam even fought a brief border war in 1979. Perhaps most important, the People's Republic of China and the Soviet Union, the world's largest and most powerful communist nations, have often experienced stormy relations. The rift in Chinese-Soviet relations has enabled the United States to follow a balance-of-power strategy by establishing diplomatic ties with the People's Republic.

The noncommunist world isn't united either. After World War II, the United States was clearly the leader of the Western democracies, but no longer. Japan and the nations of Western Europe don't necessarily want to be led, especially along paths they consider incompatible with their own interests. For example, several Western nations ignored President Carter's call for a boycott of the 1980 Moscow Olympics. President Reagan's effort to block construction of an oil pipeline between the Soviet Union and Western Europe was a complete failure. The Soviets, meanwhile, have taken advantage of Western disunity by increasing trade relations and other ties to Western Europe.

Finally, both the United States and the Soviet Union have largely lost their role as models of political and economic development for the young nations of Africa and Asia. Since the early postwar period, America has seen its international position eroded by the war in Vietnam, Watergate, the Iran-contra scandal, and economic stagnation. The Soviets, meanwhile, have had their world image tarnished by the invasions of Hungary and Czechoslovakia, the war in Afghanistan, the shooting down of a Korean passenger jet, and economic stagnation. Today, the world's developing nations are more likely to look to Japan as a model than to either the Soviet Union or the United States.

American Foreign Policy in a Changing World

During the 1970s, the administrations of Presidents Nixon, Ford, and Carter attempted to adapt American foreign policy to the realities of a changing, more complex world and to adjust to the long-term decline of the nation's economic and military power. Nixon and Henry Kissinger, who was chief foreign policy adviser to both Presidents Nixon and Ford, spoke of the end of the postwar world and emphasized what they called a realistic foreign policy designed to control America's descent into an uncertain future. The Nixon-Ford-Kissinger foreign policy sought to maintain American interests and commitments abroad but at a reduced cost. The cornerstone of this policy was the Nixon Doctrine. The **Nixon Doctrine** was a corollary to the policy of containment enunciated by President Richard Nixon providing that although the United States would help small nations threatened by communist aggression with economic and military aid, those countries must play a major role in their own defense.

Like his immediate predecessors in the White House, Jimmy Carter followed foreign policies that reflected an understanding that the international system had changed since the 1950s. His restrained response to the hostage crisis in Iran showed a recognition of the limits of American power. The Panama Canal Treaty that provided for an eventual return of sovereignty over the canal to the government of Panama represented an accommodation to the concerns of Latin Americans.

Human rights was the watchword of Carter's foreign policy. The Carter **human-rights policy** was an approach to foreign affairs that based American trade, aid, and alliances on the way other governments treated their citi-

President Nixon's visit to China in 1972 opened the door to diplomatic relations between the two nations.

zens. The policy had both an idealistic and a practical side. In the aftermath of Vietnam, Carter wanted to return an air of morality to American foreign policy. The United States would have a "foreign policy as good as the American people," Carter promised. From a practical standpoint, the president hoped to influence repressive, noncommunist governments to reform their policies. Carter recognized that harsh dictatorships are politically unstable. They invite subversion, increasing opportunities for communist influence.

Carter's critics argued that human rights was too simplistic a doctrine on which to base a global foreign-policy strategy. What if United States security interests and human rights came in conflict? Would the administration, for example, sacrifice American defense interests in South Korea in the name of human rights? The answer turned out to be no, leaving the Carter administration open to charges of hypocrisy. What's more, many observers believed the policy reflected an arrogant attitude toward the rest of the world. To them, it seemed that Carter had adopted the role of a missionary, helping the poor abroad and bringing American values to those who suffer in the dark.[10]

American Foreign Policy in the 1980s: A Resurgent America?

When Ronald Reagan came to the White House, he promised an end to the self-doubt and decline that, he said, had infected United States foreign policy in the 1970s. The problem, Reagan charged, lay not with America but with America's leaders. Reagan spoke optimistically of a resurgent America, which he called, quoting Abraham Lincoln, "the last best hope of man on earth." In contrast, he branded the Soviet Union an "evil empire."

Reagan based his foreign policy on firm opposition to Soviet power. He saw world politics as a bipolar rivalry between the United States and the Soviet Union, and he left no doubt who the bad guys were. The Soviet leaders, Reagan declared, reserved for themselves the right "to lie, to cheat, to commit any crime." To meet the challenge, Reagan called for a resolute national will and a military buildup.

The centerpiece of the president's foreign policy was known as the **Reagan Doctrine**. This was a corollary to the policy of containment enunciated by President Reagan calling for the United States to offer military aid to groups attempting to overthrow communist governments anywhere in the world. Reagan offered military aid to "liberation forces" in Nicaragua, Afghanistan, and Angola. In this fashion, Reagan hoped to increase the costs to the Soviet Union for what the president considered to be the export of revolution. Reagan hoped that the Soviets would eventually have to choose between reducing their commitments abroad and facing economic collapse at home. In the meantime, Reagan offered practically unconditional support to anticommunist governments, even if they were authoritarian governments, as in Chile, Argentina, and the Philippines.

During his first term in office, President Reagan seemed to reject the idea that the United States should adapt its policies to a changing international environment. Not only did the president ask Congress for a substantial increase in defense spending, but he was willing to flex American military muscle in certain circumstances. Reagan ordered an invasion of the Caribbean island of Grenada to overthrow a government friendly to Cuba, directed air strikes against the North African nation of Libya in retaliation for that country's alleged support of terrorism, and ordered American naval vessels to escort Kuwaiti oil tankers through the Persian Gulf, protecting them from attacks by Iran. "America is back and standing tall," boasted the president.

Nonetheless, by the mid-1980s, the key feature of American foreign policy was caution. In a number of crisis situations—the terrorist hijacking of a TWA airliner, the Soviet downing of a Korean jetliner, the loss of more than two hundred marines in a terrorist bombing in Beirut, Lebanon, and the Iraqi missile attack against the *Stark*—the Reagan administration responded with restraint. Although the White House often talked tough, the substance of Reagan's foreign policies increasingly grew to resemble the policies of the 1970s that Reagan had so roundly criticized. As two observers described it, American foreign policies were "Carterite substance concealed by Reaganite rhetoric."[11] On arms control, for example, the Reagan administration generally adhered to the weapons limits set by SALT II even though the treaty had never been ratified. Moreover, by the mid-1980s, the United States and the USSR were engaged in serious negotiations aimed at arms control and arms reductions. As for the Reagan Doctrine, the administration continued to support the contra guerrillas in Nicaragua and other anticommunist forces, but it was forced to change its policy of unconditional support for anticommunist dictators. In both the Philippines (Marcos) and Haiti (Duvalier), the administration backed local efforts to oust unpopular dictators in favor of reform-minded democratic governments.

Several factors were behind the modifications in President Reagan's foreign-policy focus. First, Congress was unwilling to support all of the president's foreign-policy initiatives. Congress consistently refused to give the contras as much aid as Reagan requested. Moreover, by Reagan's second term, the willingness of Congress to fund the president's military buildup had evaporated. Second, public opinion did not support all aspects of Reagan's foreign policies. Although the president's vision of an America standing tall was popular, polls indicated that many Americans opposed United States military involvement in Nicaragua and other trouble spots, and they feared a confrontation with the Soviet Union. Also, by the mid-1980s, polls showed that a majority of Americans believed the United States was already spending enough money for defense. Finally, firsthand experience dealing with the realities of international affairs forced Reagan to modify his foreign-policy focus. Once in office, for instance, President Reagan found that dealing with terrorism and hostage taking was as difficult as it had been for President Carter.[12]

American Foreign-Policy Options
for the 1990s

Early in his administration, President George Bush acknowledged the dramatic changes in Soviet policy, saying they were an opportunity to move "beyond containment."[13] Foreign-policy analysts offer of number of policy options to policymakers considering the course of American foreign policy for the 1990s. Evaluate the following foreign-policy alternatives in light of the assumptions they make about the nature of the international system, the role of the United States in that system, and the goals of the Soviet Union. You may also wish to consider the political feasibility of each of the policy options.

Rollback of communism.   Those who favor an American policy aimed at the rollback of communism believe that America has important interests in all corners of the world and that the Soviet Union and international communism remain the primary threats to those interests. They believe that the main thrust of American foreign policy should be to eliminate communism and promote democracy around the globe.

Global containment.   Global containment is essentially a continuation of the postwar policy of containment. Its proponents believe that America has worldwide interests and that the Soviet Union remains the principal threat to those interests. Believing the United States' ability to roll back communism is limited by budget constraints and the complexity of international affairs, the supporters of global containment favor policies designed to prevent the expansion of communism.

The realist approach.   Those who favor the so-called realist approach believe that the United States can no longer afford the luxury of trying to exert influence in all parts of the world. Instead, they argue that America should focus on deterring Soviet expansion in areas of predominant American interest, primarily the industrial areas of Europe and Asia. Consequently, they favor policies designed to deter Soviet expansion in those areas but not in the Third World. The term **Third World** refers to nonindustrialized nations that are not aligned with either the capitalist (First World) or communist (Second World) groups of countries.

Neo-isolationism.   Neo-isolationists believe that the United States can no longer afford to play an aggressive international role and that, at any rate, the Soviet Union is no longer able (or willing) to attempt expansionism. The neo-isolationists argue that American policymakers' should adopt policies aimed at avoiding war, promoting economic prosperity, and protecting United States territory.

World-order idealism.   World-order idealism differs the most dramatically from traditional American approaches to foreign policy. Its advocates think that nuclear war, ecological decay, overpopulation, and poverty are greater threats to the American way of life than communism. Consequently, they believe that American policymakers should work with other nations, including the USSR, to solve the world's problems.[14]

AMERICAN DEFENSE POLICY

Karl von Clausewitz, the nineteenth-century military strategist, once described war as diplomacy by other means. By that, he meant that defense concerns and foreign-policy issues are closely related. And so they are. Foreign-policy goals determine defense strategies. Military capabilities, meanwhile, influence a nation's foreign policy by expanding (or limiting) the options available to policymakers. Keep in mind the close interconnections between foreign-policy and defense issues as we examine American defense policy.

Defense Spending

Figure 16.1 charts American defense expenditures from 1935 through the end of the 1980s. As the graph shows, defense budgets before World War II were relatively modest, consistently falling below the $20 billion level (in 1986 dollars). During the war, defense spending skyrocketed to its highest level in American history. Although military expenditures quickly receded after the war, they never fell to their prewar level. Defense spending peaked again in the early 1950s with the Korean War and then in the late 1960s with the Vietnam War. After Vietnam, defense budgets fell until the late 1970s, when they began to turn upward again.

The upswing in defense spending from the late 1970s through the mid-1980s represented the largest peacetime military buildup in American history. Although the defense budget began to climb during the last years of the Carter presidency, the big push behind increased defense expenditures came from Ronald Reagan. During the 1980 election campaign, presidential candidate Reagan labeled the 1970s "the decade of neglect" of the nation's armed forces. He warned that the Soviet Union was ahead of the United States "in virtually every measure of military power."[15]

Once in office, Reagan proposed accelerating the military buildup begun under Carter. He asked Congress to increase military spending at a rate of 9.4 percent a year after inflation for the next five years. Although Congress refused to give the president all he wanted, it did raise the defense budget at a rate of 8 percent a year from fiscal 1981 through 1985, increasing the defense share of federal spending from 23.2 to 26.5 percent. Moreover, defense spending rose as a proportion of GNP from 5.5 to 6.6 percent.[16]

FIGURE 16.1

U.S. Defense Spending, Fiscal Years 1935–90

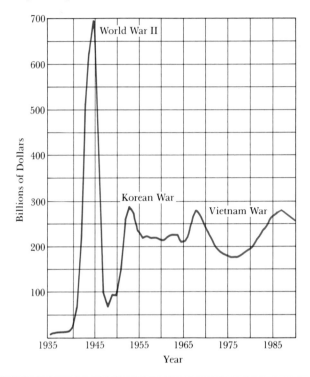

Note: In billions of constant 1986 dollars.

Data sources: U.S. Bureau of the Census, *Historical Statistics of the United States, Colonial Times to 1970s*, pts. 1 and 2 (Washington, DC: U.S. Government Printing Office, 1975), pp. 230, 1115–16; *Historical Tables, Budget of the United States Government, Fiscal Year 1986*, pp. 6.1(a)–6.1(8); William W. Kaufmann, *A Reasonable Defense* (Washington, DC: Brookings Institution,, 1986), p. 19; *CQ Weekly Report*, 10 January 1987, p. 34.

By the end of the 1980s, the American defense buildup was at an end. The reversal began in the mid-1980s under pressure of the federal budget deficit. To be sure, Reagan's spending priorities had not changed—the president's five-year plan called for a 6.5 percent annual increase after inflation in defense expenditures for every budget year from 1986 through 1990. Nonetheless, Congress, which after the 1986 elections was firmly under Democratic party control, refused to raise defense spending at a rate anywhere near what Reagan requested. To find the money to continue the defense buildup, Congress and the president would have had to agree to raise taxes, cut nondefense spending deeply, or enlarge the budget deficit. Each of these courses of action was unpopular and politically improbable. President Reagan opposed tax increases, majorities in both houses of Congress refused to make major reductions in nondefense spending, and the Gramm-Rudman Deficit Control Act stood in the way of larger budget deficits.

In the early 1990s, the issue before President Bush and Congress was how deeply to cut defense spending. More than half of the United States' defense budget is spent in some fashion on forces to defend Europe.[17] Since recent developments in the Soviet Union and Eastern Europe make a Soviet invasion of Western Europe seem highly unlikely, many observers called for reductions in defense spending.

How does American defense spending compare with that of the Soviet Union? The CIA estimates that from 1965 through 1985 the Soviet Union spent about 10 percent more on the military than America, with the United States catching up in the latter part of the 1980s.[18] Not everyone, however, agrees with CIA figures. One scholar believes that CIA estimates of Soviet defense spending are too high and that America has actually outspent the USSR over the last fifteen years.[19]

Still, the most important issue in defense isn't dollars (or rubles); it's adequacy. Are American forces capable of performing their mission? That is an exceedingly complex question, involving consideration of a range of factors and defense issues. Let's turn first to an examination of strategic forces and nuclear strategy.

Nuclear Forces and Strategy

America's **strategic forces** (that is, nuclear weaponry) include more than 14,000 nuclear warheads that can be carried to their targets through a triad of delivery systems. The **triad** refers to the three systems the United States employs to deliver nuclear warheads—including intercontinental ballistic missiles (ICBMs), submarine-launched ballistic missiles (SLBMs), and manned bombers—to their targets. The United States has a thousand ICBMs stored in missile silos and ready for launch, more than six hundred missiles on nuclear-powered submarines roaming the world's oceans, and more than three hundred manned bombers capable of delivering a nuclear payload to the Soviet Union.

Table 16.1 compares and contrasts American and Soviet strategic forces. The Soviet Union has the edge in missile launchers, with more ICBMs and SLBMs than the United States. In contrast, America has an advantage in numbers of manned bombers and in total missile warheads.

Still, numbers don't tell the whole story. Other considerations are important as well. Soviet warheads are bigger than American warheads, averaging three times the explosive power, but the United States' missiles are considered more accurate, and a larger proportion are on alert at any given time. Moreover, the United States has an advantage over the Soviet Union in both MIRV (multiple independently targetable reentry vehicle) and cruise-missile technologies. **MIRV technology** is the capacity of a missile to carry multiple nuclear warheads, each programmed to strike a different target. A cruise missile, meanwhile, is relatively small, but can carry a payload as big as the bomb that destroyed Hiroshima. A cruise missile is self-programmed so the Soviets

TABLE 16.1

Strategic Forces, United States and Soviet Union, 1989

	U.S.	USSR
ICBMs*	1,000	1,451
ICBM warheads	2,450	6,657
SLBMs†	608	942
SLBM warheads	6,208	3,806
Bombers	360	195
Bomber warheads	5,872	1,940
Total missile launchers	1,968	2,588
Total missile warheads	14,530	12,403

*ICBMs—intercontinental ballistic missiles.
† SLBMs—submarine-launched ballistic missiles.
Note: A warhead is the payload of the missile/bomb that contains the nuclear device.
Data sources: *The Military Balance, 1989–1990* (London: The International Institute for Strategic Studies, 1989), p. 212.

can't jam its radio, and it can fly at treetop level to elude radar. It is so easily launched that a B-52 bomber flying near the Soviet border could release a dozen of them. What's more, cruise missiles are relatively inexpensive—roughly a million dollars apiece.

America's nuclear strategy is based on deterrence through massive retaliation. **Deterrence** is the ability of a nation to prevent a nuclear or conventional attack on itself or its allies by the threat of nuclear retaliation. The United States has hoped to prevent aggression and preserve peace by threatening massive retaliation against aggressors. **Massive retaliation** is the doctrine that the United States will strike back against an aggressor with overwhelming force, including nuclear weapons.

Many nuclear strategists believe that nuclear weapons are so destructive that their use is unthinkable. In a macabre sense, then, nuclear weapons have promoted world peace because no American or Soviet leader acting rationally would risk initiating a nuclear holocaust. This concept is formalized in the doctrine of **mutual assured destruction (MAD)**, the belief that the United States and Soviet Union will both be deterred from launching a nuclear assault against the other for fear of being destroyed in a general nuclear war.

We can explain this concept more fully by defining first-strike and second-strike capability. A **first strike** is the initial offensive move of a general nuclear war, aimed at knocking out the other side's ability to retaliate. A **second strike** is a nuclear attack in response to an adversary's first strike. **First-strike capability** is the capacity of a nation to launch an initial nuclear assault sufficient to cripple an adversary's ability to retaliate. **Second-strike capability** is the capacity of a nation to absorb an initial nuclear attack and retain sufficient nuclear firepower to inflict unacceptable damage on its adversary. According to the principles of MAD, America's best defense against

A Boeing SM-80 Minuteman missile in its silo. America has a thousand such ICBMs in secret locations throughout the country.

nuclear attack and best deterrent to nuclear war hinge on maintaining a second-strike capability.

Today, the best guess is that both the United States and the Soviet Union have second-strike capability sufficient to deter the other from venturing a first strike. One estimate predicts that 3,350 American warheads would survive a surprise attack, carrying the equivalent of 1,060 megatons of TNT. In the meantime, the Soviets could deliver 820 warheads with the equivalent of 540 megatons after a first strike by the United States. In each case, the first nation struck would have enough nuclear firepower left to destroy the other.[20] Consequently, the United States and the Soviet Union have reached a balance of terror, in which each side is capable of destroying the other and perhaps civilization as well. As long as the balance persists, though, neither side will be tempted or frightened into launching a nuclear attack. At least that's the theory.

In the early 1980s, President Reagan proposed a controversial new nuclear force strategy based on the Strategic Defense Initiative, popularly known as Star Wars. The **Strategic Defense Initiative (SDI)** is a plan to develop a futuristic space-based ballistic missile defense system. As Reagan phrased it, SDI could supplant "mutual assured destruction" with "mutual assured survival" by creating a defensive shield that would render intercontinental ballistic missiles obsolete. No longer would the world live in fear of nuclear war. The president even promised to share SDI technology with the Soviets.

SDI has come under a great deal of criticism. Its opponents note that the technology for a space-based missile defense system is not now available and may never be. Developing SDI would be extraordinarily expensive—probably more than a trillion dollars—and no one could guarantee it would be leakproof. Moreover, the critics say, even if SDI were perfect, it would still leave the United States vulnerable to air attack and to cruise missiles fired from the sea.[21]

Because of the technical problems associated with building a leakproof missile defense, much of the present debate surrounding SDI concerns the desirability of constructing a less-than-perfect defense. The critics of SDI argue that deployment of the system would heighten the arms race, increase international tensions, reduce the chances for arms control, and increase the likelihood of a preemptive strike from the Soviet Union.[22] In contrast, supporters of SDI believe that even a somewhat effective missile defense system would strengthen America's second-strike capability. An SDI system designed to protect United States missiles, they say, would make it more difficult for the Soviets to achieve a first-strike capability.[23]

Other observers believe that the greatest utility of SDI lies in its value as a bargaining chip in arms-control negotiations. The Soviets have made clear their concern over SDI. Even if it doesn't work, the Soviets fear that American SDI research would yield technological spinoffs, further widening the technological gap between the United States and the Soviet Union. Moreover, SDI development would force the Soviets to devote even more resources to the military, thus jeopardizing *perestroika*. Consequently, a number of American arms-control experts think that SDI can best be used as a bargaining chip, with the United States agreeing to shelve plans for development in exchange for deep reductions in Soviet ICBMs.

Conventional Forces and Strategy

After World War II, American defense policy centered on the need to contain Soviet expansion. The logic of containment suggested a number of goals:

1. The maintenance of a second-strike capability. Not only does this deter against Soviet attack, but it discourages the Soviets from attempting to use nuclear blackmail to force American political concessions.
2. The defense of Western Europe. The United States cannot afford for all of Eurasia to fall under the control of a hostile power. Moreover, the United States has important economic ties to Western Europe. This goal requires that NATO be strong enough to repulse a Soviet invasion.
3. The defense of the Persian Gulf oil fields. President Carter added this objective. Although the United States gets only about 10 percent of its oil

from the Persian Gulf region, its Western European allies and Japan are dependent on oil from the area. Western economies depend on its free flow.
4. The maintenance of forces able to deal with peripheral threats to American interests in Korea or the Middle East, for example, and capable of keeping the sea lanes open.

President Reagan, you recall, proposed to extend the goals of American foreign policy to embrace the aim of rolling back communism. Accordingly, he proposed three additional missions for American armed forces.

1. The creation of a nuclear counterforce capable of defending the nation against nuclear attack—SDI.
2. The development of **conventional forces** (non-nuclear military resources) capable of carrying a war to the Soviet homeland.
3. The enhancement of the capacity of American forces to intervene against communist forces in developing nations.

For decades, defense analysts evaluated American armed forces by comparing them with Soviet and Warsaw Pact forces. Could NATO hold off a Warsaw Pact assault? Would the United States be able to defend the Persian Gulf against Soviet attack? Today, however, those sorts of comparative-force studies are out of date. The collapse of one-party communist rule in Eastern Europe virtually eliminates any prospect of a united Warsaw Pact invasion of Western Europe, at least for the foreseeable future. What's more, the current preoccupation with *perestroika* and *glasnost* has reduced the Soviets' ability and, perhaps, interest in supporting communist insurgencies in Third World nations. Though the USSR remains a world power militarily, the changes of the last few years necessitate a rethinking of American defense policy.

FOREIGN AND DEFENSE POLICYMAKING

American foreign and defense policy is made by means of a process involving the various branches of the national government as well as a number of interest groups. Let's examine the process in terms of the policymaking framework.

Agenda Setting

Events, public opinion, interest groups, Congress, and the president all play a role in setting the agenda for foreign and defense policymaking. Some issues become important items on the policy agenda because of dramatic international events—the bombing of Pearl Harbor, the launch of Sputnik, the oil embargo, the takeover of the American embassy in Teheran, Iran, or the recent developments in Eastern Europe.

Events affect the agenda for foreign and defense policymaking because of their impact on elite and mass public opinion. When the Soviets launched the Sputnik satellite, for example, the American scientific and educational communities became alarmed that the United States was falling behind the Soviet Union in science education and space technology. America's military involvement in Vietnam convinced many Americans that the United States should avoid entanglement in limited wars in distant lands. *Perestroika, glasnost*, and recent developments in Eastern Europe have convinced many Americans that the U.S. defense budget can be safely reduced.

A good many interest groups participate in foreign and defense policy-making. Dozens of corporations and their workers' unions lobby on behalf of weapons systems in which they have a financial interest. Other corporate and trade groups focus on trade policy, either seeking protection from foreign competition or working against restrictive trade policies that could threaten their export business. In the meantime, ethnic groups—African-Americans, Hispanic-Americans, Greek-Americans, Chinese-Americans, and Jews—take an interest in foreign policies affecting areas of particular interest to them. One study found, for example, that pro-Israel political action committees (PACs) gave more money to candidates for Congress in 1984 than did any group of domestic PACs.[24]

In recent years, Congress has increasingly taken the initiative on foreign and defense policy issues. During the late 1940s and 1950s, presidents could generally count on bipartisan support on foreign-policy issues. (**Bipartisanship** is the close cooperation and general agreement between the two major political parties in dealing with foreign-policy matters.) Postwar bipartisanship reflected a consensus supporting active United States involvement in world affairs and cooperation between the executive and legislative branches of government. Since the Vietnam War and the Watergate scandal, however, congressional bipartisanship on foreign-policy and defense issues has become the exception rather than the rule, especially in the House of Representatives.[25] During the Reagan years, for example, Congress enacted tough sanctions against the government of South Africa, passing the legislation over President Reagan's veto.

Despite recent congressional assertiveness in the foreign-policy arena, the president historically has played a more important role in setting the agenda for foreign and defense policies than has Congress. In 1947, for instance, the Truman administration, particularly under Secretary of State Dean Acheson, convinced congressional leaders that United States aid for Greece and Turkey was essential to American security. During the 1960s and 1970s, a series of presidents and a procession of State Department and Pentagon spokespersons worked to persuade Congress and the nation of the importance of American intervention in Vietnam.

Policy Formulation and Adoption

Constitutionally, the president and Congress share authority to formulate and adopt foreign and defense policy. The president negotiates treaties, but the treaties must be ratified by the Senate. The president has the power of diplomatic recognition, but the Senate must confirm ambassadorial appointments. The president may budget money for foreign aid and defense, but Congress must appropriate the funds. The president is commander in chief of the armed forces, but only Congress can declare war.

In practice, the president usually initiates foreign and defense policies, with Congress acting to modify or, occasionally, reject policies formulated in the executive branch. This division of labor has developed for a number of reasons. First, the executive branch is better equipped to deal with international crises than the legislative branch. Unlike Congress, the president is always "in session." The president can respond quickly to international events and speak with one voice.

Second, the president has an advantage in that secret national-security information from the CIA, military, and diplomatic corps flows directly to the White House. A clever president can keep Congress in the dark about foreign and defense developments or can release information selectively to justify policies. During the 1980 presidential campaign, for example, President Carter leaked classified information on the development of the Stealth Bomber (an aircraft able to elude radar detection) in order to counter criticism of his decision to shelve the B-1 bomber project.

Third, the general public looks to the president for leadership in foreign and defense policymaking. As a rule, the public is neither well informed nor particularly attentive to foreign affairs. In times of international crisis, Americans tend to rally around the president. One study finds, for instance, that a president enjoys a surge of popularity for roughly a thirty-day period following the visible use of military force abroad.[26]

Finally, the president has often had considerable influence on foreign and defense policymaking because Congress has allowed it. Many members of Congress aren't interested in overall foreign policy and defense strategy. Congress as an institution is decentralized, focusing on the parts of policy but seldom the big picture. Individual members, meanwhile, involve themselves primarily with the big issues that gain national attention (such as sanctions against South Africa) or with issues of primary importance to their constituents (such as Defense Department decisions on closing military bases).

Since the end of the Vietnam War, Congress has become considerably more involved in the details of foreign and defense policy than at any time in the nation's history. During the 1970s, Congress passed the War Powers Act over a presidential veto to limit the chief executive's authority to commit American forces abroad without congressional authorization. It enacted the Military Sales Act to give itself a veto on arms sales overseas. It acted to restrain the activities of the CIA, to control the spread of nuclear materials, and to restrict the development of trade relations with the Soviet Union. Congress cut American aid to Chile and South Korea and voted to ban all aid to countries engaged in a pattern of human-rights violations unless the president certified that aid would benefit the needy people of the nation. In the 1980s, Congress acted to restrict the president's use of military force in Central

America. It overrode President Reagan's veto of legislation imposing economic sanctions against the white-minority government in South Africa. Congress also pressured the White House to adopt tougher trade policies and to adhere to the weapons limits set in the unratified SALT II treaty.

Each of these congressional actions was an important policymaking step, but the impact was generally to check the actions of the president rather than serve as a blueprint for a comprehensive foreign and defense policy. As one scholar describes it, Congress is concerned with "micromanagement," examining the details of foreign and defense policy without much attention to the big picture.[27]

Most foreign policies are formulated in the executive branch. Presidents with a special interest and experience in foreign policy may take personal charge of foreign and defense policymaking. Richard Nixon and George Bush, two presidents with extensive foreign-policy experience and expertise, immersed themselves in the details of the nation's foreign policies. In contrast, Ronald Reagan came to office with almost no foreign-policy experience at all and apparently little interest in the subject. Consequently, Reagan relied heavily on aides and advisers for foreign-policy advice.

Political scientists Cecil V. Crabb, Jr., and Pat M. Holt identify four models of presidential foreign policymaking: (1) The president makes policy, often leaving the State Department in the dark. Franklin Roosevelt took this approach. (2) The president sets policy goals, but relies on the State Department for the day-to-day conduct of foreign affairs. Harry Truman followed this model. (3) The president demands consensus in support of administration policy, suppressing full and frank discussion among advisers. Lyndon Johnson practiced this method. (4) The president fosters rivalries between the State Department and the National Security Council, with decision-making centered in the White House. President Nixon took this approach.[28]

Some foreign and defense policies can be adopted in the executive branch alone, but most require congressional action as well. Foreign assistance and defense budgets must journey through the regular appropriations process. The Senate must ratify treaties and confirm appointments. In practice, Congress more frequently modifies than blocks executive-branch initiatives in foreign and defense policy. In the 1970s, for example, the Senate ratified the Panama Canal Treaty after tacking on twenty-four amendments, reservations, conditions, and understandings.

Policy Implementation and Evaluation

The executive branch is primarily responsible for the implementation of foreign policy. The State Department, Department of Defense, and CIA are prominently involved, but many other agencies and departments play a role as well. The Agriculture Department, for example, promotes the sale of American agricultural products abroad. The Department of Education, meanwhile, administers student-exchange programs.

Foreign and defense policies may not always be implemented the way the president and Congress originally intended or expected. After all, bureaucrats sometimes have priorities of their own. Also, large bureaucracies tend to develop standard operating procedures (SOPs) that they follow in performing their tasks.

President Kennedy learned this lesson during the Cuban missile crisis. According to the U.S. Navy procedures manual, naval blockades were to be established no closer than ninety miles from the blockaded coast in order to reduce the danger of attack from land-based enemy aircraft. Kennedy, however, specifically ordered the blockade set up closer to shore than the standard ninety miles. With so much at stake, Kennedy wanted to postpone as long as possible the moment when an American warship would first stop a Soviet vessel, to allow more time for the two countries to reach a compromise and avert war. Subsequently, the president was perturbed to learn that the navy had established the blockade ninety miles out after all, just as naval SOPs specify.[29]

The government has no systematic, ongoing mechanism for evaluating foreign and defense policies. Congress monitors expenditures, but limits its policy oversight to high-profile issues, such as arms control and Middle East peace prospects. Scandals, such as the Iran-contra affair, also receive considerable attention. Other efforts at evaluation take place in the executive branch, in academia, and by the news media.

In general, foreign and defense policies are probably more difficult to evaluate than policies in other areas. It's not always possible to determine whether policy goals have been met. In the absence of war, for example, any evaluation of the effectiveness of particular defense strategies has to be at least somewhat speculative. Another problem is that many of the details of policy implementation are secret. Only now, years after the events took place, is information available so that historians can begin to intelligently evaluate American foreign policy in the years immediately following World War II.

CONCLUSION: POLITICS AND FOREIGN POLICY

There's a saying that "politics stops at the water's edge." This phrase suggests that foreign and defense policy ought to be above partisan politics. Most American policymakers pay lip service to this idea and, we believe, attempt to practice what they preach. Most presidents, members of Congress, military leaders, and civilian bureaucrats try to formulate, adopt, and implement foreign and defense policies that they believe are in the national interest. Inevitably, however, politics plays a major role in foreign and defense policymaking.

First, the actors involved in foreign and defense policymaking are political. Presidents often proclaim their commitment to keeping politics out of foreign policy and may privately instruct their advisers to ignore political concerns in their advice. Nevertheless, politics often enters beneath the surface. With the Cuban missile crisis, for example, President Kennedy had to weigh the risk of blowing up the planet against the threat of political attack at home. For some months, the Kennedy administration had been fending off election-year attacks from Republicans that the president was soft on communism. Although some critics had even suggested that the Soviets were sneaking missiles into Cuba, the White House had strongly denied the allegation. Now that the administration had proof of the missiles, Kennedy had to respond vigorously or give the Republicans a major campaign issue.[30]

Kennedy faced another political dilemma in Vietnam. No president wants to be accused of letting a country "go communist," but none wants to send American soldiers into combat either. Kennedy found himself trying to walk this thin line in Vietnam. In fact, Kenneth O'Donnell, one of Kennedy's advisers, reports that the president had planned the complete withdrawal of American troops from Vietnam but decided to wait until 1965, after he was reelected.[31]

Congress, too, is political. Some members of Congress have a broad, continuing interest in foreign affairs and national security policy, but most are primarily concerned with domestic policy. Foreign and defense policies become important to them when they directly affect their constituents. In the mid-1980s, for example, members of Congress jockeyed to have a new army base built in their states (army bases bring jobs and money to a local economy). Who won? Alaska. Never mind that the purpose of the base was to train soldiers to fight in Latin America or the Middle East. Alaska got the base because the chair of the Senate Appropriations Subcommittee for Defense, Ted Stevens, was from Alaska.[32]

Second, foreign and defense policy are the objects of pressure-group politics similar to that in other areas of public policy. Multinational corporations, such as energy companies and big banks, are acutely aware of, and concerned about, American foreign policy because it affects their business abroad. Other interests are concerned with trade policy. American automobile and steel companies and their workers' unions lobby for tariffs to keep out what they regard as unfair foreign competition. In contrast, farmers and other American industries favor free trade because they benefit as exporters. Moreover, many companies, including General Dynamics, Lockheed, and McDonnell Douglas, focus their lobbying on defense policy because of their role as major defense contractors.

Third, foreign and defense policymaking, like domestic policymaking, require political bargaining and compromise. The Panama Canal Treaty, for example, ultimately passed the Senate because its backers were willing to compromise and accept reservations. The defense budget inevitably reflects the political compromises characteristic of the appropriations process. In

1986, President Reagan was forced to compromise in order to win congressional approval of aid for the contras.

Finally, consider the politics of bureaucracy. As we have said, military officers and civilian bureaucrats try to act in the national interest. As with everyone else, though, their views of the world are colored by their own experiences. Consequently, they tend to equate national security with the interests of their own organizations. In fact, a number of defense analysts believe that bureaucratic infighting and interservice rivalries seriously undermine the effectiveness of America's armed forces.

Consider the circumstances surrounding the ill-fated attempt to rescue the American hostages taken from the embassy in Teheran, Iran. Instead of assigning responsibility for the effort to a single military service, the Pentagon gave a piece of the action to every branch of the armed forces except the Coast Guard. The mission ended in disaster, when the Marine pilots of a Navy helicopter collided with an Air Force transport, primarily because personnel from different services misunderstood each other's procedures.[33]

Even the Grenada invasion, which was a political success, was nearly botched by bureaucratic mishandling. The island was defended by 679 Cubans, only 43 of whom were professional soldiers; the rest were construction workers. The Cubans had no air defenses, no combat aircraft, no missiles, no tanks, and no artillery. Nonetheless, the 7,000-man American invasion force took three days and had to be reinforced twice before taking the island. Moreover, two-thirds of the 18 Americans killed and a fifth of the 116 Americans wounded were felled by "friendly fire" or accidents. What went wrong? Once again, the problem was bureaucratic mismanagement. Even though every aspect of the invasion was land combat, the Pentagon assigned command responsibilities to the Navy, which decided to reenact D-Day. They landed forces at either end of the small island, some distance from the key targets in the center of Grenada. This strategy gave the Cubans time to prepare a defense. What's more, the Pentagon committed both Army and Marine ground forces, requiring the division of the little island into two theaters of operation. Since Army and Marine radios are incompatible, ground units could not talk with one another, creating serious problems of communications and coordination.[34]

A number of observers called for reforms in the military command structure. General David C. Jones, former chair of the Joint Chiefs of Staff, said that the Joint Chiefs system is incapable of waging war successfully and is wasteful in peacetime.[35] Professors William J. Lynn and Barry R. Posen, meanwhile, agree that the military command structure is dominated by services acting to preserve or improve their size, wealth, and autonomy. The consequences, they say, are "ineffective allocations of defense dollars, the neglect of key military missions, and peacetime command arrangements that ensure to an unreasonable degree that no senior theatre commander will have much operational control over forces other than those from his parent service."[36]

In 1986, Congress responded to the calls for reform by enacting a major overhaul of the Pentagon command structure. Congress strengthened the Joint Chiefs of Staff, streamlined the Pentagon command staff, and expanded the authority of field commanders. The reforms may have paid off during the American invasion of Panama in 1989. General Colin Powell, the chairman of the Joint Chiefs of Staff, squelched interservice rivalries by giving two Army generals clear authority to direct the attack. In comparison with the Grenada invasion, the Panamanian operation went more smoothly.[37]

As you can see, politics doesn't stop at the water's edge. Foreign and defense policy are made through the interplay of executive and legislative bodies, public and private interests, and personalities. And the process is highly political as the various participants maneuver for advantage.

KEY TERMS

balance of power

bipartisanship

Cold War

containment

conventional forces

convergence theory

détente

deterrence

diplomacy

diplomatic relations

first strike

first-strike capability

glasnost

human-rights policy

isolationism

Marshall Plan

massive retaliation

MIRV technology

mutual assured destruction (MAD)

Nixon Doctrine

North Atlantic Treaty Organization (NATO)

Organization of Petroleum Exporting Countries (OPEC)

perestroika

Reagan Doctrine

second strike

second-strike capability

Strategic Defense Initiative (SDI)

strategic forces

Third World

triad

Truman Doctrine

United Nations (UN)

Warsaw Pact

NOTES

1. Marshall I. Goldman, "The Future of Soviet Economic Reform," *Current History* 88 (October 1989): 325–28, 354.
2. Robert G. Kaiser, "The End of the Soviet Empire: Failure on a Historic Scale," *Washington Post*, National Weekly Edition, 1–7 January 1990, pp. 23–24.

3. Coil D. Blacker, "The New United States–Soviet Détente," *Current History* 88 (October 1989): 321–25, 357–59.
4. Michael Isikoff, "U.S. Manufacturers and Dealers Are Struggling to Hold Their Market Share," *Washington Post*, National Weekly Edition, 12 January 1987, p. 8.
5. *National Journal*, 8 April 1989, p. 849.
6. George F. Kennan, *American Diplomacy 1900–1950* (New York: New American Library, 1951), p. 10.
7. Ruth Leger Sivard, *World Military and Social Expenditures, 1985* (Washington, DC: World Priorities, 1985), pp. 35–36.
8. Kenneth A. Oye, "Constrained Confidence and the Evolution of Reagan Foreign Policy," in Kenneth A. Oye, Robert J. Lieber, and Donald Rothchild, eds., *Eagle Resurgent? The Reagan Era in American Foreign Policy* (Boston: Little, Brown, 1987), p. 10.
9. Ibid.
10. Stanley Hoffman, "Requiem," *Foreign Policy* 42 (Spring 1981): 3–26.
11. William D. Anderson and Sterling J. Kernek, "How 'Realistic' Is Reagan's Diplomacy?" *Political Science Quarterly* 100 (Fall 1985): 406.
12. Robert J. Lieber, "*Eagle* Revisited: A Reconsideration of the Reagan Era in U.S. Foreign Policy," *Washington Quarterly* (Summer 1989): 115–26.
13. Quoted in Strobe Talbot, "Beyond the Reagan Doctrine," *Time*, 17 July 1989, p. 68.
14. Stephen M. Walt, "The Case for Finite Containment: Analyzing U.S. Grand Strategy," *International Security* 14 (Summer 1989): 5–49.
15. *New York Times*, 23 November 1982, p. A12.
16. William W. Kaufman, *A Reasonable Defense* (Washington, DC: Brookings Institution, 1986), pp. 24–25.
17. Patrick E. Tyler and Molly Moore, "Contingencies for War, Reductions for Peace," *Washington Post*, National Weekly Edition, 1–7 January 1990, p. 8.
18. "U.S., Soviet Defense Outlays Nearly Equal in '85," *Houston Post*, 16 September 1986, p. 6B.
19. Franklin D. Holzman, "Politics and Guesswork: CIA and DIA Estimates of Soviet Military Spending," *International Security* 14 (Fall 1989), pp. 101–31.
20. Barry R. Posen and Stephen W. Van Evera, "Reagan Administration Defense Policy: Departure from Containments," in Oye, Lieber, and Rothchild, eds., *Eagle Resurgent?* p. 80.
21. James R. Schlesinger, "Rhetoric and Realities in the Star Wars Debate," *International Security* 10 (Summer 1985): 3–12.
22. Robert H. Gromoll, "SDI and the Dynamics of Strategic Uncertainty," *Political Science Quarterly* 102 (Fall 1987): 481–500.
23. Fred S. Hoffman, "The SDI in U.S. Nuclear Strategy," *International Security* 10 (Summer 1985): 13–24.
24. Eric M. Uslaner, "One Nation, Many Voices: Interest Groups in Foreign Policy Making," in Allan J. Cigler and Burdett A. Loomis, eds., *Interest Group Politics*, 2d ed. (Washington, DC: Congressional Quarterly Press, 1986), p. 252.
25. James M. McCormick and Eugene R. Wittkopf, "Bush and Bipartisanship: The Past as Prologue?" *Washington Quarterly* 13 (Winter 1990): 5–16.
26. Richard J. Stoll, "The Sound of the Guns," *American Politics Quarterly* 15 (April 1987): 223–37.
27. James M. Lindsay, "Congress and Defense Policy: 1961 to 1986," *Armed Forces & Society* 13 (Spring 1987): 371–401.

28. Cecil V. Crabb, Jr., and Pat M. Holt, *Invitation to Struggle: Congress, the President, and Foreign Policy*, 3d ed. (Washington, DC: Congressional Quarterly Press, 1989), pp. 30–33.
29. Graham T. Allison, *Essence of Decision: Explaining the Cuban Missile Crisis* (Boston: Little, Brown, 1971), pp. 129–30.
30. Morton H. Halperin, *Bureaucratic Politics and Foreign Policy* (Washington, DC: Brookings Institution, 1974), chap. 4.
31. Kenneth F. O'Donnell, "LBJ and the Kennedys," *Life*, 7 August 1970, pp. 44–56.
32. Jerry Hagstrom and Robert Guskind, "Lobbying the Pentagon," *National Journal*, 31 May 1986, pp. 1316–21.
33. Edward N. Luttwak, *The Pentagon and the Art of War: The Question of Military Reform* (New York: Simon & Schuster, 1984), pp. 44–45.
34. Ibid., pp. 52–57; Richard Gabriel, "Scenes from an Invasion," *Washington Monthly*, February 1986, pp. 34–41.
35. Quoted in Luttwak, p. 61.
36. William J. Lynn and Barry R. Posen, "The Case for JCS Reform," *International Security* 10 (Winter 1985/86), pp. 69–97.
37. "Passing the Manhood Test," *Time*, 8 January 1990, p. 43.

SUGGESTED READINGS

Beckman, Peter R., et al. *The Nuclear Predicament: An Introduction*. Englewood Cliffs, NJ: Prentice-Hall, 1989.

Crabb, Cecil V., Jr., and Holt, Pat M. *Invitation to Struggle: Congress, the President, and Foreign Policy*, 3d ed. Washington, DC: Congressional Quarterly Press, 1989.

LaFeber, Walter. *The American Age: United States Foreign Policy at Home and Abroad Since 1750*. New York: Norton, 1989.

Morris, Charles R. *Iron Destinies, Lost Opportunities: The Arms Race Between the U.S.A. and the U.S.S.R., 1945–1987*. New York: Harper & Row, 1988.

Nelson, Daniel N., and Anderson, Roger B. *Soviet-American Relations*. Wilmington, DE: SR Books, 1988.

Newsom, David D. *Diplomacy and the American Democracy*. Bloomington, IN: Indiana University Press, 1988.

Rhodes, Edward. *Power and MADness: The Logic of Nuclear Coercion*. New York: Columbia University Press, 1989.

GLOSSARY

ABILITY-TO-PAY THEORY OF TAXATION An approach to government finance that holds that taxes should be based on individuals' ability to pay.

ADMINISTRATIVE LAW Rules adopted by regulatory agencies.

ADVERSARY PROCEEDING A legal procedure in which each side in a lawsuit presents evidence and arguments to bolster its position, while rebutting evidence that might support the other side.

AFFIRMATIVE ACTION The legal requirement that companies and other organizations take positive steps to remedy the effects of past discrimination.

AGENDA BUILDING The process through which issues become matters of public concern and governmental action.

AGENTS OF SOCIALIZATION Factors that contribute to political socialization by shaping formal and informal learning.

AMICUS CURIAE BRIEF A written legal argument presented by parties not directly involved in a case.

APPEAL The taking of a case from a lower court to a higher court by the losing party in a lower court decision.

APPEALS A technical term for the Supreme Court's decision to hear arguments and make a ruling in a case.

APPROPRIATION BILL A legislative authorization to spend money for particular purposes.

APPROPRIATION PROCESS The legislative procedure through which Congress provides money for a particular purpose.

AT-LARGE ELECTION A method for choosing public officials in which every citizen of a political subdivision, such as a city, or county, or state, votes to select a public official.

ATTENTIVE PUBLIC Persons who have an active and continuing interest in a particular political issue.

AUTHORITARIANISM The concentration of political power in one person or a small group of persons.

AUTHORIZATION PROCESS The legislative process through which Congress establishes a program, defines its general purpose, devises procedures for its operation, specifies an agency to implement the program, and indicates an approximate level of funding for the program (but does not provide the money).

BABY-BOOM GENERATION The exceptionally large group of Americans born during the late 1940s, 1950s, and early 1960s.

BAD-TENDENCY TEST A standard used by the Supreme Court to determine the permissible bounds of free speech, holding that any expression that has a tendency to lead to substantial evil can be banned by the government.

BALANCE OF POWER A system of political alignments in which peace and security may be maintained through an equilibrium of forces between rival groups of nations.

BIASED SAMPLE A survey sample that tends to produce results that don't reflect the true characteristics of the universe because it is unrepresentative of the universe.

BICAMERAL Referring to a legislature with two houses.

BILL OF ATTAINDER A law that declares a person, or group of persons, guilty of a crime and inflicts punishment without benefit of judicial proceedings.

BILL OF RIGHTS A constitutional document guaranteeing individual rights and liberties.

BIPARTISANSHIP The close cooperation and general agreement between the two major political parties in dealing with foreign-policy matters.

BLOCK GRANT PROGRAM A federal grant program that provides money for a program in a broad, general policy area.

BOND A certificate of indebtedness; an IOU.

BOND ELECTION A procedure used to obtain voter approval for state or local government to go into debt.

BRACKET CREEP The phenomenon of inflation pushing taxpayers into higher and higher brackets while their real earnings do not increase.

BUDGET An estimate of the receipts and expenditures needed by government to carry out its programs in some future period, usually a fiscal year.

BUDGET DEFICIT The amount by which budget expenditures exceed budget receipts.

BUDGET SURPLUS The amount by which budget receipts exceed expenditures.

BUSINESS CYCLE The rhythmic fluctuation of a free economy, involving movements from prosperity to recession, followed by economic recovery and a return to prosperity.

CABINET The president's advisory group, composed of the executive department heads and other officials the president may choose to include, such as the ambassador to the United Nations and the national security adviser.

CAPITAL GAINS TAX A levy assessed on income from investments.

CAPITAL PUNISHMENT   The death penalty.

CAPITALISM   An economic system based on individual and corporate ownership of the means of production and based on a supply-and-demand market economy.

CAPTURED AGENCIES   Agencies that work to benefit the economic interests they regulate rather than serving the public interest.

CASH-TRANSFER PROGRAM   A public assistance program that gives money directly to eligible recipients.

CATEGORICAL GRANT PROGRAM   A federal grant-in-aid program that provides funds to state and local governments for specific purposes.

CAUCUS METHOD OF DELEGATE SELECTION   A procedure for choosing national party convention delegates that involves party voters participating in a series of precinct and district or county political meetings.

CERTIORARI   A technical term for the Supreme Court's decision to hear arguments and make a ruling in a case.

CHECKS AND BALANCES   The overlapping of the powers of the branches of government so that public officials limit the authority of one another.

CHIEF EXECUTIVE   The head of the executive branch of government.

CIVIL CASE   A legal dispute concerning a private conflict between two parties—individuals, corporations, or government agencies.

CIVIL LIBERTIES   The protection of the individual from the unrestricted power of government.

CIVIL RIGHTS   The protection of the individual from arbitrary or discriminatory acts by government or by other individuals.

CIVILIAN SUPREMACY OF THE ARMED FORCES   The constitutional concept that the armed forces should be under the direct control of civilian authorities.

CLEAR-AND-PRESENT-DANGER RULE   A test used by the Supreme Court to measure the permissible bounds of free speech, holding that government may suppress expression that is of such a nature as to create a clear and present danger of a substantive evil that Congress has a right to prevent.

CLOTURE   The procedure for ending a filibuster.

CLUSTER SAMPLING   A survey research technique for taking a sample in stages.

COATTAIL EFFECT   A political phenomenon in which a strong candidate for one office gives a boost to fellow party members on the same ballot seeking other offices.

COLD WAR   The post–World War II period of global tensions between the United States and the Soviet Union.

COMMON LAW   Law made centuries ago by English judges who decided cases on the basis of local custom and precedent.

COMPARABLE WORTH   The concept that wages should be based on the value of a job to an employer.

CONCURRENT POWERS   Powers which are jointly exercised by the national and state governments.

CONCURRING OPINION   A written judicial statement by a justice or justices that agrees with the majority opinion's ruling but disagrees with its reasoning.

CONFEDERATION   A league of nearly independent states.

CONFERENCE   A closed meeting attended only by the justices of the Supreme Court.

CONFERENCE COMMITTEE   A special, joint committee created to negotiate differences on similar pieces of legislation passed by the House and Senate.

CONSERVATISM   The defense of the status quo against major changes in political, economic, or social institutions of society. Conservatives generally oppose governmental regulation and heavy government spending while favoring low taxes and traditional values.

CONSERVATIVE COALITION   An informal alliance in Congress between conservative Democrats, mostly from the South, and Republicans.

CONSTITUENCY SERVICE   The work of members of Congress and their staffs who attend to the individual, particular needs of constituents.

CONSTITUTION   The fundamental law by which a state or nation is organized and governed.

CONSTITUTIONAL AMENDMENT   A formal, written change or addition to the nation's governing document.

CONSTITUTIONAL LAW   Law that involves the interpretation and application of the Constitution.

CONSUMER PRICE INDEX (CPI)   A measure of inflation based on changes in the cost of a hypothetical market basket of goods and services.

CONTAINMENT   The postwar American policy of keeping the Soviet Union from expanding its sphere of control.

CONTRACT CASE   A civil suit dealing with disputes over written or implied legal agreements, such as a suit over a faulty roof-repair job.

CONVENTIONAL FORCES   Non-nuclear military resources.

CONVERGENCE THEORY   The view that communism and capitalism were evolving in similar ways; as they became more alike they would no longer be a threat to one another.

COST-BENEFIT ANALYSIS An evaluation of a proposed policy or regulation based on a comparison between its expected benefits and anticipated costs.

COST-OF-LIVING ADJUSTMENT (COLA) A mechanism designed to regularly increase the size of a payment, such as a Social Security pension check, to compensate for the effects of inflation.

CRIMINAL CASE A legal dispute dealing with an alleged violation of a penal law.

CURRENT SERVICES BUDGET An estimate of the cost of continuing present government programs at current levels.

DE FACTO SEGREGATION Racial separation resulting from factors other than law, such as housing patterns.

DE JURE SEGREGATION Racial separation established by law.

DEFENDANT The party charged with a criminal offense, or the responding party in a civil case.

DELEGATED POWERS The powers of the federal government that are specifically listed in the United States Constitution.

DEMOCRACY A system of government in which the people hold ultimate political power.

DEPRESSION A severe and prolonged economic slump.

DÉTENTE A period of improved relations between the United States and the USSR from the latter 1960s until the early 1970s.

DETERRENCE The ability of a nation to prevent a nuclear or conventional attack on itself or its allies by the threat of nuclear retaliation.

DEVELOPMENTAL PROGRAMS Programs designed to help communities to improve their economic positions.

DIPLOMACY The process by which nations carry on political relations with each other.

DIPLOMATIC RELATIONS A system of official contacts between two nations in which the countries exchange ambassadors and other diplomatic personnel and operate embassies in each other's country.

DIRECT DEMOCRACY A political system in which citizens vote directly on matters of public concern.

DISFRANCHISEMENT The act of depriving someone of the right to vote.

DISSENTING OPINION A written judicial statement by a justice or justices that disagrees with the decision of the court majority.

DOCTRINE OF NATURAL RIGHTS The belief that individual rights transcend the power of government.

DOMESTIC-RELATIONS CASE A civil suit based on the law involving the relationships between husband and wife, and between parents and children, such as divorce and child custody cases.

DOUBLE JEOPARDY The government's trying a criminal defendant twice for the same offense.

DOUBLE STANDARD The judicial doctrine that the Supreme Court will accept economic legislation as constitutional unless proven otherwise, while assuming governmental restrictions of the basic freedoms guaranteed by the Bill of Rights to be unconstitutional.

DUE PROCESS OF LAW A constitutional provision holding that government should follow fair and regular procedures in actions that might lead to an individual's suffering loss of life, liberty, or property.

ECONOMICS The process that determines the production, distribution, and consumption of goods and services in a society.

ELASTIC CLAUSE A provision in the Constitution granting Congress the power to make all laws "necessary and proper" for carrying out the delegated powers.

ELECTORAL COLLEGE The system established in the Constitution for indirect selection of the president and vice-president.

ELITE THEORY (ELITISM) The view that political power in America is held by a small group of people who control politics by controlling economic resources.

EMINENT DOMAIN The authority of government to take private property for public use upon just compensation.

EMPIRICAL ANALYSIS A method of study that relies on experience and scientific observation.

ENTITLEMENT PROGRAM A government program providing benefits to all persons qualified to receive them under law.

ENUMERATED POWERS The powers of the federal government that are specifically listed in the United States Constitution.

EQUAL RIGHTS AMENDMENT (ERA) A proposed amendment to the Constitution declaring that "[e]quality of rights under the law shall not be denied or abridged by the United States or any state on account of sex."

EQUITY A branch of law that allows a judge to do what is fair in a particular case regardless of the common law.

EX POST FACTO LAW A retroactive criminal statute which operates to the disadvantage of accused persons.

EXCISE TAX A tax levied on the manufacture, transportation, sale, or consumption of a particular item or set of related items.

EXCLUSIONARY RULE The judicial doctrine stating that when the police violate an individual's constitutional rights, the evidence obtained as a result of police misconduct or error cannot be used against the defendant.

EXECUTIVE AGREEMENTS International understandings between the president and foreign nations that do not require Senate ratification.

EXECUTIVE ORDER A rule or regulation issued by an executive official to an administrative agency or executive department.

EXECUTIVE POWER The power to enforce laws.

EXTERNAL POLITICAL EFFICACY Individuals' assessment of governmental responsiveness to their demands.

EXTERNALITY A cost or benefit not taken into account by private decision-makers.

EXTRADITION The return from one state (or nation) to another of a person accused of a crime.

FEDERAL PREEMPTION OF STATE AUTHORITY An act of Congress adopting regulatory policies that overrule state policies in a particular regulatory area.

FEDERATION (FEDERAL SYSTEM) A political system that divides power between a central government, with authority over the whole nation, and a series of state governments.

FELONY A serious crime, such as murder, rape, or burglary.

FEUDALISM The system of political organization found in Europe from the ninth to about the fifteenth century that provided for a hierarchical class structure with lords, vassals, and serfs.

FILIBUSTER An attempt to defeat a bill through prolonged debate.

FIRST STRIKE The initial offensive move of a general nuclear war, aimed at knocking out the other side's ability to retaliate.

FIRST-STRIKE CAPABILITY The capacity of a nation to launch an initial nuclear assault sufficient to cripple an adversary's ability to retaliate.

FISCAL POLICY The use of government spending and taxation for the purpose of achieving economic goals.

FISCAL YEAR The budget year.

FOCUS GROUP A session in which a moderator asks a number of voters a series of political questions or shows them political commercials and asks for their reaction.

FORMULA GRANT PROGRAM A federal grant program that awards funding on the basis of a formula established by Congress for every state and/or locality that qualifies.

FRANKING PRIVILEGE A rule of Congress that grants members free postage for official business.

FREE-RIDER BARRIER TO GROUP MEMBERSHIP The concept that individuals will have little incentive to join a group and contribute resources to it if the group's benefits go to members and nonmembers alike.

FRIEND OF THE COURT BRIEF A written legal brief presented by parties not directly involved in a court case.

FROSTBELT The Midwest and Northeast (U.S.).

FULL FAITH AND CREDIT CLAUSE A constitutional provision requiring that states recognize the official acts of other states.

GENDER GAP Differences in political opinion and behavior between men and women.

GENERAL ELECTION An election to fill state and national offices held in November of even-numbered years.

GERRYMANDERING The drawing of legislative district lines for political advantage.

GLASNOST A series of political reforms initiated by Soviet leader Mikhail Gorbachev; literally, "openness."

GOVERNMENT The institution with authority to set policy for society.

GRAND JURY A body of citizens who hear evidence against persons accused of serious crimes and determine whether the evidence is sufficient to bring the person to trial.

GRANDFATHER CLAUSE A requirement that all prospective voters pay a tax or pass a test, except those whose grandfathers had been eligible to vote at some earlier date.

GRANT-IN-AID PROGRAMS Programs through which Congress makes funds available to state and local governments for expenditure in accordance with set standards and conditions.

GREAT SOCIETY Legislative program proposed by President Lyndon Johnson.

GROSS NATIONAL PRODUCT (GNP) The total value of goods and services produced by an economy in a year—a standard measure of the size of a nation's economy.

HEAD OF STATE The official head of government.

HEROIC PRESIDENT A larger-than-life president who personifies the best in American government.

HUMAN-RIGHTS POLICY An approach to foreign affairs that based American trade, aid, and alliances on the way other governments treated their citizens.

HYPOTHESIS A specific prediction about events that can be tested by experimentation and the collection and analysis of data.

IMMUNITY FROM PROSECUTION An exemption from prosecution for self-incriminating testimony given to a witness in a judicial proceeding or congressional hearing.

IMPEACH To accuse an executive or judicial officeholder of committing offenses that may warrant removal from office.

IMPERIAL PRESIDENT A president who uses the considerable power of the office in a harmful fashion.

IMPLIED POWERS Those powers of Congress not specifically mentioned in the Constitution, but derived by implication from the delegated powers.

IMPORT QUOTA A limit placed on the amount of a given product that may be imported in a year.

IMPOUNDMENT Refusal of the president to spend funds already appropriated by Congress.

IN FORMA PAUPERIS A policy of waiving filing fees for litigants with limited funds who appeal their cases to the Supreme Court.

INCREMENTALIST MODEL OF BUDGETING A budget process based on small (incremental) changes in budget categories from one budget to the next, derived from a comparison with the prior year.

INCUMBENT A current officeholder.

INDIVIDUALISM The concept that places primary emphasis on the individual rather than the group or society as a whole.

INFLATION A general increase in prices that produces a decline in the purchasing power of the currency.

INFORMATION A formal accusation made under oath by a prosecuting attorney, charging a person with a crime.

INITIATIVE A procedure whereby citizens can propose legislation by gathering a certain number of signatures of registered voters on a petition.

IN-KIND BENEFITS PROGRAM A public assistance program that distributes goods and services directly to eligible recipients.

INNER CABINET The secretary of state, the secretary of defense, the secretary of the treasury, and the attorney general.

INTEREST Money paid for the use of money.

INTEREST AGGREGATION The process of organizing the concerns of diverse groups into a workable program.

INTEREST GROUP An organization of people who join together voluntarily on the basis of some interest they share, for the purpose of influencing policy.

INTERNAL POLITICAL EFFICACY Individuals' evaluations of their own ability to influence policy.

IRON TRIANGLE A cozy, mutually beneficial, three-sided relationship among governmental agencies, interest groups, and key members of Congress.

ISOLATIONISM American foreign policy emphasizing noninvolvement in the affairs of other nations.

ISSUE NETWORK A group of political actors concerned with some aspect of public policy.

JIM CROW LAWS Legal provisions that required the social segregation of blacks in separate and generally unequal facilities.

JOINT COMMITTEE A committee that includes members from both houses of Congress.

JUDICIAL ACTIVISM The principle that judges should use their position and authority to promote desirable social ends.

JUDICIAL POWER The power to interpret laws.

JUDICIAL RESTRAINT The principle that judges should avoid substituting their policy judgments for those of legislators and executives.

JUDICIAL REVIEW The power of courts to evaluate the actions of other branches and units of government to determine whether they are consistent with the Constitution and, if they are not, to declare them null and void.

JURISDICTION The authority of a court to hear and decide a case.

KEYNESIAN ECONOMICS An economic theory that utilizes the machinery of government to guide and direct a free enterprise economy.

LABOR PRODUCTIVITY The amount of output generated per worker.

LAISSEZ FAIRE An economic philosophy holding that government intervention impedes the free-market forces that drive a healthy economy.

LAW A rule of conduct prescribed by, or accepted by, the governing authority of a state or nation and enforced by courts.

LEGAL BRIEF A written legal argument.

LEGISLATIVE POWER The power to make laws.

LEGISLATIVE VETO A provision in a bill giving one or both houses of Congress, or a congressional committee, the authority to invalidate an action by the executive branch.

LIBEL False written statements that lower a person's reputation or expose a person to hatred, contempt, or ridicule.

LIBERALISM The political view that seeks to change the political, economic, or social status quo to foster the development and well-being of the individual. Liberals usually support government regulation of business and high levels of spending for social programs. On social issues, though, such as abortion and pornography regulation, liberals tend to support the right of adult free choice against government interference.

LINE-ITEM VETO   The power of an executive to veto sections or items of an appropriation bill while signing the remainder of the bill into law.

LITERACY TEST   A legal requirement that citizens demonstrate an ability to read and write before they can register to vote.

LITIGANTS   Parties to a lawsuit.

LOBBYIST   A representative for an interest group whose job is to present that group's point of view to political decision-makers.

LOOSE CONSTRUCTION   The doctrine holding that the Constitution should be interpreted broadly.

MAJORITY LEADER   The head of the majority party in the Senate; the second-ranking member of the majority party in the House.

MAJORITY OPINION   The official decision of a court that serves as a guideline for lower courts when similar legal issues arise.

MAJORITY WHIP   Assistant to the majority leader in the House or Senate.

MANDATE   A legislative requirement placed on a lower level of government by a higher level of government that requires the lower level of government to take certain policy actions.

MARGINAL TAX RATE   The rate of tax imposed on the last dollar earned.

MARK-UP   The process in which legislators go over a bill line-by-line, revising, amending, or rewriting it.

MARSHALL PLAN   An American program that provided billions of dollars to the countries of Western Europe to rebuild their economies after World War II.

MASSIVE RETALIATION   The doctrine that the United States will strike back against an aggressor with overwhelming force, including nuclear weapons.

MATCHING FUNDS   The legislative requirement that the national government will provide money for a project or program only on condition that the state or local government involved supply a certain percentage of the total money.

MATERIAL INCENTIVES TO GROUP MEMBERSHIP Benefits that can be measured in dollars and cents.

MINORITY BUSINESS SET-ASIDE   A legal requirement that firms receiving government grants or contracts allocate a certain percentage of their purchases of supplies and services to businesses owned or controlled by members of minority groups.

MINORITY LEADER   The head of the minority party in the House or Senate.

MINORITY-VOTE DILUTION   The drawing of election district lines to thinly spread minority voters among several districts, thus reducing their electoral influence in any one district.

MINORITY-VOTE PACKING   The drawing of election district lines to cluster minority voters into one district or a small number of districts.

MINORITY WHIP   Assistant to the minority leader in the House or Senate.

MIRV TECHNOLOGY   The capacity of a missile to carry multiple nuclear warheads, each programmed to strike a different target.

MISDEMEANOR   A relatively less serious offense, such as a minor traffic violation.

MIXED ECONOMY   An economy that combines some aspects of a capitalist economy with some features of socialism.

MONETARISM   The economic theory holding that stable economic growth can best be assured through management of the money supply.

MONETARY POLICY   The control of the money supply for the purpose of achieving economic goals.

MONOPOLY   A market condition in which a single firm is the sole supplier of a good or service.

MULTIPLE REFERRAL OF LEGISLATION   A practice that allows bills to be considered jointly, sequentially, or partially by more than one committee.

MUTUAL ASSURED DESTRUCTION (MAD)   The belief that the United States and the Soviet Union will both be deterred from launching a nuclear assault against the other for fear of being destroyed in a general nuclear war.

NATIONAL DEBT   The accumulated indebtedness of the federal government.

NATIONAL SUPREMACY CLAUSE   The constitutional provision that declares that the Constitution, the laws made under it, and the treaties of the United States are the supreme law of the land.

NATURAL MONOPOLY   A monopoly bestowed by nature on a geographical area, or one that, because of the nature of an enterprise, would make competition wasteful.

NECESSARY AND PROPER CLAUSE   The constitutional provision granting Congress the power to make all laws "necessary and proper" for carrying out the delegated powers.

NEOCLASSICAL INTERNATIONAL ECONOMIC THE-ORY An economic theory holding that the openness of the American economy makes it immune to economy-wide recessions, although slumps may strike certain weak industries.

NEW DEAL The legislative program proposed by President Franklin Roosevelt.

NEW WAVE ECONOMICS An economic theory holding that the openness of the American economy makes it immune to economy-wide recessions, although slumps may strike certain weak industries.

NIXON DOCTRINE A corollary to the U.S. policy of containment enunciated by President Richard Nixon offering economic and military aid to small nations threatened by communist aggression if those countries played a major role in their own defense.

NORMATIVE ANALYSIS A method of study based on certain values.

NORMS Unwritten but expected modes of behavior.

NORTH ATLANTIC TREATY ORGANIZATION (NATO) A regional defense alliance consisting of the United States, Canada, and their Western European allies, formed after World War II to defend against a Soviet attack in Western Europe.

OFF-BUDGET OPERATIONS Loans and loan guarantees made available by the federal government (but not included in the official budget document) to a broad array of individuals and institutions.

OFFICIAL AGENDA The set of problems that government actually chooses to attempt to remedy.

OLIGOPOLY A market condition in which only a few non-competitive firms control the supply of a good or a service.

OPERATIONALIZATION The process through which a hypothesis is stated in terms that can be tested experimentally.

OPINION LEADER Someone who shapes public attitudes about an issue.

ORGANIZATION OF PETROLEUM EXPORTING COUNTRIES (OPEC) A thirteen-nation oil cartel that attempts to set world oil prices.

ORIGINAL JURISDICTION The set of cases a court may hear as a trial court.

PARDON An executive action that frees an accused or convicted person from all penalty for an offense.

PARTY PLATFORM A statement of party principles and issue positions.

PER CURIAM OPINION An unsigned written opinion issued by the Supreme Court.

PERESTROIKA The Soviet economic reform program initiated by Mikhail Gorbachev; literally, "economic restructuring."

PHILLIPS CURVE An economic model holding that unemployment goes up as the rate of inflation goes down.

PLAINTIFF The party initiating a civil suit.

PLEA BARGAINING A procedure in which a defendant agrees to plead guilty in order to receive punishment less than the maximum for an offense, or plead guilty to a lesser offense than the original charge.

PLURALIST THEORY (PLURALISM) The view that diverse groups of elites with differing interests compete with one another to control policy in different issue areas.

POCKET VETO The action of a president allowing a bill to die without signature after Congress has adjourned.

POLICE POWER The authority of states to promote and safeguard the health, morals, safety, and welfare of the people.

POLICY ADOPTION The official decision of a governmental body to accept a particular policy and put it into effect.

POLICY EVALUATION The assessment of policy.

POLICY FORMULATION The development of courses of action for dealing with problems on the official agenda.

POLICY IMPLEMENTATION The stage of the policy process in which policies are carried out.

POLICY OUTCOMES The situations that arise as a result of the impact of policy in operation.

POLICY OUTPUTS Governmental policies.

POLITICAL ACTION COMMITTEE (PAC) An organization created to raise and distribute money in election campaigns.

POLITICAL CAMPAIGN An attempt to get information to voters that will persuade them to elect a candidate or not to elect an opponent.

POLITICAL CULTURE The widely held, deeply rooted political values of a society.

POLITICAL EFFICACY The extent to which people believe they can affect the policymaking process.

POLITICAL LEGITIMACY The popular acceptance of a government and its officials as rightful authorities in the exercise of power.

POLITICAL PARTY A group of individuals who join together voluntarily to seek political office in order to make policy.

POLITICAL PATRONAGE   The power of an officeholder to award favors, such as government jobs, to political allies.

POLITICAL SCIENCE   The academic discipline that deals with the theory and practice of politics and the description and analysis of political systems and political behavior.

POLITICAL SOCIALIZATION   The process whereby individuals acquire political knowledge, attitudes, and beliefs.

POLITICS   The process that determines who shall occupy the roles of leadership in government and how the power of government shall be exercised.

POLL TAX   A tax levied on the right to vote.

POPULAR SOVEREIGNTY   The concept that ultimate political power rests with the people.

POVERTY LINE   The amount of money an individual or family needs to purchase basic necessities, such as food, clothing, health care, shelter, and transportation.

POWER OF THE PURSE   The control of the finances of government.

PRECEDENT   A court ruling that sets a basis for deciding similar cases.

PRESIDENTIAL PREFERENCE PRIMARY   A procedure for selecting national party convention delegates in which party voters cast their ballots for the presidential candidate they prefer or for delegates pledged to support that candidate.

PRIMARY ELECTION   An intraparty election held to determine the party nominees for the general-election ballot.

PRIOR RESTRAINT   Government action to prevent the publication of objectionable materials.

PRIVILEGES AND IMMUNITIES CLAUSE   A constitutional provision requiring that the citizens of one state not be discriminated against when traveling in another state.

PROBATE CASE   A civil suit dealing with the disposition of the property of a deceased individual.

PROCEDURAL DUE PROCESS   The constitutional principle that laws should be executed, administered, and interpreted in accordance with accepted standards of justice.

PROGRESSIVE TAX   A levy that taxes persons earning higher incomes at a greater rate than it does individuals making less money.

PROJECT GRANT PROGRAM   A federal grant program that requires state and local governments to compete for available federal money.

PROPERTY CASE   A civil suit over the ownership of real estate or personal possessions, such as land, jewelry, or an automobile.

PROPORTIONAL REPRESENTATION   An election system that awards legislative seats to each party approximately equal to its popular voting strength.

PROPORTIONAL TAX   A levy that taxes all persons at the same percentage rate, regardless of income.

PROSECUTOR   The attorney who tries a criminal case on behalf of the government.

PUBLIC AGENDA   The set of problems that are raised to public concern.

PUBLIC OPINION   The combined personal opinions of adults toward issues of relevance to government.

PUBLIC POLICY   The response, or lack of response, of governmental decision-makers to an issue.

PUBLIC POLICY PROCESS   The process through which public policy is made.

PUBLIC UTILITY   A privately owned business that performs an essential service for the community.

PURITANS   Seventeenth-century English religious reformers.

PURPOSIVE INCENTIVES TO GROUP MEMBERSHIP   The rewards individuals find in working together for a cause in which they believe.

RACIAL QUOTA   A legal requirement that businesses and other organizations include within their membership or employment a certain percentage of minority group members.

RACIALLY RESTRICTIVE COVENANTS   Private deed restrictions that prohibited property owners from selling or leasing property to African-Americans or other minorities.

RANDOM SAMPLE   An unbiased sample in which each member of a universe has an equal likelihood of being included.

RATIONAL-EXPECTATIONS SCHOOL OF ECONOMICS   An economic theory holding that people closely observe government policies and then react in accordance with their own self-interest, which may run counter to policy objectives.

REAGAN DOCTRINE   A corollary to the U.S. policy of containment enunciated by President Reagan offering military aid to groups attempting to overthrow communist governments anywhere in the world.

REALIGNMENT   A change in the underlying party loyalties of voters.

RECALL   A procedure which allows voters to remove elected officials from office before expiration of their terms.

RECESSION   An economic slowdown characterized by declining economic output and rising unemployment.

REDISTRIBUTIVE PROGRAMS Programs designed to benefit low-income individuals or other disadvantaged groups, such as the elderly, minorities, and the disabled.

REDISTRICT To redraw boundaries of legislative districts to reflect population movement.

REFERENDUM An election in which voters approve or reject a legislative measure.

REGRESSIVE TAX A levy whose burden falls more heavily upon low-income groups than upon wealthy taxpayers, such as a sales tax.

RELIGIOUS TEST A legal requirement that an individual express belief in a particular religious faith or in a Supreme Being as a requirement for holding public office.

REPRESENTATIVE DEMOCRACY A political system in which citizens elect representatives to make public policy decisions on their behalf.

REPRIEVE An executive action that delays punishment.

REPUBLIC A political system in which citizens elect representatives to make public policy decisions on their behalf.

RESERVED POWERS The powers of government left to the states.

RESIDUAL POWERS The powers of government left to the states.

RESPONSIBLE PARTIES Political parties that clearly spell out issue positions in their platforms and faithfully carry them out in office.

RETROSPECTIVE VOTING Citizens' choosing of candidates based on their perception of an incumbent candidate's past performance in office or the performance of the incumbent party.

REVERSE DISCRIMINATION The allegation that governmental efforts on behalf of women and minority group members effectively discriminate against white males.

RIDER A provision, unlikely to become law on its own merits, that is attached to an important bill so that it will "ride" through the legislative process.

RULE A legally binding regulation.

RULE OF FOUR Decision process used by the Supreme Court to determine which cases to consider on appeal, holding that the Court will hear a case if four of the nine justices agree.

RULE OF LAW A political doctrine that holds that the discretion of public officials in dealing with individuals is limited by the law.

RULEMAKING The regulatory process used by government agencies to enact legally binding regulations.

RUNOFF PRIMARY An election procedure requiring a second election between the two top finishers should no candidate receive a majority of the vote in the initial primary.

SAMPLE In survey research, a subset of a universe.

SCIENCE A method of study concerned with describing and explaining certain phenomena through the formulation of theories and laws.

SCIENTIFIC LAW A theory that has not been disproved and is generally accepted as correct.

SCIENTIFIC THEORY A general, logical statement of relationships among characteristics and events that explains a particular range of phenomena.

SECOND STRIKE A nuclear attack in response to an adversary's first strike.

SECOND-STRIKE CAPABILITY The capacity of a nation to absorb an initial nuclear attack and retain sufficient nuclear firepower to inflict unacceptable damage on its adversary.

SELECT COMMITTEE A legislative committee established for a limited time.

SELECTIVE INCORPORATION OF THE BILL OF RIGHTS The process through which the United States Supreme Court has interpreted the due process clause of the Fourteenth Amendment of the United States Constitution to apply most of the provisions of the national Bill of Rights to the states.

SENATORIAL COURTESY The custom that senators from the president's party have the right to veto judicial appointments from their states.

SENIORITY The length of continuous service a member has with a legislative body.

SEPARATE-BUT-EQUAL The judicial doctrine holding that separate facilities for whites and blacks satisfy the equal-protection requirement of the Fourteenth Amendment.

SEPARATION OF POWERS The division of political power among executive, legislative, and judicial branches of government.

SINGLE-ISSUE GROUP An interest group that focuses its efforts on a single issue or a group of related issues.

SINGLE-MEMBER DISTRICT ELECTION A method for choosing public officials in which a political subdivision, such as a state, is divided into districts and each district elects one official.

SLANDER False oral statements that lower a person's reputation or expose a person to hatred, contempt, or ridicule.

SOCIAL CONTRACT THEORY The philosophy that government is created through an informal contract, or compact, among the people and a formal contract (a constitution) between the people and the government.

SOCIALISM   An economic system based on governmental ownership of the means of production, such as factories, land, banks, and businesses.

SOFT MONEY   Campaign funds raised by political parties to support their presidential ticket.

SOLIDARY INCENTIVES TO GROUP MEMBERSHIP   Social benefits arising from associating with other group members.

SOVEREIGNTY   The authority of a state to exercise its legitimate powers within its boundaries, free from external interference.

SPECIAL COMMITTEE   A legislative committee established for a limited time.

SPECIAL ELECTION   An election called at a time outside the normal election calendar.

SPLIT-LEVEL REALIGNMENT   A change in voter allegiances that produces an advantage for one political party in contests for one office or set of offices while another party has the upper hand in other races.

SPLIT-TICKET VOTING   Citizens' voting for candidates of two or more parties for different offices.

SPOILS SYSTEM   The method of hiring government employees from among the friends and supporters of elected officeholders.

STAGFLATION   An economic condition in which high unemployment, reduced output, and high rates of inflation exist at the same time.

STANDING COMMITTEE   A permanent legislative committee.

STARE DECISIS   The legal principle that court decisions stand as precedents for future cases involving the same issues.

STATES' RIGHTS   An interpretation of the Constitution that would limit the implied powers of the federal government while expanding the reserved powers of the states.

STATUTORY LAW   Law written by the legislature.

STRAIGHT-TICKET VOTING   Citizens' voting for all the candidates of a single party.

STRATEGIC DEFENSE INITIATIVE (SDI)   A plan to develop a futuristic space-based ballistic missile defense system.

STRATEGIC FORCES   Nuclear weaponry.

STRICT CONSTRUCTION   The doctrine holding that the Constitution should be interpreted narrowly.

STRICT JUDICIAL SCRUTINY   The decision-rule holding that the Supreme Court will find a governmental policy unconstitutional unless government can demonstrate a compelling governmental interest justifying the action.

SUBGOVERNMENT   A cozy, mutually beneficial, three-sided relationship among government agencies, interest groups, and key members of Congress.

SUBSIDY   A financial incentive bestowed by government upon private individuals, companies, or groups to improve their economic position and accomplish some public objective.

SUBSTANTIVE DUE PROCESS   The constitutional principle that legislative and executive actions should be neither arbitrary nor unreasonable, nor should they cover subject matter beyond the reach of government.

SUFFRAGE   The right to vote.

SUNBELT   The South and Southwest (U.S.).

SUPPLY-SIDE ECONOMICS   The economic theory that focuses on factors, such as tax rates, that affect the supply of goods and services in the economy.

SURVEY RESEARCH   The measurement of public opinion.

SUSPECT CLASSIFICATION DOCTRINE   The judicial principle that certain types of distinctions among persons violate the equal protection clause of the Fourteenth Amendment unless government can demonstrate that it has a "compelling governmental interest" for making the challenged classification and that it can achieve that interest in no other way.

TABLE   To postpone consideration of a legislative measure.

TARIFF   A tax levied on imported goods.

TAX DEDUCTION   An expenditure, such as a charitable contribution, that can be subtracted from a taxpayer's gross income before computing the tax owed.

TAX EXEMPTION   The exclusion of some types of income from taxation.

TAX INCIDENCE   The point at which the actual cost of a tax falls.

TAX PREFERENCE   A tax deduction or exclusion that allows individuals to pay less tax than they would otherwise.

TEST CASE   A lawsuit initiated to assess the constitutionality of a legislative or executive act.

TEST OF UNDERSTANDING   A legal requirement that citizens must accurately explain a passage in the U.S. Constitution or a state constitution before they can register to vote.

TETHERED PRESIDENT   A president whose powers are too constrained to provide necessary policy leadership.

THIRD WORLD   Nonindustrialized nations that are not aligned with either the capitalist (First World) or communist (Second World) groups of countries.

TORT CASE   A civil suit involving personal injury or damage to property, such as a lawsuit stemming from an airplane crash.

TOTALITARIANISM   A form of authoritarianism in which the government controls nearly every aspect of people's lives.

TRADE DEFICIT   The amount by which the value of a nation's imports exceeds its exports.

TRIAD   The three systems the United States employs to deliver nuclear warheads to their targets, including intercontinental ballistic missiles (ICBMs), submarine-launched ballistic missiles (SLBMs), and manned bombers.

TRIAL   The formal examination of a civil or criminal action in accordance with law before a single judge who has jurisdiction to hear the dispute.

TRUMAN DOCTRINE   The foreign policy put forward by President Harry Truman supporting all free peoples resisting communist aggression by internal or outside forces.

TWO-PRESIDENCIES THESIS   The hypothesis that presidents have more influence over foreign affairs than they do over domestic policy.

TYRANNY OF THE MAJORITY   The abuse of the minority by the majority.

UNCONTROLLABLE EXPENDITURES   Funds that must be included in the budget because of existing contracts or laws.

UNICAMERAL   Referring to a one-house legislature.

UNITARY GOVERNMENT   A governmental system in which political authority is concentrated in a single national government.

UNITED NATIONS (UN)   An international organization founded in 1945 as a diplomatic forum to resolve conflict among the world's nations.

UNIVERSE   In survey research, the population being studied.

USE IMMUNITY   An exemption from prosecution that protects individuals from having their actual testimony used against them, but does not shelter them from a prosecution based on evidence gained by other means.

VETERANS' PREFERENCE   The system that awards extra points on civil service exams to veterans of the armed forces.

WARRANT   An official authorization for some action.

WARSAW PACT   A military alliance joining the Soviet Union and most of the countries of Eastern Europe.

WHITE PRIMARY   An electoral system used in the South that prevented the participation of blacks in the Democratic primary.

WRIT OF HABEAS CORPUS   A court order requiring government authorities either to release a person held in custody or to demonstrate that the person is detained in accordance with law.

WRIT OF MANDAMUS   A court order directing a public official to perform a specific act or duty.

ZONING   The regulation by law of the uses to which land may be put.

THE DECLARATION OF INDEPENDENCE
IN CONGRESS, JULY 4, 1776

*The unanimous Declaration
of the thirteen united States of America.*

When in the Course of human events, it becomes necessary for one people to dissolve the political bands which have connected them with another, and to assume among the Powers of the earth, the separate and equal station to which the Laws of Nature and of Nature's God entitle them, a decent respect to the opinions of mankind requires that they should declare the causes which impel them to the separation.

We hold these truths to be self-evident, that all men are created equal, that they are endowed by their Creator with certain unalienable Rights, that among these are Life, Liberty and the pursuit of Happiness. That to secure these rights, Governments are instituted among Men, deriving their just powers from the consent of the governed. That whenever any Form of Government becomes destructive of these ends, it is the Right of the People to alter or to abolish it, and to institute new Government, laying its foundation on such principles and organizing its powers in such form, as to them shall seem most likely to effect their Safety and Happiness. Prudence, indeed, will dictate that Governments long established should not be changed for light and transient causes; and accordingly all experience hath shown, that mankind are more disposed to suffer, while evils are sufferable, than to right themselves by abolishing the forms to which they are accustomed. But when a long train of abuses and usurpations, pursuing invariably the same Object evinces a design to reduce them under absolute Despotism, it is their right, it is their duty, to throw off such Government, and to provide new Guards for their future security.— Such has been the patient sufferance of these Colonies; and such is now the necessity which constrains them to alter their former Systems of Government. The history of the present King of Great Britain is a history of repeated injuries and usurpations, all having in direct object the establishment of an absolute Tyranny over these States. To prove this, let Facts be submitted to a candid world.

He has refused his Assent to Laws, the most wholesome and necessary for the public good.

He has forbidden his Governors to pass Laws of immediate and pressing importance, unless suspended in their operation till his Assent should be obtained; and when so suspended, he has utterly neglected to attend to them.

He has refused to pass other Laws for the accommodation of large districts of people, unless those people would relinquish the right of Representation in the Legislature, a right inestimable to them and formidable to tyrants only.

He has called together legislative bodies at places unusual, uncomfortable, and distant from the depository of their Public Records, for the sole purpose of fatiguing them into compliance with his measures.

He has dissolved Representative Houses repeatedly, for opposing with manly firmness his invasions on the rights of the people.

He has refused for a long time, after such dissolutions, to cause others to be elected; whereby the Legislative Powers, incapable of Annihilation, have returned to the People at large for their exercise; the State remaining in the mean time exposed to all the dangers of invasion from without, and convulsions within.

He has endeavoured to prevent the population of these States; for that purpose obstructing the Laws for Naturalization of Foreigners; refusing to pass others to encourage their migrations hither, and raising the conditions of new Appropriations of Lands.

He has obstructed the Administration of Justice, by refusing his Assent to Laws for establishing Judiciary Powers.

He has made Judges dependent on his Will alone, for the tenure of their offices, and the amount and payment of their salaries.

He has erected a multitude of New Offices, and sent hither swarms of Officers to harass our people, and eat out their substance.

He has kept among us, in times of peace, Standing Armies without the Consent of our legislatures.

He has affected to render the Military independent of and superior to the Civil Power.

He has combined with others to subject us to a jurisdiction foreign to our constitution, and unacknowledged by our laws; giving his Assent to their acts of pretended Legislation:

For quartering large bodies of armed troops among us:

For protecting them, by a mock Trial, from Punishment for any Murders which they should commit on the inhabitants of these States:

For cutting off our Trade with all parts of the world:

For imposing taxes on us without our Consent:

For depriving us in many cases, of the benefits of Trial by Jury:

For transporting us beyond Seas to be tried for pretended offences:

For abolishing the free System of English Laws in a neighbouring Province, establishing therein an Arbitrary government, and enlarging its Boundaries so as to render it at once an example and fit instrument for introducing the same absolute rule into these Colonies:

For taking away our Charters, abolishing our most valuable Laws, and altering fundamentally the Forms of our Governments:

For suspending our own Legislatures, and declaring themselves invested with Power to legislate for us in all cases whatsoever.

He has abdicated Government here, by declaring us out of his Protection and waging War against us.

He has plundered our seas, ravaged our Coasts, burnt our towns, and destroyed the lives of our people.

He is at this time transporting large armies of foreign mercenaries to compleat the works of death, desolation and tyranny, already begun with circumstances of Cruelty & perfidy scarcely paralleled in the most barbarous ages, and totally unworthy the Head of a civilized nation.

He has constrained our fellow Citizens taken Captive on the high Seas to bear Arms against their Country, to become the executioners of their friends and Brethren, or to fall themselves by their Hands.

He has excited domestic insurrections amongst us, and has endeavoured to bring on the inhabitants of our frontiers, the merciless Indian Savages, whose known rule of warfare, is an undistinguished destruction of all ages, sexes and conditions.

In every stage of these Oppressions We have Petitioned for Redress in the most humble terms: Our repeated Petitions have been answered only by repeated injury. A Prince, whose character is thus marked by every act which may define a Tyrant, is unfit to be the ruler of a free people.

Nor have we been wanting in attentions to our British brethren. We have warned them from time to time of attempts by their legislature to extend an unwarrantable jurisdiction over us. We have reminded them of the circumstances of our emigration and settlement here. We have appealed to their native justice and magnanimity, and we have conjured them by the ties of our common kindred to disavow these usurpations which, would inevitably interrupt our connections and correspondence. They too have been deaf to the voice of justice and of consanguinity. We must, therefore, acquiesce in the necessity, which denounces our Separation, and hold them, as we hold the rest of mankind, Enemies in War, in Peace Friends.

We, therefore, the Representatives of the united States of America, in General Congress, Assembled, appealing to the Supreme Judge of the world for the rectitude of our intentions, do, in the Name, and by authority of the good People of these Colonies, solemnly publish and declare, That these United Colonies are, and of Right ought to be Free and Independent States; that they are Absolved from all Allegiance to the British Crown, and that all political connection between them and the State of Great Britain, is and ought to be totally dissolved; and that as Free and Independent States, they have full power to levy War, conclude Peace, contract Alliances, establish Commerce, and to do all other Acts and Things which Independent States may of right do. And for the support of this Declaration, with a firm reliance on the Protection of Divine Providence, we mutually pledge to each other our Lives, our Fortunes and our sacred Honor.

THE CONSTITUTION OF THE UNITED STATES OF AMERICA

We the People of the United States, in Order to form a more perfect Union, establish justice, insure domestic Tranquility, provide for the common defence, promote the general Welfare, and secure the Blessings of Liberty to ourselves and our Posterity, do ordain and establish this Constitution for the United States of America.

ARTICLE I

Section 1.

All legislative Powers herein granted shall be vested in a Congress of the United States, which shall consist of a Senate and House of Representatives.

Section 2.

The House of Representatives shall be composed of Members chosen every second Year by the People of the several States, and the Electors in each State shall have the Qualifications requisite for Electors of the most numerous Branch of the State Legislature.

No Person shall be a Representative who shall not have attained to the Age of twenty five Years, and been seven Years a Citizen of the United States, and who shall not, when elected, be an Inhabitant of that State in which he shall be chosen.

Representatives and direct Taxes shall be apportioned among the several States which may be included within this Union, according to their respective Numbers, which shall be determined by adding to the whole Number of free Persons, including those bound to Service for a Term of Years, and excluding Indians not taxed, three fifths of all other Persons.[1] The actual Enumeration shall be made within three years after the first Meeting of the Congress of the United States, and within every subsequent Term of ten Years, in such Manner as they shall by Law direct. The Number of Representatives shall not exceed one for every thirty Thousand, but each State shall have at Least one Representative; and until such enumeration shall be made, the State of New Hampshire shall be entitled to chuse three, Massachusetts eight, Rhode-Island and Providence Plantations one, Connecticut five, New-York six, New Jersey four, Pennsylvania eight, Delaware one, Maryland six, Virginia ten, North Carolina five, South Carolina five, and Georgia three.

When vacancies happen in the Representation from any State, the Executive Authority thereof shall issue Writs of Election to fill such Vacancies.

The House of Representatives shall chuse their Speaker and other Officers; and shall have the sole Power of Impeachment.

Section 3.

The Senate of the United States shall be composed of two Senators from each State, chosen by the Legislature thereof, for six Years; and each Senator shall have one Vote.

Immediately after they shall be assembled in Consequence of the first Election, they shall be divided as equally as may be into three Classes. The Seats of the Senators of the first Class shall be vacated at the Expiration of the second Year, of the second Class at the Expiration of the fourth Year, and of the third Class at the Expiration of the Sixth Year, so that one third may be chosen every second Year; and if Vacancies happen by Resignation, or otherwise, during the Recess of the Legislature of any State, the Executive thereof may make temporary Appointments until the next Meeting of the Legislature, which shall then fill such Vacancies.[2]

No Person shall be a Senator who shall not have attained to the Age of thirty Years, and been nine Years a Citizen of the United States, and who shall not, when elected, be an Inhabitant of that State for which he shall be chosen.

The Vice President of the United States shall be President of the Senate, but shall have no Vote, unless they be equally divided.

The Senate shall chuse their other Officers, and also a President pro tempore, in the Absence of the Vice President, or when he shall exercise the Office of President of the United States.

The Senate shall have the sole Power to try all impeachments. When sitting for that Purpose, they shall be on Oath or Affirmation. When the President of the United States is tried the Chief Justice shall preside: And no Person shall be convicted without the Concurrence of two thirds of the Members present.

Judgment in Cases of Impeachment shall not extend further than to removal from Office, and disqualification to hold and enjoy any Office of honor, Trust or Profit under the United States; but the Party convicted shall nevertheless be liable and subject to Indictment, Trial, Judgment and Punishment, according to Law.

---

[1] "Other Persons" being black slaves. Modified by Amendment XIV, Section 2.

[2] Provisions changed by Amendment XVII.

Section 4.

The Times, Places and Manner of holding Elections for Senators and Representatives, shall be prescribed in each State by the Legislature thereof; but the Congress may at any time by Law make or alter such Regulations, except as to the Places of chusing Senators.

The Congress shall assemble at least once in every Year, and such Meeting shall be on the first Monday in December, unless they shall by Law appoint a different Day.[3]

Section 5.

Each House shall be the Judge of the Elections, Returns and Qualifications of its own Members, and a Majority of each shall constitute a Quorum to do Business; but a smaller Number may adjourn from day to day, and may be authorized to compel the Attendance of absent Members, in such Manner, and under such Penalties as each House may provide.

Each House may determine the Rules of its Proceedings, punish its Members for disorderly Behaviour, and, with the Concurrence of two thirds, expel a Member.

Each House shall keep a Journal of its Proceedings, and from time to time publish the same, excepting such Parts as may in their Judgment require Secrecy; and the Yeas and Nays of the Members of either House on any question shall, at the Desire of one fifth of those Present, be entered on the Journal.

Neither House, during the Session of Congress, shall, without the Consent of the other, adjourn for more than three days, nor to any other Place than that in which the two Houses shall be sitting.

Section 6.

The Senators and Representatives shall receive a Compensation for their Services, to be ascertained by Law, and paid out of the Treasury of the United States. They shall in all Cases, except Treason, Felony and Breach of the Peace, be privileged from Arrest during their Attendance at the Session of their respective Houses, and in going to and returning from the same; and for any Speech or Debate in either House, they shall not be questioned in any other Place.

No Senator or Representative shall, during the Time for which he was elected, be appointed to any civil Office under the Authority of the United States, which shall have been created, or the Emoluments whereof shall have been encreased during such time; and no Person holding any Office under the United States, shall be a Member of either House during his Continuance in Office.

Section 7.

All Bills for raising Revenue shall originate in the House of Representatives; but the Senate may propose or concur with Amendments as on other Bills.

Every Bill which shall have passed the House of Representatives and the Senate, shall, before it become a Law, be presented to the President of the United States; If he approve he shall sign it, but if not he shall return it, with his Objections to that House in which it shall have originated, who shall enter the Objections at large on their Journal, and proceed to reconsider it. If after such Reconsideration two thirds of that House shall agree to pass the Bill, it shall be sent, together with the Objections, to the other House, by which it shall likewise to be reconsidered, and if approved by two thirds of that House, it shall become a Law. But in all such Cases the Votes of both Houses shall be determined by yeas and Nays, and the Names of the Persons voting for and against the Bill shall be entered on the Journal of each House respectively. If any Bill shall not be returned by the President within ten Days (Sundays excepted) after it shall have been presented to him, the Same shall be a Law, in like Manner as if he had signed it, unless the Congress by their Adjournment prevent its Return, in which Case it shall not be a Law.

Every Order, Resolution, or Vote to which the Concurrence of the Senate and House of Representatives may be necessary (except on a question of Adjournment) shall be presented to the President of the United States; and before the Same shall take Effect, shall be approved by him, or being disapproved by him, shall be repassed by two thirds of the Senate and House of Representatives, according to the Rules and Limitations prescribed in the Case of a Bill.

Section 8.

The Congress shall have Power To lay and collect Taxes, Duties, Imposts and Excises, to pay the Debts and provide for the common Defence and general Welfare of the United States; but all Duties, Imposts and Excises shall be uniform throughout the United States;

To borrow Money on the credit of the United States;

To regulate Commerce with foreign Nations, and among the several States, and with the Indian Tribes;

To establish an uniform Rule of Naturalization, and uniform Laws on the subject of Bankruptcies throughout the United States;

To coin Money, regulate the Value thereof, and of foreign Coin, and fix the Standard of Weights and Measures;

To provide for the Punishment of counterfeiting the Securities and current Coin of the United States;

To establish Post Offices and post Roads;

To promote the Progress of Science and useful Arts, by securing for limited Times to Authors and Inventors the exclusive Right to their respective Writings and Discoveries;

To constitute Tribunals inferior to the supreme Court;

To define and punish Piracies and Felonies committed on the high Seas, and Offences against the Law of Nations;

To declare War, grant Letters of Marque and Reprisal, and make Rules concerning Captures on Land and Water;

To raise and support Armies, but no Appropriation of Money to that Use shall be for a longer Term than two Years;

---

[3] Provision changed by Amendment XX, Section 2.

To provide and maintain a Navy;

To make Rules for the Government and Regulation of the land and naval Forces;

To provide for calling forth the Militia to execute the Laws of the Union, suppress Insurrections and repel Invasions;

To provide for organizing, arming, and disciplining, the Militia, and for governing such Part of them as may be employed in the Service of the United States, reserving to the States respectively, the Appointment of the Officers, and the Authority of training the Militia according to the discipline prescribed by Congress;

To exercise exclusive Legislation in all Cases whatsoever, over such District (not exceeding ten Miles square) as may, by Cession of particular States, and the Acceptance of Congress, become the Seat of the Government of the United States, and to exercise like Authority over all Places purchased by the Consent of the Legislature of the State in which the Same shall be, for the Erection of Forts, Magazines, Arsenals, dock-Yards, and other needful Buildings;—And

To make all Laws which shall be necessary and proper for carrying into Execution the foregoing Powers, and all other Powers vested by this Constitution in the Government of the United States, or in any Department or Officer thereof.

Section 9.

The Migration or Importation of such Persons as any of the States now existing shall think proper to admit, shall not be prohibited by the Congress prior to the Year one thousand eight hundred and eight, but a Tax, or duty may be imposed on such Importation, not exceeding ten dollars for each Person.

The Privilege of the Writ of Habeas Corpus shall not be suspended, unless when in Cases of Rebellion or Invasion the public Safety may require it.

No Bill of Attainder or ex post facto Law shall be passed.

No Capitation, or other direct, Tax shall be laid, unless in Proportion to the Census or Enumeration herein before directed to be taken.

No Tax or Duty shall be laid on Articles exported from any State.

No Preference shall be given by any Regulation of Commerce or Revenue to the Ports of one State over those of another; nor shall Vessels bound to, or from, one State, be obliged to enter, clear, or pay Duties in another.

No Money shall be drawn from the Treasury, but in Consequence of Appropriations made by Law; and a regular Statement and Account of the Receipts and Expenditures of all public Money shall be published from time to time.

No Title of Nobility shall be granted by the United States: And no Person holding any Office of Profit or Trust under them, shall without the Consent of the Congress, accept of any present, Emolument, Office, or Title, of any kind whatever, from any King, Prince, or foreign State.

Section 10.

No State shall enter into any Treaty, Alliance, or Confederation; grant Letters of Marque and Reprisal; coin Money; emit Bills of Credit; make any Thing but gold and silver Coin a Tender in Payment of Debts; pass any Bill of Attainder, ex post facto Law, or Law impairing the Obligation of Contracts, or grant any Title of Nobility.

No State shall, without the Consent of the Congress, lay any Imposts or Duties on Imports or Exports, except what may be absolutely necessary for executing its inspection Laws; and the net Produce of all Duties and Imposts, laid by any State on Imports or Exports, shall be for the Use of the Treasury of the United States; and all such Laws shall be subject to the Revision and Control of the Congress.

No State shall, without the Consent of Congress, lay any Duty of Tonnage, keep Troops, or Ships of War in time of Peace, enter into any Agreement or Compact with another State, or with a foreign Power, or engage in War, unless actually invaded, or in such imminent Danger as will not admit of delay.

ARTICLE II

Section 1.

The executive Power shall be vested in a President of the United States of America. He shall hold his Office during the Term of four Years, and, together with the Vice President, chosen for the same Term, be elected, as follows:

Each State shall appoint, in such Manner as the Legislature thereof may direct, a Number of Electors, equal to the whole Number of Senators and Representatives to which the State may be entitled in Congress; but no Senator or Representative, or Person holding an Office of Trust or Profit under the United States, shall be appointed an Elector.

The Electors shall meet in their respective States, and vote by Ballot for two Persons, of whom one at least shall not be an Inhabitant of the same State with themselves. And they shall make a List of all the Persons voted for, and of the Number of Votes for each; which List they shall sign and certify, and transmit sealed to the Seat of the Government of the United States, directed to the President of the Senate. The President of the Senate shall, in the Presence of the Senate and House of Representatives, open all the Certificates, and the Votes shall then be counted. The Person having the greatest Number of Votes shall be the President, if such Number be a Majority of the whole Number of Electors appointed; and if there be more than one who have such Majority, and have an equal Number of Votes, then the House of Representatives shall immediately chuse by Ballot one of them for President; and if no Person have a Majority, then from the five highest on the List the said House shall in like Manner chuse the President. But in chusing the President, the Votes shall be taken by States, the Representation from each State having one Vote; A quorum for this Purpose shall consist of a Member or Members from two thirds of the States, and a Majority of all the States shall be necessary to a Choice. In every Case, after the Choice of the President, the Person having the greatest Number of Votes of the Electors shall be the Vice President. But if there should remain two or more who have equal Votes, the Senate shall chuse from them by Ballot the Vice President.[4]

The Congress may determine the Time of chusing the Electors, and the Day on which they shall give their Votes; which Day shall be the same throughout the United States.

No Person except a natural born Citizen, or a Citizen of the United States, at the time of the Adoption of this Constitution, shall be eligible to the Office of President; neither shall any Person be eligible to that Office who shall not have attained to the Age of thirty five Years, and been fourteen Years a Resident within the United States.

In Case of the Removal of the President from Office, or of his Death, Resignation, or Inability to discharge the Powers and Duties of the said Office, the Same shall devolve on the Vice President, and the Congress may by Law provide for the Case of Removal, Death, Resignation or Inability, both of the President and Vice President, declaring what Officer shall then act as President, and such Officer shall act accordingly, until the Disability be removed, or a President shall be elected.

The President shall, at stated Times, receive for his Services, a Compensation, which shall neither be encreased nor diminished during the Period for which he shall have been elected, and he shall not receive within that Period any other Emolument from the United States, or any of them.

Before he enter on the Execution of his Office, he shall take the following Oath or Affirmation: — "I do solemnly swear (or affirm) that I will faithfully execute the Office of President of the United States, and will to the best of my Ability, preserve, protect and defend the Constitution of the United States."

Section 2.

The President shall be Commander in Chief of the Army and Navy of the United States, and of the Militia of the several States, when called into the actual Service of the United States; he may require the Opinion, in writing, of the principal Officer in each of the executive Departments, upon any Subject relating to the Duties of their respective Offices, and he shall have Power to grant Reprieves and Pardons for Offences against the United States, except in Cases of Impeachment.

He shall have Power, by and with the Advice and Consent of the Senate, to make Treaties, provided two thirds of the Senators present concur; and he shall nominate, and by and with the Advice and Consent of the Senate, shall appoint Ambassadors, other public Ministers and Consuls, Judges of the supreme Court, and all other Officers of the United States, whose Appointments are not herein otherwise provided for, and which shall be established by Law: but the Congress may by Law vest the Appointment of such inferior Officers, as they think proper in the President alone, in the Courts of Law, or in the Heads of Departments.

The President shall have Power to fill up all Vacancies that may happen during the Recess of the Senate, by granting Commissions which shall expire at the end of their next Session.

Section 3.

He shall from time to time give the Congress Information of the State of the Union, and recommend to their Consideration such Measures as he shall judge necessary and expedient; he may, on extraordinary Occasions, convene both Houses, or either of them, and in Case of Disagreement between them, with Respect to the Time of Adjournment, he may adjourn them to such Time as he shall think proper; he shall receive Ambassadors and other public Ministers; he shall take Care that Laws be faithfully executed, and shall Commission all the Officers of the United States.

Section 4.

The President, Vice President and all civil Officers of the United States, shall be removed from Office on Impeachment for, and Conviction of, Treason, Bribery, or other high Crimes and Misdemeanors.

ARTICLE III

Section 1.

The judicial Power of the United States, shall be vested in one supreme Court, and in such inferior Courts as the Congress may from time to time ordain and establish. The Judges, both of the supreme and inferior Courts, shall hold their Offices during good Behaviour, and shall, at stated Times, receive for their Services, a Compensation, which shall not be diminished during their Continuance in Office.

Section 2.

The judicial Power shall extend to all Cases in Law and Equity, arising under this Constitution, the Laws of the United States, and Treaties made, or which shall be made, under their Authority;—to all Cases affecting Ambassadors, other public Ministers and Consuls;—to all Cases of admiralty and maritime Jurisdiction;—to Controversies to which the United States shall be a Party;—to Controversies between two or more states;—between a State and Citizens of another

---

[4] Provisions superseded by Amendment XII.

State;—between Citizens of different States;—between Citizens of the same State claiming Lands under Grants of different States, and between a State, or the Citizens thereof, and foreign States, Citizens or Subjects.[5]

In all Cases affecting Ambassadors, other public Ministers and Consuls, and those in which a State shall be Party, the supreme Court shall have original Jurisdiction. In all the other Cases before mentioned, the supreme Court shall have appellate Jurisdiction, both as to Law and Fact, with such Exceptions, and under such Regulations as the Congress shall make.

The Trial of all Crimes, except in Cases of Impeachment, shall be by Jury; and such Trial shall be held in the State where the said Crimes shall have been committed, but when not committed within any State, the Trial shall be at such Place or Places as the Congress may by law have directed.

Section 3.

Treason against the United States, shall consist only in levying War against them, or in adhering to their Enemies, giving them Aid and Comfort. No person shall be convicted of Treason unless on the Testimony of two Witnesses to the same overt Act, or on Confession in open Court.

The Congress shall have Power to declare the Punishment of Treason, but no Attainder of Treason shall work Corruption of Blood, or Forfeiture except during the Life of the Person attainted.

ARTICLE IV

Section 1.

Full Faith and Credit shall be given in each State to the public Acts, Records, and judicial Proceedings of every other State. And the Congress may by general Laws prescribe the Manner in which such Acts, Records and Proceedings shall be proved, and the Effect thereof.

Section 2.

The Citizens of each State shall be entitled to all Privileges and Immunities of Citizens in the several States.

A Person charged in any State with Treason, Felony, or other Crime, who shall flee from Justice, and be found in another State, shall on Demand of the executive Authority of the State from which he fled, be delivered up, to be removed to the State having Jurisdiction of the Crime.

No Person held to Service or Labour in one State, under the Laws thereof, escaping into another, shall, in Consequence of any Law or Regulation therein, be discharged from such Service or Labour, but shall be delivered up on Claim of the Party to whom such Service or Labour may be due.

---

[5] Clause changed by Amendment XI.

Section 3.

New States may be admitted by the Congress into this Union; but no new State shall be formed or erected within the jurisdiction of any other State; nor any State be formed by the Junction of two or more States, or Parts of States, without the Consent of the Legislatures of the States concerned as well as of the Congress.

The Congress shall have Power to dispose of and make all needful Rules and Regulations respecting the Territory or other Property belonging to the United States; and nothing in this Constitution shall be so construed as to Prejudice any Claims of the United States, or of any particular State.

Section 4.

The United States shall guarantee to every State in this Union a Republican Form of Government, and shall protect each of them against Invasion; and on Application of the Legislature, or of the Executive (when the Legislature cannot be convened) against domestic Violence.

ARTICLE V

The Congress, whenever two thirds of both Houses shall deem it necessary, shall propose Amendments to this Constitution, or, on the Application of the Legislatures of two thirds of the several States, shall call a Convention for proposing Amendments, which, in either Case, shall be valid to all Intents and Purposes, as Part of this Constitution, when ratified by the Legislatures of three fourths of the several states, or by Conventions in three fourths thereof, as the one or the other Mode of Ratification may be proposed by the Congress; Provided that no Amendment which may be made prior to the Year One thousand eight hundred and eight shall in any Manner affect the first and fourth Clauses in the Ninth Section of the first Article; and that no State, without its Consent, shall be deprived of its equal Suffrage in the Senate.

ARTICLE VI

All Debts contracted and Engagements entered into, before the Adoption of this Constitution, shall be as valid against the United States under this Constitution, as under the Confederation.

This Constitution, and the Laws of the United States which shall be made in Pursuance thereof; and all Treaties made, or which shall be made, under the Authority of the United States, shall be the supreme Law of the Land; and the Judges in every State shall be bound thereby, any Thing in the Constitution or Laws of any State to the Contrary notwithstanding.

The Senators and Representatives before mentioned, and the Members of the several State Legislatures, and all executive and judicial Officers, both of the United States and of the several States, shall be bound by Oath or Affirmation, to support this Constitution; but no religious Test shall ever be required as a Qualification to any Office or public Trust under the United States.

ARTICLE VII

The Ratification of the Conventions of nine States shall be sufficient for the Establishment of this Constitution between the States so ratifying the Same.

Done in Convention by the Unanimous Consent of the States present the Seventeenth Day of September in the Year of our Lord one thousand seven hundred and Eighty seven and of the Independence of the United States of America and the Twelfth[6] IN WITNESS whereof We have here unto subscribed our Names.

[names omitted]

---

[6] The Constitution was submitted on September 17, 1787, by the Constitutional Convention, was ratified by the conventions of several states at various dates up to May 29, 1790, and became effective on March 4, 1789.

AMENDMENTS TO THE CONSTITUTION
(THE FIRST TEN AMENDMENTS FORM THE BILL OF RIGHTS)

[AMENDMENT I]

Congress shall make no law respecting an establishment of religion, or prohibiting the free exercise thereof; or abridging the freedom of speech, or of the press, or the right of the people peaceably to assemble, and to petition the Government for a redress of grievances.

[AMENDMENT II]

A well regulated Militia being necessary to the security of a free State, the right of the people to keep and bear Arms, shall not be infringed.

[AMENDMENT III]

No Soldier shall, in time of peace be quartered in any house, without the consent of the Owner, nor in time of war, but in a manner to be prescribed by law.

[AMENDMENT IV]

The right of the people to be secure in their persons, houses, papers, and effects, against unreasonable searches and seizures, shall not be violated, and no Warrants shall issue, but upon probable cause, supported by Oath or affirmation, and particularly describing the place to be searched, and the persons or things to be seized.

[AMENDMENT V]

No person shall be held to answer for a capital, or otherwise infamous crime, unless on a presentment or indictment of a Grand Jury, except in cases arising in the land or naval forces, or in the Militia, when in actual service in time of War or public danger; nor shall any person be subject for the same offense to be twice put in jeopardy of life or limb; nor shall be compelled in any criminal case to be a witness against himself, nor be deprived of life, liberty, or property, without due process of law; nor shall private property be taken for public use, without just compensation.

[AMENDMENT VI]

In all criminal prosecutions, the accused shall enjoy the right to a speedy and public trial, by an impartial jury of the State and district wherein the crime shall have been committed, which district shall have been previously ascertained by law, and to be informed of the nature and cause of the accusation; to be confronted with the witnesses against him; to have compulsory process for obtaining witnesses in his favor, and to have the Assistance of Counsel for his defence.

[AMENDMENT VII]

In Suits at common law, where the value in controversy shall exceed twenty dollars, the right of trial by jury shall be preserved, and no fact tried by a jury, shall be otherwise reexamined in any court of the United States, than according to the rules of the common law.

[AMENDMENT VIII]

Excessive bail shall not be required, nor excessive fines imposed, nor cruel and unusual punishments inflicted.

[AMENDMENT IX]

The enumeration in the Constitution, of certain rights, shall not be construed to deny or disparage others retained by the people.

[AMENDMENT X]

The powers not delegated to the United States by the Constitution, nor prohibited by it to the States, are reserved to the States respectively, or to the people.[7]

[AMENDMENT XI]

The Judicial power of the United States shall not be construed to extend to any suit in law or equity, commenced or prosecuted against one of the United States by Citizens of another State, or by Citizens or Subjects of any Foreign State.[8]

[AMENDMENT XII]

The Electors shall meet in their respective states, and vote by ballot for President and Vice-President, one of whom, at least, shall not be an inhabitant of the same state with themselves; they shall name in their ballots the person voted for as President, and in distinct ballots the person voted for as Vice-President, and they shall make distinct lists of all persons voted for as President, and of all persons voted for as Vice-President, and of the number of votes for each, which lists they shall sign and certify, and transmit sealed to the seat of the government of the United States, directed to the President of the Senate;—The President of the Senate shall,

---

[7] The first ten amendments were all proposed by Congress on September 25, 1789, and were ratified and adoption certified on December 15, 1791.

[8] Proposed by Congress on March 4, 1794, and declared ratified on January 8, 1798.

in the presence of the Senate and House of Representatives, open all the certificates and the votes shall then be counted;—The person having the greatest number of votes for President, shall be the President, if such number be a majority of the whole number of Electors appointed; and if no person have such majority, then from the persons having the highest numbers not exceeding three on the list of those voted for as President, the House of Representatives shall choose immediately, by ballot, the President. But in choosing the President, the votes shall be taken by states, the representation from each state having one vote; a quorum for this purpose shall consist of a member or members from two-thirds of the states, and a majority of all the states shall be necessary to a choice. And if the House of Representatives shall not choose a President whenever the right of choice shall devolve upon them, before the fourth day of March next following, then the Vice-President shall act as President, as in the case of the death or other constitutional disability of the President.—The person having the greatest number of votes as Vice-President, shall be the Vice-President, if such number be a majority of the whole number of Electors appointed, and if no person have a majority, then from the two highest numbers on the list, the Senate shall choose the Vice-President; a quorum for the purpose shall consist of two-thirds of the whole number of Senators, and a majority of the whole number shall be necessary to a choice. But no person constitutionally ineligible to the office of President shall be eligible to that of Vice-President of the United States.[9]

[AMENDMENT XIII]

Section 1.

Neither slavery nor involuntary servitude, except as a punishment for crime whereof the party shall have been duly convicted, shall exist within the United States, or any place subject to their jurisdiction.

Section 2.

Congress shall have power to enforce this article by appropriate legislation.[10]

[AMENDMENT XIV]

Section 1.

All persons born or naturalized in the United States and subject to the jurisdiction thereof, are citizens of the United States and the State wherein they reside. No State shall make or enforce any law which shall abridge the privileges or immunities of citizens of the United States; nor shall any State deprive any person of life, liberty, or property, without due process of law; nor deny to any person within its jurisdiction the equal protection of the laws.

Section 2.

Representatives shall be apportioned among the several States according to their respective numbers counting the whole number of persons in each State, excluding Indians not taxed. But when the right to vote at any election for the choice of electors for President and Vice-President of the United States, Representatives in Congress, the Executive and Judicial officers of a State, or the members of the Legislature thereof, is denied to any of the male inhabitants of such State being twenty-one years of age and citizens of the United States, or in any way abridged, except for participation in rebellion or other crime, the basis of representation therein shall be reduced in the proportion which the number of such male citizens shall bear to the whole number of male citizens twenty-one years of age in such State.

Section 3.

No person shall be a Senator or Representative in Congress, or elector of President and Vice President or hold any office, civil or military, under the United States or under any State, who, having previously taken an oath, as a member of Congress, or as an officer of the United States, or as a member of any State legislature or as an executive or judicial officer of any State to support the Constitution of the United States, shall have engaged in insurrection or rebellion against the same, or given aid or comfort to the enemies thereof. But Congress may by a vote of two-thirds of each House, remove such disability.

Section 4.

The validity of the public debt of the United States authorized by law, including debts incurred for payment of pensions and bounties for services in suppressing insurrection or rebellion, shall not be questioned. But neither the United States nor any State shall assume or pay any debt or obligation incurred in aid of insurrection or rebellion against the United States, or any claim for the loss or emancipation of any slave; but all such debts, obligations and claims shall be held illegal and void.

Section 5.

The Congress shall have power to enforce, by appropriate legislation, the provisions of this article.[11]

---

[9] Proposed by Congress on December 9, 1803; declared ratified on September 25, 1804; supplemented by Amendments XX and XXIII.

[10] Proposed by Congress on January 31, 1865; declared ratified on December 18, 1865.

[11] Proposed by Congress on June 13, 1866; declared ratified on July 28, 1868.

[AMENDMENT XV]

Section 1.

The right of citizens of the United States to vote shall not be denied or abridged by the United States or by any State on account of race, color, or previous condition of servitude.

Section 2.

The Congress shall have power to enforce this article by appropriate legislation.[12]

[AMENDMENT XVI]

The Congress shall have power to lay and collect taxes on incomes, from whatever source derived, without apportionment among the several States, and without regard to any census or enumeration.[13]

[AMENDMENT XVII]

The Senate of the United States shall be composed of two Senators from each State, elected by the people thereof, for six years; and each Senator shall have one vote. The electors in each State shall have the qualifications requisite for electors of the most numerous branch of the State legislatures.

When vacancies happen in the representation of any State in the Senate, the executive authority of such State shall issue writs of election to fill such vacancies: *Provided*, That the legislature of any State may empower the executive thereof to make temporary appointments until the people fill the vacancies by election as the legislature may direct.

This amendment shall not be so construed as to affect the election or term of any Senator chosen before it becomes valid as part of the Constitution.[14]

[AMENDMENT XVIII]

Section 1.

After one year from the ratification of this article the manufacture, sale, or transportation of intoxicating liquors within, the importation thereof into, or the exportation thereof from the United States and all territory subject to the jurisdiction thereof for beverage purposes is hereby prohibited.

Section 2.

The Congress and the several States shall have concurrent power to enforce this article by appropriate legislation.

Section 3.

This article shall be inoperative unless it shall have been ratified as an amendment to the Constitution by the legislatures of the several States, as provided in the Constitution, within seven years from the date of the submission hereof to the States by the Congress.[15]

[AMENDMENT XIX]

The right of citizens of the United States to vote shall not be denied or abridged by the United States or by any State on account of sex.

Congress shall have power to enforce this article by appropriate legislation.[16]

[AMENDMENT XX]

Section 1.

The terms of the President and Vice President shall end at noon on the 20th day of January, and the terms of Senators and Representatives at noon on the 3d day of January, of the years in which such terms would have ended if this article had not been ratified; and the terms of their successors shall then begin.

Section 2.

The Congress shall assemble at least once in every year, and such meeting shall begin at noon on the 3d day of January, unless they shall by law appoint a different day.

Section 3.

If, at the time fixed for the beginning of the term of the President, the President elect shall have died, the Vice President elect shall become President. If a President shall not have been chosen before the time fixed for the beginning of his term, or if the President elect shall have failed to qualify, then the Vice President elect shall act as President until a President shall have qualified; and the Congress may by law provide for the case wherein neither a President elect nor a Vice President elect shall have qualified, declaring who shall then act as President, or the manner in which one who is to act shall be selected, and such person shall act accordingly until a President or Vice President shall have qualified.

Section 4.

The Congress may by law provide for the case of the death of any of the persons from whom the House of Representatives may choose a President whenever the right of choice

---

[12] Proposed by Congress on February 26, 1869; declared ratified on March 30, 1870.

[13] Proposed by Congress on July 12, 1909; declared ratified on February 25, 1913.

[14] Proposed by Congress on May 13, 1912; declared ratified on May 31, 1913.

[15] Proposed by Congress on December 18, 1917; declared ratified on January 29, 1919; repealed by Amendment XXI.

[16] Proposed by Congress on June 4, 1919; declared ratified on August 26, 1920.

shall have devolved upon them, and for the case of the death of any of the persons from whom the Senate may choose a Vice President whenever the right of choice shall have devolved upon them.

Section 5.

Sections 1 and 2 shall take effect on the 15th day of October following the ratification of this article.

Section 6.

This article shall be inoperative unless it shall have been ratified as an amendment to the Constitution by the legislatures of three-fourths of the several States within seven years from the date of its submission.[17]

[AMENDMENT XXI]

Section 1.

The eighteenth article of amendment to the Constitution of the United States is hereby repealed.

Section 2.

The transportation or importation into any States, Territory, or possession of the United States for delivery or use therein of intoxicating liquors, in violation of the laws thereof, is hereby prohibited.

Section 3.

This article shall be inoperative unless it shall have been ratified as an amendment to the Constitution by conventions in the several States, as provided in the Constitution, within seven years from the date of the submission hereof to the States by the Congress.[18]

[AMENDMENT XXII]

Section 1.

No person shall be elected to the office of the President more than twice, and no person who has held the office of President, or acted as President, for more than two years of a term to which some other person was elected President shall be elected to the office of the President more than once. But this Article shall not apply to any person holding the office of President when the Article was proposed by the Congress, and shall not prevent any person who may be holding the office of President, or acting as President, during the term within which this Article becomes operative from holding the office of President or acting as President during the remainder of such term.

Section 2.

This article shall be inoperative unless it shall have been ratified as an amendment to the Constitution by the legislatures of three-fourths of the several States within seven years from the date of its submission to the States by the Congress.[19]

[AMENDMENT XXIII]

Section 1.

The District constituting the seat of Government of the United States shall appoint in such manner as the Congress shall direct:

A number of electors of President and Vice President equal to the whole number of Senators and Representatives in Congress to which the District would be entitled if it were a State, but in no event more than the least populous State; they shall be in addition to those appointed by the States, but they shall be considered, for the purposes of the election of President and Vice President, to be electors appointed by a State; and they shall meet in the District and perform such duties as provided by the twelfth article of amendment.

Section 2.

The Congress shall have power to enforce this article by appropriate legislation.[20]

[AMENDMENT XXIV]

Section 1.

The right of citizens of the United States to vote in any primary or other election for President or Vice President, for electors for President or Vice President, or for Senator or Representative in Congress, shall not be denied or abridged by the United States or any state by reason of failure to pay any poll tax or other tax.

Section 2.

The Congress shall have the power to enforce this article by appropriate legislation.[21]

[AMENDMENT XXV]

Section 1.

In case of the removal of the President from office or his death or resignation, the Vice President shall become President.

---

[17] Proposed by Congress on March 2, 1932; declared ratified on February 6, 1933.

[18] Proposed by Congress on February 20, 1933; declared ratified on December 5, 1933.

[19] Proposed by Congress on March 24, 1947; declared ratified on March 1, 1951.

[20] Proposed by Congress on June 16, 1960; declared ratified on April 3, 1961.

[21] Proposed by Congress on August 27, 1962; declared ratified on January 23, 1963.

Section 2.

Whenever there is a vacancy in the office of the Vice President, the President shall nominate a Vice President who shall take the office upon confirmation by a majority vote of both houses of Congress.

Section 3.

Whenever the President transmits to the President pro tempore of the Senate and the Speaker of the House of Representatives his written declaration that he is unable to discharge the powers and duties of his office, and until he transmits to them a written declaration to the contrary, such powers and duties shall be discharged by the Vice President as Acting President.

Section 4.

Whenever the Vice President and a majority of either the principal officers of the executive departments or of such other body as Congress may by law provide, transmit to the President pro tempore of the Senate and the Speaker of the House of Representatives their written declaration that the President is unable to discharge the powers and duties of his office, the Vice President shall immediately assume the powers and duties of the office as Acting President.

Thereafter, when the President transmits to the President pro tempore of the Senate and the Speaker of the House of Representatives his written declaration that no inability exists, he shall resume the powers and duties of his office unless the Vice President and a majority of either the principal officers of the executive department or of such other body as Congress may by law provide, transmit within four days to the President pro tempore of the Senate and the Speaker of the House of Representatives their written declaration that the President is unable to discharge the powers and duties of his office. Thereupon Congress shall decide the issue, assembling within 48 hours for that purpose if not in session. If the Congress, within 21 days after receipt of the latter written declaration, or, if Congress is not in session, within 21 days after Congress is required to assemble, determines by two-thirds vote of both houses that the President is unable to discharge the powers and duties of his office, the Vice President shall continue to discharge the same as Acting President; otherwise, the President shall resume the powers and duties of his office.[22]

[AMENDMENT XXVI]

Section 1.

The right of citizens of the United States, who are 18 years of age or older, to vote shall not be denied or abridged by the United States or any state on account of age.

Section 2.

The Congress shall have the power to enforce this article by appropriate legislation.[23]

---

[22] Proposed by Congress July 6, 1965; declared ratified on February 10, 1967.

[23] Proposed by Congress on March 23, 1971; declared ratified on June 30, 1971.

CREDITS

PHOTOGRAPHS AND CARTOONS

Unless otherwise acknowledged, all photos are the property of ScottForesman.

Cover: Patricia Fisher/Folio Inc.

2, Adam Woolfitt/Woodfin Camp & Associates; **12,** DPI; **15,** AP/Wide World; **17,** Reuters/UPI/Bettmann Newsphotos; **25,** Charles Cherney, Copyrighted, Chicago Tribune Company, all rights reserved. Reprinted with permission; **31,** George Hall/Woodfin Camp & Associates; **38,** AP/Wide World; **42,** Painting by Howard Chandler Christy, National Geographic Photographer, George F. Mobley, Courtesy, U.S. Capitol Historical Society; **45,** Antonio Suarez, © Time Warner Inc.; **52,** UPI/Bettmann Newsphotos; **60,** UPI/Bettmann Newsphotos; **63,** Jon Blumb/Gamma-Liaison; **69,** UPI/Bettmann Newsphotos; **71,** Reprinted by permission: Tribune Media Services; **77,** Timothy A. Murphy/U.S. News & World Report; **84,** Dennis Brack/Black Star; **90,** AP/Wide World; **95,** Drawing by Mort Gerberg © 1987 The New Yorker Magazine, Inc.; **100,** Brent Jones; **110,** Jean-Claude LeJeune/Stock Boston; **112,** Reprinted by permission, Los Angeles Times Syndicate; **117,** Reprinted by permission: Tribune Media Services; **123,** UPI/Bettmann Newsphotos; **126** (all), AP/Wide World; **128,** Tannenbaum/Sygma; **133,** AP/Wide World; **138,** AP/Wide World; **142–143,** Thomas Nast from THOMAS NAST by Albert Bigelow Paine; **156,** Joe Traver/Gamma-Liaison; **161,** AP/Wide World; **167,** Bill Luckovich; **174,** Atlan/Sygma; **179,** Jerry Tomaselli, Copyrighted, Chicago Tribune Company, all rights reserved. Reprinted with permission; **181,** © 1987 Washington Post Writers; **182,** AP/Wide World; **188,** Ron Sachs/Consolidated News Service/Uniphoto; **191,** AP/Wide World; **193,** Dennis Brack/Black Star; **195,** Reprinted with permission, Copley News Service; **197,** AP/Wide World; **208,** AP/Wide World; **214,** Distributed by King Features Syndicate, Inc.; **224,** AP/Wide World; **230,** AP/Wide World; **232,** AP/Wide World; **241,** AP/Wide World; **245,** The White House; **252,** Michael Fryer, Copyrighted, Chicago Tribune Company, all rights reserved. Reprinted with permission; **259,** NASA; **260,** Jeff Jacobson; **262,** Newspaper Enterprise Association, Inc.; **271,** Dick Durrance II/ Woodfin Camp & Associates; **278,** Dennis Brack/Black Star; **283,** Steve Liss, © Time Warner Inc.; **289,** UPI/Bettmann Newsphotos; **296,** Supreme Court Historical Society; **299,** AP/Wide World; **310,** Charles Steiner/Picture Group; **313,** Larry Downing/Woodfin Camp & Associates; **329,** Linda Haas/Decisive Moment; **331,** UPI/Bettmann Newsphotos; **334,** Reprinted by permission: Tribune Media Services; **341,** UPI/Bettmann Newsphotos; **346,** George Hall/Woodfin Camp & Associates; **354,** Reprinted by permission: Tribune Media Services; **359,** Frank Hanes, Copyrighted, Chicago Tribune Company, all rights reserved. Reprinted with permission; **361,** AP/Wide World; **362,** Michael O'Brien; **364,** Brent Jones; **368,** UPI/Bettmann Newsphotos; **372,** Lawrence Manning/Black Star; **375,** Bill Levin; **382,** Bryce Flynn/Picture Group; **386,** AP/Wide World; **388,** Brent Jones; **396,** UPI/Bettmann Newsphotos; **398,** Library of Congress; **404,** Frank Johnston/Black Star; **408,** UPI/Bettmann Newsphotos; **410,** UPI/Bettmann Newsphotos; **414,** AP/Wide World; **422,** AP/Wide World; **429,** Diana Walker/Gamma-Liaison; **437,** Regis Bossu/Sygma; **441,** UPI/Bettman Newsphotos; **443,** Reprinted by permission: Tribune Media Services; **444,** AP/Wide World; **448,** Wally McNamee/ Woodfin Camp & Associates; **456,** AP/Wide World.

TABLES AND FIGURES

Page 145: Data in Table 6.1 from "Trend in Political Affiliation," THE GALLUP REPORT, April 1981, Report No. 187, p. 20. Reprinted by permission of American Institute of Public Opinion.

Page 148: Data in Table 6.2 from "Political Party Affiliation," THE GALLUP REPORT, Sept. 1988, Report No. 276, p. 6. Reprinted by permission of American Institute of Public Opinion.

Page 248: Data in Figure 9.1 from OPINION ROUNDUP, Public Opinion, Jan/Feb 1989, Vol. 11, No. 5, p. 40. Reprinted by permission of American Enterprise Institute for Public Policy Research, Washington, D.C.

INDEX

Presidential Election Year	Elected to Office			
	President	Party	Vice-President	Party
1884	Grover Cleveland	Democratic	Thomas A. Hendricks	Democratic
1888	Benjamin Harrison	Republican	Levi P. Morton	Republican
1892	Grover Cleveland	Democratic	Adlai E. Stevenson	Democratic
1896	William McKinley	Republican	Garret A. Hobart	Republican
1900	William McKinley	Republican	Theodore Roosevelt	Republican
1904	Theodore Roosevelt	Republican	Charles W. Fairbanks	Republican
1908	William Howard Taft	Republican	James S. Sherman	Republican
1912	Woodrow Wilson	Democratic	Thomas R. Marshall	Democratic
1916	Woodrow Wilson	Democratic	Thomas R. Marshall	Democratic
1920	Warren G. Harding	Republican	Calvin Coolidge	Republican
1924	Calvin Coolidge	Republican	Charles G. Dawes	Republican
1928	Herbert C. Hoover	Republican	Charles Curtis	Republican

Major Opponents		Electoral Vote		Popular Vote
For President	*Party*			
James G. Blaine	Republican	Cleveland	219	4,874,621
John P. St. John	Prohibition	Blaine	182	4,848,936
Benjamin F. Butler	Greenback	Butler	—	175,096
		St. John	—	147,482
Grover Cleveland	Democratic	B. Harrison	233	5,447,129
Clinton B. Fisk	Prohibition	Cleveland	168	5,537,857
Alson J. Streeter	Union Labor			
Benjamin Harrison	Republican	Cleveland	277	5,555,426
James B. Weaver	Populist	B. Harrison	145	5,182,600
John Bidwell	Prohibition	Weaver	22	1,029,846
William Jennings Bryan	Democratic, Populist, and National Silver Republican	McKinley	271	7,102,246
		Bryan	176	6,492,559
Joshua Levering	Prohibition			
John M. Palmer	National Democratic			
William Jennings Bryan	Democratic and Fusion Populist	McKinley	292	7,218,039
		Bryan	155	6,358,345
Wharton Barker	Anti-Fusion Populist	Woolley	—	209,004
Eugene V. Debs	Social Democratic	Debs	—	86,935
John G. Woolley	Prohibition			
Alton B. Parker	Democratic	T. Roosevelt	336	7,626,593
Eugene V. Debs	Socialist	Parker	140	5,082,898
Silas C. Swallow	Prohibition	Debs	—	402,489
		Swallow	—	258,596
William Jennings Bryan	Democratic	Taft	321	7,676,258
		Bryan	162	6,406,801
Eugene V. Debs	Socialist	Debs	—	420,380
Eugene W. Chafin	Prohibition	Chafin	—	252,821
William Howard Taft	Republican	Wilson	435	6,296,547
Theodore Roosevelt	Progressive (Bull Moose)	T. Roosevelt	88	4,118,571
		Taft	8	3,486,720
Eugene V. Debs	Socialist			
Eugene W. Chafin	Prohibition			
Charles E. Hughes	Republican	Wilson	277	9,127,695
Allen L. Benson	Socialist	Hughes	254	8,533,507
J. Frank Hanly	Prohibition			
Charles W. Fairbanks	Republican			
James M. Cox	Democratic	Harding	404	16,133,314
Eugene V. Debs	Socialist	Cox	127	9,140,884
		Debs	—	913,664
John W. Davis	Democratic	Coolidge	382	15,717,553
Robert M. LaFollette	Progressive	Davis	136	8,386,169
		LaFollette	13	4,814,050
Alfred E. Smith	Democratic	Hoover	444	21,391,993
Norman Thomas	Socialist	Smith	87	15,016,169

Presidential Election Year	Elected to Office			
	President	Party	Vice-President	Party
1932	Franklin D. Roosevelt	Democratic	John N. Garner	Democratic
1936	Franklin D. Roosevelt	Democratic	John N. Garner	Democratic
1940	Franklin D. Roosevelt	Democratic	Henry A. Wallace	Democratic
1944	Franklin D. Roosevelt	Democratic	Harry S Truman	Democratic
1948	Harry S Truman	Democratic	Alben W. Barkley	Democratic
1952	Dwight D. Eisenhower	Republican	Richard M. Nixon	Republican
1956	Dwight D. Eisenhower	Republican	Richard M. Nixon	Republican
1960	John F. Kennedy	Democratic	Lyndon B. Johnson	Democratic
1964	Lyndon B. Johnson	Democratic	Hubert H. Humphrey	Democratic
1968	Richard M. Nixon	Republican	Spiro T. Agnew	Republican
1972	Richard M. Nixon	Republican	Spiro T. Agnew	Republican
1976	Jimmy Carter	Democratic	Walter Mondale	Democratic
1980	Ronald Reagan	Republican	George Bush	Republican
1984	Ronald Reagan	Republican	George Bush	Republican
1988	George Bush	Republican	J. Danforth Quayle	Republican